Mi
Se

SYNTAX
OF THE
MOODS & TENSES
OF THE
GREEK VERB

BCP Advanced Language Series

Current and forthcoming titles:

The Greek Dialects, C.D. Buck
Greek Grammar, W. Goodwin
The Greek Language, L. Palmer
Greek Metre, D. Raven
The Greek Particles, J. Denniston
Greek Prose Style, J. Denniston
Syntax of the Moods & Tenses of the Greek Verb, W. Goodwin
Latin Grammar, B. Gildersleeve & G. Lodge
The Latin Language, L. Palmer
Latin Metre, D. Raven
A New Latin Syntax, E. Woodcock

SYNTAX
OF THE
MOODS & TENSES
OF THE
GREEK VERB

BY

W.W. Goodwin

Published by Bristol Classical Press
General Editor: John H. Betts

First published 1875 in the USA
Published in the UK by Macmillan & Co. Ltd., 1889
Reissued 1965

Paperback edition published in 1998 by
Bristol Classical Press
an imprint of
Gerald Duckworth & Co. Ltd
61 Frith Street
London W1D 3JL
e-mail: inquiries@duckworth-publishers.co.uk
Website: www.ducknet.co.uk

Reprinted 1999, 2001

A catalogue record for this book is available
from the British Library

ISBN 1-85399-555-X

Printed in Great Britain by
Antony Rowe Ltd, Eastbourne

PREFACE.

THE present work is the result of an attempt to revise the much smaller book which was first published under the same title in 1860, and again, somewhat enlarged, in 1865. When it falls to the lot of a writer to revise, under the greater sense of responsibility which doubled years and more than doubled experience have brought him, a book written in the enthusiasm of youth as an ephemeral production, he is sure to be his own severest critic; and what he begins as a revision inevitably becomes, as he proceeds, more and more a new and independent work. I cannot forget that this book is addressed in great part to a different generation of scholars from that to which the former one was offered; and a treatment of the subject which was permissible in 1860 would be far from satisfactory now. I then attempted chiefly to give "a plain and practical statement of the principles which govern the relations of the Greek Moods and Tenses," avoiding theoretical discussions as far as possible. At that time prevailing theories, based chiefly on abstract speculations, had obscured some of the most important facts in the syntax of the moods, and perhaps no better service could be rendered by a new writer than the clearing away of some of the clouds. Few younger scholars are aware how modern are many of the grammatical doctrines which are now taught in all classical schools. It is hard to believe that so elementary a principle as that by which the aorist infinitive is past in φησὶν ἐλθεῖν and future in βούλεται ἐλθεῖν was never distinctly stated until 1847, when it appeared simultaneously in the *Greek*

Syntax of Professor Madvig at Copenhagen and in the *Greek Grammar* of Professor Sophocles at Harvard University. Something more than mere statement of facts has been attempted in the present work, although nothing has been further from my thoughts than a complete theoretical discussion of all the principles which govern the use of the moods. He who ventures far upon that sea is in great danger of being lost in the fog or stranded; for, while Comparative Philology has thrown much and most welcome light on the early history of the Greek language, it has also made us more painfully aware of our ignorance, although it is a more enlightened ignorance than that of our predecessors.

Since the publication of the first edition, many most important additions have been made to our resources. Of these I can undertake to notice only a few. Delbrück's elaborate treatise on the Greek Subjunctive and Optative (in his *Syntaktische Forschungen*, vol. i.), with a comparison of Greek and Sanskrit usages, is familiar to all scholars. Whatever may be thought of Delbrück's main thesis, the distinction of the subjunctive as the mood of *will* from the optative as the mood of *wish*, none can fail to be impressed and instructed by his attractive and original treatment of the subject, which has made an epoch in grammatical science. Lange's unfinished work on the Particle Εἰ in Homer is a model of careful and thorough investigation. When I think of my deep and continued indebtedness to Lange's learned discussions, which include a treatment of all the 200 examples of εἰ with the optative in Homer, I am grieved to dissent so frequently from his most important conclusions. His chief argument is discussed in Appendix I. Schanz, in his *Beiträge zur Griechischen Syntax*, has undertaken a work of immense extent, involving an amount of labour which it is hard to over-estimate. His plan is to give full and accurate statistics of the use of every construction bearing on the history of Greek syntax, and thus to make a true historic syntax of the language a possibility. The work of collecting, classifying, and discussing the examples of different constructions has been assigned by

him to a large number of colleagues, and every year
testifies to substantial progress. The following treatises
bearing on the construction of the moods and tenses have
already been published by Schanz: Weber, *Enwickelungs-
geschichte der Absichtssätze ;* Sturm, *Geschichtliche Entwickelung der Constructionen mit* Πρίν; Schmitt, *Ueber den Ursprung des Substantivsatzes mit Relativpartikeln im Griechischen ;* Grünewald, *Der freie formelhafte Infinitiv der Limitation im Griechischen ;* Birklein, *Entwickelungsgeschichte des
substantivirten Infinitivs.* The amount of patient labour
devoted to these compilations, in which the exact number
of examples of each construction in each Greek author
before Aristotle is given, while the most important passages
are quoted and nearly all are cited, will be most gratefully
appreciated by those who would be least willing to undertake the work themselves. The results of such dry
enumerations are often interesting and surprising. No one
knows whether statistics will be dry and barren or not,
until they are collected and classified; and though it may
seem a useless task to count the examples of each of the
final particles in all Greek literature before Aristotle, it is
interesting to know that in all the Attic prose, except
Xenophon, ὡς final occurs only five or six times while ἵνα
occurs 999 times. Some of the results derived from
Weber's statistics of the use of the final particles are given
in Appendix III., and an account of Xenophon's peculiar
use of ὡς, ὡς ἄν, and ὅπως ἄν in Appendix IV., for the
benefit of those who have not Weber's book at hand, or
want the patience to follow his elaborate historical statements. Monro's *Homeric Grammar* is one of the best
results of recent English scholarship, and for the study of
Homeric usages in the moods it is invaluable. I regret
that the new edition of this book, soon to be published, has
not come in time to benefit the present work. It seems a
mere form to acknowledge my obligations to the standard
Grammars; but I must repeat my former expression of
thanks to Madvig, Krüger, and Kühner, not to mention a
host of others. To Madvig I am indebted for the first
conviction that the syntax of the Greek moods belonged

to the realm of common sense. To Krüger I have been indebted in the study of every construction; and I have still retained most of the remarks on the tenses of the indicative which were originally borrowed from him. The revised edition of Kühner's *Griechische Grammatik* has supplied a large store of examples, to which I have frequently had recourse. I am under especial obligation to him for many of the examples which illustrate the uses of the Supplementary Participle, and the corresponding uses of the infinitive with many of the same verbs. Frequent references are made in the notes to the authorities which I have mentioned, and to many others.

It is with pride and pleasure that I acknowledge my deepest indebtedness to an American scholar, whose writings have thrown light upon most of the dark places in Greek syntax. I need not say that I refer to my friend, Professor Gildersleeve of Baltimore. As editor of the *American Journal of Philology* he has discussed almost every construction of the Greek moods, and he has always left his mark. His two reviews of Weber's work on the Final Sentence in vols. iv. and vi. of his Journal may well save many scholars the trouble of reading the book itself, while they contain much new matter which is valuable to every one. The acute observation, that the use of ἄν and κέ in final constructions depends on the force of ὡς, ὅπως, and ὄφρα as conditional relative or temporal adverbs, explains much which before seemed inexplicable. His article on πρίν in vol. ii. stated important principles of classic usage which were confirmed by Sturm's statistics; and this, with the later review of Sturm's volume, has done much to correct current errors and to establish sounder views about πρίν. His articles on the Articular Infinitive in the *Transactions of the American Philological Association for* 1878 and in the third volume of his *Journal* practically anticipated the results of Birklein's statistics. I can mention further only his article in vol. vii. of the *Journal* on the Consecutive Sentence, which gives (it seems to me) the clearest statement ever made of the relations of ὥστε with the infinitive to ὥστε with the finite moods. I have expressed my indebtedness to these and other writings of Gildersleeve as occasion has required; but I have also often referred to his articles in his *Journal* by the simple mention of that periodical. I have sometimes omitted a reference where one might seem proper, lest I should appear to make him responsible for what he might deem some dangerous heresy.

I am also under the greatest obligation to my friends and colleagues in Harvard University, Professors Allen, Greenough, Lane, Lanman, White, and Wright, and Dr. Morgan, for valuable suggestions, and to most of them for important help in revising and proof-reading. I regret that I have not had the advantage of their aid in reading the proofs of the last two-thirds of the work. To my friendship of twenty-one years with Dr. Henry Jackson, of Trinity College, Cambridge, I am indebted for some of the most important suggestions which I have received since the publication of the former editions.

The Index to the Examples includes all of the more than 4800 examples quoted or cited in the main body of the work, but not those in the Appendix nor those which are given in the classified lists in the footnotes on pp. 92, 115, 152, 172, and 290. It may seem useless to index many examples which merely illustrate a common principle, like those of a simple aorist infinitive or present indicative; but it would be difficult to discriminate here, and one seldom knows what may make an example useful to another. The same consideration has induced me to give as great a variety of examples as possible, from authors of different classes, illustrating many constructions which apparently need no such aid.

It is hardly necessary to remark that the work, in its present enlarged form, is not intended for use as a grammatical text-book in the class-room, except perhaps the portion printed in the largest type. On the other hand, it is hoped that the increased fulness and the greater space given to discussions will make the work more useful for private study and for reference.

The Dramatists are cited by Dindorf's lines; except the tragic fragments, which follow Nauck's edition, and the comic fragments, which follow Kock. The lyric fragments follow Bergk's *Poetae Lyrici*. Plato is cited by the pages and letters of Stephanus, and the Orators by the numbers of the orations and the sections now in universal use. The other citations will be easily understood.

In conclusion, I must express my grateful thanks to the University Libraries of Heidelberg and Leyden, and to the Royal Library at The Hague, for the hospitality which was kindly shown me while I was correcting the proofs.

W. W. GOODWIN.

PALLANZA, LAGO MAGGIORE,
24th September 1889.

CONTENTS.

CHAPTER I.

GENERAL VIEW OF THE MOODS.

CHAPTER II.

THE TENSES.

I. TENSES OF THE INDICATIVE.

PRESENT.

IMPERFECT.

PERFECT AND PLUPERFECT.

III. TENSES OF THE PARTICIPLE.

GNOMIC AND ITERATIVE TENSES.

GNOMIC AORIST AND PERFECT.

DEPENDENCE OF MOODS AND TENSES.

CHAPTER III.

THE PARTICLE ἈΝ.

INDICATIVE WITH ἄν.

CHAPTER IV.

USE OF THE MOODS.

SECTION I.

The Potential Optative and Indicative with ἄν and κέ.

I. POTENTIAL OPTATIVE.

SECTION II.

Imperative and Subjunctive in Commands, Exhortations, and
Prohibitions.—Subjunctive and Indicative with μή and
μὴ οὐ in Cautious Assertions.—Ὅπως and ὅπως μή with
the Independent Future Indicative or Subjunctive.

SECTION III.

Subjunctive, like Future Indicative, in Independent Sentences
in Homer.—Interrogative Subjunctive.

(b) FUTURE CONDITIONS.

1. Subjunctive or Future Indicative in Protasis with a Future Apodosis.

2. Optative in Protasis and Apodosis.

II. PRESENT AND PAST GENERAL SUPPOSITIONS.

PECULIAR FORMS OF CONDITIONAL SENTENCES.

Substitution and Ellipsis in Protasis—Protasis without a Verb.

Substitution and Ellipsis in Apodosis.

Apodosis contained in Protasis.

Πρίν WITH INDICATIVE.

Πρίν WITH SUBJUNCTIVE AND OPTATIVE.

Πρὶν ἤ, πρότερον ἤ, AND πάρος.

Πρίν, πάρος, ETC. IN LEADING CLAUSE.

SECTION VIII.

Indirect Discourse.

SIMPLE SENTENCES.

Ὅπως, ὅ, οὕνεκα, AND ὁθούνεκα.

SECTION IX.

Causal Sentences.

SECTION X.

Expression of a Wish.

FUTURE WISHES.

PRESENT OR PAST WISHES (NOT ATTAINED).

Infinitive of Purpose.

Absolute Infinitive.

Infinitive in Commands, Prohibitions, Wishes, and Exclamations.

B. INFINITIVE WITH THE ARTICLE.

Articular Infinitive as Subject or Object.

Infinitive with τό after Adjectives and Nouns.

Infinitive with τοῦ, τῷ, and τό in various Constructions.

CHAPTER VI.

THE PARTICIPLE.

I. Not in Indirect Discourse.

Omission of ὤν.

Infinitive with Verbs of §§ 879-901.

II. Participle in Indirect Discourse.

CHAPTER VII.

VERBAL ADJECTIVES IN -τέος.

APPENDIX.

CHAPTER I.

GENERAL VIEW OF THE MOODS.

1. THE Mood of a verb shows the *manner* in which the assertion of the verb is made.

The Greek verb has four moods, properly so called,—the indicative, the subjunctive, the optative, and the imperative. The infinitive, which is a verbal noun, and the participle and the verbal in -τέος, which are verbal adjectives, are so closely connected with the moods in many constructions, that they are discussed with them in Syntax.

The four proper moods, as opposed to the infinitive, are sometimes called the *finite* moods. The subjunctive, optative, imperative, and infinitive, as opposed to the indicative, are sometimes called the *dependent* moods.

I. INDICATIVE.

2. The indicative, in its most primitive use, makes a simple, absolute assertion, or asks a question which includes or concerns such an assertion. *E.g.*

Γράφει, *he is writing;* ἔγραφεν, *he was writing;* ἔγραψεν, *he wrote;* γράψει, *he will write.* Γράφει; *is he writing?* ἐγράψατε; *did you write?* γράψετε; *will you write?* τί ἔγραψεν; *what did he write?*

3. The indicative may also express

(*a*) A dependent statement (or quotation) of such an absolute assertion or question. *E.g.*

Λέγει ὅτι γράφει, *he says that he is writing* (he says γράφω); λέγει ὅτι γράψει, *he says that he will write* (he says γράψω); ἐρωτᾷ τί ἐγράψαμεν, *he asks what we wrote;* ἐρωτᾷ εἰ ἔγραψα, *he asks whether I wrote.*

(*b*) A distinct statement of an object aimed at or feared. *E.g.*

Ἐπιμελεῖται ὅπως τοῦτο γενήσεται, *he takes care that this shall be done* (339); φοβούμεθα μὴ ἀμφοτέρων ἡμαρτήκαμεν, *we fear that we have missed both* (369, 2).

(*c*) A distinct supposition of an absolute statement, that is, a supposition that such a statement is, was, or will be true. *E.g.*

Εἰ γράφει, *if he is writing;* εἰ ἔγραψεν, *if he wrote;* εἰ γέγραφε, *if he has written;* εἰ γράψει, *if he shall write or if he is to write.* What is supposed in each case could be expressed by γράφει, ἔγραψεν, γέγραφε, or γράψει.

4. The past tenses of the indicative may, further, express a supposition that some statement either *had been* or *were now* true, while it is implied that really it *was not* or *is not* true. *E.g.*

Εἰ ἔγραψα, *if I had written;* εἰ ἔγραφον, *if I were now writing* or *if I had been writing;* the context indicating that really *I did not write* or *am not writing* (410). These expressions originally always referred to the past, as they do in Homer.

5. Out of the form of unreal supposition (4) were developed after Homer the use of the past tenses of the indicative with εἴθε or εἰ γάρ in wishes (732); and also the Attic construction of the past tenses of the indicative to express an unaccomplished purpose (333), where there is an assimilation of the final clause to a preceding indicative. *E.g.*

Εἰ γὰρ τοῦτο ἐποίησα, *O if I had only done this!* Εἴθε τοῦτο εἶχες, *O if you only had this!*

Εἴθε τότ' ἀπέθανον, ἵνα μὴ τοῦτο ἔπαθον, *would that I had then perished, that I might not have suffered this.*

For the indicative with ἄν or κέ, the *potential* indicative, see **243**.

II. SUBJUNCTIVE.

6. (*a*) The subjunctive, in its simplest and apparently most primitive use, seen in Homer (284), expresses futurity, like the future indicative, and has οὐ for its negative. *E.g.*

Οὐ γάρ πω τοίους ἴδον ἀνέρας οὐδὲ ἴδωμαι, *for never did I see such men nor shall I ever see them,* Il. i. 262; καί ποτέ τις εἴπῃσιν, *and some one will some time say,* Il. vi. 459.

(*b*) Though this primitive use disappears in the later language, the subjunctive still remains closely related in sense to the future indicative, and in most of its constructions can be interchanged with it.

7. The subjunctive in questions of appeal as to the future (287) has, even in Homer, developed the idea of propriety or expediency. *E.g.*

Αὖθι μένω ἦε θέω; *shall I remain here or run?* Il. x. 62. So πῇ ἴω; *whither shall I go?* Od. xv. 509. But the future indicative can be used in the same sense; as τί δῆτα δρῶμεν; μητέρ' ἢ φονεύσομεν; *what are we to do? shall we slay our mother?* EUR. El. 967. (See 68.)

8. (*a*) In exhortations and in prohibitions with μή (250-259) the subjunctive has an imperative force, and is always future; as in ἴωμεν, *let us go;* μὴ θαυμάσητε, *do not wonder.*

The future indicative occasionally occurs in prohibitions with μή (70).

(*b*) The subjunctive with μή, especially in Homer, may express a future object of fear with a desire to avert it; as in μὴ νῆας ἔλωσι, *may they not seize the ships* (*as I fear they will*). (See 261.) From such expressions combined with verbs of fearing arose the dependent use of μή with the subjunctive expressing a future object of fear; as φοβοῦμαι μὴ ἀπόληται, *I fear that he may perish.*

9. In the constructions with οὐ μή (294) the subjunctive and the future indicative are used, without apparent distinction, in a future sense; as οὐ μὴ γένηται and οὐ μὴ γενήσεται, *it will not happen.*

10. The subjunctive may express a future purpose or a future object of care or exertion. *E.g.*

Ἔρχεται ὅπως τοῦτο ἴδῃ, *he comes that he may see this* (317); ἐπιμελεῖται ὅπως τοῦτο γένηται (or γενήσεται), *he takes care that this shall be done* (339). In clauses of purpose the future indicative is sometimes used (324), and in the construction of 339 it became the regular Attic form.

11. In conditional clauses the subjunctive expresses either a future supposition (444), or a general supposition which is indefinite (never strictly present) in its time (462).

(*a*) In the former it supposes such a future case as the Homeric subjunctive (6) states; as ἐάν τις εἴπῃ, *if one shall say* (the thing supposed being εἴπῃ τις, *one will say*); here the future indicative may be used

in essentially the same sense (447). In the general condition it
supposes an event to occur at any time, as we say *if any one ever goes*
or *whoever goes*, with an apodosis expressing repetition or a general
truth ; as ἐάν τις κλέψῃ (or ὃς ἂν κλέψῃ), κολάζεται, *if any one steals*
(or *whoever steals*), *he is always punished.*

(*b*) The subjunctive in general suppositions is the only subjunctive
which does not refer to future time, and here the future indicative can
never be used. In most other languages (as in English and generally
in Latin), and sometimes in Greek, such a condition is expressed by
the present indicative, like an ordinary present supposition ; but the
Greek, in its desire to avoid a form denoting present time, generally
fell into one which it uses elsewhere only for future time. The construction, however, appears in Homer imperfectly established, except
in relative clauses (468): this indicates that it does not belong to
the primitive uses of the subjunctive. (See 17.)

For the Homeric subjunctive with κέ or ἄν in independent
sentences, which does not differ perceptibly in meaning from the future
with κέ or ἄν, see 201, 1.

III. OPTATIVE.

12. The optative is commonly a less distinct and direct
form of expression than the subjunctive, imperative, or
indicative, in constructions of the same general character as
those in which these moods are used.

13. This is seen especially in independent sentences,
where the optative either expresses a wish or exhortation,
or is used (regularly with ἄν or κέ) in a potential sense.

Thus ἴοιμεν, *may we go*, corresponds as a weaker form to ἴωμεν, *let
us go*. Corresponding to ἐξελθών τις ἰδέτω, *let some one go out and see*,
we have ἐξελθών τις ἴδοι, *may some one go out and see*, Od. xxiv. 491.
Ἕλοιτο ἄν, *he would take* or *he might take*, corresponds to the Homeric
ἕληται or ἕληταί κε, *he will take* or *he may take* (201, 1).

We find in Homer a few optatives expressing concession or permission, which have a neutral sense and can hardly be classed as
either potential or wishing. See Il. iv. 17, εἰ δ' αὖ πως τόδε πᾶσι
φίλον καὶ ἡδὺ πέλοιτο, ἦ τοι μὲν οἰκέοιτο πόλις Πριάμοιο ἄνακτος,
αὖτις δ' Ἀργείην Ἑλένην Μενέλαος ἄγοιτο, where we may translate
the apodosis either *let the city still be a habitation and let M. carry away
Helen*, or *the city may still be a habitation and M. may carry away
Helen.* In iii. 72 we have γυναῖκά τε οἴκαδ' ἀγέσθω, and in iii. 255
τῷ δέ κε νικήσαντι γυνὴ καὶ κτήμαθ' ἕποιτο, where ἀγέσθω and
ἕποιτό κε refer to essentially the same thing with ἄγοιτο in iv. 19.
Following Il. iii. 255 (above) we have οἱ δ' ἄλλοι ναίοιμεν Τροίην,
τοὶ δὲ νέονται, i.e. *the rest of us may remain dwellers in Troy, while*

they will return to Greece. From such neutral future expressions were probably developed the two distinct uses of the optative. In its hortatory sense as a form of wishing, the optative was distinguished by the use of μή as a negative ; while in its potential sense it had οὐ as its negative (as in οὐ μὴν γάρ τι κακώτερον ἄλλο πάθοιμι, *for really I can suffer nothing worse,* Il. xix. 321), and it was soon further marked by the addition of κέ or ἄν. (See Appendix I.)

14. In dependent clauses expressing purpose or the object of exertion or of fear, the optative is never an original form ; but it always represents a dependent subjunctive or future indicative (8, *b* ; 10) in the changed relation in which either of them is placed when its leading verb is changed from present or future to past time.

We represent this change in English by a change from *may* to *might,* or from *shall* or *will* to *should* or *would ;* as ἔρχεται ἵνα ἴδῃ, *he comes that he may see,* ἦλθεν ἵνα ἴδοι, *he came that he might see ;* ἐπιμελεῖται ὅπως τοῦτο γενήσεται, *he takes care that this shall be done,* ἐπεμελεῖτο ὅπως τοῦτο γενήσοιτο, *he took care that this should be done ;* φοβεῖται μὴ τοῦτο πάθῃ, *he fears that he may suffer this ;* ἐφοβήθη μὴ τοῦτο πάθοι, *he feared that he might suffer this.* Here the original subjunctive or future indicative (especially the latter) is very often used in place of the optative.

15. In all forms of indirect discourse the same principle (14) holds, that the optative after past tenses represents (in a changed relation) an indicative or a subjunctive of the direct form, which original mood is always used after present and future tenses, and may be retained after past tenses (667, 1).

Here again we see what the change is, for we represent it by our change from *is* to *was,* *have* to *had,* *shall* and *will* to *should* and *would,* etc. ; as λέγει ὅτι ἀληθές ἐστιν, *he says that it is true ;* ἔλεξεν ὅτι ἀληθὲς εἴη (or ἐστίν), *he said that it was true ;* λέγει ὅτι γράψει, *he says that he will write ;* ἔλεξεν ὅτι γράψοι (or γράψει), *he said that he would write.* So οὐκ οἶδα τί εἴπω, *I know not what I shall say ;* οὐκ ᾔδειν τί εἴποιμι (or εἴπω), *I knew not what I should say.*

16. In future conditions the optative expresses the supposition in a weakened future form, as compared with the stronger future of the subjunctive and the future indicative.

Compare ἐὰν ἔλθω, *if I (shall) go* (444), with εἰ ἔλθοιμι, *if I should go* (455). Often the form of the leading sentence (the apodosis) decides whether a given supposition shall be expressed by a subjunctive or by an optative ; thus in DEM. iv. 11 we have ἂν οὗτός τι πάθῃ, *if any-*

thing happens (shall happen) to him (Philip), depending on ποιήσετε; and in the next sentence, referring to precisely the same contingency, we have εἴ τι πάθοι, depending on two optatives with ἄν.

17. The only remaining form of dependent optative is that found in past general suppositions, as εἴ τις κλέψειεν (or ὃς κλέψειεν), ἐκολάζετο, *if ever any one stole* (or *whoever stole*), *he was (always) punished* (462; 531).

Here the optative after a past tense represents an original subjunctive after a present tense (11), differing in this from the optative in future conditions (16), which is in an original construction. The late development of this optative appears from its almost total absence in protasis with εἰ in Homer (468), where the corresponding subjunctive in protasis is also infrequent. It may therefore be disregarded in considering the primitive uses of the optative. (See 11, *b*.)

For a more full discussion of the relations of the optative to the other moods, see Appendix I.

IV. IMPERATIVE.

18. The imperative expresses a command, exhortation, entreaty, or prohibition (250 and 259). *E.g.*

Φεῦγε, *begone!* Ἐλθέτω, *let him come.* Δός μοι τοῦτο, *give me this.* Μὴ ποίει ἄδικα, *do not do what is unjust.*

CHAPTER II.

THE TENSES.

19. THERE are seven Tenses,—the present, imperfect, perfect, pluperfect, aorist, future, and future perfect. The imperfect and pluperfect occur only in the indicative; the futures are wanting in the subjunctive and imperative.

20. These tenses may express two relations. They may designate the time of an action as *present, past,* or *future;* and also its character as *going on, finished,* or simply *taking place.* The latter relation is expressed by the tenses in all the moods and in the infinitive and the participle; the former is always expressed in the indicative, and to a certain extent (to be explained below) in the dependent moods and the participle.

21. The tenses are divided into *primary* tenses, which denote present or future time, and *secondary* or *historical* tenses, which denote past time. This distinction applies properly only to the tenses of the indicative; but it may be extended to any forms of the dependent moods which have the same distinction of time as the tenses of the indicative.

The primary tenses of the indicative are the present (in its ordinary uses), perfect, future, and future perfect. The secondary tenses are the imperfect, pluperfect, and aorist (in its ordinary uses).

This distinction will be more fully explained at the end of this chapter (165-191). It must be noted that the historic present (33) is a secondary tense, and the gnomic aorist (154) is a primary tense.

22. In speaking of the time denoted by any verb, we must distinguish between time which is present, past, or future with reference to the time of speaking or writing (that is, time *absolutely* present, etc.), and time which is present, past, or future with reference to the time of some verb with which the verbal form in question is connected (that is, time *relatively* present, etc.) Thus, when we say τοῦτο ἀληθές ἐστιν, *this is true*, ἐστίν is present with reference to the time of speaking; but when we say ἔφη τοῦτο ἀληθὲς εἶναι or εἶπεν ὅτι τοῦτο ἀληθές ἐστιν (or εἴη), *he said that this was true*, (i.e. *he said "this is true"*), the present tense which we use denotes time present to the time of the leading verb, *i.e.* time *absolutely* past and only *relatively* present. The same distinction is seen between the future in τοῦτο γενήσεται, *this will happen*, and that in ἔφη τοῦτο γενήσεσθαι or εἶπεν ὅτι γενήσεται (γενήσοιτο), *he said that this would happen;* where the future in the first case is *absolutely* future, but in the other cases is only *relatively* future and may be even *absolutely* past. Again, in τοῦτο ἐγένετο, *this happened*, the aorist is absolutely past; but in ἔφη τοῦτο γενέσθαι, or εἶπεν ὅτι τοῦτο ἐγένετο (or γένοιτο), *he said that this had happened*, it denotes time past to the time of the past leading verb, and so is *doubly* past. But in connection with a future expression an aorist, though relatively past, may be absolutely future; as in PLAT. Rep. 478 D, τὸ φανέν as subject of ἔσεσθαι means *that which will hereafter have appeared.* So διαπραξάμενος in 496 E. (See 143.)

It is a special distinction between the Greek and the English idioms, that the Greek uses its verbal forms much more freely to denote merely relative time. Thus, we translate the Greek presents εἶναι and ἐστί after ἔφη or εἶπεν (above) by our *was;* the futures γενήσεσθαι and γενήσεται by *would happen;* and the aorists γενέσθαι and ἐγένετο by *had happened.* This distinction appears especially in the indicative, optative, and infinitive of indirect discourse; in future forms after past tenses in final and object clauses with ἵνα, ὅπως, etc.; and usually in the participle; but not in protasis.

I. TENSES OF THE INDICATIVE.

PRESENT.

23. The present indicative represents an action as *going on* at the time of speaking or writing; as γράφω, *I write,* or *I am writing.*

An important exception occurs when the present indicative in indirect discourse denotes time which is present relatively to the leading verb. See above, 22; 669, 2; 674, 1.

24. As the limits of such an action on either side of the
present moment are not defined, the present may express a
customary or *repeated* action or a *general truth*. *E.g.*

'Η πρύμνα τοῦ πλοίου ὃ εἰς Δῆλον 'Αθηναῖοι πέμπουσιν, *the
stern of the ship which the Athenians send to Delos* (*every year*). PLAT.
Phaed. 58 A. Τίκτει τοι κόρος ὕβριν, ὅταν κακῷ ὄλβος ἕπηται,
satiety begets insolence, whenever prosperity follows the wicked. THEOG.
153. 'Εν χρόνῳ ἀποφθίνει τὸ τάρβος ἀνθρώποισιν, *in time timidity
dies out in men.* AESCH. Ag. 857.

25. The present denotes merely the continuance or progress
of an action, without reference to its completion. It may, however, be implied by the context that the action is *not* to be
completed, so that the present denotes an *attempted* or *intended*
action. Especially δίδωμι, in the sense of *offer*, and πείθω, *try to
persuade*, are thus used. *E.g.*

Νῦν δ' ἅμα τ' αὐτίκα πολλὰ διδοῖ, *he offers many things.* Il. ix.
519. Πείθουσι ὑμᾶς ἐναντία καὶ τοῖς νόμοις καὶ τῷ δικαίῳ ψηφίσασθαι, *they are trying to persuade you to vote contrary both to the laws and
to justice.* ISAE. i. 26.

This *conative* signification is much more common in the imperfect.
See 36 and the examples.

26. The present is often used with expressions denoting past
time, especially πάλαι, in the sense of a perfect and a present
combined. *E.g.*

Κεῖνον ἰχνεύω πάλαι, *I have been tracking him a long time* (*and
still continue it*). SOPH. Aj. 20. Οὐ πάλαι σοι λέγω ὅτι ταὐτόν
φημι εἶναι; i.e. *have I not long ago told you* (*and do I not still repeat*)
that I call it the same thing? PLAT. Gorg. 489 C. Θεοὺς αἰτῶ . . .
φρουρᾶς ἐτείας μῆκος. AESCH. Ag. 1. So πολὺν χρόνον τοῦτο ποιῶ.
So in Latin, iam dudum loquor.

27. The presents ἥκω, *I am come*, and οἴχομαι, *I am gone*, are
used in the sense of the perfect. An approach to the perfect
sense is sometimes found in such presents as φεύγω, in the sense
I am banished, ἁλίσκομαι, *I am captured*, νικῶ and κρατῶ, *I am
victorious*, ἡττῶμαι, *I am conquered*, ἀδικῶ, *I have been unjust* (*I am
ἄδικος*). So the Epic ἵκω and ἱκάνω, with ὄλλυμαι and sometimes τίκτω in tragedy. *E.g.*

Οἴχεται εἰς ἅλα δῖαν, *he is gone to the divine sea.* Il. xv. 223.
Θεμιστοκλῆς ἥκω παρὰ σέ, *I, Themistocles, am come to you.* THUC. i.
137. Τοὺς ἀδίκως φεύγοντας δικαίως κατήγαγον, *they justly restored those who were unjustly banished.* PLAT. Menex. 242 B. 'Ιλίου
ἁλισκομένου, *after the capture of Ilium.* THUC. vi. 2. So ἁλισκομένου τοῦ τείχεος. HDT. i. 85. 'Οπισθε τῆς ἀνοιγομένης θύρης,
behind the open door. HDT. i. 9. Εἰ πάντα ταῦτα ἐλυμαίνετο τοῖς
ὅλοις, ἕως ἀνέτρεψε, τί Δημοσθένης ἀδικεῖ; *how is Demosthenes to*

blame? DEM. xviii. 303. Πύργων ὀλλυμένων ἐν ναυσὶν ἔβαν, *I embarked after the towers had been destroyed.* EUR. I. T. 1108. Ἥδε τίκτει σε, *this woman is thy mother.* Id. Ion. 1560.

Present participles are given in some examples here where they illustrate the meaning of the tense.

28. The Greek, like other languages, often uses such presents as *I hear, I learn, I say,* even when their action is finished before the time to which they strictly refer. *E.g.*

Εἰ στασιάζουσιν, ὥσπερ πυνθανόμεθα, *if they (the Sicilians) are in discord, as we learn.* THUC. vi. 16. Ἐπὶ πόλεις, ὡς ἐγὼ ἀκοῇ αἰσθάνομαι, μέλλομεν ἰέναι μεγάλας. Id. vi. 20.

(Εἶμι *as Future.*) **29.** The present εἶμι, *I am going,* and its compounds, have a future sense. Εἶμι thus became a future of ἔρχομαι, the future ἐλεύσομαι not being in good use in Attic prose. *E.g.*

Σεῦ ὕστερος εἶμ' ὑπὸ γαῖαν, *I shall go.* Il. xviii. 333. Εἶμι πάλιν ἐπ' ἐκεῖνα, *I shall recur to that.* PLAT. Phaed. 100 B. Ὦ φίλ', ἐγὼ μὲν ἄπειμι, σύας καὶ κεῖνα φυλάξων. Od. xvii. 593. Ἀλλ' εἴσειμι, σοῦ δ' οὐ φροντιῶ, *but I'll go in and not mind you.* AR. Nub. 125. Εἰ δ' οὗτοι ἀπίασιν, ἡμεῖς μόνοι μενοῦμεν, *but if they (shall) depart, we alone shall remain.* XEN. Cyr. iv. 5, 24.

In Homer εἶμι is used also as a present; as οἷος δ' ἀστὴρ εἶσι μετ' ἀστράσι, Il. xxii. 317. So ii. 87, xi. 415; Od. iv. 401; and often in similes. This is doubtful in Attic; as in πρόσειμι δῶμα καὶ βρέτας τὸ σόν, AESCH. Eum. 242, where πρόσειμι may be πρός + εἰμί. See Krüger and Classen on ἐπίασιν, THUC. iv. 61.

30. The future sense of εἶμι and its compounds extends to the optative, infinitive, and participle in indirect discourse, and often to the participle in other uses (especially when it expresses purpose with ὡς). *E.g.*

Προεῖπον ὅτι, εἰ μὴ παρεσόμεθα συστρατευσόμενοι, ἐκεῖνοι ἐφ' ἡμᾶς ἴοιεν, i.e. *that they would come against us.* XEN. Hell. v. 2, 13. See also v. 1, 34, where εἰ μὴ ἀπίοιεν corresponds to εἰ μὴ ἐκπέμψοιεν. As ἴοιμι in this use is equivalent to a future optative, it is naturally rare (128). Ἀπιέναι ἐνόμιζεν ὅταν βούληται, *he believed he could depart* (ἄπειμι) *whenever he pleased.* THUC. v. 7. So οὐκ ἔφασαν (ἔφη) ἰέναι, XEN. An. i. 3, 1 and 8; i. 4, 12: cf. ii. 1, 3, iii. 6, 10. Καὶ τὸ πῦρ γε αὖ προσιόντος τοῦ ψυχροῦ αὐτῷ ἢ ὑπεξιέναι ἢ ἀπολεῖσθαι. PLAT. Phaed. 103 D. (Προσιόντος is an ordinary present participle: see 31.) Οὐ γὰρ ᾔδειν ἐξιών, *for he did not know that he was to go.* AR. Pac. 1182. Ὁ δ' εἰς Πέρσας ἰὼν παρῆν συνεσκευασμένος. XEN. Cyr. iv. 5, 26. Ταῦτ' εἰπὼν ἀνιστάμην ὡς ἀπιών. PLAT. Prot. 335 C (this might come under 31). So ἀνεστήκη ὡς ἐξιών, ib. 335 D. Παρεσκευάζετο ὡς ἀπιοῦσα. XEN. Cyr. i. 3, 13. So THUC. vi. 63.

31. In the optative and infinitive not in indirect discourse, and often in the participle, the same forms of εἶμι are used as ordinary presents. *E.g*

Οὐδὲν ἂν διάφορον ποιοῖ, ἀλλ' ἐπὶ ταὐτὸν ἴοιεν. PLAT. Rep. 360 C. Εἰ πολέμιος ἴοι. Ib. 415 E. See ἴοι in Rep. 490 B, in a peculiar indirect quotation. Ὅτε ἴοι. Id. Tim. 78 C. In XEN. An. i. 3, 1, after ἰέναι as future (30), we have ἐβιάζετο ἰέναι and ἤρξατο προιέναι. Ἐξὸν αὐτῷ εἰσιόντι εἰς τὰς οἰκίας συγγίγνεσθαι ὅτῳ βούλοιτο. PLAT. Rep. 360 C. Ἀποτρεπόμενος ὁ ἀὴρ καὶ διὰ τοῦ σώματος ἔξω ἰών. Id. Tim. 79 C. So ANT. v. 78, vi. 45.

In the subjunctive and imperative there can of course be no special future sense in these verbs.

32. In animated language the present often refers to the future, to express *likelihood, intention*, or *danger*. *E g.*

Εἰ αὕτη ἡ πόλις ληφθήσεται, ἔχεται ἡ πᾶσα Σικελία, *if this city shall be captured, all Sicily is (at once) in their possession*. THUC. vi. 91. Μένομεν ἕως ἂν ἕκαστοι κατὰ πόλεις ληφθῶμεν ; *shall we wait until we are each captured, city by city?* Id. vi. 77. Εἰ δέ φησιν οὗτος, δειξάτω καὶ παρασχέσθω, κἀγὼ καταβαίνω, *and I will take my seat.* DEM. xix. 32. So ἀπόλλυμαι, *I am to perish*, LYS. xii. 14. For a similar use of the perfect, see 51. (See also 61.)

33. (*Historic Present*.) The present is often used in narration for the aorist, sometimes for the imperfect, to give a more animated statement of past events. This is called the historic present. *E.g.*

Βουλὴν ἐπιτεχνᾶται ὅπως μὴ ἁλισθεῖεν Ἀθηναῖοι, *he contrives a plan to prevent the Athenians from assembling.* HDT. i. 63. Κελεύει πέμψαι ἄνδρας· ἀποστέλλουσιν οὖν, καὶ περὶ αὐτῶν ὁ Θεμιστοκλῆς κρύφα πέμπει. THUC. i. 91. Δαρείου καὶ Παρυσάτιδος γίγνονται παῖδες δύο. XEN. AN. i. 1, 1. Τοιαῦτα τοῦ παρόντος ἡνίκ' ἡλίῳ δείκνυσι τοὔναρ ἔκλυον ἐξηγουμένου. SOPH. El. 424.

The historic present is not found in Homer.

IMPERFECT.

34. The imperfect represents an action as *going on* in past time ; as ἔγραφον, *I was writing*.

35. The imperfect is thus a present transferred to the past, retaining all the peculiarities of the present which are consistent with the change. Thus it may denote a customary or repeated action, or a series of actions ; or, if it refers to a single action (as it very frequently does), it represents it in its progress rather than as a simple past occurrence (like the aorist). In narration it dwells on the course of an event instead of merely stating its occurrence. *E.g.*

Ἐπὶ Κέκροπος ἡ Ἀττικὴ κατὰ πόλεις ᾠκεῖτο, καὶ οὐ ξυνῇεσαν βουλευσόμενοι, ἀλλ᾽ αὐτοὶ ἕκαστοι ἐπολιτεύοντο καὶ ἐβουλεύοντο. Ἐπειδὴ δὲ Θησεὺς ἐβασίλευσεν, ἐς τὴν νῦν πόλιν οὖσαν ξυνῴκισε πάντας. THUC. ii. 15. (Here the imperfects refer to the state of the country or to customs ; the aorists state events, ἐβασίλευσε, *became king*, ξυνῴκισε, *collected into one state*.) Καὶ παραστὰς ὁ μὲν ἔνθεν ὁ δ᾽ ἔνθεν, ἐβόων, ἐξέκρουόν με, τελευτῶντες ἐχλεύαζον· ὑμεῖς δ᾽ ἐγελᾶτε, καὶ οὔτ᾽ ἀκούειν ἠθέλετε οὔτε πιστεύειν ἐβούλεσθε, *they kept on shouting*, etc., *and you laughed*, etc. DEM. xix. 23. Ἐπειρώμην τι λέγειν τούτων ὧν εἰς τὴν βουλὴν ἀπήγγειλα. Ibid. Πότερον ταῦτα πάντα ποιῶν ἠδίκει καὶ παρεσπόνδει καὶ ἔλυε τὴν εἰρήνην ἢ οὔ; *in doing all these things was he acting unjustly and breaking the peace*, etc.? Id. xviii. 71 ; see also ib. 69. (Compare τὴν εἰρήνην ἔλυσε τὰ πλοῖα λαβών, of the event, ib. 73.) Παρελθὼν ἐπὶ Θρᾴκης Βυζαντίους ἠξίου συμπολεμεῖν. Ib. 87. Ὑμεῖς γὰρ ταῦτ᾽ ἐπράττετε, καὶ ταῦτα πᾶσιν ὑμῖν ἤρεσκεν (of a course of action). Id. xix. 189. Ἐπειδὴ γὰρ εἷλεν Ὄλυνθον Φίλιππος, Ὀλύμπια ἐποίει, εἰς δὲ τὴν θυσίαν πάντας τοὺς τεχνίτας συνήγαγεν. Ib. 192. Εἶτα τότ᾽ οὐκ ἔλεγες παραχρῆμα ταῦτα οὐδ᾽ ἐδίδασκες ἡμᾶς; *did you then not tell this at once on the spot, or instruct us?* Ib. 25.

The same action (as in the last two examples) could easily have been mentioned, without reference to its continuance, as a mere *event*. For the relations of the imperfect to the aorist, see 56.

36. The imperfect, like the present (25), sometimes denotes *attempted* action, being here strictly an *imperfect* tense. So especially ἐδίδουν and ἔπειθον. *E.g.*

(Φίλιππος) Ἀλόννησον ἐδίδου, *Philip offered Halonnesus* (lit. *tried to give it*). AESCHIN. iii. 83. Ἕκαστος ἔπειθεν αὐτὸν ὑποστῆναι τὴν ἀρχήν, *each one tried to persuade him to undertake the command*. XEN. An. vi. 1, 19.

Κῦμα ἵστατ᾽ ἀειρόμενον, κατὰ δ᾽ ᾕρεε Πηλείωνα, *and was about to overpower the son of Peleus*. Il. xxi. 327. Ἐμισθοῦτο παρ᾽ οὐκ ἐκδιδόντος τὴν αὐλήν, *he tried to hire the yard of one who refused to let it*. HDT. i. 68. Πέμψαντες ἐς Σάρδις χρυσὸν ὠνέοντο, *they sent to Sardis and wanted to buy gold*. HDT. i. 69. Ἐπεθύμησε τῆς χλανίδος, καὶ αὐτὴν προσελθὼν ὠνέετο, *he took a fancy* (aor.) *to the cloak, and tried to buy it*. HDT. iii. 139. Ἃ ἐπράσσετο οὐκ ἐγένετο, *what was attempted did not happen*. THUC. vi. 74. So προσετίθει, *she wanted to add*, AR. Nub. 63.

37. When the present has the force of the perfect (27), the imperfect has regularly the force of a pluperfect. *E.g.*

Ὁ ὄχλος κατὰ θέαν ἧκεν, *the crowd had come to look on*. THUC. vi. 31. Ἐπεὶ ᾤχεο νηὶ Πύλονδε, *after thou wast gone by ship to Pylos*. Od. xvi. 24.

38. The imperfect sometimes denotes *likelihood, intention,* or *danger* in past time (see 32). *E.g.*

Ἐπειδὴ τῷ ψεύδεσθαι ἀπώλλυτο, *when he was on the point of ruin through his deceit.* ANT. v. 37. Καὶ τἄμ᾽ ἔθνησκε τέκν᾽, ἀπωλλύμην δ᾽ ἐγώ, *and my children were about to die, and I was about to perish.* EUR. H. F. 538. Ἐκαινόμην ξίφει, *I was to be slain,* Id. I. T. 27.

39. The imperfect ἦν (generally with ἄρα) may express a *fact* which is just recognised as such by the speaker or writer, having previously been denied, overlooked, or not understood. *E.g.*

Ὦ πόποι, οὐκ ἄρα πάντα νοήμονες οὐδὲ δίκαιοι ἦσαν Φαιήκων ἡγήτορες ἠδὲ μέδοντες, i.e. *they are not, as I once imagined.* Od. xiii. 209. Οὐκ ἄρα μοῦνον ἔην ἐρίδων γένος, ἀλλ᾽ ἐπὶ γαῖαν εἰσὶ δύω, *there is not after all merely one race of discords, but there are two on earth.* HES. Op. 11. Ὅδ᾽ ἦν ἄρα ὁ ξυλλαβών με, *this is then the one who seized me.* SOPH. Ph. 978. Οὐ σὺ μόνος ἄρ᾽ ἦσθ᾽ ἔποψ; *are you not then the only epops (as I thought)?* AR. Av. 280. Ἆρ᾽ οὐ τόδε ἦν τὸ δένδρον, ἐφ᾽ ὅπερ ἦγες ἡμᾶς; *is not this then the tree to which you were bringing us?* PLAT. Phaedr. 230 A.

Other imperfects are rare ; as ἠπίστω, XEN. Hell. iii. 4, 9.

40. In like manner the imperfect may express something which is the result of a previous discussion, with reference to which the past form is used. This is sometimes called the *philosophic* imperfect. *E.g.*

Ἦν ἡ μουσικὴ ἀντίστροφος τῆς γυμναστικῆς, εἰ μέμνησαι, *music then (as we proved) corresponds, if you remember, to gymnastics.* PLAT. Rep. 522 A. Καὶ δίκαιον δὴ φήσομεν ἄνδρα εἶναι τῷ αὐτῷ τρόπῳ, ᾧπερ καὶ πόλις ἦν δικαία, *and now we shall say that a man is just in the same way in which also a state was (shown to be) just.* Ib. 441 D. Διαφθεροῦμεν ἐκεῖνο, ὃ τῷ μὲν δικαίῳ βέλτιον ἐγίγνετο, τῷ δὲ ἀδίκῳ ἀπώλλυτο, *we shall destroy that which (as we proved) becomes better by justice and is ruined by injustice.* PLAT. Crit. 47 D.

41. The Greek sometimes uses an idiom like the English *he was the one who did it* for *he is the one who did it;* as ἦν ὁ τὴν γνώμην ταύτην εἰπὼν Πείσανδρος, THUC. viii. 68 ; τίς ἦν ὁ βοηθήσας τοῖς Βυζαντίοις καὶ σώσας αὐτούς; DEM. xviii. 88.

PERFECT AND PLUPERFECT.

42. The perfect represents an action as already finished at the *present* time ; as γέγραφα, *I have written* (that is, *my writing is now finished*).

43. The pluperfect represents an action as already finished at a given *past* time ; as ἐγεγράφειν, *I had written* (that is, *my writing was finished at some specified past time*).

44. The perfect, although it implies the performance of the action in past time, yet states only that it *stands completed* at the *present* time. This explains why the perfect is classed with the present as a primary tense, that is, as a tense of *present* time.

45. The perfect and the pluperfect may be expressed by the perfect participle with the present and imperfect of εἰμί. Here, however, each part of the compound generally retains its own signification, so that this form expresses more fully the continuance of the *result* of the action of the perfect to the *present* time, and of that of the pluperfect to the *past* time referred to. *E.g.*

Πεποιηκώς ἐστιν (or ἦν), *he is* (or *was*) *in the condition of having done,—he has done* (or *had done*). Ἐμοῦ οἱ νόμοι οὐ μόνον ἀπεγνωκότες εἰσὶ μὴ ἀδικεῖν, ἀλλὰ καὶ κεκελευκότες ταύτην τὴν δίκην λαμβάνειν, *it is the laws which not only have acquitted me of injustice, but have commanded me to inflict this punishment*. LYS. i. 34. Ἐτόλμα λέγειν ὡς ἐγὼ τὸ πρᾶγμ᾽ εἰμὶ τοῦτο δεδρακώς, *he dared to say that I was the one who had done this deed*. DEM. xxi. 104. In DEM. xviii. 23, οὔτε γὰρ ἦν πρεσβεία πρὸς οὐδένα ἀπεσταλμένη τότε τῶν Ἑλλήνων means *for there was no embassy then out on a mission to any of the Greeks*; whereas ἀπέσταλτο would have given the meaning *no embassy had ever been sent out* (see 831).

This of course does not apply to cases where the compound form is the only one in use, as in the third person plural of the perfect and pluperfect passive and middle of mute and liquid verbs.

46. On the other hand, although the simple form very often implies the continuance of the result of the action down to the present time or to a specified past time, it does so less distinctly than the compound form, and *not necessarily* (see the last two examples below). *E.g.*

Ἐπιμελῶς οἱ θεοὶ ὧν οἱ ἄνθρωποι δέονται κατεσκευάκασιν, *the Gods have carefully provided what men need*. XEN. Mem. iv. 3, 3. Τῶν ποιητῶν τινες ὑποθήκας ὡς χρὴ ζῆν καταλελοίπασιν, *some of the poets have left us suggestions how to live*. ISOC. ii. 3. Ἀκήκοα μὲν τοὔνομα, μνημονεύω δ᾽ οὔ, *I have heard the name, but I do not remember it*. PLAT. Theaet. 144 B. Ἃ σοι τύχη κέχρηκε, ταῦτ᾽ ἀφείλετο, *Fortune has taken back what she has lent you*. MEN. Fr. 598.

47. Ἔχω with the aorist and sometimes the perfect participle may form a periphrastic perfect (831). In tragedy and in Herodotus this is often fully equivalent to our perfect with *have;* elsewhere, especially in Attic prose, the participle and ἔχω are more or less distinct in their force. Still, this is the beginning of the modern perfect. *E.g.*

Ποίῳ σὺν ἔργῳ τοῦτ᾽ ἀπειλήσας ἔχεις; *have you made this threat?* SOPH. O. C. 817. Τὸν μὲν προτίσας, τὸν δ᾽ ἀτιμάσας ἔχει; Id. Ant. 22 ; see ib. 32. Ἡμᾶς πρᾶγος ἄσκοπον ἔχει περάνας. Id. Aj. 21. Ηὐδᾶτο γὰρ ταῦτ᾽, οὐδέ πω λήξαντ᾽ ἔχει, i.e. *the story has not yet ceased to be told*. Id. O. T. 731; see Tr. 37, ταρβήσασ᾽ ἔχω. Ὃς σφε νῦν ἀτιμάσας ἔχει. EUR. Med. 33; see ib. 90. Ἄρεως τε

μοῖραν μεταλαβὼν ἔχει τινά. Id. Bacch. 302. Σὺ θαυμάσας ἔχω
τόδε. SOPH. Ph. 1362 ; so PLAT. Phaedr. 257 C (in poetic language).
Οἷά μοι βεβουλευκὼς ἔχει. SOPH. O. T. 701 (after στήσας ἔχεις
in 699). Ὅστις γ᾽ ἔχει μου ᾽ξαρπάσας τὸ παιδίον, whoever has
snatched away (though here ἔχει may mean keeps). AR. Th. 706.
Ἐγκλῄσασ᾽ ἔχει τὰ σιτία. Id. Eccl. 355. Ὑπὲρ τῶν Ἑλλήνων
τοὺς σὺ δουλώσας ἔχεις, i.e. whom you hold in slavery or whom you
have enslaved. HDT. i. 27. Ἀμφοτέρων με τούτων ἀποκλῃίσας
ἔχεις. Id. i. 37 ; so i. 41. Ἀλαζόνι ἐπιτρέψαντες ἡμέας αὐτοὺς
ἔχομεν, we have entrusted ourselves, etc. Id. vi. 12. Πολλὰ χρήματα
ἔχομεν ἀνηρπακότες. XEN. An. i. 3, 14 (here ἔχομεν expresses
possession). See THUC. i. 68 ; DEM. ix. 12, xxvii. 17.

The beginning of this usage appears in HES. Op. 42 :—

Κρύψαντες γὰρ ἔχουσι θεοὶ βίον ἀνθρώποισι.

48. Εἶχον or ἔσχον with the participle may form a periphrastic
pluperfect in the same way (47). *E.g.*

Ὃν γ᾽ εἶχον ἤδη χρόνιον ἐκβεβληκότες. SOPH. Ph. 600.
See HDT. i. 28, 73, and 75 ; XEN. An. iv. 7, 1.

49. (*a*) The perfect of many verbs has the signification of a
present, which may usually be explained by the peculiar meaning
of the verbs. Thus θνῄσκειν, *to die,* τεθνηκέναι, *to be dead ;* καλ-
εῖν, *to call,* κεκλῆσθαι, *to be called* or *named ;* γίγνεσθαι, *to become,*
γεγονέναι, *to be ;* μιμνῄσκειν, *to remind,* μεμνῆσθαι, *to remember ;*
εἰδέναι, *to know ;* ἱστάναι, *to place,* ἑστάναι, *to stand.* So βεβηκέναι,
to stand ; ἐγνωκέναι, *to know ;* ἠμφιέσθαι, *to wear ;* κεκτῆσθαι, *to
possess ;* πεποιθέναι, *to trust ;* πεφυκέναι, *to be* (*by nature*) ; etc.

(*b*) The pluperfect of such verbs has the signification of the
imperfect ; as οἶδα, *I know,* ᾔδειν, *I knew.*

50. In epistles, the perfect and aorist are sometimes used where we
might expect the present, the writer transferring himself to the time
of the reader. *E.g.*

Ἀπέσταλκά σοι τόνδε τὸν λόγον, *I send you this speech.* ISOC. i. 2.
Μετ᾽ Ἀρταβάζου, ὅν σοι ἔπεμψα, πρᾶσσε. THUC. i. 129. (Here
ὃν ἔπεμψα refers to the man who was to carry the letter.) So *scripsi*
and *misi* in Latin.

51. The perfect sometimes refers to the future, to denote certainty
or likelihood that an action will immediately take place, in a sense
similar to that of the present (32), but with more emphasis, as the
change in time is greater. *E.g.*

Ὥστ᾽ εἴ με τόξων ἐγκρατὴς αἰσθήσεται, ὄλωλα, *I shall perish at
once.* SOPH. Ph. 75. Κἂν τοῦτο νικῶμεν, πάνθ᾽ ἡμῖν πεποίηται.
XEN. An. i. 8, 12. So *perii* in Latin.

52. In a somewhat similar sense (51), the pluperfect may express
the immediate or sudden occurrence of a past action. This occurs
especially in Homer and Herodotus. *E.g.*

Οὐδ' ἀπίθησεν μύθῳ 'Αθηναίης· ἡ δ' Οὐλυμπόνδε βεβήκειν, and she was gone to Olympus. Il. i. 221. 'Η μὲν θαμβήσασα πάλιν οἰκόνδε βεβήκειν. Od. i. 360. Τὸν δ' ἔλιπε ψυχή, κατὰ δ' ὀφθαλμῶν κέχυτ' ἀχλύς. Il. v. 696. "Αλλοι δὲ ἡγεμόνας ἔχοντες ὡρμέατο ἐπὶ τὸ ἱρόν, i.e. they were on their way (at once). HDT. viii. 35 ; see ix. 61.

For the gnomic perfect, see 154 and 155.

AORIST.

53. The aorist indicative expresses the simple *occurrence* of an action in past time ; as ἔγραψα, *I wrote*.

54. This fundamental idea of *simple occurrence* remains the essential characteristic of the aorist through all the dependent moods, however indefinite they may be in regard to time. The *aorist* takes its name (ἀόριστος, *unlimited, unqualified*) from its thus denoting merely the occurrence of an action, without any of the limitations (ὅροι) as to *completion, continuance, repetition*, etc., which belong to other tenses. It corresponds to the ordinary preterite (e.g. *did, went, said*) in English, whereas the Greek imperfect corresponds generally to the forms *I was doing*, etc. Thus, ἐποίει τοῦτο is he was doing this or he did this habitually ; πεποίηκε τοῦτο is he has already done this ; ἐπεποιήκει τοῦτο is he had already (at some past time) done this ; but ἐποίησε τοῦτο is simply he did this, without qualification of any kind.

55. The aorist of verbs which denote a *state* or *condition* generally expresses the entrance into that state or condition. *E.g.* Βασιλεύω, I am king, ἐβασίλευσα, I became king ; ἄρχω, I hold office, ἦρξα, I took office ; πλουτῶ, ἐπλούτησα, I became rich. Τῇ ἀληθείᾳ συνῴκει καὶ οὐδέπω καὶ τήμερον ἀπολέλοιπεν· ἀλλὰ παρὰ ζῶντος Τιμοκράτους ἐκείνῳ συνῴκησε, she was his wife in good faith, and has not yet even to this day been divorced ; but she went to live with him from Timocrates while T. was still living. DEM. xxx. 33.

56. The aorist is distinguished from the imperfect by· expressing only the occurrence of an action or the entrance into a state or condition, while the imperfect properly represents an action or state as going on or as repeated. See the examples of the imperfect and aorist in 35, and compare συνῴκει and συνῴκησε in DEM. xxx. 33 (in 55). The aorist is therefore more common in rapid narration, the imperfect in detailed description. It must be remembered that the same event may be looked upon from different points of view by the same person ; thus in DEM. xviii. 71 and 73 (quoted in 35) ἔλυε τὴν εἰρήνην and τὴν εἰρήνην ἔλυσε refer to the same thing, once as an act in progress, and once as a fact accomplished. No amount of duration in an act, therefore, can make the aorist an improper form to express it, provided it is stated as a single past event viewed as a whole. Thus ἐβασί-λευϑε δέκα ἔτη (see HDT. ii. 157) means *he had a reign of ten years,* (which is viewed as a single past event), while ἐβασίλευε δέκα ἔτη might refer to the same reign in the sense *he was reigning during ten years.* The aorist may refer even to a series of repetitions ; but it takes them collectively as a whole, while the imperfect would take them separately as individuals. See DEM. xviii. 80, μετὰ ταῦτα δὲ τοὺς ἀποστόλους ἅπαντας ἀπέστειλα, *and afterwards I sent out all the naval armaments ;* and xviii. 60, ἃ μὲν πρὸ τοῦ πολιτεύεσθαι καὶ δημηγορεῖν ἐμὲ προὔλαβε καὶ κατέσχε Φίλιππος, *the (succession of) advantages which Philip secured during the period before I entered public life,* emphatically opposed (as a whole) to Philip's many failures after that time, which are mentioned in ἃ δὲ καὶ διεκωλύθη. If the orator had wished to dwell on the number of the advantages or failures, or on their duration, he could have used the imperfect. See the last example under 35.

57. Since the same event may thus be stated by the aorist or the imperfect according to the writer's point of view, it is natural that it should occasionally be a matter of indifference which form is used, especially when the action is of such a nature that it is not important to distinguish its duration from its occurrence. For example, this distinction can seldom be important in such expressions as *he said, he commanded ;* and we find ἔλεγον and ἐκέλευον in the historians where no idea of duration can have been in mind. See οἱ δ᾽ ἐκέλευόν τε ἐπιέναι, καὶ παρελθόντες οἱ Ἀθηναῖοι ἔλεγον τοιάδε, THUC. i. 72, followed, at the end of the speech in 79, by τοιαῦτα δὲ οἱ Ἀθηναῖοι εἶπον and Ἀρχίδαμος ἔλεξε τοιάδε. In such cases as the following (cited with others by Krüger) it was not important to the narrative whether the idea of duration was included in the expression or not : βάλλετο and βάλετο, Il. ii. 43 and 45 ; θῆκεν and τίθει, xxiii. 653 and 656 ; δῶκε and δίδου, vii. 303 and 305 ; ἔλιπεν and λεῖπε, ii. 106 and 107 ; compare also μίστυλλον with ἔπειραν, ὤπτησαν, and ἐρύσαντο, i. 465 and 466. In all these cases the fundamental distinction of the tenses, which was inherent in the form, remained ; only it happened that either of the two distinct forms expressed the meaning which was here needed equally well. It must not be thought, from these occasional examples, that the Greeks of any period were not fully alive to the distinction of the two tenses and could not use it with skill and nicety. But the Greeks, like other workmen, did not care to use their finest tools on every occasion ; and it is often necessary to remember this if we would avoid hair-splitting.

58. The aorist, expressing simply a past occurrence, is sometimes used where we should expect a perfect or pluperfect, the action being merely referred to the past without the more exact specification which these tenses would give. *E.g.*

Τῶν οἰκετῶν οὐδένα κατέλιπεν, ἀλλ᾽ ἅπαντα πέπρακεν, *he (has) left none of the servants, but has sold everything.* AESCHIN. i. 99. Ἐτράποντο ἐς τὸν Πάνορμον, ὅθενπερ ἀνηγάγοντο, *they turned towards Panormus, whence they (had) set sail.* THUC. ii. 92. Κῦρον δὲ μεταπέμπεται ἀπὸ τῆς ἀρχῆς ἧς αὐτὸν σατράπην ἐποίησεν, *from the dominion of which he (had once) made him satrap.* XEN. An. i. 1, 2.

59. The aorist is generally used with ἐπεί or ἐπειδή, *after that,* the aorist with the particle being equivalent to our pluperfect. So after ἕως and πρίν, *until. E.g.*

Ἐπειδὴ ἐτελεύτησε Δαρεῖος καὶ κατέστη Ἀρταξέρξης, *after Darius (had) died and Artaxerxes had become established.* XEN. An. i. 1, 3. Οὐ πρόσθεν ἐξενεγκεῖν ἐτόλμησαν πρὸς ἡμᾶς πόλεμον πρὶν τοὺς στρατηγοὺς ἡμῶν συνέλαβον, *they did not dare to bring war upon us until they (had) seized our generals.* Ib. iii. 2, 29. But the pluperfect may still be used after ἐπεί or ἐπειδή, to give additional emphasis to the doubly past action ; as in DEM. xviii. 42, ἐπειδὴ ἐξηπάτησθε μὲν ὑμεῖς, ἐξηπάτηντο δὲ οἱ Φωκεῖς καὶ ἀνῄρηντο αἱ πόλεις, τί ἐγένετο ;

So in Latin we have generally postquam *venit,* but occasionally postquam *venerat.*

60. The aorist is sometimes used colloquially by the poets (especially the dramatists), when a sudden action, which *is just taking place,* is spoken of as if it had already happened. *E.g.*

Ἐπῄνεσ᾽ ἔργον καὶ πρόνοιαν ἣν ἔθου, *I must approve your act,* etc. SOPH. Aj. 536. Ἥσθην ἀπειλαῖς, ἐγέλασα ψολοκομπίαις, *I am amused by your threats, I cannot help laughing,* etc. AR. Eq. 696.

61. The aorist sometimes refers vividly to the future, like the present (32) or perfect (51); as ἀπωλόμην εἴ με λείψεις, *I perish if you leave me.* EUR. Alc. 386 : so Med. 78. See also ὤλετο, Il. ix. 413 and 415.

62. In questions with τί οὐ, expressing surprise that something is not already done, and implying an exhortation to do it, the aorist is sometimes used strangely like a future. *E.g.*

Τί οὖν οὐ διηγήσω ἡμῖν τὴν ξυνουσίαν ; *why then don't you tell us about the meeting ?* PLAT. Prot. 310 A. Τί οὖν οὐ καὶ Πρόδικον καὶ Ἱππίαν ἐκαλέσαμεν ; *why then don't we call Prodicus and Hippias too ?* Ib. 317 D. So τί οὖν οὐ . . . ἐσκέψω ; Id. Soph. 251 E. See also SOPH. O. T. 1003.

For the gnomic aorist see 154.

FUTURE.

63. The future denotes that an action is to take place

in time to come; as γράψω, *I shall write* or *I shall be writing*, sometimes *I will write*; πείσεται, *he will suffer*, sometimes *he shall suffer*.

64. In indirect discourse and in all final constructions the future expresses time future relatively to the leading verb. See 22.

65. The future may represent an action in its duration, its mere occurrence, or its inception; as ἕξω, *I shall have*, or *I shall obtain;* τοῦτο δώσω, *I shall give this;* ἄρξω, *I shall rule*, or *I shall obtain power* (cf. 55). *E.g.*

Πραγματεύονται ὅπως ἄρξουσιν, *they take trouble to gain power.* XEN. Rep. Lac. xiv. 5. Ἆρ᾽ οὐ (διαιρετέον) οἵτινες ἄρξουσίν τε καὶ ἄρξονται; *must we not distinguish between those who are to rule and those who are to be ruled?* PLAT. Rep. 412 B. Πῇ στασιάσουσιν οἱ ἐπίκουροι καὶ οἱ ἄρχοντες; *how will they fall into faction?* Ib. 545 D (see below, ὅπως δὴ πρῶτον στάσις ἔμπεσε).

66. The future may be used in a *gnomic* sense, denoting that something will always happen when an occasion offers. *E.g.*

Ἀνὴρ ὁ φεύγων καὶ πάλιν μαχήσεται. MEN. Mon. 45. "*He that fights and runs away may turn and fight another day.*"

67. The future is sometimes used to express what will hereafter be proved or be recognised as a truth. Compare the use of the imperfect in 40. *E.g.*

Φιλόσοφος ἡμῖν ἔσται ὁ μέλλων καλὸς κἀγαθὸς ἔσεσθαι φύλαξ, *he will prove to be a philosopher.* PLAT. Rep. 376 C.

68. The future is sometimes used in questions of doubt, where the subjunctive is more common (287). *E.g.*

Τί δῆτα δρῶμεν; μητέρ᾽ ἢ φονεύσομεν; *what shall we do? shall we kill our mother?* EUR. El. 967: so Ion. 758. Ποῖ τρέψομαι; *whither shall I turn?* Id. Hipp. 1066. Εἶτ᾽ ἐγώ σου φείσομαι; AR. Ach. 312. Τί οὖν ποιήσομεν; πότερον εἰς τὴν πόλιν πάντας τούτους παραδεξόμεθα; *what then shall we do? Are we to receive all these into the state?* PLAT. Rep. 397 D.

69. The second person of the future may express a concession or permission; and it often expresses a command, like the imperative. *E.g.*

Πρὸς ταῦτα πράξεις οἷον ἂν θέλῃς, *you may act as you please.* SOPH. O. C. 956. Πάντως δὲ τοῦτο δράσεις, *but by all means do this.* AR. Nub. 1352. So in the common imprecations, ἀπολεῖσθε, οἰμώξεσθε, *may you perish*, etc. Χειρὶ δ᾽ οὐ ψαύσεις ποτέ. EUR. Med. 1320. Compare the Latin facies ut sciam, *let me know;* abibis, *depart.*

70. In a few instances the future indicative with μή expresses a prohibition, like the imperative or subjunctive with μή (259). *E.g.*

Ταύτην, ἄν μοι χρῆσθε συμβούλῳ, φυλάξετε τὴν πίστιν πρὸς

τοῦτον τὸν Θρᾷκα, καὶ μὴ βουλήσεσθε εἰδέναι, κ.τ.λ., *if you follow my advice, hold fast to this security* (69), *and do not wish to know*, etc. DEM. xxiii. 117. 'Εὰν δὲ εὖ φρονῆτε, καὶ νυνὶ τοῦτο φανερὸν ποιήσετε, καὶ μηδεμίαν αὐτοῖς ἄδειαν δώσετε. LYS. xxix. 13. Ξένον ἀδικήσεις μηδέποτε καιρὸν λαβών. MEN. Mon. 397. So probably οὐ σῖγα; μηδὲν τῶνδ' ἐρεῖς κατὰ πτόλιν, *silence ! say nothing of all this in the city.* AESCH. Sept. 250. (See 279.)

71. The future sometimes denotes a present intention, expectation, or necessity that something shall be done, in which sense the periphrastic form with μέλλω (73) is more common. *E.g.*

Τί διαφέρουσι τῶν ἐξ ἀνάγκης κακοπαθούντων, εἴ γε πεινήσουσι καὶ διψήσουσι καὶ ῥιγήσουσι καὶ ἀγρυπνήσουσι; *if they are to endure hunger and thirst*, etc. XEN. Mem. ii. 1, 17. (Here εἰ μέλλουσι πεινῆν καὶ διψῆν, etc., would be more common, as in the last example under 73.) Αἶρε πλῆκτρον, εἰ μαχεῖ, *raise your spur, if you are going to fight.* AR. Av. 759. The distinction between this and the ordinary future (63) is important in conditional sentences (see 407).

72. A still more emphatic reference to a present intention is found in the question τί λέξεις; *what do you mean to say ?* often found in tragedy; as ὤμοι, τί λέξεις; ἦ γὰρ ἐγγύς ἐστί που; EUR. Hec. 1124. So Hec. 511, 712 ; Hipp. 353 ; Ion. 1113 ; SOPH. Ph. 1233.

For the future in protasis, see 447 and 407 ; in relative clauses expressing a purpose, 565 ; with ἄν, 196 ; with οὐ μή, 294-301.

73. (Μέλλω *with the Infinitive.*) A periphrastic future is formed by μέλλω and the present or future (seldom the aorist) infinitive. This form sometimes denotes mere futurity, and sometimes intention, expectation, or necessity. *E.g.*

Μέλλει τοῦτο πράττειν (or πράξειν), *he is about to do this*, or *he intends to do this*. So in Latin, *facturus est* for *faciet.* Μέλλω ὑμᾶς διδάξειν ὅθεν μοι ἡ διαβολὴ γέγονε. PLAT. Ap. 21 B. Οὐκοῦν δεήσει τοῦ τοιούτου τινὸς ἀεὶ ἐπιστάτου, εἰ μέλλει ἡ πολιτεία σώζεσθαι; *if the constitution is to be preserved.* PLAT. Rep. 412 A. (See 71.)

74. Although the present and the future infinitive were preferred with μέλλω (73), the aorist was still used by some writers, as by Euripides. See AESCH. Prom. 625 (μέλλω παθεῖν); EUR. Ion. 80 (μέλλω τυχεῖν), 760 (θανεῖν μέλλω), El. 17 (μέλλοντα θανεῖν), Phoen. 300 (μέλλεις θιγεῖν) ;—where the metre allows no change.

75. The future infinitive with μέλλω forms the only regular exception to the general principle which restricts the use of the future infinitive to indirect discourse (see 86 ; 112).

76. The imperfect (seldom the aorist) of μέλλω with the infinitive expresses *past* intention, expectation, or necessity. *E.g.*

Κύκλωψ, οὐκ ἄρ᾽ ἔμελλες ἀνάλκιδος ἀνδρὸς ἑταίρους ἔδμεναι ἐν
σπῆϊ γλαφυρῷ, *so you were not after all to eat*, etc. (cf. 39). Od. ix.
475. See Il. ii. 36. Ἐμελλόν σ᾽ ἄρα κινήσειν ἐγώ, *I thought I
should start you off.* AR. Nub. 1301. Ἐπιστάτην λαβεῖν, ὃς ἔμελλεν
αὐτῷ καλῷ τε κἀγαθῷ ποιήσειν. PLAT. Ap. 20 A. Ἐμέλλησαν
ἐμβάλλειν. THUC. i. 134.

FUTURE PERFECT.

77. The future perfect denotes that an action will be
already finished at some future time.   It is thus a perfect
transferred to the future.   *E.g.*

Καί με ἐὰν ἐξελέγξῃς, οὐκ ἀχθεσθήσομαί σοι, ἀλλὰ μέγιστος
εὐεργέτης παρ᾽ ἐμοὶ ἀναγεγράψει, *you will have been enrolled as my
greatest benefactor.* PLAT. Gorg. 506 C.   Ἢν δὲ μὴ γένηται, μάτην ἐμοὶ
κεκλαύσεται, σὺ δ᾽ ἐγχανὼν τεθνήξεις, *I shall then have had my
whippings for nothing, and you will have died grinning.* AR. Nub. 1435.

78. The future perfect often denotes the continuance of an
action, or the permanence of its results, in future time.   *E.g.*

Δύναμιν, ἧς ἐς ἀίδιον τοῖς ἐπιγιγνομένοις μνήμη καταλελεί-
ψεται, *power, the memory of which will be left to our posterity for ever.*
THUC. ii. 64.   (Compare 105.)

79. The future perfect sometimes denotes certainty or likelihood that an action will *immediately* take place, which idea is
still more vividly expressed by the perfect (51).   *E.g.*

Εἰ δὲ παρελθὼν εἰς ὁστισοῦν δύναιτο διδάξαι, πᾶς ὁ παρὼν φόβος
λελύσεται, *all the present fear will be at once dispelled.* DEM. xiv. 2.
(Here the inferior Mss. have λέλυται, which would be like ὄλωλα,
quoted in 51.)   Φράζε, καὶ πεπράξεται, *speak, and it shall be no
sooner said than done.* AR. Plut. 1027.   Εὐθὺς Ἀριαῖος ἀφεστήξει,
ὥστε φίλος ἡμῖν οὐδεὶς λελείψεται. XEN. An. ii. 4, 5.

80. The future perfect can be expressed by the perfect
participle and ἔσομαι.   In the active voice this is the only form
in use, except in a few cases (chiefly ἑστήξω and τεθνήξω).   *E.g.*

Ἂν ταῦτ᾽ εἰδῶμεν, καὶ τὰ δέοντα ἐσόμεθα ἐγνωκότες καὶ
λόγων ματαίων ἀπηλλαγμένοι, *we shall have already resolved to do
our duty and shall have been freed from vain reports.* DEM. iv. 50.
(See 45 and 831.)

81. A similar circumlocution with the aorist participle and ἔσομαι
is sometimes found, especially in the poets.   *E.g.*

Οὐ σιωπήσας ἔσει; SOPH. O. T. 1146.   Λυπηθεὶς ἔσει. SOPH. O.
C. 816.   (See 47 and 831.)

82. When the perfect is used in the sense of a present (49), the

future perfect is its regular future ; as κεκλήσομαι, μεμνήσομαι, ἀφε-
στήξω, *I shall be named, I shall remember, I shall withdraw,* etc.

83. In many other verbs, the future perfect differs very slightly,
if at all, from an ordinary future. Thus πεπράσομαι is the regular
future passive of πιπράσκω. Still, where there is another future, the
future perfect is generally more emphatic.

84. It must be remembered that, in most cases in which the Latin
or the English would use a future perfect in a dependent clause, the
Greek uses an aorist or even a perfect subjunctive. (See 90 and 103,
with the examples.)

II. TENSES OF THE DEPENDENT MOODS.

85. The distinctions of time which mark the various tenses
in the indicative are retained when the optative and infinitive
represent the indicative in indirect discourse, and usually in the
participle. But in other constructions these distinctions of time
disappear in the dependent moods, and the tenses here differ
only in their other character of denoting the *continuance*, the
completion, or simply the *occurrence* of an action (20). The infinitive with ἄν is not included in this statement (see Chap. III.)

The tenses in these two uses must, therefore, be discussed
separately.

A. NOT IN INDIRECT DISCOURSE.

86. In the subjunctive and imperative, and also in the
optative and infinitive not in indirect discourse (666 ; 684),
the tenses chiefly used are the present and the aorist. The
perfect is used here only when the completion of the action
is to be emphasized (see 102-110). For the occasional
future, see 111-113 ; 130-132.

PRESENT AND AORIST.

87. The present and aorist here differ only in this, that
the present expresses an action in its *duration*, that is, as
going on or *repeated*, while the aorist expresses simply its
occurrence, the time of both tenses being otherwise precisely the same. *E.g.*

Ἐὰν ποιῇ τοῦτο, *if he shall be doing this,* or *if he shall do this*
(*habitually*) ; ἐὰν ποιήσῃ τοῦτο, (simply) *if he shall do this;* εἰ
ποιοίη τοῦτο, *if he should be doing this,* or *if he should do this (habitu-*

ally) ; εἰ ποιήσεις τοῦτο, *if he should do this;* ποίει τοῦτο, *do this* (*habitually*) ; ποίησον τοῦτο, *do this.*   Οὕτω νικήσαιμί τ᾽ ἐγὼ καὶ νομιζοίμην σοφός, *on this condition may I gain the victory* (aor.) *and be considered* (pres.) *wise.* AR. Nub. 520.   Βούλεται τοῦτο ποιεῖν, *he wishes to do this* (*habitually*) ; βούλεται τοῦτο ποιῆσαι, (simply) *he wishes to do this.*   For other examples see below.

This is a distinction entirely unknown to the Latin, which has (for example) only one form, *si faciat*, corresponding to εἰ ποιοίη and εἰ ποιήσειεν, and only *facere* to correspond to both ποιεῖν and ποιῆσαι (as used above).

88. It is sometimes difficult here, as in the corresponding case of the imperfect and the aorist indicative (56 ; 57), to see any decisive reason for preferring one tense to the other ; and it can hardly be doubted that the Greeks occasionally failed to make use of this, as well as of other fine distinctions, when either form would express the required sense equally well, although they always had the distinction ready for use when it was needed.   Compare the present and the aorist subjunctive and optative in the following examples :—

Ἐὰν γάρ τί σε φανῶ κακὸν πεποιηκώς, ὁμολογῶ ἀδικεῖν· ἐὰν μέντοι μηδὲν φαίνωμαι κακὸν πεποιηκὼς μηδὲ βουληθείς, οὐ καὶ σὺ ὁμολογήσεις μηδὲν ὑπ᾽ ἐμοῦ ἀδικεῖσθαι; *if I shall appear* (aor.) *to have done you any wrong,* and *if I shall appear* (pres.) *to have done you no wrong.* XEN. Cyr. v. 5, 13.   Εἰ μὲν γὰρ προσδέξαιτο Φωκέας συμμάχους . . . εἰ δὲ μὴ προσδέχοιτο, κ.τ.λ. DEM. xix. 318.   Εἴ τινες πολλῶν θανάτων ἦσαν αἴτιοι, (ἵνα) πάντων τούτων δεκαπλασίας ἀλγηδόνας ὑπὲρ ἑκάστου κομίσαιντο, καὶ αὖ εἴ τινες εὐεργεσίας εὐεργετηκότες εἶεν, (ἵνα) κατὰ ταὐτὰ τὴν ἀξίαν κομίζοιντο, *if any had caused many deaths, that they might receive* (aor.)· *suffering for all these, tenfold for each ; and again, if they had done kind services to any, that they might in like manner receive* (pres.) *their due reward.* PLAT. Rep. 615 B.   In the last example, it is obvious that the change from κομίσαιντο to κομίζοιντο is connected with the change from εἰ ἦσαν to εἰ εὐεργετηκότες εἶεν ; but it is questionable whether the latter change is the cause or the effect, and it is also quite as hard to see the reason for this change in the protasis, when both conditions are equally general, as for that in the final clause.   Probably no two scholars would agree in the reasons which they might assign for the use of the tenses in these examples.   It is certain, however, that either present or aorist would express the meaning equally well in all these cases.

Subjunctive and Imperative.

89. The present and aorist subjunctive and imperative are always future, except that in general conditions (462 ; 532) the subjunctive is general in its time.   In all final constructions the subjunctive is future relatively to the leading verb. The following examples will show the distinction of the two tenses :—

Πειθώμεθα πάντες· φεύγωμεν σὺν νηυσὶ φίλην ἐς πατρίδα γαῖαν, let us all be persuaded; let us fly, etc. Il. ii. 139. Τί φῶ; τί δρῶ; what shall I say? what shall I do? Πῶς οὖν περὶ τούτων ποιῶμεν; how then shall we act about this? PLAT. Phil. 63 A.

Ἀναλογισώμεθα τὰ ὡμολογημένα ἡμῖν, let us enumerate the points which have been conceded by us. PLAT. Prot. 332 D. Μηδὲν φοβηθῇς, fear not. But μηδὲν φοβοῦ, be not timid. Τί ποιήσω; what shall I do (in this case)? But τί ποιῶ; what shall I do (generally)? Οὐ μὴ τοῦτο εἴπῃς, you shall not say this. Οὐ μὴ γένηται, it will not happen. So in the Homeric οὐδὲ ἴδωμαι, nor shall I ever see (6).

Ἂν δέ τις ἀνθιστῆται, πειρασόμεθα χειροῦσθαι, but if any one shall stand opposed to us, we will try to subdue him. XEN. An. vii. 3, 11. Κἂν πόλεμος ᾖ, ἕως ἂν ἐπ᾽ ἄλλον ἔχωμεν στρατεύεσθαι, σοῦ τε καὶ τῶν σῶν ἀφεξόμεθα, and if there shall be war, so long as we shall be able, etc. XEN. Hell. iv. 1, 38. Ἀλλ᾽ ᾗ ἂν γιγνώσκω βέλτιστα ἐρῶ, but I will speak as I shall think best. THUC. vi. 9. Οὓς ἂν βούλῃ ποιήσασθαι φίλους, ἀγαθόν τι λέγε περὶ αὐτῶν πρὸς τοὺς ἀπαγγέλλοντας, whomsoever you shall wish, etc. ISOC. i. 33. Ἅπας λόγος, ἂν ἀπῇ τὰ πράγματα, μάταιόν τι φαίνεται καὶ κενόν, all speech, if (wherever) deeds are wanting, appears vain and empty. DEM. ii. 12. Συμμαχεῖν τούτοις ἐθέλουσιν ἅπαντες, οὓς ἂν ὁρῶσι παρεσκευασμένους, all are willing to be allied to those whom they see prepared. DEM. iv. 6.

Ὡς ἂν εἴπω πειθώμεθα, let us obey as I shall direct. Il. ix. 704. Ἢν ἐγγὺς ἔλθῃ θάνατος, οὐδεὶς βούλεται θνήσκειν, if death comes near (the moment that death comes near), no one wants to die. EUR. Alc. 671. Ἢν τὴν εἰρήνην ποιησώμεθα, μετὰ πολλῆς ἀσφαλείας τὴν πόλιν οἰκήσομεν, if we (shall) make the peace, etc. ISOC. viii. 20. Ὃν μὲν ἂν ἴδῃ ἀγνῶτα (sc. ὁ κύων), χαλεπαίνει· ὃν δ᾽ ἂν γνώριμον (sc. ἴδῃ); ἀσπάζεται, i.e. whomsoever the dog sees (at any time). PLAT. Rep. 376 A.

Δοκεῖ μοι κατακαῦσαι τὰς ἁμάξας, ἵνα μὴ τὰ ζεύγη ἡμῶν στρατηγῇ, ἀλλὰ πορευώμεθα ὅπῃ ἂν τῇ στρατιᾷ συμφέρῃ, it seems good to me to burn the wagons, that our beasts of burden may not be our generals, and that we may go on whithersoever it may be best for the army. XEN. An. iii. 2, 27. Καὶ γὰρ βασιλεὺς αἱρεῖται, οὐχ ἵνα ἑαυτοῦ καλῶς ἐπιμελῆται, ἀλλ᾽ ἵνα καὶ οἱ ἑλόμενοι δι᾽ αὐτὸν εὖ πράττωσι. XEN. Mem. iii. 2, 3.

Δέδοικα μὴ ἐπιλαθώμεθα τῆς οἴκαδε ὁδοῦ, I fear lest we may forget the road home. XEN. An. iii. 2, 25. Διανοεῖται αὐτὴν λῦσαι, ὡς μὴ διαβῆτε ἀλλ᾽ ἀποληφθῆτε, i.e. he intends to destroy the bridge, that you may not pass over but be caught. Ib. ii. 4, 17.

Φεῦγε, begone; χαιρόντων, let them rejoice; μὴ νομίζετε, do not believe. Εἰπέ μοι, tell me; δότε μοι τοῦτο, give me this. Σφενδόνην τίς μοι δότω, let some one give me a sling. AR. Av. 1187.

90. When the aorist subjunctive depends on ἐπειδάν (or ἐπάν, ἐπήν), *after that*, it is referred by this meaning of the particle to time *preceding* the action of the leading verb, so that ἐπειδὰν τοῦτο ἴδω, ἥξω means *after I (shall) have seen this, I will come;* and ἐπειδὰν τοῦτο ἴδω, ἀπέρχομαι, *after I have seen this, I (always) depart.* In such cases it may be translated by our future perfect when the leading verb is future, and by our perfect when the leading verb denotes a general truth and is translated by the present. As the subjunctive here can never depend upon a verb of simply *present* time, it can never refer to time absolutely *past;* and we use the perfect indicative in translating such an aorist after a verb expressing a general truth, merely because we use the present in translating the leading verb, although this is properly not present but general in its time.

In like manner, after ἕως, πρίν, and other particles signifying *until, before that,* and even after the relative pronoun or ἐάν, the aorist subjunctive may be translated by our future perfect or perfect, when the context shows that it refers to time preceding that of the leading verb. *E.g.*

Χρὴ δέ, ὅταν μὲν τιθῆσθε τοὺς νόμους, ὁποῖοί τινές εἰσι σκοπεῖν, ἐπειδὰν δὲ θῆσθε, φυλάττειν καὶ χρῆσθαι, *while you are enacting laws, you must look to see of what kind they are; but after you have enacted them, you must guard and use them.* DEM. xxi. 34. (Here the present τιθῆσθε with ὅταν, *while,* refers to an action continuing through the time of the leading verb; but θῆσθε with ἐπειδάν, *after that,* refers to time *past* relatively to the leading verb.)   Ταῦτα, ἐπειδὰν περὶ τοῦ γένους εἴπω, τότε, ἂν βούλησθε ἀκούειν, ἐρῶ, *when I shall have spoken about my birth, then, if you desire to hear, I will speak of these things.* DEM. lvii. 16. (Here the aorist εἴπω, though absolutely future, denotes time *past* with reference to ἐρῶ.)   Ἐπειδὰν διαπράξωμαι ἃ δέομαι, ἥξω, *when I shall have accomplished what I desire, I will come.* XEN. An. ii. 3, 29.   Ἐπειδὰν δὲ κρύψωσι γῇ, ἀνὴρ ἡρημένος ὑπὸ τῆς πόλεως λέγει ἐπ᾽ αὐτοῖς ἔπαινον τὸν πρέποντα, *when they have covered them with earth,* etc. THUC. ii. 34.   Ἕως ἂν σῴζηται τὸ σκάφος, τότε χρὴ προθύμους εἶναι· ἐπειδὰν δὲ ἡ θάλαττα ὑπέρσχῃ, μάταιος ἡ σπουδή, *as long as the vessel remains in safety* (present); *but the moment that the sea has overwhelmed it* (aorist). DEM. ix. 69.   Ἕως ἂν ἐκμάθῃς, ἔχ᾽ ἐλπίδα, *until you have learnt fully, have hope.* SOPH. O. T. 834. Μία δὲ κλίνη κενὴ φέρεται τῶν ἀφανῶν, οἳ ἂν μὴ εὑρεθῶσιν ἐς ἀναίρεσιν, *and one bier is always carried empty, in honour of the missing, whose bodies are not (have not been) found.* THUC. ii. 34.   Διανοεῖται, ἃ ἂν ἄλλοι τῇ ἀρετῇ καταπράξωσι, τούτων ἰσομοιρεῖν; i.e. *he thinks of having an equal share in those things which others by their valour have acquired?* XEN. Cyr. ii. 3, 5.   Πάνθ᾽ ὅσ᾽ ἂν ἐκ πολέμου γιγνομένης εἰρήνης προεθῇ, ταῦτα τοῖς ἀμελήσασιν ἀπόλλυται, *all things which are (or have been) abandoned when peace is made are always lost to those who abandoned them.* DEM. xix. 151. Ἦν δ' ἄρα καί του πείρᾳ σφαλῶσιν, ἀντελπίσαντες ἄλλα ἐπλήρωσαν τὴν χρείαν, *if they have been disappointed in anything, they always supply the deficiency,* etc. (154 and 171). THUC. i. 70. Οὐχὶ παύσομαι, πρὶν ἄν σε τῶν σῶν κύριον στήσω τέκνων, *I will not cease before I have (shall have) made you master of your children.* SOPH. O. C. 1040. Μὴ στέναζε πρὶν μάθῃς, *do not groan until you have heard.* SOPH. Ph. 917.

91. This use of the aorist subjunctive (90) sometimes seems to approach very near to that of the perfect subjunctive (103); and we often translate both by the same tense. But in the perfect, the idea of an action *completed* at the time referred to is expressed by the *tense* of the verb, without aid from any particle or from the context; in the aorist, the idea of relative past time can come *only* from the particle or the context. (See 103 with examples, and 104.) The Greek often uses the less precise aorist subjunctive and optative (see 95) where the perfect would be preferred but for its cumbrous forms; and we sometimes give the aorist more precision than really belongs to it in itself by translating it as a perfect or future perfect. (See the last six examples under 90.) The following example illustrates the distinction between the perfect and aorist subjunctive :—

Ὃν μὲν ἂν ἴδῃ ἀγνῶτα (ὁ κύων), χαλεπαίνει· ὃν δ' ἂν γνώριμον (ἴδῃ), ἀσπάζεται, κἂν μηδὲν πώποτε ὑπ' αὐτοῦ ἀγαθὸν πεπόνθῃ, *whomsoever he sees whom he knows, he fawns upon, even if he has hitherto received no kindness from him.* PLAT. Rep. 376 A. Compare this with ἐὰν ἀγαθόν τι πάθῃ ὑπό τινος, ἀσπάζεται, *if he ever happens to receive any kindness from any one, he always fawns upon him;* and ἐπειδὰν ἀγαθόν τι πάθῃ, ἀσπάζεται, *after he has received any kindness, he always fawns upon him.*

92. The present subjunctive with μή or ὅπως μή after verbs of *fearing,* though it generally refers to a future object of fear, may also denote what may hereafter *prove to be* an object of fear. *E.g.*

Δέδοικα μὴ ἀληθὲς ᾖ, *I fear it may prove true.* DEM. ix. 1. Δεινῶς ἀθυμῶ, μὴ βλέπων ὁ μάντις ᾖ, *lest the prophet may prove to have his sight* (cf. the following δείξεις δὲ μᾶλλον). SOPH. O. T. 747 ; so Ant. 1114. Ὅρα μὴ περὶ τοῖς φιλτάτοις κυβεύῃς, *beware lest it may prove that you are staking what is dearest.* PLAT. Prot. 314 A. Ὅρα ὅπως μὴ παρὰ δόξαν ὁμολογῇς. Id. Crit. 49 C. In all these cases the present indicative would be required if the object of fear were really present (369, 1).

Compare the examples of the perfect subjunctive in 103.

93. In a few passages of Homer the aorist subjunctive with μή seems to express a similar fear that something may prove to have already happened ; as δείδοικα μή σε παρείπῃ, *I fear it may prove that she persuaded you,* Il. i. 555. So Il. x. 98, μὴ κοιμήσωνται ἀτὰρ λάθωνται, and x. 538, δείδοικα μή τι πάθωσι, *I fear lest it may prove that they have met some harm.* The reference to the past here cannot come from any past force of the aorist subjunctive itself, but is probably an inference drawn from the context. As the later language would use a perfect subjunctive in such cases, these aorists seem to be instances of an earlier laxity of usage, like the use of ἀπόλοιτό κε for both *would have perished* and *would perish* (440).

In Il. x. 537 there is a similar case of the aorist optative in a wish: αἲ γὰρ δὴ ὧδ' ἄφαρ ἐκ Τρώων ἐλασαίατο μώνυχας ἵππους, i.e. *may it prove that they have driven the horses away from the Trojans* (95).

Optative.

94. The present and aorist optative in independent sentences (in wishes and with ἄν), and in all conditional sentences except past general conditions (462; 532), express future time, the relation of which to the future expressed by other moods is explained in 12, 13, and 16. (Some Homeric present or past unreal conditions and present wishes are exceptions: see 438-441.) In all final constructions the optative (which is used only after past tenses) represents the subjunctive after primary tenses, and is future relatively to the leading verb. *E.g.*

Εἴθε τοῦτο εἴη (utinam sit), *O that this may be.* Εἴθε μὴ ταῦτα πάσχοιεν, *may they not suffer these things* (with a view to the progress of their suffering). But εἴθε μὴ ταῦτα πάθοιεν, *may they not suffer these things* (viewed collectively). Εἴθε σὺ τοιοῦτος ὢν φίλος ἡμῖν γένοιο, *may you become a friend to us.* XEN. Hell. iv. 1, 38. Μὴ γένοιτο, *may it not happen.* See examples of the optative with ἄν below.

Οὐ γὰρ ἂν ἐπαινοίη με, εἰ ἐξελαύνοιμι τοὺς εὐεργέτας, *for he would not praise me, if I should banish my benefactors.* XEN. An. vii. 7, 11. Εἴης φορητὸς οὐκ ἄν, εἰ πράσσοις καλῶς, *you would not be endurable, if you should be in prosperity* (at any time). AESCH. Prom. 979. Πῶς γὰρ ἄν τις, ἅ γε μὴ ἐπίσταιτο, ταῦτα σοφὸς εἴη; *for how could any one be wise in that which he did not understand* (i.e. εἴ τινα μὴ ἐπίσταιτο)? XEN. Mem. iv. 6, 7. Ἀλλ' εἴ τι μὴ φέροιμεν, ὤτρυνεν φέρειν, *but if we neglected to bring anything, he always exhorted us to bring it.* EUR. Alc. 755. Οὐκ ἀπελείπετο ἔτι αὐτοῦ, εἰ μή τι ἀναγκαῖον εἴη, *he never left him, unless there was some necessity for it.* XEN. Mem. iv. 2, 40.

Εἰ ἔλθοι, πάντ' ἂν ἴδοι, *if he should go, he would see all.* Εἰ ἔλθοι, πάνθ' ἑώρα, *if ever* (whenever) *he went, he* (always) *saw all.* Οὐδ' εἰ πάντες ἔλθοιεν Πέρσαι, πλήθει γε οὐχ ὑπερβαλοίμεθ' ἂν τοὺς πολεμίους, *not even if all the Persians should come, should we surpass the enemy in numbers.* XEN. Cyr. ii. 1, 8. Ὅτε ἔξω τοῦ δεινοῦ γένοιντο καὶ ἐξείη πρὸς ἄλλους ἄρχοντας ἀπιέναι, πολλοὶ αὐτὸν ἀπέλειπον, *but when they were come out of danger and it was in their power* (present) *to go to other commanders,* (in all such cases) *many left him.* Id. An. ii. 6, 12. Ἄνευ γὰρ ἀρχόντων οὐδὲν ἂν οὔτε καλὸν οὔτε ἀγαθὸν γένοιτο, *nothing could be done,* etc. Ib. iii. 1, 38. Οὐκ οἶδα ὅ τι ἄν τις χρήσαιτο αὐτοῖς, *I do not know what use any one could make of them.* Ib. iii. 1, 40.

Τούτου ἐπεθύμει, ἵνα εὖ πράττοι, *he desired this in order that he might be in prosperity.* Ἐφοβεῖτο μὴ τοῦτο ποιοῖεν, *he feared lest they should do this (habitually).* Δῆλος ἦν ἐπιθυμῶν ἄρχειν, ὅπως πλείω λαμβάνοι, ἐπιθυμῶν δὲ τιμᾶσθαι, ἵνα πλείω κερδαίνοι· φίλος τε ἐβούλετο εἶναι τοῖς μέγιστα δυναμένοις, ἵνα ἀδικῶν μὴ διδοίη δίκην. XEN. An. ii. 6, 21. (Here the aorist optative would have referred to *single acts* of *receiving, getting gain,* and *suffering punishment,* while the present refers to a *succession* of cases, and to a whole course of conduct.)

Ἦν ὁ Φίλιππος ἐν φόβῳ μὴ ἐκφύγοι τὰ πράγματ' αὐτόν, *Philip was in fear lest the control of affairs might escape him.* DEM. xviii. 33.

95. The aorist optative with ἐπειδή or ἐπεί, *after that,* is referred by the meaning of the particle to time preceding that of the leading verb, like the aorist subjunctive in 90 ; so that ἐπειδὴ ἴδοι ἀπῄει means *after he had seen he (always) went away.* This gives the aorist in translation the force of a pluperfect. So after words meaning *until,* and in the other cases mentioned in 90. *E.g.*

Οὓς μὲν ἴδοι εὐτάκτως ἰόντας, τίνες τε εἶεν ἠρώτα, καὶ ἐπεὶ πύθοιτο ἐπῄνει, *he asked any whom he saw marching in good order, who they were; and after he had ascertained, he praised them.* XEN. Cyr. v. 3, 55. Περιεμένομεν ἑκάστοτε ἕως ἀνοιχθείη τὸ δεσμωτήριον· ἐπειδὴ δὲ ἀνοιχθείη, εἰσῇειμεν παρὰ τὸν Σωκράτη, *we waited each morning until the prison was opened (or had been opened); and after it was opened, we went in to Socrates.* PLAT. Phaed. 59 D. In PLAT. Rep. 331 C, εἴ τις λάβοι παρὰ φίλου ἀνδρὸς σωφρονοῦντος ὅπλα, εἰ μανεὶς ἀπαιτοῖ, is thus given by Cicero (Offic. iii. 95): Si gladium quis apud te sanae mentis *deposuerit, repetat* insaniens; and there can be no doubt that εἰληφὼς εἴη (the equivalent of *deposuerit*) would have been more exact than λάβοι in Greek (see 91). For a peculiar aorist optative in Il. x. 537, see above (93, end).

Infinitive.

96. A present or aorist infinitive (without ἄν) not in indirect discourse is still a verbal noun so far that it expresses no time except such as is implied in the context. Thus, when it depends on a verb of *wishing* or *commanding* or any other verb whose natural object is a future action, or when it expresses purpose, it is future without regard to its tense; as, in βούλομαι νικᾶν (or νικῆσαι), *I wish to be victorious* (or *to gain victory*), the infinitive expresses time only so far as the noun νίκην would in βούλομαι νίκην. Likewise, when the present or aorist infinitive (without ἄν) has the article, except in the rare cases in which it stands in indirect discourse (794), it has no reference to time in itself; as in τὸ γνῶναι ἐπιστήμην λαβεῖν ἐστιν, *to learn is to obtain knowledge*, where γνῶναι expresses time only as the noun γνῶσις would in its place. *E.g.*

Ἔξεστι μένειν, *it is possible to remain.* Ἐξέσται τοῦτο ποιεῖν, *it will be possible to do this.* Δέομαι ὑμῶν μένειν, *I beg you to remain.* Τί τὸ κωλῦον ἔτ᾽ αὐτὸν ἔσται βαδίζειν ὅποι βούλεται, *what will there be to prevent him from going whither he pleases ?* DEM. i. 12. Ἐκέλευσα αὐτὸν τοῦτο ποιεῖν, *I commanded him to do this.* Ἐβούλετο σοφὸς εἶναι, *he wished to be wise.* Δεινός ἐστι λέγειν, *he is skilled in speaking.* Ὥρα βαδίζειν, *it is time to be going.* Πᾶν ποιοῦσιν ὥστε δίκην μὴ διδόναι, *they do everything so as to avoid being punished.* PLAT. Gorg. 479 C. Τὸ μὲν οὖν ἐπιτιμᾶν ἴσως φήσαι τις ἂν ῥᾴδιον εἶναι, τὸ δ᾽ ὅ τι δεῖ πράττειν ἀποφαίνεσθαι, τοῦτ᾽ εἶναι συμβούλου, *some one may say that finding fault is easy, but that showing what ought to be done is the duty of an adviser.* DEM. i. 16. (Ἐπιτιμᾶν, ἀποφαίνεσθαι, and πράττειν belong here ; but εἶναι in both cases is in indirect discourse, 117.) Οὐ πλεονεξίας ἕνεκεν ταῦτ᾽ ἔπραξεν, ἀλλὰ τῷ δικαιότερα τοὺς Θηβαίους ἢ ὑμᾶς ἀξιοῦν, *he did this not from love of gain, but because of the Thebans making juster demands than you.* Id. vi. 13. Ἐτειχίσθη δὲ Ἀταλάντη νῆσος, τοῦ μὴ λῃστὰς κακουργεῖν τὴν Εὔβοιαν, *in order to prevent pirates from ravaging Euboea.* THUC. ii. 32.

Πόλεώς ἐστι θάνατος ἀνάστατον γενέσθαι, *it is death for a city to be laid waste.* LYCURG. 61. Ὥσπερ τῶν ἀνδρῶν τοῖς καλοῖς κἀγαθοῖς αἱρετώτερόν ἐστι καλῶς ἀποθανεῖν ἢ ζῆν αἰσχρῶς, οὕτω καὶ τῶν πόλεων ταῖς ὑπερεχούσαις λυσιτελεῖν (ἡγοῦντο) ἐξ ἀνθρώπων ἀφανισθῆναι μᾶλλον ἢ δούλαις ὀφθῆναι γενομέναις, *as it is preferable for honourable men to die* (aor.) *nobly rather than to continue living* (pres.) *in disgrace, so also they thought that it was better* (pres.) *for the pre-eminent among states to be (at once) made to disappear* (aor.) *from among men, than to be (once) seen* (aor.) *to fall into slavery.* ISOC. iv. 95. Πέμπουσιν ἐς τὴν Κέρκυραν πρέσβεις, δεόμενοι μὴ σφᾶς περιορᾶν φθειρομένους, ἀλλὰ τούς τε φεύγοντας ξυναλλάξαι σφίσι καὶ τὸν τῶν βαρβάρων πόλεμον καταλῦσαι, *asking them not to allow them to be destroyed, but to bring their exiles to terms with them, and to put an end to the barbarians' war.* THUC. i. 24. Τὸ γὰρ γνῶναι ἐπιστήμην που λαβεῖν ἐστιν, *to learn is to obtain knowledge.* PLAT. Theaet. 209 E. Πάντες τὸ καταλιπεῖν αὐτὰ πάντων μάλιστα φεύγομεν, *we all try most of all to avoid leaving them behind.* XEN. Mem. ii. 2, 3. Οὐ γὰρ τὸ μὴ λαβεῖν τἀγαθὰ οὕτω γε χαλεπὸν ὥσπερ τὸ λαβόντα στερηθῆναι λυπηρόν. Id. Cyr. vii. 5, 82. Τοῦ πιεῖν ἐπιθυμία, *the desire of obtaining drink.* THUC. vii. 84. Κελεύει αὐτὸν ἐλθεῖν, *he commands him to go.* Ἐκέλευσεν αὐτὸν ἐλθεῖν, *he commanded him to go.* Κελεύσει αὐτὸν ἐλθεῖν, *he will command him to go.* Πρὸς τῷ μηδὲν ἐκ τῆς πρεσβείας λαβεῖν, τοὺς αἰχμαλώτους ἐλύσατο, *besides receiving nothing from the embassy, he ransomed the captives.* DEM. xix. 229. Ει πρὸ τοῦ τοὺς Φωκέας ἀπολέσθαι ψηφίσαισθε βοηθεῖν, *if before the destruction of the Phocians you should vote to go to their assistance.* Id. xviii. 33. Τὰς αἰτίας προύγραψα, τοῦ μή τινα ζητῆσαί ποτε ἐξ ὅτου τοσοῦτος πόλεμος κατέστη, *that no one may ever ask the reason why,* etc. THUC. i. 23. Τὸν ὑπὲρ τοῦ μὴ γενέσθαι ταῦτ᾽ ἀγῶνα, *the contest to prevent these from being done.* DEM. xviii. 201.

No account is here taken of the infinitive with ἄν (204).

97. The distinction between the present and aorist infinitive is well illustrated by Aristotle, when he says of pleasure, Eth. x. 3, 4, ἡσθῆναι μὲν γὰρ ἔστι ταχέως ὥσπερ ὀργισθῆναι, ἥδεσθαι δ᾽ οὔ, οὐδὲ πρὸς ἕτερον· βαδίζειν, δὲ καὶ αὔξεσθαι καὶ πάντα τὰ τοιαῦτα. μεταβάλλειν μὲν οὖν εἰς τὴν ἡδονὴν ταχέως καὶ βραδέως ἔστιν, ἐνεργεῖν δὲ κατ᾽ αἰτὴν οὐκ ἔστι ταχέως, λέγω δ᾽ ἥδεσθαι. *We may* BECOME *pleased* (ἡσθῆναι) *quickly, as we may get angry quickly; but we cannot* BE *pleased* (ἥδεσθαι) *quickly, even as compared with another person, although we can thus walk and grow and do such things. We may then change into a state of pleasure quickly or slowly, but we cannot actually enjoy the pleasure, I mean* BE PLEASED (ἥδεσθαι), *quickly.*

So in PLAT. Theaet. 155 C, Socrates says, ἄνευ τοῦ γίγνεσθαι γενέσθαι ἀδύνατον (sc. ἐμὲ ἐλάττω), i.e. *without going through the process of becoming* (γίγνεσθαι) *smaller, it is impossible for me to get* (γενέσθαι) *smaller.*

98. Χράω, ἀναιρέω, θεσπίζω, and other verbs signifying *to give an oracular response,* generally take the present or the aorist infinitive, expressing the command or warning of the oracle, where we might expect the future in indirect discourse (135). These verbs here take the ordinary construction of verbs of *commanding, advising,* and *warning.* E.g.

Λέγεται δὲ ᾽Αλκμαίωνι τὸν ᾽Απόλλω ταύτην τὴν γῆν χρῆσαι οἰκεῖν, *it is said that Apollo gave a response to Alcmaeon that he should inhabit this land* (warned him to inhabit it). THUC. ii. 102. Χρωμένῳ δὲ τῷ Κύλωνι ἀνεῖλεν ὁ θεὸς ἐν τῇ τοῦ Διὸς τῇ μεγίστῃ ἑορτῇ καταλαβεῖν τὴν ᾽Αθηναίων ἀκρόπολιν, *that he should seize.* Id. i. 126. ᾽Εκέχρητο γὰρ τοῖσι Σπαρτιήτῃσι, ἢ Λακεδαίμονα ἀνάστατον γενέσθαι ἢ τὸν βασιλέα σφέων ἀπολέσθαι. HDT. vii. 220. Εθέσπισε κομίσαι καὶ εἰσιδεῖν. EUR. I. T. 1014. ῾Ως χρησμοῦ ὄντος τὴν πόλιν διαφθαρῆναι, *as if there were an oracle dooming the city to perish.* PLAT. Rep. 415 C. Πολλάκι γάρ οἱ ἔειπε νούσῳ ὑπ᾽ ἀργαλέῃ φθίσθαι ἢ ὑπὸ Τρώεσσι δαμῆναι, *the diviner told him that he must either die by painful disease, or perish at the hands of the Trojans.* Il. xiii. 667. But we find ἀνεῖλεν ἔσεσθαι, THUC. i. 118; χρήσαντος κρατήσειν, LYCURG. 99; ἐκέχρηστο βασιλεύσειν, HDT. ii. 147; as indirect discourse.

99. Even verbs of *saying* and *thinking*, as λέγω when it signifies *to command*, and δοκεῖ, *it seems good*, may take the present or aorist infinitive not in indirect discourse, like other verbs of the same meaning. Εἶπον seldom takes the infinitive, except when it signifies *to command* (753). The context will always distinguish these cases from indirect quotations. *E.g.*

Τούτοις ἔλεγον πλεῖν, *I told them to sail.* DEM. xix. 150. (Τού-τους ἔλεγον πλεῖν would mean *I said that they were sailing.*) Εἰπὼν μηδένα παριέναι εἰς τὴν ἀκρόπολιν, *having given orders that no one should pass into the citadel.* XEN. Hell. v. 2, 29. Ὦ φίλοι, ἤδη μέν κεν ἐγὼν εἴποιμι καὶ ἄμμιν μνηστήρων ἐς ὅμιλον ἀκοντίσαι, *now I would command you to join me in hurling*, etc. Od. xxii. 262. Παραδοῦναι λέγει, *he tells us to give her up (he says, give her up).* AR. Av. 1679. Δοκεῖ ἡμῖν τοῦτο ποιεῖν (or ποιῆσαι) *it pleases us to do this.* (But δοκεῖ μοι ὑμᾶς τοῦτο ποιεῖν (or ποιῆσαι) generally means *it seems to me that you are doing this*, or *did this.*) Ἔδοξε in the sense *it was resolved*, introducing a decree, is followed by the present or aorist (not future) infinitive.

100. Verbs of *hoping, expecting, promising*, and *swearing* form an intermediate class between those that take the infinitive in indirect discourse and other verbs (136). When they refer to a future object, they naturally take the future infinitive, but may also have the present or aorist infinitive (not in indirect discourse) like verbs of *wishing*, etc. Thus *he promised to give* may be ὑπέσχετο διδόναι (or δοῦναι) as well as ὑπέσχετο δώσειν.

To facilitate comparison, the examples of the present and aorist infinitive thus used are given with those of the future in 136.

101. The present αἴτιός εἰμι, *I am the cause*, is often used with reference to the past, where logically a past tense would be needed ; as αἴτιός ἐστι τούτῳ θανεῖν, *he is the cause of his death*, instead of αἴτιος ἦν τούτῳ θανεῖν, *he was the cause of his death.* This may make an ordinary aorist infinitive appear like a verb of past time. *E.g.*

Αἴτιοι οὖν εἰσι καὶ ὑμῖν πολλῶν ἤδη ψευσθῆναι καὶ δὴ ἀδίκως γέ τινας ἀπολέσθαι, *they are the cause why you were deceived and some even perished* (i.e. *they caused you to be deceived and some even to perish*). LYS. xix. 51. Τεθνᾶσιν· οἱ δὲ ζῶντες αἴτιοι θανεῖν, *they are dead ; and the living are the causes of their death.* SOPH. Ant. 1173. Ἦ μοι μητρὶ μὲν θανεῖν μόνῃ μεταίτιος. Id. Tr. 1233.

PERFECT.

102. As the perfect indicative represents an act as finished at the *present* time, so the perfect of any of the dependent moods properly represents an act as *finished* at the time (present, past, or future) at which the present of that mood would represent it as going on.

103. The perfect subjunctive and optative are very often expressed in the active, and almost always in the passive and middle, by the perfect participle with ὦ and εἴην; and this combination of a present and a perfect makes the time denoted especially clear. Where the present would denote *future* time, the perfect denotes *future-perfect* time. *E.g.*

Τὸ χρόνον γεγενῆσθαι πολὺν δέδοικα μή τινα λήθην ὑμῖν πεποιήκῃ, *I fear lest the lapse of a long time that has occurred may (when you come to decide the case) prove to have caused in you some forgetfulness* (see 91). DEM. xix. 3. (Μὴ ποιῇ would mean *lest it may cause*, the time being the same as before.) Χρὴ αὐτὰ [ἃ τελευτήσαντα ἑκάτερον περιμένει] ἀκοῦσαι, ἵνα τελέως ἑκάτερος αὐτῶν ἀπειλήφῃ τὰ ὀφειλόμενα, *we must hear what awaits each of them after death, that (when we have finished) each may have fully received his deserts.* PLAT. Rep. 614 A. Τοὺς μὲν ἄλλους, κἂν δεδωκότες ὦσιν εὐθύνας, τὴν ἀειλογίαν ὁρῶ προτεινομένους, *I see that other men, even if they have already rendered their accounts,*—i.e. *if they are (in the state of) persons who have rendered their accounts,*—*always offer a perpetual reckoning.* DEM. xix. 2. Ἀνδρεῖόν γε πάνυ νομίζομεν, ὃς ἂν πεπλήγῃ πατέρα, *we always consider one very manly who has (may have) beaten his father.* AR. AV. 1350. Νόμον θήσειν μηδενὶ τῶν Ἑλλήνων ὑμᾶς βοηθεῖν ὃς ἂν μὴ πρότερος βεβοηκὼς ὑμῖν ᾖ, *to enact a law that you shall assist no one of the Greeks who shall not previously have assisted you.* DEM. xix. 16. (Ὃς ἂν μὴ πρότερος βοηθῇ would mean *who shall not previously assist you.*) Ἔδεισαν μὴ λύσσα ἡμῖν ἐμπεπτώκοι, *they feared lest madness might prove to have fallen upon us.* XEN. An. v. 7, 26. (Μὴ ἐμπίπτοι would mean *lest it might fall upon us.*) Ἐδεήθην τῶν δικαστῶν μηδὲν τοιοῦτον πρᾶξαι, ἵν᾽ ἐγὼ μηδένα Ἀθηναίων ἀπεκτονὼς εἴην, *that I might not be in the position of having put an Athenian to death.* DEM. liii. 18. Ἢν γὰρ εὑρεθῇ λέγων σοὶ ταῦτ᾽, ἔγωγ᾽ ἂν ἐκπεφευγοίην πάθος, *I should (in that case) have escaped harm.* SOPH. O. T. 839. Πῶς οὐκ ἂν οἰκτρότατα πάντων ἐγὼ πεπονθὼς εἴην, εἰ ἐμὲ ψηφίσαιντο εἶναι ξένον; *how should I not have suffered the most pitiable of all things, if they should vote me to be an alien?* DEM. lvii. 44. (This could have been expressed, with a very slight difference in meaning, πῶς οὐ πεπονθὼς ἔσομαι, ἐὰν ψηφίσωνται; *how shall I not have suffered,* etc.) Εἰ ὁτιοῦν πεπονθὼς ἑκάτερος ἡμῶν εἴη, οὐ καὶ ἀμφότεροι ἂν τοῦτο πεπόνθοιμεν; *if each of us should have suffered anything whatsoever, would not both of us have suffered it?* PLAT. Hipp. M. 301 A. Οὐκ ἂν διὰ τοῦτό γ᾽ εἶεν οὐκ εὐθὺς δεδωκότες, *this, at least, cannot be the reason why they did not pay it at once;* lit. *they would not (on inquiry) prove to have not paid it at once on this account.* DEM. xxx. 10.

104. The perfect subjunctive in protasis corresponds exactly to the

Latin future perfect indicative ; but the Greek seldom uses this cumbrous perfect, preferring the less precise aorist (91). The perfect optative, in both protasis and apodosis, corresponds to the Latin perfect subjunctive ; but it is seldom used, for a similar reason (95).

The perfect optative can hardly be accurately expressed in English. For when we use the English forms *would have suffered* and *should have suffered* to translate the perfect optative, these are merely vaguer expressions for *will* and *shall have suffered*. (See the examples above.) *I should have suffered* is commonly past in English, being equivalent to ἔπαθον ἄν; but here it is future, and is therefore liable to be misunderstood. There is no more reference to past time, however, in the perfect optative with ἄν, than there is in the future perfect indicative (77) in such expressions as μάτην ἐμοὶ κεκλαύσεται, *I shall have had my whippings for nothing* (referring to those received in his boyhood), Ar. Nub. 1436.

105. The perfect imperative is most common in the third person singular of the passive, where it expresses a command that something just done or about to be done shall be *decisive* and *final*. It is thus equivalent to the perfect participle with ἔστω. *E.g.*

Ταῦτα μὲν δὴ ταύτῃ εἰρήσθω, *let so much have been thus said,* (= εἰρημένα ἔστω), i.e. *let what has been thus said be sufficient.* Plat. Crat. 401 D. But ὅμως δὲ εἰρήσθω ὅτι, κ.τ.λ., *still let as much as this (which follows) be said (once for all), that,* etc. Id. Rep. 607 C. Περὶ τῶν ἰδίων ταῦτά μοι προειρήσθω, *let this have been said (once for all) by way of introduction.* Isoc. iv. 14. Ταῦτα πεπαίσθω τε ὑμῖν, καὶ ἴσως ἱκανῶς ἔχει, *let this be the end of the play,* etc. Plat. Euthyd. 278 D. Τετάχθω ἡμῖν κατὰ δημοκρατίαν ὁ τοιοῦτος ἀνήρ, *let such a man remain (where we have placed him), corresponding to democracy.* Id. Rep. 561 E. Ἀπειργάσθω δὴ ἡμῖν αὕτη ἡ πολιτεία, *let this now be a sufficient description of this form of government.* Ib. 553 A. Μέχρι τοῦδε ὡρίσθω ὑμῶν ἡ βραδυτής, *at this point let the limit of your sluggishness be fixed.* Thuc. i. 71.

The third person plural in the same sense could be expressed by the perfect participle with ἔστων, as in Plat. Rep. 502 A, οὗτοι τοίνυν τοῦτο πεπεισμένοι ἔστων, *grant then that these have been persuaded of this.*

106. On this principle the perfect imperative is used in mathematical language, to imply that something is to be considered as proved or assumed *once for all*, or that lines drawn or points fixed are to remain as data for a following demonstration. *E.g.*

Εἰλήφθω ἐπὶ τῆς ΑΒ τυχὸν σημεῖον τὸ Δ, καὶ ἀφῃρήσθω ἀπὸ τῆς ΑΓ τῇ ΑΔ ἴσῃ ἡ ΑΕ, *let any point Δ be assumed as taken in the line ΑΒ, and ΑΕ equal to ΑΔ as cut off from ΑΓ.* Eucl. i. Pr. 9.

107. The perfect imperative of the *second* person is rare ; when it is used, it seems to be a little more emphatic than the present or aorist. *E.g.*

'Ηὲ σὺ τόνδε δέδεξο. Il. v. 228. Μὴ πεφόβησθε, *do not be afraid.*
Thuc. vi. 17. Μόνον σὺ ἡμῖν πιστὰ θεῶν πεποίησο καὶ δεξιὰν δός,
only make us (*immediately* or *once for all*) *solemn pledges and give the right
hand.* Xen. Cyr. iv. 2, 7. Πέπαυσο, *stop! not another word!* Dem.
xxiv. 64.

108. In verbs whose perfect has the force of a present (49) the
perfect imperative is the ordinary form ; as μέμνησο, κεκλήσθω,
ἔσταθι, ἐστάτω, τέθναθι, τεθνάτω, ἴστω. So κεχήνατε, Ar. Ach. 133 ;
μὴ κεκράγατε, Vesp. 415. The perfect imperative active seems to
have been used only in such verbs. Occasionally we find the periphrastic form with the participle and εἰμί, as ἔστω ξυμβεβηκυῖα,
Plat. Leg. 736 B.

109. The perfect infinitive not in indirect discourse
generally represents an act as *finished* when the present
would represent it as *going on* (96). *E.g.*

Οὐδὲ βουλεύεσθαι ἔτι ὥρα, ἀλλὰ βεβουλεῦσθαι· τῆς γὰρ
ἐπιούσης νυκτὸς πάντα ταῦτα δεῖ πεπρᾶχθαι, *it is no longer time
even to be deliberating, but* (*it is time*) *to have done deliberating ; for
all this must be finished within the coming night.* Plat. Crit. 46 A.
Καὶ μὴν περὶ ὧν γε προσετάξατε προσήκει διῳκηκέναι, *and it is his
duty to have attended to the business about which you gave him instructions.*
Dem. xix. 6. (This refers to an ambassador presenting his accounts on
his return.) Ξυνετύγχανε πολλαχοῦ διὰ τὴν στενοχωρίαν τὰ μὲν
ἄλλοις ἐμβεβληκέναι τὰ δ' αὐτοὺς ἐμβεβλῆσθαι, δύο τε περὶ
μίαν ξυνηρτῆσθαι, *it often befell them to have made an attack on one
side and* (*at the same time*) *to have been attacked themselves on the other,*
etc. Thuc. vii. 70. 'Ανάγκη γὰρ τὰ μὲν μέγιστ' αὐτῶν ἤδη κατα-
κεχρῆσθαι μικρὰ δέ τινα παραλελεῖφθαι, *for it must be that the
most important subjects have been used up, and that only unimportant ones
have been left.* Isoc. iv. 74. Οὐκ ἤθελον ἐμβαίνειν διὰ τὸ καταπε-
πλῆχθαι τῇ ἥσσῃ, *they were unwilling to embark on account of having
been terrified by the defeat.* Thuc. vii. 72. Τὸ γὰρ πολλὰ ἀπολωλεκέναι κατὰ τὸν πόλεμον τῆς ἡμετέρας ἀμελείας ἄν τις θείη δικαίως,
τὸ δὲ μήτε πάλαι τοῦτο πεπονθέναι πεφηνέναι τέ τινα ἡμῖν
συμμαχίαν τούτων ἀντίρροπον, τῆς παρ' ἐκείνων εὐνοίας εὐεργέτημ'
ἄν ἔγωγε θείην, *for our having lost many things during the war one might
justly charge upon our neglect ; but our never having suffered this before,
and the fact that an alliance has now appeared to us to make up for these
losses, I should consider a benefaction,* etc. Dem. i. 10. (Compare
γεγενῆσθαι in the first example under 103.) Ἔφθασαν παροικοδομή-
σαντες, ὥστε μηκέτι μήτε αὐτοὶ κωλύεσθαι ὑπ' αὐτῶν, ἐκείνους τε
καὶ παντάπασιν ἀπεστερηκέναι . . . σφᾶς ἀποτειχίσαι, i.e. *they
carried their own wall first beyond that of the Athenians, so as no longer to
be themselves interfered with by them, and so as to have effectually prevented
them from walling them in.* Thuc. vii. 6. 'Επεμελήθη καὶ τῶν λοιπῶν,
ὥστε τῶν παρόντων τοῖς ἀνθρώποις ἀγαθῶν μηδὲν μὲν ἄνευ τῆς πόλεως

εἶναι, τὰ δὲ πλεῖστα διὰ ταύτην γεγενῆσθαι. Isoc. iv. 38. Τοιαῦτα
καὶ τοσαῦτα κατεσκεύασυν ἡμῖν, ὥστε μηδενὶ τῶν ἐπιγιγνομένων
ὑπερβολὴν λελεῖφθαι, *they made such and so great acquisitions as to
have no possibility of surpassing them left to any one who should come
after them.* Dem. iii. 25. Δίδομεν αὐτοῖς προῖκα συγκεκόφθαι, *we
allow them to have cut us up for nothing* (i.e. *we make no account of
their having done so*). Ar. Nub. 1426.

See [Aristot.] Eth. Nic. vi. 2, 6 : οὐκ ἔστι δὲ προαιρετὸν οὐδὲν
γεγονός, οἷον οὐδεὶς προαιρεῖται Ἴλιον πεπορθηκέναι, *but nothing
past can be purposed ; for example, nobody purposes to have sacked Ilium,*
i.e. the expression προαιροῦμαι Ἴλιον πεπορθηκέναι would be nonsense.
This illustrates well the restricted use of the perfect infinitive.

110. The perfect infinitive sometimes signifies that the action is
to be *decisive* and *permanent* (like the perfect imperative, 105); and
sometimes it seems to be merely more emphatic than the present or
aorist infinitive. *E.g.*

Εἶπον τὴν θύραν κεκλεῖσθαι, *they ordered that the door should be
shut (and remain so).* Xen. Hell. v. 4, 7. Βουλόμενος ἀγῶνι καὶ δικαστηρίῳ μοι διωρίσθαι παρ' ὑμῖν ὅτι τἀναντία ἐμοὶ καὶ τούτοις
πέπρακται, i.e. *wishing to have it once for all settled in your minds.*
Dem. xix. 223. Θελούσας πρὸς πύλαις πεπτωκέναι, *eager to fall
before the gates.* Aesch. Sept. 462. Ἤλαυνεν ἐπὶ τοὺς Μένωνος, ὥστ'
ἐκείνους ἐκπεπλῆχθαι καὶ τρέχειν ἐπὶ τὰ ὅπλα, *he marched against
the soldiers of Menon, so that they were (once for all) thoroughly frightened
and ran to arms.* Xen. An. i. 5, 13. (Here ἐκπεπλῆχθαι is merely
more emphatic than the present or aorist would be.)

FUTURE.

111. The future is used in the dependent moods only in the
optative and the infinitive, and in these it is never regular except
in indirect discourse and kindred constructions and in the periphrastic form with μέλλω (73).

For the future optative in indirect discourse see 128-134 ; for the
future infinitive in indirect discourse see 135 and 136.

112. In constructions out of indirect discourse the present
and aorist infinitive can always refer to future time if the context
requires it (96), so that the future infinitive is here rarely needed.
Therefore, after verbs which naturally have a future action as
their object but yet do not introduce indirect discourse,—as those
of *commanding, wishing,* etc. (684),—the present or aorist infinitive
(not the future) is regularly used. Thus the Greek expresses
they wish to do this not by βούλονται τοῦτο ποιήσειν, but by
βούλονται τοῦτο ποιεῖν (or ποιῆσαι). So the infinitive in
other future expressions, as after ὥστε and in its final sense, is

generally present or aorist. (For the single exception after μέλλω, see 73.)

113. On the other hand, when it was desired to make the reference to the future especially prominent, the future infinitive could be used exceptionally in ₂!! these cases. Thus we sometimes find the future after verbs signifying *to be able, to wish, to be unwilling*, and the like ; sometimes also in a final sense or with ὥστε and ἐφ᾽ ᾧτε; and sometimes when the infinitive with the article refers to future time. This use of the future is a partial adoption of the form of indirect discourse in other constructions. It was a particularly favourite usage with Thucydides. *E.g.*

Ἐδεήθησαν δὲ καὶ τῶν Μεγαρέων ναυσὶ σφᾶς ξυμπροπέμψειν, *they asked the Megareans also to escort them with ships.* THUC. i. 27. Ἐβούλοντο προτιμωρήσεσθαι. Id. vi. 57. So ἐπιχειρήσειν ἐθελήσεις; AESCHIN. iii. 152. Τὸ στόμα αὐτοῦ διενοοῦντο κλήσειν. THUC. vii. 56. Ἐφιέμενοι μὲν τῆς πάσης ἄρξειν, βοηθεῖν δὲ ἅμα εὐπρεπῶς βουλόμενοι τοῖς ἑαυτῶν ξυγγενέσι καὶ ξυμμάχοις. Id. vi. 6. (Here βοηθεῖν is regular.) Τοῦ ταῖς ναυσὶ μὴ ἀθυμεῖν ἐπιχειρήσειν, *to prevent them from being without spirit to attack them in ships.* Id. vii. 21. Οὔτ᾽ ἀποκωλύσειν δύνατοι ὄντες. Id. iii. 28. Εἰ σέ γ᾽ ἐν λόγοις πείσειν δυνησόμεσθα. SOPH. Ph. 1394. Εἴ τις εἰς τοῦτο ἀναβάλλεται ποιήσειν τὰ δέοντα, *if any one postpones doing his duty as far as this.* DEM. iii. 9. (The ordinary construction would be ἀναβάλλεται ποιεῖν or ποιῆσαι.) Οὔτε τῶν προγόνων μεμνῆσθαι [δεῖ] οὔτε τῶν λεγόντων ἀνέχεσθαι, νόμον τε θήσειν καὶ γράψειν, κ.τ.λ. DEM. xix. 16. (Here we have δεῖ θήσειν.) Πολλοῦ δέω ἐμαυτόν γε ἀδικήσειν καὶ κατ᾽ ἐμαυτοῦ ἐρεῖν αὐτός. PLAT. Ap. 37 B.

Τοὺς ὁμήρους παρέδοσαν τῷ Ἀργείων δήμῳ διὰ ταῦτα διαχρήσεσθαι, *that they might put them to death.* THUC. vi. 61. So πεύσεσθαι, Id. iii. 26. Ἐφ᾽ ᾧτε βοηθήσειν. AESCHIN. iii. 114 (see 610). Ἀποδείξω αὐτὸν τὴν προῖκα οὐ δεδωκότα οὕτω μεγάλοις τεκμηρίοις ὥστε ὑμᾶς ἅπαντας εἴσεσθαι. DEM. xxx. 5 : so xxix. 5. Ἐλπίδι τὸ ἀφανὲς τοῦ κατορθώσειν ἐπιτρέψαντες, *having committed to hope what was uncertain in the prospect of success.* THUC. ii. 42. (Here κατορθώσειν is more explicit than the present κατορθοῦν would be : τὸ ἀφανὲς τοῦ κατορθοῦν would mean simply *what was uncertain in regard to success.*) Τοῦ ἐς χεῖρας ἐλθεῖν πιστότερον τὸ ἐκφοβήσειν ἡμᾶς ἀκινδύνως ἡγοῦνται, *they feel more confidence in the prospect of frightening us without risk than in meeting us in battle.* Id. iv. 126. Τὸ μὲν οὖν ἐξελέγξειν αὐτὸν θαρρῶ καὶ πάνυ πιστεύω, *I have courage and great confidence as to my convicting him.* DEM. xix. 3. (Here most of the ordinary Mss. read ἐξελέγχειν.)

See also THUC. iv. 115 and 121, v. 35, vii. 11, viii. 55 and 74 ; and Krüger's note on i. 27, where these passages are cited. In several of these there is some Ms. authority for the aorist infinitive.

114. The future perfect infinitive occurs only in indirect discourse (137), except in verbs whose perfect has the sense of a present (82).

B. OPTATIVE AND INFINITIVE OF INDIRECT DISCOURSE.

115. When the optative and infinitive are in indirect discourse, each tense represents the *corresponding tense* of the direct discourse; the present including also the imperfect, and the perfect also the pluperfect.

See the general principles of indirect discourse (667). The optative is included here only as it is used after past tenses to represent an indicative or subjunctive of the direct discourse. No cases of the optative or infinitive with ἄν are considered here : for these see Chapter III. For the meaning of the term "indirect discourse" as applied to the infinitive, see 684.

PRESENT OPTATIVE.

116. The present optative in indirect discourse may represent the following forms of direct discourse :—

1. The present indicative of a leading verb. *E.g.*

Περικλῆς προηγόρευε, ὅτι Ἀρχίδαμός οἱ ξένος εἴη, *Pericles announced that Archidamus was his friend* (*i.e.* he said ξένος μοί ἐστιν). Thuc. ii. 13. Ἔγνωσαν ὅτι κενὸς ὁ φόβος εἴη, *they learned that their fear was groundless* (*i.e.* they learned κενός ἐστιν ὁ φόβος). Xen. An. ii. 2, 21. Ἐπυνθάνετο εἰ οἰκοῖτο ἡ χώρα, *he asked whether the country was inhabited* (*i.e.* he asked the question οἰκεῖται ἡ χώρα;). Xen. Cyr. iv. 4, 4.

2. The present indicative or subjunctive of a dependent verb. *E.g.*

Εἶπεν ὅτι ἄνδρα ἄγοι ὃν εἶρξαι δέοι, *he said that he was bringing a man whom it was necessary to confine* (he said ἄνδρα ἄγω ὃν εἶρξαι δεῖ). Xen. Hell. v. 4, 8. Ἡγεῖτο ἅπαν ποιήσειν αὐτὸν εἴ τις ἀργύριον διδοίη, *he believed that the man would do anything if one were to give him money* (he believed ἅπαν ποιήσει ἐάν τις ἀργύριον διδῷ). Lys. xii. 14.

3. The present subjunctive in a question of appeal (287). *E.g.*

Κλέαρχος ἐβουλεύετο, εἰ πέμποιέν τινας ἢ πάντες ἴοιεν, *Clearchus was deliberating whether they should send a few or should all go.* Xen. An. i. 10, 5. (The question was, πέμπωμέν τινας ἢ πάντες ἴωμεν; *shall we send a few, or shall we all go?* See 677.) The context will always make it clear whether the optative represents a subjunctive (as here) or an indicative (1).

4. The imperfect indicative of a leading verb. *E.g.*

᾿Απεκρίναντο ὅτι οὐδεὶς μάρτυς παρείη, *they replied that no witness had been present* (when a certain payment was made). DEM. xxx. 20. (They said οὐδεὶς παρῆν.)

This is the rare imperfect optative (673). The imperfect indicative is regularly retained in such cases, and is always retained in a *dependent* clause of a quotation (689, 2).

PRESENT INFINITIVE.

117. (*As Present.*) The present infinitive in indirect discourse generally represents a present indicative of the direct form. *E.g.*

Φησὶ γράφειν, *he says that he is writing;* ἔφη γράφειν, *he said that he was writing;* φήσει γράφειν, *he will say that he is (then) writing.* (In all three cases he says γράφω.) ᾿Αρρωστεῖν προφασίζεται, *he pretends that he is sick;* ἐξώμοσεν ἀρρωστεῖν τουτονί, *he took his oath that this man was sick.* DEM. xix. 124. Οὐκ ἔφη αὐτὸς ἀλλ᾿ ἐκεῖνον στρατηγεῖν, *he said that not he himself, but Nicias, was general;* i.e. he said οὐκ ἐγὼ αὐτὸς ἀλλ᾿ ἐκεῖνος στρατηγεῖ. THUC. iv. 28. See other examples under 683.

118. Verbs of *hoping* and *swearing* may thus take the present infinitive in indirect discourse. This must be distinguished from the more common use of the present and aorist infinitive (not in indirect discourse) after these verbs, referring to the future (100; 136). *E.g.*

᾿Ελπίζων εἶναι ἀνθρώπων ὀλιβώτατος, ταῦτα ἐπειρώτα, *he asked this, trusting that he was the most happy of men.* HDT. i. 30. So i. 22, ἐλπίζων σιτοδείην τε εἶναι ἰσχυρὴν καὶ τὸν λεὼν τετρῦσθαι. Ξυνὰ δ᾿ ἐλπίζω λέγειν, *and I hope I speak for the common good.* AESCH. Sept. 76. ᾿Ομνύντες βλέπειν τὸν οὐκέτ᾿ ὄντα ζῶντ᾿ ᾿Αχιλλέα πάλιν, i.e. *swearing that they saw Achilles alive again.* SOPH. Ph. 357.

Compare the first two examples with ἐλπίζει δύνατος εἶναι, *he hopes to be able,* PLAT. Rep. 573 C; and the last with ὀμόσαι εἶναι μὲν τὴν ἀρχὴν κοινήν, πάντας δ᾿ ὑμῖν ἀποδοῦναι τὴν χώραν, *to swear that the dominion shall be common, and that all shall surrender the land,* DEM. xxiii. 170. (See 136 and the examples.)

119. (*As Imperfect.*) The present infinitive may also represent an imperfect indicative of the direct discourse, thus supplying the want of an imperfect infinitive. *E.g.*

Τίνας οὖν εὐχὰς ὑπολαμβάνετ᾽ εὔχεσθαι τοῖς θεοῖς τὸν Φίλιππον ὅτ᾽ ἔσπενδεν; *what prayers then do you suppose Philip made to the Gods when he was pouring his libations?* DEM. xix. 130. (Here the temporal clause ὅτ᾽ ἔσπενδεν shows that εὔχεσθαι is past.) Πότερ᾽ οἴεσθε πλέον Φωκέας Θηβαίων ἢ Φίλιππον ὑμῶν κρατεῖν τῷ πολέμῳ; *do you think that the superiority of the Phocians over the Thebans or that of Philip over you was the greater in the war* (the war being then past)? DEM. xix. 148. (Here the direct discourse would be ἐκράτουν and ἐκράτει.) Πῶς γὰρ οἴεσθε δυσχερῶς ἀκούειν Ὀλυνθίους, εἴ τίς τι λέγοι κατὰ Φιλίππου κατ᾽ ἐκείνους τοὺς χρόνους ὅτ᾽ Ἀνθεμοῦντα αὐτοῖς ἀφίει; ... ἆρα προσδοκᾶν αὐτοὺς τοιαῦτα πείσεσθαι (sc. οἴεσθε); ... ἆρ᾽ οἴεσθε, ὅτε τοὺς τυράννους ἐξέβαλλε, (τοὺς Θετταλοὺς) προσδοκᾶν, κ.τ.λ.; *for how unwillingly do you think the Olynthians used to hear it, if any one said anything against Philip in those times when he was ceding Anthemus to them, etc. ? Do you think they were expecting to suffer such things? Do you think that the Thessalians, when he was expelling the despots, were expecting, etc. ?* DEM. vi. 20 and 22. (The direct questions were πῶς ἤκουον εἰ λέγοι; and προσεδόκων;) Καὶ γὰρ τοὺς ἐπὶ τῶν προγόνων ἡμῶν λέγοντας ἀκούω τούτῳ τῷ ἔθει χρῆσθαι, *I hear that they used to follow this custom.* DEM. iii. 21. Τὰ μὲν πρὸ Ἕλληνος οὐδὲ εἶναι ἡ ἐπίκλησις αὕτη (sc. δοκεῖ), *in the times before Hellen this name does not appear to have even existed.* THUC. i. 3. Again, in the same sentence of Thucydides, παρέχεσθαι, *to have furnished.* Μηδὲν οἴου ἄλλο μηχανᾶσθαι ἢ ὅπως ... δέξοιντο, ἵνα ... γίγνοιτο. PLAT. Rep. 430 A. Μετὰ ταῦτα ἔφη σφᾶς μὲν δειπνεῖν, τὸν δὲ Σωκράτη οὐκ εἰσιέναι· τὸν οὖν Ἀγάθωνα πολλάκις κελεύειν μεταπέμψασθαι τὸν Σωκράτη, ἓ δὲ οὐκ ἐᾶν. PLAT. Symp. 175 C. (He said, ἐδειπνοῦμεν, ὁ δὲ Σ. οὐκ εἰσῄει· ὁ οὖν Ἀ. ἐκέλευεν· ἐγὼ δὲ οὐκ εἴων.) Συντυχεῖν γὰρ (ἔφη) Ἀτρεστίδᾳ παρὰ Φιλίππου πορευομένῳ, καὶ μετ᾽ αὐτοῦ γύναια καὶ παιδάρια βαδίζειν, *for he said that he had met* (aor.) *Atrestidas coming from Philip, and that there were walking with him* (impf.), *etc.* DEM. xix. 305. Τοῦτ᾽ ἐγώ φημι δεῖν ἐμὲ μὴ λαθεῖν, *I say that this ought not to have escaped my notice.* DEM. xviii. 190. (The direct form was τοῦτ᾽ ἔδει ἐμὲ μὴ λαθεῖν, 415.)

The imperfect infinitive is found even in Homer; as καὶ σὲ, γέρον, τὸ πρὶν μὲν ἀκούομεν ὄλβιον εἶναι, *we hear that you were once prosperous.* Il. xxiv. 543. So Il. v. 639; Od. viii. 181, 516.

For the imperfect participle, see 140.

120. This use of the present infinitive as an imperfect must be carefully distinguished from its ordinary use after past tenses, where we translate it by the imperfect, as in ἔφη τὸ στράτευμα μάχεσθαι, *he said that the army was fighting.* This has sometimes been called an imperfect infinitive; but here μάχεσθαι refers to time *present* relatively to ἔφη; whereas, if it had been used as an imperfect, it would have referred to time *past* relatively to ἔφη, as in ἔφη τὸ στράτευμα τῇ προτεραίᾳ μάχεσθαι, *he said that the army had been fighting on the day* *before.* In the former case the direct discourse was μάχεται, in the latter it was ἐμάχετο. Such an *imperfect* infinitive differs from the aorist in the same construction only by expressing the duration or repetition of an action (as in the indicative) ; it gives, in fact, the only means of representing in the infinitive what is usually expressed by λέγει ὅτι ἐποίει, *he says that he was doing,* as opposed to λέγει ὅτι ἐποίησεν, *he says that he did.* (For the similar use of the present optative to represent the imperfect, see 116, 4.) This construction is never used unless the context makes it certain that the infinitive represents an imperfect and not a present, so that no ambiguity can arise. See the examples.

So sometimes in Latin : Q. Scaevolam memoria teneo bello Marsico, cum esset summa senectute, cotidie *facere* omnibus conveniendi potestatem sui. CIC. Phil. viii. 31. So Q. Maximum accepimus facile *celare, tacere, dissimulare, insidiari, praeripere* hostium consilia. CIC. de Off. i. 108.

PERFECT OPTATIVE.

121. The perfect optative in indirect discourse may represent—

1. The perfect indicative of a leading verb. *E.g.*

Ἔλεγε ὅσα ἀγαθὰ Κῦρος Πέρσας πεποιήκοι, *he told how many services Cyrus had done the Persians.* HDT. iii. 75. (Πεποιήκοι here represents πεποίηκε.) Οὗτοι ἔλεγον ὡς πεντακόσιοι αὐτοῖς εἴησαν ἐκ τοῦ Πειραιῶς δεδεκασμένοι. LYS. xxix. 12. (Here the direct discourse was πεντακόσιοί εἰσιν δεδεκασμένοι.)

2. The perfect indicative or subjunctive of a dependent verb. *E.g.*

Εἶπεν ὅτι Δέξιππον οὐκ ἐπαινοίη εἰ ταῦτα πεποιηκὼς εἴη (he said οὐκ ἐπαινῶ εἰ ταῦτα πεποίηκε, *I do not approve him if he has done this*). XEN. An. vi. 6, 25.

Ἐλέγομεν ὅτι ἕνα ἕκαστον ἓν δέοι ἐπιτηδεύειν, εἰς ὃ αὐτοῦ ἡ φύσις ἐπιτηδειοτάτη πεφυκυῖα εἴη (we said ἕκαστον ἓν δεῖ ἐπιτηδεύειν, εἰς ὃ ἂν πεφυκὼς ᾖ, *each one is to practise one thing, for which his nature is best fitted;* though this might be πέφυκε, like πεποίηκε in the first example). PLAT. Rep. 433 A.

PERFECT INFINITIVE.

122. The perfect infinitive in indirect discourse generally represents a perfect indicative of the direct form. *E.g.*

Φησὶ τοῦτο πεπραχέναι, *he says that he has done this;* ἔφη τοῦτο πεπραχέναι, *he said that he had done this;* φήσει τοῦτο πεπραχέναι, *he will say that he has done this* (the direct form in each case being πέπραχα). Ἔφη χρήμαθ' ἑαυτῷ τοὺς Θηβαίους ἐπικεκηρυχέναι, *he said that the Thebans had offered a reward for his seizure.* DEM. xix. 21. In AR. Nub. 1277, προσκεκλῆσθαί μοι δοκεῖς (according to MSS. Rav. and Ven.), *you seem to me to be sure to be summoned to court (to be as good as already summoned)*, the infinitive represents a perfect indicative referring to the future (51). There is probably a regard to the perfect of the preceding verse, σεσεῖσθαί μοι δοκεῖς. So THUC. ii. 8 : ἐν τούτῳ τε κεκωλῦσθαι ἐδόκει ἑκάστῳ τὰ πράγματα ᾧ μή τις αὐτὸς παρέσται, *and each man thought that things were the same as stopped in that matter in which he was not himself to take part.* After a verb of *swearing* : ὤμνυε μηδὲν εἰρηκέναι περὶ αὐτοῦ φαῦλον, DEM. xxi. 119. After ἐλπίζω : ἐλπίζων τὸν λεὼν τετρῦσθαι, HDT. i. 22 (see 118, above).

123. The perfect infinitive rarely represents a pluperfect of the direct form. *E.g.*

Λέγεται ἄνδρα ἐκπεπλῆχθαι πολύν τινα χρόνον ἐπὶ τῷ κάλλει τοῦ Κύρου, *it is said that a man had been struck with amazement for some time at the beauty of Cyrus* (i.e. ἐξεπέπληκτο). XEN. Cyr. i. 4, 27. Ἀντέλεγον, λέγοντες μὴ ἐπηγγέλθαι πω τὰς σπονδὰς ὅτ' ἐσέπεμψαν τοὺς ὁπλίτας, *saying that the truce had not yet been proclaimed* (ἐπήγγελτο). THUC. v. 49.

AORIST OPTATIVE.

124. The aorist optative in indirect discourse may represent—

1. The aorist indicative of a leading verb. *E.g.*

Ἔλεξαν ὅτι πέμψειε σφᾶς ὁ βασιλεύς, *they said that the king had sent them* (i.e. they said ἔπεμψεν ἡμᾶς ὁ βασιλεύς). XEN. Cyr. ii. 4, 7. Τότε ἐγνώσθη ὅτι οἱ βάρβαροι τὸν ἄνθρωπον ὑποπέμψαιεν, *then it became known that the barbarians had sent the man.* XEN. An. ii. 4, 22. Ἐτόλμα λέγειν ὡς πολλὰ τῶν ἐμῶν λάβοιεν, *he dared to say that they had taken* (ἔλαβον) *much of my property.* DEM. xxvii. 49. Ἠρώτων αὐτὸν εἰ ἀναπλεύσειεν ἔχων ἀργύριον, *I asked him whether he had set sail with money* (i.e. I asked him the question, ἀνέπλευσας ;). DEM. l. 55. (This form is rare ; see 125.) Ἐπειρώτα τίνα ἴδοι, *he asked whom he had seen* (i.e. τίνα εἶδες, *whom did you see?*). HDT. i. 31. So i. 116 : εἴρετο κόθεν λάβοι.

2. The aorist subjunctive of a dependent verb. *E.g.*

Εὔξαντο σωτήρια θύσειν ἔνθα πρῶτον εἰς φιλίαν γῆν ἀφίκοιντο, *they vowed that they would make thank offerings for their deliverance wherever they should first enter a friendly land* (i.e. ἔνθα ἂν . . . ἀφικώμεθα, θύσομεν). XEN. An. v. 1, 1 (see iii. 2, 9).

An aorist indicative in a dependent clause of a quotation is regularly retained (689, 3).

3. The aorist subjunctive in a question of appeal (287). *E.g.*

Οἱ Ἐπιδάμνιοι τὸν θεὸν ἐπήροντο εἰ παραδοῖεν Κορινθίοις τὴν πόλιν, *they asked whether they should deliver up their city to the Corinthians* (i.e. *they asked the question,* παραδῶμεν τὴν πόλιν; *shall we deliver up our city?*). Thuc. i. 25. Ἐσκόπουν ὅπως κάλλιστ᾽ ἐνέγκαιμ᾽ αὐτόν, *I looked to see how I could best endure him* (i.e. *I asked,* πῶς ἐνέγκω αὐτόν; *how can I endure him?*). Eur. Hipp. 393. Διεσιώπησε σκοπῶν ὅ τι ἀποκρίναιτο, *he continued silent, thinking what he should answer* (i.e. *thinking* τί ἀποκρίνωμαι;). Xen. Mem. iv. 2, 10. (See 677.)

125. The context must decide whether an aorist optative in an indirect question represents the aorist subjunctive (as in 3) or the aorist indicative (as in the last examples under 1). Thus the first example under 3 might mean *they asked whether they had given up their city,* παρέδομεν τὴν πόλιν; But in most cases the aorist subjunctive is the direct form implied, and an aorist indicative used in a direct question is generally retained ; εἰ ἀναπλεύσειεν in 1 is, therefore, exceptional.

AORIST INFINITIVE.

126. The aorist infinitive in indirect discourse represents an aorist indicative of the direct form. *E.g.*

Φησὶν τοῦτο ποιῆσαι, *he says that he did this* (i.e. *he says* τοῦτο ἐποίησα) ; ἔφη τοῦτο ποιῆσαι, *he said that he had done this* (i.e. *he said* τοῦτο ἐποίησα); φήσει τοῦτο ποιῆσαι, *he will say that he did this* (i.e. *he will say* τοῦτο ἐποίησα). Ὁ Κῦρος λέγεται γενέσθαι Καμβύσεω, *Cyrus is said to have been the son of Cambyses.* Xen. Cyr. i. 2, 1. Παλαιότατοι λέγονται ἐν μέρει τινὶ τῆς χώρας Κύκλωπες οἰκῆσαι, *the Cyclops are said to have settled most anciently in a part of the country.* Thuc. vi. 2. Ἦσαν ὕποπτοι αὐτοῖς μὴ προθύμως σφίσι πέμψαι ἃ ἔπεμψαν, *they were suspected by them of not having sent to them with alacrity what they did send.* Thuc. vi. 75.

127. Although the usage of the language is very strict, by which the aorist infinitive after verbs of *saying, thinking,* etc. is past, as representing an aorist indicative, still several passages are found, even in the best authors, in which an aorist infinitive after such verbs as νομίζω, οἴομαι, and even φημί refers to future time. Many critics, especially Madvig,[1] deny the existence of this anomaly, and emend the offending aorists to the future or insert ἄν. If they are allowed (and most of the passages still stand uncorrected in many editions), they must be treated as strictly exceptional ; and no principle, and no consistent exception to the general principle, can be based on them. *E.g.*

Φάτο γὰρ τίσασθαι ἀλείτας, *for he said that he should punish the*

---

[1] See Madvig's *Bemerkungen über einige Puncte der griechischen Wortfügungslehre,* pp. 34-44 : *Griech. Syntax,* § 172 *a, Anm.*

offenders. Od. xx. 121. (In Π iii. 28, we have in most Mss. and editions φάτο γὰρ τίσεσθαι ἀλείτην, in precisely the same sense; but Bekker has τίσασθαι.) So ἐφάμην τίσασθαι in Il. iii. 366. Καὶ αὐτῷ οὐ μέμψασθαι Ἀπρίην (sc. ἀπεκρίνατο)· παρέσεσθαι γὰρ καὶ αὐτὸς καὶ ἄλλους ἄξειν, and (he answered) that Apries should not have reason to blame him; for he not only would be present himself, but would bring others. HDT. ii. 162. (Notice the strange transition from the aorist (?) to the two futures.) Φησὶν οὐδὲ τὴν Διὸς Ἔριν πέδῳ σκήψασαν ἐμποδὼν σχεθεῖν. AESCH. Sept. 429. Οἶμαι γάρ νιν ἱκετεῦσαι τάδε, I think of imploring. EUR. I. A. 462. (Hermann reads ἱκετεύσειν by conjecture.) Ἐνόμισαν ἐπιθέμενοι ῥᾳδίως κρατῆσαι, they thought they should gain the victory. THUC. ii. 3. Νομίζω, ἢν ἱππεὺς γένωμαι, ἄνθρωπος πτηνὸς γενέσθαι. XEN. Cyr. iv. 3, 15. Οὐκ ἔφασαν ἐπιτρέψαι ταῦτα γενέσθαι, they said they would not permit this to happen. LYS. xiii. 15 ; same in xiii. 47. Τοῦτο δὲ οἴεταί οἱ μάλιστα γενέσθαι, εἰ σοὶ συγγένοιτο, and he thinks that this would be most likely to happen to him if he should join himself with you. PLAT. Prot. 316 C. (Here we should expect γενέσθαι ἄν, to correspond to εἰ συγγένοιτο.)

AR. Nub. 1141 is commonly quoted in this list, as having δικάσασθαί φασί μοι in all Mss.; but in the year 1872 I found δικάσεσθαι in Cod. Par. 2712 (Brunck's A) and by correction in 2820, so that this emendation (as it is commonly thought to be) is confirmed.

It may be thought that the aorist is less suspicious in the Homeric passages than in Attic Greek, where the uses of indirect discourse are more precisely fixed.

FUTURE OPTATIVE.

128. The future optative is used chiefly in indirect discourse after past tenses, to represent a future indicative of the direct form. Even here the future indicative is generally retained (670, *b*). *E.g.*

Ὑπειπὼν τἄλλα ὅτι αὐτὸς τἀκεῖ πράξοι, ᾤχετο, *having suggested as to what remained, that he would himself attend to things there, he departed.* THUC. i. 90. (Here πράξοι represents πράξω of the direct discourse, for which we might have πράξει in the indirect form. See, in the same chapter, ἀποκρινάμενοι ὅτι πέμψουσιν, *having replied that they would send*, where πέμψοιεν might have been used.) Εἴ τινα φεύγοντα λήψοιτο, προηγόρευεν ὅτι ὡς πολεμίῳ χρήσοιτο. XEN. Cyr. iii. 1, 3. (Here the announcement was εἴ τινα λήψομαι, ὡς πολεμίῳ χρήσομαι.) Ἔλεγεν ὅτι ἕτοιμος εἴη ἡγεῖσθαι αὐτοῖς εἰς τὸ Δέλτα, ἔνθα πολλὰ λήψοιντο. XEN. An. vii. 1, 33. (He said ἕτοιμός εἰμι . . . ἔνθα λήψεσθε.) Here belongs the rare use after ἐλπίς in THUC. vi. 30, μετ᾽ ἐλπίδος τε ἅμα καὶ ὀλοφυρμῶν, τὰ μὲν ὡς κτήσοιντο, τοὺς δ᾽ εἴ ποτε ὄψοιντο, i.e. *(they sailed) with hope and lamentations at once,—hope that they might acquire Sicily, lamentations at the thought whether they should ever see their friends again* (ὀψόμεθα;).

129. The future optative occurs first in Pindar, in an indirect question, ἐκέλευσεν διακρῖναι ἄντινα σχήσοι τις ἡρώων, *to decide which maiden each of the heroes should take* (τίνα σχήσει;), Py. ix. 126. It is used chiefly by the Attic prose writers, as the correlative of the future indicative, that tense having had no corresponding optative form in the older language, as the present, perfect, and aorist indicative and subjunctive had. It is never used with ἄν.

130. Apart from its use after verbs of *saying* and *thinking*, the future optative is found in object clauses with ὅπως after verbs of *striving*, etc. (339). Here its use is closely akin to that in indirect discourse, as it always represents thought which was originally expressed by the future indicative. *E.g.*

Ἐπεμελεῖτο ὅπως μήτε ἄσιτοι μήτε ἄποτοι ἔσοιντο, *he took care that they should be neither without food nor without drink* (his thought was ὅπως μήτε . . . ἔσονται). XEN. Cyr. viii. 1, 43. Ἐπεμελήθη ὅπως οἱ στρατιῶται τοὺς πόνους δυνήσοιντο ὑποφέρειν. XEN. Ag. ii. 8. Μηδὲν οἴου ἄλλο μηχανᾶσθαι, ἢ ὅπως ἡμῖν ὅτι κάλλιστα τοὺς νόμους δέξοιντο ὥσπερ βαφήν. PLAT. Rep. 430 A. See Tim. 18 C, μηχανωμένους ὅπως μηδεὶς γνώσοιτο, νομιοῦσι δὲ πάντες (where γνώσοιτο represents γνώσεται, while the next word νομιοῦσι is retained in the indicative). Ἐσκόπει ὁ Μενεκλῆς ὅπως μὴ ἔσοιτο ἄπαις, ἀλλ' ἔσοιτο αὐτῷ ὅστις ζῶντά τε γηροτροφήσοι καὶ τελευτήσαντα θάψοι αὐτόν, καὶ εἰς τὸν ἔπειτα χρόνον τὰ νομιζόμενα αὐτῷ ποιήσοι, *Menecles took thought that he might not be childless, but might have some one to support his old age while he lived and to bury him when he died*, etc. ISAE. ii. 10 (see 134). Other examples are XEN. Cyr. viii. 1, 10; Hell. vii. 5, 3; Oec. vii. 5; PLAT. Ap. 36 C; ISOC. xxi. 13; ISAE. vi. 35; DEM. xxvii. 40 (ὅπως μισθώσοιτο, in the MSS.) In XEN. Hell. ii. 1, 22 we have ὡς with the future optative: προεῖπεν ὡς μηδεὶς κινήσοιτο ἐκ τῆς τάξεως μηδὲ ἀνάξοιτο.

In all such cases the future indicative is generally retained (340).

131. The future optative is found in four passages after verbs of *fearing*, three times with μή, and once with ὅπως μή :—

Κατέβαλε τὸ Ἡρακλεωτῶν τεῖχος, οὐ τοῦτο φοβούμενος, μή τινες πορεύσοιντο ἐπὶ τὴν ἐκείνου δύναμιν, *not fearing this, lest any should march into his dominions*. XEN. Hell. vi. 4, 27. So XEN. Mem. i. 2, 7. Ἀλλὰ καὶ τοὺς θεοὺς ἂν ἔδεισας παρακινδυνεύειν, μὴ οὐκ ὀρθῶς αὐτὸ ποιήσοις. PLAT. Euthyphr. 15 D. Οὐ μόνον περὶ τῆς βασάνου καὶ τῆς δίκης ἐδεδοίκει, ἀλλὰ καὶ περὶ τοῦ γραμματείου, ὅπως μὴ ὑπὸ τοῦ Μενεξένου συλληφθήσοιτο. ISOC. xvii. 22. (Here the fear was expressed originally by ὅπως μὴ συλληφθήσεται, 370.)

As μή with the future indicative is rare after verbs of *fearing* (367), it is still rarer with the future optative after such verbs.

132. No case is quoted of the future optative in a pure final clause, except a peculiar one with μή in PLAT. Rep. 393 E : 'Αγαμέμνων ἠγρίαινεν, ἐντελλόμενος νῦν τε ἀπιέναι καὶ αὖθις μὴ ἐλθεῖν, μὴ αὐτῷ τό τε σκῆπτρον καὶ τὰ τοῦ θεοῦ στέμματα οὐκ ἐπαρκέσοι. (Another reading, ἐπαρκέσειεν, of inferior authority, is adopted by Bekker.) If ἐπαρκέσοι is retained (as it is by most editors), it can be explained only by assuming that Plato had in his mind μὴ οὐκ ἐπαρκέσει as the direct form. Μή final with the future indicative occurs in Aristophanes, Homer, and Theognis (see 324) ; there is therefore no objection to μὴ ἐπαρκέσοι as representing μὴ ἐπαρκέσει. We must remember that Plato is here paraphrasing Homer (Il. i. 25-28), but by no means literally. The Homeric line is Μή νύ τοι οὐ χραίσμῃ σκῆπτρον καὶ στέμμα θεοῖο (see 263).

133. As ἵνα never takes the future indicative, it can never have the future optative.

134. A future optative rarely occurs in a relative clause of purpose after a past tense ; as αἱρεθέντες ἐφ᾽ ᾧτε συγγράψαι νόμους, καθ᾽ οὕστινας πολιτεύσοιντο, *having been chosen for the purpose of making a code of laws, by which they were to govern.* XEN. Hell. ii. 3, 11. (Here we have an indirect expression of the thought of those who chose the Thirty, of which the direct form is found in ii. 3, 2, ἔδοξε τριάκοντα ἄνδρας ἑλέσθαι, οἳ τοὺς πατρίους νόμους ξυγγράψουσι, καθ᾽ οὓς πολιτεύσουσι.) See ISAE. ii. 10 (quoted in 130).

FUTURE INFINITIVE.

135. The future infinitive is regularly used only in indirect discourse (111, 112), where it always represents a future indicative of the direct form. *E.g.*

Γράψειν φησίν, *he says that he will write;* γράψειν ἔφη, *he said that he would write;* γράψειν φήσει, *he will say that he will write :* all representing γράψω, *I will write.* Πολλούς γε ἔσεσθαι ἔλεγον τοὺς ἐθελήσοντας, *they said that there would be many who would be willing.* XEN. Cyr. iii. 2, 26.

136. Verbs of *hoping, expecting, promising, swearing,* and a few others of like meaning, form an intermediate class between those which take the infinitive in indirect discourse (with the time of its tense preserved) and those which do not. When these refer to a future object, they regularly take the future infinitive in indirect discourse ; but they also allow the aorist and even the present infinitive (not in indirect discourse), like verbs of *wishing,* etc. Examples are given of different verbs of this class with both constructions :—

Τρωσὶν δ᾽ ἔλπετο θυμὸς νῆας ἐνιπρήσειν κτενέειν θ᾽ ἥρωας 'Αχαιούς. Il. xv. 701. 'Εέλπετο κῦδος ἀρέσθαι, *he was hoping to obtain glory.* Il. xii. 407. Ἤλπιζον γὰρ μάχην ἔσεσθαι, *for they expected that there would be a battle.* THUC. iv. 71. Ἐν ἐλπίδι ὢν τὰ τείχη αἱρήσειν. THUC. vii. 46. Ἐλπίζει δυνατὸς εἶναι ἄρχειν, *he hopes to be able to rule.* PLAT. Rep. 573 C. (Compare εἶναι in HDT. i. 22 and 30, quoted in 118.) Πάλιν ἔμολ' ἃ πάρος οὔποτε ἤλπισεν παθεῖν. EUR. H. F. 746. Εἰ γὰρ κρατήσειαν τῷ ναυτικῷ, τὸ Ῥήγιον ἤλπιζον ῥᾳδίως χειρώσασθαι, *they hoped to subdue Rhegium.* THUC. iv. 24. Οὐδ' ἂν ἐλπὶς ἦν αὐτὰ βελτίω γενέσθαι, *there would not be even a hope of their becoming better.* DEM. iv. 2. Besides these constructions, ἐλπίζω (or ἐλπίς) has the infinitive with ἄν in THUC. vii. 61 ; ὡς with the future indicative in EUR. El. 919, with the future optative in THUC. vi. 30 (see 128), with the aorist optative and ἄν in THUC. v. 9 ; ὅπως with the future indicative in SOPH. El. 963, EUR. Her. 1051.

Τὸν στρατηγὸν προσδοκῶ ταῦτα πράξειν. XEN. An. iii. 1, 14. Μενέλεων προσδόκα μολεῖν, *expect M. to come.* AESCH. Ag. 675. Προσδοκῶν ῥᾳδίως ὑμᾶς ἐξαπατῆσαι. ISAE. xi. 22.

Ὑπό τ' ἔσχετο καὶ κατένευσεν δωσέμεναι. Il. xiii. 368. Ἐκ τούτου ὑπέσχετο μηχανὴν παρέξειν. XEN. Cyr. vi. 1, 21. Σὺ γὰρ ὑπέσχου ζητήσειν. PLAT. Rep. 427 E. Ὑποσχόμενος μὴ πρόσθεν παύσασθαι πρὶν αὐτοὺς καταγάγοι οἴκαδε, *having promised not to stop until he had restored them to their homes.* XEN. An. i. 2, 2. Ὑπέσχετο μοι βουλεύσεσθαι. Ib. ii. 3, 20.

Ὡμολόγησα εἰς τήμερον παρέσεσθαι. PLAT. Symp. 174 A. Ὁμολογήσαντε ποιήσειν τὸ κελευόμενον. Id. Phaedr. 254 B. So ANT. vi. 23 ; AND. i. 62. Compare φαμὲν τούτον ὡμολογηκέναι ταῦτα ποιήσειν with φάσκοντές σε ὡμολογηκέναι πολιτεύεσθαι, PLAT. Crit. 51 E and 52 D. See Crit. 52 C ; and compare ξυνέθου πολιτεύεσθαι, ib. 52 D. Ἐπείσθην τὴν σύνοδον τῇ ὀγδόῃ ὁμολογῆσαι ποιήσασθαι. DEM. xlii. 12.

Ἠγγυᾶτο μηδὲν αὐτοὺς κακὸν πείσεσθαι, *he pledged himself that they should suffer no harm.* XEN. An. vii. 4, 13. Προσαγαγὼν ἐγγυητὰς ἦ μὴν πορεύεσθαι, *having given securities as a pledge that he would go.* Id. Cyr. vi. 2, 39.

Καὶ δή μοι γέρας αὐτὸς ἀφαιρήσεσθαι ἀπειλεῖς. Il. i. 161. So xv. 179 ; Od. xi. 313 ; HDT. vi. 37 ; EUR. Med. 287. Ἠπείλησεν νῆας ἅλαδ' ἑλκέμεν. Il. ix. 682. Ἠπείλησαν ἀποκτεῖναι ἅπαντας τοὺς ἐν τῇ οἰκίᾳ. XEN. Hell. v. 4, 7.

Τάχα οὐδένα εἰκὸς σὺν αὐτῷ βουλήσεσθαι εἶναι, *it is likely that soon nobody will want to be with him.* XEN. Cyr. v. 3, 30. Ἐκ μὲν τοῦ κακῶς πράττειν τὰς πόλεις μεταβολῆς τυχεῖν ἐπὶ τὸ βέλτιον εἰκός ἐστιν, ἐκ δὲ τοῦ παντάπασι γενέσθαι ἀνάστατον καὶ τῶν κοινῶν ἐλπίδων στερηθῆναι. LYCURG. 60.

Ὄμοσσον ἦ μήν μοι ἀρήξειν. Il. i. 76 ; so x. 321. Ὀμόσας ἀπάξειν οἴκαδ', ἐς Τροίαν μ' ἄγει, SOPH. Ph. 941 ; cf. Ph. 594, 623. Ὀμόσαντες ταύταις ἐμμενεῖν. XEN. Hell. v. 3, 26. Ἀναγκάζει τὸν Κερσοβλέπτην ὀμόσαι εἶναι μὲν τὴν ἀρχὴν κοινήν, πάντας δ' ὑμῖν ἀποδοῦναι τὴν χώραν. DEM. xxiii. 170.

FUTURE PERFECT.

137. The future perfect of the dependent moods is rare, except in verbs whose perfect has the meaning of a present (49), where it is an ordinary future (82).

When it occurs in other verbs, it is only in the infinitive of indirect discourse. *E.g.*

Ταῦτα (ἔφη) πεπράξεσθαι δυοῖν ἢ τριῶν ἡμερῶν, *he said that we should see these things already accomplished within two or three days.* DEM. xix. 74. (Here the direct discourse was πεπράξεται ταῦτα, *these things will have been already accomplished.*)

III. TENSES OF THE PARTICIPLE.

138. The tenses of the participle generally express time present, past, or future relatively to the time of the verb with which they are connected.

The uses of the participle with ἄν are not included here. For these see Chapter III.

PRESENT PARTICIPLE.

139. The present participle generally represents an action as going on at the time of its leading verb. *E.g.*

Τοῦτο ποιοῦσιν νομίζοντες δίκαιον εἶναι, *they do this thinking it is just.* Ἐποίουν νομίζοντες, *they were doing it in the thought,* etc. Ἐποίησαν νομίζοντες, *they did it in the thought,* etc. Ποιήσουσιν νομίζοντες, *they will do it in the thought,* etc. Ταῦτ᾽ ἐπράχθη Κόνωνος στρατηγοῦντος, *these things were done when Conon was general.* ISOC. ix. 56. (Στρατηγοῦντος is present relatively to ἐπράχθη.) Καίτοι ταῦτα πράττων τί ἐποίει; *now in doing this what was he doing?* DEM. ix. 15. Ταῦτα περιδεῖν γιγνόμενα, *to see this go on.* DEM. xviii. 63.

140. The present participle is also used as an imperfect, like the present infinitive (119). With the participle this use is not confined (as it is with the infinitive) to indirect discourse. *E.g.*

Οἱ συμπρεσβεύοντες καὶ παρόντες καταμαρτυρήσουσιν, *those who were his colleagues on the embassy and who were present will testify.* DEM. xix. 129. (Here the embassy is referred to as a well-known event in the past.) Φαίνεται γὰρ ἡ νῦν Ἑλλὰς καλουμένη οὐ πάλαι βεβαίως οἰκουμένη, ἀλλὰ μεταναστάσεις τε οὖσαι τὰ πρότερα, καὶ ῥᾳδίως ἕκαστοι τὴν ἑαυτῶν ἀπολείποντες, i.e. *the following things are evident,* Ἑλλὰς οὐ πάλαι βεβαίως ᾠκεῖτο, ἀλλὰ μεταναστάσεις

ἦσαν, καὶ ἕκαστοι τὴν ἑαυτῶν ἀπέλειπον. Thuc. i. 2. Οἶδα τὸν
Σωκράτην δεικνύντα τοῖς ξυνοῦσιν ἑαυτὸν καλὸν κἀγαθὸν ὄντα·
οἶδα δὲ κἀκείνω σωφρονοῦντε ἔστε Σωκράτει συνήστην. Xen.
Mem. i. 2, 18. (The direct discourse was ἐδείκνυ and ἐσωφρονείτην.)

In Thuc. iv. 3, ἡ Πύλος ἐστὶν ἐν τῇ Μεσσηνίᾳ ποτὲ οὔσῃ γῇ,
Pylos is in the country which was once Messenia, οὔσῃ is imperfect, and
denotes time absolutely past, as is shown by ποτέ, without which it
would be the country which is (now) Messenia.

141. An attributive present participle (824) occasionally refers to
time *absolutely* present, even when the leading verb is not present.
This is always denoted by νῦν or some other word in the context. *E.g.*

Τὴν νῦν Βοιωτίαν καλουμένην ᾤκησαν, they settled in the country
now called Boeotia. Thuc. i. 12. Ὁ τοίνυν Φίλιππος ἐξ ἀρχῆς, οὔπω
Διοπείθους στρατηγοῦντος, οὐδὲ τῶν ὄντων ἐν Χερρονήσῳ νῦν
ἀπεσταλμένων, Σέρρειον καὶ Δορίσκον ἐλάμβανε, Philip then in the
beginning, when Diopeithes was not yet general, and when the soldiers who
ARE NOW in the Chersonese had not yet been sent out, seized upon Serrium
and Doriscus. Dem. ix. 15. (Here στρατηγοῦντος is present to the
time of ἐλάμβανε, while ὄντων is present to the time of speaking.)

For a corresponding use of the aorist participle, see 152.

PERFECT PARTICIPLE.

142. The perfect participle in all its uses represents an
action as already finished at the time of its leading verb.
E.g.

Ἐπαινοῦσι τοὺς εἰρηκότας, they praise those who have spoken.
Ἐπῄνεσαν τοὺς εἰρηκότας, they praised those who had spoken. Ἐπαι-
νέσουσι τοὺς εἰρηκότας, they will praise those who will (then) have
spoken. Ἐπέδειξα οὐδὲν ἀληθὲς ἀπηγγελκότα (Αἰσχίνην), I showed
that Aeschines had announced nothing that was true (i.e. I showed, οὐδὲν
ἀληθὲς ἀπήγγελκεν). Dem. xix. 177. Τοὺς δεσμώτας μετεμέλοντο
ἀποδεδωκότες, they repented of having restored the captives. Thuc. v.
35. Τῆς Αἰολίδος χαλεπῶς ἔφερεν ἀπεστερημένος, he took it hard
that he had been deprived of Aeolis. Xen. Hell. iii. 2, 13.

AORIST PARTICIPLE.

143. The aorist participle generally represents an action
as past with reference to the time of its leading verb. *E.g.*

Ταῦτα ποιήσαντες ἀπελθεῖν βούλονται, having done this, they (now)
wish to go away. Ταῦτα εἰπόντες ἀπῆλθον, having said this, they
went away. Οὐ πολλοὶ φαίνονται ξυνελθόντες, not many appear
to have joined in the expedition. Thuc. i. 10. Βοιωτοὶ ἐξ Ἄρνης
ἀναστάντες τὴν Βοιωτίαν ᾤκησαν, Boeotians who had been driven

from Arne settled Boeotia. THUC. i. 12. Ἔφαμεν οὔτε ἐπιστήμην οὔτε
ἄγνοιαν ἐπ' αὐτῷ ἔσεσθαι, ἀλλὰ τὸ μεταξὺ αὖ φανὲν ἀγνοίας καὶ
ἐπιστήμης, i.e. *we said that it would be the province of neither knowledge nor
ignorance, but of that which should have appeared* (φανέν) *in due course
between these.* PLAT. Rep. 478 D. (Here φανέν is past to ἔσεσθαι,
though absolutely future ; see 22.) Ἀφίκετο δεῦρο τὸ πλοῖον, γνόντων τῶν Κεφαλλήνων, ἀντιπράττοντος τούτου, ἐνταῦθα καταπλεῖν
αὐτό, *the vessel arrived here, the Cephallenians having determined that it
should return to this port, although this man opposed it.* DEM. xxxii. 14.
(Here γνόντων denotes time *past* relatively to ἀφίκετο, and ἀντιπράττοντος time *present* relatively to γνόντων, which is its leading verb.)

144. When the aorist participle is used with any form of
λανθάνω, *to escape the notice of,* τυγχάνω, *to happen,* and φθάνω, *to
anticipate,* except the present and imperfect, it does not denote
time past with reference to the verb, but coincides with it in time.
Thus ἔλαθον ἀπελθόντες means *they went away secretly* (= ἀπῆλθον
λάθρα) ; οὐκ ἔφθησαν ἀπελθόντες, *no sooner were they gone* (= οὐ
πρότερον ἀπῆλθον) ; ἔτυχον εἰσελθόντες, *they came in by chance,* or
they happened to come in (= εἰσῆλθον τύχῃ). *E.g.*

Τοὺς δ' ἔλαθ' εἰσελθὼν Πρίαμος, *and Priam entered unnoticed by
them.* Il. xxiv. 477; so xvii. 2 and 89. Ἔλαθεν (αὐτὴν) ἀφθέντα πάντα
καὶ καταφλεχθέντα, *everything took fire and was consumed before she
knew it.* THUC. iv. 133. Λανθάνει (historic present) στήλην παίσας.
SOPH. El. 744. Ἔφθη ὀρεξάμενος, *he aimed a blow first.* Il. xvi. 322.
Αὐτοὶ φθήσονται αὐτὸ δράσαντες, *they will do it first themselves.*
PLAT. Rep. 375 C. Οὐ γὰρ ἔφθη μοι συμβᾶσα ἡ ἀτυχία, καὶ εὐθὺς
ἐπεχείρησαν, κ.τ.λ., *for no sooner did this misfortune come upon me, than
they undertook, etc.* DEM. lvii. 65. Στρατιὰ οὐ πολλὴ ἔτυχε μέχρι
Ἰσθμοῦ παρελθοῦσα, *an army of no great size had by chance marched
as far as the Isthmus.* THUC. vi. 61. Ἔτυχε δὲ κατὰ τοῦτο τοῦ
καιροῦ ἐλθών, *and he happened to come just at that moment.* Id.
vii. 2. Ὀλίγα πρὸς τὰ μέλλοντα τυχεῖν πράξαντες (sc. ἡγοῦνται),
*they think that it was their fortune to accomplish only a little in comparison
with their expectations.* Id. i. 70. So τοῦτ' ἔτυχον λαβών, *I happened
to take this,* AR. Eccl. 375.

Ὁππότερός κε φθῇσιν ὀρεξάμενος χρόα καλόν, *whichever shall
first hit, etc.* Il. xxiii. 805. Βουλοίμην ἂν λαθεῖν αὐτὸν ἀπελθών,
I should like to get away without his knowing it. XEN. An. i. 3, 17.
Τοὺς ἀνθρώπους λήσομεν ἐπιπεσόντες. Ib. vii. 3, 43. Εὐλαβεῖσθαι
παρεκελεύεσθε ἀλλήλοις, ὅπως μὴ πέρα τοῦ δέοντος σοφώτεροι γενόμενοι λήσετε διαφθαρέντες, *you exhorted one another to take care not
to become wise overmuch and so get corrupted unawares.* PLAT. Gorg.
487 D. (Here γενόμενοι is an ordinary aorist, past with reference to
the future phrase λήσετε διαφθαρέντες.)

The last four examples show that this use of the aorist participle is
allowed even when both participle and verb refer to the future.

145. The aorist participle has the same use with συμπίπτω, *to happen*, in Herodotus (890). *E.g.*

Καὶ τόδε ἕτερον συνέπεσε γενόμενον, *and this other event occurred (as it chanced)*. HDT. ix. 101.

So συγκυρέω in HDT. viii. 87 (see 889).

146. An aorist participle with the present or imperfect of any of the above verbs (144) cannot coincide with the verb in time, and retains its own reference to past time. This combination seldom occurs.[1] *E.g.*

Ὅπερ λαβοῦσα τυγχάνει μήτηρ χεροῖν, *which, as it happens, the mother has taken in her hands (happens to have taken)*. EUR. Bacch. 1140. Ἄριστα τυγχάνουσι πράξαντες, *it happens that they fared the best*. ISOC. iv. 103. Δικαίως ἂν τὴν αὐτὴν εὐεργεσίαν ἀπολάβοιμεν, ἥνπερ αὐτοὶ τυγχάνομεν εἰς ὑμᾶς ὑπάρξαντες, *we should justly receive back the same kindness which it is our own fortune to have first shown to you (we happen to have begun)*. Id. xiv. 57. Πρὸς τί τοῦτ᾽ εἰπὼν κυρεῖς; *wherefore did you chance to speak thus (does it chance that you spoke)?* SOPH. El. 1176. Ποῦ κυρεῖ ἐκτόπιος συθείς; Id. O. C. 119. Ὅρα καθ᾽ ὕπνον μὴ καταυλισθεὶς κυρῇ, *see lest it may chance that he has retired to sleep within*. Id. Ph. 30. Compare συνεκύρησε παραπεσοῦσα, *happened to collide*. HDT. viii. 87 (889). Μῖξις μία λύπης τε καὶ ἡδονῆς ξυμπίπτει γενομένη, *i.e. happens to have occurred* (Badham proposes γιγνομένη). PLAT. Phil. 47 D.

Οὐδ᾽ ἄρα Κίρκην ἐξ Ἀίδεω ἐλθόντες ἐλήθομεν, *nor was it unknown to Circe that we had returned from Hades*. Od. xii. 16. Ὅσοι ἐτύγχανον οὕτως ἀθρόοι ξυνεξελθόντες, *all who happened to have thus come out together*. THUC. iii. 111. Εἴ τί που αἰγῶν περιλειφθὲν ἐτύγχανε γένος, *if any race of goats happened to have been left*. PLAT. Leg. 677 E. Ἀρισταγόρῃ δὲ συνέπιπτε τοῦ αὐτοῦ χρόνου πάντα συνελθόντα, *and it was the fortune of A. that all these came to him at the same time*. HDT. v. 36. (Here it is difficult to distinguish the doubly past time ; but the analogy of the other examples, and the difficulty of conceiving an imperfect and aorist as coincident in time, seem decisive.) Ὀρθῶς σφι ἡ φήμη συνέβαινε ἐλθοῦσα, *rightly, as it happened, had the report come to them*. Id. ix. 101. Just below : τῆς αὐτῆς ἡμέρης συνέβαινε γίνεσθαι, *i.e. they* (the battles of Plataea and Mycale) *happened to fall on the same day*.

In LYS. xii. 27 we have the aorist and perfect participles together with ἐτύγχανε, each expressing its own time : ὅστις ἀντειπών γε ἐτύγχανε καὶ γνώμην ἀποδεδειγμένος, *who chanced to have spoken in opposition and to have shown his opinion*.

It appears from these examples that the aorist participle can coincide in its time only with forms which have a similar aoristic or complexive meaning, while in other cases the verb and participle are distinct in time.

---

[1] For the examples of τυγχάνω here given I am indebted to an unpublished paper on this construction by Dr. James R. Wheeler, in which notice of this peculiarity is taken for the first time (so far as I am aware).

147. 1. The perfect participle can always be used with the verbs of 144 to denote an action which is completed at the time of the leading verb. This is the most common way of expressing past time in the participle here. *E.g.*

Ἐτύγχανον ἄρτι παρειληφότες τὴν ἀρχήν, *they happened to have just received their authority.* THUC. vi. 96. Ἐάν τις ἠδικηκώς τι τυγχάνῃ τὴν πόλιν, *if it ever happens that one has wronged the city.* DEM. xviii. 123. So THUC. i. 103 (see 887).

2. The present participle with these verbs is regular, representing an action as *going on* at the time of the verb. See PLAT. Crit. 49 B and the four following examples (with others), in 887.

148. In many constructions in which the aorist participle follows a verb in the sense of the ordinary object infinitive (not in indirect discourse), it does not refer to past time, but differs from the present participle only as the aorist infinitive in such a construction would differ from the present (96). This applies especially to the participle with περιορῶ and ἐφορῶ (περιεῖδον, ἐπεῖδον), in the sense of *allow, not interfere with,* and ὁρῶ (εἶδον) *permit* and *see* (cf. 884 and 885). *E.g.*

Προσδεχόμενος τοὺς Ἀθηναίους κατοκνήσειν περιιδεῖν αὐτὴν [τὴν γῆν] τμηθεῖσαν, ἀνεῖχεν, *expecting that they would be unwilling to see their land ravaged,* etc. THUC. ii. 18. But in ii. 20 we find the aorist infinitive, ἤλπιζεν τὴν γῆν οὐκ ἂν περιιδεῖν τμηθῆναι, *would not let their land be ravaged,* referring to precisely the same event from another point of view (see 903, 6). Μὴ περιίδητε ἡμέας διαφθαρέντας, *do not look on and see us destroyed.* HDT. iv. 118. Οὐ μή σ' ἐγὼ περιόψομαι ἀπελθόντα, *I will by no means let you go.* AR. Ran. 509. Ἔτλησαν ἐπιδεῖν ἐρήμην μὲν τὴν πόλιν γενομένην τὴν δὲ χώραν πορθουμένην, ἅπαντα δὲ τὸν πόλεμον περὶ τὴν πατρίδα τὴν αὑτῶν γιγνόμενον. ISOC. iv. 96. (Here the aorist participle denotes the *laying waste* of the city (as a single act), while the presents denote the continuous *ravaging* of the country and the gradual *coming on* of a state of war. This is precisely the difference between the present and aorist infinitive in similar constructions.) Ἐπεῖδον τὴν ἑαυτῶν πατρίδα ἀνάστατον γενομένην. ANT. v. 79.

Εἰ κεῖνόν γε ἴδοιμι κατελθόντ' Ἄιδος εἴσω, *if I should see him go down and enter Hades.* Il. vi. 284. Μή μ' ἰδεῖν θανόνθ' ὑπ' ἀστῶν, *not to see me killed by the citizens.* EUR. Or. 746. Διὰ τὸ σωφρονεῖν τῷ πώποτ' εἶδες ἤδη ἀγαθόν τι γενόμενον; AR. Nub. 1061. Ὅταν αὐτὸν ἴδῃ ἐξαίφνης πταίσαντα πρὸς τῇ πόλει καὶ ἐκχέαντα τά τε αὑτοῦ καὶ ἑαυτόν, . . . ἢ ἀποθανόντα ἢ ἐκπεσόντα ἢ ἀτιμωθέντα καὶ τὴν οὐσίαν ἅπασαν ἀποβαλόντα. PLAT. Rep. 553 A. So Rep. 498 D, Prot. 324 B ; AESCH. Supp. 423 ; SOPH. Ant. 476.

So after ἀκούω ; as αἴ κ' ἐθέλῃσ' εἰπόντος ἀκουέμεν, *in case he will hear me speak,* Il. vi. 281. Τοσαῦτα φωνήσαντος εἰσηκούσαμεν, *so much we heard him say.* SOPH. O. C. 1645. So also πραθέντα τλῆναι, *endured to be sold,* AESCH. Ag. 1041 ; σπείρας ἔτλα, Sept. 754 :

for τλάω with the regular infinitive, see Isoc. iv. 96, quoted above. So μένειν νοστήσαντα ἄνακτα, *to await the king's return*, Il. xiii. 38.

149. The aorist participle loses its reference to past time also in the peculiar construction in which the participle with its noun has the force of the infinitive with its subject; as μετὰ Συρακούσας οἰκισθεί-σας, *after the founding of Syracuse* (= μετὰ τὸ Συρακούσας οἰκισθῆναι), THUC. vi. 3. See examples in 829 (*b*).

150. An aorist participle denoting that in which the action of a verb of past time consists (845) may express time coincident with that of the verb, when the actions of the verb and the participle are practically one.[1] *E.g.*

Νεῦσ᾽ ἐπὶ οἷ καλέσας, *he called him to him by a nod.* Od. xvii. 330. Βῆ ἀΐξασα. Il. ii. 167. Εὖ γ᾽ ἐποίησας ἀναμνήσας με, *you did well in reminding me.* PLAT. Phaed. 60 C. Μή τι ἐξαμάρτητε ἐμοῦ κατα-ψηφισάμενοι, *lest you make any mistake in condemning me.* Id. Ap. 30 D. Παῖδα κατακανὼν ξυήλῃ πατάξας, *having killed a child by the stroke of a dagger.* XEN. An. iv. 8, 25. Ἤδη πώποτε οὖν ἦ δακοῦσα κακόν τί σοι ἔδωκεν ἦ λακτίσασα; *did your mother ever do you any harm by biting or kicking you?* Id. Mem. ii. 2, 7. Πέμπει ὡς τὸν Ἀστύοχον κρύφα ἐπιστείλας ὅτι Ἀλκιβιάδης αὐτῶν τὰ πράγματα φθείρει, i.e. *he sends a private message*, etc. THUC. viii. 50. After a perfect: ὅσ᾽ ἡμᾶς ἀγαθὰ δέδρακας εἰρήνην ποιήσας, *what blessings you have done us in making a peace!* AR. Pac. 1199.

The following examples among many in the New Testament illustrate the usage :—

Ἀποκριθεὶς εἶπεν ἐν παραβολαῖς αὐτοῖς, λέγων, *he answered and spake to them in parables, and said.* MATTH. xxii. 1. (Λέγων is the ordinary present, less closely connected with εἶπον than ἀποκριθείς.) Προσευξάμενοι εἶπαν, *they prayed and said.* Act. Apost. i. 24. Καλῶς ἐποίησας παραγενόμενος, *thou hast well done that thou art come.* Ib. x. 33.

151. In such passages as ὡμολόγησαν τοῖς Ἀθηναίοις τείχη τε περιελόντες καὶ ναῦς παραδόντες φόρον τε ταξάμενοι, THUC. i. 108, the aorist participle is past with reference to the time of the *beginning* of the peace to which ὡμολόγησαν refers, and the meaning is, *they obtained terms of peace, on condition that they should first (before the peace began) tear down their walls*, etc. Such passages are THUC. i. 101, 108, 115, 117. See Krüger's note on i. 108, and Madvig's *Bemer-kungen*, p. 46. Madvig quotes, to confirm this view, LYS. xii. 68: ὑπέσχετο εἰρήνην ποιήσειν μήτε ὅμηρα δοὺς μήτε τὰ τείχη καθελὼν μήτε τὰς ναῦς παραδούς, i.e. *he promised to make a peace without giving pledges*, etc.

152. An attributive aorist participle occasionally refers to

---

[1] See the discussion of this, with especial reference to the New Testament, where examples of this kind are frequent, by Professor W. G. Ballantine, in the *Bibliotheca Sacra* for October 1884, p. 787.

time *absolutely* past, without regard to the time of its verb.
E.g.

'Ηγεμόνα παρεχόμενοι Μεγάπανον τὸν Βαβυλῶνος ὕστερον τούτων
ἐπιτροπεύσαντα, i.e. *they had as their leader Megapanus, who after
this was made governor of Babylon.* HDT. vii. 62. (Here the aorist
participle is past at the time of writing only; it is even future compared
with the time of παρεχόμενοι.) So in vii. 106 : κατέλιπε δὲ ἄνδρα
τοιόνδε Μασκάμην γενόμενον, and *he left M.* (*in authority*), *who* (*afterwards*) *proved himself such a man* (the evidence of his later merits follows
in a relative sentence).

For the corresponding use of the present participle see 141.

For the use of the aorist infinitive and participle with ἄν, see 207
and 215. For the aorist participle with ἔχω and εἶχον as a circumlocution for the perfect and pluperfect, as θαυμάσας ἔχω and εἶχον, see
47 and 48. For the rare use of the aorist participle with ἔσομαι for
the future perfect, see 81. For the aorist participle in protasis, see
472 and 841.

FUTURE PARTICIPLE.

153. The future participle represents an action as future
with reference to the time of its leading verb. *E.g.*

Τοῦτο ποιήσων ἔρχεται, *he is coming to do this;* τοῦτο ποιήσων
ἦλθεν, *he came to do this.* Πεμφθήσεται ταῦτα ἐρῶν, *he will be sent
to say this.* Οἶδα αὐτὸν τοῦτο ποιήσοντα, *I know that he will do this;*
οἶδα τοῦτο ποιήσων, *I know that I shall do this;* ἤδειν αὐτὸν τοῦτο
ποιήσοντα, *I knew that he would do* 's.

For the various uses of the future participle, and examples, see
Chapter VI.

GNOMIC AND ITERATIVE TENSES.

GNOMIC AORIST AND PERFECT.

154. The aorist and sometimes the perfect indicative are
used in animated language to express *general truths.* These
are called the *gnomic aorist* and the *gnomic perfect,* and are
usually to be translated by our present.

155. These tenses give a more vivid statement of general
truths, by employing a distinct case or several distinct cases in
the past to represent (as it were) all possible cases, and implying
that what has occurred is likely to occur again under similar
circumstances. *E.g.*

Κάτθαν' ὅμως ὅ τ' ἀεργὸς ἀνὴρ ὅ τε πολλὰ ἐοργώς, *the idle man
and he who has laboured much alike must die.* Il. ix. 320. Ὅστε καὶ
ἄλκιμον ἄνδρα φοβεῖ καὶ ἀφείλετο νίκην, *who terrifies even a valiant*

man and snatches his victory away. Il. xvii. 177 (see 157, below). Βία καὶ μεγάλαυχον ἔσφαλεν ἐν χρόνῳ. PIND. Py. viii. 15. Σοφοὶ δὲ μέλλοντα τριταῖον ἄνεμον ἔμαθον, οὐδ᾽ ὑπὸ κέρδει βλάβεν. Id. Nem. vii. 17. Καὶ δὴ φίλον τις ἔκταν᾽ ἀγνοίας ὕπο, *and now one may kill a friend through ignorance.* AESCH. Supp. 499. Ἀλλὰ τὰ τοιαῦτα εἰς μὲν ἅπαξ καὶ βραχὺν χρόνον ἀντέχει, καὶ σφόδρα γε ἤνθησεν ἐπὶ ταῖς ἐλπίσιν, ἂν τύχῃ, τῷ χρόνῳ δὲ φωρᾶται καὶ περὶ αὐτὰ καταρρεῖ. DEM. ii. 10 (see 157 and 171). Ἢν ἄρα σφαλῶσιν, ἀντελπίσαντες ἄλλα ἐπλήρωσαν τὴν χρείαν, *they supply the deficiency* (*as often as one occurs*). THUC. i. 70. Ἢν δέ τις τούτων τι παραβαίνῃ, ζημίαν αὐτοῖς ἐπέθεσαν, i.e. *they impose a penalty upon every one who transgresses.* XEN. Cyr. i. 2, 2. Δεινῶν τ᾽ ἄημα πνευμάτων ἐκοίμισε στένοντα πόντον. SOPH. Aj. 674. Μί᾽ ἡμέρα τὸν μὲν καθεῖλεν ὑψόθεν, τὸν δ᾽ ἦρ᾽ ἄνω. EUR. Fr. 424. Ὅταν ὁ Ἔρως ἐγκρατέστερος γένηται, διαφθείρει τε πολλὰ καὶ ἠδίκησεν. PLAT. Symp. 188 A. Ὅταν τις ὥσπερ οὗτος ἰσχύσῃ, ἡ πρώτη πρόφασις καὶ μικρὸν πταῖσμα ἅπαντα ἀνεχαίτισε καὶ διέλυσεν. DEM. ii. 9.

Ἐπειδάν τις παρ᾽ ἐμοῦ μάθῃ, ἐὰν μὲν βούληται, ἀποδέδωκεν ὃ ἐγὼ πράττομαι ἀργύριον· ἐὰν δὲ μή, ἐλθὼν εἰς ἱερὸν ὀμόσας, ὅσου ἂν φῇ ἄξια εἶναι τὰ μαθήματα, τοσοῦτον κατέθηκεν. PLAT. Prot. 328 B. (Here the perfect and aorist, according to the Mss., are used in nearly the same sense, *he pays*. But Sauppe reads ἀπέδωκεν for ἀποδέδωκεν.) Πολλοὶ διὰ δόξαν καὶ πολιτικὴν δύναμιν μεγάλα κακὰ πεπόνθασιν, i.e. *many always have suffered, and many do suffer.* XEN. Mem. iv. 2, 35. Τὸ δὲ μὴ ἐμποδὼν ἀνανταγωνίστῳ εὐνοίᾳ τετίμηται. THUC. ii. 45.

The gnomic *perfect* is not found in Homer.

156. The sense as well as the origin of the gnomic aorist is often made clearer by the addition of such words as πολλάκις, ἤδη, or οὔπω. Such examples as these form a simple transition from the common to the gnomic use of the aorist :—

Πολλὰ στρατόπεδα ἤδη ἔπεσεν ὑπ᾽ ἐλασσόνων, i.e. *many cases have already arisen,* implying *it often happens.* THUC. ii. 89. Μέλλων γ᾽ ἰατρὸς, τῇ νόσῳ διδοὺς χρόνον, ἰάσατ᾽ ἤδη μᾶλλον ἢ τεμὼν χρόα, *the slow physician, by giving the disease time, may work more cures than he who cuts too deep.* EUR. Fr. 1057. Πολλάκις ἔχων τις οὐδὲ τἀναγκαῖα νῦν αὔριον ἐπλούτησ᾽, ὥστε χἀτέρους τρέφειν, i.e. *cases have often occurred in which such a man has become rich the next day,* etc. PHIL. Fr. 120. Ἀθυμοῦντες ἄνδρες οὔπω τρόπαιον ἔστησαν. PLAT. Criti. 108 C. Οὐδεὶς ἐπλούτησεν ταχέως δίκαιος ὤν, *no man ever became rich suddenly who was just.* MEN. Fr. 294. Compare DEM. iv. 51. (See Krüger, § 53, 10, A. 2.)

157. General truths are more commonly expressed in Greek, as in English, by the present. The present and aorist appear together above, in nearly the same sense ; the gnomic aorist is, however, commonly distinguished from the present by referring to a single or a sudden occurrence, while the present (as usual) implies duration.

Thus in DEM. ii. 10, above, the aorist ἤνθησεν implies a sudden *blossoming out* with hopes, as opposed to the continuance or repetition expressed by ἀντέχει, *hold out*, φωρᾶται, *are detected*, and καταρρεῖ, *fall in ruin*.

158. An aorist somewhat resembling the gnomic is very common in Homeric *similes*, where it is usually to be translated by the present. *E.g.*

Ἤριπε δ' ὡς ὅτε τις δρῦς ἤριπεν, *and he fell, as when an oak falls*, (literally, *as when an oak once fell*). Il. xiii. 389.

This can better be seen in the longer and more complicated examples which are quoted under 547 and 548.

159. The gnomic aorist is found in indirect discourse in the infinitive and participle, and even in the optative. *E.g.*

(a) Ὅπου δ' ὑβρίζειν δρᾶν θ' ἃ βούλεται παρῇ,
    ταύτην νόμιζε τὴν πόλιν χρόνῳ ποτὲ
    ἐξ οὐρίων δραμοῦσαν ἐς βυθὸν πεσεῖν,

but where man is permitted to insult and to work his own will, believe that that state, though it may run before fair breezes, must in time sink to the depths. SOPH. Aj. 1082. (Here πεσεῖν represents ἔπεσεν of the direct form, which can be only gnomic.) Εἴ σοι δέος παρέστηκεν ἡγουμένῳ χαλεπὸν εἶναι φιλίαν συμμένειν, καὶ διαφορᾶς γενομένης κοινὴν ἀμφοτέροις καταστῆναι τὴν συμφοράν, *if you fear, thinking that it is hard for friendship to abide, and that when a quarrel occurs the calamity that arises is common to both* (the direct form would be χαλεπόν ἐστιν, καὶ κοινὴ κατέστη ἡ συμφορά). PLAT. Phaedr. 232 B. Ἡγουμένης δὴ ἀληθείας οὐκ ἄν ποτε φαῖμεν αὐτῇ χορὸν κακῶν ἀκολουθῆσαι, *now when truth leads, we never could say that a chorus of evils accompany her* (ἠκολούθησεν). PLAT. Rep. 490 C.

(b) Σμικρῷ χαλινῷ δ' οἶδα τοὺς θυμουμένους ἵππους καταρτυθέντας, *and I know that high-spirited horses are tamed by a small bit.* SOPH. Ant. 478. Οἶδα δὲ τοὺς τοιούτους ἐν μὲν τῷ κατ' αὐτοὺς βίῳ λυπηροὺς ὄντας, τῶν δὲ ἔπειτα ἀνθρώπων προσποίησιν ξυγγενείας τισὶ καὶ μὴ οὖσαν καταλιπόντας, *I know that such men, although in their own lifetimes they are offensive, yet often leave to some who come after them a desire to claim connexion with them, even where there is no ground for it.* THUC. vi. 16.

(c) A clear case of the gnomic aorist in the optative is seen in PLAT. Rep. 490 B, in the peculiar *oratio obliqua* introduced by ἀπολογησόμεθα ὅτι (in A), which implies a philosophic imperfect (40) and thus takes the optative. We have πεφυκὼς εἴη, ἐμμένοι, ἴοι, etc., representing πέφυκε, ἐμμένει, εἶσι, etc.; and afterwards γνοίη τε καὶ ἀληθῶς ζῴη καὶ τρέφοιτο (representing ἔγνω τε καὶ ἀληθῶς ζῇ καὶ τρέφεται), i.e. *he attains knowledge* (aor.), *and then truly lives and is nourished* (pres.), where the gnomic force of the aorist is plain. (See 676.)

160. The gnomic perfect is found in the infinitive of indirect discourse in DEM. ii. 18 : εἰ δέ τις σώφρων ἢ δίκαιος, παρεῶσθαι καὶ ἐν οὐδενὸς εἶναι μέρει τὸν τοιοῦτον (φησίν), *such a man (he says) is always thrust aside and is of no account.*

161. The imperfect was probably never used in a gnomic sense, except where the form is aoristic in other respects, as ἔκλυον in Il. i. 218, ix. 509; cf. xiv. 133.

ITERATIVE IMPERFECT AND AORIST WITH Ἄν.—IONIC
ITERATIVE FORMS IN -σκον AND -σκόμην.

162. The imperfect and aorist are sometimes used with the adverb ἄν to denote a customary action, being equivalent to our narrative phrase *he would often do this* or *he used to do it. E.g.*

Διηρώτων ἂν αὐτοὺς τί λέγοιεν, *I used to ask them (I would ask them) what they said.* PLAT. Ap. 22 B. Εἴ τινες ἴδοιέν πῃ τοὺς σφετέρους ἐπικρατοῦντας, ἀνεθάρσησαν ἄν, *whenever any saw their friends in any way victorious, they would be encouraged* (i.e. *they were encouraged in all such cases*). THUC. vii. 71. Πολλάκις ἠκούσαμεν ἄν τι κακῶς ὑμᾶς βουλευσαμένους μέγα πρᾶγμα, *we used very often to hear you,* etc. AR. Lys. 511. Εἴ τις αὐτῷ περί του ἀντιλέγοι μηδὲν ἔχων σαφὲς λέγειν, ἐπὶ τὴν ὑπόθεσιν ἐπανῆγεν ἂν πάντα τὸν λόγον, *he always brought the whole discussion back to the main point.* XEN. Mem. iv. 6, 13. Ὁπότε προσβλέψειέ τινας τῶν ἐν ταῖς τάξεσι, τοτὲ μὲν εἶπεν ἄν· ὦ ἄνδρες, κ.τ.λ. τοτὲ δ᾿ αὖ ἐν ἄλλοις ἂν ἔλεξεν. Id. Cyr. vii. 1, 10. So HDT. ii. 109, iii. 51 and 148.

This construction must be distinguished from the potential indicative with ἄν (243). See, however, 249. For the iterative imperfect and aorist with ἄν transferred to the infinitive, see 210.

163. The Ionic iterative imperfect and aorist in -σκον and -σκόμην express the repetition of such actions as the ordinary imperfect and aorist express. *E.g.*

Ἄλλους μὲν γὰρ παῖδας ἐμοὺς πόδας ὠκὺς Ἀχιλλεὺς πέρνασχ᾿, ὅν τιν᾿ ἕλεσκε. Il. xxiv. 751. Ὅκως ἔλθοι ὁ Νεῖλος ἐπὶ ὀκτὼ πήχεας, ἄρδεσκε Αἴγυπτον τὴν ἔνερθε Μέμφιος. HDT. ii. 13.

164. Herodotus sometimes uses the iterative forms in -σκον and -σκόμην with ἄν in the construction of 162. He uses this form of the aorist in only two passages, in both with ἄν. *E.g.*

Φοιτέουσα κλαίεσκε ἂν καὶ ὀδυρέσκετο. iii. 119. Ἐς τούτους ὅκως ἔλθοι ὁ Σκύλης, τὴν μὲν στρατιὴν καταλείπεσκε ἐν τῷ προαστείῳ, αὐτὸς δὲ ὅκως ἔλθοι ἐς τὸ τεῖχος, λάβεσκε ἂν Ἑλληνίδα ἐσθῆτα. iv. 78. So λάβεσκον ἄν, iv. 130. See Krüger, II. § 53, 10, 5.

DEPENDENCE OF MOODS AND TENSES.

165. In dependent sentences, where the construction allows both the subjunctive and the optative, the subjunctive is used if the leading verb is primary, and the optative if it is secondary. (See 21.) *E.g.*

Πράττουσιν ἃ ἂν βούλωνται, *they do whatever they please;* but ἔπραττον ἃ βούλοιντο, *they did whatever they pleased.*

166. In like manner, where the construction allows both the indicative and the optative, the indicative follows primary, and the optative follows secondary tenses. *E.g.*

Λέγουσιν ὅτι τοῦτο βούλονται, *they say that they wish for this;* ἔλεξαν ὅτι τοῦτο βούλοιντο, *they said that they wished for this.*

167. To these fundamental rules we find one special exception. In indirect discourse of all kinds (including sentences denoting a *purpose* or *object* after ἵνα, ὅπως, μή, etc.) either an indicative or a subjunctive may depend upon a secondary tense, so that the mood and tense actually used by the speaker may be retained in the indirect form. (See 667, 1.) *E.g.*

Εἶπεν ὅτι βούλεται, for εἶπεν ὅτι βούλοιτο, *he said that he wished* (i.e. *he said* βούλομαι). Ἐφοβεῖτο μὴ τοῦτο γένηται, for ἐφοβεῖτο μὴ τοῦτο γένοιτο, *he feared lest it should happen* (i.e. *he thought,* φοβοῦμαι μὴ γένηται). (See 318.)

168. An only *apparent* exception occurs when either a potential optative or indicative with ἄν, or an optative expressing a wish, stands in a dependent sentence. In both these cases the original form is retained without regard to the leading verb. It is obvious that a change of mood would in most cases change the whole nature of the expression. *E.g.*

Ἐγὼ οὐκ οἶδ᾽ ὅπως ἄν τις σαφέστερον ἐπιδείξειεν, *I do not know how any one could show this more clearly.* DEM. xxvii. 48. Δεῖ γὰρ ἐκείνῳ τοῦτο ἐν τῇ γνώμῃ παραστῆσαι, ὡς ὑμεῖς ἐκ τῆς ἀμελείας ταύτης τῆς ἄγαν ἴσως ἂν ὁρμήσαιτε. DEM. iv. 17. Εἰ δ᾽ ὑμεῖς ἄλλο τι γνώσεσθε, ὃ μὴ γένοιτο, τίνα οἴεσθε αὐτὴν ψυχὴν ἕξειν; DEM. xxviii. 21.

A few other unimportant exceptions will be noticed as they occur.

169. It is therefore important to ascertain which tenses (in all the moods) are followed, in dependent sentences, as primary tenses by the indicative or subjunctive, and which as secondary tenses by the optative.

INDICATIVE.

170. In the indicative the general rule holds, that the present, perfect, future, and future perfect are primary, and the imperfect, pluperfect, and aorist are secondary tenses.

171. But the historical present is a secondary tense, as it refers to the past; and the gnomic aorist is a primary tense, as it refers to the present.

See HDT. i. 63 (under 33), where the optative follows an historical present; and DEM. ii. 10, THUC. i. 70, XEN. Cyr. i. 2, 2 (under 155), where the subjunctive follows gnomic aorists.

172. The imperfect indicative in the protasis or apodosis of an unfulfilled condition (410) and in its potential use (243), when it refers to *present* time, is a primary tense. *E.g.*

Ἔγραφον ἂν ἡλίκα ὑμᾶς εὖ ποιήσω, εἰ εὖ ᾔδειν, *I would tell you in my letter how great services I would render you, if I knew,* etc. DEM. xix. 40. Πάνυ ἂν ἐφοβούμην, μὴ ἀπορήσωσι λόγων. PLAT. Symp. 193 E. Ἐφοβούμην ἂν σφόδρα λέγειν, μὴ δόξω, κ.τ.λ., *I should be very much afraid to speak, lest I should seem,* etc. PLAT. Theaet. 143 E. Ταῦτ' ἂν ἤδη λέγειν ἐπεχείρουν, ἵν' εἰδῆτε. DEM. xxiii. 7 (for the construction here see 336). See XEN. An. v. 1, 10; DEM. xvi. 12.

173. On the other hand, the aorist indicative in the same constructions (172), and also the imperfect when it refers to the *past*, are secondary tenses. *E.g.*

Ἀλλὰ καὶ τοὺς θεοὺς ἂν ἔδεισας παρακινδυνεύειν, μὴ οὐκ ὀρθῶς αὐτὸ ποιήσοις. PLAT. Euthyph. 15 D. Ἀλλ' οὐδὲ μετὰ πολλῶν μαρτύρων ἀποδιδοὺς εἰκῇ τις ἂν ἐπίστευσεν, ἵν' εἴ τις γίγνοιτο διαφορὰ, κομίσασθαι ῥᾳδίως παρ' ὑμῖν δύνηται. DEM. xxx. 20. (Here the subjunctive δύνηται is properly used after a past tense (318), but the optative shows that the leading verb is secondary.) See ἵνα γίγνοιντο, after an imperfect with ἄν, PLAT. Men. 89 B.

Χρῆν ἐπείρεσθαι κότερα τὴν ἑωυτοῦ ἢ τὴν Κύρου λέγοι ἀρχήν, *he ought to have asked whether the oracle meant his own or Cyrus's empire.* HDT. i. 91.

SUBJUNCTIVE AND IMPERATIVE.

174. All the tenses of the subjunctive and imperative are *primary*, as they refer to future or to present time (89). *E.g.*

Ἔπεσθ' ὅπῃ ἄν τις ἡγῆται, *follow whithersoever any one leads the way.* THUC. ii. 11. Σκοπῶμεν εἰ πρέπει ἢ οὔ. PLAT. Rep. 451 D.

175. But when a subjunctive depends upon a past tense, as often happens in final clauses (318), it may be followed by an optative; as in XEN. Hell. vi. 5, 21, ἦγε τὴν ταχίστην εἰς τὴν Εὔταιαν, βουλόμενος ἀπαγαγεῖν τοὺς ὁπλίτας πρὶν καὶ τὰ πυρὰ τῶν πολεμίων ἰδεῖν, ἵνα μή τις εἴπῃ ὡς φεύγων ἀπαγάγοι, *he led on, wishing to lead off his soldiers before they even saw the enemies' fires, that no one might say that he had led them off in flight* (187). With the other reading, ἵνα μή τις εἴποι, the example would illustrate 176 A (below).

OPTATIVE.

176. As the optative refers sometimes to the future and
sometimes to the past, it exerts upon a dependent verb sometimes the force of a primary, and sometimes that of a secondary
tense.

A. When it refers to the past, as in general suppositions with
εἰ and relatives after past tenses, or when it takes its time from
a past verb (as in a final clause), it has the force of a secondary
tense.

B. When it refers to the future, as in future conditions, in
its use with ἄν, and in wishes, it is properly to be considered
primary. In many cases, however, a double construction is here
allowed. On the principle of assimilation the Greeks preferred
the optative to the subjunctive in certain clauses depending on
an optative, the dependent verb referring to the future like the
leading verb, and differing little from a subjunctive in such a
position. A dependent indicative is, however, very seldom
assimilated to a leading optative. Such assimilation of a dependent verb to an optative takes place (1) *regularly* in protasis
and conditional relative clauses depending on an optative of
future time ; (2) *seldom* in final and object clauses after ἵνα,
ὅπως, μή, etc. ; (3) *very rarely* in the case of the indicative in
indirect quotations or questions, but (4) more freely in the case
of the subjunctive in indirect questions.

These four classes of sentences which depend on an optative
referring to the future are treated separately below (I.–IV.)

177. I. (*a*) In protasis and conditional relative sentences
depending upon an optative which *refers to the future*, the optative
rather than the subjunctive is regularly used to express a
future condition. *E.g.*

Εἴης φορητὸς οὐκ ἄν, εἰ πράσσοις καλῶς, *you would be unendur-
able, if you should be prosperous.* AESCH. Prom. 979. Ἀνδρὶ δέ κ᾽ οὐκ
εἴξειε μέγας Τελαμώνιος Αἴας, ὃς θνητός τ᾽ εἴη καὶ ἔδοι Δημήτερος
ἀκτήν. Il. xiii. 321. Πῶς γὰρ ἄν τις, ἅ γε μὴ ἐπίσταιτο, ταῦτα
σοφὸς εἴη; *for how could any one be wise in those things which he did
not understand?* XEN. Mem. iv. 6, 7. Δέοιτο ἂν αὐτοῦ μένειν, ἔστε
σὺ ἀπέλθοις. Id. Cyr. v. 3, 13. Εἰ ἀποθνήσκοι μὲν πάντα ὅσα τοῦ
ζῆν μεταλάβοι, ἐπειδὴ δὲ ἀποθάνοι μένοι ἐν τούτῳ, ἆρ᾽ οὐ πολλὴ
ἀνάγκη τελευτῶντα πάντα τεθνάναι; *if all things partaking of life
should die, and after dying should remain dead, must it not very certainly
follow that all things would finally be dead?* PLAT. Phaed. 72 C. Ὡς
ἀπόλοιτο καὶ ἄλλος ὅ τις τοιαῦτά γε ῥέζοι, *may any other man
also perish who shall do such things.* Od. i. 47. Τεθναίην, ὅτε μοι
μηκέτι ταῦτα μέλοι, *may I die, when I (shall) no longer care for these !*

MIMN. Fr. i. 2. (Here ὅταν μηκέτι μέλῃ might be used without change of meaning. See the second example under *b*.)

178. (*b*) On the other hand, the dependent verb is sometimes in the subjunctive or future indicative, on the ground that it follows a tense of future time, especially when the leading verb is an optative with ἄν used in its sense approaching that of the future indicative (235). *E.g.*

Ἢν οὖν μάθῃς μοι τοῦτον, οὐκ ἂν ἀποδοίην, *if then you should (shall) learn this for me, I would not pay*, etc. AR. Nub. 116. Ἢν σε ἀφέλωμαι, κάκιστ᾽ ἀπολοίμην. Id. Ran. 586. Ἐγὼ δὲ ταύτην μὲν τὴν εἰρήνην, ἕως ἂν εἷς Ἀθηναίων λείπηται, οὐδέποτ᾽ ἂν συμβουλεύσαιμι ποιήσασθαι τῇ πόλει, *I would never advise the city to make this peace, as long as a single Athenian shall be (should be or was) left.* DEM. xix. 14. (Here ἕως λείποιτο would be the common form.) Ὥσπερ ἂν ὑμῶν ἕκαστος αἰσχυνθείη τὴν τάξιν λιπεῖν ἣν ἂν ταχθῇ ἐν τῷ πολέμῳ, *as each one of you would be ashamed to leave the post at which he may be (might be) placed in war.* AESCHIN. iii. 7. (Here ἣν ταχθείη would be the more common expression.) Τῶν ἀτοπωτάτων ἂν εἴη, εἰ ταῦτα δυνηθεὶς μὴ πράξει, *it would be one of the strangest things if, when he gets the power, he fails (shall fail) to do this.* DEM. i. 26.

179. It will be understood that no assimilation to the optative can take place when the protasis is present or past, as a change to the optative here would involve a change of time. See 561.

180. II. (*a*) In final and object clauses with ἵνα, ὡς, ὅπως, ὄφρα, and μή, the subjunctive (or future indicative) is generally used after a potential optative with ἄν or after an optative in protasis referring to the future. *E.g.*

Ἦ ῥά κε νῦν ἅμ᾽ ἡμῖν οἴκαδ᾽ ἕποιο, ὄφρα ἴδῃ, κ.τ.λ. Od. xv. 431. So Od. vi. 57, xvi. 87 ; Il. xxiv. 264. Δι᾽ ὠτὸς ἂν παῦρα συμφέροι, ὡς ὀρούσῃ. SOPH. El. 1439. Τίς αὐτὸν ἂν καλέσειεν, ὡς ἴδῃ με; EUR. Bacch. 1258. Ὀκνοίην ἂν εἰς τὰ πλοῖα ἐμβαίνειν, μὴ καταδύσῃ· φοβοίμην δ᾽ ἂν τῷ ἡγεμόνι ἕπεσθαι, μὴ ἡμᾶς ἀγάγῃ ὅθεν οὐχ οἷόν τε ἔσται ἐξελθεῖν. XEN. An. i. 3, 17. Τίς οὐκ ἂν φεύγοι, ἵνα μηδ᾽ ἄκων αὐτῇ περιπέσῃ; DEM. xxv. 33. Οἴομαι ἂν ὑμᾶς μέγα ὀνῆσαι τὸ στράτευμα, εἰ ἐπιμεληθείητε ὅπως ἀντὶ τῶν ἀπολωλότων ὡς τάχιστα στρατηγοὶ καὶ λοχαγοὶ ἀντικατασταθῶσιν. XEN. An. iii. 1, 38. Εἰ δὲ καὶ ὅπως εἰρήνη ἔσται φανεροὶ εἴητε ἐπιμελούμενοι. Id. Vect. v. 10 (see 180, *b*).

(*b*) The only examples of the optative here are one in Aristophanes, one in Plato, and six in Xenophon [1] :—

Διὰ τοῦτ᾽ εἰκότως βούλοιντ᾽ ἂν ἡμᾶς ἐξολωλέναι, ἵνα τὰς τελετὰς λάβοιεν. AR. Pac. 411. Οὐκ ἄν πω πάνυ γε μέγα τι εἴη, εἰ βουκόλους . . . προσθεῖμεν, ἵνα οἱ γεωργοὶ ἐπὶ τὸ ἀροῦν ἔχοιεν

---

[1] See Weber, *Absichtssätze*, pp. 220, 221 ; 245-247. I have assumed that Weber's collection of examples is complete.

βοῦς. PLAT. Rep. 370 D. Πειρῴμην (ἂν) μὴ πρόσω ὑμῶν εἶναι, ἵνα,
εἴ πυυ καιρὸς εἴη, ἐπιφανείην. XEN. Cyr. ii. 4, 17. So Cyr. i. 6,
22 ; An. ii. 4, 3, iii. 1, 18 (with various readings in last two). Ἡ
φυλακὴ γελοία τις ἂν φαίνοιτο, εἰ μὴ σύγε ἐπιμελοῖο ὅπως ἔξωθέν
τι εἰσφέροιτο. XEN. Oecon. vii. 39. Εἰ δὲ καὶ ὅπως τὸ ἐν Δελφοῖς
ἱερὸν αὐτόνομον γένοιτο φανεροὶ εἴητε ἐπιμελούμενοι. XEN. Vect.
v. 9 ; but in the next sentence, ὅπως εἰρήνη ἔσται (see 180, a).

181. (c) After an optative in a wish twelve examples of these clauses
with the optative and ten with the subjunctive are cited from Homer
and the lyric and tragic poets. These are

Τάχιστά μοι ἔνδον ἑταῖροι εἶεν, ἵν᾽ ἐν κλισίῃ λαρὸν τετυκοίμεθα
δόρπον. Od. xiv. 407. So xviii. 368, xx. 79. (Subjunctive in Il. xvi.
99, xxiv. 74 ; Od. iv. 735, xviii. 202.) So THEOG. 885, 1119 ; PIND.
Py. v. 120 (?). (Subj. PIND. Nem. viii. 35.) Ἔλθοι ὅπως γένοιτο
τῶνδ᾽ ἐμοὶ λυτήριος. AESCH. Eum. 297. Γενοίμαν ἵν᾽ ὑλᾶεν ἔπεστι
πόντου πρόβλημ᾽ ἁλίκλυστον, τὰς ἱερὰς ὅπως προσείποιμεν
Ἀθήνας. SOPH. Aj. 1217 ; so Ph. 324 and Tr. 953. (Subj. SOPH.
Tr. 1109.) Εἴ μοι γένοιτο φθόγγος ἐν βραχίοσι, ὡς πάνθ᾽ ὁμαρτῇ
τῶν ἔχοιντο γουννάτων. EUR. Hec. 836 ; so Hipp. 732. (Subjunctives
in EUR. Hel. 174, Suppl. 621, I.T. 439, Ion. 671.)

182. No case of either subjunctive or optative after an optative in
a wish in prose is cited by Weber. Perhaps one may be found in
DEM. xviii. 89, where Cod. Σ reads, ὧν διαμάρτοιεν, καὶ μετάσχοιεν
ὧν ὑμεῖς οἱ τὰ βέλτιστα βουλόμενοι τοὺς θεοὺς αἰτεῖτε, μὴ μεταδοῖεν
ὑμῖν ὧν αὐτοὶ προῄρηνται, which can best be translated, *in which
(hopes) may they be disappointed ; and may they (rather) share the blessings
for which you, who wish for the best, pray the Gods, lest they involve you
in the evils which they have chosen for themselves.* Μή with the subjunctive
in this sense occurs twice in Demosthenes, xix. 225, xxxviii. 26. The
alternative, if we keep this reading, is to make μὴ μεταδοῖεν an independent wish, as if it were μηδὲ μεταδοῖεν, the usual reading.

183. In relative sentences expressing a purpose the future indicative
is regularly retained after optatives and even after past tenses of
the indicative (566). For exceptional cases of the optative in this
construction see 573 and 574, with 134.

184. III. In indirect quotations and questions depending
upon an optative which refers to the future, the indicative is
the only form regularly used to represent an *indicative* of the
direct discourse. E.g.

Οὐ γὰρ ἂν τοῦτό γ᾽ εἴποις, ὡς ἔλαθεν. AESCHIN. ii. 151. Ἐκεῖνο
λέγειν ἂν ἐπιχειρήσειε Λεπτίνης, ὡς αἱ λειτουργίαι εἰς πένητας
ἀνθρώπους ἔρχονται (187). DEM. xx. 18 ; so xvi. 4. Εἰ ἀποδειχθείη
τίνα χρὴ ἡγεῖσθαι τοῦ λαισίου. XEN. An. iii. 2, 36.

185. But in DEM. xvi. 5 we find the optative in an indirect quotation : οὐ γὰρ ἐκεῖνό γ᾽ ἂν εἴποιμεν, ὡς ἀνταλλάξασθαι βουλοίμεθ᾽
ἀντιπάλους Λακεδαιμονίους ἀντὶ Θηβαίων. There are no other

readings, and we must call it an exceptional case of assimilation (*we could not say this, that we wished*, etc.) unless we emend it either by reading βουλόμεθα (as proposed by Madvig, *Bemerk.* p. 21) or by inserting ἄν. In PLAT. Rep. 515 D, we find in the best Mss. τί ἄν οἴει αὐτὸν εἰπεῖν, εἴ τις αὐτῷ λέγοι ὅτι τότε μὲν ἑώρα φλυαρίας, νῦν δὲ ὀρθότερα βλέποι; *what do you think he would say, if any one should tell him that all that time he had been seeing foolish phantoms, but that now he saw more correctly?* (Some Mss. read βλέπει.)

In Il. v. 85, Τυδείδην οὐκ ἂν γνοίης ποτέροισι μετείη, the optative represents μέτεστιν in the direct question; but οὐκ ἂν γνοίης here refers to the past, meaning *you would not have known* (442).

186. IV. In indirect questions depending on an optative, the optative may represent an interrogative subjunctive (287) of the direct question. *E.g.*

Οὐκ ἂν ἔχοις ἐξελθὼν ὅ τι χρῷο σαυτῷ, *if you should withdraw, you would not know what to do with yourself.* PLAT. Crit. 45 B. Οὐκ ἂν ἔχοις ὅ τι χρήσαιο σαυτῷ, ἀλλ᾽ ἰλιγγιῴης ἂν καὶ χασμῷο οὐκ ἔχων ὅ τι εἴποις. Id. Gorg. 486 B. The direct questions here were τί χρῶμαι;—τί χρήσωμαι;—τί εἴπω; The subjunctive can always be retained in this construction, even after past tenses (677).

INFINITIVE AND PARTICIPLE.

187. The present, perfect, and future of the infinitive and participle, and the aorist infinitive when it is not in indirect discourse, regularly denote time which is relative to that of the leading verb. They therefore merely *transmit* the force of that verb, as primary or secondary, to the dependent clauses. *E.g.*

Βούλεται λέγειν τί τοῦτό ἐστιν, *he wishes to tell what this is.* Ἐβούλετο λέγειν τί τοῦτο εἴη, *he wished to tell what this was.* Φησὶν ἀκηκοέναι τί ἐστιν, *he says he has heard what it is.* Ἔφη ἀκηκοέναι τί εἴη, *he said he had heard what it was.* Φησὶ ποιήσειν ὅ τι ἂν βούλησθε, *he says he will do whatever you may wish.* Ἔφη ποιήσειν ὅ τι βούλοισθε, *he said he would do whatever you might wish.*

Μένουσιν βουλόμενοι εἰδέναι τί ἐστι. Ἔμενον βουλόμενοι εἰδέναι τί εἴη. Μένουσιν ἀκηκοότες τί ἐστιν. Ἔμενον ἀκηκοότες τί εἴη, *they waited, having heard what it was* (τί ἐστίν;). Μένουσιν ἀκουσόμενοι τί ἐστιν. Ἔμενον ἀκουσόμενοι τί εἴη.

Βούλεται γνῶναι τί τοῦτό ἐστιν, *he wishes to learn what this is.* Ἐβούλετο γνῶναι τί τοῦτο εἴη, *he wished to learn what this was.*

Οὐδενὶ πώποτε τούτων δεδώκατε τὴν δωρεὰν ταύτην οὐδ᾽ ἂν δοίητε, ἐξεῖναι τοὺς ἰδίους ἐχθροὺς ὑβρίζειν αὐτῶν ἑκάστῳ, ὁπότ᾽ ἂν βούληται καὶ ὃν ἂν δύνηται τρόπον. DEM. xxi. 170. Οὔθ᾽ ὑμῖν οὔτε Θηβαίοις οὔτε Λακεδαιμονίοις οὐδεπώποτε συνεχώρηθη τοῦθ᾽ ὑπὸ τῶν Ἑλλήνων, ποιεῖν ὅ τι βούλοισθε, *never was this granted you*, etc., *to do whatever you pleased.* Id. ix. 23. Here ποιεῖν denotes a habit,

and is followed by the optative (532); if the leading verb were συγ-
χωρεῖται, we should have ποιεῖν ὅ τι ἂν βούλησθε. Compare the
two subjunctives in the preceding example.

188. The present infinitive and participle representing the imperfect
(without ἄν), and the perfect representing the pluperfect, are secondary
tenses in themselves, without regard to the leading verb. *E.g.*

Πῶς γὰρ οἴεσθε δυσχερῶς ἀκούειν, εἴ τίς τι λέγοι; *how unwillingly do you think they heard it, when any one said anything?* DEM. vi.
20. So PLAT. Rep. 430 A. See these and other examples under 119.
For the perfect see XEN. Cyr. i. 4, 27, and THUC. v. 49, under 123.

189. The aorist infinitive in indirect discourse is a past tense
in itself, and is therefore secondary. *E.g.*

Φησὶ γνῶναι τί τοῦτο εἴη, *he says that he learned what this was.*
Ἔφη γνῶναι τί τοῦτο εἴη, *he said that he had learned what this was.*

Φησὶ γὰρ ὁμολογῆσαί με τοῦ κλήρου τῷ παιδὶ τὸ ἡμικλήριον
μεταδώσειν εἰ νικήσαιμι τοὺς ἔχοντας αὐτόν (*he says I promised,
μεταδώσω ἐὰν νικήσω*). ISAE. xi. 24. Θαλῆν Θρᾷττά τις θεραπαινὶς
ἀποσκῶψαι λέγεται, ὡς τὰ μὲν ἐν οὐρανῷ προθυμοῖτο εἰδέναι, τὰ
δ' ἔμπροσθεν αὐτοῦ λανθάνοι αὐτόν. PLAT. Theaet. 174 A. Ἆρά σοι
δοκῶ οὐ μαντικῶς ἃ νῦν δὴ ἔλεγον εἰπεῖν, ὅτι Ἀγάθων θαυμαστῶς
ἐροῖ ἐγὼ δ' ἀπορήσοιμι; Id. Symp. 198 A. In all these cases
the optative depends on the aorist infinitive as a *past* tense.

190. The aorist participle properly refers to time past relatively
to the leading verb. It is therefore secondary when the leading
verb is past or present, so that the participle refers to time
absolutely past; but it may be primary when the leading verb
is future, if the participle refers to time absolutely future. *E.g.*

Ἴστε ἡμᾶς ἐλθόντας ἵνα τοῦτο ἴδοιμεν, *you know that we came
that we might see this.*

Ψήφων δὲ δείσας μὴ δεηθείη ποτὲ
      ἵν' ἔχοι δικάζειν, αἰγιαλὸν ἔνδον τρέφει,
and once he took fright lest he might sometime lack pebbles (for votes) *to
enable him to be a judge, and so he keeps a beach on the premises.* AR.
Vesp. 109. Πρὸς ὀργὴν ἐκφέρει, μεθεῖσά μοι λέγειν ἃ χρῄζοιμι,
you rush into a passion, after you gave me leave to say what I wished (i.e.
ἃ ἂν χρῄζῃς). SOPH. El. 628.
Ὑπειπὼν τἆλλα ὅτι αὐτὸς τἀκεῖ πράξοι, ᾤχετο. THUC. i. 90.
Τῇ μάστιγι τυπτέσθω πληγὰς ὑπὸ κήρυκος ἐν τῇ ἀγορᾷ, κηρύξαντος
ὧν ἕνεκα μέλλει τύπτεσθαι, i.e. *let the crier flog him, after proclaiming*
(having proclaimed) *for what he is to be flogged.* PLAT. Leg. 917 E.

191. The tenses of the infinitive and participle with ἄν are
followed, in dependent clauses, by those constructions that
would follow the finite moods which they represent, if these
stood in the same position. See Chapter III.

CHAPTER III.

THE PARTICLE ʼAN.

192. The adverb ἄν (with the epic κέ, Doric κά) has two uses, which must be distinguished.

1. In one use, it denotes that the action of the verb to which it is joined is dependent upon some condition, expressed or implied. This is its force with the secondary tenses of the indicative, and with the optative, infinitive, and participle : with these it belongs strictly to the verb, to which it gives a potential force, like our *would*.

2. In its other use, it is joined regularly to εἰ, *if*, to relative and temporal words, and sometimes to the final particles ὡς, ὅπως, and ὄφρα, when any of these are followed by the subjunctive. Here, although as an adverb it qualifies the verb, it is so closely connected with the relative or particle, that it often coalesces with it, forming ἐάν, ἤν, ἄν ὅταν, ὁπόταν, ἐπειδάν, ἐπάν or ἐπήν (Ionic ἐπεάν).

These statements include only the constructions which are in good use in Attic Greek. For the epic use of κέ or ἄν with the subjunctive in a potential sense (as with the optative) see 201, 1; for κέ or ἄν with the future indicative see 196.

193. There is no word or expression in English which can be used separately to translate ἄν. In its first use (192, 1) we express it by the form of the verb which we use; as ἔλθοι ἄν, *he would go;* ἦλθεν ἄν, *he would have gone.* In its second use, with the subjunctive, it generally has no force that can be made perceptible in translation.

The peculiar use of ἄν can be understood only by a study of the various constructions in which it occurs. These are enumerated below, with references (when it is necessary) to the more full explanation of each in Chapter IV.

194. No theory of the origin of either ἄν or κέ has yet helped to explain their meaning, however valuable the discussion of the question may have been to comparative philology. It seems to be clear that κέ is the older particle; it occurs 621 times in Homer while ἄν occurs 155 times; in Pindar the two are nearly balanced; ἄν has a preference for negative sentences, being very often attached to the negative; ἄν is more emphatic, as appears indeed from its fixed accent, while κέ is enclitic; κέ is much more frequent than ἄν in relative clauses in Homer.[1] But, practically, it is still safe to assume that the two particles are used in substantially the same sense in all epic and lyric poetry. In Herodotus and Attic Greek only ἄν is used.

INDICATIVE WITH ἌΝ.

195. The present and perfect indicative are never used with ἄν.

This seems to occur chiefly when Plato and Aristotle use κἄν εἰ (= καὶ ἄν, εἰ) like καὶ εἰ, without regard to the mood of the verb which is to follow, to which κἄν really belongs. See PLAT. Men. 72 C, κἄν εἰ πολλαί εἰσιν, ἔν γέ τι εἶδος ταὐτὸν πᾶσαι ἔχουσι, i.e. *even if they are many, still (it would seem to follow that) they all have one and the same form.* So Rep. 579 D, Soph. 247 E. So ARISTOT. Pol. iii. 6, 1, κἄν εἰ πλείους, with σκεπτέον ἐστίν.

Examples of a different class (without κἄν εἰ) are obviously corrupt, and have now almost disappeared from our texts. One of the last relics, PLAT. Leg. 712 E, ἐγὼ δὲ οὕτω νῦν ἐξαίφνης ἂν ἐρωτηθεὶς ὄντως ὅπερ εἶπον, οὐκ ἔχω εἰπεῖν, is now simply emended by reading ἀνερωτηθείς.

196. The future indicative is often used with κέ or ἄν by the early poets, especially Homer. The addition of ἄν seems to make the future more contingent than that tense naturally is, sometimes giving it a force approaching that of the optative with ἄν. *E.g.*

Ἀλλ' ἴθ', ἐγὼ δέ κέ τοι Χαρίτων μίαν ὁπλοτεράων δώσω, ὀπυιέμεναι καὶ σὴν κεκλῆθαι ἄκοιτιν, *I will give you one of the younger Graces,* etc. Il. xiv. 267. Καί κέ τις ὧδ' ἐρέει Τρώων ὑπερηνορεόντων, *and some one will* (or *may*) *thus speak.* Il. iv. 176. Ὁ δέ κεν κεχολώσεται ὅν κεν ἵκωμαι, *and he may be angry to whom I come.* Il. i. 139. Εἰ δ' ἄγε, τοὺς ἂν ἐγὼν ἐπιόψομαι· οἱ δὲ πιθέσθων. Il. ix. 167. Πάρ' ἔμοι γε καὶ ἄλλοι, οἵ κέ με τιμήσουσι, *others, who will honour*

---

[1] See Monro, *Homeric Grammar*, pp. 265-267. For Pindar, see Gildersleeve in *Am. Jour. Phil.* iii. pp. 446-455, where may be found a complete enumeration of the passages in Pindar containing either ἄν (30 cases) or κέ (33 cases).

mc. Il. i. 174. Εἰ δ᾽ Ὀδυσεὺς ἔλθοι καὶ ἵκοιτ᾽ ἐς πατρίδα γαῖαν, αἶψά κε σὺν ᾧ παιδὶ βίας ἀποτίσεται ἀνδρῶν. Od. xvii. 539. Here ἀποτίσεταί κε, which may be aorist subjunctive (201, 1), is used nearly in the sense of the optative, corresponding to the optatives in the protasis.

Κέ is much more common with the future than ἄν.

197. The use of ἄν with the future indicative in Attic Greek is absolutely denied by many critics, and the more careful revision of the texts has greatly diminished the number of examples cited in support of it. Still, in several passages, even of the best prose, we must either emend the text against the Mss., or admit the construction as a rare exception. *E.g.*

Αἰγυπτίους δὲ οὐχ ὁρῶ ποίᾳ δυνάμει συμμάχῳ χρησάμενοι μᾶλλον ἂν κολάσεσθε τῆς νῦν σὺν ἐμοὶ οὔσης. ΧΕΝ An. ii. 5, 13. Ἔφη οὖν τὸν ἐρωτώμενον εἰπεῖν, οὐχ ἥκει, φάναι, οὐδ᾽ ἂν ἥξει δεῦρο, *he said that the one who was asked replied, " He hasn't come, and he won't come this way."* PLAT. Rep. 615 D. (The only other reading is ἥξοι. The colloquial style here makes ἄν less objectionable ; see SOPH. Ant. 390, quoted in 208.) Ἔφη λέγων πρὸς ὑμᾶς ὡς, εἰ διαφευξοίμην, ἤδη ἂν ὑμῶν οἱ υἱεῖς πάντες παντάπασι διαφθαρήσονται. Id. Ap. 29 C. Κἂν ἔτ᾽ ἔτι φόνιον ὄψομαι αἷμα (so the Mss.). ΕΥΡ. El. 484.

See 208 and 216, on the future infinitive and participle with ἄν.

198. The most common use of ἄν with the indicative is with the secondary tenses, generally the imperfect and aorist, in the apodosis of an unfulfilled condition (410) or in a potential sense (243).

199. The imperfect and aorist indicative are sometimes used with ἄν in an iterative sense (162), which construction must not be confounded with that just mentioned (198).

SUBJUNCTIVE AND OPTATIVE WITH ἌΝ.

200. In Attic Greek ἄν is regularly used with the subjunctive in protasis and in conditional relative sentences, and sometimes in final clauses with ὡς and ὅπως, being always closely joined with the particle or the relative ; but never in independent sentences. See 325, 381, and 522.

201. 1. In epic poetry, when the independent subjunctive has nearly the sense of the future indicative (284), it sometimes takes κέ or ἄν. This forms a future potential expression, nearly equivalent to the future indicative with κέ or ἄν, and sometimes approaching the optative with κέ or ἄν. *E.g.*

Εἰ δέ κε μὴ δώῃσιν, ἐγὼ δέ κεν αὐτὸς ἕλωμαι, *and if he does not give her up, I will take her myself.* Il. i. 324 ; see also i. 137.

See 285 and 452. For the variety of nearly equivalent future potential forms which the Homeric language presents, reduced to one in Attic Greek, see 235.

2. The epic language has κέ or ἄν with the subjunctive in the constructions of 192, 2 ; but its use of κέ or ἄν in conditions is less strict, and that with final particles is more free, than the Attic use of ἄν.

See 325-328 ; 450-454 ; 468-471 ; 538-541.

202. The optative with ἄν forms the apodosis of the less vivid future condition (like the English form with *would* or *should*), or has a potential sense. *E.g.*

Εἰ τοῦτο ποιήσειεν, ἄθλιος ἂν εἴη, *if he should do this, he would be wretched.* Ἡδέως ἂν ἐροίμην αὐτόν, *I should like to ask him.* (See 233 and 455.)

For construction of ἄν or κέ with εἰ or the final particles and the optative, see 460 ; and 329, 330, 349, 350, 351.

203. As the future optative came into common use after the future indicative with ἄν (196) was nearly extinct, it was never used with ἄν.

Infinitive with ἌΝ.

204. The infinitive can be used with ἄν in all cases in which a finite verb would have ἄν if it stood in its place.

This is found chiefly in indirect discourse, in which each tense of the infinitive with ἄν represents the *corresponding tenses* of the indicative or optative with ἄν in the direct form. The context must decide whether the indicative or optative is represented in each case.

205. (*Present.*) The present infinitive, which represents also the imperfect (119), when used with ἄν, may be equivalent either to the imperfect indicative with ἄν or to the present optative with ἄν. It can represent no other form, as no other form of these tenses has ἄν joined with the verb in a finite mood. *E.g.*

Φησὶν αὐτοὺς ἐλευθέρους ἂν εἶναι, εἰ τοῦτο ἔπραξαν, *he says that they would (now) be free, if they had done this* (εἶναι ἄν representing ἦσαν ἄν). Φησὶν αὐτοὺς ἐλευθέρους ἂν εἶναι, εἰ τοῦτο πράξειαν, *he says that they would (hereafter) be free, if they should do this* (εἶναι ἄν representing εἴησαν ἄν). Οἴεσθε γὰρ τὸν πατέρα οὐκ ἂν φυλάτ-τειν καὶ τὴν τιμὴν λαμβάνειν τῶν ξύλων; *do you think he would not have taken care and have received the pay for the timber?* DEM. xlix. 35. (Here the direct discourse would be ἐφύλαττεν ἂν καὶ ἐλάμβανεν.)

Μαρτυρίῳ ἐχρῶντο, μὴ ἂν τούς γε ἰσοψήφους ἄκοντας, εἰ μή τι ἠδίκουν οἷς ἐπῇεσαν, ξυστρατεύειν, *they used us as an argument, that people who had an equal vote with themselves (like us) would not be serving with them against their will, unless those whom they attacked were guilty of some wrong.* Thuc. iii. 11.   Οἶμαι γὰρ ἂν οὐκ ἀχαρίστως μοι ἔχειν, *for I think it would not be a thankless labour* (οὐκ ἂν ἔχοι). Xen. An. ii. 3, 18.

206. (*Perfect.*) The perfect infinitive, which represents also the pluperfect (123), when used with ἄν, may be equivalent either to the pluperfect indicative with ἄν or to the perfect optative with ἄν.   *E.g.*

Εἰ μὴ τὰς ἀρετὰς ὑπὲρ αὐτῶν ἐκείνας οἱ Μαραθῶνι καὶ Σαλαμῖνι παρέσχοντο, . . . πάντα ταῦθ᾽ ὑπὸ τῶν βαρβάρων ἂν ἑαλωκέναι (sc. φήσειεν ἄν τις), *if those at Marathon and Salamis had not exhibited those deeds of valour in their behalf, any one would say that all these would have been captured by the barbarians.* Dem. xix. 312.   (Here ἑαλωκέναι ἄν represents ἑαλώκεσαν ἄν.)   Ἀλλ᾽ οὐκ ἂν ἡγοῦμαι αὐτοὺς δίκην ἀξίαν δεδωκέναι, εἰ ἀκροασάμενοι αὐτῶν καταψηφίσαισθε, *but I do not believe they would (then) have suffered sufficient punishment, if you after hearing them should condemn them.* Lys. xxvii. 9.   (Here the protasis in the optative shows that δεδωκέναι ἄν represents δεδωκότες ἂν εἶεν (103); but if the protasis were εἰ κατεψηφίσασθε, *if you had condemned them*, δεδωκέναι ἄν would represent ἐδεδώκεσαν ἄν, *they would have suffered*.)   See also, in xxvii. 8, οὐκ ἂν ἀπολωλέναι, ἀλλὰ δίκην δεδωκέναι, representing perfect optatives with ἄν.   Ἀνδραποδώδεις ἂν δικαίως κεκλῆσθαι (ἡγεῖτο). Xen. Mem. i. 1, 16.   (Here κεκλῆσθαι ἄν represents κεκλημένοι ἂν εἶεν.)

These constructions are of course rare, as are the forms of the finite moods here represented.

207. (*Aorist.*) The aorist infinitive with ἄν may be equivalent either to the aorist indicative with ἄν or to the aorist optative with ἄν.   *E.g.*

Οὐκ ἂν ἡγεῖσθ᾽ αὐτὸν κἂν ἐπιδραμεῖν; *do you not believe that (if this had been so) he would even have run thither?* i.e. οὐκ ἂν ἐπέδραμεν; Dem. xxvii. 56.   Ἄνευ δὲ σεισμοῦ οὐκ ἄν μοι δοκεῖ τὸ τοιοῦτο ξυμβῆναι γενέσθαι (οὐκ ἂν ξυμβῆναι representing οὐκ ἂν ξυνέβη), *but unless there had been an earthquake, it does not seem to me that such a thing could by any chance have happened.* Thuc. iii. 89.   Τοὺς Ἀθηναίους ἤλπιζεν ἴσως ἂν ἐπεξελθεῖν καὶ τὴν γῆν οὐκ ἂν περιιδεῖν τμηθῆναι (i.e. ἴσως ἂν ἐπεξέλθοιεν καὶ οὐκ ἂν περιίδοιεν). Id. ii. 20.   Οὐδ᾽ ἂν κρατῆσαι αὐτοὺς τῆς γῆς ἡγοῦμαι (i.e. κρατήσειαν ἄν). Id. vi. 37.

208. (*Future.*) The future infinitive with ἄν can be equivalent only to the Homeric construction of the future indicative with ἄν.   But as ἄν is not found in Homer with the future infinitive, this construction rests chiefly on the authority of passages in Attic writers, and is subject to the same doubts and suspicions as the future indicative with ἄν in those writers. (See 197.) Unless we exterminate the latter, there can be no objection to this as its representative. In the following passages it is still retained on the best Ms. authority.

Νομίζοντες, εἰ ταύτην πρώτην λάβοιεν, ῥᾳδίως ἂν σφίσι τἆλλα προσχωρήσειν. THUC. ii. 80. (Here the direct discourse would regularly have had either the future indicative without ἄν, or the aorist optative with ἄν.) The same may be said of THUC. v. 82, νομίζων μέγιστον ἂν σφᾶς ὠφελήσειν (where one Ms. reads by correction ὠφελῆσαι). See also THUC. vi. 66 ; viii. 25 and 71 ; and PLAT. Crit. 53 D ; Crat. 391 A. Σχολῇ ποθ᾽ ἥξειν δεῦρ᾽ ἂν ἐξηύχουν ἐγώ, I declared that I should be very slow to come hither again. SOPH. Ant. 390. (Here the colloquial style may account for ἥξειν ἄν, as for ἥξει ἄν in PLAT. Rep. 615 D, unless we take ἄν with ἐξηύχουν. See 197.) In PIND. Ol. i. 108, we have εἰ δὲ μὴ ταχὺ λίποι, ἔτι γλυκυτέραν κεν ἔλπομαι σὺν ἅρματι θοῷ κλείξειν.

As the future optative is never used with ἄν (203), this can never be represented by the future infinitive with ἄν.

209. The infinitive with ἄν is rare in the early poets, occurring but once in Homer, Il. ix. 684 (quoted under 683), and three times in Pindar, Pyth. vii. 20 (present), Pyth. iii. 110 (aorist), and Ol. i. 108 (future, quoted in 208).

210. The infinitive with ἄν sometimes represents an iterative imperfect or aorist indicative with ἄν (162). This must be carefully distinguished from the potential use. E.g.

Ἀκούω Λακεδαιμονίους τότε ἐμβαλόντας ἂν καὶ κακώσαντας τὴν χώραν ἀναχωρεῖν ἐπ᾽ οἴκου πάλιν, I hear that the Lacedaemonians at that time, after invading and ravaging the country, used to return home again. DEM. ix. 48. (Here ἀναχωρεῖν ἄν represents ἀνεχώρουν ἄν in its iterative sense, they used to return.) Φασὶ μὲν γὰρ αὐτὸν ἐρεπτόμενον τὰ τῶν ἐχόντων ἀνέρων οὐκ ἂν ἐξελθεῖν ἀπὸ τῆς σιπύης· τοὺς δ᾽ ἀντιβολεῖν ἂν ὁμοίως, they say that, when he was feeding on men of wealth, he never would get away from the meal-tub ; and they all alike used to implore him (οὐκ ἂν ἐξῆλθεν, οἱ δὲ ἠντιβόλουν ἄν). AR. Eq. 1295.

211. The infinitive with ἄν, in the cases already mentioned, stands in indirect discourse after a verb of *saying* or *thinking*. Sometimes, however, it is found in other constructions, where the present or aorist infinitive (without ἄν) would be expected. In such cases there is an approach to the usage of indirect discourse, so far at least that the infinitive with ἄν has the force of the corresponding tense of the indicative or optative. E.g.

Τὰ δὲ ἐντὸς οὕτως ἐκαίετο, ὥστε ἥδιστα ἂν ἐς ὕδωρ ψυχρὸν σφᾶς αὐτοὺς ῥίπτειν, so that they would most gladly have thrown themselves into cold water (ῥίπτειν ἄν here being equivalent to ἔρριπτον ἄν). THUC. ii. 49. Μιᾶς τρέφει πρὸς νυκτός, ὥστε μήτ᾽ ἐμὲ μήτ᾽ ἄλλον,

ὅστις φῶς ὁρᾷ, β λ ά ψ α ι ποτ᾽ ἄν, *so that you could harm* (βλάψειας ἄν)
neither me nor any other who beholds the light. SOPH. O.T. 374. So Tr.
669. Ἔφθασαν παρελθόντες τὴν τῶν Ἀθηναίων οἰκοδομίαν, ὥστε
μηκέτι μήτε αὐτοὶ κωλύεσθαι ὑπ᾽ αὐτῶν, ἐκείνους τε καὶ παντάπασιν
ἀπεστερηκέναι, εἰ καὶ κρατοῖεν, μὴ ἂν ἔτι σφᾶς ἀποτειχίσαι, *so as
to be no longer themselves obstructed by them, and so as to have deprived
them absolutely of the power of ever again walling them in, even if they
should be victorious.* THUC. vii. 6. Ὑσομεν τὴν νύκτα πᾶσαν· ὥστ᾽
ἴσως βουλήσεται κ ἂ ν ἐν Αἰγύπτῳ τ υ χ ε ῖ ν ὧν μᾶλλον ἢ κρῖναι κακῶς,
*we will rain all night long, so that perhaps he will wish to have the luck to
be* (*that he might by chance find himself*) *in Egypt rather than to judge
unfairly.* AR. Nub. 1130. (Here τυχεῖν ἄν follows βούλομαι like the
future infinitive in THUC. vi. 57 : see 113.) We have ἐλπίζω followed
by the infinitive and ἄν in THUC. vii. 61, τὸ τῆς τύχης κ ἂ ν μεθ᾽ ἡμῶν
ἐλπίσαντες στῆναι, *hoping that fortune may take sides with us* (σταίη
ἄν). See also SOPH. El. 1482, ἀλλά μοι πάρες κ ἂ ν σμικρὸν ε ἰ π ε ῖ ν,
but permit me at least to say a little (*that I might say even a little,*
εἴποιμι ἄν).

See the corresponding use of the future infinitive in similar expressions, where there is the same approach to indirect discourse (113).

212. Even the infinitive with the article occasionally takes ἄν, as in
ANT. v. 8, τοῦτο ὑμᾶς διδάξω, οὐ τῷ φεύγειν ἂν τὸ πλῆθος τὸ ὑμέτερον,
this I will teach you, not because I would avoid your people. In SOPH.
Ant. 236, τῆς ἐλπίδος τὸ μὴ π α θ ε ῖ ν ἂν ἄλλο, *the hope that I could
not suffer anything else,* the construction is practically that of indirect
discourse (794).

PARTICIPLE WITH ἌΝ.

213. When the participle is used with ἄν, each tense
represents the corresponding tenses of the indicative or
optative with ἄν.

The participle with ἄν is not, like the infinitive with ἄν, found
chiefly in indirect discourse ; but ἄν is more frequently added to
an *attributive* or a *circumstantial* participle (822) to give it a potential
force equivalent to that of the indicative or optative with ἄν.
The participle with ἄν is not found in Homer or Pindar.

214. (*Present.*) The present participle (like the present
infinitive) with ἄν represents the imperfect indicative or the
present optative with ἄν. E.g.

Οἶδα αὐτοὺς ἐλευθέρους ἂν ὄντας, εἰ τοῦτο ἔπραξαν, *I know they
would* (*now*) *be free, if they had done this.* Οἶδα αὐτοὺς ἐλευθέρους ἂν
ὄντας, εἰ τοῦτο πράξειαν, *I know they would* (*hereafter*) *be free, if they
should do this.* (In the former ὄντας ἄν represents ἦσαν ἄν, in the
latter εἴησαν ἄν.) Τῶν λαμβανόντων δίκην ὄντες ἂν δικαίως (i.e.
ἦμεν ἄν), *whereas we should justly be among those who inflict punishment.*

DEM. lvii. 3. Ὅπερ ἔσχε μὴ κατὰ πόλεις αὐτὸν ἐπιπλέοντα τὴν Πελοπόννησον πορθεῖν, ἀδυνάτων ἂν ὄντων (ὑμῶν) ἐπιβοηθεῖν, *when you would have been unable to bring aid* (ἀδύνατοι ἂν ἦτε). THUC. i. 73. Πόλλ' ἂν ἔχων ἕτερ' εἰπεῖν περὶ αὐτῆς παραλείπω, *although I might be able to say many other things about it, I omit them.* DEM. xviii. 258. Ἀπὸ παντὸς ἂν φέρων λόγου δικαίου μηχάνημα ποικίλον (i.e. ὃς ἂν φέροις), *thou who wouldst derive,* etc. SOPH. O. C. 761.

215. (*Aorist.*) The aorist participle with ἄν represents the aorist indicative or the aorist optative with ἄν. *E.g.*

Οὔτε ὄντα οὔτε ἂν γενόμενα λογοποιοῦσιν, *they relate things which are not real, and which never could happen* (i.e. οὐκ ἂν γένοιτο). THUC. vi. 38. Ἐφ' ἡμῶν οὐ γεγονὸς οὐδ' οἶδα εἰ γενόμενον ἄν, (a thing) *which has not occurred in our day, and I doubt whether it ever could occur* (γένοιτο ἄν). PLAT. Rep. 414 C. Ἀλλὰ ῥᾳδίως ἂν ἀφεθεὶς, εἰ καὶ μετρίως τι τούτων ἐποίησε, προείλετο ἀποθανεῖν, *whereas he might easily have been acquitted,* etc. XEN. Mem. iv. 4, 4. Καὶ εἰ ἀπήχθησθε ὥσπερ ἡμεῖς, εὖ ἴσμεν μὴ ἂν ἧσσον ὑμᾶς λυπηροὺς γενομένους τοῖς ξυμμάχοις, καὶ ἀναγκασθέντας ἂν ἢ ἄρχειν, κ.τ.λ. (i.e. οὐκ ἂν ἐγένεσθε, καὶ ἠναγκάσθητε ἄν), *if you had become odious as we have, we are sure that you would have been no less oppressive to your allies, and that you would have been forced,* etc. THUC. i. 76. Ὁρῶν τὸ παρατείχισμα ἁπλοῦν ὂν καὶ, εἰ ἐπικρατήσειέ τις τῆς ἀναβάσεως, ῥᾳδίως ἂν αὐτὸ ληφθέν (i.e. ῥᾳδίως ἂν ληφθείη), *seeing that it would easily be taken,* etc. Id. vii. 42. So ὡς τάχ' ἂν συμβάντων, DEM. xxiii. 58 (see 918).

216. (*Future.*) A few cases of the future participle with ἄν, representing the future indicative with ἄν, are found in Attic writers. These rest on the same authority as those of the future indicative and the future infinitive with ἄν (197 and 208). *E.g.*

Ἀφίετε ἢ μὴ ἀφίετε, ὡς ἐμοῦ οὐκ ἂν ποιήσοντος ἄλλα, οὐδ' εἰ μέλλω πολλάκις τεθνάναι (i.e. οὐκ ἂν ποιήσω ἄλλα): so all Mss. PLAT. Ap. 30 B. Τοὺς ὁτιοῦν ἂν ἐκείνῳ ποιήσοντας ἀνῃρηκότες ἐκ τῆς πόλεως ἔσεσθε. DEM. xix. 342. (Here most Mss., including Σ, have ποιήσοντας, but A has ποιήσαντας.) Πάλαι τις ἡδέως ἂν ἴσως ἐρωτήσων κάθηται, *many a one has long been sitting here who perhaps would be very glad to ask* (so all Mss.). DEM. ix. 70.

217. The participle with ἄν can never represent a protasis, because there is no form of protasis which could be represented by a participle, where ἄν is separable from the conditional particle. (See 224.)

POSITION OF ἌΝ.

218. 1. When ἄν is used with the subjunctive, if it does not coalesce with the relative or particle into one word (as in ἐάν, ὅταν, etc.), it is generally separated from it only by such monosyllables as μέν, δέ, τέ, γάρ, καί, νύ, πέρ, etc., rarely τὶς.

See examples under 444 and 529.

2. In Homer and Hesiod two such words may precede κέ; as εἴ περ γάρ κεν, εἰ γάρ νύ κε, εἰ γάρ τίς κε, ὃς μὲν γάρ κε. This is rare with ἄν in prose ; see DEM. iv. 45, ὅποι μὲν γὰρ ἄν. Exceptional are ὅποι τις ἄν, οἶμαι, προσθῇ, DEM. ii. 14 ; ὅ τι ἄλλο ἂν δοκῇ ὑμῖν, XEN. Cyr. iv. 5, 52. The strange καθ' ὧν μηνύῃ ἄν τις, ANT. v. 38, is now corrected to ἂν μηνύῃ, but still stranger is ὅποσον ἡ φάρυγξ ἂν ἡμῶν χανδάνῃ (?), AR. Ran. 259.

219. When ἄν is used with the optative or indicative, it may either stand near the verb, or be attached to some other emphatic word. Particularly, it is very often placed directly after interrogatives, negatives, adverbs of *time, place*, etc., and other words which especially affect the sense of the sentence. *E.g.*

Ἀλλὰ τίς δὴ θεῶν θεραπεία εἴη ἂν ἡ ὁσιότης ; PLAT. Euthyph. 13 D. Ἀλλ᾽ ὁμῶς τὸ κεφάλαιον αὐτῶν ῥᾳδίως ἂν εἴποις. Id. 14 A. Οὐκ ἂν δὴ τόνδ᾽ ἄνδρα μάχης ἐρύσαιο μετελθών, Τυδείδην, ὃς νῦν γε ἂν καὶ Διὶ πατρὶ μάχοιτο ; Il. v. 456. Πῶς ἂν τὸν αἱμυλώτατον, ἐχθρὸν ἄλημα, τούς τε δισσάρχας ὀλέσσας βασιλῆς, τέλος θάνοιμι καὐτός. SOPH. Aj. 389. Πολλὰ κἂν ἄκων ἔδρων. Id. O. T. 591. Τάχιστ᾽ ἄν τε πόλιν οἱ τοιοῦτοι ἑτέρους πείσαντες ἀπολέσειαν. THUC. ii. 63.

220. 1. By a peculiar usage, ἄν is often separated from its verb by such verbs as οἴομαι, δοκῶ, φημί, οἶδα, etc. In such cases care must be taken to connect the ἄν with the verb to which it really belongs. *E.g.*

Καὶ νῦν ἡδέως ἄν μοι δοκῶ κοινωνῆσαι, and now I think I should gladly take part (ἄν belonging to κοινωνῆσαι). XEN. Cyr. viii. 7, 25. So AESCHIN. iii. 2 (end). Οὐδ᾽ ἂν ὑμεῖς οἶδ᾽ ὅτι ἐπαύσασθε πολεμοῦντες, nor would you (I am sure) have ceased fighting. DEM. vi. 29. Πότερα γὰρ ἂν οἴεσθε ῥᾷον εἶναι ; DEM. xlix. 45. Ἐκλέξαντα ἃ μήτε προῄδει μηδεὶς μήτ᾽ ἂν ᾠήθη τήμερον ῥηθῆναι, selecting what nobody knew beforehand and nobody thought would be mentioned to-day. DEM. xviii. 225. (Here ῥηθῆναι ἄν = ῥηθείη ἄν. If ἄν were taken with ᾠήθη, the meaning would be, what nobody would have thought had been mentioned.) Τί οὖν ἄν, ἔφην, εἴη ὁ Ἔρως; PLAT. Symp. 202 D.

2. Especially irregular are such expressions as οὐκ οἶδα ἂν εἰ, or οὐκ ἂν οἶδα εἰ, followed by an optative or indicative to which the ἄν belongs. *E.g.*

Οὐκ οἶδ᾽ ἂν εἰ πείσαιμι, I do not know whether I could persuade him. EUR. Med. 941. (The more regular form would be οὐκ οἶδα εἰ πείσαιμι ἄν.) So Alc. 48. Οὐκ ἂν οἶδ᾽ εἰ δυναίμην. PLAT. Tim. 26 B. Οὐκ οἶδ᾽ ἂν εἰ ἐκτησάμην παῖδα τοιοῦτον. XEN. Cyr. v. 4, 12. So οὐκ ἂν οἶδ᾽ ὅ τι ἄλλο εἶχον ψηφίσασθαι, I do not know what other vote I could have given (τί ἄλλο εἶχον ἂν ψηφίσασθαι ;), DEM. xlv. 7.

221. (Τάχ᾽ ἄν.) Among the words to which ἄν is very frequently joined is τάχα, perhaps (i.e. *quickly, soon*), the two forming τάχ᾽ ἄν, which expression is sometimes supposed to mean *perhaps*. But τάχ' ἄν cannot be used unless the ἄν belongs in its ordinary sense to the verb of the sentence.

Thus τάχ' ἄν γένοιτο means *it might perhaps happen*, and τάχ' ἄν ἐγένετο means *it might perhaps have happened ;* but the latter can never mean *perhaps it happened*, like ἴσως ἐγένετο. Τάχα alone often means *perhaps*, as in XEN. An. v. 2, 17. Aristotle writes τάχα and ἄν separately in the same sense as τάχ' ἄν; as τάχα δὲ καὶ μᾶλλον ἄν ταύτην ὑπολάβοι, Eth. Nic. i. 5, 6.

222. Ἄν never begins a sentence, or a clause before which a comma could stand. But it may directly follow a parenthetic clause, provided some part of its own clause precedes. *E.g.*

Ἀλλ' ὦ μέλ' ἄν μοι σιτίων διπλῶν ἔδει, AR. Pac. 137. So τὸ μέλλον, ἐπεὶ γένοιτ', ἄν κλύοις (or without the commas), *the future you can hear when it comes*, AESCH. Ag. 250.

REPETITION OF Ἄν.

223. Ἄν is sometimes used twice, or even three times, with the *same verb*. This may be done in a long sentence, to make the conditional force felt through the whole, especially when the connexion is broken by intermediate clauses. It may also be done in order to emphasise particular words with which ἄν is joined, and to make them prominent as being affected by the contingency. *E.g.*

Ὥστ' ἄν, εἰ σθένος λάβοιμι, δηλώσαιμ' ἄν οἷ' αὐτοῖς φρονῶ. SOPH. El. 333. Οὔ τἂν ἑλόντες αὖθις ἀνθαλοῖεν ἄν. AESCH. Ag. 340. Ἄλλους γ' ἄν οὖν οἰόμεθα τὰ ἡμέτερα λαβόντας δεῖξαι ἄν μάλιστα εἴ τι μετριάζομεν. THUC. i. 76. (See 220.) Οὔτ' ἄν κελεύσαιμ', οὔτ' ἄν, εἰ θέλοις ἔτι πράσσειν, ἐμοῦ γ' ἄν ἡδέως δρῴης μέτα. SOPH. Ant. 69. Λέγω καθ' ἕκαστον δοκεῖν ἄν μοι τὸν αὐτὸν ἄνδρα παρ' ἡμῶν ἐπὶ πλεῖστ' ἄν εἴδη καὶ μετὰ χαρίτων μάλιστ' ἄν εὐτραπέλως τὸ σῶμα αὔταρκες παρέχεσθαι. THUC. ii. 41. (Here ἄν is used three times, belonging to παρέχεσθαι.) Ὑμῶν δὲ ἔρημος ὢν οὐκ ἄν ἱκανὸς οἶμαι εἶναι οὔτ' ἄν φίλον ὠφελῆσαι οὔτ' ἄν ἐχθρὸν ἀλέξασθαι. XEN. An. i. 3, 6. (Here ἄν is used three times, belonging to εἶναι.) Οὐκ ἄν ἡγεῖσθ' αὐτὸν κἄν ἐπιδραμεῖν; DEM. xxvii. 56.

224. A participle representing a protasis (472) is especially apt to have an emphatic ἄν near it. This, by showing that the verb is to form an apodosis, tends to point out the participle as conditional in an early part of the sentence. *E.g.*

Νομίσατε τό τε φαῦλον καὶ τὸ μέσον καὶ τὸ πάνυ ἀκριβὲς ἄν ξυγ-κραθὲν μάλιστ' ἄν ἰσχύειν, *believe that these, if they should be united, would be especially strong*, THUC. vi. 18. (Here ξυγκραθέν, not with ἄν, is equivalent to εἰ ξυγκραθείη.) Ἀγῶνας ἄν τίς μοι δοκεῖ, ἔφη, ὦ πάτερ, προειπὼν ἑκάστοις καὶ ἆθλα προτιθεὶς μάλιστ' ἄν

ποιεῖν εὖ ἀσκεῖσθαι, *it seems to me, said he, father, that if any one
should proclaim contests,* etc., *he would cause,* etc. XEN. Cyr. i. 6, 18.
(Here the protasis implied in the participles is merely emphasised by
ἄν, which belongs to ποιεῖν.) See also λέγοντος ἄν τινος πιστεῦσαι
οἴεσθε; (i.e. εἴ τις ἔλεγεν, ἐπίστευσαν ἄν;) *do you think they would
have believed it, if any one had told them?* DEM. vi. 20. (Here ἄν stands
near λέγοντος only to point this out as the protasis to which its own
verb πιστεῦσαι is the apodosis, with which ἄν is not repeated.)

225. (*a*) Repetition of κέ is rare ; yet it sometimes occurs. *E.g.*

Τῷ κε μάλ᾽ ἤ κεν ἔμεινε καὶ ἐσσύμενός περ ὁδοῖο,
ἤ κέ με τεθνηυῖαν ἔνι μεγάροισιν ἔλειπεν. Od iv. 733.

(*b*) On the other hand, Homer sometimes joins ἄν and κέ in the
same sentence for emphasis. *E.g.*

Καρτεραὶ, ἃς οὔτ᾽ ἄν κεν Ἄρης ὀνόσαιτο μετελθὼν
οὔτε κ᾽ Ἀθηναίη λαοσσόος. Il. xiii. 127.

226. When an apodosis consists of several *co-ordinate* clauses
with the same mood, ἄν is generally used only in the first and
understood in the others, unless it is repeated for emphasis or
for some other special reason. *E.g.*

Οὐδ᾽ ἄν ἐμὲ, ἡνίκα δεῦρο ἀποπλεῖν ἐβουλόμην, κατεκώλυεν, οὐδὲ
τοιαῦτα λέγειν τούτῳ προσέταττεν, ἐξ ὧν ἥκισθ᾽ ὑμεῖς ἐμέλλετ᾽
ἐξιέναι. DEM. xix. 51. (Here ἄν is understood with προσέταττεν.)
Οὕτω δὲ δρῶν οὐδὲν ἄν διάφορον τοῦ ἑτέρου ποιοῖ, ἀλλ᾽ ἐπὶ ταὐτὸν
ἴοιεν ἀμφότεροι. PLAT. Rep. 360 C. Οὐκοῦν κἂν, εἰ πρὸς αὐτὸ τὸ
φῶς ἀναγκάζοι αὐτὸν βλέπειν, ἀλγεῖν τε ἂν τὰ ὄμματα καὶ φεύγειν
ἀποστρεφόμενον (οἴει); Ib. 515 E. (Κἂν belongs to the infinitives ; 223.)
See also XEN. An. ii. 5, 14. Πάντα ᾕρει ὁ Φίλιππος, πολλὰ λέγοντος
ἐμοῦ καὶ θρυλοῦντος ἀεὶ, τὸ μὲν πρῶτον ὡς ἂν εἰς κοινὸν γνώμην ἀπο-
φαινομένου, μετὰ ταῦτα δ᾽ ὡς ἀγνοοῦντας διδάσκοντος, τελευτῶντος δὲ
ὡς ἂν πρὸς πεπρακότας αὑτοὺς καὶ ἀνοσιωτάτους ἀνθρώπους οὐδὲν
ὑποστελλομένου. DEM. xix. 156. The clauses with ὡς represent (1) ὡς
ἔλεγον ἄν εἰ ἐφαινόμην, *as I should have spoken if I had been merely
informing my colleagues;* (2) ὡς ἔλεγον (ἄν) εἰ ἀγνοοῦντας ἐδίδασκον, *as
I should have spoken if I had been instructing ignorant men;* (3) ὡς
λέγοιμι ἄν, *as I should speak to men who had sold themselves,* etc. In
the second clause, the construction remaining the same, ἄν is omitted ;
but in the third, where an optative is implied, ἄν reappears.

In PLAT. Rep. 398 A, we find ἄν used with two co-ordinate optatives,
understood with a third, and repeated again with a fourth to avoid
confusion with a dependent optative in a relative clause. Ἄν may be
understood with an optative even in a separate sentence, if the construction is continued from a sentence in which ἄν is used with the
optative ; as in PLAT. Rep. 352 E: Ἔσθ᾽ ὅτῳ ἄν ἄλλῳ ἴδοις ἤ
ὀφθαλμοῖς; Οὐ δῆτα. Τί δέ; ἀκούσαις ἄλλῳ ἤ ὠσίν; So with
πράττοι after γάρ, ib. 439 B.

ELLIPTICAL USES OF ἌΝ.

227. Ἄν is sometimes used elliptically without a verb, when one can be supplied from the context. *E.g.*

Οἱ οἰκέται ῥέγκουσιν· ἀλλ' οὐκ ἂν πρὸ τοῦ (sc. ἔρρεγκον), *the slaves are snoring; but they wouldn't have been doing so at this hour in old times.* AR. Nub. 5. Ὡς οὔτ' ἂν ἀστῶν τῶνδ' ἂν ἐξείποιμί τῳ, οὔτ' ἂν τέκνοισι τοῖς ἐμοῖς (sc. ἐξείποιμι), στέργων ὅμως. SOPH. O. C. 1528. Τί ἂν δοκεῖ σοι Πρίαμος (sc. πρᾶξαι), εἰ τάδ' ἤνυσεν; *but what think you Priam would have done if he had accomplished what you have?* AESCH. Ag. 935. Σώφρων μὲν οὐκ ἂν μᾶλλον, εὐτυχὴς δ' ἴσως (sc. οὖσα). EUR. Alc. 182 : cf. AR. Eq. 1252. (See 483.)

So πῶς γὰρ ἄν (sc. εἴη); *how could it?* πῶς οὐκ ἄν; and similar phrases ; especially ὥσπερ ἂν εἰ (also written as one word, ὡσπερανεί), in which the ἄν belongs to the verb that was originally understood after εἰ; as φοβούμενος ὥσπερ ἂν εἰ παῖς, *fearing like a child* (originally for φοβούμενος ὥσπερ ἂν ἐφοβεῖτο εἰ παῖς ἦν). PLAT. Gorg. 479 A. See DEM. xviii. 194 : τί χρὴ ποιεῖν; ὥσπερ ἂν εἴ τις ναύκληρον πάντ' ἐπὶ σωτηρίᾳ πράξαντα . . . τῆς ναυαγίας αἰτιῷτο, *what are we to do? (We are to do) just what a shipowner would do* (ποιοῖ ἄν) *if any one should blame him for the wreck of his ship,* etc. See φήσειεν ἄν, which explains the omitted verb, just afterwards.

228. Κἄν in both its meanings (as καί with the adverb ἄν, and as καί with ἄν = ἐάν) may stand without a verb. *E.g.*

Ἀλλ' ἄνδρα χρὴ δοκεῖν πεσεῖν ἂν κἂν ἀπὸ σμικροῦ κακοῦ. SOPH. Aj. 1077. (Here κἄν, for καὶ ἄν, which we may express by *even* or *though it be,* belongs to πεσεῖν understood.) Ἱκανῶς οὖν τοῦτο ἔχομεν, κἂν εἰ πλεοναχῇ σκοποῖμεν; *are we then satisfied of this (and should we be so) even if we were to look at it in various ways?* PLAT. Rep. 477 A. (We must supply ἱκανῶς ἔχοιμεν with κἄν.) See different cases of κἂν εἰ in 195, in which a verb follows to which ἄν cannot belong.

Καὶ ὅποι τις ἄν, οἶμαι, προσθῇ κἂν μικρὰν δύναμιν, πάντ' ὠφελεῖ, *and, I think, wherever we add even (though it be) a little power, it all helps.* DEM. ii. 14. (Here κἄν = καὶ ἄν τις προσθῇ, *even though we add.*) Μέτρησον εἰρήνης τί μοι, κἂν πέντ' ἔτη, *measure me out some peace, even if it be only for five years* (καὶ ἂν μετρήσῃς), AR. Ach. 1021.

229. Ἄν may be used with a relative without a verb, as it is with εἰ (in ἄν = εἰ ἄν) in the last examples (228). So in XEN. An. i. 3, 6, ὡς ἐμοῦ οὖν ἰόντος ὅπῃ ἂν καὶ ὑμεῖς, οὕτω τὴν γνώμην ἔχετε (i.e. ὅπῃ ἂν καὶ ὑμεῖς ἴητε), *be of this mind, that I shall go wherever you go.*

CHAPTER IV.

USE OF THE MOODS.

230. This chapter treats of all constructions which require any other form of the finite verb than the simple indicative in absolute assertions and direct questions (2). The infinitive and participle are included here so far as either of them is used in indirect discourse, in protasis or apodosis, and in other constructions (as with πρίν and ὥστε) in which the finite moods also are used.

231. These constructions are discussed under the following heads :—

I. The potential optative and indicative.

II. The imperative and subjunctive in commands, exhortations, and prohibitions.—Subjunctive and indicative with μή and μὴ οὐ in cautious assertions.—Ὅπως and ὅπως μή with the independent future indicative or subjunctive.

III. The subjunctive (like the future indicative) in independent sentences.—The interrogative subjunctive.

IV. Οὐ μή with the subjunctive or future indicative.

V. Final and object clauses after ἵνα, ὡς, ὅπως, ὄφρα, and μή.

VI. Conditional sentences.

VII. Relative and temporal sentences, including consecutive sentences with ὥστε, etc.

VIII. Indirect discourse.

IX. Causal sentences.

X. Expressions of a wish.

SECTION I.

The Potential Optative and Indicative.

232. We find fully established in the Homeric language a use of the optative and the past tenses of the indicative with ἄν or κέ, which expresses the action of the verb as dependent on circumstances or conditions; as ἔλθοι ἄν, *he might (could or would) go;* ἦλθεν ἄν, *he might (could or would) have gone.* Such an optative or indicative is called *potential.*

I. POTENTIAL OPTATIVE.

233. It has already been seen (13) that Homer sometimes uses the optative in a weak future sense, without κέ or ἄν, to express a concession or permission. Such neutral forms seem to form a connecting link between the simple optative in wishes and the optative with ἄν, partaking to a certain extent of the nature of both. (For a full discussion of these forms and their relations, see Appendix I.) Such expressions seem to show that the early language used forms like ἔλθοιμι and ἴδοιμι in two senses, *I may go* and *I may see,* or *may I go* and *may I see,* corresponding to ἔλθω and ἴδω in their two Homeric senses *I shall go* and *I shall see* (284), or *let me go* and *let me see* (257).

234. The neutral optatives like Il. iv. 18 are rare even in Homer, the language having already distinguished the two meanings in sense, and marked them in most cases by external signs. The optative expressing what may happen in the future took the particle κέ or ἄν, and was negatived by οὐ, denoting the relations which we express by our potential mood with *may, can, might, could, would,* and *should.* Thus ἕλοιμί κε ἢ κεν ἀλοίην, *I may slay or I may be slain,* Il. xxii. 253; ἀνὴρ δέ κεν οὔ τι Διὸς νόον εἰρύσσαιτο, *a man cannot contend against the will of Zeus,* Il. viii. 143.[1] On the other hand, the simple optative (without κέ or ἄν) was more and more restricted to the expression of a wish or exhortation, and was negatived by μή; as μὴ γένοιτο, *may it not happen,* πίθοιό μοι, *listen to me* (Od. iv. 193), as opposed to οὐκ ἂν γένοιτο, *it could not happen.* The potential forms ἔλθοιμι ἄν

---

[1] When the idea of *ability, possibility,* or *necessity* is the chief element in the expression, and is not (as above) merely auxiliary, it is expressed by a special verb like δύναμαι, δεῖ, or χρή. Especially, the idea of *obligation* is generally expressed by δεῖ or χρή with the infinitive; as τοῦδε χρὴ κλύειν, *him we must obey,* SOPH. Ant. 666.

and ἴδοιμι ἄν differ from the more absolute future indicative and the old subjunctive forms ἔλθω and ἴδω, *I shall go* and *I shall see*, by expressing a future act as dependent on some future circumstances or conditions, which may be more or less distinctly implied. The freedom of the earlier language extended the use of the potential optative to present and sometimes even to past time. See 438 and 440.

235. In most cases the limiting condition involved in the potential optative is not present to the mind in any definite form, and can be expressed in English only by such words as *perchance, possibly,* or *probably,* or by the auxiliaries *could, would, should, might,* etc. with the vague conditions which these imply (like *if he should try, if he pleased, if he could, if what is natural should happen,* etc.) Sometimes a more general condition is implied, like *in any possible case;* as οὐκ ἂν δεχοίμην τοῦτο, *I would not accept this (on any terms);* here the expression becomes nearly absolute, and may often be translated by our future, as οὐκ ἂν μεθείμην τοῦ θρόνου, *I will not give up the throne* (AR. Ran. 830), or (in positive sentences) by *must,* as πάντες θαυμάζοιεν ἂν τοῦτο, *all must admire this.*

The optative thus used with no conscious feeling of any *definite* condition, but still implying that the statement is conditioned and not absolute, is the simplest and most primitive potential optative. It is equivalent to the Latin potential subjunctive, as *credas, dicas, cernas, putes,* etc., *you may believe, say, perceive, think,* etc. The Homeric language has six forms, all expressing futurity with different degrees of absoluteness and distinctness; as ὄψομαι, ὄψομαί κε, ἴδωμαι, ἴδωμαί κε, ἰδοίμην, ἰδοίμην κε (or ἄν), containing every step from *I shall see* to *I should see.* Of these only the first and the last (with a tradition of the second) survived the Homeric period, and the others (especially the fifth) were already disappearing during that period (240), being found unnecessary as the language became settled, and as the optative with κέ or ἄν became more fixed as a future potential form.

236. In the following examples of the potential optative no definite form of condition is present to the mind :—

Ἐμοὶ δὲ τότ᾽ ἂν πολὺ κέρδιον εἴη, but it *would at that time (be likely to) profit me far more.* Il. xxii. 108. Φεύγωμεν· ἔτι γάρ κεν ἀλύξαιμεν κακὸν ἦμαρ, *let us flee; for perchance we may still escape the evil day.* Od. x. 269. Πλησίον ἀλλήλων· καί κεν διοϊστεύσειας, *the rocks are close together : you might perhaps shoot an arrow across the space.* Od. xii. 102. So Od. xxiii. 125. Οὐκοῦν πόροις ἂν τήνδε δωρεὰν ἐμοί; *would you then grant me this favour?* AESCH. Prom. 616. So

πᾶν γὰρ ἂν ·πύθοιό μου, *for you can learn anything* (*you please*) *from
me.* Ib. 617. Τί τόνδ᾽ ἂν εἴποις ἄλλο; *what else could you say of
this man?* SOPH. Ant. 646. So Ant. 552 and 652. Πολλὰς ἂν
εὕροις μηχανάς, *you can find many devices.* EUR. And. 85.
Ἔψομαί
τοι καὶ οὐκ ἂν λειφθείην, *I will follow you and in no case will I
be left behind.* HDT. iv. 97. Οἱ μὲν (sc. λέγοντες) ὡς οὐδενὶ ἂν τρόπῳ
ἔλθοιεν οἱ Ἀθηναῖοι. THUC. vi. 35. Ἔνθα πολλὴν μὲν σωφροσύνην
καταμάθοι ἄν τις. XEN. An. i. 9, 3. So Mem. i. 3, 5, iii. 5, 1 and 7.
Δὶς ἐς τὸν αὐτὸν ποταμὸν οὐκ ἂν ἐμβαίης, *you cannot step twice into
the same river* (saying of Heraclitus). PLAT. Crat. 402 A. Οὐ μὴν
ἔστι καλλίων ὁδὸς οὐδ᾽ ἂν γένοιτο, *there is none and there could be
none.* Id. Phil. 16 B; so 64 B. Ἀκούοις ἄν, *you can hear.* Id. Rep.
487 E. Δειξάτω ὡς οἱ Θετταλοὶ νῦν οὐκ ἂν ἐλεύθεροι γένοιντο
ἄσμενοι, *let him show that they would not now gladly become free.* DEM.
ii. 8. Ἡδέως δ᾽ ἂν ἔγωγ᾽ ἐροίμην Λεπτίνην, *but I would gladly ask
Leptines.* Id. xx. 129. Εἰ ἠγνόησε ταῦτα, γένοιτο γὰρ ἂν καὶ τοῦτο,
if he did not know this,—and it might easily so happen. Ib. 143. Οὔτ᾽
ἂν οὗτος ἔχοι λέγειν οὔθ᾽ ὑμεῖς πεισθείητε. Id. xxii. 17. Ποῖ οὖν
τραποίμεθ᾽ ἂν ἔτι; *in what other direction could we possibly turn?*
PLAT. Euthyd. 290 A. Οὐκ ἂν μεθείμην τοῦ θρόνου, *I will not give
up the throne.* AR. Ran. 830. So οὐκ ἂν δεχοίμην, AESCH. Eum. 228.
Τίς οὐκ ἂν ἀγάσαιτο τῶν ἀνδρῶν ἐκείνων τῆς ἀρετῆς; *who would not
admire the valour of these men?* (i.e. *every one must admire their valour*).
DEM. xviii. 204.

Βουλοίμην ἄν, *I should like*, is used like *velim*. For ἐβουλόμην ἄν,
vellem, see 246.

237. The potential optative in the second person may have
the force of a mild command or exhortation. *E.g.*

Σὺ μὲν κομίζοις ἂν σεαυτὸν ᾗ θέλεις, *you may take yourself off
whither you please* (a milder expression than κόμιζε σεαυτόν). SOPH.
Ant. 444. So Ant. 1339. Κλύοις ἂν ἤδη, Φοῖβε προστατήριε,
hear me now. Id. El. 637. Χωροῖς ἂν εἴσω. Id. Ph. 674.

So probably Il. ii. 250: τῷ οὐκ ἂν βασιλῆας ἀνὰ στόμ᾽ ἔχων
ἀγορεύοις, *therefore you must not take kings upon your tongue and talk* (or
do not take, etc.)

238. Occasionally the potential optative expresses what may
hereafter prove to be true or to have been true. *E.g.*

Ποῦ δῆτ᾽ ἂν εἶεν οἱ ξένοι; *where may the strangers be?* (i.e. *where is
it likely to turn out that they are?*) SOPH. El. 1450. Ἡ γὰρ ἐμὴ (sc.
σοφία) φαύλη τις ἂν εἴη, *for it may turn out that my wisdom is of a
mean kind.* PLAT. Symp. 175 E. Ἑλλήνων τινάς φασι ἁρπάσαι
Εὐρώπην· εἴησαν δ᾽ ἂν οὗτοι Κρῆτες, *and these would prove to be
Cretans* (or *to have been Cretans*). HDT. i. 2. Αὗται δὲ οὐκ ἂν πολλαὶ
εἴησαν, *and these* (the islands) *would not prove to be many.* THUC. i. 9.

This has nothing to do with the Homeric use of the optative with
κέ or ἄν in a present or a past sense (438; 440). See the similar use
of the subjunctive with μή after verbs of fearing (92).

239. The potential optative may express every grade of potentiality from the almost pure future οὐκ ἂν μεθείμην, *I will not give up (under any circumstances)*, to οὐκ ἂν δικαίως ἐς κακὸν πέσοιμί τι, *I could not justly fall into any trouble*, SOPH. Ant. 240, where δικαίως points to the substance of a limiting condition, *if justice should be done.* From this the step is but slight to such cases as οὔτε ἐσθίουσι πλείω ἢ δύνανται φέρειν · διαρραγεῖεν γὰρ ἄν, *they do not eat more than they can carry ; for (if they should) they would burst*, XEN. Cyr. viii. 2, 21, where εἰ . . . ἐσθίοιεν is necessary to complete the sense and is clearly understood from the preceding words. A final step in the same direction is taken when the condition is actually stated as part of the sentence. As ἔλθοι ἄν means *he would go* (under some future circumstances), if these limiting circumstances are to be definitely expressed it is natural to use the corresponding form of condition, εἰ with the optative, as εἰ κελεύσειας ἔλθοι ἄν, *if you should command he would go.* The protasis is thus assimilated to the apodosis in form, as it conforms to it in sense and general character. So when a conclusion is to follow such a condition as εἰ κελεύσειας, the corresponding optative with ἄν, *i.e.* the potential optative, is naturally chosen, although nothing but regard to harmony and symmetry makes either *if you should command he will go* or *if you command he would go*, or the equivalent Greek forms, objectionable. In fact, these very forms are far more common in the more fluid Homeric language than in the fixed and regular style of Attic prose. There is, therefore, no necessary or logical bond of union between two forms like εἰ κελεύσειας and ἔλθοι ἄν. This connexion is, indeed, far more the effect of assimilation in form, as appears especially when the apodosis contains an optative in a wish ; as in ὡς ἀπόλοιτο καὶ ἄλλος ὅτις τοιαῦτά γε ῥέζοι, *may another perish also who shall do the like* (Od. i. 47), where if ἀπολέσθω had been used we should naturally have had ῥέζῃ.

For examples of the optative with ἄν or κέ with a definite protasis expressed or implied in the context, see 455 and 472.

240. The use of ἄν or κέ with the potential optative had already become fixed in the Homeric language. A few cases of "neutral optatives" in Homer, which seem to show an early potential use without κέ or ἄν, have been given above (13). Besides these, a few more distinctly potential optatives without ἄν or κέ occur in Homer, but they are exceptions to the general usage even there. Such are the following :—

Οὔ τι κακώτερον ἄλλο πάθοιμι. Il. xix. 321. Τούτου γε σπομένοιο καὶ ἐκ πυρὸς αἰθομένοιο ἄμφω νοστήσαιμεν. Il. x. 246. 'Ρεῖα θεὸς γ᾽ ἐθέλων ἀμείνονας δωρήσαιτο. Il. x. 556 : see Od. iii. 231. Χερμάδιον λάβε, ὃ οὐ δύο γ᾽ ἄνδρε φέροιεν. Il. v. 302 : so xx. 285.

Οὔ τίς πείσειε γυναῖκα. Od. xiv. 122. So also Il. vii. 48, xiv. 190, xv. 45, 197.

See, further, HES. Theog. 723 and 725 ; PIND. Ol. x. 21, Py. iv. 118.

241. Some cases of the optative without ἄν occur with the indefinite ἔστιν ὅς in Homer, and with ἔστιν ὅστις, ἔστιν ὅπως, ἔστιν ὅποι, in the Attic poets. These form a class by themselves. *E.g.*

Οὐκ ἔσθ' ὃς σῆς γε κύνας κεφαλῆς ἀπαλάλκοι. Il. xxii. 348. Οὐ γὰρ ἔην ὅς τίς σφιν ἐπὶ στίχας ἡγήσαιτο. Il. ii. 687. Οὐκ ἔσθ' ὅπως λέξαιμι τὰ ψευδῆ καλά. AESCH. Ag. 620. Οὐκ ἔσθ' ὅτῳ μείζονα μοῖραν νείμαιμ' ἢ σοι. Id. Prom. 292. Οὐκ ἔστιν ὅστις πλὴν ἐμοῦ κείραιτό νιν. Id. Cho. 172. Ἔστ' οὖν ὅπως Ἄλκηστις ἐς γῆρας μόλοι; EUR. Alc. 52. Ἔσθ' ὅποι τις στείλας παραλῦσαι ψυχάν; Ibid. 113.

242. On the other hand, a few other cases in the Attic poets are mere anomalies, even if we admit that the text is sound. *E.g.*

Τεὰν, Ζεῦ, δύνασιν τίς ἀνδρῶν ὑπερβασία κατάσχοι; *what transgression of man can check thy power?* SOPH. Ant. 605. Ἀλλ' ὑπέρτολμον ἀνδρὸς φρόνημα τίς λέγοι; AESCH. Cho. 594. Πῶς οὖν τάδ', ὡς εἴποι τις, ἐξημάρτανες ; *i.e. as one might say.* (?) EUR. Andr. 929. Θᾶσσον ἢ λέγοι τις πώλους ἐστήσαμεν. Id. Hipp. 1186. Ὥσπερ εἴποι τις τόπος, *as one would say* τόπος. (?) AR. Av. 180. The cases cited from Attic prose are now generally admitted to be corrupt. See Krüger, ii. 54, 3, Anm. 8.

II. POTENTIAL INDICATIVE.

243. As the potential optative represents a future act as dependent on future circumstances (234), so the potential indicative originally represents a past act as dependent on past circumstances. Therefore, while ἦλθεν means *he went*, ἦλθεν ἄν means *he would have gone (under some past circumstances).* It is probable that no definite limiting circumstances were present to the mind when this form first came into use, so that ἦλθεν ἄν naturally signified merely that *it was likely, possible,* or *probable that he went* or (as we express it) that *he might have gone* or *would have been likely to go,* sometimes that *he must have gone.*

In this sense it appears as a past form of the potential optative, *e.g.* of ἔλθοι ἄν in the sense *he might perchance go* or *he would be likely to go* (in the future). The same relation appears in Latin, where *credas, putes, cernas, dicas, you would be likely to believe, think,* etc., are transferred to past time as *crederes, putares, cerneres, diceres, you would have believed, thought,* etc.[1] Here *putet* and

---

[1] We are probably justified in assuming that the past meaning which here appears in *crederes,* etc. is the original meaning of the Latin imperfect subjunctive in this use, as it certainly is that of the Greek imperfect indicative with ἄν. See 435.

putaret are precisely equivalent to οἴοιτο ἄν, *he would be likely to think*, and ᾤετο ἄν, *he would have been likely to think.*

244. We find the potential indicative in its simplest use (last mentioned)—with no reference to any definite condition, but merely expressing past possibility, probability, or necessity—in all classes of Greek writers. *E.g.*

Οὐδ᾽ ἂν ἔτι φράδμων περ ἀνὴρ Σαρπηδόνα δῖον ἔγνω, *no longer would even a shrewd man have known Sarpedon.* Il. xvi. 638. Ὑπό κεν ταλασίφρονά περ δέος εἷλεν, *fear might have seized even a man of stout heart.* Il. iv. 421. See other Homeric examples below.

Ἀλλ᾽ ἦλθε μὲν δὴ τοῦτο τοὔνειδος τάχ᾽ ἂν ὀργῇ βιασθὲν μᾶλλον ἢ γνώμῃ φρενῶν, *but this reproach may perhaps have come from violence of wrath*, etc. Soph. O. T. 523. (Here τάχ᾽ ἂν ἦλθε expresses past possibility, with no reference to any definite condition, unfulfilled or otherwise.) Θεοῖς γὰρ ἦν οὕτω φίλον τάχ᾽ ἄν τι μηνίουσιν εἰς γένος πάλαι, *for perchance it may have been thus pleasing to Gods who of old bore some wrath against our race.* Id. O. C. 964. (According to the common punctuation τάχ᾽ ἄν would be taken with μηνίουσιν, = οἳ τάχ᾽ ἄν τι ἐμήνιον, *who may perchance have borne some wrath*, see Plat. Phaedr. 265 B, below ; but the analogy of O. T. 523 favours the other interpretation.) Πρὸς ποῖον ἂν τόνδ᾽ αὐτὸς Ὀδυσσεὺς ἔπλει; i.e. *who might this man have been to whom Ulysses was sailing?* Id. Ph. 572. Ὁ θεασάμενος πᾶς ἄν τις ἀνὴρ ἠράσθη δάιος εἶναι, *every man who saw this drama* (the " Seven against Thebes ") *would have been eager to be a warrior.* Ar. Ran. 1022. (This is the past form of πᾶς ἄν τις ἐρασθείη δάιος εἶναι, *every one would be eager*, having no more reference to an unfulfilled condition than the latter has.) Διέβησαν, ὡς μὲν εἰκὸς καὶ λέγεται, ἐπὶ σχεδιῶν, τάχα ἂν δὲ καὶ ἄλλως πως ἐσπλεύσαντες, i.e. *while they probably crossed on rafts, they may perhaps have crossed in some other way by sailing* (διέβησαν with τάχα ἄν in the latter clause meaning *they may have*, or *might have, perhaps crossed under other* (possible) *circumstances*). Thuc. vi. 2. Ἐπερρώσθη δ᾽ ἄν τις ἐκεῖνο ἰδών, *and any one would have been encouraged who saw that.* Xen. Hell. iii. 4, 18. Θᾶττον ἢ ὥς τις ἂν ᾤετο, *sooner than one would have thought.* Id. An. i. 5, 8. Ἔνθα δὴ ἔγνω ἄν τις ὅσον ἄξιον εἴη τὸ φιλεῖσθαι ἄρχοντα, *there any one might have learned*, etc. Id. Cyr. vii. 1, 38. Ἐν ταύτῃ τῇ ἡλικίᾳ λέγοντες πρὸς ὑμᾶς ἐν ᾗ ἂν μάλιστα ἐπιστεύσατε, *talking to you at that age at which you would have been most likely to have put trust in them.* Plat. Ap. 18 C. Ἴσως μὲν ἀληθοῦς τινος ἐπαπτόμενοι, τάχα δ᾽ ἂν καὶ ἄλλοσε παραφερόμενοι, μυθικόν τινα ὕμνον προσεπαίσαμεν Ἔρωτα, *while perhaps we were clinging to some truth, although perchance we may have been led aside into some error* (παραφερόμενοι ἄν = παρεφερόμεθα ἄν), *we celebrated Eros in a mythical hymn.* Id. Phaedr. 265 B. Τί γὰρ καὶ βουλόμενοι μετεπέμπεσθ᾽ ἂν αὐτοὺς ἐν τούτῳ τῷ καιρῷ; *for with what wish even could you possibly have been summoning them at this time?* Dem. xviii. 24. Πῶς ἂν ὁ μὴ παρὼν μηδ᾽ ἐπιδημῶν ἐγώ τί σε ἠδίκησα; i.e. *how was I likely to do you any wrong?* Id. xxxvii. 57. Τὸν χορὸν συνέλεξα ὥσπερ ἂν ἥδιστα καὶ ἐπιτηδειότατα ἀμφοτέροις ἐγίγνετο, *I collected the chorus in the way which was likely to be most agreeable and convenient to both.* ANT. vi. 11.

Two Homeric examples are peculiar in their reference to time :—
Ἀλλὰ τάχιστα πείρα ὅπως κεν δὴ σὴν πατρίδα γαῖαν ἵκηαι· ἢ γάρ μιν ζωόν γε κιχήσεαι, ἤ κεν Ὀρέστης κτεῖνεν ὑποφθάμενος, σὺ δέ κεν τάφου ἀντιβολήσαις, *but strive with all speed to come to your father-land; for either you will find him* (Aegisthus) *alive* (and so can kill him yourself), *or else Orestes may have already killed him before you come, and then you can go to his funeral.* Od. iv. 544. (Here ἤ κεν κτεῖνεν, by a change in the point of view, expresses what will be a past possibility at the time of the arrival of Menelaus, to which time the following optative is future.) Καὶ γὰρ Τρῶάς φασι μαχητὰς ἔμμεναι ἄνδρας, οἵ κε τάχιστα ἔκριναν μέγα νεῖκος, *for they say that the Trojans are men of war, who would most speedily have decided a mighty strife* (implying that they would therefore speedily decide any impending strife). Od. xviii. 261. (This was said by Ulysses *before* he went to Troy. See 249.)

245. In most cases of the past tenses of the indicative with ἄν there is at least an implied reference to some supposed circumstances different from the real ones, so that ἦλθεν ἄν commonly means *he would have gone (if something had not been as it was).* When we speak of a past event as subject to conditions, we are apt to imply that the conditions were not fulfilled, as otherwise they would not be alluded to. This reference to an unfulfilled condition, however, does not make it necessary that the action of the potential indicative itself should be unreal, although this is generally the case. (See 412.) The unfulfilled past condition to which the potential indicative refers may be as vague and indistinct as the future condition to which the potential optative refers (235); as *if he had wished, if he had tried, if it had been possible, in any case,* and others which are implied in our auxiliaries *might, could, would, should,* etc., but are seldom expressed by us in words. Compare οὐδὲν ἂν κακὸν ποιήσειαν, *they could do no harm* (i.e. *if they should try*), with οὐδὲν ἂν κακὸν ἐποίησαν, *they could have done no harm* (i.e. *if they had tried*). *E.g.*

Οὐ γάρ κεν δυνάμεσθα θυράων ὑψηλάων ἀπώσασθαι λίθον, *for we could not have moved the stone from the high doorway.* Od. ix. 304. Μένοιμ' ἄν· ἤθελον δ' ἂν ἐκτὸς ὢν τυχεῖν, *I will remain; but I should have preferred to take my chance outside.* SOPH. Aj. 88. Τούτου τίς ἂν σοι τἀνδρὸς ἀμείνων εὑρέθη; *who could have been found, etc.?* Ib. 119. Ἔκλυον ἂν ἐγὼ οὐδ' ἂν ἤλπισ' αὐδάν, *I heard a voice which I could never even have hoped to hear.* Id. El. 1281. Δὺ' ἐξέλεξας, οἷν ἐγὼ ἥκιστ' ἂν ἠθέλησ' ὀλωλότοιν κλύειν. Id. Ph. 426. Κλύειν ἂν οὐδ' ἅπαξ ἐβουλόμην, *I should have wished not to hear it even once.* Ib. 1239. Οὐκ ἔσθ' ὅπως ἔτεκεν ἂν ἡ Διὸς δάμαρ Λητὼ τοσαύτην

ἀμαθίαν, *under no circumstances would Leto have been the mother of so
great ignorance.* EUR. I. T. 385. Οἰκεῖα πράγματ᾽ εἰσάγων, ἐξ ὧν γ᾽
ἂν ἐξηλεγχόμην, *by which I might have been exposed.* AR. Ran. 959.
Τότε ὀψὲ ἦν, καὶ τὰς χεῖρας οὐκ ἂν καθεώρων, *it was then dark, and
they would not have seen the show of hands* (in voting). XEN. Hell. i. 7, 7.
Ποίων δ᾽ ἂν ἔργων ἢ πόνων ἢ κινδύνων ἀπέστησαν; *from what
acts, etc., would they have shrunk back* (i.e. *if they had been required of
them*)? ISOC. iv. 83.   Πρὸ πολλῶν μὲν ἂν χρημάτων ἐτιμησάμην
τοσοῦτον δύνασθαι τὴν φιλοσοφίαν· ἴσως γὰρ οὐκ ἂν ἡμεῖς πλεῖστον
ἀπελείφθημεν, οὐδ᾽ ἂν ἐλάχιστον μέρος ἀπελαύσαμεν αὐτῆς·
ἐπειδὴ δ᾽ οὐκ οὕτως ἔχει, βουλοίμην ἂν παύσασθαι τοὺς φλυαροῦν-
τας. Id. xiii. 11.   Οἳ ἐποίησαν μὲν οὐδὲν ἂν κακόν, μὴ παθεῖν δ᾽
ἰφυλάξαντ᾽ ἂν ἴσως, τούτους ἐξαπατᾶν αἱρεῖσθαι, *these who could
have done him no harm, but who might perhaps have guarded themselves
against suffering any.* DEM. ix. 13.   Τότε δ᾽ αὐτὸ τὸ πρᾶγμ᾽ ἂν ἐκρί-
νετο ἐφ᾽ αὑτοῦ, *but the case would then have been decided on its own
merits.* Id. xviii. 224: so 101.   Πῶς ἂν οὖν ὑβριστικώτερον ἄνθρωπος
ὑμῖν ἐχρήσατο; Id. xix. 85.   Οὗ μεῖζον οὐδὲν ἂν κατέλιπεν ὄνειδος.
Id. xlv. 35.   Ἃ δ᾽ ἡμῖν δικαίως ἂν ὑπῆρχεν ἐκ τῆς εἰρήνης, ταῦτ᾽
ἀνθ᾽ ὧν ἀπέδοντο αὐτοὶ λογίζεσθαι· ἀλλὰ ταῦτα μὲν ἦν ἂν ὁμοίως
ἡμῖν, ἐκεῖνα δὲ τούτοις ἂν προσῆν εἰ μὴ διὰ τούτους, *but* (*it is not
right*) *to set off against what they themselves sold what would justly have
been ours by the peace; but these would have been ours all the same* (*in
any case*), *while the others would have been added* (*or would now be added*)
to them had it not been for these men. Id. xix. 91.   (Here ὑπῆρχεν ἄν
and ἦν ἄν refer to an actual fact, the possession of certain places; the
apodosis προσῆν ἄν refers to something which was prevented from
becoming a fact.   This passage shows the natural steps from the
potential form to the apodosis.   See 247.)

246. When no definite condition is understood with the
potential indicative, the imperfect with ἄν regularly refers to
past time, according to the older usage (435), like the aorist;
as in the examples above.

The imperfect referring to present time, which is common
in apodosis after Homer (410), appears in these potential expressions chiefly in a few simple phrases, especially in ἐβουλόμην ἄν,
vellem, I should wish, I should like (also *I should have liked*).
Even in Homer the construction with ὤφελον and the infinitive
(424), which includes a form of potential indicative (415; 416),
sometimes refers to present time.   *E.g.*

Ἐγὼ δ᾽ ἐβουλόμην ἂν αὐτοὺς ἀληθῆ λέγειν· μετῆν γὰρ ἂν καὶ
ἐμοὶ τούτου τἀγαθοῦ οὐκ ἐλάχιστον μέρος. νῦν δὲ οὔτε πρὸς τὴν
πόλιν αὐτοῖς τοιαῦτα ὑπάρχει οὔτε πρὸς ἐμέ, *and I should like it if they
spoke the truth; for* (*were that so*) *no small part of this advantage would
be mine: but this is not true of them, etc.* LYS. xii. 22.   Μειδίαν, ὃν
ἐβουλόμην ἂν πολλῶν ἕνεκεν ζῆν, *Midias, whom for many reasons I*

should like to have alive. AESCHIN. iii. 115. See LYCURG. 3. (For
ἐβουλόμην ἄν as past, see SOPH. Ph. 1239, quoted in 245.) See also
AR. Nub. 680, ἐκεῖνο δ᾽ ἦν ἂν καρδόπη, Κλεωνύμη, *and this would be*
καρδόπη, etc. For βουλοίμην ἄν, *velim*, see 236.
For ὤφελον and the infinitive as present in Homer, see 424.

247. It is but a slight step from the potential forms quoted
in 245 and 246 to those which form the conclusion to an unfulfilled condition definitely implied in the context. After Homer
the imperfect with ἄν may here refer to present time. *E.g.*

Ἀλλά κε κεῖνα μάλιστα ἰδὼν ὀλοφύραο θυμῷ, *but you would have*
lamented most in your heart if you had seen this (ἰδών = εἰ εἶδες). Od. xi.
418. Οὐδέ κεν αὐτὸς ὑπέκφυγε κῆρα μέλαιναν, ἀλλ᾽ Ἥφαιστος
ἔρυτο, *nor would he by himself have escaped, but Hephaestus rescued him.*
Il. v. 22. Ἀλλ᾽ εἰκάσαι μὲν, ἡδύς· οὐ γὰρ ἂν κάρα πολυστεφὴς ὧδ᾽
εἷρπε, *but, as it seems, he has good news; for (otherwise) he would not be*
coming with head thus thickly crowned. SOPH. O. T. 83 ; so O. C. 125,
146. Πολλοῦ γὰρ ἂν τὰ ὄργανα ἦν ἄξια, *for instruments would be*
worth much (if they had this power). PLAT. Rep. 374 D. Ἥγετε τὴν
εἰρήνην ὅμως· οὐ γὰρ ἦν ὅ τι ἂν ἐποιεῖτε, *for there was nothing that*
you could have done (if you had not kept the peace). DEM. xviii. 43.
Σημεῖον δέ· οὐ γὰρ ἂν δεῦρ᾽ ἧκον ὡς ὑμᾶς, *for (otherwise) they would*
not have come hither to you. Id. xix. 58. Τότε Φιλίππῳ προδεδωκέναι
πάντας ἂν ἔσχεν αἰτίαν, *in that case she (Athens) would have had*
the blame of having betrayed all to Philip. Id. xviii. 200. See other
examples in 472.

248. The final step is taken when an unreal condition is
expressed as part of the sentence, forming the protasis to which
the potential indicative is the apodosis ; as ἦλθεν ἄν εἰ ἐκέλευσα,
he would have gone if I had commanded him. The dependent
protasis, by a natural assimilation, has a past tense of the indicative corresponding to the form of the apodosis. On the other
hand, when an unreal condition has been expressed, as εἰ ἐκέλευσα,
the potential indicative is the natural form to state what *would*
have been the result if the condition had been fulfilled. (See 390,
2 ; and 410.) The potential indicative does not change its
essential nature by being thus made part of an unreal conditional
expression, and it is not necessarily implied that its action did
not take place (see 412). Although the latter is generally
implied or inferred, while the reverse seldom occurs, still it is
important to a true understanding of the nature of the indicative
with ἄν to remember that it is not essential or necessary for it either
to refer to an unreal condition or to denote in itself what is
contrary to fact.

For a periphrastic form of potential indicative with ἔδει, χρῆν, etc.,
with the infinitive, see 415.

For the Homeric use of the present optative with κέ or ἄν as a present potential form (like the later imperfect with ἄν), see 438.

For the rare Homeric optative with κέ in the sense of the past tenses of the indicative with κέ or ἄν, see 440.

249. From the primitive use of the past tenses of the indicative to express what *was likely to occur under past circumstances*, we may explain the iterative use of these tenses with ἄν (162), which is generally thought to have no connection with the potential indicative with ἄν. Thus ἦλθεν ἄν, meaning originally *he would have gone (under some past circumstances)*, might easily come to have a frequentative sense, *he would have gone (under all circumstances* or *whenever occasion offered)*, and hence to mean *he used to go*. See SOPH. Ph. 443, ὃς οὐκ ἄν εἵλετ᾽ εἰσάπαξ εἰπεῖν, ὅπου μηδεὶς ἐῴη, (Thersites) *who used never to be content to speak but once when all forbade him* (lit. *when nobody permitted him*). Originally οὐκ ἄν εἵλετο would mean *he would not have been content (under any circumstances)*, hence *he was never content*. The optative ἐῴη (532) shows the nature of the expression here. See the examples under 162, and the last example under 244.

This construction is not Homeric; but it is found in Herodotus and is common in Attic Greek. There is no difficulty in understanding it as an offshoot of the potential indicative, when it is seen that the latter did not involve originally any denial of its own action.

SECTION II.

The Imperative and Subjunctive in Commands, Exhortations, and Prohibitions.—Subjunctive and Indicative with μή and μὴ οὐ in Cautious Assertions.—Ὅπως and ὅπως μή with the Independent Future Indicative, etc.

IMPERATIVE IN COMMANDS, ETC.

250. The imperative is used to express a command, an exhortation, or an entreaty. *E.g.*

Λέγε, *speak thou.* Φεῦγε, *begone!* Ἐλθέτω, *let him come.* Χαιρόντων, *let them rejoice.* Ἔρχεσθον κλισίην Πηληιάδεω Ἀχιλῆος. Il. i. 322. Ζεῦ, θεωρὸς τῶνδε πραγμάτων γενοῦ. AESCH. Cho. 246.

For prohibitions, *i.e.* negative commands, see 259 and 260.

251. The imperative is often emphasised by ἄγε or ἄγετε, φέρε, ἴθι, δεῦρο or δεῦτε, *come, look here;* or by εἰ δ᾽ ἄγε (474). Ἄγε, φέρε, and ἴθι may be singular when the imperative is plural, and in the second person when the imperative is in the third. *E.g.*

Εἴπ' ἄγε μοι καὶ τόνδε, φίλον τέκος, ὅς τις ὅδ' ἐστίν. Il. iii. 192.
'Αλλ' ἄγε μίμνετε πάντες, ἐυκνήμιδες 'Αχαιοί. Il. ii. 331. Βάσκ'
ἴθι, οὖλε ὄνειρε, θοὰς ἐπὶ νῆας 'Αχαιῶν. Il. ii. 8. "Αγε δὴ ἀκούσατε.
Xen. Ap. 14. "Αγετε δειπνήσατε. Xen. Hell. v. 1, 18. Φέρ' εἰπὲ
δή μοι. Soph. Ant. 534. Φέρε δή μοι τόδε εἰπέ. Plat. Crat. 385 B.
"Ιθι δὴ λέξον ἡμῖν πρῶτον τοῦτο. Xen. Mem. iii. 3, 3. "Ιθι νυν
παρίστασθον. Ar. Ran. 1378. "Ιθι νυν λιβανωτὸν δεῦρό τις καὶ πῦρ
δότω. Ib. 871. Καί μοι δεῦρο, ὦ Μέλητε, εἰπέ. Plat. Ap. 24 C.
Δεῦτε, λείπετε στέγας. Eur. Med. 894.

252. The poets sometimes use the *second* person of the imperative with πᾶς in hasty commands. *E.g.*

"Ακουε πᾶς, *hear, every one!* Ar. Thes. 372. Χώρει δεῦρο πᾶς
ὑπηρέτης· τόξευε, παῖε· σφενδόνην τίς μοι δότω. Id. Av. 1186. "Αγε
δὴ σιώπα πᾶς ἀνήρ. Id. Ran. 1125.

253. The imperative is sometimes used by the dramatists
after οἶσθ' ὅ and similar interrogative expressions, the imperative
being really the verb of the relative clause.[1] The difficulty of
translating such expressions is similar to that of translating
relatives and interrogatives with participles. *E.g.*

'Αλλ' οἶσθ' ὃ δρᾶσον; τῷ σκέλει θένε τὴν πέτραν, *but do you know
what you must do?—strike the rock with your leg!* Ar. Av. 54. Οἶσθ'
ὅ μοι σύμπραξον; *do you know what you must do for me?* Eur. Her.
451. Οἶσθά νυν ἅ μοι γενέσθω; δεσμὰ τοῖς ξένοισι πρόσθες, *do
you know what must be done for me?—put bonds on the strangers.* Id.
I. T. 1203. Οἶσθ' ὡς ποίησον; *do you know how you must act?* Soph.
O. T. 543. (Compare Eur. Cyc. 131, οἶσθ' οὖν ὃ δράσεις; *do you
know what you are to do?*)

The English may use a relative with the imperative, as in *which do
at your peril.* See Hdt. i. 89, κάτισον φυλάκους, οἳ λεγόντων ὡς
ἀναγκαίως ἔχει. So Soph. O. C. 473.

A peculiar interrogative imperative is found in μὴ ἐξέστω; *is it
not to be allowed?* Plat. Polit. 295 E; and ἐπανερωτῶ εἰ κείσθω, *I
ask whether it is to stand,* Id. Leg. 800 E. (See 291.)

254. The imperative sometimes expresses a mere assumption, where
something is supposed to be true for argument's sake. *E.g.*

Πλούτει τε γὰρ κατ' οἶκον, εἰ βούλει, μέγα, καὶ ζῆ τύραννον
σχῆμ' ἔχων, i.e. *grant that you are rich and live in tyrant's state* (lit. *be
rich,* etc.) Soph. Ant. 1168. Προσειπάτω τινὰ φιλικῶς ὅ τε ἄρχων
καὶ ὁ ἰδιώτης, *suppose that both the ruler and the private man address one
in a friendly way.* Xen. Hier. viii. 3.

FIRST PERSON OF SUBJUNCTIVE AS IMPERATIVE.

255. The want of a first person in the imperative is supplied

---

[1] See Postgate in *Transactions of the Cambridge Philological Society*, III.
1, pp. 50-55.

by the first person of the subjunctive, which expresses both
positive and negative exhortations and appeals (the negative
with μή). Ἄγε, ἄγετε, εἰ δ᾽ ἄγε, φέρε, ἴθι, δεῦρο, and δεῦτε (251)
may precede this subjunctive ; so sometimes ἔα, *permit, let.*

256. The first person plural is most common, and generally
expresses an exhortation of the speaker to others to join him in
doing or in not doing some act. *E.g.*

Ἴωμεν, *let us go; μὴ ἴωμεν, let us not go.* Οἴκαδέ περ σὺν νηυσὶ
νεώμεθα, τόνδε δ᾽ ἐῶμεν, *let us sail homeward with our ships, and
leave him.* Il. ii. 236. Ἀλλ᾽ ἄγε μηκέτι ταῦτα λεγώμεθα, *but come,
let us no longer talk thus.* Il. xiii. 292 ; so ii. 435. Ἀλλ᾽ ἄγε δὴ καὶ
νῶι μεδώμεθα θούριδος ἀλκῆς. Il. iv. 418. Εἰ δ᾽ ἄγετ᾽ ἀμφὶ πόλιν
σὺν τεύχεσι πειρηθῶμεν. Il. xxii. 381; so 392. Δεῦτε, φίλοι,
τὸν ξεῖνον ἐρώμεθα. Od. viii. 133. Μὴ δή πω λύωμεθα ἵππους,
ἀλλ᾽ ἰόντες Πάτροκλον κλαίωμεν. Il. xxiii. 7. Ἀλλ᾽ εἰ δοκεῖ,
πλέωμεν, ὁρμάσθω ταχύς. Soph. Ph. 526. Ἐπίσχετον, μάθωμεν.
Ib. 539. Φέρε δὴ διαπεράνωμεν λόγους. Eur. And. 333. Δεῦρό
σου στέψω κάρα. Id. Bacch. 341. Ἐπίσχες, ἐμβάλωμεν εἰς ἄλλον
λόγον. Id. El. 962. Παρῶμέν τε οὖν ὥσπερ Κῦρος κελεύει, ἀσκῶ-
μέν τε δι᾽ ὧν μάλιστα δυνησόμεθα κατέχειν ἃ δεῖ, παρέχωμέν τε
ἡμᾶς αὐτούς, κ.τ.λ. Xen. Cyr. viii. 1, 5. Μή ποτε φῶμεν ἕνεκα
τούτων μηδὲν μᾶλλόν ποτε ψυχὴν ἀπόλλυσθαι. Plat. Rep. 610 B.
Ἔα δὴ νῦν ἐν σοὶ σκεψώμεθα. Id. Soph. 239 B.

257. The less common first person singular is, in *affirmative*
exhortations, generally preceded by a word like ἄγε, etc. (251),
or by some other command, and the speaker appeals to himself
to do something or to others for permission to do it. In *negative*
appeals with μή the first person singular is rare and poetic ; the
speaker may call on others to avert some evil from himself, or
he may utter a threat or a warning. *E.g.*

Ἀλλ᾽ ἄγε δὴ τὰ χρήματ᾽ ἀριθμήσω καὶ ἴδωμαι, *come, let me
count the things and see.* Od. xiii. 215. Ἀλλ᾽ ἄγεθ᾽ ὑμῖν τεύχε᾽ ἐνείκω θωρηχθῆναι. Od. xxii. 139. Θάπτε με ὅττι τάχιστα, πύλας
Ἀίδαο περήσω, *bury me as quickly as possible; let me pass the gates of
Hades.* Il. xxiii. 71. Ἀλλ᾽ ἄγε νῦν ἐπίμεινον, ἀρήια τεύχεα δύω. Il.
vi. 340. Φέρε ἀκούσω, *come, let me hear.* Hdt. i. 11. Σῖγα, πνοὰς
μάθω · φέρε πρὸς οὓς βάλω. Eur. H. F. 1059. Ἐπίσχετ᾽, αὐδὴν
τῶν ἔσωθεν ἐκμάθω. Id. Hipp. 567. Λέγε δή, ἴδω. Plat. Rep.
457 C.

Μή σε, γέρον, κοίλησιν ἐγὼ παρὰ νηυσὶ κιχείω, *let me not find
you at the ships!* Il. i. 26. Μή σευ ἀκούσω εὐχομένου. Il. xxi. 475.
Ἀλλά μ᾽ ἔκ γε τῆσδε γῆς πόρθμευσον ὡς τάχιστα, μήδ᾽ αὐτοῦ θάνω.
Soph. Tr. 801. Ὦ ξεῖνοι, μὴ δῆτ᾽ ἀδικηθῶ. Id. O. C. 174.

258. In the first person (255-257) both present and aorist subjunctive are used with μή, the distinction of 259 applying only to the

second and third persons. In affirmative exhortations the second and third persons of the subjunctive are not regularly used, the imperative being the only recognised form. But in SOPH. Ph. 300, φέρ᾽, ὦ τέκνον, νῦν καὶ τὸ τῆς νήσου μάθῃς (if the text is sound), the positive μάθῃς seems strangely to follow the analogy of the negative μὴ μάθῃς. Nauck reads μάθε here. See also τὸ ψάφισμα ἀνατεθᾷ in an inscription quoted in Appendix I. p. 385.

IMPERATIVE AND SUBJUNCTIVE IN PROHIBITIONS.

259. In prohibitions, in the second and third persons, the *present* imperative or the *aorist* subjunctive is used with μή and its compounds. The distinction of tense here is solely the ordinary distinction between the present and aorist (87), and has no reference to the moods. *E.g.*

Μὴ ποίει τοῦτο, do not do this (habitually), or do not go on doing this (or stop doing this); μὴ ποιήσῃς τοῦτο, (simply) do not do this. Ἐξαύδα, μὴ κεῦθε νόῳ, ἵνα εἴδομεν ἄμφω. Il. i. 363. Ἀτρείδη, μὴ ψεύδε᾽ ἐπιστάμενος σάφα εἰπεῖν. Il. iv. 404. Ἀργεῖοι, μή πώ τι μεθίετε θούριδος ἀλκῆς. Il. iv. 234. Εἰπέ μοι εἰρομένῳ νημερτέα, μηδ᾽ ἐπικεύσῃς. Od. xv. 263. Ἤδη νῦν σῷ παιδὶ ἔπος φάο, μηδ᾽ ἐπίκευθε (compare the last example). Od. xvi. 168. Τῷ νῦν μή μοι μᾶλλον ἐν ἄλγεσι θυμὸν ὀρίνῃς. Il. xxiv. 568. See Il. xxiv. 778. Μὴ δή με ἕλωρ Δαναοῖσιν ἐάσῃς κεῖσθαι. Il. v. 684. Κλῦθι μηδὲ μεγήρῃς. Od. iii. 55. Μή πως ἀνδράσι δυσμενέεσσιν ἕλωρ καὶ κύρμα γένησθε, do not become prey and spoil to hostile men. Il. v. 487. Μή ποτε ἀπὸ πᾶσαν ὀλέσσῃς ἀγλαΐην. Od. xix. 81. Ὑμεῖς δὲ τῇ γῇ τῇδε μὴ βαρὺν κότον σκήψησθε, μὴ θυμοῦσθε, μηδ᾽ ἀκαρπίαν τεύξητε. AESCH. Eum. 800. Ὃν μήτ᾽ ὀκνεῖτε, μήτ᾽ ἀφῆτ᾽ ἔπος κακόν. SOPH. O. C. 731. Μὴ θῆσθε νόμον μηδένα, ἀλλὰ τοὺς βλάπτοντας ὑμᾶς λύσατε. DEM. iii. 10. (Here θέσθε would not be allowed; but λύσατε, an affirmative command, is regular.) Μὴ κατὰ τοὺς νόμους δικάσητε· μὴ βοηθήσητε τῷ πεπονθότι δεινά· μὴ εὐορκεῖτε. Id. xxi. 211. Μὴ πρίῃ, παῖ, δᾷδα. AR. Nub. 614. Καὶ μηδεὶς ὑπολάβῃ με βούλεσθαι λαθεῖν. Isoc. v. 93. Καὶ μηδεὶς οἰέσθω μ᾽ ἀγνοεῖν. Id. iv. 73.

260. The *third* person of the aorist imperative is sometimes used with μή in prohibitions; but the *second* person with μή is very rare and only poetic. *E.g.*

Μηδ᾽ ἡ βία σε μηδαμῶς νικησάτω. SOPH. Aj. 1334. Μηδέ σοι μελησάτω. AESCH. Prom. 332; so 1002. Καὶ μηδεὶς ὑμῶν προσδοκησάτω ἄλλως. PLAT. Ap. 17 C.

Τῷ μή μοι πατέρας ποθ᾽ ὁμοίῃ ἔνθεο τιμῇ. Il. iv. 410; see Od. xxiv. 248. Μή πω καταδύσεο μῶλον Ἄρηος. Il. xviii. 134. Μὴ ψεῦσον, ὦ Ζεῦ, μή μ᾽ ἔλῃς ἄνευ δορός in SOPH. Peleus, Frag. 450, is parodied in AR. Thes. 870, μὴ ψεῦσον, ὦ Ζεῦ, τῆς ἐπιούσης ἐλπίδος.

INDEPENDENT SUBJUNCTIVE WITH μή IMPLYING FEAR (HOMERIC).

261. In the following Homeric examples the independent subjunctive with μή expresses apprehension, coupled with a desire to avert the object of fear, both ideas being inherent in the construction. The third person is the most common here.

Μὴ δὴ νῆας ἕλωσι καὶ οὐκέτι φευκτὰ πέλωνται, *may they not (as I fear they may) seize the ships and make it no longer possible to escape.* Il. xvi. 128. Μὴ δή μοι τελέσωσι θεοὶ κακὰ κήδεα θυμῷ, *may the Gods not bring to pass (as I fear they may) bitter woes for my soul.* Il. xviii. 8. Μή τι χολωσάμενος ῥέξῃ κακὸν υἷας Ἀχαιῶν, *may he not (as I fear he may) in his wrath do anything to harm the sons of the Achaeans.* Il. ii. 195. Ὦ μοι ἐγώ, μή τίς μοι ὑφαίνῃσιν δόλον αὖτε ἀθανάτων. Od. v. 356. Μή πώς μ' ἐκβαίνοντα βάλῃ λίθακι προτὶ πέτρῃ κῦμα μέγ' ἁρπάξαν, μελέη δέ μοι ἔσσεται ὁρμή, *I fear that some great wave may dash me against a solid rock, and my effort will (then) be in vain* (the expression of fear being merged in an assertion). Od. v. 415. See also Il. xxi. 563 ; Od. v. 467, xvii. 24, xxii. 213. Τῶν εἴ κεν πάντων ἀντήσομεν, μὴ πολύπικρα καὶ αἰνὰ βίας ἀποτίσεαι ἐλθών, i.e. *I fear you may punish their violence only to our bitter grief (and may you not do this).* Od. xvi. 255. Μή τι κακὸν ῥέξωσι καὶ ἡμέας ἐξελάσωσιν, ἄλλων δ' ἀφικώμεθα γαῖαν, *may they not (as I fear) do us some harm and drive us out, and may we not come to some land of others.* Od. xvi. 381. Μή μιν ἐγὼ μὲν ἵκωμαι ἰών, ὁ δέ μ' οὐκ ἐλεήσει, *I fear I may approach him as I come, while he will not pity me.* Il. xxii. 122 (see Od. v. 415, above). Μή τοι κατὰ πάντα φάγωσιν κτήματα δασσάμενοι, σὺ δὲ τηϋσίην ὁδὸν ἔλθῃς. Od. xv. 12.

The present subjunctive occurs in Od. xv. 19, μή τι φέρηται, and in xvi. 87, μή μιν κερτομέωσιν. See also πέλωνται in Il. xvi. 128, above. (See 258.)

In these examples sometimes the fear itself, and sometimes the desire to avert its object, is more prominent.

262. (a) By prefixing δείδω or φοβοῦμαι to any of the subjunctives with μή in 261, we get the full construction with verbs of fearing ; as δείδω μὴ νῆας ἕλωσι, *I fear they may seize the ships,* in which μὴ ἕλωσι represents an original construction which at first followed δείδω paratactically—*I fear: may they not seize the ships*—and afterwards became welded with it as a dependent clause. So if δείδω were removed from a sentence like δείδω μή τι πάθῃσιν, Il. xi. 470, we should have an independent clause like those quoted above. See μὴ δαμάσσῃ and δείδω μὴ γένωμαι, Od. v. 467 and 473.

(b) In like manner, by prefixing other verbs than those of fearing to such clauses, the original negative final clause with μή is developed ; as μαχούμεθα μὴ νῆας ἕλωσι, *we will fight that they may not seize the ships.* Again, if the loading clause were removed from a sentence like αὐτοῦ μίμν᾽ ἐπὶ πύργῳ, μὴ παῖδ᾽ ὀρφανικὸν θήῃς χήρην τε γυναῖκα, *remain here on the tower, lest you make your child an orphan and your wife a widow,* Il. vi. 431, there would remain μή . . . θήῃς, *do not make,* or *may you not make,* in the originally independent form, like the clauses with μή in 261. (See 307.)

263. (Mὴ οὐ *with the Subjunctive.*) The clause with μή expressing desire to avert an object of fear, in its original simple form as well as in the developed final construction, may refer to a negative object, and express fear that something *may not* happen. Here μὴ οὐ is used with the subjunctive, like *ne non* in Latin.

Thus μὴ νῆας ἕλωσι being *may they not seize the ships,* μὴ οὐ νῆας ἕλωσι would be *may they not fail to seize the ships,* implying fear that they *may not* seize them. Homer has one case of μὴ οὐ after a verb of fearing : δείδω μὴ οὐ τίς τοι ὑπόσχηται τόδε ἔργον, Il. x. 39. He has several cases of μή οὐ in final clauses and one in an object clause (354). Il. i. 28, μή νύ τοι οὐ χραίσμῃ σκῆπτρον καὶ στέμμα θεοῖο, is often cited as a case of independent μὴ οὐ, meaning *beware lest the staff and fillet of the God shall prove of no avail to you.* So Delbrück (I. p. 119), who nevertheless quotes Il. i. 565, ἀλλ᾽ ἀκέουσα κάθησο ἐμῷ δ᾽ ἐπιπείθεο μύθῳ, μή νύ τοι οὐ χραίσμωσιν ὅσοι θεοί εἰσ᾽ ἐν Ὀλύμπῳ, as containing a dependent final clause. In the two other cases of μὴ οὐ with the subjunctive in Homer, Il. xv. 164 (an object clause, see 354), and xxiv. 569 (final), the dependence of the clause with μὴ οὐ is even more obvious ; and in Il. xxiv. 584 we have in μὴ οὐκ ἐρύσαιτο the decisive proof that this clause is felt to be dependent in the change from the subjunctive to the optative after a past tense. It is therefore more than doubtful whether μὴ οὐ χραίσμῃ in Il. i. 28 is not dependent on μή σε κιχείω in vs. 26. Plato in paraphrasing this passage (Rep. 393 E) takes the clause as final and dependent (see 132). But, whether we have a case of independent μὴ οὐ with the subjunctive in Homer or not, there can be no doubt that this is the original form from which came the dependent final clause with μὴ οὐ.

264. After Homer we have the independent clause with μή in Aeschylus, Ag. 134 and 341 ; in Euripides we have independent μή in Alc. 315 (μὴ σοὺς διαφθείρῃ γάμους), Orest. 776 (μὴ λάβωσί σ᾽ ἄσμενοι), H. F. 1399 (αἷμα μὴ σοῖς ἐξομόρξωμαι πέπλοις), and μὴ οὐ in Tro. 982 (μὴ οὐ πείσῃς σοφούς), besides Rhes. 115 (μὴ οὐ μόλῃς). Aristophanes, Eccl. 795, has a doubtful μὴ οὐ λάβῃς (Heindorf and Meineke, for Mss. λάβοις). Besides these few cases, we have in Plato three of μή with the subjunctive implying apprehension in the Homeric sense (261) : Euthyd. 272 C (μὴ οὖν τις ὀνειδίσῃ), Symp. 193 B (μή μοι ὑπολάβῃ), Leg. 861 E (μή τις οἴηται).

Euripides and Herodotus are the first after Homer to use μὴ οὐ in *dependent* clauses of fear (306).

SUBJUNCTIVE WITH μή AND μὴ οὐ IN CAUTIOUS ASSERTIONS.

265. In Herodotus v. 79 we have ἀλλὰ μᾶλλον μὴ οὐ τοῦτο ᾖ τὸ μαντήιον, but I suspect rather that this may prove not to be the meaning of the oracle. This is the first example of a construction, very common in Plato, used also by Aristotle, and found once in Demosthenes, in which μή with the subjunctive expresses a suspicion that something *may be* (or *may prove to be*) true, and μὴ οὐ with the subjunctive a suspicion that something *may not be* true ; the former amounting to a cautious assertion, the latter to a cautious negation. Examples from Plato are :—

Μὴ ἀγροικότερον ᾖ τὸ ἀληθὲς εἰπεῖν, I am afraid the truth may be too rude a thing to tell. Gorg. 462 E. Μὴ ὡς ἀληθῶς ταῦτα σκέμματα ᾖ τῶν ῥᾳδίως ἀποκτιννύντων, I suspect these may prove to be considerations for those, etc. Crit. 48 C. Μὴ φαῦλον ᾖ καὶ οὐ καθ᾽ ὁδόν, I think it will be bad and not in the right way (i.e. μὴ οὐ ᾖ). Crat. 425 B. Ἀλλὰ μὴ οὐχ οὕτως ἔχῃ, ἀλλ᾽ ἀναγκαῖον ᾖ εἰδότα τίθεσθαι (i.e. μὴ ᾖ). Crat. 436 B. Ἀλλὰ μὴ οὐ τοῦτ᾽ ᾖ χαλεπὸν, θάνατον ἐκφυγεῖν, but I suspect this may not be the hard thing, to escape death. Ap. 39 A. Ἡμῖν μὴ οὐδὲν ἄλλο σκεπτέον ᾖ, I am inclined to think we have nothing else to consider. Crit. 48 C. Μὴ οὐ δέῃ ὑπολογίζεσθαι, I think there will be no need of taking into account, etc. Crit. 48 D. Μὴ οὐκ ᾖ διδακτὸν ἀρετή, it will probably turn out that virtue is not a thing to be taught. Men. 94 E. Ἀλλὰ μὴ οὐχ οὗτοι ἡμεῖς ὦμεν, but I think we shall not prove to be of this kind. Symp. 194 C.[1]

See also Aristotle, Eth. x. 2, 4, μὴ οὐδὲν λέγωσιν (v. l. λέγουσίν), there can hardly be anything in what they say. (See 269.)

In DEM. i. 26 we have μὴ λίαν πικρὸν εἰπεῖν ᾖ, I am afraid it may be too harsh a thing to say.

The present subjunctive here, as in dependent clauses of fear (92), may refer to what *may prove* true.

266. In these cautious assertions and negations, although no desire of the speaker to avert an object of fear is implied, there is always a tacit allusion to such a desire on the part of some person who is addressed or referred to, or else an ironical pretence of such a desire of the speaker himself.

267. The subjunctive with μή in this sense is sometimes found in dependent clauses. *E.g.*

Ὅρα μὴ ἄλλο τι τὸ γενναῖον καὶ τὸ ἀγαθὸν ᾖ τοῦ σῴζειν καὶ σῴζεσθαι, see to it lest (it prove true that) these may be different things, etc. PLAT. Gorg. 512 D. The common translation, *see whether they may*

---

[1] Other examples in Plato are Phaed. 67 B, 69 A ; Theaet. 188 D ; Crat. 429 C, 432 A, 432 B, 435 C, 438 C, 440 C ; Men. 89 C, 94 B ; Lys. 209 A, 219 D, 220 A ; Symp. 214 C ; Parm. 130 D, 132 B, 134 E, 136 D ; Leg. 635 E ; Theag. 122 B ; Amat. 137 B. See Weber (pp. 191, 192), who gives these examples in Plato, with HDT. v. 79 and DEM. i. 26, as the only cases of independent μή or μὴ οὐ in this peculiar sense before Aristotle.

not be different, gives the general sense, but not the construction, which
is simply that of μὴ ἄλλο τι ᾖ (265) transferred to a dependent clause.

268. In a few cases Plato has μή with the subjunctive in a cautious
question with a negative answer implied. As μὴ ἄλλο τι ᾖ τοῦτο
means *this may possibly be something else,* so the question μὴ ἄλλο τι ᾖ
τοῦτο ; means *can this possibly be something else?* The four examples
given by Weber are :—

Μή τι ἄλλο ᾖ παρὰ ταῦτα; *can there be any other besides these?* Rep.
603 C. Ἆρα μὴ ἄλλο τι ᾖ θάνατος ἢ τοῦτο ; *is it possible that death
can prove to be anything but this?* Phaed. 64 C. So μή τι ἄλλο ᾖ ᾖ ἤ,
κ.τ.λ.; Parm. 163 D. Ἀλλὰ μὴ ἐμὴ περιεργία ᾖ καὶ τὸ ἐρωτῆσαί
σε περὶ τούτου ; *but can it be that even asking you about this is inquisi-
tiveness on my part?* Sisyph. 387 C (this can be understood positively,
it may be that it is, etc.).

In XEN. Mem. iv. 2, 12, the same interrogative construction occurs
with μὴ οὐ : μὴ οὖν οὐ δύνωμαι ἐγὼ τὰ τῆς δικαιοσύνης ἔργα
ἐξηγήσασθαι; *do you suspect that I shall be unable to explain the works
of Justice?*

In PLAT. Phil. 12 D we have πῶς γὰρ ἡδονή γε ἡδονῇ μὴ οὐχ
ὁμοιότατον ἂν εἴη ; *for how could one pleasure help being most like
another?* Here εἴη ἄν takes the place of ᾖ, and πῶς shows that the
original force of μή is forgotten.

INDICATIVE WITH μή AND μὴ οὐ IN CAUTIOUS ASSERTIONS.

269. The present or past tenses of the indicative with μή or
μὴ οὐ may express a similar cautious assertion or suspicion about
a present or past act. As φοβοῦμαι μὴ πάσχει (or ἔπαθεν) means
I fear that he is suffering (or *suffered*), so μὴ πάσχει or μὴ ἔπαθεν
may mean *I suspect he is suffering* or *I suspect he suffered,* and μὴ
οὐ πάσχει or μὴ οὐκ ἔπαθεν may mean *I suspect he does not* (or *did
not*) *suffer.* (Cf. 265.) *E.g.*

Μὴ γὰρ τοῦτο μὲν, τὸ ζῆν ὁποσονδὴ χρόνον, τόν γε ὡς ἀληθῶς
ἄνδρα ἐατέον ἐστὶ καὶ οὐ φιλοψυχητέον (i.e. καὶ μὴ οὐ φιλ.), *for I am
of the opinion that this, merely living for a certain time, is what one who
is truly a man should disregard, and that he should not be fond of life.*
PLAT. Gorg. 512 D. (This passage is often strangely emended and
explained.) Ἀλλ᾽ ἄρα μὴ οὐ τοιαύτην ὑπολαμβάνεις σου τὴν
μάθησιν ἔσεσθαι, *I suspect that you do not think your learning will be like
this.* Id. Prot. 312 A. Ἀλλὰ μὴ τοῦτο οὐ καλῶς ὡμολογήσαμεν,
but perhaps we did not do well in assenting to this. Id. Men. 89 C.
(This may be interrogative (268) : *can it be that we did not do well,* etc. ?)
So Aristotle, Eth. x. 1, 3, μή ποτε δὲ οὐ καλῶς λέγεται, *but it
may be that this is not well said* : compare x. 2, 4, quoted in 265.

270. Apart from independent sentences with μὴ οὐ (263-269),
this double negative occurs chiefly in ordinary clauses after
verbs of fearing where the object of fear is negative (305 ; 365).

"Οπως AND ὅπως μή WITH THE INDEPENDENT
FUTURE INDICATIVE, ETC.

271. The Athenians developed a colloquial use of ὅπως or
ὅπως μή with the future indicative to express either a positive
exhortation or command or a prohibition. Thus ὅπως τοῦτο ἐρεῖς,
see that you say this, is a familiar way of saying εἰπὲ τοῦτο. So
ὅπως μὴ τοῦτο ἐρεῖς is equivalent to μὴ τοῦτο εἴπῃς. This expression was probably suggested and certainly encouraged by the
common Attic construction of ὅπως and the future after verbs of
striving, taking care, etc. (339); so that it is common to explain
this form by an ellipsis of σκόπει in σκόπει ὅπως τοῦτο ἐρεῖς, *see to
it that you say this*. But we may doubt whether any definite
leading verb was ever in mind when these familiar exhortations
were used (see 273).

272. The earliest example is AESCH. Prom. 68, ὅπως μὴ σαυτὸν
οἰκτιεῖς ποτε, *beware lest at some time you may have yourself to pity*, which
conveys a warning, like μή σε κιχείω, Il. i. 26. In AESCH. Ag. 600,
we have the first person singular with ὅπως (used like the subjunctive
in 257): ὅπως δ' ἄριστα τὸν ἐμὸν αἰδοῖον πόσιν σπεύσω δέξασθαι
(not mentioned by Weber). In Sophocles there is only one case, O. T.
1518, γῆς μ' ὅπως πέμψεις ἄποικον, *send me forth an exile from the
land* (like πέμψον με). Five examples in Euripides are simple
exhortations, as ἀλλ' ὅπως ἀνὴρ ἔσει, *but see that you are a man*, Cycl.
595; so also Cycl. 630, H. F. 504, I. T. 321, Or. 1060 (with doubtful
construction): one conveys a warning, Bacch. 367, Πενθεὺς δ' ὅπως μὴ
πένθος εἰσοίσει δόμοις τοῖς σοῖσι, *beware lest Pentheus bring sorrow*
(πένθος) *into your house*.

273. We find the greater part of the examples of 271 in
the colloquial language of Aristophanes,[1] who often uses the
imperative and ὅπως with the future as equivalent constructions
in the same sentence. *E.g.*

Κατάθου σὺ τὰ σκεύη ταχέως, χὤπως ἐρεῖς ἐνταῦθα μηδὲν
ψεῦδος, *put down the packs quickly, and tell no lies here*. Ran. 627.
Ἀλλ' ἔμβα χὤπως ἀρεῖς τὴν Σώτειραν. Ib. 377. See also Eq. 453,
495, Eccl. 952, Ach. 955. Νῦν οὖν ὅπως σώσεις με, *so now save me*.
Nub. 1177. "Οπως παρέσει μοι καὶ σὺ καὶ τὰ παιδία, *be on hand,
you and your children* (an invitation). Av. 131. "Αγε νυν ὅπως εὐθέως
ὑφαρπάσει. Nub. 489.

274. (Examples from Prose.) "Οπως οὖν ἔσεσθε ἄνδρες ἄξιοι τῆς
ἐλευθερίας, *prove yourselves men worthy of freedom*. XEN. An. i. 7, 3.

---

[1] See Weber, pp. 85, 95, 113, 124, for the history of this usage. Weber cites 41
examples from Aristophanes, besides Ach. 343; 13 from Plato, whose extra-
ordinary use of the independent sentence with μή has been noticed; 7 from
Xenophon, 9 from Demosthenes, 2 from Lysias, and one from Isaeus.

Ὅπως μοι, ὦ ἄνθρωπε, μὴ ἐρεῖς ὅτι ἔστι τὰ δώδεκα δὶς ἕξ, see that you do not tell me that twice six are twelve. PLAT. Rep. 337 B : so 336 D. Φέρε δὴ ὅπως μεμνησόμεθα ταῦτα. Id. Gorg. 495 D. Ὅπως γε, ἄν τι τούτων γίγνηται, τούτους ἐπαινέσεσθε καὶ τιμήσετε καὶ στεφανώσετε, ἐμὲ δὲ μή· καὶ μέντοι κἄν τι τῶν ἐναντίων, ὅπως τούτοις ὀργιεῖσθε. DEM. xix. 45. Ὅπως τοίνυν περὶ τοῦ πολέμου μηδὲν ἐρεῖς, see therefore that you say nothing about the war. Ib. 94. One case occurs in Herodotus in iii. 142. (See also 280, below.)

275. Although the second person is naturally most common in these expressions, the first and third persons also occur. *E.g.*

Ὅπως δὲ τὸ σύμβολον λαβόντες ἔπειτα πλησίον καθεδούμεθα. AR. Eccl. 297. Οἴμοι τάλας, ὁ Ζεὺς ὅπως μή μ᾽ ὄψεται, don't let Zeus see me! Id. Av. 1494. Καὶ ὅπως, ὥσπερ ἐρωτῶσι προθύμως, οὕτω καὶ ποιεῖν ἐθελήσουσιν. DEM. viii. 38. (See also 278.)

276. Ἄγε and φέρε (251) sometimes introduce this construction. See examples above (273 and 274).

277. In a few cases the prohibition with ὅπως μή takes the form of a warning. Besides AESCH. Prom. 68 and EUR. Bacch. 367, quoted above, see XEN. Cyr. i. 3, 18, ὅπως οὖν μὴ ἀπολεῖ μαστιγούμενος, look out that you are not flogged to death. So PLAT. Prot. 313 C, quoted in 283.

278. Ὅπως μή with the future indicative or the subjunctive sometimes occurs in independent sentences implying a desire to avert something that is not desired, like μή with the subjunctive in Homer and sometimes in Attic Greek (261 ; 264). *E.g.*

Ὅπως μὴ αἰσχροὶ μὲν φανούμεθα ἀσθενεῖς δὲ ἐσόμεθα, let us not appear base and be weak (as I fear we may). XEN. Cyr. iv. 2, 39. Ὅπως μὴ ἀναγκάσωμεν (so most MSS.) αὐτούς, κἂν μὴ βούλωνται, ἀγαθοὺς γενέσθαι, there is danger of our compelling them to become brave, even against their will. Ib. iv. 1, 16. Καὶ ὅπως γε μηδὲ τὸ χωρίον ἡδέως ὁρῶσιν ἔνθα κατέκανον ἡμῶν τοὺς συμμάχους, and let us not allow them even to enjoy the sight of the place where they slew our allies. Ib. v. 4, 21. Ὅπως μὴ φήσῃ τις ἡμᾶς ἡδυπαθεῖν, take care lest any one say of us, etc. Id. Symp. iv. 8. Ἀλλ᾽ ὅπως μὴ οὐχ οἷός τ᾽ ἔσομαι, προθυμούμενος δὲ γέλωτα ὀφλήσω, but I am afraid that I shall not have the power, but that in my zeal I shall make myself ridiculous. PLAT. Rep. 506 D. So Men. 77 A.

279. These cases (278) are analogous to those of ὅπως μή with the future indicative or the subjunctive after verbs of fearing, in place of the simple μή (370). They are also a connecting link between the subjunctive with μή in prohibitions and the rare future indicative with μή in the same sense ; as ταύτην φυλάξετε τὴν πίστιν, καὶ μὴ βουλήσεσθε εἰδέναι, hold fast to this security, and do not wish to know, etc., DEM. xxiii. 117 (see other examples in 70).

280. In a few cases ὅπως μή with the subjunctive expresses a cautious assertion, where the simple μή is generally used (265). *E.g.*

Καὶ ὅπως μὴ ἐν μὲν τοῖς ζωγραφήμασιν ᾖ τοῦτο, and it may be that this will prove true in the case of pictures. PLAT. Crat. 430 D. Weber (p. 264) quotes HDT. vi. 85 for this sense : ὅκως ἐξ ὑστέρης μή τι ὑμῖν, ἢν ταῦτα ποιήσητε, πανώλεθρον κακὸν ἐς τὴν χώρην ἐμβάλωσι, it is not unlikely that they will turn about and bring some fatal harm on your country ; but this can be understood like the examples in 278.

281. Ὡς ἂν σκοποὶ νῦν ἦτε τῶν εἰρημένων, mind now and guard what I have said (i.e. be watchful to do it), SOPH. Ant. 215, must be brought under this head (271). In the early stage of the Attic construction of ὅπως with the future, of which only two cases occur in Aeschylus and one in Sophocles (272), ὡς ἂν ἦτε was here used like ὅπως ἔσεσθε. Compare ἐπιμελεῖσθαι ὡς ἂν πραχθῇ, XEN. Hipp. ix. 2 (see 351).

282. In AR. Ach. 343 is the single case of ὅπως μή with a present tense, expressing a suspicion and apprehension concerning a present ground of fear : ἀλλ᾽ ὅπως μή 'ν τοῖς τρίβωσιν ἐγκάθηνταί που λίθοι, but I am afraid they now have stones hidden somewhere in their cloaks. This bears the same relation to the common ὅπως μή with the future (272) that φοβοῦμαι μὴ πάσχουσιν, I fear that they are suffering (369, 1), bears to φοβοῦμαι μὴ πάσχωσιν, I fear that they may suffer (365) ; and the same that μὴ τοῦτο ἐατέον ἐστί (269) bears to μὴ σκεπτέον ᾖ (265).

283. Positive independent sentences with ὅπως all have the future indicative, the regular form in dependent object clauses of this nature (339). Among the 33 independent clauses with ὅπως μή which are cited (excluding AR. Ach. 343) ten have the subjunctive, and four others have more or less Ms. support for the subjunctive. Of the ten, the two quoted in 280, and the three from Xenophon quoted in 278, are either in cautious assertions or in sentences implying fear or the averting of danger, where the subjunctive is the regular form. The other five express warning, and are quoted here :—

Οπως δὲ τοῦτο μὴ διδάξῃς μηδένα, but be sure that you teach this to nobody. AR. Nub. 824. Καὶ ὅπως γε μὴ ὁ σοφιστὴς ἐξαπατήσῃ ἡμᾶς, and do not let the sophist cheat us. PLAT. Prot. 313 C. Ἀλλ᾽ ὅπως μή τι ἡμᾶς σφήλῃ τὸ ἀεὶ τοῦτο. Id. Euthyd. 296 A. "Οπως μηδείς σε πείσῃ, do not let anybody persuade you, etc. Id. Charm. 157 B. Καὶ ὅπως μὴ ποιήσητε ὃ πολλάκις ὑμᾶς ἔβλαψεν, and see that you do not do what has often harmed you. DEM. iv. 20.

Four of these subjunctives are of the σ- class, easily confounded with the future indicative, and the judgment of scholars on these has depended to a great extent upon their opinion about the admissibility of the subjunctive with ὅπως and ὅπως μή in dependent object clauses (339). This question will be discussed in 364. But it may fairly be claimed, independently of the main question, that these cases of ὅπως μή with the subjunctive in *prohibitions* are supported by the analogy of μή with the subjunctive in the same sense. Thus μὴ διδάξῃς, do not teach, makes ὅπως μὴ διδάξῃς in the same sense much more

natural than the positive ὅπως διδάξῃς would be, for which there is no
such analogy and little or no Ms. authority. On this ground the
examples are given above as they stand in the Mss.

SECTION III.

Subjunctive, like the Future Indicative, in Independent
Sentences.—Interrogative Subjunctive.

HOMERIC SUBJUNCTIVE.

284. In the Homeric language the subjunctive (generally
the aorist) may be used in independent sentences, with the
force of a future indicative. The negative is οὐ. *E.g.*

Οὐ γάρ πω τοίους ἴδον ἀνέρας οὐδὲ ἴδωμαι, *for I never yet saw nor
shall I ever see such men.* Il. i. 262. Ὑμῖν ἐν πάντεσσι περικλυτὰ
δῶρ᾽ ὀνομήνω, *I will enumerate the gifts before you all.* Il. ix. 121.
Δύσομαι ἐς Ἀίδαο καὶ ἐν νεκύεσσι φαείνω, *I will descend to Hades
and shine among the dead* (said by the Sun). Od. xii. 383. (Here the
future δύσομαι and the subjunctive φαείνω do not differ in force.)
Μνήσομαι οὐδὲ λάθωμαι Ἀπόλλωνος ἑκάτοιο, *I will remember and
will not forget the far-shooting Apollo.* Hymn. Ap. 1. Αὐτοῦ οἱ θάνατον
μητίσομαι, οὐδέ νυ τόν γε γνωτοί τε γνωταί τε πυρὸς λελάχωσι
θανόντα, i.e. *they shall not give his dead body the honour of a funeral
pyre.* Il. xv. 349. Εἰ δέ κε τεθνηῶτος ἀκούσω, σῆμά τέ οἱ χεύω καὶ
ἐπὶ κτέρεα κτερεΐξω, *I will raise a mound for him, and pay him
funeral honours.* Od. ii. 222. Οὐ γάρ τίς με βίῃ γε ἑκὼν ἀέκοντα
δίηται. Il. vii. 197. Καί ποτέ τις εἴπῃσιν, *and some one will say.*
Il. vi. 459. (In vs. 462, referring to the same thing, we have ὥς ποτέ
τις ἐρέει.) Οὐκ ἔσθ᾽ οὗτος ἀνὴρ οὐδ᾽ ἔσσεται οὐδὲ γένηται, ὅς
κεν Τηλεμάχῳ σῷ υἱέι χεῖρας ἐποίσει. Od. xvi. 437. Οὐδέ μιν ἀν-
στήσεις· πρὶν καὶ κακὸν ἄλλο πάθῃσθα, *nor will you bring him back
to life; sooner will you suffer some new evil besides.* Il. xxiv. 551 (the
only example of the second person).

285. This Homeric subjunctive, like the future indicative, is
sometimes joined with κέ or ἄν in a potential sense. This en-
abled the earlier language to express an apodosis with a sense
between that of the optative with ἄν and that of the simple
future indicative, which the Attic was unable to do. (See 201
and 452.) *E.g.*

Εἰ δέ κε μὴ δώῃσιν, ἐγὼ δέ κεν αὐτὸς ἕλωμαι, *but if he does not
give her up, I will take her myself.* Il. i. 324. (Here ἕλωμαί κεν has a
shade of meaning between ἑλοίμην κεν, *I would take,* and αἱρήσομαι, *I*

will take, which neither Attic Greek nor English can express. See 235, end.) Τὴν μὲν πέμψω, ἐγὼ δέ κ᾿ ἄγω Βρισηίδα, *her I will send; but I shall take Briseis.* Il. i. 184. Νῦν δ᾿ ἂν πολλὰ πάθῃσι φίλου ἀπὸ πατρὸς ἁμαρτών, *but now he must suffer much*, etc. Il. xxii. 505. Ἧις ὑπεροπλίῃσι τάχ᾿ ἄν ποτε θυμὸν ὀλέσσῃ, *by his own insolence he may perchance lose his life.* Il. i. 205.

286. In the following cases the subjunctive and the optative with κέ or ἄν are contrasted :—

Ἄλλον κ᾿ ἐχθαίρῃσι βροτῶν, ἄλλον κε φιλοίη, *one mortal he (a king) will hate, and another he may love.* Od. iv. 692. Εἴ τίς σε ἴδοιτο, αὐτίκ᾿ ἂν ἐξείποι· Ἀγαμέμνονι, καί κεν ἀνάβλησις λύσιος νεκροῖο γένηται, *if any one should see you, he would straightway tell Agamemnon, and there might (may) be a postponement*, etc. Il. xxiv. 653. Εἰ μὲν δὴ ἀντίβιον σὺν τεύχεσι πειρηθείης, οὐκ ἄν τοι χραίσμῃσι βιὸς καὶ ταρφέες ἰοί. Il. xi. 386. Compare ἤν χ᾿ ὑμῖν σάφα εἴπω ὅτε πρότερός γε πυθοίμην, (a message) *which I will (would) tell you plainly so soon as I shall (should) hear it*, Od. ii. 43, with ἤν χ᾿ ἡμῖν σάφα εἴποι ὅτε πρότερός γε πύθοιτο, ii. 31,—both referring to the same thing.

INTERROGATIVE SUBJUNCTIVE.

287. The first person of the subjunctive is used in *questions of appeal*, where the speaker asks himself or another *what he is to do.* The negative is μή. In Attic Greek this subjunctive is often introduced by βούλει or βούλεσθε, sometimes in poetry by θέλεις or θέλετε. *E.g.*

Εἴπω τοῦτο; *shall I say this?* or βούλει εἴπω τοῦτο; *do you wish that I should say this?* Μὴ τοῦτο ποιῶμεν (or ποιήσωμεν); *shall we not do this?* Τί εἴπω; or τί βούλεσθε εἴπω; *what shall I say?* or *what do you want me to say?*

Πῇ τ᾿ ἄρ᾿ ἐγὼ, φίλε τέκνον, ἴω; τεῦ δώμαθ᾿ ἵκωμαι; ἦ ἰθὺς σῆς μητρὸς ἴω καὶ σοῖο δόμοιο; *whither shall I go? to whose house shall I come?* etc. Od. xv. 509. Ἦ αὐτὸς κεύθω; φάσθαι δέ με θυμὸς ἀνώγει. Od. xxi. 194. Ὦ Ζεῦ, τί λέξω; ποῖ φρενῶν ἔλθω, πάτερ; SOPH. O. C. 310. Ὤμοι ἐγὼ, πᾶ βῶ; πᾶ στῶ; πᾶ κέλσω; EUR. Hec. 1056. Ποῖ τράπωμαι; ποῖ πορευθῶ; Ib. 1099. Εἴπω τι τῶν εἰωθότων, ὦ δέσποτα; *shall I make one of the regular jokes?* AR. Ran. 1. Τίνα γὰρ μάρτυρα μείζω παράσχωμαι; i.e. *how shall I bring forward a greater witness?* DEM. xix. 240. Μηδ᾿, ἐάν τι ὠνῶμαι, ἔρωμαι ὁπόσου πωλεῖ; *may I not ask*, etc.? Μηδ᾿ ἀποκρίνωμαι οὖν, ἄν τίς με ἐρωτᾷ νέος, ἐὰν εἰδῶ; *and may I not answer*, etc.? XEN. Mem. i. 2, 36. Μὴ ἀποκρίνωμαι, ἀλλ᾿ ἕτερον εἴπω; PLAT. Rep. 337 B. So μὴ φῶμεν; Ib. 554 B. Μισθωσώμεθα οὖν κήρυκα, ἢ αὐτὸς ἀνείπω; Ib. 580 B. Μεθύοντα ἄνδρα πάνυ σφόδρα δέξεσθε συμπότην, ἢ ἀπίωμεν; *will you receive him, or shall we go away?* Id. Symp. 212 E. Ἄρα μὴ αἰσχυνθῶμεν τὸν Περσῶν βασιλέα μιμή-

σασθαι; shall we then be ashamed to imitate the king of the Persians?
—we shall not be ashamed; shall we? XEN. Oec. iv. 4.
Ποῦ δὴ βούλει καθιζόμενοι ἀναγνῶμεν; where wilt thou that we
sit down and read? PLAT. Phaedr. 228 E. (So ib. 263 E.) Βούλει
οὖν ἐπισκοπῶμεν ὅπου ἤδη τὸ δυνατόν ἐστι; XEN. Mem. iii. 5, 1.
Βούλει λάβωμαι δῆτα καὶ θίγω τί σου; SOPH. Phil. 761. Βού-
λεσθ᾽ ἐπεισπέσωμεν; EUR. Hec. 1042. Θέλεις μείνωμεν αὐτοῦ
κἀνακούσωμεν γόων; SOPH. El. 81. Τί σοι θέλεις δῆτ᾽ εἰκάθω;
Id. O. T. 650. Θέλετε θηρασώμεθα Πενθέως Ἀγαύην μητέρ᾽ ἐκ
βακχευμάτων, χάριν τ᾽ ἄνακτι θῶμεν; EUR. Bacch. 719. Βούλεσθε
τὸ ὅλον πρᾶγμα ἀφῶμεν καὶ μὴ ζητῶμεν; AESCHIN. i. 73.

So with κελεύετε : Ἀλλὰ πῶς; εἴπω κελεύετε καὶ οὐκ ὀργιεῖσθε;
do you command me to speak, and will you not be angry? DEM. ix. 46.

In PLAT. Rep. 372 E, we find εἰ δ᾽ αὖ βούλεσθε καὶ φλεγμαί-
νουσαν πόλιν θεωρήσωμεν, οὐδὲν ἀποκωλύει, but if, again, you will
have us examine an inflamed state, there is nothing to prevent. This
shows that βούλεσθε is not parenthetical, but is felt to be the leading
verb on which the subjunctive depends (see 288). In Phaed. 95 E,
ἵνα μή τι διαφύγῃ ἡμᾶς, εἴ τέ τι βούλει προσθῇς ἢ ἀφέλῃς, the subjunctives may depend on ἵνα.

288. Εἰ βούλεσθε θεωρήσωμεν, if you wish us to examine, quoted
in 287, shows that we have in βούλεσθε with the subjunctive a
parataxis not yet developed into a leading and a dependent clause. It
is probable that nothing like this was felt in the simple subjunctive
as it is found in Homer. The original interrogative subjunctive is
probably the interrogative form corresponding to the subjunctive in
exhortations (256) ; ἔλθωμεν, let us go, becoming ἔλθωμεν; shall we
go? (See Kühner, § 394, 5.) When βούλει and βούλεσθε were first
introduced in appeals to others, the two questions were doubtless felt
to be distinct ; as βούλεσθε; εἴπω; do you wish? shall I speak?—
which were gradually welded into one, do you wish that I speak?
Compare in Latin cave facias,—visne hoc videamus? etc. No conjunction
could be introduced to connect βούλει or θέλεις to the subjunctive
in classic Greek, as these verbs could have only the infinitive ; but in
later Greek, where ἵνα could be used after θέλω, the construction was
developed into θέλετε ἵνα εἴπω ; do you wish me to speak? See πάντα
ὅσα ἂν θέλητε ἵνα ποιῶσιν ὑμῖν οἱ ἄνθρωποι, whatsoever ye would that
men should do unto you, N. T. MATTH. vii. 12. So θέλω ἵνα δῷς μοι
τὴν κεφαλὴν Ἰωάννου τοῦ βαπτιστοῦ. MARC. vi. 25. These forms
appear in the New Testament side by side with the old construction
without ἵνα ; as τί σοι θέλεις ποιήσω; what wilt thou that I should do
unto thee? with the answer, ἵνα ἀναβλέψω, that I may receive my sight,
LUC. xviii. 41. So βούλεσθε ὑμῖν ἀπολύσω τὸν βασιλέα τῶν
Ἰουδαίων; IOH. xviii. 39.

From θέλετε ἵνα εἴπω; comes the modern Greek θέλετε νὰ εἴπω;
will you that I speak? and probably also the common future θὰ εἴπω,
I shall speak (if θά represents θέλω νά).

289. The *third* person of the subjunctive is sometimes used in these questions of appeal, but less frequently than the first, and chiefly when a speaker refers to himself by τὶς. *E.g.*

Πότερόν σέ τις, Αἰσχίνη, τῆς πόλεως ἐχθρὸν ἢ ἐμὸν εἶναι φῇ; i.e. *shall we call you the city's enemy, or mine?* DEM. xviii. 124. Εἶτα ταῦθ᾽ οὗτοι πεισθῶσιν ὑπὲρ αὐτῶν σε ποιεῖν, καὶ τὰ τῆς σῆς πονηρίας ἔργα ἐφ᾽ ἑαυτοὺς ἀναδέξωνται; i.e. *are these men to believe,* etc. ; *and are they to assume,* etc.? Id. xxii. 64. Τί τις εἶναι τοῦτο φῇ; Id. xix. 88. Πῶς τίς τοι πείθηται; *how can any one obey you?* Il. i. 150. Θύγατερ, ποῖ τις φροντίδος ἔλθῃ; SOPH. O. C. 170. Ποῖ τις οὖν φύγῃ; Id. Aj. 403. Πόθεν οὖν τις ταύτης ἄρξηται μάχης; PLAT. Phil. 15 D.

Πῶς οὖν ἔτ᾽ εἴπῃς ὅτι συνέσταλμαι κακοῖς; EUR. H. F. 1417, the only case of the second person, is probably corrupt. Dindorf reads ἂν εἴποις.

290. The subjunctive is often used in the question τί πάθω; *what will become of me?* or *what harm will it do me?* literally, *what shall I undergo? E.g.*

Ὤ μοι ἐγώ, τί πάθω; τί νύ μοι μήκιστα γένηται; Od. v. 465. So Il. xi. 404. Τί πάθω; τί δὲ δρῶ; τί δὲ μήσωμαι; AESCH. Sept. 1057. Τί πάθω τλήμων; Id. Pers. 912 ; AR. Pl. 603. Τί πάθω; τί δὲ μήσομαι; οἴμοι. SOPH. Tr. 973. Τὸ μέλλον, εἰ χρή, πείσομαι· τί γὰρ πάθω; *I shall suffer what is to come, if it must be ; for what harm can it do me?* EUR. Ph. 895. (The difference between τί πάθω; and πάσχω in its ordinary use is here seen.) Ὡμολόγηκα· τί γὰρ πάθω; PLAT. Euthyd. 302 D. So in the plural, τί γὰρ πάθωμεν μὴ βουλομένων ὑμέων τιμωρέειν; HDT. iv. 118.

291. (*Negative* μή.) The negative μή of the interrogative subjunctive is explained by the origin of the construction (288). If ἔλθωμεν; *shall we go?* is the interrogative of ἔλθωμεν, *let us go,* then μὴ ἔλθωμεν; *shall we not go?* is the interrogative of μὴ ἔλθωμεν, *let us not go,* and implies (addressed to others) *do you wish not to have us go?* This is still more evident when βούλεσθε is prefixed to the subjunctive (288). Similar to this interrogative form of the subjunctive of exhortation is the rare interrogative imperative (also negatived by μή); as ἂν ὁ μετὰ τέχνης γράψας ἀφίκηται, μὴ ἐξέστω δὴ ἕτερα προστάττειν; i.e. *is he not to be allowed to give other orders?* PLAT. Polit. 295 E, where μὴ ἐξέστω; is the interrogative of μὴ ἐξέστω, *let him not be allowed,* as μὴ ἔλθωμεν; (above) is that of μὴ ἔλθωμεν, *let us not go.* See also the indirect question in PLAT. Leg. 800 E, ἐπανερωτῶ πάλιν, τῶν ἐκμαγείων ταῖς ᾠδαῖς εἰ πρῶτον ἐν τοῦθ᾽ ἡμῖν ἀρέσκον κ εῖσθω, *I ask again, whether first this is to stand approved by us as one of our models for songs.* We cannot express such an imperative precisely in English ; and there is the same difficulty with οἶσθ᾽ ὃ δρᾶσον; etc., in **253.** See also ὥστε with imperative forms (602).

292. 1. When the future indicative is used in the sense of the interrogative subjunctive (68), it may be negatived by μή; as πῶς οὖν μήτε ψεύσομαι φανερῶς; *how then shall I escape telling an open lie?* (where there is some Ms. authority for ψεύσωμαι), DEM. xix. 320 (see Shilleto's note).

2. A similar use of μή is found with the potential optative (with ἄν) in questions, if the idea of *prevention* is involved in it; as τί οὖν οὐ σκοποῦμεν πῶς ἂν αὐτῶν μὴ διαμαρτάνοιμεν; *why then do we not consider how we can avoid mistaking them?* (the direct question here would differ little from πῶς μὴ διαμαρτάνωμεν;). XEN. Mem. iii. 1, 10. So πῶς ἄν τις μὴ θυμῷ λέγοι περὶ θεῶν; *how can one help being excited when he speaks of Gods?* PLAT. Leg. 887 C. Sometimes such an optative with μή is in a second clause, preceded by a positive question, so that the harshness of μὴ ἄν with the optative is avoided; as τί ἂν λέγοντες εἰκὸς ἢ αὐτοὶ ἀποκνοῖμεν ἢ πρὸς τοὺς ἐκεῖ ξυμμάχους σκηπτόμενοι μὴ βοηθοῖμεν; i.e. *what good ground can we give for holding back ourselves, or what decent excuse can we make to our allies there for withholding our aid from them?* THUC. vi. 18. So τίνα ἂν τρόπον ἐγὼ μέγα δυναίμην καὶ μηδείς με ἀδικοῖ; *in what way can I have great power and prevent any one from doing me wrong?* PLAT. Gorg. 510 D. See also ISOC. v. 8, xv. 6. In DEM. xxi. 35, πότερα μὴ δῷ διὰ τοῦτο δίκην ἢ μείζω δοίη δικαίως; *shall he escape punishment for this, or would he rather deserve a still greater penalty?*—δοίη is used as if οὐκ ἂν δοίη had preceded (Schaefer inserts κἄν).

In PLAT. Phaed. 106 D is the singular expression, σχολῇ γὰρ ἄν τι ἄλλο φθορὰν μὴ δέχοιτο, εἴ γε τὸ ἀθάνατον ἀίδιον ὂν φθορὰν δέξεται, *for hardly can anything else escape from admitting destruction if the immortal, which is eternal, is to admit it.* This differs from the preceding interrogative examples merely in the substitution of σχολῇ, *hardly,* for πῶς or τίνα τρόπον.

293. As οὐ cannot be used with the interrogative subjunctive, μή here sometimes introduces a question which expects an affirmative answer. See XEN. Mem. i. 2, 36, and PLAT. Rep. 337 B, 554 B, quoted in 287; and compare XEN. Oec. iv. 4 (ibid.), where a negative answer is expected. In PLAT. Rep. 552 E, we must read μὴ οἰώμεθα (not οἰόμεθα, Herm.), *shall we not think?* as the answer must be affirmative (see Stallbaum's note).

SECTION IV.

Οὐ μή with the Subjunctive and the Future Indicative.

294. The subjunctive and the future indicative are used with the double negative οὐ μή in independent sentences, sometimes expressing a denial, like the future indicative with οὐ, and sometimes a prohibition, like the imperative or subjunctive with μή. The compounds of both οὐ and μή can be used here as well as the simple forms.

For a discussion of the origin of this construction, and of the relation of the sentences of denial to those of prohibition, see Appendix II.

295. (*Denial.*) The subjunctive (usually the aorist), and sometimes the future indicative, with οὐ μή may have the force of an emphatic future with οὐ. Thus οὐ μὴ τοῦτο γένηται, sometimes οὐ μὴ τοῦτο γενήσεται, means *this surely will not happen.* E.g.

(*Aor. Subj.*) Καὶ τῶνδ᾽ ἀκούσας οὔ τι μὴ ληφθῶ δόλῳ, I shall not be caught by any trick. AESCH. Sept. 38. So Sept. 199, Supp. 228. Οὐ μὴ πίθηται, he will not obey. SOPH. Ph. 103. Οὐ γάρ σε μὴ γνῶσι. Id. El. 42. Καὶ οὔ τι μὴ λάχωσι τοῦδε συμμάχου. Id. O. C. 450. Οὗτοι σ᾽ Ἀχαιῶν, οἶδα, μή τις ὑβρίσῃ. Id. Aj. 560. Ὁ δ᾽ οὐ πάρεστιν, οὐδὲ μὴ μόλῃ ποτέ, but he is not here, and he never will come. EUR. H. F. 718. Κοὐ μή ποθ᾽ ἁλῶ. AR. Ach. 662. Τῶν ἦν κρατήσωμεν, οὐ μή τις ἡμῖν ἄλλος στρατὸς ἀντιστῇ κοτε ἀνθρώπων. HDT. vii. 53. So i. 199. Οὐ μή ποτε ἐσβάλωσιν. THUC. iv. 95; cf. v. 69. Οὐ μή σε κρύψω πρὸς ὅντινα βούλομαι ἀφικέσθαι. XEN. Cyr. vii. 3, 13. Ὡς οἱ Ἀρμένιοι οὐ μὴ δέξωνται τοὺς πολεμίους. Ib. iii. 2, 8 (see 296, b). Ἂν καθώμεθα οἴκοι, οὐδέποτ᾽ οὐδὲν ἡμῖν οὐ μὴ γένηται τῶν δεόντων. DEM. iv. 44; so ix. 75. Οὔτε γὰρ γίγνεται οὔτε γέγονεν οὐδὲ οὖν μὴ γένηται ἀλλοῖον ἦθος πρὸς ἀρετήν, for there is not, nor has there been, nor will there ever be, etc. PLAT. Rep. 492 E. (Here οὐδὲ μὴ γένηται seems merely more emphatic than the ordinary οὐδὲ γενήσεται.)

(*Aor. Subj. 2d Pers.*) Οὐ γάρ τι μᾶλλον μὴ φύγῃς τὸ μόρσιμον, for you shall none the more escape your fate. AESCH. Sept. 281. Ἀλλ᾽ οὐ ποτ᾽ ἐξ ἐμοῦ γε μὴ πάθῃς τόδε. SOPH. El. 1029. Οὐ μή ποτ᾽ ἐς τὴν Σκῦρον ἐκπλεύσῃς ἔχων. Id. Ph. 381. Ἀλλ᾽ οὔ τι μὴ φύγητε λαιψηρῷ ποδί. EUR. Hec. 1039. Κοὐχὶ μὴ παύσησθε, you will never cease. AR. Lys. 704.

(*Pres. Subj.*) Ἢν γὰρ ἅπαξ δύο ἢ τριῶν ἡμερῶν ὁδὸν ἀπόσχωμεν, οὐκέτι μὴ δύνηται βασιλεὺς ἡμᾶς καταλαβεῖν. XEN. An. ii. 2, 12. So οὐ μὴ δύνωνται, Id. Hier. xi. 15. Πρὸς ταῦτα κακούργει καὶ συκοφάντει, εἴ τι δύνασαι· ἀλλ᾽ οὐ μὴ οἷός τ᾽ ᾖς, but you will not be able. PLAT. Rep. 341 B. Οὐ γὰρ μὴ δυνατὸς ὦ. Id. Phil. 48 D. In the much-discussed passage, SOPH. O. C. 1023, ἄλλοι γὰρ οἱ σπεύδοντες, οὓς οὐ μή ποτε χώρας φυγόντες τῆσδ᾽ ἐπεύχωνται θεοῖς, for there are others in eager pursuit; and they (the captors) will never (be in a condition to) be thankful to the Gods for escaping these and getting out of this land, the chief force is in φυγόντες, as if it were οὐ μὴ φύγωσι ὥστε ἐπεύχεσθαι θεοῖς, the present subjunctive expressing a state of thankfulness.

(*Fut. Ind.*) Οὔ σοι μὴ μεθέψομαί ποτε. SOPH. El. 1052. Οὔ
τοι μήποτέ σ᾽ ἐκ τῶν ἑδράνων, ὦ γέρον, ἄκοντά τις ἄξει. Id. O. C.
176; so οὐκ οὖν μὴ ὁδοιπορήσεις, O. C. 848. Μὰ τὸν Ἀπόλλω οὐ
μή σ᾽ ἐγὼ περιόψομἀπελθόντ᾽ (i.e. περιόψομαι ἀπελθόντα). AR. Ran.
508. Τοὺς πονηροὺς οὐ μή ποτε βελτίους ποιήσετε. AESCHIN. iii.
177.

296. Οὐ μή with the subjunctive or the future indicative can
stand in various dependent sentences :—

(*a*) Especially in indirect discourse; as εὖ γὰρ οἶδ᾽ σαφῶς ὅτι ταῦθ᾽
. . . οὐ μὴ 'πιλάθῃ. AR. Pac. 1302. So XEN. Cyr. viii. 1, 5, Hell. iv. 2,
3; PLAT. Rep. 499 B. See also THUC. v. 69. We have οὐ μή with
the future optative after ὡς, representing the future indicative of the
direct form, in SOPH. Ph. 611: τά τ᾽ ἄλλα πάντ᾽ ἐθέσπισεν, καὶ τἀπὶ
Τροίας πέργαμ᾽ ὡς οὐ μή ποτε πέρσοιεν εἰ μὴ τόνδε ἄγοιντο. (The
direct discourse was οὐ μή ποτε πέρσετε ἐὰν μὴ τόνδε ἄγησθε.) In
a similar construction in XEN. Hell. i. 6, 32, the future indicative is
retained after a past tense: εἶπεν ὅτι ἡ Σπάρτη οὐδὲν μὴ κάκιον οἰκιεῖται αὑτοῦ ἀποθανόντος. In EUR. Phoen. 1590, we have the future
infinitive of indirect discourse with οὐ μή: εἶπε Τειρεσίας οὐ μή ποτε,
σοῦ τήνδε γῆν οἰκοῦντος, εὖ πράξειν πόλιν, representing οὐ μὴ εὖ
πράξει πόλις.

(*b*) In causal sentences with ὡς; as AR. Av. 461: λέγε θαρρήσας,
ὡς τὰς σπονδὰς οὐ μὴ πρότερον παραβῶμεν, *for we will not break the
truce before you have spoken.* So XEN. Cyr. iii. 2, 8 (see 295).

(*c*) In consecutive sentences with ὥστε; as PLAT. Phaedr. 227 D:
οὕτως ἐπιτεθύμηκα ἀκοῦσαι, ὥστ᾽, ἐὰν ποιῇ τὸν περίπατον Μέγαράδε,
οὐ μή σου ἀπολειφθῶ.

In AESCH. Ag. 1640, τὸν δὲ μὴ πειθάνορα ζεύξω βαρείαις οὔτι μὴ
σειραφόρον κριθῶντα πῶλον, and *I will yoke him who is not obedient
under a heavy yoke,* (and I will let him run) *by no means as a wanton
colt in traces,* οὔτι μή belongs grammatically to ζεύξω, though its
position makes it affect the following words in sense: cf. καὶ μὴν τόδ᾽
εἰπὲ μὴ παρὰ γνώμην ἐμοί, Ag. 931, where the force of μή falls on
the words that follow it. See Paley's note on Ag. 1640 (1618).

297. (*Prohibition.*) In the dramatic poets, the second
person singular of the future indicative (occasionally of the
subjunctive) with οὐ μή may express a strong *prohibition.*
Thus οὐ μὴ λαλήσεις means *you shall not prate,* or *do not
prate,* being nearly equivalent to μὴ λάλει or μὴ λαλήσῃς.
E.g.

Ὦ παῖ, τί θροεῖς; οὐ μὴ παρ᾽ ὄχλῳ τάδε γηρύσει, *do not (I beg
you) speak out in this way before the people.* EUR. Hipp. 213. Ὦ θύγατερ, οὐ μὴ μῦθον ἐπὶ πολλοὺς ἐρεῖς. Id. Supp. 1066. Οὐ μὴ γυναικῶν δειλὸν εἰσοίσεις λόγον, *do not adopt the cowardly language of
women.* Id. And. 757. Οὐ μὴ ἐξεγερεῖς τὸν ὕπνῳ κάτοχον κἀκ-

κινήσεις κἀναστήσεις φοιτάδα δεινὴν νόσον, ὦ τέκνον, do not wake him and arouse, etc. SOPH. Tr. 978. (Here οὐ μή belongs to three verbs.) Τί ποιεῖς; οὐ μὴ καταβήσει, don't come down. AR. Vesp. 397. Ποῖος Ζεύς; οὐ μὴ ληρήσῃς· οὐδ᾽ ἔστι Ζεύς, Zeus indeed! Don't talk nonsense; there isn't any Zeus. Id. Nub. 367. (Here all Mss. have ληρήσῃς. See Nub. 296, quoted in 298; and section 301 below.)

298. A prohibition thus begun by οὐ μή with the future or subjunctive may be continued by μηδέ with another future form. An affirmative command may be added to the prohibition by a future or an imperative with ἀλλά or δέ. E.g.

Οὐ μὴ καλεῖς μ᾽, ὦνθρωφ᾽, ἱκετεύω, μηδὲ κατερεῖς τοὔνομα, do not call to me, I implore you, nor speak my name. AR. Ran. 298. Οὐ μὴ προσοίσεις χεῖρα μηδ᾽ ἅψει πέπλων, do not bring your hand near me nor touch my garments. EUR. Hipp. 606. Οὐ μὴ προσοίσεις χεῖρα, βακχεύσεις δ᾽ ἰών, μηδ᾽ ἐξομόρξει μωρίαν τὴν σὴν ἐμοί, do not bring your hand near me; but go and rage, and do not wipe off your folly on me. Id. Bacch. 343. (Here μηδέ continues the original prohibition as if there had been no interruption.) Οὐ μὴ λαλήσεις, ἀλλ᾽ ἀκολουθήσεις ἐμοί, do not prate, but follow me. AR. Nub. 505. Οὐ μὴ διατρίψεις, ἀλλὰ γεύσει τῆς θύρας, do not delay, but taste of the door. Id. Ran. 462. Οὐ μὴ φλυαρήσεις ἔχων, ὦ Ξανθία, ἀλλ᾽ ἀράμενος οἴσεις πάλιν τὰ στρώματα. Ib. 524. Οὐ μὴ δυσμενὴς ἔσει φίλοις, παύσει δὲ θυμοῦ καὶ πάλιν στρέψεις κάρα, . . . δέξει δὲ δῶρα καὶ παραιτήσει πατρός, be not inimical to friends, but cease your rage, etc. EUR. Med. 1151. Οὐ μὴ σκώψῃς μηδὲ ποιήσῃς (so all the Mss.) ἅπερ οἱ τρυγοδαίμονες οὗτοι, ἀλλ᾽ εὐφήμει, do not scoff, nor do what these wretches do; but keep silence! AR. Nub. 296. (Here the imperative is used precisely like the future with ἀλλά or δέ in the preceding examples.)

The clause with μηδέ is here a continuation of that with οὐ μή, οὐ belonging to both. The future in the clause with ἀλλά or δέ is like that in πάντως τοῦτο δράσεις, by all means do this, AR. Nub. 1352 (see 69). A single οὐ μή may introduce a prohibition consisting of several futures connected by καί, as in SOPH. Tr. 978 (quoted in 297).

299. Sometimes οὐ with the future indicative in a question implying an affirmative answer (thus equivalent to an exhortation) is followed by μή or μηδέ with the future in a question implying a negative answer (and thus equivalent to a prohibition). Here there is no case of οὐ μή. E.g.

Οὐ σῖγ᾽ ἀνέξει, μηδὲ δειλίαν ἀρεῖς; will you not keep silence, and not become a coward? SOPH. Aj. 75. (Here μὴ δειλίαν ἀρεῖς; is an independent question, will you be a coward ? = do not be a coward.) Οὐ θᾶσσον οἴσεις, μηδ᾽ ἀπιστήσεις ἐμοί; will you not extend your hand, and not distrust me ? Id. Tr. 1183. Οὐκ εἶ σύ τ᾽ οἴκους, σύ τε Κρέων κατὰ στέγας, καὶ μὴ τὸ μηδὲν ἄλγος εἰς μέγ᾽ οἴσετε; Id. O. T. 637.

300. All the examples under 297 and 298 are usually printed as interrogative, in accordance with Elmsley's doctrine, stated in his note to EUR. Med. 1120 (1151) and in the *Quarterly Review* for June 1812. He explains οὐ μὴ λαλήσεις; as meaning *will you not stop prating?* (lit. *will you not not prate?*) ; and when a second clause in the future with μηδέ or ἀλλά follows, he extends the interrogative force of οὐ also to this. But this explanation requires an entirely different theory to account for οὐ μή in clauses of denial (295), where no question is possible. Moreover, the five examples of the second person of the subjunctive quoted under 295, taken in connection with those in 297 and 298, are sufficient to show the impossibility of separating the two constructions in explanation. One of the examples in 298 (AR. Nub. 296), where the imperative εὐφήμει follows in the clause with ἀλλά, seems decisive against the interrogative theory. The examples under 299 are really interrogative ; but they consist practically of an exhortation followed by a prohibition (both being interrogative), and contain no construction with οὐ μή at all.

301. In most modern editions of the classics the subjunctive is not found in the construction of 297 ; and in many cases the first aorist subjunctive in -σῃς has been emended to the future, against the authority of the Mss., in conformity to Dawes's rule. (See 364.) Thus, in AR. Nub. 296 and 367 the Mss. have the subjunctive ; and in 296, οὐ μὴ σκώψῃς could not be changed to οὐ μὴ σκώψεις, as the future of σκώπτω is σκώψομαι. Elmsley's emendation σκώψει, which is adopted by most editors, requires a greater change than should be made merely to sustain an arbitrary rule, which rests on no apparent principle. If both constructions (295 and 297) are explained on the same principle, there is no longer any reason for objecting to the subjunctive with οὐ μή in prohibitions ; and it seems most probable that both future indicative and subjunctive were allowed *in both constructions*, but that the subjunctive was more common in clauses of denial, and the future in clauses of prohibition.

SECTION V.

Final and Object Clauses after Ἵνα, Ὡς, Ὅπως, Ὄφρα, and Μή.

CLASSIFICATION.—NEGATIVES.

302. The final particles are ἵνα, ὡς, ὅπως, and (in epic and lyric poetry) ὄφρα, *that, in order that.* To these must be added μή, *lest,* which became in use a negative final particle.

303. The clauses which are introduced by these particles, all of which are sometimes called *final clauses*, may be divided into three classes :—

A. Pure final clauses, in which the end or purpose of the action of any verb may be expressed; as ἔρχεται ἵνα τοῦτο ἴδῃ, *he is coming that he may see this;* ἀπέρχεται ἵνα μὴ τοῦτο ἴδῃ, *he is departing that he may not see this;* ἦλθεν ἵνα τοῦτο ἴδοι, *he came that he might see this.* Here all the final particles are used, but with different frequency in various classes of writers (see 311-314).

B. Object clauses with ὅπως or ὅπως μή after verbs of *striving*, etc. ; as σκόπει ὅπως γενήσεται, *see that it happens;* σκόπει ὅπως μὴ γενήσεται, *see that it does not happen.* These clauses express the direct object of the verb of *striving*, etc., so that they may stand in apposition to an object accusative like τοῦτο ; as σκόπει τοῦτο, ὅπως μή σε ὄψεται, *see to this, viz., that he does not see you.* They also imply the end or purpose of the action of the leading verb, and to this extent they partake of the nature of final clauses.

C. Clauses with μή after verbs of *fearing*, etc.; as φοβοῦμαι μὴ τοῦτο γένηται, *I fear that this may happen;* ἐφοβήθη μὴ τοῦτο γένοιτο, *he feared that this might happen.* These clauses have in use become object clauses, though in their origin they are of a very different nature (262; 307).

304. Although the object clauses of class B partake slightly of the nature of final clauses, so that they sometimes allow the same construction (the subjunctive for the future indicative), still the distinction between classes A and B is very strongly marked. An object clause, as we have seen, can stand in apposition to a preceding τοῦτο ; whereas a final clause would stand in apposition to τούτου ἕνεκα, as ἔρχεται τούτου ἕνεκα, ἵνα ἡμῖν βοηθήσῃ, *he comes for this purpose, viz., that he may assist us.* The two can be combined in one sentence ; as σπουδάζει ὅπως πλουτήσει, ἵνα τοὺς φίλους εὖ ποιῇ, *he is eager to be rich, that he may benefit his friends.*

Care must be taken not to mistake the nature of an object clause with ὅπως when its subject is attracted by the leading verb ; as σκόπει τὴν πόλιν ὅπως σωθήσεται for σκόπει ὅπως ἡ πόλις σωθήσεται, *see that the city is saved.* So also when an object clause of the active construction becomes a subject clause in the equivalent passive form ; as ἐπράττετο ὅπως συμμαχίαν εἶναι ψηφιεῖσθε, *it was brought about that*

you should vote to have an alliance made (AESCHIN. iii. 64), which
represents the active construction ἔπραττον ὅπως ψηφιεῖσθε.

305. The regular negative after ἵνα, ὡς, ὅπως, and ὄφρα is μή;
but after μή, *lest*, οὐ is used. *E.g.*

Ἀπέρχεται, ἵνα μὴ τοῦτο ἴδῃ, *he is departing that he may not see this.*
Φοβεῖται μὴ οὐ τοῦτο γένηται, *he is afraid that this may not happen.*

306. This use of μὴ οὐ (305) occurs in Homer in a few final clauses
(263) and once after δείδω (Il. x. 39). After this it is confined to
clauses after verbs of fearing, with the exception of XEN. Mem. ii. 2,
14, Cyneg. vii. 10, and the peculiar μὴ οὐκ ἐπαρκέσοι in PLAT. Rep.
393 E (132). This use of οὐ after μή is naturally explained by the
origin of the dependent clause with μή (262) ; but after μή had come
to be felt as a conjunction and its origin was forgotten, the chief
objection to μὴ . . . μή was probably in the sound, and we find a
few cases of it where the two particles are so far apart that the repetition
is not offensive. Such a case is XEN. Mem. i. 2, 7 : ἐθαύμαζε δ' εἴ τις
φοβοῖτο μὴ ὁ γενόμενος καλὸς κἀγαθὸς τῷ τὰ μέγιστα εὐεργετήσαντι
μὴ τὴν μεγίστην χάριν ἔξοι, where we should expect μὴ οὐχ ἔξοι.
So THUC. ii. 13 : ὑποτοπήσας μὴ . . . παραλίπῃ καὶ μὴ δῃώσῃ. So
in a final clause, μὴ . . . μὴ προσδέχοιτο, PLAT. Euthyd. 295 D.

DEVELOPMENT OF CLAUSES WITH ἵνα, ὡς, ὅπως, ὄφρα, AND μή.

307. The development of final clauses and of clauses with μή
after verbs of fearing from an original *parataxis*, or co-ordination
of two independent sentences, is especially plain in dependent
negative clauses with the simple μή. Thus ἀπόστιχε, μή τι νοήσῃ
Ἥρη, *withdraw, lest Hera notice anything* (Il. i. 522), presents the
form of an original paratactic expression, which would mean
withdraw :—may not (or *let not*) *Hera notice anything*, the latter
clause being like μὴ δὴ νῆας ἕλωσι, *may they not take the ships* (Il.
xvi. 128), and μὴ δή μοι τελέσωσι θεοὶ κακὰ κήδεα (Il. xviii. 8).
(See 261.) Such sentences as these last imply fear or anxiety
lest the event may happen which μή with the subjunctive expresses a desire to avert ; and in a primitive stage of the
language they might naturally be preceded by a verb of fearing,
to which the (still independent) subjunctive with μή would stand in
the relation of an explanatory clause defining the substance of the
fear. Thus δείδω·—μὴ νῆας ἕλωσι would originally be two independent sentences, *I fear :—may they not take the ships ;* but would
in time come to be felt as a single sentence, equivalent to our
I fear that (lest) they may take the ships. After φοβοῦμαι μὴ τοῦτο
πάθωσιν (for example) was domesticated in the sense *I fear lest
they may suffer this*, the second clause followed the ordinary course,
and began to be felt as a thoroughly dependent clause ; and when

the leading verb became past, the subjunctive became optative, as ἐφοβήθην μὴ τοῦτο πάθοιεν, *I feared lest they might suffer this.* When this stage is reached, all feeling of the original independence may be said to have vanished and a dependent clause is fully established. As this decisive evidence of complete dependence is constantly found in the Homeric language, we cannot suppose that such an expression as δείδοικα μή τι πάθωσιν (Il. x. 538) was still felt to be composed of two independent sentences, although the original paratactic form is precisely preserved. Indeed, we have no evidence that the step from parataxis to hypotaxis was taken after the Greek language had an independent existence.[1]

308. It was a simple and natural step to extend the construction thus established to present and past objects of fear, although we cannot assume for the primitive language such independent indicatives with μή as we find later (see 269). In Homer we find δείδω μὴ θεὰ νημερτέα εἶπεν, *I fear that the Goddess spoke the truth* (Od. v. 300). This use was greatly extended in Attic Greek (see 369).

309. This simple construction of a dependent verb introduced by μή with no connecting conjunction remained the established form after verbs of fearing in all periods of the language ; and occasional exceptions, like μὴ φοβοῦ ὡς ἀπορήσεις, *do not fear that you will be at a loss* (371), οὐ φοβεῖ ὅπως μὴ ἀνόσιον πρᾶγμα τυγχάνῃς πράττων ; (370), and οὐ φοβούμεθα ἐλασσώσεσθαι, *we are not afraid that we shall have the worst of it* (372), in place of the regular μὴ ἀπορήσῃς, μὴ τυγχάνῃς, μὴ ἐλασσωθῶμεν, only prove the rule. The original independent sentence with μή, expressing an object of fear which is desired to avert, like μὴ νῆας ἕλωσι, is well established in Homer and appears occasionally in the Attic poets (261 ; 264). But in Plato it suddenly appears as a common construction, expressing, however, not an object of fear but an object of suspicion or surmise (265), so that μή with the subjunctive is a cautious expression of a direct assertion ; as μὴ ἀγροικότερον ᾖ τὸ ἀληθὲς εἰπεῖν, *I rather think the truth may be too rude to tell* (Gorg. 462 E).

310. In like manner, the simple negative form of the pure final clause, as ἀπόστιχε, μή τι νοήσῃ Ἥρη (quoted above), was already established in Homer, the negative μή serving as a connective, so that the want of a final conjunction was not felt. Here also the feeling of dependence is shown by the subjunctive becoming optative when the leading verb is past ; as in φεύξομαι μή τίς με ἴδῃ and ἔφυγον μή τίς με ἴδοι. But it is obvious that

[1] See Brugmann, *Griechische Grammatik*, p. 122.

only negative purpose could bo oxpressed by this simple form, in which μή could serve as a connective. We find, it is true, a few positive sentences in which a purpose is implied by the mere sequence of two clauses; as ἀλλ' ἄγε νῦν ἰθὺς κίε Νέστορος ἱπποδάμοιο· εἴδομεν (subj.) ἥν τινα μῆτιν ἐνὶ στήθεσσι κέκευθεν, i.e. *go straightway to Nestor : let us know what counsel he buries in his breast* (Od. iii. 17), and θάπτε με ὅττι τάχιστα· πύλας Ἀίδαο περήσω, *bury me as quickly as possible : let me pass the gates of Hades* (Il. xxiii. 71). But these disconnected expressions, with no particle to unite them, could never satisfy the need of a positive sentence of purpose. To supply this want, several final particles were developed, and were already in familiar use in Homer. These are ἵνα, ὡς, ὅπως, and ὄφρα, which will be discussed separately.

311. (Ἵνα.) Ἵνα is the only purely *final* particle, having nothing of the relative character of ὡς and ὅπως, or of the temporal character of ὄφρα. Its derivation is uncertain. It appears in Homer as a fully developed final conjunction, and occasionally also in the sense of *where* (Od. ix. 136) and *whither* (Od. xix. 20). It is overshadowed in epic and lyric poetry by ὄφρα, and in tragedy by ὡς ; but Aristophanes uses it in three-fourths of his final sentences, and in Plato and the orators it has almost exterminated the other final particles. As ἵνα is purely final, both in use and in feeling, it never takes ἄν or κέ, which are frequently found with the other final particles, especially with the relative ὡς.

312. (Ὡς.) 1. Ὡς is originally an adverb of manner, derived from the stem ὁ- of the relative ὅς, like οὕτως from the stem of οὗτος. As a relative it means originally *in which way, as ;* as an indirect interrogative it means *how,* whence comes its use in indirect discourse (663, 2). Since purpose can be expressed by a relative pronoun, which in Homer regularly takes the subjunctive (568), as ἡγεμόν' ἐσθλὸν ὄπασσον, ὅς κέ με κεῖσ' ἀγάγῃ, *send me a good guide, to lead me thither* (Od. xv. 310), so can it be by the relative adverb of manner, as κρῖν' ἄνδρας κατὰ φῦλα, κατὰ φρήτρας, ὡς φρήτρη φρήτρηφιν ἀρήγῃ, φῦλα δὲ φύλοις, *divide the men in that way by which clan may help clan,* etc., i.e. *(so) divide them that clan may help clan,* etc. (Il. ii. 362). Here the original force of ὡς can be seen ; but in Od. xvii. 75, ὄτρυνον ἐμὸν ποτὶ δῶμα γυναῖκας, ὥς τοι δῶρ' ἀποπέμψω, *in order that I may send you the gifts,* the final force is as strong as if we had ἵνα ἀποπέμψω.

2. Ὡς, however, always retained so much of its original relative nature that it could take κέ or ἄν in a final sentence with the subjunctive, like other final relatives, which in Homer hardly ever omit κέ before a subjunctive (568). Compare ὅς κέ με κεῖσ'

ἀγάγῃ (above) with the equivalent ὥς κέ με κεῖσ' ἀγάγῃ. The final clause thus receives a conditional *form*, with which it must have received originally more or less conditional force.[1] Thus an expression like πείθεο ὡς ἂν κῦδος ἄρηαι probably meant originally *obey in whatever way you may gain glory*, or *obey in some way in which you may gain glory*, ὡς ἂν ἄρηαι being chiefly a conditional relative clause (529); but before the Homeric usage was established, the final element had so far obliterated the relative, that the conditional force of ὡς ἄν must have been greatly weakened. The expression in Homer (Il. xvi. 84) may have meant *obey that (if so be) you may gain me glory*. (See examples under 326.) The same is true of the less common use of κέ or ἄν with ὄφρα and ὅπως in Homer (327 ; 328). How far the original conditional force survived in the Attic ὡς ἄν and ὅπως ἄν with the subjunctive, especially in ὅπως ἄν of Attic prose, is a question which at this distant day we have hardly the power to answer, and each scholar will be guided by his own feeling as he reads the expressions. (See 326 ; 328 ; 348.) It certainly can be seen in some of Xenophon's uses of ὡς ἄν with the subjunctive ; see Cyr. ii. 4, 28, and Eques. i. 16, quoted in Appendix IV.

3. Ὡς and ὥς κε with the subjunctive are used in Homer also in object clauses after verbs of *planning, considering,* etc. (341), where ὅπως with the future indicative is the regular Attic form. Ὡς (with ὡς ἄν) is by far the most common final particle in tragedy ; it seldom occurs in Aristophanes and Herodotus ; while in Attic prose it almost entirely disappears,[2] except in Xenophon, with whom it is again common, though less so than ὅπως or ἵνα. (See Weber's tables in Appendix III.)

313. (Ὅπως.) 1. Ὅπως is related to ὡς as ὁπότε to ὅτε, being the adverb of the relative stem ὁ- and the indefinite stem πο- combined.[3] Like ὡς, it is originally a relative adverb, meaning *as ;* and it can always be used in this sense, as in οὕτως ὅπως

---

[1] See Gildersleeve in *Am. Jour. Phil.* iv. p. 422.

[2] Weber (p. 174) quotes two passages of Demosthenes as examples of final ὡς with the future indicative, a construction otherwise unknown in Attic prose : ὡς δὲ σαφῶς γνώσεσθε ὅτι ἀληθῆ λέγω, ἐγὼ ὑμῖν ἐρῶ, xxiv. 146 ; and ὡς δὲ καταφανὲς ἔσται ὅτι πρότερον ἀναισχυντοῦντες περιεγένοντο, ἀναγίγνωσκε τὰς μαρτυρίας, xliii. 42. But compare the common formula of the orators ὡς (or ὅτι) ἀληθῆ λέγω, λαβὲ τὴν μαρτυρίαν (or κάλει τοὺς μάρτυρας), *e.g.* in DEM. xxvii. 28, with the occasional full form, ἵνα εἰδῆτε ταῦτα ὅτι ἀληθῆ λέγω, λαβὲ τὴν μαρτυρίαν, DEM. xlv. 19 ; so xviii. 305. See also ὡς εἰκότα ποιοῦμεν, καὶ τάδ' ἐννοήσατε (sc. ἵνα εἰδῆτε), XEN. Hell. ii. 3, 33. This common ellipsis shows that in DEM. xliii. 42 we can easily supply a final clause like ἵνα εἰδῆτε before ὡς καταφανὲς ἔσται, *that you may know how it is to be established*, etc. In xxiv. 146 there is no need even of an ellipsis, as we can translate *how you are to know that I speak the truth, I will explain to you*.

[3] See Delbrück, *Conj. u. Opt.* p. 61.

δύνανται, *thus as they can*, Thuc. vii. 67.   Then it is used in
indirect questions, in the sense of ὅτῳ τρόπῳ, *how, in what way*,
and is followed by the future indicative; as σκοπεῖν ὅπως ἡ
πόλις σωθήσεται, *to see how the city can be saved*.   So τοῖς γεγενη-
μένοις πονηροῖς, ὅπως μὴ δώσουσι δίκην, ὁδὸν δείκνυσι, *he shows
those who have been rascals how they can avoid suffering punishment*
(= ὅτῳ τρόπῳ μὴ δώσουσι), Dem. xxiv. 106.   Then, by a slight
modification in sense, it may denote *also* the object to which the
striving, etc., is directed; so that σκοπεῖν (or σκοπεῖν τοῦτο) ὅπως
ἡ πόλις σωθήσεται may mean *to see* (*to this, viz.*) *that the city shall
be saved*.   Here, however, the subjunctive is sometimes allowed,
as the interrogative force of ὅπως is lost sight of and its force as
a final particle, *in order that*, begins to appear.   From this it
becomes established as a final particle, and denotes the *purpose*
in ordinary final clauses.   From the original force of ὅπως as a
relative, used in indirect questions in the sense of *how*, we must
explain its occasional use in indirect questions in the sense of ὡς
(706).

The interrogative force of ὅπως can be seen from passages in which
other interrogative words take its place in the same sense; as Dem.
xvi. 19, σκοπεῖν ἐξ ὅτου τρόπου μὴ γενήσονται (φίλοι), *to see in
what way they can be prevented from becoming friends*; and Thuc. i. 65,
ἔπρασσεν ὅπη ὠφελία τις γενήσεται, *he negotiated to have some help
come* (*how some help should come*).   So Thuc. iv. 128, ἔπρασσεν ὅτῳ
τρόπῳ τάχιστα τοῖς μὲν ξυμβήσεται τῶν δὲ ἀπαλλάξεται.[1]

2. Although ὅπως is fully established in the Homeric language,
both in its half-interrogative use after verbs of *planning*, etc.
(341), and also in its final sense, it seldom occurs in Homer in
either construction.   It first becomes frequent in the Attic poets.
In Thucydides and Xenophon it is the most common final
particle; and in these writers, as in tragedy, its final use greatly
exceeds its use in object clauses.   The latter, however, far exceeds the final use in Herodotus, Plato, and the orators; but
here ἵνα has gained almost undisputed possession of the field
as a final particle.

3. Ὅπως never takes κέ or αν in pure final clauses in Homer.
Ὅπως ἄν with the subjunctive appears for the first time in
final clauses in Aeschylus (328), and afterwards maintains itself
vigorously by the side of the simple ὅπως.   In object clauses
ὅπως κε with the subjunctive is found in a few places in Homer,
and ὅπως ἄν in a few in the Attic poets, while ὅπως ἄν in these
clauses in prose is found chiefly in Plato and Xenophon (348).

314.   (Ὄφρα.)   The most common final particle in Homer

---

[1] See Madvig's *Syntax*, § 123.

is ὄφρα, which is originally a temporal particle, meaning *while* (*so long as*) and then *until*. From the last meaning the final force was naturally developed, as the idea of *until*, when it looks forward to the future, may involve that of aiming at an object to be attained, as in English *we shall fight until we are free*. Another temporal particle meaning both *while* and *until*, ἕως, is used in a final sense in a few passages of the Odyssey (614, 2). Both of the temporal uses of ὄφρα appear in full vigour in Homer; but its final character must have been more distinctly marked at an earlier period than that of either ὡς or ὅπως, so that it seldom took either κέ or ἄν before the subjunctive.

Ὄφρα is found only in epic and lyric poetry.

315. (*Negative Final Clauses.*) The need of these final particles was first felt, as has been shown (310), in positive clauses of purpose, as a negative purpose could always be expressed by the simple μή, which thus became in use a conjunction. Still the final particles were as well suited to negative as to positive final clauses, and they could always be prefixed to μή, which thus was restored to its natural place as a negative adverb. Thus φεύξομαι ἵνα μή τίς με ἴδῃ has the same meaning as the older φεύξομαι μή τίς με ἴδῃ, *I shall flee, that no one may see me*.

The history of the Greek language shows a gradual decrease of final μή and an increase of the final particles with μή in negative final clauses.[1] The tendency in this direction was so strong that ὅπως μή sometimes took the place of μή even after verbs of *fearing*, to express the object of the fear (370), while it became the regular form after verbs of *striving*, etc., to express the object aimed at (339).

The different origin of the negative final clause (with ἵνα μή, etc.) and of the clause with μή explains the fact that, while clauses introduced by the final particles are negatived by μή, those introduced by μή, *lest*, are negatived by οὐ. (See 306.)

316. Finally, the Attic Greek took the last step in developing the final clause, by using the past tenses of the indicative with ἵνα, ὡς, and ὅπως to express a purpose which failed of attainment because of the failure of the action of the leading sentence; as τί μ' οὐκ ἔκτεινας, ὡς μήποτε τοῦτ' ἔδειξα; *why did you not kill me, that I might never have shown this?* (See 333.)

---

[1] In Homer, Hesiod, and the lyric poets we find 131 cases of simple μή and 50 of the final particles with μή; in tragedy the proportion is 76 : 59; in Aristophanes it is 8 : 55; in Herodotus, 8 : 53. In Attic prose (except in Plato and Xenophon) the simple μή in final clauses almost vanishes. Thucydides has only 4 or 5 cases; the ten orators only 4 (Demosthenes 2, Isocrates 1, Isaeus 1); Plato 24; and Xenophon 12.

A. PURE FINAL CLAUSES.

317. Pure final clauses regularly take the subjunctive if the leading verb is primary, and the optative if the leading verb is secondary. *E.g.*

Νῦν δ' ἔρχεσθ' ἐπὶ δεῖπνον, ἵνα ξυνάγωμεν Ἄρηα. Il. ii. 381. Σοὶ δ' ὧδε μνηστῆρες ὑποκρίνονται, ἵν' εἰδῇς αὐτὸς σῷ θυμῷ εἰδῶσι δὲ πάντες Ἀχαιοί. Od. ii. 111. Εἴπω τι δῆτα κἄλλ', ἵν' ὀργίζῃ πλέον ; SOPH. O. T. 364. Καὶ γὰρ βασιλεὺς αἱρεῖται, οὐχ ἵνα ἑαυτοῦ καλῶς ἐπιμελῆται, ἀλλ' ἵνα καὶ οἱ ἑλόμενοι δι' αὐτὸν εὖ πράττωσι. XEN. Mem. iii. 2, 3. Δοκεῖ μοι κατακαῦσαι τὰς ἁμάξας, ἵνα μὴ τὰ ζεύγη ἡμῶν στρατηγῇ. Id. An. iii. 2, 27. Πρὸς τοὺς ζῶντας, ἵνα μηδὲν ἀλλ' εἴπω, τὸν ζῶντα ἐξέταζε. DEM. xviii. 318. (Here the final clause depends on some implied expression like *I say this*.) Ὤρνυθ', ἵν' ἀθανάτοισι φόως φέροι ἠδὲ βροτοῖσιν. Od. v. 2. Φίλος ἐβούλετο εἶναι τοῖς μέγιστα δυναμένοις, ἵνα ἀδικῶν μὴ διδοίη δίκην. XEN. An. ii. 6, 21. Τὸ ψήφισμα τοῦτο γράφω (hist. pres.), ἵν' οὕτω γίγνοινθ' οἱ ὅρκοι, καὶ μὴ κύριος τῆς Θρᾴκης καταρσταίη. DEM. xviii. 27.

Βουλὴν δ' Ἀργείοις ὑποθησόμεθ', ἥ τις ὀνήσει, ὡς μὴ πάντες ὄλωνται ὀδυσσαμένοιο τεοῖο. Il. viii. 36. Διανοεῖται αὐτὴν (γέφυραν) λῦσαι, ὡς μὴ διαβῆτε, ἀλλ' ἐν μέσῳ ἀποληφθῆτε. XEN. An. ii. 4, 17. Πέμνε δ' Εὔρυτον, ὡς Αὐγέαν λάτριον μισθὸν πράσσοιτο. PIND. Ol. x. (xi.) 31. Καί σ' ἐξέπεμπον, ὡς μόνη κλύοις. SOPH. Ant. 19. Ἔπεμψα ὡς πύθοιτο. Id. O. T. 71. Τοῦτο δ'ὅπερ ἕνεκα φίλων ᾤετο δεῖσθαι, ὡς συνεργοὺς ἔχοι. XEN. An. i. 9, 21. Τὸν δὲ μνηστῆρες λοχῶσιν, ὅπως ἀπὸ φῦλον ὄληται ἐξ Ἰθάκης. Od. xiv. 181. Μέθες τόδ' ἄγγος νῦν, ὅπως τὸ πᾶν μάθῃς. SOPH. El. 1205. Εἰς καιρὸν ἥκεις, ὅπως τῆς δίκης ἀκούσῃς. XEN. Cyr. iii. 1, 8. Παρακαλεῖς ἰατροὺς, ὅπως μὴ ἀποθάνῃ. Id. Mem. ii. 10, 2. Οἶμαι δὲ ταῦτα γίγνεσθαι, οὐχ ὅπως τοὺς αὐτοὺς χοροὺς κρίνωσιν οἱ πολῖται, οὐδ' ὅπως τοὺς αὐτοὺς αὐλητὰς ἐπαινῶσιν, οὐδ' ὅπως τοὺς αὐτοὺς ποιητὰς αἱρῶνται, οὐδ' ἵνα τοῖς αὐτοῖς ἥδωνται, ἀλλ' ἵνα τοῖς νόμοις πείθωνται. Id. Mem. iv. 4, 16. Ἐν χείρεσσιν ἔθηκεν, ὅπως ἔτι πῆμα φύγοιμι. Od. xiv. 312. Ἀφικόμην, ὅπως σοῦ πρὸς δόμους ἐλθόντος εὖ πράξαιμί τι. SOPH. O. T. 1005. Ἐπρεσβεύοντο ἐγκλήματα ποιούμενοι, ὅπως σφίσιν ὅτι μεγίστη πρόφασις εἴη τοῦ πολεμεῖν. THUC. i. 126. Κεφαλῇ κατανεύσομαι, ὄφρα πεποίθῃς. Il. i. 524. Ὄρσεο δὴ νῦν, ξεῖνε, πόλινδ' ἴμεν, ὄφρα σε πέμψω. Od. vi. 255. Αὐτὰρ ἐμοὶ γέρας αὐτίχ' ἑτοιμάσατ', ὄφρα μὴ οἶος Ἀργείων ἀγέραστος ἔω. Il. i. 118. Δόμον Φερσεφόνας ἐλθέ, ὄφρ' ἰδοῖσ' υἱὸν εἴπῃς. PIND. Ol. xiv. 20. Ὡς ὁ μὲν ἔνθα κατέσχετ' ἐπειγόμενός περ ὁδοῖο, ὄφρ' ἕταρον θάπτοι καὶ ἐπὶ κτέρεα κτερίσειεν. Od. iii. 284. Ἀλλὰ σὺ μὲν νῦν αὖτις ἀπόστιχε, μή τι νοήσῃ Ἥρη · ἐμοὶ δέ κε ταῦτα μελήσεται ὄφρα τελέσσω. Il. i. 522. Οὐ δῆτ' αὐτὸν ἄξεις δεῦρο, μή τις ἀναρπάσῃ ; SOPH. Aj. 986. Λυσιτελεῖ ἐᾶσαι ἐν τῷ

παρόντι, μὴ καὶ τοῦτον πολέμιον προσθώμεθα. ΧΕΝ. Cyr. ii. 4, 12.
Λέγεται εἰπεῖν ὅτι ἀπιέναι βούλοιτο, μὴ ὁ πατήρ τι ἄχθοιτο καὶ ἡ
πόλις μέμφοιτο. Ib. i. 4, 25. Λοῦσαι κέλετ', ὡς μὴ Πρίαμος ἴδοι
υἱόν, μὴ ὁ μὲν ἀχνυμένη κραδίῃ χόλον οὐκ ἐρύσαιτο. Il. xxiv. 582.
For the relative frequency of the final particles, see Appendix III.

318. As final clauses after past tenses express some
person's previous purpose or motive, they allow the double
construction of indirect discourse (667, 1); so that, instead
of the optative, they can have the *mood* and *tense* which
the person himself would have used in conceiving the purpose. Thus we can say either **ἦλθεν ἵνα ἴδοι**, *he came that
he might see*, or **ἦλθεν ἵνα ἴδῃ**, because the person himself
would have said **ἔρχομαι ἵνα ἴδω**, *I come that I may see*.

Hence the subjunctive in final clauses after past tenses
is very common, in some writers even more common than
the regular optative. *E.g.*

Ἐπεκλώσαντο δ' ὄλεθρον ἀνθρώποις, ἵνα ᾖσι καὶ ἐσσομένοισιν
ἀοιδή. Od. viii. 579. Ἀχλὺν δ' αὖ τοι ἀπ' ὀφθαλμῶν ἕλον, ἣ πρὶν
ἐπῆεν, ὄφρ' εὖ γιγνώσκῃς ἠμὲν θεὸν ἠδὲ καὶ ἄνδρα. Il. v. 127.
Ἀριστεὺς ξυνεβούλευεν ἐκπλεῦσαι, ὅπως ἐπὶ πλέον ὁ σῖτος ἀντίσχῃ.
Thuc. i. 65. Ἦλθον πρεσβευσόμενοι, ὅπως μὴ σφίσι τὸ Ἀττικὸν
(ναυτικὸν) προσγενόμενον ἐμπόδιον γένηται. Id. i. 31. Ἐχώρουν
ἐκ τῶν οἰκιῶν, ὅπως μὴ κατὰ φῶς θαρσαλεωτέροις οὖσι προσφέρων-
ται καὶ σφίσιν ἐκ τοῦ ἴσου γίγνωνται, ἀλλ' ἥσσους ὦσι. Id. ii.
3. Καὶ ἐπίτηδές σε οὐκ ἤγειρον, ἵνα ὡς ἥδιστα διάγῃς. PLAT.
Crit. 43 B. Πλοῖα κατέκαυσεν ἵνα μὴ Κῦρος διαβῇ. ΧΕΝ. An.
i. 4, 18. Ταύτας ἵνα κωλύηθ' οἱ νόμοι συνήγαγον ὑμᾶς, οὐχ ἵνα
κυρίας τοῖς ἀδικοῦσι ποιῆτε. DEM. xix. 1. Καὶ περὶ τούτων ἐμνή-
σθην, ἵνα μὴ ταὐτὰ πάθητε. Id. iii. 6. (Here the purpose was conceived in the form ἵνα μὴ ταὐτὰ πάθωσιν.)

319. This principle applies also to clauses with ὅπως after verbs of
striving (339) and with μή after verbs of *fearing*, etc. (365).

320. This is a favourite construction with certain authors, especially
Thucydides, who also, on the same principle, prefers the indicative
and subjunctive to the optative in ordinary indirect discourse after
past tenses (670). The early poets, on the other hand, especially
Homer, use it very sparingly.[1]

----

[1] Weber, p. 243, gives a comparison of the usage of various writers, showing that the proportion of subjunctives to optatives after past tenses in pure
final clauses and after verbs of fearing is as follows:—in *Homer* 35 : 156,
Pindar 2 : 10, Aeschylus 2 : 9, Sophocles 2 : 23, Euripides 31 : 65, Aristophanes
13 : 37, Herodotus 86 : 47, *Thucydides* 168 : 60, Lysias 22 : 19, Isocrates 21 : 17,
Isaeus 8 : 17, *Demosthenes* 40 : 40, Aeschines 13 : 7, Plato 22 : 79, Xenophon
45 : 265. In all writers before Aristotle 528 : 894. In the Attic writers and
Herodotus, excluding Xenophon, the two are just equal, 441.

321. The subjunctive thus used for the optative makes the language more vivid, by introducing more nearly the original form of thought of the person whose purpose is stated. As the two forms are equally correct, we sometimes find both in the same sentence, just as we find the indicative and optative interchanged in indirect discourse (670 ; see 677 and 690). *E.g.*

Ἐξακοσίους λογάδας ἐξέκριναν, ὅπως τῶν τε Ἐπιπολῶν εἶησαν φύλακες καὶ, ἦν ἐς ἄλλο τι δέῃ, ταχὺ ξυνεστῶτες παραγίγνωνται, i.e. *they selected them, that they might be guards of Epipolae, and that they might be on hand if they should be needed for anything else.* Thuc. vi. 96.

Παρανῖσχον δὲ φρυκτοὺς, ὅπως ἀσαφῆ τὰ σημεῖα τοῖς πολεμίοις ᾖ καὶ μὴ βοηθοῖεν, *they raised fire-signals at the same time, in order that the enemy's signals might be unintelligible to them, and that they (the enemy) might not bring aid.* Id. iii. 22.

A common interpretation of the latter and of similar passages, that " the subjunctive mood indicates the *immediate*, and the optative the *remote* consequence of the action contained in the principal verbs, the second being a consequence of the first " (Arnold), manifestly could not apply to the first example.

322. The use of the optative for the subjunctive in final clauses after primary tenses is, on the other hand, very rare, and is to be viewed as a mere irregularity of construction.   See ἄξω τῆλ' Ἰθάκης, ἵνα μοι βίοτον πολὺν ἄλφοι, Od. xvii. 250 ; ὅππως μαχέοιντο, Il. i. 344 ; and vii. 340, xviii. 88. So Soph. El. 56, O. C. 11 ; Hdt. ii. 93 (ἵνα μὴ ἁμάρτοιεν). Most of these are emended by various editors ; and no good reason for the anomaly appears in any of them.

323. Sometimes the optative is properly used after a leading verb which implies a reference to the past as well as the present. *E.g.*

Τοῦτον ἔχει τὸν τρόπον ὁ νόμος, ἵνα μηδὲ πεισθῆναι μηδ' ἐξαπατηθῆναι γένοιτ' ἐπὶ τῷ δήμῳ. Dem. xxii. 11. (Here ἔχει implies also the past existence of the law ; the idea being, *the law was made as it is, so that it might not be possible,* etc.) So Dem. xxiv. 145, 147. In Dem. iii. 34 ἵνα τοῦθ' ὑπάρχοι depends on a past verb of *saying* to be mentally supplied. In Ar. Ran. 23, τοῦτον δ' ὀχῶ, ἵνα μὴ ταλαιπωροῖτο μηδ' ἄχθος φέροι, *I am letting him ride, that he might not be distressed,* etc., the meaning of ὀχῶ goes back to the time when Dionysus first let the slave mount the ass.

324. (*Future Indicative.*) The future indicative occasionally takes the place of the subjunctive in pure final clauses. It occurs chiefly with ὅπως, very seldom with ὄφρα, ὡς, and μή, and never with ἵνα.[1]   It has essentially the same force as the subjunctive. *E.g.*

[1] Weber cites the following cases, in addition to those given above. For ὅπως : Aesch. Cho. 265, Suppl. 449 ; Soph. Aj. 698 (?) ; Eur. El. 835 ; Ar. Vesp. 528, Pac. 309, 431, Lys. 1093, Thesm. 431, 653, 285 (?), Eccl. 783, 997 ; Andoc. i. 89 ; Xen. Hipp. i. 18, Mem. ii. 1, 1 (παιδεύειν ὅπως ἔσται ?). In Xen. Cyr. ii. 1, 4 and 21 the Mss. vary : in Cyr. iii. 3, 42 ὅπως is probably independent.   For ὄφρα : Il. viii. 110 ; Od. iv. 163, xvii. 6.   For ὡς : Eur.

Αἰεὶ δὲ μαλακοῖσι καὶ αἱμυλίοισι λόγοισι θέλγει, ὅπως 'Ιθάκης
ἐπιλήσεται. Od. i. 56. Μὴ πρόσλευσσε, ἡμῶν ὅπως μὴ τὴν τύχην
διαφθερεῖς. Soph. Ph. 1068. 'Απομυκτέον δέ σοί γ', ὅπως λήψει
πιεῖν. Eur. Cycl. 561. 'Αρδῶ σ' ὅπως ἀμβλαστανεῖς. Ar. Lys.
384. 'Επ' αὐτοὺς τοὺς προλόγους σου τρέψομαι, ὅπως τὸ πρῶτον τῆς
τραγῳδίας μέρος πρώτιστον βασανιῶ. Ar. Ran. 1120. Προιέναι
(δεῖ) τῶν τόπων ἐνθυμούμενον, ὅπως μὴ διαμαρτήσεται. Xen.
Cyneg. ix. 4. Χρὴ ἀναβιβάζειν ἐπὶ τὸν τροχὸν τοὺς ἀναγραφέντας,
ὅπως μὴ πρότερον νὺξ ἔσται πρὶν πυθέσθαι τοὺς ἄνδρας ἅπαντας.
And. i. 43.
Θάρσυνον δέ οἱ ἦτορ ἐνὶ φρεσὶν, ὄφρα καὶ ῞Εκτωρ εἴσεται. Il.
xvi. 242. ῾Ως τί ῥέξομεν; that we may do what? Soph. O. C. 1724.
῞Ωστ' εἰκὸς ἡμᾶς μὴ βραδύνειν ἐστὶ, μὴ καί τις ὄψεται χημῶν ἴσως
κατείπῃ. Ar. Eccl. 495. So μὴ κεχολώσεται, Il. xx. 301.

῎Αν or κέ in Final Clauses with Subjunctive.

325. The final particles which have a relative origin, ὡς,
ὅπως, and ὄφρα, sometimes have ἄν or κέ in final clauses with
the subjunctive. They did this originally in their capacity as
conditional relatives; and it is probable that at first κέ or ἄν
with the relative gave the clause a combined final and conditional
force, in which the conditional element gradually grew weaker
as the relative particles came to be felt chiefly or only as final
particles (312, 2). ῞Ινα and μή never take ἄν or κέ in this way.[1]

326. (῾Ως.) 1. ῞Ως κε and ὡς ἄν are together much more
common in Homer with the subjunctive than simple ὡς. ῾Ως ἄν
with the subjunctive is not uncommon in the Attic poets, and it
occurs in Herodotus; but (like ὡς itself) it almost disappears in
Attic prose. E.g.

Πείθεο, ὡς ἄν μοι τιμὴν μεγάλην καὶ κῦδος ἄρηαι, obey, that
thou mayest gain for me great honour and glory. Il. xvi. 84. Αὐτάρ οἱ
προφρὼν ὑποθήσομαι, ὥς κε μάλ' ἀσκηθὴς ἢν πατρίδα γαῖαν ἵκηται.
Od. v. 143. Παίσατε, ὥς χ' ὁ ξεῖνος ἐνίσπῃ οἶσι φίλοισιν. Od.
viii. 251. 'Αλλ' ἴθι, μή μ' ἐρέθιζε, σαώτερος ὥς κε νέηαι, that
thou mayest go the more safely. Il. i. 32. Προσδεόμεθα . . . συμπέμψαι
ἡμῖν, ὡς ἄν μιν ἐξέλωμεν ἐκ τῆς χώρης. Hdt. i. 36. Τοὺς ἐμοὺς
λόγους θυμῷ βάλ', ὡς ἄν τέρματ' ἐκμάθῃς ὁδοῦ. Aesch. Prom.
705. 'Αλλ' ἐάσωμεν, φίλοι, ἔκηλον αὐτὸν, ὡς ἄν εἰς ὕπνον πέσῃ.

Bacch. 784. For μή: Od. xxiv. 544; Theog. 1307; Ar. Eccl. 488. Only four
undoubted examples occur in prose.
[1] In the single case of κέ with ἵνα, Od. xii. 156, ἀλλ' ἐρέω μὲν ἐγὼν, ἵνα
εἰδότες ἤ κε θάνωμεν, ἤ κεν ἀλευάμενοι θάνατον καὶ κῆρα φύγωμεν, ἵνα κε is not
used like ὥς κε, etc., above, but ἵνα is followed by a potential subjunctive
with κέ (285). The repetition of κέ removes the case from the class under
consideration. ῞Ινα in its sense of where may have ἄν (see Soph. O. C. 405).
Μή, lest, may have ἄν with the optative after verbs of fearing (368).

SOPH. Ph. 825. Καθείρξατ᾽ αὐτὸν, ὡς ἂν σκότιον εἰρορᾷ κνέψυς.
EUR. Bacch. 510. Τουτὶ λαβών μου τὸ σκιάδειον ὑπέρεχε ἄνωθεν,
ὡς ἂν μή μ᾽ ὁρῶσιν οἱ θεοί. AR. Av. 1508.

2. In Attic prose ὡς ἄν with the subjunctive is found only in
Xenophon and in one passage of Thucydides.

The last is THUC. vi. 91 : (πέμψετε) ἄνδρα Σπαρτιάτην ἄρχοντα, ὡς
ἂν τούς τε παρόντας ξυντάξῃ καὶ τοὺς μὴ θέλοντας προσαναγκάσῃ.
See XEN. An. ii. 5, 16, ὡς δ᾽ ἂν μάθῃς, ἀντάκουσον. So An. vi. 3,
18. See other examples of Xenophon's peculiar use of ὡς ἄν with the
subjunctive in Appendix IV.

327. (Ὄφρα.) Ὄφρα κε and ὄφρ᾽ ἄν have the subjunctive in
a few final clauses in Homer. *E.g.*

Οὗτος νῦν σοι ἅμ᾽ ἕψεται, ὄφρα κεν εὕδῃ σοῖσιν ἐνὶ μεγάροισιν. Od.
iii. 359. Ἴομεν, ὄφρα κε θᾶσσον ἐγείρομεν ὀξὺν Ἄρηα. Il. ii. 440.
Τὸν ξεῖνον ἄγ᾽ ἐς πόλιν, ὄφρ᾽ ἂν ἐκεῖθι δαῖτα πτωχεύῃ. Od. xvii. 10.

For ὄφρα κε and ὄφρ᾽ ἄν with the optative, see 329, 1.

328. (Ὅπως.) Ὅπως does not occur in Homer in pure final
clauses with either κέ or ἄν. Ὅπως ἄν final with the subjunctive
appears first in Aeschylus, and remains in good use in Attic
poetry and prose, being almost the only final expression found
in the formal language of the Attic inscriptions. One case of
ὅκως ἄν occurs in Herodotus. *E.g.*

Φύλασσε τὰν οἴκῳ καλῶς, ὅπως ἂν ἀρτίκολλα συμβαίνῃ τάδε,
watch what goes on in the house, that these things may work harmoniously.
AESCH. Cho. 579 : so Prom. 824, Eum. 573, 1030, Suppl. 233. Ἴσθι
πᾶν τὸ δρώμενον, ὅπως ἂν εἰδὼς ἧμιν ἀγγείλῃς σαφῆ. SOPH. El. 40.
Τοῦτ᾽ αὐτὸ νῦν δίδασχ᾽, ὅπως ἂν ἐκμάθω. Id. O. C. 575. Οὐκ ἄπιθ᾽,
ὅπως ἂν οἱ Λάκωνες καθ᾽ ἡσυχίαν ἀπίωσιν; AR. Lys. 1223. Ταῦτα
δὲ ἐποίεε τῶνδε εἵνεκεν, ὅκως ἂν ὁ κῆρυξ ἀγγείλῃ Ἀλυάττῃ. HDT. i.
22 (see 318). Διὰ τῆς σῆς χώρας ἄξεις ἡμᾶς, ὅπως ἂν εἰδῶμεν, κ.τ.λ.
XEN. Cyr. v. 2, 21. Καί φατε αὐτὸν τοιοῦτον εἶναι, ὅπως ἂν
φαίνηται ὡς κάλλιστος καὶ ἄριστος. PLAT. Symp. 199 A. Ἄν γέ
τινας ὑποπτεύῃ ἐλεύθερα φρονήματα ἔχοντας μὴ ἐπιτρέψειν αὐτῷ
ἄρχειν, (πολέμους κινεῖ) ὅπως ἂν τούτους μετὰ προφάσεως ἀπολ-
λύῃ, *that he may destroy them.* Id. Rep. 567 A. Εὐσεβοῦμεν καὶ τὴν
δικαιοσύνην ἀσκοῦμεν, οὐχ ἵνα τῶν ἄλλων ἔλαττον ἔχωμεν, ἀλλ᾽
ὅπως ἂν ὡς μετὰ πλείστων ἀγαθῶν τὸν βίον διάγωμεν. ISOC. iii.
2 (ἵνα and ὅπως ἄν may here be compared in sense : see 312, 2).
Τὴν πόλιν συνέχειν, ὅπως ἂν μίαν γνώμην ἔχωσιν ἅπαντες καὶ μὴ
τοῖς ἐχθροῖς ἡδονὴν ποιῶσιν. DEM. xix. 298 : so xiv. 23.

Ἄν or κέ in Final Clauses with Optative.

329. 1. (Ὡς and ὄφρα in Homer and ὡς and ὅκως in Herodotus.) In Homer ὡς κε and ὡς ἄν sometimes have the optative in final

clauses after both primary and secondary tenses. Ὄφρα κε and ὄφρ' ἄν occur each once in Homer with the optative after past tenses. Herodotus has ὡς ἄν and ὅκως ἄν with the optative after past tenses, and ὅκως ἄν once after a present tense. This optative with κέ or ἄν after primary tenses is certainly potential as well as final; and this analogy makes it difficult or impossible to take it in any other sense after secondary tenses, though here the potential force is less obvious.

(a) After primary tenses six cases occur in the Odyssey and one in Herodotus :—

Ἀπερρίγασι νέεσθαι ὥς κ' αὐτὸς ἐεδνώσαιτο θύγατρα, they dread to go to him that he may settle (if he will) the bridal gifts of his daughter, lit. that he would settle, etc. Od. ii. 53. Κνυζώσω δέ τοι ὄσσε, ὡς ἄν ἀεικέλιος φανείης, I will dim your eyes, to the end that you might appear unseemly. Od. xiii. 401. Δύο δοῦρε καλλιπέειν, ὡς ἄν ἐπιθύσαντες ἐλοίμεθα. Od. xvi. 297. Τῷ κε τάχα γνοίης φιλότητά τε πολλά τε δῶρα ἐξ ἐμεῦ, ὡς ἄν τίς σε συναντόμενος μακαρίζοι, so that one would call you blessed. Od. xvii. 164 (= xv. 537, xix. 310). Ἡγείσθω ὀρχηθμοῖο, ὥς κέν τις φαίη γάμον ἔμμεναι ἐκτὸς ἀκούων, let him lead off the dance, so that any one who should hear without would say there was a marriage. Od. xxiii. 134. Ἴσχεσθε πτολέμου, ὥς κεν ἀναιμωτί γε διακρινθεῖτε τάχιστα. Od. xxiv. 531.

Κελεύει σε τὸ παιδίον θεῖναι, ὅκως ἄν. τάχιστα διαφθαρείη, he bids you so expose the child that he˙would be likely to perish most speedily. HDT. i. 110.

(b) After past tenses the following cases occur¹ :—

Ὕε δ' ἄρα Ζεὺς συνεχές, ὄφρα κε θᾶσσον ἁλίπλοα τείχεα θείη. Il. xii. 25. Ἐώλπειν σε Φθίηνδε νέεσθαι, ὡς ἄν μοι τὸν παῖδα Σκυρόθεν ἐξαγάγοις, i.e. I hoped for your coming, that you might perchance bring my son away from Scyros. Il. xix. 330. Καί μιν μακρότερον καὶ πάσσονα θῆκεν ἰδέσθαι, ὥς κεν Φαιήκεσσι φίλος πάντεσσι γένοιτο. Od. viii. 20. Τύμβον χεύαμεν, ὥς κει τηλεφανὴς ἐκ ποντόφιν ἀνδράσιν εἴη. Od. xxiv. 83. Σὺ δέ με προίεις, ὄφρ' ἄν ἐλοίμην δῶρα (Bekker ἀνελοίμην). Ib. 333.

Λέγεται διώρυχα ὀρύσσειν, ὅκως ἄν τὸ στρατόπεδον ἱδρυμένον κατὰ νώτου λάβοι, i.e. he is said to have dug (119) a channel, in order that the river might flow behind the army. HDT. i. 75. Ταῦτα δὲ περὶ

¹ It must be confessed that there are some difficult questions concerning these optatives with κέ or ἄν in final clauses after past tenses. It may perhaps be thought that the subjunctive after ὥς κε, ὅκως ἄν, etc., has been changed to the optative after a past tense retaining κέ or ἄν without effect on the verb. Compare ἕως ἄν with the optative (613, 4 ; 702). Would ὅκως ἄν in HDT. i. 22 (quoted in 328) have changed its nature if ἀγγείλῃ had been changed to ἀγγείλειε ? On the other hand, can we separate the optatives in HDT. i. 75 and 99 (in b) from the optative in i. 110 (in a) ? The potential view seems, on the whole, much the more natural ; but the potential force can be expressed in English only with great difficulty, owing to the ambiguity of our auxiliaries might, would, should, etc.

ἑωυτὸν ἐπέμνυε τῶνδε εἵνεκεν, ὅκως ἂν μὴ ὁρέονιες οἱ ὑμήλικες
λυπεοίατο καὶ ἐπιβουλεύοιεν, ἀλλ᾽ ἑτεροῖός σφι δοκέοι εἶναι
μὴ ὁρῶσι, *in order that his companions might not be offended by seeing
him and plot against him, but that he might appear to them to be of
another nature when they did not see him.* Id. i. 99. Πορφύρεον εἷμα
περιβαλόμενος, ὡς ἂν πυνθανόμενοι πλεῖστοι συνέλθοιεν. Id. i.
152. Τὸ ὕδωρ τότε ἐπῆκαν, ὡς ἂν χαραδρωθείη ὁ χῶρος, *they let
in the water, in order that the country might be gullied.* Id. vii. 176.
Περιέπεμπον ἔξωθεν Σκιάθου, ὡς ἂν μὴ ὀφθείησαν περιπλέουσαι
Εὔβοιαν. Id. viii. 7. Ἤλαυνον τοὺς ἵππους, ὡς ἂν τὸν νεκρὸν ἀνε-
λοίατο. Id. ix. 22. Μετακινέεσθαι ἐδόκεε τότε, ὡς ἂν μὴ ἰδοίατο
οἱ Πέρσαι ἐξορμεομένους. Ib. 51.

2. Ὡς ἄν with the optative in Attic prose is found chiefly in
Xenophon. It is never strictly final; but ὡς is relative or interrogative, and the optative with ἄν is potential. *E.g.*

῎Εδοξεν αὐτῷ τοῦτο ποιῆσαι, ὡς ὅτι ἥκιστα ἂν ἐπιφθόνως σπανιός
τε καὶ σεμνὸς φανείη, *he decided to do this in such a way that he might
appear,* etc. (i.e. *in the way by which*). XEN. Cyr. vii. 5, 37. (Here the
separation of ἄν from ὡς makes the potential character plainer.) Ὡς
δ᾽ ἂν καὶ οἱ πόδες εἷεν τῷ ἵππῳ κράτιστοι, εἰ μέν τις ἔχει ῥάῳ
ἄσκησιν, κ.τ.λ., *as to means by which the horse's feet could be kept
strongest.* Id. Hipp. i. 16. See other examples in Appendix IV. This
is the same relative use of ὡς with the potential optative which we
find in DEM. vi. 3, ὡς μὲν ἂν εἴποιτε δικαίους λόγους ἄμεινον
Φιλίππου παρεσκεύασθε· ὡς δὲ κωλύσαιτ᾽ ἂν ἐκεῖνον πράττειν
ταῦτα, παντελῶς ἀργῶς ἔχετε, *as to means by which you could make just
speeches, you are better equipped than Philip; but as to steps by which you
could prevent him from doing what he does, you are wholly inactive.* See
also DEM. vi. 37, ὡς δ᾽ ἂν ἐξετασθείη μάλιστ᾽ ἀκριβῶς, μὴ γένοιτο,
*as to any means by which the truth could be tested most thoroughly,—may
this never come !*

330. Ὅπως ἄν with a final potential optative occurs once in
Thucydides, four times in Xenophon, and once in Aeschylus.

Τὰς πρῴρας κατεβύρσωσαν, ὅπως ἂν ἀπολισθάνοι ἡ χεὶρ ἐπι-
βαλλομένη, *they covered the prows with hides, that the (iron) hand when
thrown on might be likely to slip off.* THUC. vii. 65. ῎Εδωκε χρήματα
᾽Ανταλκίδᾳ, ὅπως ἄν, πληρωθέντος ναυτικοῦ ὑπὸ Λακεδαιμονίων, οἱ
᾽Αθηναῖοι μᾶλλον τῆς εἰρήνης προσδέοιντο. XEN. Hell. iv. 8, 16.
(Here πληρωθέντος ναυτικοῦ, *if a navy should be manned,* stands as
protasis to προσδέοιντο ἄν.) ῞Οπως δ᾽ ἂν ὡς ἐρρωμενέστατον τὸ στρά-
τευμα ποιήσαιτο, ἐξ ἄλλων πόλεων ἠγυρολόγει. Ib. iv. 8, 30.
Πᾶσιν ἐδίδου βοῦς τε, ὅπως ἂν θύσαντες ἐστιῷντο, καὶ ἐκπώματα.
Id. Cyr. viii. 3, 33 (one Ms. omits ἄν). Τὴν λείαν ἀπέπεμψε δια-
τίθεσθαι Ἡρακλείδην, ὅπως ἂν μισθὸς γένοιτο τοῖς στρατιώταις.
Id. An. vii. 4, 2 (most Mss. have ὅπως γένηται). So AESCH. Ag. 364.
In these cases the final force is equally strong with the potential.

Elliptical Constructions.

331. In colloquial Greek we often find ἵνα τί; *that what?*—where τί takes the place of a final clause, which generally appears in the answer to the question. *E.g.*

ΒΛ. ἵνα τί; ΠΡ. δῆλον τουτογί· ἵνα ... ἔχωσιν. Ar. Eccl. 719. So Nub. 1192, Pac. 409. So Dem. xix. 257 : ἵνα τί; ἵν' ὡς μετὰ πλείστης συγγνώμης παρ' ὑμῶν κατηγορῶ. Just before this we have διὰ τί; ἵνα μήτε ἐλέου μήτε συγγνώμης τύχῃ. So Plat. Ap. 26 C.

332. A final clause may stand without a leading verb expressed, when the omission can easily be supplied ; as ὅτι ἦρξα, μὴ ἀποδημήσω; ἵνα γε μὴ προλαβὼν χρήματα τῆς πόλεως ἢ πράξεις δρασμῷ χρήσῃ, *because I held an office, may I not leave the country?* *No : that you may not take to flight,* etc. Aeschin. iii. 21.

SECONDARY TENSES OF INDICATIVE IN FINAL CLAUSES.

333. In Attic Greek the secondary tenses of the indicative are used in final clauses with ἵνα, sometimes with ὅπως or ὡς, to denote that the purpose is dependent upon some unaccomplished action or unfulfilled condition, and therefore *is not* or *was not* attained.

The tenses of the indicative differ here as in conditional sentences, the imperfect (the most frequent tense) referring to present time or to continued or repeated action in past time, the aorist and pluperfect to past time (410). Thus ἵνα τοῦτο ἔπραττεν means *in order that he might be doing this (but he is not doing it)*, or *that he might have been doing this (but he was not)* ; ἵνα τοῦτο ἔπραξεν means *that he might have done this (but he did not)* ; ἵνα τοῦτο ἐπεπράχει means *that he might have done this (but he has not)*. *E.g.*

Οὐκ ἂν ἐσχόμην, ἵν' ἦ τυφλός τε καὶ κλύων μηδέν, *in that case I should not have forborne (to destroy my hearing), so that I might (now) be both blind and devoid of hearing* (implying that really he is not so). Soph. O. T. 1387. Φεῦ, φεῦ, τὸ μὴ τὰ πράγματ' ἀνθρώποις ἔχειν φωνήν, ἵν' ἦσαν μηδὲν οἱ δεινοὶ λόγοι, *Alas! alas! that the facts have no voice for men, so that words of eloquence might be as nothing.* Eur. Fr. (Hipp.) 442. Ἐβουλόμην μὲν ἕτερον ἂν τῶν ἠθάδων λέγειν τὰ βέλτισθ', ἵν' ἐκαθήμην ἥσυχος. Ar. Eccl. 151. Ἐχρῆν εἰσκαλέσαντας μάρτυρας πολλοὺς παρασημήνασθαι κελεῦσαι τὰς διαθήκας, ἵν', εἴ τι ἐγίγνετο ἀμφισβητήσιμον, ἦν εἰς τὰ γράμματα ταῦτ' ἐπανελθεῖν. Dem. xxviii. 5. (This implies that they did not have the will thus sealed, so that it is *not now possible* to refer to it in case of dispute.) Ἐξήτησεν ἄν με τὸν παῖδα, ἵν' εἰ μὴ παρεδίδουν μηδὲν δίκαιον λέγειν ἐδόκουν. Dem. xxix. 17. Ἐχρῆν αὐτοὺς τὴν προτέραν ζήτησιν ζητεῖν, ἵνα ἀπηλλάγμεθα τούτου τοῦ δημαγωγοῦ, they ought to have made the previous investigation, in order that we might have been already freed from this demagogue (but we have not been freed from him). DIN. i. 10.   See LYS. i. 40 and 42 ; ISOC. ix. 5, xviii. 51. Ἀλλὰ σὲ ἐχρῆν ἡμῖν συγχωρεῖν, ἵνα συνουσία ἐγίγνετο, but you ought to give way to us, that our conversation might not be interrupted (as it is). PLAT. Prot. 335 C.

Τί δῆτ' οὐκ ἔρριψ' ἐμαυτὴν τῆσδ' ἀπὸ πέτρας, ὅπως τῶν πάντων πόνων ἀπηλλάγην ; why did I not throw myself from this rock, that I might have been freed from all my toils ? AESCH. Prom. 747 : so Cho. 195.   See SOPH. El. 1134.   Οὐκοῦν ἐχρῆν σε Πηγάσου ξεῦξαι πτερόν, ὅπως ἐφαίνου τοῖς θεοῖς τραγικώτερος ; AR. Pac. 135.

Τί μ' οὐ λαβὼν ἔκτεινας εὐθύς, ὡς ἔδειξα μήποτε ἐμαυτὸν ἀνθρώ-ποισιν ἔνθεν ἦ γεγώς ; that I might never have shown, as I have done. SOPH. O. T. 1391.   Εἰ γάρ μ' ὑπὸ γῆν ἦκεν, ὡς μήτε θεὸς μήτε τις ἄλλος τοῖσδ' ἐπεγήθει, would that he had sent me under the earth, so that neither any God nor any one else should be rejoicing at these things (as they are). AESCH. Prom. 152.   Ἔδει τὰ ἐνέχυρα τότε λαβεῖν, ὡς μηδ' εἰ ἐβούλετο ἐδύνατο ἐξαπατᾶν. XEN. An. vii. 6, 23 (the only case in Xenophon).

334. This construction is the result of an assimilation, which makes more distinct the connection in thought between the two clauses.   It is especially common after secondary tenses implying unfulfilled conditions and unaccomplished wishes.

335. Ἄν cannot properly be added to the indicative in this construction.   In the two examples in which it is found, it would seem that the construction has slipped into an apodosis, or that copyists have been misled by the resemblance to an apodosis and inserted ἄν.

Ζῶντι ἔδει βοηθεῖν, ὅπως ὅτι δικαιότατος ὢν καὶ ὁσιώτατος ἔζη τε ζῶν καὶ τελευτήσας ἀτιμώρητος ἂν κακῶν ἁμαρτημάτων ἐγίγνετο, in order that he might thus live while he lives, and (so that) after death he would be (as a consequence of such a life) free from punishment (?). PLAT. Leg. 959 B.   Τόν γε πράττοντά τι δίκαιον οὐ προσῆκεν ἀπορεῖν ἀλλ' εὐθὺς λέγειν, ἵνα μᾶλλον ἂν ἐπιστεύετο ὑφ' ὑμῶν, (possibly) that the result might be that he would be (in that case) the more trusted by you. ISAE. xi. 6.

336. The indicative can never be used in this construction, unless the final clause refers to present or past time, and unless also it is distinctly implied that the purpose is not (or was not) attained.   If the purpose is future (at the time of speaking), or if it is left uncertain whether the object is or was attained, it must be expressed in the ordinary way by the subjunctive or optative, even though it depends on one of the class of verbs mentioned above.   Both constructions may occur in the same sentence.   E.g.

Οὓς (τῶν νέων τοὺς ἀγαθοὺς) ἡμεῖς ἂν ἐφυλάττομεν ἐν ἀκροπόλει, ἵνα μηδεὶς αὐτοὺς διέφθειρεν, ἀλλ' ἐπειδὴ ἀφίκοιντο εἰς τὴν ἡλικίαν, χρήσιμοι γίγνοιντο ταῖς πόλεσιν, *we should guard (in that case) in the Acropolis, that no one might corrupt them (as some now corrupt them), and that when (in the future) they should become of age they might become useful to their states.* PLAT. Men. 89 B. (Here it is not implied that they never become useful, this depending partly on the future.) Ταῦτ᾽ ἂν ἤδη λέγειν πρὸς ὑμᾶς ἐπεχείρουν, ἵν᾽ εἰδῆτε πολλοῦ δεῖν ἄξιον ὄντα τυχεῖν τοῦ ψηφίσματος αὐτὸν τουτονί, *I should (if that were so) be now undertaking to explain this to you, that you might (after hearing me) know that he is far from deserving the honour of the proposed decree.* DEM. xxiii. 7. Καίτοι χρῆν σε ἢ τοῦτον μὴ γράφειν ἢ ἐκεῖνον λύειν, οὐχ, ἵνα ὃ βούλει σὺ γένηται, πάντα συνταράξαι, i.e. *you ought not to have confused everything in order that what you want might be done.* DEM. xxiv. 44.

337. Clauses with μή after verbs of fearing are never thus assimilated to a preceding indicative, as there is no reference here to the attainment of a purpose.

338. A purpose can be expressed in various forms besides that of the final clause ; as by the relative with the future indicative, or in Homer with the subjunctive (565 ; 568) ; by the infinitive (770) or the infinitive with ὥστε or ὡς (587, 3) ; by the future participle (840) ; by ὑπέρ with the genitive of the articular infinitive (802).

B. OBJECT CLAUSES WITH Ὅπως AND Ὅπως μή AFTER VERBS OF STRIVING, ETC.

339. In Attic Greek and in Herodotus, object clauses with ὅπως and ὅπως μή after verbs signifying *to strive, to plan, to care for, to effect,* regularly have the future indicative after primary tenses to express the object aimed at. The subjunctive also is used, but less frequently than the future indicative.

After secondary tenses the future optative may be used, corresponding to the future indicative after primary tenses ; but generally the future indicative is retained, as the original form of the thought (319). The other tenses of the optative are sometimes used, to correspond to the same tenses of the subjunctive, or the subjunctive itself may be retained (318). *E.g.*

Ἐπιμελεῖται ὅπως (or ὅπως μή) γενήσεται or γένηται, *he takes care that it may (or may not) happen.* Ἐπεμελεῖτο ὅπως γενήσεται, γενήσοιτο, or γένοιτο, *he took care that it should happen.*

(Fut.) Τὸ μὲν καλῶς ἔχον ὅπως χρονίζον εὖ μενεῖ βουλευτέον, *we must take counsel that what is well shall continue to be well.* AESCH. Ag. 846. Διδοὺς δὲ τόνδε φράζ᾽ ὅπως μηδεὶς βροτῶν κείνου πάροιθεν ἀμφιδύσεται χροΐ. SOPH. Tr. 604. Σοὶ δὴ μέλειν χρὴ τἄλλ᾽ ὅπως ἕξει καλῶς. EUR. I. T. 1051. Εἰρήνη δ᾽ ὅπως ἔσται προτιμῶσ᾽ οὐδέν, *but that there shall be peace they care not.* AR. Ach. 26. Σοὶ μελέτω ὅκως μή σε ὄψεται. HDT. i. 9. Ὅρα ὅκως μὴ ἀποστήσονται. Id. iii. 36. Χρὴ ὁρᾶν τοὺς Ἀργείους ὅπως σωθήσεται ἡ Πελοπόννησος. THUC. v. 27. Ὥσπερ τὸν ποιμένα δεῖ ἐπιμελεῖσθαι ὅπως σῶαί τε ἔσονται αἱ οἶες καὶ τὰ ἐπιτήδεια ἕξουσιν, οὕτω καὶ τὸν στρατηγὸν ἐπιμελεῖσθαι δεῖ ὅπως σῷοί τε οἱ στρατιῶται ἔσονται καὶ τὰ ἐπιτήδεια ἕξουσι, καὶ οὗ ἕνεκα στρατεύονται τοῦτο ἔσται. XEN. Mem. iii. 2, 1. Καλῶς δὲ δημαγωγήσεις, ἢν σκοπῇς ὅπως οἱ βέλτιστοι μὲν τὰς τιμὰς ἕξουσιν, οἱ δ᾽ ἄλλοι μηδὲν ἀδικήσονται. ISOC. ii. 16. Φρόντιζ᾽ ὅπως μηδὲν ἀνάξιον τῆς τιμῆς ταύτης πράξεις. Ib. 37. Τί μάλιστ᾽ ἐν ἅπασι διεσπούδασται τοῖς νόμοις; ὅπως μὴ γενήσονται οἱ περὶ ἀλλήλους φόνοι. DEM. xx. 157. Μίκραν πρόνοιαν ἔχειν ὑμῖν ὁ θεὶς τὸν νόμον δοκεῖ ὅπως κύριος ἔσται καὶ μήτε συγχυθήσεται μήτ᾽ αὖ μεταποιηθήσεται; Id. xxiii. 62. Καλὸν τὸ παρασκευάζειν ὅπως ὡς βέλτισται ἔσονται τῶν πολιτῶν αἱ ψυχαί. PLAT. Gorg. 503 A. Δεῖ εὐλαβεῖσθαι, μάλιστα μὲν ὅπως μὴ ἐγγενήσεσθον, ἂν δὲ ἐγγένησθον, ὅπως ὅτι τάχιστα ἐκτετμήσεσθον. Id. Rep. 564 C.

(Subj.) Χρὴ φυλάσσειν καὶ προκαταλαμβάνειν ὅπως μηδ᾽ ἐς ἐπίνοιαν τούτου ἴωσι. THUC. iii. 46. (Παρασκευάζεσθαι) ὅπως σὺν θεῷ ἀγωνιζώμεθα. XEN. Cyr. i. 5, 14. Οὐ γὰρ ὅπως πλείονος ἄξιος γένηται ἐπιμελεῖται, ἀλλ᾽ ὅπως αὐτὸς ὅτι πλεῖστα ὡραῖα καρπώσεται (subj. and fut. combined). Id. Symp. viii. 25. Οὐ φυλάξεσθ᾽ ὅπως μὴ δεσπότην εὕρητε. DEM. vi. 25. Ἄλλου του ἐπιμελήσει ἢ ὅπως ὅτι βέλτιστοι οἱ πολῖται ὦμεν; PLAT. Gorg. 515 B. Ὅρα ὅπως μὴ παρὰ δόξαν ὁμολογῇς. Id. Crit. 49 C.

(Fut. Opt.) Ἔζη ὑπὸ πολλῆς ἐπιμελείας ὅπως ὡς ἐλάχιστα μὲν ὄψοιτο, ἐλάχιστα δ᾽ ἀκούσοιτο, ἐλάχιστα δ᾽ ἔροιτο. XEN. Oec. vii. 5. (After a primary tense this would be ὅπως ὄψεται, ἀκούσεται, ἔρηται. But Cobet reads ἐροίη.) Ἐπεμελεῖτο ὅπως μὴ ἄσιτοί ποτε ἔσοιντο. Id. Cyr. viii. 1, 43. See the examples under 130.

(Fut. Indic. after past tenses.) Ἔπρασσον ὅπως τις βοήθεια ἥξει. THUC. iii. 4. Προθυμηθέντος ἑνὸς ἑκάστου ὅπως ἡ ναῦς προέξει. Id. vi. 31. Εὐλαβεῖσθαι παρεκελεύεσθε ἀλλήλοις, ὅπως μὴ λήσετε διαφθαρέντες. PLAT. Gorg. 487 D. Οὐδ᾽ ὅπως ὀρθὴ πλεύσεται προείδετο, ἀλλὰ τὸ καθ᾽ αὑτὸν ὅπως ἐπὶ τοῖς ἐχθροῖς ἔσται παρεσκεύασεν. DEM. xix. 250 ; so xix. 316.

(Pres. or Aor. Opt.) Ἐπεμέλετο αὐτῶν, ὅπως ἀεὶ ἀνδράποδα διατελοῖεν. XEN. Cyr. viii. 1, 44. Ἀπεκρίνατο, ὅτι αὐτῷ μέλοι ὅπως καλῶς ἔχοι. Id. An. i. 8, 13. Ἐμεμελήκει δὲ αὐτοῖς ὅπως ὁ ἱππαγρέτης εἰδείη οὓς δέοι πέμπειν. Id. Hell. iii. 3, 9.

(Subj. after past tenses.) Φρουρήσουσ᾽ (ἦξα) ὅπως Αἴγισθος ἡμᾶς μὴ λάθῃ. SOPH. El. 1402. So HDT. ii. 121. Ἔπρασσεν ὅπως

πόλεμος γένηται. Thuc. i. 57. Ἔπρασσον ὅπως ἀποστήσωσιν
Ἀθηναίων τὴν πόλιν. Id. iii. 70. Ὠνεῖται παρ᾽ αὐτῶν ὅπως μὴ
ἀπίωμεν (v.l. ἄπιμεν) ἐκ Μακεδονίας, he bribed them to effect that we
should not leave Macedonia (after historic present). Dem. xviii. 32.

340. It will thus be seen that the future indicative is the most
common form in these sentences, after both primary and secondary
tenses ; the future optative, which is theoretically the regular form
after secondary tenses, being rarely used. (See 128.)

Homeric and other early Usages.

341. In Homer, verbs signifying *to plan, to consider*, and *to try*,
chiefly φράζομαι, βουλεύω, μερμηρίζω, and πειρῶ, have ὅπως or ὡς
with the subjunctive after primary tenses, and the optative
(never future) and sometimes the subjunctive (318) after
secondary tenses. Κέ is almost always used here with ὡς and
the subjunctive, less frequently with ὅπως (313, 3).

342. The original relative and interrogative force of ὅπως
and ὡς is more apparent here than in the Attic construction of
ὅπως with the future indicative, especially after verbs of *considering ;* though after πειρῶ the dependent clause comes nearer
the later meaning. *E.g.*

Αὐτοὶ δὲ φραζώμεθ᾽ ὅπως ὄχ᾽ ἄριστα γένηται, *let us ourselves
consider how the very best things may be done.* Od. xiii. 365. Φραζόμεθ᾽
(imperfect) Ἀργείοισιν ὅπως ὄχ᾽ ἄριστα γένοιτο. Od. iii. 129.
Φράζεσθαι ὅππως κε μνηστῆρας κτείνῃς. Od. i. 295. Περιφρα-
ζώμεθα πάντες νόστον, ὅπως ἔλθῃσιν, i.e. *how he may come.* Od.
i. 76. Φράζωμεσθ᾽ ὥς κέν μιν πεπίθωμεν. Il. ix. 112. Φράσσεται
ὥς κε νέηται, ἐπεὶ πολυμήχανός ἐστιν. Od. i. 205. Ἄμα πρόσσω
καὶ ὀπίσσω λεύσσει ὅπως ὄχ᾽ ἄριστα γένηται, i.e. *he looks to see
how, etc.* Il. iii. 110. Ἐνόησε θεὰ ὡς Ὀδυσεὺς ἔγροιτο. Od. vi. 112.
Οὐ γὰρ δὴ τοῦτον μὲν ἐβούλευσας νόον αὐτή, ὡς ἦ τοι κείνους
Ὀδυσεὺς ἀποτίσεται ἐλθών; Od. v. 23. Βούλευον ὅπως ὄχ᾽ ἄριστα
γένοιτο. Od. ix. 420. Ἦλθον, εἴ τινα βουλὴν εἴποι ὅπως Ἰθάκην
ἐς παιπαλόεσσαν ἱκοίμην. Od. xi. 479. Μερμήριζεν ὅπως ἀπο-
λοίατο πᾶσαι νῆες. Od. ix. 554. Μερμήριζε κατὰ φρένα ὡς Ἀχιλῆα
τιμήσῃ (or τιμήσει), i.e. *how he might honour Achilles.* Il. ii. 3.
Ἀλλ᾽ ἄγε μῆτιν ὕφηνον ὅπως ἀποτίσομαι αὐτούς. Od. xiii. 386.
Ὥρμηνεν ἀνὰ θυμὸν ὅπως παύσειε πόνοιο δῖον Ἀχιλλῆα. Il. xxi.
137. Μνησόμεθ᾽ ὥς χ᾽ ὁ ξεῖνος ἣν πατρίδα γαῖαν ἵκηται, μηδέ τι
μεσσηγύς γε κακὸν καὶ πῆμα πάθῃσιν. Od. vii. 192. In Hymn.
Ap. Pyth. 148 we have τεχνήσομαι ὥς κε γένηται. Πείρα ὅπως
κεν δὴ σὴν πατρίδα γαῖαν ἵκηαι, i.e. *try to find means by which you
may go, etc.* Od. iv. 545. Πειρᾷ ὥς κε Τρῶες ὑπερφίαλοι ἀπό-
λωνται. Il. xxi. 459. Τοῖσι δὲ πόλλ᾽ ἐπέτελλε πειρᾶν ὡς πε-

πίθοιεν ἀμύμονα Πηλείωνα. Il. ix. 179. In Il. xv. 104 we have φραζέσθω μή μ' οὐδὲ ταλάσσῃ μεῖναι (354). For a full citation of the Homeric examples with ὅπως and ὡς, see Appendix III. 3.

343. The frequent addition of κέ to ὡς or ὅπως in Homer shows the relative origin of the construction (312, 2).

For ὅκως ἄν in Herodotus, see 350 ; for ὅπως ἄν in this construction in Attic writers, see 348, 349.

344. In Homer ὅπως takes the future indicative chiefly when it is merely an indirect interrogative, with no reference to purpose, as in Il. ii. 252, οὐδέ τί πω σάφα ἴδμεν ὅπως ἔσται τάδε ἔργα, *we do not yet even know certainly how these things are to be;* or in Od. xiii. 376, φράζευ ὅπως μνηστῆρσιν ἀναιδέσι χεῖρας ἐφήσεις, *consider how you will lay hands on the shameless suitors.* See Il. ix. 251 ; Od. xx. 38. In Od. xx. 28 the future indicative is retained after a past tense, there being as yet no future optative (128); ἔνθα καὶ ἔνθα ἑλίσσετο μερμηρίζων ὅππως δὴ μνηστῆρσιν ἀναιδέσι χεῖρας ἐφήσει. Ὅπως may take the future (like other tenses) as a simple relative ; as in Il. i. 136, ὅπως ἀντάξιον ἔσται, *as shall be an equivalent.*

345. Ὄφρα has the subjunctive in an object clause in Il. vi. 361, ἤδη γάρ μοι θυμὸς ἐπέσσυται, ὄφρ' ἐπαμύνω Τρώεσσι, and the optative in Od. iv. 463, τίς συμφράσσατο βουλὰς ὄφρα μ' ἕλοις; In Il. i. 523, ἐμοὶ δέ κε ταῦτα μελήσεται ὄφρα τελέσσω, ὄφρα may mean *until.*

346. The single object clause of this class in Pindar is Pyth. i. 72, νεῦσον ἄμερον ὄφρα κατ' οἶκον ὁ Φοῖνιξ ὁ Τυρσανῶν τ' ἀλάλατος ἔχῃ, *grant that the Phoenician, with the Etruscan war-cry, may keep quiet at home.* (See 359.)

347. As relics of the Homeric usage we find ὡς with the subjunctive in sentences of this class in EUR. Med. 461, I. T. 467, PLAT. Rep. 349 C ; and with the optative in AESCH. Prom. 203 (see 353, below). Herodotus has ὡς with the future indicative in iii. 84, 159, vii. 161 (in the last ὡς στρατηγήσεις γλίχεαι). Herodotus has ὡς ἄν with the subjunctive in iii. 85, μηχανῶ ὡς ἄν σχῶμεν τοῦτο τὸ γέρας, which is cited as the solitary case of ὡς ἄν in these object clauses after Homer, except in Xenophon (351). See also AESCH. Sept. 627, Eum. 771 ; SOLON xiii. 38 ; SOPH. Ant. 215 (in 281, above).

Ὅπως ἄν *in Attic Greek and Herodotus.*
Ὡς *and* ὡς ἄν *in Xenophon.*

348. The Attic writers sometimes use ὅπως ἄν with the subjunctive in these object clauses. This occurs chiefly in Aristophanes, Xenophon, and Plato. *E.g.*

Σκόπει ὅπως ἄν ἀποθάνωμεν ἀνδρικώτατα, *see that we die most manfully.* AR. Eq. 80. Διαμηχανήσομαι ὅπως ἄν ἱστίον σαπρὸν λάβῃς,

I will contrive that (somehow?) you get a rotten mast. Ib. 917. So AR.
Nub. 739, Eccl. 623, Ach. 1060, Eq. 926. Μᾶλλον ἢ πρόσθεν εἰσῄει
αὐτοὺς ὅπως ἂν καὶ ἔχοντές τι οἴκαδε ἀφίκωνται. XEN. An. vi. 1,
17. (Here some word like ἐπιμέλεια is understood as the subject of
εἰσῄει.) Τῶν ἄλλων ἐπιμελεῖται ὅπως ἂν θηρῶσιν. Id. Cyr. i. 2,
10. Ἐκέλευσε τὸν Φεραύλαν ἐπιμεληθῆναι ὅπως ἂν οὕτω γένηται
αὔριον ἡ ἐξέλασις. Ib. viii. 3, 6 : so v. 5, 48. See also XEN. Cyneg.
vi. 23 ; Eques. iv. 3. Ἢ ἄλλου ἐφιέμενοι δικάσουσιν ἢ τούτου, ὅπως
ἂν ἕκαστοι μήτ᾽ ἔχωσι τἀλλότρια μήτε τῶν αὐτῶν στέρωνται;
PLAT. Rep. 433 E. Πάντα ποιοῦντας ὅπως ἂν σφίσι τὸ πηδάλιον
ἐπιτρέψῃ. Ib. 488 C. Ἐὰν δ᾽ ἔλθῃ, μηχανητέον ὅπως ἂν διαφύγῃ
καὶ μὴ δῷ δίκην ὁ ἐχθρός. Id. Gorg. 481 A.

Besides the examples cited above, Weber gives fifteen of Plato, and
the following : SOPH. Tr. 618 ; EUR. I. A. 539 ; ISAE. vii. 30 ; DEM.
xvi. 17, xix. 299. He adds HDT. i. 20, where ὅκως ἄν is certainly
final.

349. The only case of ὅπως ἄν with the optative in an object
clause in Attic Greek, except in Xenophon (351), is PLAT. Lys. 207 E,
προθυμοῦνται ὅπως ἂν εὐδαιμονοίης, which is potential and on the
Xenophontic model (see 351, 2). In DEM. xxxv. 29, ἐκελεύομεν
τούτους ἐπιμελεῖσθαι ὅπως ἂν ὡς τάχιστ᾽ ἀπολάβοιμεν τὰ χρήματα, Cod. A reads ἀπολάβωμεν.

350. Herodotus has ὅκως ἄν with the potential optative four times
after past tenses. *E.g.*

Προθυμεομένου δὲ Λοξίεω ὅκως ἂν γένοιτο, *being zealous that it
might (in some way) be done.* i. 91. So ii. 126, iii. 44, v. 98.

351. (*Xenophon.*) Although Xenophon generally follows the
Attic usage in these object clauses (339), he yet violates this
signally by having ὡς and ὡς ἄν with both subjunctive and
optative, and ὅπως ἄν with the optative ; and further by having
the optative with ὡς ἄν and ὅπως ἄν after both primary and
secondary tenses. He also has ὡς twice with the future indicative (like ὅπως) and once with the future optative.

1. Ὡς or ὡς ἄν with the subjunctive, ὡς with the future
indicative, and ὡς with the optative, are used by Xenophon like
ὅπως in the construction of 339. *E.g.*

Ἐπιμελοῦνται ὡς ἔχῃ οὕτως. Oec. xx. 8. (Here the regular
Attic usage requires ὅπως ἕξει.) Ἐπιμελεῖσθαι ὡς ἂν πραχθῇ, *to
take care that they shall be done.* Hipp. ix. 2. Ἐπεμέλοντο ὡς μὴ
κωλύοιντο. Cyr. vi. 3, 2. Ὡς δὲ καλῶς ἕξει τὰ ὑμέτερα, ἐμοὶ
μελήσει. Ib. iii. 2, 13. Προεῖπεν ὡς μηδεὶς κινήσοιτο μηδὲ ἀνάξοιτο. Hell. ii. 1, 22 (see 355).

For Xenophon's regular use of ὅπως in all these constructions, see
examples under 339. For his regular use of ὅπως ἄν with the subjunctive, see 348.

2. When the optative follows ὡς ἄν or ὅπως ἄν, it is always potential, and the original relative and interrogative force of ὡς and ὅπως plainly appears. *E.g.*

Ἐπιμέλονται ὡς ἂν βέλτιστοι εἶεν οἱ πολῖται, *they take care that the citizens may be best (to see how they might be best).* Cyr. i. 2, 5. Ὡς ἂν ἀσφαλέστατά γ᾿ εἰδείην ἐποίουν, *I took steps that (by which) I might know most accurately.* Ib. vi. 3, 18. Σκοπῶ ὅπως ἂν ὡς ῥᾷστα διάγοιεν, *I am considering how they might live the easiest lives.* Symp. vii. 2. (Cf. PLAT. Lys. 207 E, quoted in 349.)

For a full enumeration of all the irregular passages of this class in Xenophon, see Appendix IV.

Negative Object Clauses.

352. None of the object clauses with ὅπως or ὡς in Homer (341) are negative, except that Od. vii. 192 combines ὡς κε ἵκηται with μηδέ τι πάθῃσιν. Negative object clauses are expressed in Homer, like most negative final clauses (315), by the simple μή with the subjunctive or optative, as in Il. v. 411, φραζέσθω μή τίς οἱ ἀμείνων σεῖο μάχηται, and Il. xv. 164, xxii. 358, Od. xvii. 595, all with φράζομαι μή and the subjunctive. So μέμβλετο τεῖχος μὴ Δαναοὶ πέρσειαν, Il. xxi. 517. These examples show a common origin with clauses after verbs of fearing, but the optative in the last example indicates that the original parataxis is no longer felt.

353. The earliest example of a negative object clause with a final particle and μή is AESCH. Prom. 203, σπεύδοντες (past) ὡς Ζεὺς μήποτ᾿ ἄρξειεν θεῶν. In all the Attic writers and in Herodotus the development of the negative object clause with ὅπως μή and the future keeps pace with that of the negative final clause with ἵνα μή, etc.

354. (Μή for ὅπως μή in Object Clauses.) Verbs of this class (339) which imply *caution*, especially ὁρῶ and σκοπῶ, may have the simple μή with the subjunctive (rarely with the future indicative), even in Attic prose, like ordinary verbs of fear and caution (365), as well as ὅπως μή with the future. Such verbs belong equally to the two classes B and C (303). *E.g.*

Σκόπει μή σοι πρόνοι᾿ ᾖ τοῦ θεοῦ φυλακτέα. SOPH. O. C. 1180. Ὅρα σὺ μὴ νῦν μέν τις εὐχερὴς παρῇς. Id. Ph. 519. Ὅρα μὴ παρὰ γνώμην πέσῃς. EUR. H. F. 594. Σκόπει τάδε, μὴ νῦν φυγόντες εἶθ᾿ ἁλῶμεν ὕστερον. Id. And. 755. Τηροῦ μὴ λάβῃς ὑπώπια. AR. Vesp. 1386. Ὅρα μὴ μάτην κόμπος ὁ λόγος οὗτος εἰρημένος ᾖ, i.e. *lest this may prove to have been spoken,* etc. HDT. vii. 103. Ὅρα μὴ πολλῶν ἑκάστῳ ἡμῶν χειρῶν δεήσει. XEN. Cyr. iv. 1, 18. Σκοπεῖ δὴ μὴ τούτοις αὐτὸν ἐξαιτήσηται καὶ καταγελάσῃ. DEM. xxi. 151. Ὅρα οὖν μή τι καὶ νῦν ἐργάσηται. PLAT. Symp. 213 D. So Il. xv. 164 (see 342).

See the corresponding use of ὅπως μή for μή after verbs of fearing (370).

Ὅπως after Verbs of Asking, Commanding, etc.

355. Verbs of *asking, entreating, exhorting, commanding,* and *forbidding,* which regularly take an object infinitive, sometimes have an object clause with ὅπως or ὅπως μή in nearly or quite the same sense. *E.g.*

Διδοὺς δὲ τόνδε φράζ᾽ ὅπως μηδεὶς βροτῶν κείνου πάροιθεν ἀμφι-δύσεται χροΐ, i.e. *tell him that no one shall put on the robe before himself.* Soph. Tr. 604 : so Aj. 567. Λακεδαιμονίων ἐδέοντο τὸ ψήφισμ᾽ ὅπως μεταστραφείη. Ar. Ach. 536. Καί σ᾽ αἰτῶ βραχὺ, ὅπως ἔσομαί σοι Φανός. Id. Eq. 1256. Ὅκως ἑωυτῶν γένηται τὸ ἔργον παρακελευσάμενοι, ἔργου εἴχοντο προθυμότερον. Hdt. ix. 102. Τὸ Πάνακτον ἐδέοντο Βοιωτοὺς (?) ὅπως παραδώσουσι Λακεδαιμονίοις. Thuc. v. 36. Ὅπως μὲν μὴ ἀποθάνῃ ἠντιβόλει καὶ ἱκέτευεν, Lys. i. 29. Παραιτεῖσθαι ὅπως αὐτῶν μὴ καταψηφίσησθε. Ant. i. 12. Δεήσεται δ᾽ ὑμῶν ὅπως δίκην μὴ δῷ. Ib. 23 : so αἰτοῦμαι ὅπως δῷ, Ibid. Διακελεύονται ὅπως τιμωρήσεται πάντας τοὺς τοιούτους. Plat. Rep. 549 E. Παραγγέλλει ὅπως μὴ ἔσονται. Ib. 415 B. Ἔμοιγε ἀπηγόρευες ὅπως μὴ τοῦτο ἀποκρινοίμην (fut. opt.) Ib. 339 A. Ἀπειρημένον αὐτῷ ὅπως μηδὲν ἐρεῖ ὧν ἡγεῖται, *when he is forbidden to say a word of what he believes.* Ib. 337 E.

356. This is rare in Homer ; but twice in the Odyssey λίσσομαι has an object clause with ὅπως :—

Λίσσεσθαι δέ μιν αὐτὸς ὅπως νημερτέα εἴπῃ, *and implore him yourself to speak the truth.* Od. iii. 19. (Compare the regular construction, οὐδέ σε λίσσομαι μένειν. Il. i. 174.) Λίσσετο δ᾽ αἰεὶ Ἥφαιστον κλυτοεργὸν ὅπως λύσειεν Ἄρηα, *he implored him to liberate Ares.* Od. viii. 344.

357. Λίσσομαι with ἵνα and the subjunctive is found in Od. iii. 327 : λίσσεσθαι δέ μιν αὐτὸς ἵνα νημερτὲς ἐνίσπῃ, *and implore him yourself that he may speak the truth.* With this we may compare Dem. xvi. 28, δῆλοι ἔσονται οὐχ ἵνα Θεσπιαὶ κατοικισθῶσι μόνον ποιούμενοι τὴν σπουδήν, *it will be evident that they take an interest not merely in having Thespiae established;* in both cases the object clause falls into the construction of a pure final clause. This is very rare in classic Greek ; but it reappears in the later language, as in the New Testament: thus ἐντολὴν καινὴν δίδωμι ὑμῖν, ἵνα ἀγαπᾶτε ἀλλήλους, *a new commandment I give unto you, that ye love one another,* Ioh. Evang. xiii. 34. So ἐδεήθην ἵνα ἐκβάλλωσιν, Luc. ix. 40. Compare the Latin, *rogat ut liceat.*

358. In Od. xvii. 362 we find ὤτρυν᾽ ὡς ἂν πύρνα κατὰ μνηστῆ-ρας ἀγείροι, *she exhorted him that he should collect bread among the suitors.* (See 329, 1.)

359. The singular case of ὡς with the subjunctive in Il. i. 558, τῇ σ᾽ οἴω κατανεῦσαι ἐτήτυμον, ὡς Ἀχιλῆα τιμήσῃς, ὀλέσῃς δὲ πολέας ἐπὶ νηυσὶν Ἀχαιῶν, i.e. *I believe that you promised by your nod to honour*

Achilles, etc. has the appearance of indirect discourse; but probably κατανεύω ὡς is used with the same feeling as λίσσομαι ὅπως in 356, *promising to act* here taking the same construction as *entreating to act.* See PIND. Py. i. 72 (in 346). Ὡς, as an adverb of manner, is here clearly on its way to its use in indirect discourse. Some read τιμήσεις and ὀλέσεις.

360. A singular use of ὅπως and the future indicative with δεῖ σε in place of the regular infinitive occurs in SOPH. Aj. 556, δεῖ σε ὅπως δείξεις, for δεῖ σε δεῖξαι, and Ph. 54, τὴν Φιλοκτήτου σε δεῖ ψυχὴν ὅπως λόγοισιν ἐκκλέψεις λέγων. So Cratinus, Fr. 108, δεῖ σ' ὅπως εὐσχήμονος ἀλεκτρυόνος μηδὲν διοίσεις. This would be like δέομαι ὅπως (355) except for the object σέ, which is like σέ in δεῖ σε τούτου, the ὅπως clause representing the genitive.

Object Infinitive and Indirect Questions.

361. Some verbs which regularly take an object clause with ὅπως sometimes take an object infinitive, which may have the article τοῦ or τό. (See 373 and 374.) *E.g.*

Ἀεί τινα ἐπεμέλοντο σφῶν αὐτῶν ἐν ταῖς ἀρχαῖς εἶναι, *they always took care that one of their own number should be in the offices* (where we should expect ὅπως τις ἔσται or ἔσοιτο). THUC. vi. 54. Οὐδ' ἐπεμελήθην τοῦ διδασκαλόν μοί τινα γενέσθαι τῶν ἐπισταμένων. XEN. Mem. iv. 2, 4. Τὸ μὲν οὖν λεκτικοὺς γίγνεσθαι τοὺς συνόντας οὐκ ἔσπευδεν. Ib. iv. 3, 1. (See 793.)

362. Verbs signifying *to see* or *look out* (like σκοπῶ) may be followed by an indirect question with εἰ, *whether;* as εἰ ξυμπονήσεις καὶ ξυνεργάσει σκόπει, *see whether you will assist me,* etc. SOPH. Ant. 41.

For independent clauses with ὅπως and ὅπως μή with the future, often explained by an ellipsis of σκόπει or σκοπεῖτε, see 271-283.

Aorist Subjunctive in -σω and -σωμαι.—Dawes's Canon.

363. When an aorist subjunctive active or middle was to be used with ὅπως or ὅπως μή in any construction, the second aorist was preferred to a first aorist in -σω or -σωμαι, if both forms were in use. This preference arose from the great similarity in form between these sigmatic aorists and the future indicative (as between βουλεύσῃ and βουλεύσει, βουλεύσηται and βουλεύσεται). This made it natural also for a writer to avoid those forms of the subjunctive which were nearly identical with the future indicative where the latter could be used as well. This of course does not apply to the first aorist subjunctive passive, which has no resemblance to the future; and there is no reason for applying it to liquid aorists like μείνω and σφήλω.

364. The general rule laid down by Dawes more than a century ago (*Misc. Crit.* pp. 222 and 228), the so-called *Canon Davesianus*, which declared the first aorist subjunctive active and middle a solecism after ὅπως μή and οὐ μή, was extended by others so as to include ὅπως (without μή), and the Greek authors were thoroughly emended to conform to it. As this rule has no other foundation than the accidental circumstance just mentioned (363), it naturally fails in many cases, in some of which even emendation is impossible. In the first place, there is no reason for applying the rule to pure final clauses, in which the future indicative is exceptional (324); and here it is now generally abandoned in theory, though not always in practice. There is, therefore, no objection whatever to such sentences as these : ὧν ἕνεκα ἐπιταθῆναι, ὅπως ἀπολαύσωμεν καὶ ὅπως γενώμεθα, XEN. Cyr. vii. 5, 82 ; ἐκκλησίαν ξυνήγαγον, ὅπως ὑπομνήσω καὶ μέμψωμαι, THUC. ii. 60 ; and τὴν ἀγορὰν ἐπὶ τὴν θάλασσαν κομίσαι, ὅπως παρὰ τὰς ναῦς ἀριστοποιήσωνται, καὶ δι᾽ ὀλίγου τοῖς Ἀθηναίοις ἐπιχειρῶσιν, THUC. vii. 39, in which the best Mss. have the subjunctive. Indeed, where the reading is doubtful, the subjunctive should be preferred in these cases. Secondly, in independent prohibitions with ὅπως μή, although the future is the regular form, there is less objection to the subjunctive (even the first aorist) than in positive commands with simple ὅπως, since the analogy of the common μὴ ποιήσῃς τοῦτο, do not do this, supports ὅπως μὴ ποιήσῃς τοῦτο in the same sense (283). There is no such analogy, however, to justify such a positive command as ὅπως ποιήσῃς τοῦτο, do this, and this form has much less manuscript authority to rest on. Thirdly, in the case of οὐ μή, if both constructions (denials and prohibitions) are explained on the same principle, no reason exists for excluding the subjunctive from either ; and it cannot be denied that both the first and the second aorist subjunctive are amply supported by the manuscripts. (See 301.) Fourthly, in object clauses with ὅπως there is so great a preponderance of futures over subjunctives, that the presumption in all doubtful cases is here in favour of the future, as it is in favour of the subjunctive in pure final clauses. A much stronger case, therefore, is made out by those who (like Weber and most modern editors) change all sigmatic aorist subjunctives in this construction to futures. Some cases, however, resist emendation ; as XEN. An. v. 6, 21, κελεύουσι προστατεῦσαι ὅπως ἐκπλεύσῃ ἡ στρατιά, where we cannot read ἐκπλεύσει, as the future is ἐκπλεύσομαι or ἐκπλευσοῦμαι. In DEM. i. 2, all Mss. except one read παρασκευάσασθαι τὴν ταχίστην ὅπως ἐνθένδε βοηθήσητε καὶ μὴ πάθητε ταὐτόν, and it seems very arbitrary to change βοηθήσητε to βοηθήσετε and leave πάθητε. But a few cases like these weigh little against the established usage of the language, and we must perhaps leave the venerable *Canon Davesianus* undisturbed in the single department of object clauses with ὅπως, although we may admit an occasional exception even there.

See *Transactions of the American Philological Association for* 1869-70, pp. 46-55, where this question is discussed more fully.

C. CLAUSES WITH μή AFTER VERBS OF FEARING, ETC.

365. Verbs and phrases which express or imply *fear, caution,* or *danger* take μή, *lest* or *that,* with the subjunctive if the leading verb is primary, and with the optative if the leading verb is secondary. The subjunctive can also follow secondary tenses to retain the mood in which the object of the fear originally occurred to the mind.

Mή (like Latin *ne*) denotes fear that something *may happen* which is *not desired;* μὴ οὐ (*ut = ne non*) denotes fear that something *may not happen* which *is desired. E.g.*

Φοβοῦμαι μὴ γένηται (vereor *ne* accidat), *I fear that it may happen:* φοβοῦμαι μὴ οὐ γένηται (vereor *ut* accidat), *I fear that it may not happen.* Δείδω μὴ θήρεσσιν ἕλωρ καὶ κύρμα γένωμαι. Od. v. 473. Δείδω μὴ οὔ τίς τοι ὑπόσχηται τόδε ἔργον. Il. x. 39. (This is the only case of μὴ οὐ in these sentences in Homer. The next that are found are EUR. And. 626, El. 568, Phoen. 263. See 264, above.) Οὐ φοβῇ μή σ᾽ ᾿Αργος ἀποκτεῖναι θέλῃ. EUR. Or. 770. Ποῖον ἔθνος οὐ δοκεῖ ὑπερητήσειν φοβούμενον μή τι πάθῃ; XEN. Cyr. i. 6, 10. Φροντίζω μὴ κράτιστον ᾖ μοι σιγᾶν. Id. Mem. iv. 2, 39. Φυλαττόμενος μὴ δόξῃ μανθάνειν τι. Ib. iv. 2, 3. Δέδοικα μὴ οὐδ᾽ ὅσιον ᾖ ἀπαγορεύειν. PLAT. Rep. 368 B. Τὰ περὶ τῆς ψυχῆς πολλὴν ἀπιστίαν παρέχει τοῖς ἀνθρώποις, μὴ ἐπειδὰν ἀπαλλαγῇ τοῦ σώματος οὐδαμοῦ ἔτι ᾖ, ἀλλὰ διαφθείρηταί τε καὶ ἀπολλύηται. Id. Phaed. 70 A. Οὐκοῦν νῦν καὶ τοῦτο κίνδυνος, μὴ λάβωσι προστάτας αὐτῶν τινας τούτων, *there is danger of this, that they may take,* etc. XEN. An. vii. 7, 31. Κίνδυνός ἐστι, μὴ μεταβάλωνται καὶ γένωνται μετὰ τῶν πολεμίων. ISOC. xiv. 38. ᾿Οκνῶ μή μοι ὁ Λυσίας ταπεινὸς φανῇ. PLAT. Phaedr. 257 C. Εὐλαβοῦ δὲ μὴ φανῇς κακὸς γεγώς. SOPH. Tr. 1129. Οὐδὲν δεινοὶ ἔσονται μὴ βοηθέωσι ταύτῃ. HDT. vii. 235. ῾Υποπτεύομεν καὶ ὑμᾶς μὴ οὐ κοινοὶ ἀποβῆτε. THUC. iii. 53. Αἰσχυνόμενος μὴ φορτικῶς σκοπῶμεν. PLAT. Theaet. 183 E. Οἱ μῦθοι στρέφουσιν αὐτοῦ τὴν ψυχήν, μὴ ἀληθεῖς ὦσι, *torment his soul with fear lest they may prove true* (92). Id. Rep. 330 D.

Δείσας μή πώς οἱ ἐρυσαίατο νεκρὸν ᾿Αχαιοί. Il. v. 298. ῎Αζετο γὰρ μὴ Νυκτὶ θοῇ ἀποθύμια ἔρδοι. Il. xiv. 261. ᾿Εγὼ γὰρ ἤμην ἐκπεπληγμένη φόβῳ, μή μοι τὸ κάλλος ἄλγος ἐξεύροι ποτέ. SOPH. Tr. 24. ῎Εδεισαν οἱ ῞Ελληνες μὴ προσάγοιεν πρὸς τὸ κέρας καὶ αὐτοὺς κατακόψειαν. XEN. An. i. 10, 9. Οὐκέτι ἐπετίθεντο, δεδοικότες μὴ ἀποτμηθείησαν. Ib. iii. 4, 29. ῎Εδεισαν μὴ λύττα τις ὥσπερ κυσὶν ἡμῖν ἐμπεπτώκοι. Ib. v. 7, 26. ῾Υποπτεύσας μὴ τὴν θυγατέρα λέγοι, ἤρετο, *having suspected that he might mention his daughter.* Id. Cyr. v. 2, 9. ᾿Ηθύμησάν τινες, ἐννοούμενοι μὴ τὰ ἐπιτήδεια οὐκ ἔχοιεν ὁπόθεν λαμβάνοιεν. Id. An. iii. 5, 3. Οὐδεὶς

γὰρ κίνδυνος ἐδόκει εἶναι μή τις ἄνω πορευομένων ἐκ τοῦ ὄπισθεν ἐπί-
σποιτο. Ib. iv. 1, 6.

Οἱ Φωκαιέες τὰς νήσους οὐκ ἐβούλοντο πωλέειν, δειμαίνοντες μὴ
ἐμπόριον γένωνται. HDT. i. 165. Τῷ γὰρ δεδιέναι μὴ λόγοις ἦσ-
σους ὦσι, τολμηρῶς πρὸς τὰ ἔργα ἐχώρουν. THUC. iii. 83. Περιδεὴς
γενόμενος μὴ ἐπιπλεύσωσιν αἱ νῆες. Id. iii. 80. Ἔδεισα μὴ
Τροίαν ἀθροίσῃ καὶ ξυνοικίσῃ πάλιν. EUR. Hec. 1138. Οἱ θεώμενοι
ἐφοβοῦντο μή τι πάθῃ. XEN. Symp. ii. 11. Δῆλος ἦν πᾶσιν
(Κῦρος) ὅτι ὑπερεφοβεῖτο μή οἱ ὁ πάππος ἀποθάνῃ. Id. Cyr. i.
4, 2.

For the present subjunctive in these sentences denoting what *may
hereafter prove* to be an object of fear, see 92.

366. The manner in which this complex sentence expressing fear
was developed from an independent sentence like μὴ νῆας ἕλωσι, *may
they not seize the ships*, and a preceding verb of fearing like δείδω, the
two gradually becoming one sentence, has already been explained (307).
As the fear and the desire to avert the cause of fear are both implied
in μή with the subjunctive, it is not strange that this expression can
follow verbs like ὁρῶ and οἶδα which do not imply fear in themselves;
as ἐξελθών τις ἴδοι, μὴ δὴ σχεδὸν ὦσι κιόντες, *let some one go out and see
that they do not approach near* (cf. videat ne accedant) ; originally, *let
some one go out and look to it : may they not approach*, Od. xxiv. 491.
So οὐδέ τι ἴδμεν, μή πως καὶ διὰ νύκτα μενοινήσωσι μάχεσθαι, *nor do
we know any way to prevent their being impelled to fight even during the
night ;* originally, *nor have we any knowledge : may they not be impelled
to fight*, Il. x. 100. See also PLAT. Phaed. 91 D, τόδε ἄδηλον παντί,
μὴ πολλὰ σώματα κατατρίψασα ἡ ψυχὴ τὸ τελευταῖον αὐτὴ ἀπολλύηται, i.e. *no one knows any security against the soul itself finally perishing*,
etc. The indirect question sometimes used in translating such a clause
with μή, as *whether they may not approach* or *whether they may not be
impelled*, is merely an attempt to express the hesitation which the
apprehension involves, as there can be, of course, no real indirect
question. See especially the cases of μή with the present indicative
(369, 1), which are often called interrogative. See the corresponding
construction in 492.

367. (*Future Indicative.*) Sometimes, though seldom, μή has
the future indicative after verbs of fearing. The examples are :—

Φρὴν ἀμύσσεται φόβῳ, μὴ πόλις πύθηται . . . καὶ τὸ Κισσίων
πόλισμ᾽ ἀντίδουπον ἄσεται, βυσσίνοις δ᾽ ἐν πέπλοις πέσῃ λακίς.
AESCH. Pers. 115. Ταῦτ᾽ οὖν φοβοῦμαι, μὴ πόσις μὲν Ἡρακλῆς ἐμὸς
καλεῖται (fut.), τῆς νεωτέρας δ᾽ ἀνήρ. SOPH. Tr. 550. Δέδοικα μὴ
ἄλλου τινὸς μεθέξω. XEN. Cyr. ii. 3, 6. Φοβοῦμαι δὲ μή τινας
ἡδονὰς ἡδοναῖς εὑρήσομεν ἐναντίας. PLAT. Phil. 13 A. Ἀλλὰ
(φοβερὸν καὶ σφαλερὸν) μὴ σφαλεὶς κείσομαι. Id. Rep. 451 A.
(The last two examples are not given by Weber.)

For three cases of μή with the future optative after past tenses of
verbs of fearing, representing the future indicative, see 131.

368. The particles ἄν and κέ are never used with μή and the subjunctive. But a potential optative with ἄν can follow μή after a verb expressing fear or anxiety, after both primary and secondary tenses (168). *E.g.*

Δέδοικα γὰρ μὴ πρῷ λέγοις ἄν τὸν πόθον τὸν ἐξ ἐμοῦ, *I fear that you might perhaps tell.* SOPH. Tr. 631. Οὔτε προσδοκία οὐδεμία (ἦν) μὴ ἄν ποτε οἱ πολέμιοι ἐπιπλεύσειαν. THUC. ii. 93. Ἐκεῖνο ἐννοῶ μὴ λίαν ἄν ταχὺ σωφρονισθείην, *lest (in that case) I should be very soon brought to my senses.* XEN. An. vi. 1, 28. Δεδιότες μὴ καταλυθείη ἄν ὁ δῆμος. LYS. xiii. 51.

369. (*Present and Past Tenses of Indicative with μή.*) Verbs of fearing may refer to present or past objects. (See 308.) Μή can therefore be used with the present and past tenses of the indicative after these verbs.

1. Μή with the present indicative expresses a fear that something *is now going on. E.g.*

Δέδοικα μὴ πληγῶν δέει, *I am afraid that you need blows.* AR. Nub. 493. Ὁρῶμεν μὴ Νικίας οἴεταί τι λέγειν, *let us be cautious lest Nicias is thinking that he says something.* PLAT. Lach. 196 C. (Here οἴηται would have meant *lest Nicias may think*, in the future.) Ὅρα μὴ ἐκεῖνον κωλύει. Id. Charm. 163 A. Φοβεῖσθε μὴ δυσκολώτερόν τι νῦν διάκειμαι ἢ ἐν τῷ πρόσθεν βίῳ, *you are afraid that I am now in a more peevish state of mind than I used to be in* (where the subjunctive would have been future, *lest I may hereafter be*). Id. Phaed. 84 E. Ἐπίσχες, ὡς ἄν προὐξερευνήσω στίβον, μή τις πολιτῶν ἐν τρίβῳ φαντάζεται, κἀμοὶ μὲν ἔλθῃ φαῦλος ὡς δούλῳ ψόγος. EUR. Phoen. 92. (Here μὴ φαντάζεται means *lest any one is now to be seen;* and μὴ ἔλθῃ, *lest any report may come hereafter.*) Ἀλλ' εἰσόμεσθα μή τι καὶ κατάσχετον κρυφῇ καλύπτει καρδίᾳ θυμουμένη, δόμους παραστείχοντες. SOPH. Ant. 1253. (The idea is, *we shall learn the result of our anxiety lest she is concealing*, etc.[1]) Κἀμαντῆς πέρι θέλω πυθέσθαι, μὴ 'πὶ τοῖς πάλαι κακοῖς προσκείμενόν τι πῆμα σὴν δάκνει φρένα, *and I wish to inquire about myself, (in fear) lest*, etc. EUR. Her. 481. Ἄναξ, ἐμοί τοι, μή τι καὶ θεήλατον τοὔργον τόδ', ἡ ξύννοια βουλεύει πάλαι. SOPH. Ant. 278. (The idea is, *my mind has long been deliberating in anxiety lest this is the work of the Gods*, ἐστίν being understood after μή.[2]) Ὅρα, φυλάσσου, μή τις ἐν στίβῳ βροτῶν (sc. ἐστιν). EUR. I. T. 67.

---

[1] In this passage and the following, if anywhere, it would seem necessary to admit the *interrogative* force often ascribed to μή. But here, as elsewhere, it is plain that the dependent clause with μή expresses the object of an apprehension. To establish μή as an interrogative, meaning *whether*, μή should not only follow a verb like οἶδα, but also be followed by a clause expressing no object of *apprehension*, like εἰσόμεσθα μὴ οἱ φίλοι ζῶσιν, *we shall learn whether our friends are now living;* but no such example can be found in classic Greek. The use of εἰ, *whether*, after verbs of fearing (376) shows how the Greeks expressed an indirect question in such cases.

[2] That this is the correct explanation, and that we need not emend the

2. Μή with the perfect indicative expresses a fear that something *has already happened.* The difference between this and the perfect subjunctive is often very slight, the latter expressing rather a fear that something may hereafter prove to have happened (103). *E.g.*

Νῦν δὲ φοβούμεθα μὴ ἀμφοτέρων ἅμα ἡμαρτήκαμεν, *but now we fear that we have missed both at once.* THUC. iii. 53. (The perfect subjunctive here would mean *lest it may hereafter prove that we have missed.*) Δέδοικα μὴ λελήθαμεν (τὴν εἰρήνην) ἐπὶ πολλῷ ἄγοντες, *I fear that we have been unconsciously enjoying peace borrowed at high interest.* DEM. xix. 99. Φοβοῦμαι μὴ λόγοις τισὶ ψευδέσιν ἐντετυχή- καμεν. PLAT. Lys. 218 D.

3. Μή can be used with the imperfect or the aorist indicative, to express fear that something *happened in past time.*

Δείδω μὴ δὴ πάντα θεὰ νημερτέα εἶπεν, *I fear that all that the Goddess said was true.* Od. v. 300. Ἀλλ᾽ ὅρα μὴ παίζων ἔλεγεν, *but be careful lest he was speaking in jest.* PLAT. Theaet. 145 B.

370. (Ὅπως μή *for* μή *with Verbs of Fearing.*) Verbs denoting *fear* and *caution* are sometimes followed by an object clause with ὅπως μή and the future indicative, the subjunctive, or the optative, like verbs of *striving*, etc. (339). It will be noticed that ὅπως μή here is exactly equivalent to μή in the ordinary construction, so that φοβοῦμαι ὅπως μὴ γενήσεται (or γένηται) means *I fear that it will happen* (not *I fear that it will not happen*). *E.g.*

Δέδοικ᾽ ὅπως μὴ ᾽κ τῆς σιωπῆς τῆσδ᾽ ἀναρρήξει (Laur. ἀναρρήξῃ) κακά, *I fear that a storm of evil will burst forth from this silence.* SOPH. O. T. 1074 (the earliest example). Τοῦ δαίμονος δέδοιχ᾽ ὅπως μὴ τεύξομαι κακοδαίμονος, *I fear that the luck that I shall get will be bad luck.* AR. Eq. 112. Εὐλαβούμενοι ὅπως μὴ οἰκήσομαι. PLAT. Phaed. 91 C. Δέδοικα ὅπως μὴ ἀνάγκη γενήσεται, *I fear that there may be a necessity.* DEM. ix. 75. Οὐ φοβεῖ ὅπως μὴ ἀνόσιον πρᾶγμα τυγ- χάνῃς πράττων; PLAT. Euthyph. 4 E. Φυλάττου ὅπως μὴ εἰς τοὐναντίον ἔλθῃς. XEN. Mem. iii. 6, 16. Ἡδέως ἂν (θρέψαιμι τὸν ἄνδρα), εἰ μὴ φοβοίμην ὅπως μὴ ἐπ᾽ αὐτόν με τράποιτο. Ib. ii. 9, 3. Τοῖς πρεσβυτέροις ἀντιπαρακελεύομαι μὴ καταισχυνθῆναι ὅπως μὴ δόξει μαλακὸς εἶναι, i.e. *not to be shamed into fear lest he may seem to be weak.* THUC. vi. 13.

Compare the corresponding use of μή for ὅπως μή in ordinary object clauses, especially with ὁρῶ and σκοπῶ, which belong equally to both classes, B and C. (See 354.)

371. (*Indirect Discourse with* ὡς *or* ὅπως.) In curious contrast

passage so as to read τοὔργον τόδ᾽ ᾗ, ξύννοια βουλεύει πάλαι, is suggested by the scholion: ἡ σύννοια μοι βουλεύεται καὶ οἴεται μὴ καὶ θεηλατόν ἐστι τὸ πρᾶγμα. So perhaps we should read φοβεῖσθαι μή τι δαιμόνιον τὰ πράγματα ἐλαύνει (vulg. ἐλαύνῃ) in DEM. ix. 54 (with Cod. A). But the subjunctive in both passages might be explained on the principle of 92.

with the preceding construction with ὅπως μή for μή (370) is that by which verbs of fearing sometimes take the construction of ordinary indirect discourse. Here ὡς and even ὅπως, *that*, may introduce the object of the fear, thus taking the place of μή in the common construction. This apparently occurs only when the leading verb is negatived. *E.g.*

Μὴ δείσῃς ποθ' ὡς γέλωτι τοὐμὸν φαιδρὸν ὄψεται κάρα, *do not fear that she will ever see my face joyful* (= μὴ ἴδῃ). Soph. El. 1309 : so 1426. Ἀνδρὸς μὴ φοβοῦ ὡς ἀπορήσεις ἀξίου, *do not fear that you will be at a loss.* Xen. Cyr. v. 2, 12. (Here the direct discourse would be ἀπορήσω, *I shall be at a loss.*) Μὴ δείσητε ὡς οὐχ ἡδέως καθευδήσετε, *do not fear that you will not sleep sweetly.* Id. vi. 2, 30. (Here μὴ οὐχ would be the ordinary expression.) Οὐ τοῦτο δέδοικα, ὡς ἐὰν ἀκροᾶσθε αὐτῶν ἀποψηφιεῖσθε, *I have no fear of this, that you will acquit them if you hear them.* Lys. xxvii. 9. Μὴ τρέσῃς ὅπως σέ τις ἀποσπάσει βίᾳ, *that any one shall tear you away by force.* Eur. Her. 248. Μὴ φοβεῦ μήτε ἐμέ, ὥς σεο πειρώμενος λέγω λόγον τόνδε, μήτε γυναῖκα τὴν ἐμήν, μή τί τοι ἐξ αὐτῆς γένηται βλάβος, *do not fear either that I am saying this to try you* (ὡς λέγω), *or lest any harm shall come* (μὴ γένηται). Hdt. i. 9. (Here the two constructions after φοβεῦ make the principle especially clear.)

In all these cases μή or ὅπως μή would be regular, and exactly equivalent to ὡς and ὅπως here. In the same way, we say in English *he fears lest this may happen* and *he fears that this may happen* in the same sense. In Greek we might have μὴ τρέσῃς ὅπως μή σέ τις ἀποσπάσει (370) in the same sense as μὴ τρέσῃς ὅπως σέ τις ἀποσπάσει (above).

372. (*Infinitive.*) The future infinitive may stand in indirect discourse after verbs of fearing, to represent a future indicative of the direct course. *E.g.*

Οὐ φοβούμεθα ἐλασσώσεσθαι, *we are not afraid that we shall have the worst of it.* Thuc. v. 105. (Here μή with the subjunctive would be the regular form.)

373. The present or aorist infinitive (*without* μή), not in indirect discourse, may follow verbs of fearing, to denote the *direct object* of the fear; as in English, *I fear to go.* This infinitive may have the article. *E.g.*

Φοβοῦμαι οὖν διελέγχειν σε, μὴ ὑπολάβῃς, κ.τ.λ., *I am afraid to refute you, lest you may suspect*, etc. Plat. Gorg. 457 E. Φοβήσεται ἀδικεῖν, *he will be afraid to do wrong.* Xen. Cyr. viii. 7, 15. (But φοβήσεται μὴ ἀδικῇ, *he will fear that he may do wrong.*) Δεδιέναι φασκόντων Κερκυραίων ἔχειν αὐτόν. Thuc. i. 136. Οὐ κατέδεισαν ἐσελθεῖν. Id. iv. 110. Πέφρικα Ἐρινὺν τελέσαι τὰς κατάρας, *I shudder at the idea of the Fury fulfilling the curses.* Aesch. Sept. 720. (But in vs. 790, τρέω μὴ τελέσῃ means *I tremble lest she may fulfil*

them.) See also XEN. An. i. 3, 17. Τὸ ἀποθνῄσκειν οὐδεὶς φοβεῖται, τὸ δὲ ἀδικεῖν φοβεῖται. PLAT. Gorg. 522 E.

374. Verbs of *caution* may be followed by an infinitive (with or
without μή), which sometimes has the article; the infinitive or the
infinitive with μή having the same meaning as a clause with μή and
the subjunctive or optative. *E.g.*

Πῶς οὐκ ἄξιον αὐτόν γε φυλάξασθαι τοιοῦτον γενέσθαι; *why
ought he not to guard against becoming such a man himself?* XEN. Mem.
i. 5, 3. (Here γενέσθαι is equivalent to μὴ γένηται.) Φυλαττόμενος
τὸ λυπῆσαί τινα, *taking care to offend no one.* DEM. xviii. 258.
Φυλάσσειν μηδένα περαιοῦσθαι, *to guard against any one's crossing over.*
THUC. vii. 17. Φυλαττόμενον καὶ προορώμενον μὴ καταισχῦναι
ταύτην. DEM. xxv. 11. (For μή in this construction see 815, 1.)
In THUC. vii. 77, we find the infinitive with ὥστε after φυλάσσω.

375. Κίνδυνός ἐστι, the principal expression denoting *danger*, which
takes μή and a finite verb, is quite as regularly followed by the infinitive. *E.g.*

Οὐ σμικρὸς κίνδυνός ἐστιν ἐξαπατηθῆναι, *there is no little danger
of their being deceived.* PLAT. Crat. 436 B.

Κινδυνεύω is regularly followed by the infinitive (747).

376. (*Indirect Questions.*) Verbs of *fearing* may be followed by an
indirect question introduced by εἰ, *whether,* or by some other interrogative. Ὅπως as an interrogative here must not be confounded
with ὅπως as a conjunction. *E.g.*

Οὐ δέδοικα εἰ Φίλιππος ζῇ, ἀλλ᾽ εἰ τῆς πόλεως τέθνηκε τὸ τοὺς
ἀδικοῦντας μισεῖν καὶ τιμωρεῖσθαι, *I have no fear (on the question)
whether Philip is alive; but I have fear (about this), whether our city's
habit of hating and punishing evil-doers is dead.* DEM. xix. 289. Φόβος
εἴ μοι ζῶσιν οὓς ἐγὼ θέλω. EUR. Her. 791. Φέρουσά σοι νέους ἥκω
λόγους, φόβῳ μὲν εἴ τις δεσποτῶν αἰσθήσεται, *through fear whether
any one will perceive it* (where μὴ αἴσθηται would have meant *lest any
one shall perceive it*). EUR. Andr. 60. See XEN. Cyr. vi. 1, 17. Φο-
βοῦνται ὅποι ποτὲ προβήσεται ἡ τοῦ ἀνδρὸς δύναμις. XEN. Hell. vi.
1, 14. (The direct question would be ποῖ προβήσεται;) Τὴν θεὸν
δ᾽ ὅπως λάθω δέδοικα, *I am in fear (about the question) how I shall
escape the Goddess.* EUR. I. T. 995. (The direct question was πῶς
λάθω; 287.) So SOPH. Ph. 337. Ἀπορoῦντες πῶς χρὴ ἀπειθεῖν,
φοβούμενοι δὲ πῶς χρὴ ἀπειλοῦντι ὑπακοῦσαι. XEN. Cyr. iv. 5, 19.

377. (*Causal* ὅτι.) Verbs of *fearing* may be followed by ὅτι, *because,*
and an ordinary causal sentence with the indicative (713). *E.g.*

Οὐκ ἄξιον διὰ τοῦτο φοβεῖσθαι τοὺς πολεμίους, ὅτι πολλοὶ τυγ-
χάνουσιν ὄντες, *to fear them, because they happen to be many.* ISOC.
vi. 60. Φοβουμένης τῆς μητρὸς, ὅτι τὸ χωρίον ἐπυνθάνετο νοσῶδες
εἶναι. Id. xix. 22. Ὅτι δὲ πολλῶν ἄρχουσι, μὴ φοβηθῆτε, ἀλλὰ
πολὺ μᾶλλον διὰ τοῦτο θαρρεῖτε, *do not be afraid because they rule
many,* etc. XEN. Hell. iii. 5, 10. Ἐφοβεῖτο, ὅτι ὀφθήσεσθαι ἔμελλε
τὰ βασίλεια οἰκοδομεῖν ἀρχόμενος, *he was afraid, because he was about*

to be seen, beginning to build the palace. Id. Cyr. iii. 1, 1. Φοβούμενος
τὸ κάεσθαι καὶ τὸ τέμνεσθαι, ὅτι ἀλγεινόν, *fearing them because they
are painful.* PLAT. Gorg. 479 A. So THUC. vii. 67.

SECTION VI.

Conditional Sentences.

378. A conditional sentence consists of two clauses, a
dependent clause containing the condition, which usually
precedes and is called the *protasis*, and the leading clause
containing the conclusion, which is called the *apodosis.*
The protasis is regularly introduced by the particle εἰ, *if*,
negatively εἰ μή.

379. Αἰ is a Doric and Aeolic form for εἰ, and is sometimes used in
epic poetry in the forms αἴθε and αἰ γάρ, and less frequently in αἴ κε.[1]

380. The name protasis is often restricted to clauses introduced by a particle meaning *if.* But it applies equally to all
conditional relative and temporal clauses (520), and it properly
includes all clauses which naturally precede their leading clauses
in the order of thought, as ἐπεὶ ᾔσθετο τοῦτο, ἀπῆλθεν, *after he
perceived this, he departed.* Such a clause may still be called a
protasis, even when it follows its leading clause, provided the
order of thought is not changed.

381. The adverb ἄν (epic κέ or κέν, Doric κά) is regularly joined with εἰ in the protasis when the verb is in
the subjunctive, εἰ with ἄν (ă) forming the compound ἐάν,
ἤν, or ἄν (ā). (See 200.) The simple εἰ is used in the
protasis with the indicative and the optative.

The same adverb ἄν is regularly used in the apodosis
with the optative, and also with the past tenses of the indicative when non-fulfilment of the condition is implied.

382. The only Ionic contraction of εἰ ἄν is ἤν, which is used in
Homer and Herodotus. The Attic Greek has ἐάν, ἤν, and ἄν (ā); but

---

[1] Αἰ for εἰ is usually left in Homer by editors as the Mss. give it. But
Bekker (*Homerische Blätter*, pp. 61, 62) quotes Heyne with approval, who
says that no human being can tell why we have αἰ in one place and εἰ in
another. Bekker cites, to illustrate this, αἴθ' οὕτως χόλον τελέσει' Ἀγαμέμνων,
Il. iv. 178, and εἴθ' ὥς τοι γούναθ' ἕποιτο, iv. 313; also αἴ κε θεὸς ἵκηται, Il. v.
129, followed immediately by ἀτὰρ εἴ κε Ἀφροδίτη ἔλθησ' ἐς πόλεμον. Bekker
in his last edition of Homer (1858) gives only εἰ, εἴθε, and εἰ γάρ, without
regard to the Mss. ; and he is followed by Delbrück.

ἄν, *if*, was probably never used by the tragedians or by Thucydides, although the Mss. have it in a few cases.

383. The negative particle of the protasis is regularly μή, that of the apodosis is οὐ.

384. When οὐ is found in a protasis, it is generally closely connected with a particular word (especially the verb), with which it forms a single negative expression; so that its negative force does not (like that of μή) affect the protasis *as a whole*. *E.g.*

Πάντως δήπου (οὕτως ἔχει), ἐάν τε σὺ καὶ Ἄνυτος οὐ φῆτε ἐάν τε φῆτε, *if you deny it, as well as if you admit it.* PLAT. Apol. 25 B. Εἰ τοὺς θανόντας οὐκ ἐᾷς (= κωλύεις) θάπτειν, *if you forbid burying the dead.* SOPH. Aj. 1131. Εἰ μὲν οὐ πολλοὶ (= ὀλίγοι) ἦσαν, καθ' ἕκαστον ἂν περὶ τούτων ἠκούετε, *if there were only a few,* etc. LYS. xiii. 62: cf. 76. Τῶνδε μὲν οὐδὲν ἴσον ἐστὶν, εἴγε ἀφ' ἡμῶν γε τῶν ἐν μέσῳ οὐδεὶς οὐδέποτε ἄρξεται, *there is no fairness in this, if (it is the plan, that) no one is ever to begin with us.* XEN. Cyr. ii. 2, 3.

In all these cases μή could be used, even where οὐ seems especially proper; as in ἄν τ' ἐγὼ φῶ ἄν τε μὴ φῶ, *whether I admit or deny it,* DEM. xxi. 205. See EUR. Hipp. 995, οὐδ' ἦν σὺ μὴ φῇς. The use of μή or οὐ was determined by the feeling of the speaker at the moment as to the scope of his negation. The following example makes the difference between οὐ and μή particularly clear, οὐ affecting merely the verb, and μή affecting the whole clause (including the οὐ): εἰ μὴ Πρόξενον οὐχ ὑπεδέξαντο, ἐσώθησαν ἄν, *if it had not been that they did not receive Proxenus, they would have been saved,* DEM. xix. 74.

385. Εἰ οὐ with the indicative is sometimes found in Homer where the Attic Greek would have εἰ μή; as in εἰ δέ μοι οὐκ ἐπέεσσ' ἐπιπείσεται ἀλλ' ἀλογήσει, Il. xv. 162. See also Il. xx. 129; Od. ii. 274, xii. 382.

386. After verbs expressing *wonder, delight,* and similar emotions (494), where a protasis seems to take the place of a causal sentence, εἰ οὐ can be used, on the principle of 384, though here μή is more common. See examples of εἰ μή under 494; and for εἰ οὐ see Isoc. i. 44, μὴ θαυμάσῃς εἰ πολλὰ τῶν εἰρημένων οὐ πρέπει σοι. See also 387.

387. When two clauses introduced by μέν and δέ depend upon a *single* εἰ which precedes them both, οὐ is used even more frequently than μή; as such clauses have their own construction independently of the εἰ, which merely introduces each of them *as a whole*, not affecting the construction of particular words. *E.g.*

Δεινὸν ἂν εἴη, εἰ οἱ μὲν ἐκείνων ξύμμαχοι ἐπὶ δουλείᾳ τῇ αὐτῶν φέροντες οὐκ ἀπεροῦσιν, ἡμεῖς δ' ἐπὶ τῷ αὐτοὶ σῴζεσθαι οὐκ ἄρα

δαπανήσομεν, it would be a hard thing, if (it is a fact that) their allies
will not refuse, etc. while we will not contribute. THUC. i. 121. Εἶτ'
οὐκ αἰσχρὸν, εἰ τὸ μὲν Ἀργείων πλῆθος οὐκ ἐφοβήθη τὴν Λακεδαιμονίων ἀρχὴν ὑμεῖς δὲ βάρβαρον φοβήσεσθε; is it not then disgraceful,
if (it is true that), while the Argive people did not fear, you are going to
be afraid, etc. DEM. xv. 23. See also PLAT. Phaed. 97 A; LYS. xxx.
32; ISAE. vi. 2; DEM. xxxviii. 18; AESCHIN. iii. 242.

CLASSIFICATION OF CONDITIONAL SENTENCES.

388. The most obvious natural distinction is that of (a)
present and past conditions and (b) *future* conditions. Present and
past conditions (a) are divided into two classes by distinguishing
(1) those which imply nothing as to the fulfilment of the condition from (2) those which imply that the condition is not or
was not fulfilled. Future conditions (b) have two classes (1, 2),
distinguished by the manner in which the supposition is stated.
Class 1 of present and past conditions is further distinguished
on the ground of the *particular* or *general* character of the supposition, as explained below in II. (394).

389. Excluding from the class (a) 1 the present and past
general suppositions which have a peculiar construction (395,
a and b), we have—

I. Four Forms of Ordinary Conditions.

(a) PRESENT AND PAST CONDITIONS.

390. In present or past conditions, the question of fulfilment
has already been decided, but we may or may not wish to imply
by our form of statement how this has been decided. In Greek
(as in English or Latin) we may, therefore, state such a condition
in either of two ways :—

1. We may *simply state* a present or past condition, implying
nothing as to its fulfilment ; as *if he is* (now) *doing this*, εἰ τοῦτο
πράσσει,—*if he was doing it*, εἰ ἔπρασσε,—*if he did it*, εἰ ἔπραξε,
—*if he has* (already) *done it*, εἰ πέπραχε,—*if he had* (already) *done
it* (at some past time), εἰ ἐπεπράχει. The apodosis here expresses simply what *is* (*was* or *will be*) the result of the fulfilment of the condition. Thus we may say :—

Εἰ πράσσει τοῦτο, καλῶς ἔχει, *if he is doing this, it is well; εἰ*
πράσσει τοῦτο, ἡμάρτηκεν, *if he is doing this, he has erred; εἰ*
πράσσει τοῦτο, καλῶς ἕξει, *if he is doing this, it will be well.*   Εἰ
ἔπραξε (or ἔπρασσε) τοῦτο, καλῶς ἔχει (εἶχεν, ἔσχεν, or ἕξει), *if he
did this, it is* (*was* or *will be*) *well.*   Εἰ πέπραχε τοῦτο, καλῶς ἕξει, *if*

he has done this, it will be well. So with the other tenses of the indicative in the apodosis. (See 402.)

So in Latin : *Si hoc facit, bene est ; Si hoc fecit, bene erit ;* etc.

2. On the other hand, we may state a present or past condition so as to imply that it *is not* or *was not* fulfilled ; as *if he were (now) doing this,* εἰ τοῦτο ἔπρασσε;—*if he had done this,* εἰ τοῦτο ἔπραξε (both implying the opposite). The apodosis here expresses what *would be* (or *would have been*) the result if the condition *were* (or *had been*) fulfilled. The adverb ἄν in the apodosis distinguishes these forms from otherwise similar forms under (*a*) 1. Thus we may say :—

Εἰ ἔπρασσε τοῦτο, καλῶς ἂν εἶχεν, *if he were (now) doing this, it would be well ;* or *if he had been doing this, it would have been well.*

Εἰ ἔπραξε τοῦτο, καλῶς ἂν ἔσχεν (or ἂν εἶχεν), *if he had done this, it would have been well* (or *it would now be well*). On the other hand, εἰ ἔπραξε τοῦτο, καλῶς ἔσχεν (without ἄν) would mean *if he did this, it was well.* (See 410.)

In Latin : *Si hoc faceret, bene esset* (present); *Si hoc fecisset, bene fuisset* (past).

391. The Greek has no form implying that a condition *is* or *was* fulfilled, and it is hardly conceivable that any language should find such a form necessary or useful.

(*b*) FUTURE CONDITIONS.

392. The question as to the fulfilment of a future condition is still undecided. We may state such a condition in Greek (as in English and Latin) in either of two ways :—

1. We may say *if he shall do this,* ἐὰν πράσσῃ (or πράξῃ) τοῦτο (or, still more vividly, εἰ πράξει τοῦτο), making a distinct supposition of a future case. The apodosis expresses what *will be* the result if the condition shall be fulfilled. Thus we may say :—

’Εὰν πράσσῃ (or πράξῃ) τοῦτο, καλῶς ἕξει, *if he shall do this* (or *if he does this*), *it will be well* (sometimes also εἰ πράξει τοῦτο). (See 444 and 447.) In Latin: *Si hoc faciet* (or *si hoc fecerit*), *bene erit.*

2. We may also say *if he should do this,* εἰ πράσσοι (or πράξειε) τοῦτο, still supposing a case in the future, but less distinctly and vividly than before. The apodosis corresponds to this in form (with the addition of ἄν), and expresses what *would be* the result if the condition should be fulfilled. Thus we may say :—

Εἰ πράσσοι (or πράξειε) τοῦτο, καλῶς ἂν ἔχοι, *if he should do this, it would be well.* (See 455.) In Latin : *Si hoc faciat, bene sit.*

393. The Latin commonly employs the future indicative, *si hoc faciet* (corresponding strictly to εἰ τοῦτο πράξει, *if he shall do this*), or the future perfect, *si hoc fecerit*, to express the form of protasis which the Greek expresses by ἐάν and the subjunctive (ἐὰν τοῦτο πράσσῃ or πράξῃ) ; and it uses the form *si hoc faciat* to represent the Greek εἰ τοῦτο πράσσοι, *if he should do this*.

II. *Present and Past General Suppositions.*

394. The supposition contained in a protasis may be either *particular* or *general*.

A particular supposition refers to a *definite* act or to several definite acts, supposed to occur at some definite time (or times); as *if he (now) has this, he will give it; if he had it, he gave it; if he had had the power, he would have helped me; if he shall receive it (or if he receives it), he will give it; if he should receive it, he would give it.* So *if he always acts justly* (or *if he never commits injustice*), *I honour him; if he acted justly on all these occasions, he will be rewarded.*

A general supposition refers indefinitely to any act or acts of a given class which may be supposed to occur or to have occurred at any time ; as *if ever he receives anything, he (always) gives it; if ever he received anything, he (always) gave it; if he had (on any occasion) had the power, he would (always) have helped me; if ever any one shall (or should) wish to go, he will (or would) always be permitted.* So *if he ever acts justly, I (always) honour him; if he ever acted justly, he was (always) rewarded.*

395. Although this distinction is seen in all classes of conditions, present, past, and future (as the examples show), it is only in present and past conditions which do not imply non-fulfilment (*i.e.* in those of 390, 1) that the Greek distinguishes general from particular suppositions in *construction*. Here, however, we have two classes of conditions which contain only general suppositions.

(*a*) When the apodosis has a verb of present time expressing a customary or repeated action, the protasis may refer (in a general way) to any act or acts of a given class which may be supposed to occur at any time within the period represented in English as present.   Thus we may say :—

Ἐάν τις κλέπτῃ, κολάζεται, *if (ever) any one steals, he is (in all such cases) punished; ἐάν τις πράσσῃ* (or πράξῃ) *τοιοῦτόν τι*, χαλεπαίνομεν αὐτῷ, *if (ever) any one does such a thing, we are (always) angry with him; ἐάν τις τούτου πίῃ, ἀποθνῄσκει, if any one (ever) drinks of this, he dies.* (See 462.)

(*b*) When the apodosis has a verb of past time expressing a customary or repeated action, the protasis may refer (in a general way) to any act or acts of a given class which may be supposed to have occurred at any time in the past. Thus we may say :—

Εἴ τις κλέπτοι, ἐκολάζετο, *if* (*ever*) *any one stole, he was* (*in all such cases*) *punished ;* εἴ τις πράσσοι (or πράξειε) τοιοῦτόν τι, ἐχαλεπαίνομεν αὐτῷ, *if* (*ever*) *any one did such a thing, we were* (*always*) *angry with him ;* εἴ τις τούτου πίοι, ἀπέθνῃσκεν, *if any one* (*ever*) *drank of this, he died.* (See 462.)

396. Although the Latin sometimes agrees with the Greek in distinguishing general conditions from ordinary present and past conditions, using *si faciat* and *si faceret* in a general sense, like ἐὰν πράσσῃ and εἰ πράσσοι above, it yet commonly agrees with the English in not recognising the distinction, and uses the indicative alike in both classes. Even the Greek sometimes (especially in poetry) neglects the distinction, and uses the indicative in these general conditions (467).

397. In external form the general present condition coincides with the more vivid future condition, 392, 1, as both are expressed by ἐάν and the subjunctive, the form of the apodosis alone distinguishing them. But in sense there is a much closer connexion between the general present condition and the ordinary present condition expressed by εἰ and the present indicative, 390, 1, with which in most languages (and sometimes even in Greek) it coincides also in form (see 396). On the other hand, ἐάν with the subjunctive in a future condition agrees substantially in sense with εἰ and the *future* indicative (447), and is never interchangeable with εἰ and the *present* indicative.

ORIGIN OF THE GREEK CONDITIONAL SENTENCE.—EARLY
COMBINATIONS OF εἰ WITH κέ OR ἄν.

398. It is impossible to discuss intelligently the origin of the conditional sentence until the etymology and original meaning of the particles εἰ, αἰ, ἄν, and κέ are determined. On these questions we have as yet little or no real knowledge. The theory of εἰ or αἰ which identifies it with the pronominal stem *sva* (σϝε), Oscan *svai*, and Latin *si*, is perhaps the most common. By this the original meaning of εἰ, or rather of one of its remote ancestors in some primitive language, would be *at a certain time* (or *place*), *in a certain way*.[1] But, even on this theory, we can hardly imagine any form of εἰ as existing in the *Greek* language until the word had passed at least into the relative stage, with the force of *at which time* (or *place*), *in which way, under which circumstances.* It cannot be denied that the strong analogy

---

[1] See Delbrück, *Conj. u. Opt.*, pp. 70, 71, who terms this a " wahrscheinliche positive Vermuthung."

between conditional and relative sentences and the identity of most of their forms give great support to any theory by which the conditional sentence is explained as an outgrowth of the relative, so that the conditional relative sentence is made the original conditional construction. Thus εἰ ἦλθεν might at some time have meant *in the case in which he went*, and εἰ ἔλθῃ, *in the case in which he shall go* (or *in case he shall go*), etc. But here we are on purely theoretical ground ; and we must content ourselves practically with the fact, that in the earliest Greek known to us εἰ was fully established in its conditional sense, like our *if* and Latin *si*.

399. The regular types of the conditional sentence, which are given above (390-395) as they appear in Attic prose, have been mainly sifted from a rich variety of forms which are found in earlier Greek. In Homer we have all tenses of the indicative used as in Attic Greek, except that the imperfect has not yet come to express an unreal *present* condition, but is still confined to the past. The future indicative sometimes has κέ in protasis, and the future with κέ or ἄν can stand in apodosis. The subjunctive in protasis can have εἴ κε (even εἰ ἄν), ἤν, or εἰ alone ; and it can stand in a future apodosis either alone or with ἄν or κέ (like the optative). The optative sometimes has εἴ κε in protasis, and occasionally stands in apodosis without ἄν or κέ. Once we find εἴ κε with the aorist indicative (Il. xxiii. 526).

Thus, while we have in Attic prose two stereotyped forms of future conditional sentences, ἐὰν (ἤν, ἄν) δῷ, ἐλοῦμαι and εἰ δοίη, ἐλοίμην ἄν, we have in Homer ἤν δῷ, εἴ κε δῷ, εἰ δῷ, and εἰ δοίη, εἴ κε δοίη, in protasis ; and ἐλοῦμαι, ἐλοῦμαί κε, ἔλωμαι, ἔλωμαί κε, and ἐλοίμην κε (or ἄν), rarely ἐλοίμην alone, in apodosis ; with every variety of combination of these. (For the details and examples, see 450-454 and 460.)

400. There is a tendency in Homer to restrict the subjunctive with simple εἰ (without κέ or ἄν) to general conditions (468), and a similar but less decided tendency to restrict the subjunctive with conditional relatives without κέ or ἄν to the generic relative construction (538). But the general condition with εἰ appears in Homer in a primitive stage, compared with the corresponding relative construction, which is fully developed. Both subjunctive and optative are freely used in general relative conditions in Homer, as in Attic Greek ; while in general conditions with εἰ the subjunctive occurs only nineteen times and the optative only once (468). On the supposition that the clause with εἰ is derived from the relative clause, this would appear as the ordinary process of development.

401. It is perhaps the most natural view of the various conditional expressions, εἰ, εἴ κε, εἰ ἄν, etc. to suppose that at some early stage the Greek had two perfectly analogous forms in future conditions, one with two subjunctives, and one with two optatives, e.g. εἰ δῷ τοῦτο, ἕλωμαι and εἰ δοίη τοῦτο, ἐλοίμην. The particle κέ would then begin to be allowed in both of these conditions and conclusions, giving to each more distinctly its force as a protasis or an apodosis.[1] It would thus be allowed to say εἴ κε δῷ τοῦτο, ἕλωμαί κε and εἴ κε δοίη τοῦτο, ἐλοίμην κε, both of which forms actually occur in Homer. Gradually the tendencies of the language restricted the use of κέ more and more to the subjunctive in protasis and the optative in apodosis, although for a time the usage was not strict. This state of transition appears in Homer, who preserves even a case of an otherwise extinct use of εἴ κε with the aorist indicative. Shortly before this stage, however, a new tendency was making itself felt, to distinguish the present general condition from the particular in form, the way being already marked out by the conditional relative sentence. As this new expression was to be distinguished from both the really present condition εἰ βούλεται and the future εἴ κε βούληται, the half-way form εἰ βούληται (which had nearly given place to εἴ κε βούληται in future conditions) came into use in the sense *if he ever wishes.*[2] This would soon develop a corresponding form for use after past tenses, εἰ βούλοιτο, *if he ever wished,* of which we see only the first step in Homer, Il. xxiv. 768. (See 468.) It would hardly be possible to keep the two uses of εἰ with the subjunctive distinct in form, and in time the form with κέ (or ἄν) was established in both (381). But we see this process too in transition in Homer, where εἴ κε or some form of εἰ ἄν is used in all future conditions except nine, and has intruded itself into five of the nineteen general conditions. We must suppose a corresponding process in regard to κέ or ἄν in conditional relative clauses to have gone on before the Homeric period, with more complete results.[3] In Attic Greek, except in a few poetic passages, the usage is firmly

---

[1] As I do not profess to have any distinct theory of the origin or the original meaning of either κέ or ἄν, I have not attempted to define their force, except so far as they emphasise what we see by usage may be implied by the sentence without their aid.

[2] Monro (*Hom. Gr.* p. 263) thinks "the primary use of ἄν or κέν is to show that the speaker is thinking of *particular* instances or occasions." If this is so, we should expect these particles to be first used in future conditions, while the later general conditions would first take the simple εἰ, as is here supposed.

[3] See *Am. Jour. Phil.* iii. pp. 441, 442, where Gildersleeve refers to the use of εἰ, ὅτε, etc. with the optative in oratio obliqua, representing ἐάν, ὅταν, etc. with the subjunctive in the direct form, as evidence of an old use of εἰ, ὅτε, etc. with the subjunctive.

established by which the subjunctive in protasis requires ἄν in both particular and general conditions.

I. FOUR FORMS OF ORDINARY CONDITIONAL SENTENCES.

(a) PRESENT AND PAST CONDITIONS.

1. *Simple Suppositions (chiefly Particular).*

402. When the protasis *simply states* a present or past particular supposition, implying nothing as to the fulfilment of the condition, it takes a present or past tense of the indicative with εἰ. Any form of the verb may stand in the apodosis to express the result if the condition is or was fulfilled. *E.g.*

Εἰ ἐβρόντησε, καὶ ἤστραψεν, *if it thundered, it also lightened.* (This implies no opinion of the speaker as to the reality of the thunder.) Εἰ δ᾽ οὕτω τοῦτ᾽ ἐστὶν, ἐμοὶ μέλλει φίλον εἶναι. Il. i. 564. Εἰ τότε κοῦρος ἔα, νῦν αὖτέ με γῆρας ὀπάζει. Il. iv. 321. Εἰ μάλα καρτερός ἐσσι, θεός πού σοι τό γ᾽ ἔδωκεν. Il. i. 178. Εἰ δὲ χρὴ καὶ πὰρ σοφὸν ἀντιφερίξαι, ἐρέω, *but if I must match myself against the wise one, I will speak.* PIND. Py. ix. 54. Εἰ θεοί τι δρῶσιν αἰσχρὸν, οὐκ εἰσὶν θεοί, *if Gods do aught that is base, they are not Gods.* EUR. Bell. Fr. 294. Εἰ ἐγὼ Φαῖδρον ἀγνοῶ, καὶ ἐμαυτοῦ ἐπι- λέλησμαι· ἀλλα γὰρ οὐδέτερά ἐστι τούτων, *if I do not know Phaedrus, I have forgotten myself; but neither of these is the case.* PLAT. Phaedr. 228 A. Εἰ μὲν (᾽Ασκληπιὸς) θεοῦ ἦν, οὐκ ἦν αἰσχροκερδής· εἰ δ᾽ αἰσχροκερδὴς, οὐκ ἦν θεοῦ. Id. Rep. 408 C. Εἰ δὲ ἐκεῖνος ἀσθε- νέστερος ἦν, ἑαυτῷ τοῦ πάθους αἴτιον ἡγήσατο. DEM. xxiii. 54.

403. The imperative, the subjunctive in exhortations or pro- hibitions, the optative in wishes, the potential optative or in- dicative with ἄν, or the infinitive may stand in the apodosis. *E.g.*

᾽Αλλ᾽ εἰ δοκεῖ σοι, στεῖχε, *if thou art resolved, go.* SOPH. Ant. 98. (Here ἐὰν δοκῇ would refer to the future, while εἰ δοκεῖ is strictly present in its time. Cf. Ant. 76.) ᾽Αλλ᾽ εἰ δοκεῖ, πλέωμεν, ὁρμάσθω ταχύς. Id. Ph. 526. Εἰ μὲν ἴστε με τοιοῦτον, . . . μηδὲ φωνὴν ἀνάσχησθε. DEM. xviii. 10. ᾽Αλλ᾽ εἴ που πτωχῶν γε θεοὶ καὶ ἐρινύες εἰσὶν, ᾽Αντίνοον πρὸ γάμοιο τέλος θανάτοιο κιχείη. Od. xvii. 475. ᾽Αλλ᾽ εἰ δοκεῖ σοι ταῦθ᾽, ὑπαί τις ἀρβύλας λύοι τάχος, *but if this pleases you, let some one quickly loose my shoes.* AESCH. Ag. 944. Κάκωτ᾽ ἀπολοίμην, Ξανθίαν εἰ μὴ φιλῶ. AR. Ran. 579. Πολλὴ γὰρ ἂν εὐδαιμονία εἴη περὶ τοὺς νέους, εἰ εἷς μὲν μόνος αὐτοὺς διαφθείρει οἱ δ᾽ ἄλλοι ὠφελοῦσιν. PLAT. Ap. 25 B. See also Il. vi. 128, εἰ . . . εἰλήλουθας, οὐκ ἄν . . . μαχοίμην. Τὸν ῾Υπερείδην, εἴπερ ἀληθῆ μου νῦν κατηγορεῖ, μᾶλλον ἂν εἰκότως ἢ τόνδ᾽ ἐδίωκεν, *if he is now bringing true charges against me, he would have prosecuted Hypereides with much more reason than he does this man.* DEM. xviii. 223. (See 479, 2; 503.)

404. This form of condition may be used even when the supposition is notoriously contrary to fact, if the speaker does not wish to imply this by the construction; as in DEM. xviii. 12, τῶν μέντοι κατηγοριῶν, . . . εἴπερ ἦσαν ἀληθεῖς, οὐκ ἔνι τῇ πόλει δίκην ἀξίαν λαβεῖν, *but if the charges were true* (= *erant*, not *essent*), *the state cannot obtain adequate satisfaction.* So in English, we can say *if three times six are twenty* as well as *if three times six were twenty*, or *if all men are liars* as well as *if all men were liars*,—from different points of view.

405. A present or past general supposition is sometimes expressed by the indicative : see examples in 467. Here the Greek neglects the distinction which it regularly makes between general and particular suppositions of this class.

406. Pindar uses these simple conditions with εἰ and the indicative more than all other forms.[1] But among his forty-eight cases are many general conditions (467), which most writers would have expressed by the subjunctive.

407. (*Future Indicative in Present Suppositions.*) Even the future indicative with εἰ may be used in a present condition, if it expresses merely a *present* intention or necessity that something shall be done hereafter ; as when εἰ τοῦτο ποιήσει means *if he is (now) about to do this,* and not (as it does in an ordinary future condition) *if he shall do this (hereafter).* E.g.

Αἶρε πλῆκτρον, εἰ μαχεῖ, *raise your spur, if you are going to fight.* AR. Av. 759. (Εἰ μαχεῖ in protasis commonly means *if you shall fight*, like ἐὰν μάχῃ.) Ἦ νῦν ἐγὼ μὲν οὐκ ἀνήρ, αὕτη δ᾽ ἀνήρ, εἰ ταῦτ᾽ ἀνατὶ τῇδε κείσεται κράτη, i.e. *if this is to pass unpunished.* SOPH. Ant. 484. Τί διαφέρουσι τῶν ἐξ ἀνάγκης κακοπαθούντων, εἴ γε πεινήσουσι καὶ διψήσουσι καὶ ῥιγώσουσι καὶ ἀγρυπνήσουσι καὶ τἆλλα πάντα μοχθήσουσιν ἑκόντες ; *how do they differ, etc., if they are to suffer hunger, thirst, etc.?* XEN. Mem. ii. 1, 17. So εἰ πόλεμός τε δαμᾷ καὶ λοιμὸς Ἀχαιούς, *if both war and pestilence are to lay the Achaeans low,* Il. i. 61 ; and εἰ διαβληθήσομαι, *if I am to be slandered,* EUR. Hec. 863. In Il. v. 715, ἦ ῥ᾽ ἅλιον τὸν μῦθον ὑπέστημεν Μενελάῳ, . . . εἰ οὕτω μαίνεσθαι ἐάσομεν οὖλον Ἀρῆα, *vain is the word we pledged, if we are to permit,* etc., the verb of the apodosis is past, showing that the condition is not future.

408. It is important to notice that a future indicative of this kind could not be changed to a subjunctive with ἐάν without an entire change of sense and time. It must therefore be distinguished from the future in *future* conditions, where it is generally interchangeable with

[1] See *Am. Jour. Phil.* iii. p. 438.

the subjunctive (447). Here it is nearly equivalent to the periphrastic
future expressed by μέλλω and the infinitive (73), in which the tense
of μέλλω (as in εἰ μέλλουσι τοῦτο ποιεῖν = εἰ τοῦτο ποιήσουσιν)
shows that the condition is really present and not future. So with
the Latin periphrastic future, *si hoc facturus est*.

409. A present condition may be expressed by a potential optative
in the protasis, and a present or past condition by a potential indicative ;
as εἴπερ ἄλλῳ τῳ ἀνθρώπων π ε ι θ ο ί μ η ν ἄ ν, καὶ σοὶ πείθομαι, *if (it is
true that) I would trust any one of mankind, I trust you*, PLAT. Prot. 329
B ; εἰ τοῦτο ἰσχυρὸν ἦν ἄ ν τούτῳ τεκμήριον, κἀμοὶ γενέσθω τεκμήριον,
ὅτι, κ.τ.λ., *if (it is true that) this would have been a strong proof for him
(if he had used it), so let it be a proof for me, that*, etc., DEM. xlix. 58.
(See 458, and other examples in 506.)

2. *With Supposition contrary to Fact.*

410. When the protasis states a present or past supposition, implying that the condition *is not* or *was not* fulfilled, and the apodosis expresses what *would be* (or *would
have been*) the result if that condition were (or had been)
fulfilled, the past tenses of the indicative are used in both
protasis and apodosis, and the apodosis contains the adverb ἄν.

The imperfect here, in either protasis or apodosis, refers
to present time or to an act as going on or repeated in
past time, the aorist to a simple occurrence in past time,
and the (rare) pluperfect to an act completed in past or
present time. *E.g.*

Εἰ τοῦτο ἔπρασσε, καλῶς ἄ ν εἶχ ε ν, *if he were (now) doing this,
it would be well* (implying that he *is not* doing it).   This may also mean
if he had been doing this, it would have been well (implying that he *was
not* doing it).   The context must decide, in each case, to which time
the imperfect refers.   Εἰ τοῦτο ἔπραξε, καλῶς ἄ ν ἔσχ ε ν, *if he had
done this, it would have been well* (implying that he *did not* do it).   Εἰ
τοῦτο ἐπεπράχ ε ι, καλῶς ἄ ν εἶχ ε ν, *if he had finished doing this (now
or at any past time), it would be well* (implying either *he has not* or *he
had not finished it*).

(*Impf. of Present Time.*)   Εἰ δέ μ' ὧδ' ἀεὶ λόγους ἐξῆρχ ε ς, οὐκ ἄ ν
ἦσθα λυπηρὰ κλύειν, *if you always began your talk to me in this way,
you would not be offensive to listen to* (as you are). SOPH. El. 556.   So
El. 992, 1331, O. T. 1511 ; and AESCH. Sept. 662, Ag. 1395.   Καὶ
νῦν εἰ φοβερόν τι ἐνωρῶμεν, πᾶν ἄ ν σοι προεφράζομεν, *if we saw
any cause of alarm, we should tell it all to you*. HDT. i. 120.   Ταῦτα οὐκ
ἂν ἐδύναντο ποιεῖν, εἰ μὴ καὶ διαίτῃ μετρίᾳ ἐχρ ῶ ν τ ο, *they would not
be able to do this, if they did not lead an abstemious life*. XEN. Cyr. i. 2,

16. Εὖ ἴσθ' ὅτι εἴ τι ἐμοῦ ἐκήδου, οὐδενὸς ἂν οὕτω με ἀποστερεῖν ἐφυλάττου ὡς ἀξιώματος καὶ τιμῆς, *if you cared for me at all, you would take precaution,* etc. Ib. v. 5, 34. Πολὺ ἂν θαυμαστότερον ἦν, εἰ ἐτιμῶντο, *it would be much more wonderful, if they were honoured.* Plat. Rep. 489 B. Λέγουσι πάντα ᾗ ἔχει· καίτοι εἰ μὴ ἐτύγχανεν αὐτοῖς ἐπιστήμη ἐνοῦσα, οὐκ ἂν οἷοί τ' ἦσαν τοῦτο ποιήσειν, *they tell everything as it is: and yet if knowledge did not chance to be in them, they could not do this.* Id. Phaed. 73 A. Οὐχ οὕτω δ' ἂν προθύμως ἐπὶ τὸν πόλεμον ὑμᾶς παρεκάλουν, εἰ μὴ τὴν εἰρήνην ἑώρων αἰσχρὰν ἐσομένην, *I should not exhort you, did I not see (as I do),* etc. Isoc. vi. 87.

(*Impf. of Past Time.*) Καὶ ταῦτ' ἂν οὐκ ἔπρασσον, εἰ μή μοι πικρὰς αὐτῷ τ' ἀρὰς ἠρᾶτο, *and this I should never have done, had he not invoked bitter curses on myself.* Soph. O. C. 951. Οὐκ ἂν νήσων ἐκράτει, εἰ μή τι καὶ ναυτικὸν εἶχεν, *he would not have been master of islands, if he had not had also some naval force* (implying ναυτικὸν εἶχεν and νήσων ἐκράτει, *he had a navy, for he was master of islands*). Thuc. i. 9. (Ταῦτα) οὐκ ἂν προέλεγεν, εἰ μὴ ἐπίστευεν ἀληθεύσειν, *he would not have declared these things* (referring to several), *had he not been confident that he should speak the truth.* Xen. Mem. i. 1, 5. Εἰ ἦσαν ἄνδρες ἀγαθοὶ, ὡς σὺ φῇς, οὐκ ἄν ποτε ταῦτα ἔπασχον, *if they had been good men, as you say, they would never have suffered these things* (referring to several cases). Plat. Gorg. 516 E.

(*Aorist of Past Time.*) Εἰ μὴ ὅρκοις ᾑρέθην, οὐκ ἄν ποτ' ἔσχον μὴ οὐ τάδ' ἐξειπεῖν πατρί, *had I not been bound by oaths, I should never have refrained,* etc. Eur. Hipp. 657. Καὶ ἴσως ἂν διὰ ταῦτ' ἀπέθανον, εἰ μὴ ἡ ἀρχὴ διὰ ταχέων κατελύθη. Plat. Ap. 32 D. Τί ποτ' ἂν ἔπαθον ὑπ' αὐτῶν, εἰ πλείω χρόνον ἐπετροπεύθην; εἰ κατελείφθην μὲν ἐνιαύσιος, ἒξ ἔτη δὲ προσεπετροπεύθην ὑπ' αὐτῶν, οὐδ' ἂν τὰ μικρὰ ταῦτα παρ' αὐτῶν ἀπέλαβον. Dem. xxvii. 63. Εἰ τοίνυν ὁ Φίλιππος τότε ταύτην ἔσχε τὴν γνώμην, οὐδὲν ἂν ὧν νυνὶ πεποίηκεν ἔπραξεν, οὐδὲ τοσαύτην ἐκτήσατο δύναμιν. Id. iv. 5.

(*Different tenses in Protasis and Apodosis.*) Εἰ μὴ ὑμεῖς ἤλθετε, ἐπορευόμεθα ἂν ἐπὶ βασιλέα, *if you had not come, we should (now) be on our way to the King.* Xen. An. ii. 1, 4. Ὃ εἰ ἀπεκρίνω, ἱκανῶς ἂν ἤδη παρὰ σοῦ τὴν ὁσιότητα ἐμεμαθήκη, *if you had given this answer, I should have already learned,* etc. Plat. Euthyph. 14 C. Λοιπὸν δ' ἂν ἦν ἡμῖν ἔτι περὶ τῆς πόλεως διαλεχθῆναι τῆς ἡμετέρας, εἰ μὴ προτέρα τῶν ἄλλων τὴν εἰρήνην ἐπεποίητο. (This implies ἀλλὰ τὴν εἰρήνην προτέρα πεποίηται.) Isoc. v. 56. Εἰ γὰρ ἐκ τοῦ παρεληλυθότος χρόνου τὰ δέοντα οὗτοι συνεβούλευσαν, οὐδὲν ἂν ὑμᾶς νῦν ἔδει βουλεύεσθαι, *if they had given the necessary advice in time past, there would now be no need of your deliberating.* Dem. iv. 1. Τῶν ἀδικημάτων ἂν ἐμέμνητο τῶν αὑτοῦ, εἴ τι περὶ ἐμοῦ γ' ἔγραφεν. Id. xviii. 79.

These examples show the fully developed construction, as it appears in the Attic writers and in Herodotus. For the more primitive Homeric usage, see 435 and 438.

411. This construction is equivalent to that of the Latin imperfect and pluperfect subjunctive in protasis and apodosis. With regard to the tenses, the Latin imperfect subjunctive represents the Greek imperfect indicative referring to present time, and rarely that referring to past time; while the Latin pluperfect subjunctive represents the Greek aorist and pluperfect indicative, and also most cases of the Greek imperfect referring to past time.

412. 1. It will be seen that, when this construction is used, it is usually implied not merely that the condition of the protasis is not (or was not) fulfilled but *also* that the action of the apodosis does not (or did not) take place; thus εἰ τοῦτο εἶπον, ἐπείσθη ἄν, *if I had said this, he would have been persuaded*, generally implies not merely that *I did not say this* but also that *he was not persuaded*. But this denial of the apodosis is not an essential character of the construction, as we can see if we change the apodosis to οὐκ ἄν ἐπείσθη, *he would not have been persuaded*, when it is not implied that *he really was persuaded*. We have seen that there is nothing in the nature of the potential indicative which makes a denial of its action necessary (244); and when this form is made the apodosis of an unreal condition, it simply states that something would happen (or would have happened) in a case which did not arise. Denial of the apodosis can follow as a logical inference from denial of the protasis only in the rare cases in which the unreal condition is the only one under which the action of the apodosis could have taken place, as when we say *if the moon had entered the earth's shadow, she would have been eclipsed*, where the denial of either clause carries with it by necessity the denial of the other. But if we say *if it had rained, the ground would be wet*, the denial of the protasis cuts off only one of many conditions under which the ground might be wet. Such sentences as this are, however, very common, though they are not used to prove the opposite of the apodosis (that *the ground is not wet*); but they are arguments in which the apodosis is assumed to be false (on the ground of observation or experience), and from this it is argued that the assumption of the protasis is false; that is, *since the ground is not wet* (as we can see), *it cannot have rained*, which is a good argument. This is the case in Thuc. i. 9, and Plat. Gorg. 516 E (quoted in 410, above); where it is argued that Agamemnon *had a navy* because this was a necessary condition of his ruling islands, and that certain persons were *not good men* because they suffered what they did, the facts of ruling islands and of suffering being assumed in the argument as established on independent evidence. In other cases, where it is stated that the apodosis would follow as a consequence from the fulfilment of the condition, as in Soph. Aj. 45, κἂν ἐξεπράξατ᾽ εἰ κατημέλησ᾽ ἐγώ, *he would even have accomplished it, if I had been careless*, whatever negation of the apodosis is implied (here οὐκ ἐξεπράξατο) comes from a feeling that when the only condition under which it is stated that an action would have taken place fails, there is no reason for believing it to have taken place at all. We may doubt whether any

negation of the apodosis is implied in the *form of expression* in such
cases.   Certainly, in many cases in which the apodosis states a consequence which would follow from the action of an unreal protasis,
this negation is assumed as already known apart from the construction ; thus in SOPH. El. 556 (quoted in 410) the apodosis means *you
would not then be offensive to listen to*, and the only ground on which
we mentally add *as you now are* is our knowledge of Clytaemnestra's
feeling towards Electra.   If the sentence were *if all men began their
speeches politely, they would not be offensive*, we should not think of
supplying *as they now are* without some knowledge of the facts.

2. When the sentence merely affirms or denies that one act, if it
had occurred, would be accompanied by another act, and there is no
necessary relation between the two acts as cause and effect, and there is
no argument drawn from the admitted unreality of the conclusion to
prove the opposite of the condition, no denial of the apodosis is implied
in the expression, although we may know from the context or in some
other way that the action of the apodosis does not (or did not) occur.
Thus in PLAT. Ap. 17 D, εἰ τῷ ὄντι ξένος ἐτύγχανον ὤν, ξυνεγιγνώσκετε δήπου ἄν μοι εἰ ἐν ἐκείνῃ τῇ φωνῇ ἔλεγον, etc., *if I were really a
foreigner, you would surely pardon me if I spoke in my own dialect*, etc.,
it is not implied that *now you do not pardon me*.   We should rather
say that nothing at all is implied beyond the statement *you would
pardon me in that case*.   If the apodosis were *you would not be angry
with me*, the impossibility of understanding *but now you are angry* would
make this plainer.   Again, in XEN. Ἀn. vi. 1, 32, οὐδ' ἂν ἔγωγε
ἐστασίαζον εἰ ἄλλον εἵλεσθε, *neither should I* (any more than Xenophon)
be quarrelsome if you had chosen another man, nothing like στασιάζω is
implied ; on the other hand, any such implication as οὐ στασιάζω
must come from the circumstances of the case, not from the form of
expression.   In SOPH. O. T. 220, οὐ γὰρ ἂν μακρὰν ἴχνευον αὐτός, if
the protasis is εἰ ἴχνευον αὐτός, *if I were undertaking the search by myself*
(*alone*), the apodosis *I should not be very far on the track* does not imply
μακρὰν ἰχνεύω, or anything more than the sentence states.   (See 511.)
Again, in SOPH. Tr. 896, εἰ παροῦσα πλησία ἔλευσσες οἷ' ἔδρασε,
κἄρτ' ἂν ᾤκτισας, the statement does not imply οὐκ ᾤκτισας, although
this may be true.

3. Further, in concessive sentences introduced by καὶ εἰ or εἰ, *even
if* or *although*, or οὐδ' εἰ, *not even if*, where it is stated that something
would be true even in a supposed case (which does not arise), we have
what amounts to a statement that the thing in question would be true
in any case.   Here, therefore, the action of the apodosis is distinctly
affirmed ; as in ISOC. xxi. 11, Νικίας μὲν, εἰ καὶ τὸν ἄλλον χρόνον
εἴθιστο συκοφαντεῖν, τότ' ἂν ἐπαύσατο· Εὐθύνους δὲ, καὶ εἰ μηδὲ
πώποτε διενοήθη ἀδικεῖν, τότ' ἂν ἐπήρθη, i.e. *N. would then have
stopped, while E. would have been urged on, in any case*.   So DEM. xxx.
14, and xl. 23.   See PLAT. Rep. 620 D, τὰ αὐτὰ ἂν ἔπραξε καὶ πρώτη
λαχοῦσα (= καὶ εἰ πρώτη ἔλαχεν), *it would have done the same even if
it had drawn the first choice*.

413. In the unreal conditional sentence, therefore, the unreality of the supposition is always implied, and that of the apodosis is generally either assumed or implied. The implied opposite of an imperfect is always a present or imperfect, that of an aorist is an aorist, and that of a pluperfect is usually a perfect or pluperfect. Thus εἰ ἔπρασσε, when it means *if he were doing*, implies ἀλλ᾽ οὐ πράσσει, *but really he is not doing;* when it means *if he had been doing*, it implies ἀλλ᾽ οὐκ ἔπρασσε, *but really he was not doing:* εἰ μὴ ἔπραξεν, *if he had not done*, implies ἀλλ᾽ ἔπραξεν, *but really he did do:* εἰ ἐπεποιήκει τοῦτο, *if he had already done this*, implies either ἀλλ᾽ οὐ πεποίηκεν, *but really he has not done it*, or ἀλλ᾽ οὐκ ἐπεποιήκει, *but really he had not done it*, according to the context. The aorist, however, is very often used here, as elsewhere, where the pluperfect would express the time intended more exactly ; as in the sentence quoted in 410 from DEM. iv. 5, οὐδὲν ἂν ὧν νυνὶ πεποίηκεν ἔπραξεν, where the perfect πεποίηκεν shows that the pluperfect might have been used for ἔπραξεν (see 58).

414. Sometimes an aorist not referring to past time is found in the apodosis, after a protasis in the imperfect referring to the present. This occurs chiefly in Plato, and generally with εἶπον ἄν, ἀπεκρινάμην ἄν, or a similar verb, meaning *I should at once reply*. The aorist excludes the idea of duration which the imperfect would express, and for the same reason it cannot be strictly present ; in effect it does not differ much from an aorist optative with ἄν, the apodosis really being *the result* (in the case supposed) *would be* (ἦν ἄν) *that I should reply* (εἴποιμι ἄν), etc. E.g.

Εἰ μὲν οὖν σύ με ἠρώτας; τι τῶν νῦν δή, εἶπον ἄν, κ.τ.λ., *if then you were asking me any one of the questions before us, I should (at once) say*, etc. PLAT. Euthyph. 12 D. Ὥσπερ ἂν εἰ ἐτύγχανεν ὢν ὑποδημά-των δημιουργός, ἀπεκρίνατο ἂν δή πού σοι ὅτι σκυτοτόμος, *as, if he chanced to be a maker of shoes, he would answer that he was a cobbler.* Id. Gorg. 447 D. See also PLAT. Symp. 199 D, Men. 72 B, Theag. 123 B ; ANT. Tetr. A. β. 13. In PLAT. Prot. 311 B, C, we have εἴ τίς σε ἤρετο, τί ἂν ἀπεκρίνω; with the answer εἶπον ἂν ὡς, κ.τ.λ., twice, referring to present time ; but in D, εἰ οὖν τις ἡμᾶς ἔροιτο (future), followed by τί ἂν αὐτῷ ἀποκριναίμεθα ;

An example of this is found in SOPH. Ant. 755 : εἰ μὴ πατὴρ ἦσθ᾽, εἶπον ἄν σ᾽ οὐκ εὖ φρονεῖν, *if you were not my father, I should say you were not right in mind.* See EUR. Alc. 125, ἦλθεν ἄν, i.e. *(the result would be that) she would return.* So Alc. 360.

APODOSIS WITHOUT ἄν.—Ἔδει, χρῆν, ETC. WITH THE INFINITIVE.

415. A peculiar form of potential indicative without ἄν con-sists of an infinitive depending on the imperfect of a verb of *obligation, propriety,* or *possibility,* like ἔδει, χρῆν or ἐχρῆν, εἰκὸς ἦν, or προσῆκεν. This expression refers to past or present time, and generally implies a denial of the action of the infinitive. Thus ἔδει τοῦτον ἀποθανεῖν in this idiomatic use means *he ought to have perished (but did not)* ; ἔδει ἡμᾶς τοῦτο ποιεῖν means *we ought to be doing this (but we are not)* or *we ought to have done this (but we did not do it).*

This combination contains in other words what might have been expressed substantially by a past indicative with ἄν of the verb of the infinitive, qualified by an adverb or other expression denoting obligation, propriety, or possibility: thus ἔδει τοῦτον ἀποθανεῖν is (as a construction) equivalent to οὗτος δικαίως (or ἀξίως) ἂν ἀπέθανεν, *he would justly have perished,* and εἰκὸς ἦν σε τοῦτο παθεῖν is equivalent to τοῦτο εἰκότως ἂν ἔπαθες, *you would properly have suffered this* (implying οὐκ ἔπαθες). Strictly, the expression involves also an unreal protasis, as (in the last case) εἰ τὸ εἰκὸς ἔπαθες, which with the apodosis τοῦτο ἔπαθες ἄν appears substantially in εἰκὸς ἦν σε τοῦτο παθεῖν. (See 511.)

When the present infinitive is used, the expression is present or past ; with the aorist infinitive it is always past.

416. The following imperfects may take the infinitive in this sense : ἔδει, χρῆν or ἐχρῆν, εἰκὸς ἦν, προσῆκεν, ἐνῆν, ἐξῆν, ἦν (or ὑπῆρχεν[1]), *it was possible, one might,* the impersonal ἦν with adjectives or nouns expressing obligation, propriety, possibility, and similar ideas, as δίκαιον ἦν, ἄξιον ἦν, καλὸν (κάλλιον,[2] κρεῖττον,[3] κράτιστον [4]) ἦν, αἰσχρὸν ἦν, προσῆκον ἦν, οὐ θαυμαστὸν ἦν,[5] ἀσφαλέστερον ἦν,[6] ἴσον ἦν,[7] εὔλογον ἦν,[8] συγγνωστὸν ἦν, οἷός τ᾽ ἦν, ἔργον ἦν, ἦν with the verbal in -τέος,—also ἔπρεπεν, συνέφερεν,[9] ἐλυσιτέλει,[10] with other verbs of the same nature. To these must be added the expressions specially mentioned below in 424-431.

417. These are all originally expressions of past necessity, obligation, etc., involving no reference to any condition (unfulfilled or otherwise) ; and in this sense they may always be used, as in DEM. xix. 124, ἔδει μένειν, *he was obliged to stay (and did stay),* and HDT. i. 8, χρῆν γὰρ Κανδαύλῃ γενέσθαι κακῶς, *for C. was doomed to fall into trouble.* It is only by idiomatic usage that the denial of the action of the infinitive comes to be implied in them, and that a past tense comes to express present time, both of which characteristics are found in Greek, Latin, and English ; as ἔδει σε αὐτὸν φιλεῖν, *debebas eum colere, you ought to love him* (but

---

[1] See ISOC. v. 34.   [2] ISAE. ii. 15 ; ARISTOT. Eth. x. 9, 18 (p. 1181 *a*, 4).
[3] DEM. xx. 23.   [4] ISOC. xx. 14.   [5] DEM. xviii. 248.   [6] LYS. vii. 24.
[7] ANT. v. 13.   [8] ARISTOT. Eth. x. 9, 19 (p. 1181 *a*, 6).   [9] LYS. xiii. 28.
[10] DEM. lix. 112. The imperfects not included in these references will be found among the examples in 419-422. The above list could doubtless be greatly extended.

you do not), *ought* being the past of *owe*. The infinitive is felt to
be negatived, even when the negative belongs to the leading verb.

418. Like the potential indicative, this form of expression
can either (1) be used alone, with no external protasis expressed
or distinctly implied, as in χρῆν σε ἐλθεῖν, *you ought to have gone ;*
or (2) stand as apodosis to an unreal protasis, as in εἰ ἐκέλευσε,
χρῆν σε ἐλθεῖν, *if he had commanded it, you ought to have gone.*

419. I. When these expressions are used alone, the denial of
the action of the infinitive is always implied. *E.g.*

Τούσδε γὰρ μὴ ζῆν ἔδει, *for these ought not to be living (as they
are).* SOPH. Ph. 418. "Εδει μὲν τοὺς λέγοντας ἅπαντας μήτε πρὸς
ἔχθραν ποιεῖσθαι λόγον μηδένα μήτε πρὸς χάριν, i.e. *the speakers
ought not to say a word out of regard either to enmity or to favour (and
yet they do so).* DEM. viii. 1. Σιγήσας ἡνίκ᾽ ἔδει λέγειν, *keeping
silence when he ought to speak.* Id. xviii. 189 : cf. xviii. 191.

Χρῆν γάρ σε μήτ᾽ αὐτόν ποτ᾽ εἰς Τροίαν μολεῖν, ἡμᾶς τ᾽ ἀπείρ-
γειν, *for you ought yourself never to have gone to Troy, and you ought
(now) to keep me away from it.* SOPH. Ph. 1363. See AESCH. Ag. 879,
Cho. 930 ; SOPH. El. 1505. Θανεῖν, θανεῖν σε, πρέσβυ, χρῆν πάρος
τέκνων. EUR. And. 1208. Τί ἐχρῆν με ποιεῖν; μὴ προσάγειν
γράψαι (τοὺς πρέσβεις); *what ought I to have done (which I did not
do)? Ought I not to have proposed (as I did) to invite the ambassadors?*
DEM. xviii. 28. Ἐχρῆν μὲν οὖν καὶ δίκαιον ἦν τοὺς τὸν στέφανον
οἰομένους δεῖν λαβεῖν αὐτοὺς ἀξίους ἐπιδεικνύναι τούτου, μὴ ἐμὲ
κακῶς λέγειν· ἐπειδὴ δὲ τοῦτο παρέντες ἐκεῖνο ποιοῦσιν, κ.τ.λ., i.e.
*those who think they ought to receive the crown ought to show that they
deserve it themselves, and not be abusing me ; but since now they have
neglected the former and do the latter,* etc. Id. li. 3.

Σφῷν δ᾽, ὦ τέκν᾽, οὓς μὲν εἰκὸς ἦν πονεῖν τάδε, *those of you who
ought to be bearing these labours.* SOPH. O. C. 342. Πρὸς τούτους τὸν
ἀγῶνα καταστῆναι, οὓς εἰκὸς ἦν τῷ μὲν τεθνεῶτι τιμωροὺς γενέσθαι τῷ δ᾽ ἐπεξιόντι βοηθούς, *who properly should have come forward
to avenge the dead and to help the prosecutor.* ANT. i. 2. Εἰ ὑπὸ τῶν
πολεμίων μὲν ἐσώθημεν, οὓς εἰκὸς ἦν διακωλύειν μὴ σῴζεσθαι,
i.e. *who would naturally have tried to prevent us from being saved.* LYS.
xx. 36. See DEM. xl. 30. Καὶ μάλιστα εἰκὸς ἦν ὑμᾶς προορᾶ-
σθαι αὐτὰ καὶ μὴ μαλακῶς, ὥσπερ νῦν, ξυμμαχεῖν. THUC. vi. 78.
(The orator adds, ἀλλ᾽ οὔθ᾽ ὑμεῖς νῦν γέ πω οὔθ᾽ οἱ ἄλλοι ἐπὶ ταῦτα
ὥρμησθε.) Μένειν γὰρ ἐξῆν τῷ κατηγοροῦντι τῶν ἄλλων, *he might
have stood his ground* (but really he ran away). DEM. iii. 17 : cf. xviii.
14, xxvii. 58 ; LYS. xii. 31.

Τὴν διαθήκην ἠφάνικατε, ἐξ ἧς ἦν εἰδέναι περὶ πάντων τὴν
ἀλήθειαν, *you have concealed the will, from which we (now) might know
the truth about the whole matter.* DEM. xxviii. 10. Τῆς ἡμετέρας ἔχθρας
ἡμᾶς ἐφ᾽ ἡμῶν αὐτῶν δίκαιον ἦν τὸν ἐξετασμὸν ποιεῖσθαι, i.e.
we should justly settle up our quarrel by ourselves. Id. xviii. 16 : cf. 13,

where δίκαιον ἦν is understood with χρῆσθαι, *he would justly have used them.* Πράττων πολὺ βέλτιον ἢ σὲ προσῆκον ἦν (sc. πράττειν), *being much better off than you deserve to be.* Id. xlv. 69. Καὶ μὴν ἄξιόν γ᾽ ἦν ἀκοῦσαι, *indeed, it was worth your while to hear them* (ἀξίως ἂν ἠκούσατε). PLAT. Euthyd. 304 D. The person addressed had just said οὐκ οἷός τ᾽ ἦ κατακούειν.

Ἄλλῳ ἔπρεπεν λέγειν ἃ λέγεις, *another would have becomingly said what you say* (ἄλλος ἂν ἔλεγε πρεπόντως). PLAT. Rep. 474 D. Τὸ δυσχερέστατον τῶν ὀνομάτων, ὃ τῶν φθονούντων ἔργον ἦν λέγειν, ἀλλ᾽ οὐ τῶν προεστώτων τῆς τοιαύτης παιδεύσεως, *the most disagreeable of names* (Sophist), *which the envious ought to use rather than those who stand at the head of the business in question.* ISOC. xiii. 19.

420. II. When this form is made the apodosis of an unreal condition (expressed or distinctly implied), it states that what the infinitive denotes would necessarily, properly, or possibly be done (or have been done) if the case supposed were a real one. The chief force of the apodosis here always lies in the infinitive, while the leading verb acts as an auxiliary (which we can generally express by *ought, might,* or *could,* or by an adverb), modifying the idea of the infinitive more or less in different cases. But when the chief stress is laid on the necessity, propriety, or possibility of the act, and not on the act itself, so that the real apodosis is in the leading verb, this takes ἄν, like any other imperfect in such an apodosis (423). In some cases, however, even when no ἄν is added, the force of the infinitive is so modified by the idea of the leading verb that the opposite of the apodosis (which is generally inferred) cannot be expressed without including both ideas (see examples in 422, 1).

421. In the following examples the infinitive represents the real apodosis, and its action is denied as when no protasis is added (419):—

Εἰ ἐπ᾽ ἡμέας μούνους ἐστρατηλάτεε ὁ Πέρσης, χρῆν αὐτὸν πάντων τῶν ἄλλων ἀπεχόμενον ἰέναι οὕτω ἐπὶ τὴν ἡμετέρην· καὶ ἂν ἐδήλου πᾶσι ὡς ἐπὶ Σκύθας ἐλαύνει, *if the Persian were making his expedition against us alone, he should leave all others and be marching directly into our country; then he would show everybody that he was marching against Scythians.* HDT. iv. 118. Δεῖν (= ἔδει) δὲ, εἴπερ ἦν δυνατὸν, ἄνευ τῶν ἄλλων αὐτὸ λέγεσθαι· νῦν δὲ ἀδύνατον. PLAT. Theaet. 202 A. Χρῆν σ᾽, εἴπερ ἦσθα μὴ κακὸς, πείσαντά με γαμεῖν γάμον τόνδ᾽, ἀλλὰ μὴ σιγῇ φίλων, i.e. *if you were not base, you should have made this marriage with my consent, and not* (as you do) *in secret from your friends.* EUR. Med. 586. Εἴ τινα (προῖκα) ἐδίδου, εἰκὸς ἦν καὶ τὴν δοθεῖσαν ὑπὸ τῶν παραγενέσθαι φασκόντων μαρτυρεῖσθαι, i.e. *if he had given any dowry, it would naturally have been attested by witnesses.* ISAE. iii. 28. See Id. iv. 18. Ἐμὲ εἰ μὲν ἐν ἄλλαις τισὶν ἡμέραις ἠδίκησέ τι τούτων ἰδιώτην ὄντα, ἰδίᾳ καὶ δίκην προσῆκεν αὐτῷ διδόναι, i.e. *in that case he would properly have given satisfaction by a private suit* (as if he had said προσηκόντως ἰδίᾳ δίκην ἂν ἐδίδου). DEM. xxi. 33 ; see xxxiii. 25 and 38. Οὐ γὰρ ἐνῆν μὴ παρακρουσθέντων ὑμῶν (= εἰ μὴ παρεκρούσθητε) μεῖναι Φιλίππῳ, *for Philip could not have remained (as he did) unless you had been deceived.* Id. xix. 123. Εἰ ἦσαν ἄνδρες, ὥσπερ φασὶν, ἀγαθοὶ, ὅσῳ ἀληπτότεροι ἦσαν τοῖς πέλας, τοσῷδε φανερωτέραν ἐξῆν αὐτοῖς τὴν ἀρετὴν δεικνύναι, i.e. *in that case they might all the more plainly manifest their virtue (which they do not do).* THUC. i. 37. Εἰ ἐβούλετο δίκαιος εἶναι, ἐξῆν αὐτῷ μισθῶσαι τὸν οἶκον, ἢ γῆν πριάμενος ἐκ τῶν προσιόντων τοὺς παῖδας τρέφειν, i.e. *he might have let the house, or have bought land and supported the children from the income.* LYS. xxxii. 23. Ἐν αὐτῇ τῇ δίκῃ ἐξῆν σοι φυγῆς τιμήσασθαι, εἰ ἐβούλου. PLAT. Crit. 52 C. (See ISOC. xvii. 29.) Πολλοῖς δόξω, ὡς οἷός τ᾽ ὤν σε σῴζειν εἰ ἤθελον ἀναλίσκειν χρήματα, ἀμελῆσαι, *many will think that, whereas I might have saved you if I had been willing to spend money, I neglected it.* Ib. 44 B.

422. 1. In the following examples the idea of the infinitive is so modified by that of the leading verb, that the real apodosis (the opposite of which is implied) includes both ideas ; but the chief force still remains in the infinitive, so that no ἄν is added.

Εἰ γὰρ ὑπὸ ὀδόντος τοι εἶπε τελευτήσειν με, χρῆν δή σε ποιέειν τὰ ποιέεις· νῦν δὲ ὑπὸ αἰχμῆς, *for if the dream had said that I was to be killed by a tooth, then you would properly do what you now do ; but it really said I was to be killed by a spear.* HDT. i. 39. (Here the real apodosis is not in ποιέεις alone, which is affirmed in τὰ ποιέεις, but in the combined idea *you would do with propriety ;* and it is the opposite of this which is implied. Χρῆν ἄν, which might have been used, would throw the main force on the χρῆν, with the meaning *it would be your duty to do.*) Εἰ μὲν οὖν ἅπαντες ὡμολογοῦμεν Φίλιππον τῇ πόλει πολεμεῖν, οὐδὲν ἄλλο ἔδει τὸν παριόντα λέγειν καὶ συμβουλεύειν ἢ ὅπως ἀσφαλέστατα αὐτὸν ἀμυνούμεθα, i.e. *if then we were all agreed that Philip is at war with us, the speaker ought to say nothing else and to give no other advice than this,* etc. (but it is added that, as there is a difference of opinion, it is necessary, ἀνάγκη ἐστίν, to speak on another subject also). DEM. ix. 6. (This implies not *he does speak,* etc., but *he is bound to speak,* etc. ῎Εδει ἄν would merely have thrown the balance of force upon the necessity, whereas now it falls on the speaking and advising.) Εἰ γὰρ παρ᾽ ἐμοὶ ἐτέθη τὸ γραμματεῖον, ἐνῆν αἰτιάσασθαι Ἀπατουρίῳ ὡς ἐγὼ ἠφάνικα τὰς συνθήκας, *for if the account-book had been given me to keep, A. might possibly have charged me with putting the contract out of the way* (implying that, as it was, *he could not charge me with this).* Id. xxxiii. 37. Εἰ μὲν ἑώρα μεταμέλον τῇ πόλει τῶν πεπραγμένων, οὐκ ἄξιον ἦν θαυμάζειν αὐτοῦ, *if he had seen that the state repented of her acts, we should have no good reason for being surprised at him* (implying *we now have good reason for surprise,* ἀξίως θαυμάζομεν). ISOC. xviii. 21.

The preceding examples confirm the reading of the best Mss. in

EUR. Med. 490, εἰ γὰρ ἦσθ᾽ ἄπαις ἔτι, συγγνωστὸν ἦν σοι τοῦδ᾽ ἐρασθῆναι λέχους, which may be translated, *for if you had remained still childless, you might pardonably have become enamoured of this new marriage*, the apodosis being equivalent to ἠράσθης ἄν with an adverb meaning *pardonably* (*if you had done what would have been pardonable*). This implies not *you were not enamoured*, but *you were not pardonably enamoured*. If no protasis had been added, συγγνωστὸν ἦν ἐρασθῆναι (in its potential sense) must have meant *you might pardonably have become enamoured* (*but you did not*), and then ἄν would have been required to give the sense *it would have been pardonable* (*but is not so*). The other reading, συγγνώστ᾽ ἂν ἦν, would make the same change in the balance of force that χρῆν ἄν, ἔδει ἄν, ἐνῆν ἄν, and ἄξιον ἄν ἦν would make in the preceding examples.

2. In concessive sentences introduced by καὶ εἰ, *even if*, οὐδ᾽ εἰ, *not even if*, or εἰ, *although*, containing unreal conditions, where the action of the apodosis is not denied but affirmed (see 412, 3), the real apodosis may be represented by an infinitive and a leading verb like ἔδει, ἐξῆν, etc. combined. *E.g.*

Οὐκ ἐξῆν αὐτῷ δικάζεσθαι περὶ τῶν τότε γεγενημένων, οὐδ᾽ εἰ πάντα ταῦτ᾽ ἦν πεποιηκὼς ἅ φησιν οὗτος, *he could not maintain a suit about what was then done, even if I had really done what he says I did* (implying οὐκ ἔξεστιν αὐτῷ δικάζεσθαι, but with the chief force on δικάζεσθαι). ISOC. xviii. 19.   Οὐδ᾽ εἰ γνήσιοι ἦσαν εἰσποιητοὶ δὲ, ὡς οὗτοι ἔφασαν, οὐδ᾽ οὕτω προσῆκεν αὐτοὺς Εὐκτήμονος εἶναι, *not even if they were genuine sons and were afterwards adopted into another family, would they now properly belong to E.'s house* (implying *they do not properly belong there*). ISAE. vi. 44.   See also HDT. vii. 56 ; DEM. xviii. 199, xxiii. 107.

Οὐδ᾽ εἰ γὰρ ἦν τὸ πρᾶγμα μὴ θεήλατον, ἀκάθαρτον ὑμᾶς εἰκὸς ἦν οὕτως ἐᾶν, *for even if the duty were not urged upon you by a God, you ought not to leave the guilt unpurged as you do*. SOPH. O. T. 255. (Here the apodosis as a whole is affirmed, although the infinitive itself, *not to leave*, is denied. So in the two following examples.) Καλὸν δ᾽ ἦν, εἰ καὶ ἡμαρτάνομεν, τοῖσδε εἶξαι τῇ ἡμετέρᾳ ὀργῇ, ἡμῖν δ᾽ αἰσχρὸν (sc. ἦν) βιάσασθαι τὴν μετριότητα, *if we had even been in the wrong, they might fairly have yielded to our wrath, while we could not have done violence to their moderation without disgrace*. THUC. i. 38.   Ἄξιον ἦν, εἰ καὶ μηδὲν αὐταῖς πρότερον ὑπῆρχεν ἀγαθὸν, (ταύτας) τῆς μεγίστης δωρεᾶς παρὰ τῶν Ἑλλήνων τυχεῖν, i.e. *these cities, even if they had had no other merit to rely on, deserved to receive (ought to have received) the greatest reward from the Greeks* (which, it is said, they did not receive). ISOC. xii. 71.

423. (Ἔδει ἄν, etc.)   The examples in 421, 1 and 2, show that the common rule for distinguishing ἔδει etc. with the infinitive (without ἄν) from ἔδει ἄν etc. with the infinitive,—that the former is used when the action of the infinitive is denied, the

latter when the obligation, propriety, or possibility is denied,
—often cannot be applied, though as a working rule it can be
used in the great majority of cases. While there are many
sentences in which either form would express the required sense,
the essential distinction is, that the form without ἄν is used when
the chief force of the apodosis falls on the infinitive, the leading
verb being an auxiliary (see 420); but the leading verb takes
ἄν when the chief force falls on the necessity, propriety, or
possibility of the act, rather than on the act itself.

The following examples will illustrate the form with ἄν :—

Εἰ μὲν γὰρ ἐγὼ ἔτι ἐν δυνάμει ἦν τοῦ ῥᾳδίως πορεύεσθαι πρὸς τὸ
ἄστυ, οὐδὲν ἄν σε ἔδει δεῦρο ἰέναι· ἀλλ' ἡμεῖς ἂν παρὰ σὲ ἦμεν·
νῦν δέ σε χρὴ πυκνότερον δεῦρο ἰέναι, i.e. in that case there would be
no need (as there now is) of your coming hither. PLAT. Rep. 328 C. Τῷ
μὲν πατρὶ αὐτῆς, εἰ παῖδες ἄρρενες μὴ ἐγένοντο, οὐκ ἂν ἐξῆν ἄνευ
ταύτης διαθέσθαι, her father, if he had had no male children, would not
have been allowed to leave her out of his will (implying ἀλλ' ἐξῆν). ISAE.
x. 13. Εἰ οὖν παρεκαλοῦμεν ἀλλήλους ἐπὶ τὰ οἰκοδομικὰ, πότερον
ἔδει ἂν ἡμᾶς σκέψασθαι ἡμᾶς αὐτοὺς καὶ ἐξετάσαι εἰ ἐπιστάμεθα τὴν
τέχνην; ἔδει ἂν ἢ οὔ; i.e. in that case would it be needful or not to
examine ourselves and inquire whether we understand the art? PLAT. Gorg.
514 A. See also DEM. iv. 1, quoted in 410.

A comparison of these examples with those in 422, 1, will show
the distinction between the two forms and also the narrowness of the
line which sometimes separates them.

For a discussion of χρῆν and χρῆν ἄν in DEM. xviii. 195, and of
χρῆν and ἐχρῆν ἄν in LYS. xii. 32 and 48, and for other remarks on
these constructions, see Appendix V.

424. 1. The imperfect ὤφελλον or ὄφελλον of ὀφέλλω (Epic
of ὀφείλω), owe, debeo, and the aorist ὤφελον or ὄφελον are sometimes used with the infinitive in Homer like χρῆν, ἔδει, etc. in
the later construction (415). E.g.

Τιμήν πέρ μοι ὄφελλεν Ὀλύμπιος ἐγγυαλίξαι Ζεὺς ὑψιβρε-
μέτης· νῦν δ' οὐδέ με τυτθὸν ἔτισεν, i.e. Zeus ought to have secured
me honour; but now he has not honoured me even a little. Il. i. 353.
Νῦν ὄφελεν κατὰ πάντας ἀριστῆας πονέεσθαι λισσόμενος, now
ought he to be labouring among all the nobles, beseeching them. Il. x. 117.
Ἀλλ' ὤφελεν ἀθανάτοισιν εὔχεσθαι, but he ought to have prayed to
the Gods. Il. xxiii. 546. For the reference to present time in Il. x.
117, see 246 and 734.

2. From this comes the common use of this form in expressions of a wish, in Homer and in Attic Greek; as ὤφελε Κῦρος
ζῆν, would that Cyrus were living (lit. Cyrus ought to be living),
XEN. An. ii. 1, 4. (See 734.)

425. Similar to this is the occasional use of ἐβουλόμην (without ἄν) and the infinitive, to express what some one *wishes were now true* (but which *is not true*). *E.g.*

’Εβουλόμην μὲν οὖν καὶ τὴν βουλὴν καὶ τὰς ἐκκλησίας ὀρθῶς διοικεῖσθαι καὶ τοὺς νόμους ἰσχύειν, *I would that both the Senate and the assemblies were rightly managed, and that the laws were in force* (implying the opposite of ὀρθῶς διοικεῖσθαι and ἰσχύειν). This is analogous to ὤφελεν εἶναι, *would that it were*, and ἔδει εἶναι, *it ought to be* (but *is not*). AESCHIN. iii. 2. ’Εβουλόμην μὲν οὐκ ἐρίζειν ἐνθάδε, *I would that I were not contending here* (as *I am*), or *I would not be contending here*. AR. Ran. 866. ’Εβουλόμην τὴν δύναμιν τοῦ λέγειν ἐξ ἴσου μοι καθεστάναι τῇ συμφορᾷ, *I would that power of speech equal to my misfortune were granted me.* ANT. v. i. ’Εβουλόμην κἀγὼ τἀληθῆ πρὸς ὑμᾶς εἰπεῖν δυνηθῆναι, *I would that I had found the power to tell you the truth.* ISAE. x. 1. ’Εβουλόμην μηδ’ ὑφ’ ἑνὸς ἀδικεῖσθαι τῶν πολιτῶν, *I would I had not been wronged by a single one of the citizens.* Id. Frag. 4 (Scheibe): see Frag. 22.

426. ’Εβουλόμην ἄν, vellem, *I should wish* or *I should have liked,* can always be used as a potential indicative, like ἔδει ἄν etc. (423): see AR. Eccl. 151 ; AESCHIN. iii. 115. (See 246.)

427. (*a*) The aorist of κινδυνεύω is used with the infinitive, as a periphrasis for the verb of the infinitive with ἄν. *E.g.*

Ἡ πόλις ἐκινδύνευσε πᾶσα διαφθαρῆναι εἰ ἄνεμος ἐπεγένετο, *the city ran the risk of being utterly destroyed if a wind had arisen.* THUC. iii. 74. Εἰ μὴ ἐξεφύγομεν εἰς Δελφοὺς ἐκινδυνεύσαμεν ἀπολέσθαι, *we ran the risk of perishing had we not fled to Delphi,* i.e. *we should very probably have perished if we had not fled.* AESCHIN. iii. 123. For ἐκινδύνευσα ἄν see (*b*) below.

So with κίνδυνος ἦν : as in AND. ii. 12, εἰ τότε τὰ ἐπιτήδεια μὴ εἰσήχθη, οὐ περὶ τοῦ σῶσαι τὰς ’Αθήνας ὁ κίνδυνος ἦν αὐτοῖς μᾶλλον ἤ, κ.τ.λ., i.e. *they ran a risk, in case the supplies had not then been brought in, not so much about saving Athens, as,* etc.

(*b*) When the chief force of the apodosis lies in ἐκινδύνευσα, even though the meaning is not much affected by the distinction in form, ἄν is used (as with ἔδει etc. in 423). So in XEN. An. iv. 1, 11, εἰ πλείους συνελέγησαν, ἐκινδύνευσεν ἂν πολὺ διαφθαρῆναι τοῦ στρατεύματος, *if more had been collected, there would have been danger of much of the army being destroyed.*

428. (*a*) The imperfect of μέλλω with the infinitive may express a past *intention* or *expectation* which was not realised, and so take the place of the verb of the infinitive with ἄν. *E.g.*

Ἦ μάλα δὴ ’Αγαμέμνονος φθίσεσθαι κακὸν οἶτον ἔμελλον, εἰ μὴ . . . ἔειπες, i.e. *I should have perished like A.* (lit. *I was to have perished*), *if thou hadst not spoken.* Od. xiii. 383. Μέλλεν μέν ποτε οἶκος ὅδ’ ἀφνειὸς καὶ ἀμύμων ἔμμεναι· νῦν δ’ ἑτέρως ἐβόλοντο θεοί, *this house was to have been rich and glorious; but now the Gods have willed it otherwise.* Od. i. 232. Οὐ συστρατεύσειν ἔμελλον, *they were*

not going to join him, or *they would not have joined him* (in that case).
DEM. xix. 159 ; see xviii. 172. Ἧττον τὸ ἀδίκημα πολλῶν οὐσῶν
ἔμελλε δῆλον ἔσεσθαι, *the offence would have been less plain when
there were many (olive trees).* LYS. vii. 24. See THUC. v. 38, μέλλοντες
πρότερον, εἰ ταῦτα ἔπεισαν, πειράσεσθαι. Compare the Latin :
Hoc facturi erant, nisi venisset, *they were to have done this (would have
done this), had he not come.*[1]

(b) A single case of ἄν with ἔμελλεν occurs in AND. i. 21 : εἰ καὶ
πατὴρ ἐβούλετο ὑπομένειν, τοὺς φίλους ἂν οἴεσθε . . . ἐπιτρέπειν
αὐτῷ, ἀλλ᾽ οὐκ ἂν παραιτεῖσθαι καὶ δεῖσθαι ἀπιέναι ὅπου ἂν ἔμελλεν
σωθήσεσθαι; i.e. *to depart to a place where he would have been likely to
be safe.* Most critics repudiate this ἄν; but it seems perfectly analogous
to ἄν with ἔδει, χρῆν, etc. (423).

429. Similar is the use of ἔφην in Od. iv. 171 : καί μιν ἔφην
ἐλθόντα φιλήσεμεν ἔξοχον ἄλλων, εἰ νῶιν νόστον ἔδωκεν (Ζεύς), i.e.
*I intended to love him (and should have done so) had Zeus granted us a
return.*

430. An analogous case is LYS. xii. 60 : ἀπολέσαι παρεσκευάζοντο τὴν πόλιν εἰ μὴ δι᾽ ἄνδρας ἀγαθούς, *they were preparing to
destroy the city (and would have destroyed it) had it not been for good men.*

431. A few expressions which have no dependent infinitive
are practically equivalent to a potential indicative with ἄν, and
so can stand as the apodosis of an unreal condition. *E.g.*

Τούτῳ δ᾽ εἰ μὴ ὡμολόγουν ἃ οὗτος ἐβούλετο, οὐδεμίᾳ ζημίᾳ ἔνοχος
ἦν, *but if they had not acknowledged to him what he wanted, he was liable
to no charge* (i.e. *he could not have been accused*). LYS. vii. 37. Ὧς, εἰ
μὲν τὸ ἐπ᾽ αὐτοφώρῳ μὴ προσεγέγραπτο, ἔνοχος ὢν (= ἦν) τῇ ἀπα-
γωγῇ, *assuming that, if the words ἐπ᾽ αὐτοφώρῳ had not been added, he
might properly have been tried by ἀπαγωγή.* Id. xiii. 85. Πιστεύοντος
γὰρ ἐμοῦ ἐμοὶ εἰδέναι ἃ λέγω, καλῶς εἶχεν ἡ παραμυθία, i.e. *for if I
trusted* (= εἰ ἐπίστευον) *to any knowledge of my own about what I am
saying, the consolation which you offer would encourage me* (lit. *your consolation was good* on that supposition). PLAT. Rep. 450 D. (We might
have had καλὸν ἦν σε παραμυθεῖσθαι in the same sense.) Εἰ τὸ κωλῦσαι τὴν τῶν Ἑλλήνων κοινωνίαν ἐπεπράκειν ἐγὼ Φιλίππῳ, σοὶ τὸ
μὴ σιγῆσαι λοιπὸν ἦν, *in that case it remained for you not to keep
silent* (i.e. *you should not have kept silent*). DEM. xviii. 23. (The article
with σιγῆσαι only slightly distinguishes this from the examples under
421.)

432. The same explanation applies to other cases in which a
rhetorical omission of ἄν in apodosis is commonly assumed ; as in

---

[1] This use of ἔμελλον with the infinitive corresponds precisely to the
Sanskrit use of the *past future* tense in the sense of the Greek aorist indicative
with ἄν. Thus "*if he had said* (avakṣyat) *this, he would have slain* (ahaniṣyat)
Indra" (*Çat. Brahm.* i. 6, 3¹⁰), where the two verbs are augmented past
futures, meaning literally *he was going to say* and *he was going to slay.* See
Whitney's *Sanskrit Grammar*, § 950.

EUR. Hec. 1113, εἰ δὲ μὴ Φρυγῶν πύργους πεσόντας ᾖσμεν Ἑλλήνων δορί, φόβον παρέσχεν οὐ μέσως ὅδε κτύπος, *but if we had not known that the Phrygian towers had fallen, this noise gave us cause for terror in earnest* (i.e. *would easily have terrified us*).

433. Occasionally a protasis takes the place of the infinitive in the construction of 419. *E.g.*

Ἐπεὶ τόδε κέρδιον ἦεν, εἰ νόστησ' Ὀδυσεὺς καὶ ὑπότροπος ἵκετο δῶμα, *for it had been a greater gain if Ulysses had returned* (for κέρδιον ἦεν Ὀδυσέα νοστῆσαι). Od. xx. 331. Compare MATTH. Ev. xxvi. 24, καλὸν ἦν αὐτῷ, εἰ οὐκ ἐγεννήθη ὁ ἄνθρωπος ἐκεῖνος, *it had been good for that man if he had not been born* (for καλὸν ἦν αὐτῷ μὴ γεννηθῆναι). Εἰ δὲ ἀποφεύξεται, κρείττων ἦν ὁ ἀγὼν μὴ γεγενημένος (= εἰ μὴ ἐγεγένητο), *but if he is acquitted, it were better that the trial had never taken place* (for κρεῖττον ἦν τὸν ἀγῶνα μὴ γεγενῆσθαι). AESCHIN. i. 192. This occasional substitution of a protasis does not indicate that the infinitive in κρεῖττον ἦν αὐτῷ ἐλθεῖν, *he had better have gone*, was felt as a protasis. We could substitute for this English *it were better if he had gone*, but only by a change of construction.

HOMERIC PECULIARITIES.

434. In Homer the construction of the unreal conditional sentence is not completely developed. It is not improbable that in the primitive language the optative could express in a rough way both present and past unreal conditions, and in Homer the present unreal condition is still expressed only by the present optative (438).

435. The aorist indicative in Homer, both in protasis and in apodosis with ἄν or κέ, is used as in Attic Greek; but the imperfect is always past, never present.[1] *E.g.*

Καί νύ κε δὴ ξιφέεσσ' αὐτοσχεδὸν οὐτάζοντο, εἰ μὴ κήρυκες ἦλθον, *they would have wounded each other, had not heralds come.* Il. vii. 273. Ἔνθα κε λοιγὸς ἔην καὶ ἀμήχανα ἔργα γένοντο, εἰ μὴ ἄρ' ὀξὺ νόησε πατὴρ ἀνδρῶν τε θεῶν τε, *then there would have been*, etc. Il. viii. 130. So viii. 366. Καί νύ κε δὴ προτέρω ἔτ' ἔρις γένετ' ἀμφοτέροισιν, εἰ μὴ Ἀχιλλεὺς αὐτὸς ἀνίστατο καὶ κατέρυκεν. Il. xxiii. 490. See Il. xi. 504; Od. xvi. 221, xxiv. 51.

---

[1] Mr. Monro (*Hom. Gr.* p. 236) doubts this statement, and refers to Od. iv. 178, καί κε θάμ' ἐνθάδ' ἐόντες ἐμισγόμεθ', οὐδέ κεν ἡμέας ἀλλὸ διέκρινεν, as a case in which "the imperfect ἐμισγόμεθα takes in the present time, *we should* (from that time till now) *have been meeting.*" It seems to me that, according to the Homeric usage, we can find no more in θάμα ἐμισγόμεθά κε than *we should have had frequent meetings*, and the rest comes from the context. In any case, this use is far removed from the Attic ἐπορευόμεθα ἂν ἐπὶ βασιλέα, *we should* (*now*) *be on our way to the King* (410). A nearer approach to the later use perhaps appears in Il. xxiv. 220, εἰ μὲν γάρ τις μ' ἄλλος ἐκέλευεν, *if any other* (*had ?*) *commanded me.* But see Il. ii. 80.

Καί νύ κ' ἔτι πλέονας Λυκίων κτάνε δῖος Ὀδυσσεὺς, εἰ μὴ ἄρ' ὀξὺ
νόησε μέγας κορυθαίολος Ἕκτωρ, i.e. *Ulysses would have killed still
more, had not Hector perceived him.* Il. v. 679.   Καί νύ κεν ἤια πάντα
κατέφθιτο καὶ μένε' ἀνδρῶν, εἰ μή τίς με θεῶν ὀλοφύρατο καί μ'
ἐσάωσεν. Od. iv. 363.

But ὤφελον with the present infinitive may be present, even in
Homer, both as a potential expression (424) and in wishes (734).

436. We find the imperfect referring to present time in Theognis :
see vs. 905, εἰ μὲν γὰρ κατιδεῖν βιότου τέλος ἦν, εἰκὸς ἂν ἦν. See
Pind. Nem. iv. 13.

437. In Il. xxiii. 526, εἴ κε is found with the aorist indicative in
protasis, κέ apparently adding nothing to the sense :—

> Εἰ δέ κ' ἔτι προτέρω γένετο δρόμος ἀμφοτέροισιν,
> Τῷ κέν μιν παρέλασσ' οὐδ' ἀμφήριστον ἔθηκεν.

438. (*Optative in present unreal Conditions.*)   In Homer a
present unfulfilled condition is regularly expressed by the present
optative with εἰ, and its apodosis (if present) by the present
optative with κέ or ἄν.

The only instance of this form in both protasis and apodosis is Il.
xxiii. 274, εἰ μὲν νῦν ἐπὶ ἄλλῳ ἀεθλεύοιμεν Ἀχαιοί, ἦ τ' ἂν ἐγὼ
τὰ πρῶτα λαβὼν κλισίηνδε φεροίμην, *if we were now contending in
honour of any other (than Patroclus), I should take the first prize and bear
it to my tent.*   Twice we have the optative with ἄν in apodosis with
the regular imperfect or aorist indicative (past) in the protasis : Il. ii.
80, εἰ μέν τις τὸν ὄνειρον ἄλλος ἔνισπεν, ψεῦδός κεν φαῖμεν καὶ
νοσφιζοίμεθα μᾶλλον, *if any other had told the dream, we should call
it a lie and rather turn away from it;* and the same apodosis after εἴ
τίς μ' ἄλλος ἐκέλευεν, in Il. xxiv. 222.   In Od. ii. 184, οὐκ ἂν τόσσα
θεοπροπέων ἀγόρευες, οὐδέ κε Τηλέμαχον κεχολωμένον ὧδ' ἀνιείης,
we have first the imperfect with ἄν as a past apodosis, (*in that case) you
would not have made this speech with all its divination;* and then the
present optative with κέ as present, *nor would you be urging Telemachus
on, as you now are;* both referring to an unfulfilled past condition, *if
you had perished,* suggested by καταφθίσθαι ὤφελες in vs. 183.

439. See the corresponding use of the present optative in Homer
to express an unaccomplished present wish (739).   In both wishes and
conditional sentences, it must be remembered, the use of the optative
in its ordinary future sense is completely established in Homer. See
examples in 455 and 722.

440. (*Optative in past unreal Apodosis.*)   Homer has four cases of
the optative with κέ (three aorist and one present) in the apodosis
referring to the past, with the regular indicative in the protasis expressing a past unfulfilled condition. These are—

Καί νύ κεν ἐνθ' ἀπόλοιτο ἄναξ ἀνδρῶν Αἰνείας, εἰ μὴ ἄρ' ὀξὺ
νόησε Διὸς θυγάτηρ Ἀφροδίτη, *Aeneas would have perished, had not
Aphrodite quickly perceived him.* Il. v. 311.   Καί νύ κεν ἐνθ' ἀπόλοιτο

Ἄρης ἆτος πολέμοιο, εἰ μὴ Ἡριβοία Ἑρμέῃ ἐξήγγειλεν. Il. v. 388.
Οὔ κε θανόντι περ ὧδ' ἀκαχοίμην, εἰ μετὰ οἷς ἑτάροισι δάμη Τρώων
ἐνὶ δήμῳ, I should not have felt so grieved if he had perished, θανόντι
(= εἰ ἔθανεν) being further explained by εἰ . . . δάμη. Od. i. 236.
Ἔνθα κε ῥεῖα φέροι κλυτὰ τεύχεα, εἰ μή οἱ ἀγάσσατο Φοῖβος Ἀπόλλων, he would easily have borne away the famous armour had not
Phoebus Apollo grudged him. Il. xvii. 70.   Here ἀπώλετο, ἀκαχόμην,
and ἔφερε would be the regular forms even in Homer, corresponding
to the regular protases.

441. In the transitional state of the Homeric language we see that
the past tenses of the indicative had fully established themselves in
the protasis of past unreal conditions, but not so thoroughly in the
apodosis, where the optative occasionally occurs.   In present unreal
conditions, the optative alone is used in both protasis and apodosis.

442. Besides the full conditional sentences above quoted, we find
in Homer many potential optatives with κέ or ἄν which seem to
belong to the borderland between past and future conclusions, and are
not definitely fixed in the past (like the apodoses in 440) by a past tense
in the protasis.

Such are especially φαίης κε, as in Il. iii. 220, xv. 697, and οὐδέ
κε φαίης, as in Il. iv. 429, xvii. 366, Od. iii. 124, Il. iii. 392.   In
the first four cases it seems most natural to translate them as past,
you would have said, nor would you have said; but in the last two cases
it is more natural to translate *nor would you say* (future), and so with
φαίην κεν, Il. vi. 285.   But in the fluid state of the language which
allowed both ἀπώλετό κε and ἀπόλοιτό κε to mean *he would have
perished,* and φέροι κε to mean both *he would carry* (fut.) and *he would
have carried,* according to the protasis which was used with them, it
is easy to understand how φαίης κε (without a protasis) might have a
vague potential force, *you might perchance say,* which could be felt as
either past or future as the context demanded.   We must, therefore,
hold that the optative with κέ in such cases expresses merely what
could happen, without any limitations of time except such as are
imposed by the context ; and according to the limitations thus imposed
we translate such optatives (with more exactness than they really
possess) either as past or as future.   In one case the feeling of past
time is seen in the dependent verb: Il. v. 85, Τυδεΐδην δ' οὐκ ἄν
γνοίης ποτέροισι μετείη, *you would not have known to what side he
belonged.*   (This occurs in the same book of the Iliad with both the
examples of ἀπόλοιτό κε for ἀπώλετο κε.)
Other examples are the following :—

Οὐκ ἄν ἔπειτ' Ὀδυσῆί γ' ἐρίσσειεν βροτὸς ἄλλος, *no other mortal
could then vie with Ulysses* (after a past verb). Il. iii. 223.   Ἔνθ' οὐκ
ἄν βρίζοντα ἴδοις Ἀγαμέμνονα δῖον. Il. iv. 223.   Ἔνθ' οὔ κεν ῥέα
ἵππος ἐσβαίη, πεζοὶ δὲ μενοίνεον εἰ τελέουσιν (the connection with
μενοίνεον gives ἐσβαίη a past direction). Il. xii. 58.   Ἔνθα κ' ἔπειτα
καὶ ἀθάνατός περ ἐπελθὼν θηήσαιτο ἰδὼν καὶ ταρφθείη φρεσὶν

ἦσιν. Od. v. 73. Ὡς οὐκ ἂν ἔλποιο νεώτερον ἀντιάσαντα, i.e. *as you would not expect* (?) *a younger person to do.* Od. vii. 293. Οὐδέ κεν ἴρηξ κίρκος ὁμαρτήσειεν. Od. xiii. 86. Further, compare Od. ix. 241 with Il. i. 271 and v. 303.

HOMERIC USAGES IN HERODOTUS AND IN ATTIC GREEK.

443. (*a*) Herodotus has a few cases of the potential optative with the same vague reference to time which has been noticed in Homer (442), and we may sometimes translate these, like those in Homer, by past expressions. *E.g.*

Τάχα δὲ ἂν καὶ οἱ ἀποδόμενοι λέγοιεν ἀπικόμενοι ἐς Σπάρτην ὡς ἀπαιρεθείησαν ὑπὸ Σαμίων, *and perhaps those who sold it* (the cup) *might come to Sparta and tell that they had been robbed of it.* HDT. i. 70 (see Stein's note). All that the optative itself seems to express is that this would be a natural story for them to tell. In vii. 214, εἰδείη μὲν γὰρ ἂν καὶ ἐὼν μὴ Μηλιεὺς ταύτην τὴν ἄτραπον Ὀνήτης, εἰ τῇ χώρῃ πολλὰ ὁμιληκὼς εἴη, *for Onetes, even if he was not a Malian, might know this path, supposing him to have had much acquaintance with the country,* the optative in protasis (expressing no condition contrary to fact) shows that εἰδείη ἄν is not felt to be past. See also vii. 180, τάχα δ᾽ ἄν τι ἐπαύροιτο; viii. 136, τάχ᾽ ἂν προλέγοι, *might perhaps warn him;* ix. 71, ταῦτα ἂν εἴποιεν, *they might say this.*

For εἴησαν δ᾽ ἂν οὗτοι Κρῆτες, HDT. i. 2, and similar expressions, see 238.

(*b*) In EUR. Med. 568, οὐδ᾽ ἂν σὺ φαίης εἴ σε μὴ κνίζοι λέχος, the condition seems to be present and contrary to fact, like εἰ μὴ ἔκνιζεν. See also PLAT. Menex. 240 D, ἐν τούτῳ δὴ ἄν τις γενόμενος γνοίη οἷοι ἄρα ἐτύγχανον ὄντες, κ.τ.λ. Such examples are extremely rare in Attic Greek.

(*b*) FUTURE CONDITIONS.

1. *Subjunctive or Future Indicative in Protasis with a future Apodosis.*

444. When a supposed future case is stated distinctly and vividly (as *if I shall go* or *if I go* in English) the protasis generally takes the subjunctive with ἐάν, ἤν, or ἄν (ᾱ) (Epic εἴ κε or αἴ κε). The apodosis takes the future indicative or some other form expressing future time, to denote what *will be* the result if the condition of the protasis is fulfilled. *E.g.*

Ἐάν τι λάβω, δώσω σοι, *if I* (shall) *receive anything, I will give it to you.* Ἐάν τι λάβῃς, δός μοι, *if you receive anything, give it to me.* Εἰ δέ κεν ὡς ἔρξῃς καί τοι πείθωνται Ἀχαιοί, γνώσῃ ἔπειθ᾽ ὅς θ᾽ ἡγεμόνων κακὸς ὅς τέ νυ λαῶν, *but if you shall do thus and the Achaeans obey you, you will then learn both which of the leaders and which of the soldiers is bad.* Il. ii. 364. Αἴ κ᾽ αὐτὸν γνώω νημερτέα πάντ᾽ ἐνέποντα, ἕσσω μιν χλαῖνάν τε χιτῶνά τε, εἵματα καλά. Od. xvii. 549. So αἴ κε δῶσι, Il. i. 128. Εἰ μέν κεν Μενέλαον Ἀλέξανδρος καταπέφνῃ, αὐτὸς ἔπειθ᾽ Ἑλένην ἐχέτω καὶ κτήματα πάντα, ἡμεῖς δ᾽ ἐν νήεσσι νεώμεθα ποντοπόροισιν· εἰ δέ κ᾽ Ἀλέξανδρον κτείνῃ ξανθὸς Μενέλαος, Τρῶας ἔπειθ᾽ Ἑλένην καὶ κτήματα πάντ᾽ ἀποδοῦναι. Il. iii. 281. Here ἐχέτω, νεώμεθα (subj. in exhortation), and ἀποδοῦναι (infin. for imperative) are in the apodosis. Αἴκα τῆνος ἕλῃ κεραὸν τράγον, αἶγα τὺ λαψῇ. THEOC. i. 4. Ἂν δέ τις ἀνθιστῆται, σὺν ὑμῖν πειρασόμεθα χειροῦσθαι, *if any one shall stand opposed to us, with your help we will try to overcome him.* XEN. An. vii. 3, 11. Κἂν μὴ νῦν ἐθέλωμεν ἐκεῖ πολεμεῖν αὐτῷ, ἐνθάδ᾽ ἴσως ἀναγκασθησόμεθα τοῦτο ποιεῖν, *and if we shall not now be willing to fight him there, we shall perhaps be forced to do so here.* DEM. iv. 50. (Here νῦν refers to time immediately following the present : *if we are not now willing* would be εἰ μὴ νῦν ἐθέλομεν.) Ἢν γὰρ ταῦτα καλῶς ὁρισώμεθα, ἄμεινον βουλευσόμεθα καὶ περὶ τῶν ἄλλων. ISOC. viii. 18. Ἢν δὲ τὴν εἰρήνην ποιησώμεθα, καὶ τοιούτους ἡμᾶς αὐτοὺς παράσχωμεν, μετὰ πολλῆς ἀσφαλείας τὴν πόλιν οἰκήσομεν. Id. viii. 20. Ἐὰν οὖν ἴῃς νῦν, πότε ἔσει οἴκοι; XEN. Cyr. v. 3, 27. Καὶ χρῶ αὐτοῖς, ἐὰν δέῃ τι, *and use them, if there shall be any need.* Ib. v. 4, 30. Ἢν μὲν πόλεμον αἱρῆσθε, μηκέτι ἥκετε δεῦρο ἄνευ ὅπλων, εἰ σωφρονεῖτε· ἢν δὲ εἰρήνης δοκῆτε δεῖσθαι, ἄνευ ὅπλων ἥκετε· ὡς δὲ καλῶς ἕξει τὰ ὑμέτερα, ἢν φίλοι γένησθε ἐμοὶ μελήσει. Ib. iii. 2, 13. Ἐὰν γάρ τί σε φανῶ κακὸν πεποιηκώς, ὁμολογῶ ἀδικεῖν· ἐὰν μέντοι μηδὲν φαίνωμαι κακὸν πεποιηκὼς μηδὲ βουληθείς, οὐ καὶ σὺ αὖ ὁμολογήσεις μηδὲν ὑπ᾽ ἐμοῦ ἀδικεῖσθαι; Ib. v. 5, 13. (Here ὁμολογῶ, *I am ready to confess,* refers to the future.) Ἐὰν μὴ ἢ οἱ φιλόσοφοι βασιλεύσωσιν ἢ οἱ βασιλῆς φιλοσοφήσωσιν, οὐκ ἔστι κακῶν παῦλα ταῖς πόλεσιν, *unless either the philosophers shall become kings or the kings philosophers, there is no escape from troubles for states.* PLAT. Rep. 473 D. Δίδωσ᾽ ἑκὼν κτείνειν ἑαυτόν, ἢν τάδε ψευσθῇ λέγων, *he offers himself willingly to suffer death in case he shall be proved false in this that he says.* SOPH. Ph. 1342. Μηχανητέον, ἐάν τε χρυσίον ἡρπακὼς ᾖ πολύ, μὴ ἀποδῷ τοῦτο, ἐάν τε θανάτου ἄξια ἠδικικὼς ᾖ, ὅπως μὴ ἀποθανεῖται, *if he shall (prove to) have stolen much gold, we must contrive that he shall not restore it ; and if he shall have committed crimes deserving death, that he shall not die.* PLAT. Gorg. 481 A (for the perfects see 103). Ἢν σε τοῦ λοιποῦ ποτ᾽ ἀφέλωμαι χρόνου, κάκιστ᾽ ἀπολοίμην, i.e. *may I perish, if I ever take them away.* AR. Ran. 586. (See 181.)

445. It will be seen that the apodosis here (444) may consist of any future expression, — the future indicative, the imperative, the subjunctive in exhortations and prohibitions, the infinitive in any future sense, the potential optative with ἄν, or the optative in a wish. It may also contain a present indicative including a reference to the future, like χρή or δεῖ or the verbal in τέος, or the present used emphatically for the future, like ὁμολογῶ above quoted (444) from XEN. Cyr. v. 5, 13, or παυλά ἐστι in PLAT. Rep. 473 D.

446. The English, especially the colloquial language, seldom expresses the distinction between this form of the future condition and the present condition (402). Thus modern custom allows us to use the inexact expression *if he wishes*, not merely for εἰ βούλεται, *if he now wishes*, but also for ἐὰν βούληται, *if he shall wish*. The sense, however, generally makes the distinction in time clear.

It is worth noting that the Authorised Version of the English New Testament never uses forms like *if he does, if he is*, in either future or present conditions, even when the Greek has the present indicative with εἰ; but it has either the subjunctive or the future indicative in future conditions, and the subjunctive in present conditions. The Revised Version, on the other hand, admits the present indicative (as *if he is*) in present conditions, but not consistently. See LUC. xxiii. 35, εἰ οὗτός ἐστιν ὁ Χριστός, A. V. *if he be Christ*, R. V. *if this is the Christ;* but in MATTH. vi. 23, εἰ οὖν τὸ φῶς τὸ ἐν σοὶ σκότος ἐστίν, both versions have *if therefore the light that is in thee be darkness.* See also Cor. ii. v. 17.

447. (*Future Indicative in Protasis.*) The future indicative with εἰ is often used in the protasis to express a future condition. This is a still stronger form of expression than the subjunctive, though it sometimes alternates with it in the same sentence. Both, however, correspond to the English *if I shall do this, if I do this*, etc. The future, as an emphatic form, is especially common when the condition contains a strong appeal to the feelings or a threat or warning.[1] It is thus a favourite construction with the tragedians. *E.g.*

Εἰ γὰρ Ἀχιλλεὺς οἶος ἐπὶ Τρώεσσι μαχεῖται, οὐδὲ μίνυνθ᾽ ἕξουσι ποδώκεα Πηλεΐωνα, *if Achilles shall fight alone against the Trojans, not even a little while will they keep back the swift son of Peleus.* Il. xx. 26. Εἰ δὲ σύ γ᾽ ἐς πόλεμον πωλήσεαι, ἦ τέ σ᾽ ὀίω ῥιγήσειν πόλεμόν γε, καὶ εἴ χ᾽ ἑτέρωθι πύθηαι, *if you shall mingle in the battle, verily do I believe you will shudder at the very name of battle, even if you hear it elsewhere (away from the war).* Il. v. 350. Εἰ δέ μοι οὐ τίσουσι βοῶν ἐπιεικέ᾽ ἀμοιβήν, δύσομαι εἰς Ἀίδαο καὶ ἐν νεκύεσσι φαείνω, *but if*

---

[1] In "minatory and monitory conditions": see Gildersleeve in *Trans. of Am. Phil. Assoc. for* 1876, p. 13. This article contains an enumeration of all the cases of ἐάν with the subjunctive in future conditions and of εἰ with the future indicative in the three tragedians. It appears that in Aeschylus there are 22 cases of the future and only 8 of the subjunctive; in Sophocles 67 futures and 55 subjunctives; in Euripides 131 futures and 177 subjunctives. If we omit the futures which are equivalent to μέλλω with an infinitive, for which the subjunctive could not be substituted (see 407), we have in Aeschylus 15 futures in future conditions and 8 subjunctives; in Sophocles 46 and 55; in Euripides 98 and 177. In Attic prose Thucydides and Lysias have the largest proportion of futures; but in prose, as in Aristophanes, the subjunctives always preponderate.

they do not pay me a proper requital for my cattle, I (the Sun) *will descend to Hades and shine among the dead.* Od. xii. 382. Εἰ δὲ πρὸς τούτοισι ἔτι τελευτήσει τὸν βίον εὖ, οὗτος ἐκεῖνος τὸν σὺ ζητεῖς ὄλβιος κεκλῆσθαι ἄξιός ἐστι, *and if besides he shall still end his life well, he is that happy man you are seeking.* HDT. i. 32. Ἀλλ' εἴ σε μάρψει ψῆφος, ἀλλ' ἐρεῖς τάχα, *but if the judgment shall lay hold of you, you will soon tell another story.* AESCH. Eum. 597. See Prom. 311, Sept. 196, Suppl. 472, 474, 924, Cho. 683. Εἰ ταῦτα λέξεις, ἐχθαρεῖ μὲν ἐξ ἐμοῦ. SOPH. Ant. 93. See Ant. 229, 324, O. T. 843, 846, O. C. 628, Ph. 75, El. 465, 834, 1004. Εἰ τῷδ' ἀρκέσεις, κακὸς φανεῖ, *if you aid this man,* ·*you will appear base.* EUR. Hec. 1233. Μὴ ζώην, εἰ μὴ φάσγανον σπάσω. Id. Or. 1147. See Hec. 802, Or. 157, 272, 1212, Med. 346, 352, 381. Εἰ μὴ καθέξεις γλῶσσαν, ἔσται σοι κακά. EUR. Aeg. Fr. 5. Εἰ δὲ μὴ τοῦτ' ἐπιδείξει, πῶς χρὴ ταύτῃ τῇ προκλήσει προσέχειν ὑμᾶς τὸν νοῦν. DEM. xxvii. 52. Εἰ δ' ὑμεῖς ἄλλο τι γνώσεσθε, ὃ μὴ γένοιτο, τίνα οἴεσθε αὐτὴν ψυχὴν ἕξειν; *but if you shall give any other judgment,* etc. Id. xxviii. 21. (Referring to the same thing, xxvii. 67, Demosthenes had said ἐὰν γὰρ ἀποφύγῃ με οὗτος, ὃ μὴ γένοιτο, τὴν ἐπωβελίαν ὀφλήσω.) Ἢν ἐθέλωμεν ἀποθνήσκειν ὑπὲρ τῶν δικαίων, εὐδοκιμήσομεν· εἰ δὲ φοβησόμεθα τοὺς κινδύνους, εἰς πολλὰς ταραχὰς καταστήσομεν ἡμᾶς αὐτούς. ISOC. vi. 107. Here what is feared is expressed by the emphatic future as a warning, while the alternative that is preferred has the subjunctive. See also DEM. xviii. 176, where εἰ προαιρήσομεθ' ἡμεῖς, εἴ τι δύσκολον πέπρακται Θηβαίοις πρὸς ἡμᾶς, τούτου μεμνῆσθαι, *if we shall prefer to remember every unpleasant thing the Thebans have ever done to us,* is vividly stated by the future, as this is the course which the orator specially fears and wishes to warn the people against; while he puts his own proposition into the milder subjunctive form, ἢν μέντοι πεισθῆτ' ἐμοὶ καὶ πρὸς τῷ σκοπεῖν ἀλλὰ μὴ φιλονεικεῖν γένησθε. See also ISOC. xv. 130. In other cases it is difficult to detect any distinction, as in DEM. xxvii. 67 and xxviii. 21 (above), and in HDT. i. 71; cf. Il. i. 135 and 137.

448. The future in protasis is also appropriately used when a future apodosis is implied in a past tense; as in SOPH. O. T. 843, εἰ λέξει τὸν αὐτὸν ἀριθμόν, οὐκ ἐγὼ 'κτάνον, *if he shall tell the same number* (it will follow that) *I did not kill him.* So EUR. Med. 1249.

449. This use of the future must be distinguished from its use in present conditions (407), where it is equivalent to μέλλω and the infinitive and cannot be interchanged with the subjunctive.

HOMERIC PECULIARITIES.

In the Homeric language the following peculiarities appear in this construction:—

450. By far the most common Homeric form with the sub-

junctive in future conditions is εἴ κε, often εἰ μέν κε, εἰ δέ κε, etc.
(218). Ἦν also is frequent, being the only Homeric contraction
of εἰ ἄν. Εἰ δ᾽ ἄν occurs in Il. iii. 288, and εἴ περ ἄν in Il. v.
224 and 232. Ἦν περ γάρ κ᾽ ἐθέλωσιν is found in Od. xviii.
318.

451. Εἴ κε or αἴ κε is sometimes found even with the future
indicative in Homer. *E.g.*

Αἴ κεν ἄνευ ἐμέθεν Ἰλίου πεφιδήσεται οὐδ᾽ ἐθελήσει ἐκπέρσαι, ἴστω τοῦτο. Il. xv. 213. (See 196.)

452. The subjunctive with κέ is sometimes used in the apodosis
instead of the future indicative, thus making the apodosis correspond in form to the protasis. *E.g.*

Εἰ δέ κε μὴ δώῃσιν, ἐγὼ δέ κεν αὐτὸς ἕλωμαι, and *if he do not
give her up, I will take her myself.* Il. i. 324 (compare i. 137). This
gives a form with two subjunctives analogous to that which has the
optative in both protasis and apodosis (460). See 399. (For δέ in
apodosis see 512.)

For the Epic use of the future indicative with κέ or ἄν in apodosis,
see 196.

453. The simple εἰ (without κέ or ἄν) is sometimes used with
the subjunctive in future conditions in Homer, apparently in the
same sense as εἴ κε or ἦν. *E.g.*

Εἴ περ γάρ σε κατακτάνῃ, οὔ σ᾽ ἔτ᾽ ἐγώ γε κλαύσομαι. Il. xxii.
86. Εἰ δ᾽ αὖ τις ῥαίῃσι θεῶν ἐνὶ οἴνοπι πόντῳ, τλήσομαι ἐν στήθεσσιν ἔχων ταλαπενθέα θυμόν. Od. v. 221. So Il. i. 341, v. 258, xii.
223, 245 ; Od. i. 204, i. 188, xii. 348. Only these nine cases occur,
and the more common use of the simple εἰ with the subjunctive in
Homer is in general suppositions (see 468).

454. 1. This Homeric use of the simple εἰ with the subjunctive in future conditions was allowed by poetic license in a few
passages of the Attic drama, chiefly in tragedy, even in the
dialogue. *E.g.*

Εἰ γὰρ θάνῃς καὶ τελευτήσας ἀφῇς. SOPH. Aj. 496. Δυστάλαινα
τἄρ᾽ ἐγὼ εἴ σου στερηθῶ. Id. O. C. 1443. So Ant. 887. Εἰ μή σ᾽
ἐκφάγω ἐκ τῆσδε τῆς γῆς, οὐδέποτε βιώσομαι. AR. Eq. 698. So
AESCH. Pers. 791 ; EUR. Or. 1534, I. A. 1240, εἰ πεισθῇς (Mss.) ;
all in dialogue. In Sappho 118, 1 we have αἴ τις ἔρηται.

2. In Attic prose, this construction is extremely rare and always
doubtful. The Mss., however, have it in a few passages, as THUC. vi.
21 : Οὐ ναυτικῆς στρατιᾶς μόνον δεῖ, ἀλλὰ καὶ πεζὸν πολὺν ξυμπλεῖν,
ἄλλως τε καὶ εἰ ξυστῶσιν αἱ πόλεις φοβηθεῖσαι. (Here a few
inferior Mss. read ἤν.)

2. *Optative in Protasis and Apodosis.*

455. When a supposed future case is stated less distinctly and vividly than the subjunctive would state it (as *if I should go* in English), the protasis takes the optative with εἰ. The apodosis takes the optative with ἄν to denote what *would be* the result if the condition of the protasis should be fulfilled. *E.g.*

Εἰ ἔλθοι, πάντ᾽ ἂν ἴδοι, *if he should go, he would see all.* Εἴ σ᾽ οὕτως ἐθέλοι φιλέειν κήδοιτό τε θυμῷ, τῷ κέν τις κείνων γε καὶ ἐκλελάθοιτο γάμοιο, *if she should be willing thus to love you,* etc., *then some of them would cease even to think of marriage.* Od. iii. 223. Ἦ κεν γηθήσαι Πρίαμος Πριάμοιό τε παῖδες, ἄλλοι τε Τρῶες μέγα κεν κεχαροίατο θυμῷ, εἰ σφῶιν τάδε πάντα πυθοίατο μαρναμένοιιν. Il. i. 255. ᾽Αλλ᾽ εἴ μοί τι πίθοιο, τό κεν πολὺ κέρδιον εἴη. Il. vii. 28. Εἴης φορητὸς οὐκ ἄν, εἰ πράσσοις καλῶς, *you would not be bearable if you should ever be in prosperity.* AESCH. Prom. 979. Οἶκος δ᾽ αὐτὸς, εἰ φθογγὴν λάβοι, σαφέστατ᾽ ἂν λέξειεν. Id. Ag. 37. Οὐδὲ γὰρ ἂν Μήδοκός με ὁ βασιλεὺς ἐπαινοίη, εἰ ἐξελαύνοιμι τοὺς εὐεργέτας. XEN. An. vii. 7, 11. Οὐδ᾽ εἰ πάντες ἔλθοιεν Πέρσαι, πλήθει γε οὐχ ὑπερβαλοίμεθ᾽ ἂν τοὺς πολεμίους. Id. Cyr. ii. 1, 8. Οὐ πολλὴ ἂν ἀλογία εἴη, εἰ φοβοῖτο τὸν θάνατον ὁ τοιοῦτος; PLAT. Phaed. 68 B. Εἰ δέ τις τοὺς κρατοῦντας τοῦ πλήθους ἐπ᾽ ἀρετὴν προτρέψειεν, ἀμφοτέρους ἂν ὀνήσειε. ISOC. ii. 8. Εἴ τις τῶν σοι συνόντων ἐπαρθείη ποιεῖν ἃ σὺ τυγχάνεις εὐλογῶν, πῶς οὐκ ἂν ἀθλιώτατος εἴη; Id. xi. 47. Πῶς οὖν οὐκ ἂν οἰκτρότατα πάντων ἐγὼ πεπονθὼς εἴην, εἰ ἐμὲ ψηφίσαιντο εἶναι ξένον; *how then should I not have suffered* (lit. *be hereafter in the condition of having suffered) the most pitiable of all things, if they should vote me a foreigner?* DEM. lvii. 44. (See 103 for other examples of the perfect optative.)

456. This form of the conditional sentence in its fully developed use, as it appears in Attic Greek, must be carefully distinguished from that of 410 ; the more so, as we often translate both εἴη ἄν and ἦν ἄν by the same English expression, *it would be;* although the latter implies that the supposition of the protasis is a false one, while the former implies no opinion of the speaker as to the truth of the supposition. We have seen (438-440) that the more primitive Homeric language had not yet fully separated these two constructions, and still used the optative in the apodosis of present, and sometimes of past, unreal conditions.

On the other hand, the distinction between this form and that of 444 is less marked, and it is sometimes of slight importance which of the two is used. As it is often nearly indifferent in English whether we say *if we shall go* (or *if we go*) *it will be well,* or *if we should go it would be well,* so may it be in Greek whether we say ἐὰν ἔλθωμεν

καλῶς ἕξει or εἰ ἔλθοιμεν καλῶς ἂν ἔχοι.   In writing Greek, this
distinction can generally be made by first observing the form of the
apodosis in English; if that is expressed by *should* or *would*, it is to
be translated by the Greek optative with ἄν; if it is expressed by
shall or *will*, by the future indicative.   Other forms of the apodosis,
as the imperative, will present no difficulty.   The form to be used
in the protasis will then appear from the principles of the dependence
of moods (170-178); the optative will require another optative with
εἰ in the dependent protasis, while the future indicative or any other
primary form will require a subjunctive with ἐάν or a future indicative
with εἰ.

457. In indirect discourse after past tenses we often find an optative
in protasis, which merely represents the same tense of the subjunctive
or indicative in the direct discourse.   See 667, 1; 689 ; 694.

For the occasional omission of ἄν in an apodosis of this kind, see
240-242.

458. The potential optative with ἄν may stand in the protasis
with εἰ; as in εἰ ἔλθοιμι ἄν, *supposing that I would go*, easily distinguished from εἰ ἔλθοιμι, *supposing that I should go*.   Such an expression does not belong here, but is really a present condition.   (See
409; 506.)

459. The future optative cannot be used in protasis or apodosis,
except in indirect discourse to represent a future indicative of the
direct discourse.   (See 128 and 203.)

HOMERIC PECULIARITIES.

460. Εἴ κε with the optative is sometimes found in Homer,
and εἴ περ ἄν occurs once.[1]   This is a mark of the unsettled usage
of the earlier language, in which κέ or ἄν was not yet required
with the subjunctive in protasis, and was still allowed with the
optative or indicative (401).   It is difficult to see any essential
difference between these protases with εἴ κε and those with the
simple εἰ and the optative.   *E.g.*

Εἰ δέ κεν Ἄργος ἱκοίμεθ' Ἀχαιικόν, οὖθαρ ἀρούρης, γαμβρός
κέν μοι ἔοι, *and if we should ever come to Achaean Argos, then he would
(shall) be my son-in-law.* Il. ix. 141 ; cf. ix. 283, and Od. xii. 345, xix.
589.   Πῶς ἂν ἐγώ σε δέοιμι μετ' ἀθανάτοισι θεοῖσιν, εἴ κεν Ἄρης
οἴχοιτο χρέος καὶ δεσμὸν ἀλύξας. Od. viii. 352.   Τῶν κέν τοι χαρίσαιτο πατὴρ ἀπερείσι' ἄποινα, εἴ κεν ἐμὲ ζωὸν πεπύθοιτ' ἐπὶ
νηυσὶν Ἀχαιῶν. Il. vi. 49.   The distinction between these cases and
those of 458 is obvious.

In Il. i. 60, εἴ κεν with the optative forms a subordinate protasis,

---

[1] See the examples in Lange, *Partikel EI*, pp. 185, 186.   There are
twenty-six cases of εἴ κε with the optative in Homer, and one of εἴ περ ἄν (Il.
ii. 597) ; besides Il. v. 273 (= viii. 196) and Od. xvii. 223, mentioned in the
text (461).

with a remoter and less emphatic supposition than the main protasis εἰ δαμᾷ (future); νῦν ἄμμε πάλιν πλαγχθέντας οἴω ἂψ ἀπονοστήσειν, εἴ κεν θάνατόν γε φύγοιμεν, εἰ δὴ ὁμοῦ πόλεμός τε δαμᾷ καὶ λοιμὸς Ἀχαιούς, *now I think we shall be driven back and shall return home again—that is, supposing us to escape death—if both war and pestilence are at the same time to destroy the Achaeans.* In Il. ii. 597 we have εἴ περ ἂν αὐταὶ Μοῦσαι ἀείδοιεν. These constructions are never negative.

461. In the strange protasis, εἰ τούτω κε λάβοιμεν, Il. v. 273 and viii. 196, the separation of εἰ from κέ might compel us to recognise a potential force, *if we could (possibly) secure these;* but the difference between this and the Attic examples of εἰ with the potential optative and ἄν (458 ; 506), and the difficulty of seeing any difference between this and εἰ τούτω λάβοιμεν, *if we should secure these,* induced Bekker to read εἰ τούτω γε λάβοιμεν here, and also τόν γ᾽ εἴ μοι δοίης (for τόν κ᾽ εἰ) in Od. xvii. 223.

The Homeric use of the optative in present and past unreal conditional sentences has been discussed (438).

II. PRESENT AND PAST GENERAL SUPPOSITIONS.

462. In present or past general suppositions, the apodosis expresses a *customary* or *repeated* action or a *general truth* in present or past time, and the protasis refers in a general way to *any* act or acts of a given class. Here the protasis has the subjunctive with ἐάν after present tenses, and the optative with εἰ after past tenses. The apodosis has the present or imperfect indicative, or some other form which implies repetition. *E.g.*

Ἢν ἐγγὺς ἔλθῃ θάνατος, οὐδεὶς βούλεται θνήσκειν, *if (or when) death comes near, no one is (ever) willing to die.* EUR. Alc. 671. Ἢν μὲν ἄδῃ καὶ νήφουσι, χρέωνται αὐτῷ· ἢν δὲ μὴ ἄδῃ, μετιεῖσι. HDT. i. 133. Διατελεῖ μισῶν, οὐκ ἢν τίς τι αὐτὸν ἀδικῇ, ἀλλ᾽ ἐάν τινα ὑποπτεύσῃ βελτίονα ἑαυτοῦ εἶναι, *he continues to hate, not if any one wrongs him, but if he ever suspects that any one is better than himself.* XEN. Cyr. v. 4, 35. Ἅπας λόγος, ἂν ἀπῇ τὰ πράγματα, μάταιόν τι φαίνεται καὶ κενόν, *all speech, if deeds are wanting, appears mere emptiness and vanity.* DEM. ii. 12. Ἐὰν δὲ δόξῃ τὰ δίκαια ἐγκαλεῖν καὶ ἕλῃ τὸν δεδρακότα τοῦ φόνου, οὐδ᾽ οὕτω κύριος γίγνεται τοῦ ἀλόντος. Id. xxiii. 69 (so 74, 75, 76).

Ἀλλ᾽ εἴ τι μὴ φέροιμεν, ὤτρυνεν φέρειν, *but if we ever stopped bringing him food, he always urged us to bring it.* EUR. Alc. 755. Εἴ τις ἀντείποι, εὐθὺς τεθνήκει, *if any one objected, he was a dead man at once* (52). THUC. viii. 66. Εἴ τινα πυνθάνοιτο ὑβρίζοντα, τοῦτον ἐδικαίευ. HDT. i. 100. Εἰ δέ τινας θορυβουμένους αἴσθοιτο, τὸ αἴτιον τούτου σκοπῶν κατασβεννύναι τὴν ταραχὴν ἐπειρᾶτο, *whenever he saw any making a disturbance, he always tried*, etc. XEN. Cyr. v. 3, 55. Οὐκ ἀπελείπετο ἔτι αὐτοῦ, εἰ μή τι ἀναγκαῖον εἴη, *he never left him, unless there was some necessity for it*. Id. Mem. iv. 2, 40. *Ἦν τοῖς μὲν ὀφθαλμοῖς ἐπικούρημα τῆς χιόνος, εἴ τις μέλαν τι ἔχων πρὸ τῶν ὀφθαλμῶν πορεύοιτο, τῶν δὲ ποδῶν εἴ τις κινοῖτο.* Id. An. iv. 5, 13. Ἐπειδὴ δὲ εἶδον αὐτὸν τάχιστα, συλλαβόντες ἄγουσιν ἄντικρυς ὡς ἀποκτενοῦντες, οὗπερ καὶ τοὺς ἄλλους ἀπέσφαττον εἴ τινα λῃστὴν ἢ κακοῦργον συλλάβοιεν, i.e. *where they had been in the habit of killing any others whom they took.* LYS. xiii. 78.

463. This optative referring to past time must be especially distinguished from the optative in ordinary protasis referring to the future (455). Εἰ and ἐάν in this construction are often almost equivalent to ὅτε or ὅταν (which are the more common expressions), and the protasis has precisely the same construction as the relative sentences of 532.

464. The present and aorist subjunctive and optative here do not differ except as explained in 87. The future optative of course is never used here (128).

465. The examples in 462 exhibit the ordinary Attic usage. In Homer we find this construction in a partially developed state : see 468.

466. The gnomic aorist (154) and other gnomic and iterative expressions (162 ; 163) may be used in the apodosis of these general conditions. The gnomic aorist, as a primary tense, is followed by the subjunctive. *E.g.*

Ἦν σφαλῶσιν, ἀντελπίσαντες ἄλλα ἐπλήρωσαν τὴν χρείαν, if they fail, they always supply the deficiency, etc. THUC. i. 70. *Ἦν δέ τις τούτων τι παραβαίνῃ, ζημίαν αὐτοῖς ἐπέθεσαν, they (always) impose a penalty upon every one who transgresses.* XEN. Cyr. i. 2, 2. Εἴ τινες ἴδοιέν πῃ τοὺς σφετέρους ἐπικρατοῦντας, ἀνεθάρσησαν ἄν, *whenever any saw their friends in any way victorious, they would be encouraged (i.e. they were encouraged in all such cases).* THUC. vii. 71. See XEN. Mem. iv. 6, 13, quoted in 162.

467. (*Indicative.*) The indicative is sometimes found in the place of the subjunctive or optative in these general conditions, that is, these follow the construction of ordinary present and past suppositions, as in Latin and English. Here the speaker refers to one of the cases in which the event may occur, as if it were the only one,—that is, he states the *general* supposition as if it were *particular. E.g.*

Μοῖραι δ' ἀφίσταντ', εἴ τις ἔχθρα πέλει ὁμογόνοις, αἰδῶ καλύψαι, *the Fates stand aloof to hide their shame, if there is enmity among kindred.* PIND. Py. iv. 145 ; cf. Ol. i. 64. (See 406.) Εἴ τις δύο ἢ καὶ πλέους

τις ἡμέρας λογίζεται, μάταιός ἐστιν, if any one ever counts upon two
or even more days, he is a fool. SOPH. Tr. 944. Ἐλευθέρως πολιτεύο-
μεν, οὐ δι' ὀργῆς τὸν πέλας, εἰ καθ' ἡδονήν τι δρᾷ, ἔχοντες, i.e. not
(having a habit of) being angry with our neighbour if he ever acts as he
pleases. THUC. ii. 37. (Here the indicative δρᾷ is used as if some
particular act of one neighbour, and not any act of any neighbour,
were in mind.) Εἰ γάρ τις ἐν δημοκρατίᾳ τετιμημένος τολμᾷ
βοηθεῖν τοῖς παράνομα γράφουσιν, καταλύει τὴν πολιτείαν ὑφ' ἧς
τετίμηται. AESCHIN. iii. 196. Εἴ τίς τι ἐπηρώτα, ἀπεκρίνοντο, if any
one asked anything, they replied (to all such). THUC. vii. 10. Ἐμίσει
οὐκ εἴ τις κακῶς πάσχων ἠμύνετο, ἀλλ' εἴ τις εὐεργετούμενος ἀχάρι-
στος φαίνοιτο. XEN. Ag. xi. 3. Here, without any apparent reason,
the writer changes from the indicative to the optative. (See 534.)

HOMERIC AND OTHER POETIC PECULIARITIES.

468. In Homer the subjunctive appears in protasis in general
suppositions (462) only nineteen times, and the optative only
once. Here the subjunctive generally (in fourteen cases) has
the simple εἰ (without κέ or ἄν). E.g.

Εἴ περ γάρ τε χόλον γε καὶ αὐτῆμαρ καταπέψῃ, ἀλλά γε καὶ
μετόπισθεν ἔχει κότον, ὄφρα τελέσσῃ, for even if he swallows his wrath
for the day, still he keeps his anger hereafter, until he accomplishes its object.
Il. i. 81. Τῶν οὔ τι μετατρέπομ' οὐδ' ἀλεγίζω, εἴ τ' ἐπὶ δεξί'
ἴωσι, εἴ τ' ἐπ' ἀριστερά, I do not heed them nor care for them, whether they
go to the right or to the left. Il. xii. 238. So Il. iv. 262, x. 225, xi. 116,
xvi. 263, xxi. 576, xxii. 191 (the last four in similes); Od. i. 167,
vii. 204, xii. 96, xiv. 373, xvi. 98 (= 116).

Ἦν ποτε δασμὸς ἵκηται, σοὶ τὸ γέρας πολὺ μεῖζον, if ever a
division comes, your prize is always much greater. Il. i. 166. So Od. xi.
159, ἢν μή τις ἔχῃ. Besides these two cases of ἤν, Homer has two
of εἴ κε, Il. xi. 391, xii. 302; and one of εἴ περ ἄν, Il. iii. 25 (five in
all).

The single case of εἰ with the optative in a past general condition
in Homer is Il. xxiv. 768: ἀλλ' εἴ τίς με καὶ ἄλλος ἐνίπτοι, ἀλλὰ
σὺ τόν γε κατέρυκες, but if any other upbraided me, you (always) re-
strained him.

469. Pindar has only eight cases of the subjunctive in protasis.
These all have general suppositions and all have the simple εἰ;[1] as
πολλοὶ δὲ μέμνανται, καλὸν εἴ τι ποναθῇ, but many remember it if a
noble work is done, Ol. vi. 11.

470. The other lyric and elegiac poets show no preference for the
simple εἰ. The following cases may be cited: CALL. i. 13 εἰ ᾖ (but ἤν

[1] Am. Jour. Phil. iii. p. 443. The examples are Ol. vi. 11; Pyth. iv.
266, 273 (perhaps also 263); Nem. vii. 11, ix. 46; Isth. iii. 58, iv. 12; Frag.
171 (Böckh), 5. The references to the other poets in 470 and 471 do not
profess to be complete.

in 17); TYRT. xii. 35 εἰ φύγῃ (but ἦν xi. 16); SOT. iv. 30 εἰ ᾖ ? (but ἦν xii. 1, xiii. 29); THEOG. 121, 122 εἰ λελήθῃ . . . ἔχῃ, and 321 εἰ ὀπάσσῃ (but ἦν 93, 186, 379, 697, 929, 932, 1355, 1356, 1385); all (both εἰ and ἦν) in general conditions. See SIM. AMORG. vii. 15, 69, 97 (ἦν).

471. In the Attic poets we find a few cases of the simple εἰ in general conditions. *E.g.*

Ἀλλ' ἄνδρα, κεἴ τις ᾖ σοφός, τὸ μανθάνειν πόλλ' αἰσχρὸν οὐδὲν καὶ τὸ μὴ τείνειν ἄγαν. SOPH. Ant. 710. So Aj. 521 ; O. T. 198, 874 ; O. C. 509 ; AESCH. Supp. 91, Eum. 234.

For the simple εἰ in future conditions, see 453 ; 454. For the probable relation of εἰ to εἴ κε, ἤν, ἐάν, etc., see 401.

PECULIAR FORMS OF CONDITIONAL SENTENCES.

Substitution and Ellipsis in Protasis.—Protasis without a Verb.

472. Often the protasis is not expressed in its regular form with εἰ or ἐάν, but is contained in a participle, or implied in an adverb like οὕτως or δικαίως, in a preposition with its case, or in some other form of expression. When a participle represents the protasis (841), its *tense* is always that in which the verb itself would have stood in the indicative, subjunctive, or optative. The present (as usual) includes the imperfect, and the perfect includes the pluperfect. *E.g.*

Τοῦτο ποιοῦντες εὖ πράξουσιν (i.e. ἐὰν ποιῶσιν), *if they (shall) do this, they will prosper.* Τοῦτο ποιήσαντες εὖ πράξουσιν (i.e. ἐὰν ποιήσωσιν). Τοῦτο ποιοῦντες εὖ ἂν πράττοιεν (i.e. εἰ ποιοῖεν), *if they should do this, they would prosper.* Τοῦτο ποιήσαντες εὖ ἂν πράττοιεν (i.e. εἰ ποιήσαιεν). Τοῦτο ποιοῦντες εὖ ἂν ἔπραττον (i.e. εἰ ἐποίουν), *if they were doing this (or if they had been doing this), they would be in prosperity.* Τοῦτο ποιήσαντες εὖ ἂν ἔπραττον (i.e. εἰ ἐποίησαν), *if they had done this, they would be in prosperity.*

Πῶς δῆτα δίκης οὔσης ὁ Ζεὺς οὐκ ἀπόλωλεν τὸν πατέρ' αὐτοῦ δήσας; i.e. *how is it that Zeus has not been destroyed, if Justice exists?* AR. Nub. 904. (Here δίκης οὔσης represents εἰ δίκη ἐστίν.) Ἀλλ' εἰσόμεσθα δόμους παραστείχοντες (ἐὰν παραστείχωμεν), *but we shall know, if we enter the house.* SOPH. Ant. 1255. Σὺ δὲ κλύων εἴσει τάχα (ἐὰν κλύῃς), *but you will soon know, if you listen.* AR. Av. 1390. So μὴ μαθών, *unless I learn,* for ἐὰν μὴ μάθω, Nub. 792. Καί κεν τοῦτ' ἐθέλοιμι Διός γε διδόντος ἀρέσθαι (Διὸς δίδοντος = εἰ Ζεὺς διδοίη), *and this I should like to obtain, if Zeus would only give it.* Od. i. 390. Τοιαῦτά τἂν γυναιξὶ συνναίων ἔχοις (εἰ συνναίοις), *such things would you suffer, if you should live with women.* AESCH. Sept. 195. Οὐδ' ἂν σιωπήσαιμι τὴν ἄτην ὁρῶν στείχουσαν ἀστοῖς (i.e. εἰ ὁρῴην). SOPH. Ant. 185. Ἀθηναίων δὲ τὸ αὐτὸ τοῦτο παθόντων, διπλασίαν ἂν τὴν δύναμιν εἰκάζεσθαι (οἶμαι), but *if the Athenians should ever suffer this* (παθόντων = εἰ πάθοιεν), *I think it would be inferred that their power was twice as great.* Thuc. i. 10. (Here only the context shows that παθόντων does not represent εἰ ἔπαθον, *if they had ever suffered.*) Πρὶν γενέσθαι ἠπίστησεν ἄν τις ἀκούσας (i.e. εἰ ἤκουσεν), *before it happened, any one would have disbelieved such a thing if he had heard it.* Thuc. vii. 28. Οὐ γὰρ ἂν μεταπείθειν ὑμᾶς ἐζήτει μὴ τοιαύτης οὔσης τῆς ὑπαρχούσης ὑπολήψεως, *for he would not be seeking to change your minds, if such were not the prevailing opinion* (i.e. εἰ μὴ τοιαύτη ἦν). Dem. xviii. 228. Ἔστιν οὖν ὅπως ταῦτ᾽ ἄν, ἐκεῖνα προειρηκὼς, ὁ αὐτὸς ἀνὴρ μὴ διαφθαρεὶς ἐτόλμησεν εἰπεῖν; *is it possible then that the same man, after saying that, would have dared to say this unless he had been corrupted* (εἰ μὴ διεφθάρη)? Id. xix. 308. Μὴ κατηγορήσαντος Αἰσχίνου μηδὲν ἔξω τῆς γραφῆς οὐδ᾽ ἂν ἐγὼ λόγον οὐδένα ἐποιούμην ἕτερον (εἰ μὴ κατηγόρησεν). Id. xviii. 34. Τὰ αὐτὰ ἂν ἔπραξε καὶ πρώτη λαχοῦσα (i.e. εἰ πρώτη ἔλαχεν), *it (the soul) would have done the same, even if it had had the first choice by the lot.* Plat. Rep. 620 D. Μαμμᾶν δ᾽ ἂν αἰτήσαντος ἧκόν σοι φέρων ἂν ἄρτον, *and if you ever asked for something to eat, I used to come bringing you bread.* Ar. Nub. 1383. (Here αἰτήσαντος represents εἰ αἰτήσειας in a *general* supposition, 462. For ἧκον ἄν see 162.)

Οὔτε ἐσθίουσι πλείω ἢ δύνανται φέρειν, διαρραγεῖεν γὰρ ἄν· οὔτ᾽ ἀμφιέννυνται πλείω ἢ δύνανται φέρειν, ἀποπνιγεῖεν γὰρ ἄν, *they do not eat more than they can bear, for (if they should) they would burst,* etc. Xen. Cyr. viii. 2, 21. Αὐτοὶ ἂν ἐπορεύθησαν ᾗ οἱ ἄλλοι· τὰ δ᾽ ὑποζύγια οὐκ ἦν ἄλλῃ ἢ ταύτῃ ἐκβῆναι, *they would have gone themselves where the others went; but the animals could not go otherwise than as they did.* Id. An. iv. 2, 10. So ᾗ γὰρ ἂν λωβήσαιο, Il. i. 232.

Ἡμῖν δ᾽ ἐξ πολλῆς ἂν περιουσίας νεῶν μόλις τοῦτο ὑπῆρχε καὶ μὴ ἀναγκαζομένοις, ὥσπερ νῦν, πάσαις φυλάσσειν, *but we should hardly have this advantage if we had a great superiority in number of ships* (= εἰ πολλὴν περιουσίαν εἴχομεν) *and if we were not compelled* (εἰ μὴ ἠναγκαζόμεθα), *as we are, to use our whole fleet in guarding.* Thuc. vii. 13. Τὸ μὲν ἐπ᾽ ἐκείνῳ πολλάκις ἂν διελύθησαν, *if it had depended on him, they often would have been disbanded.* Isoc. iv. 142. Διά γε ὑμᾶς αὐτοὺς πάλαι ἂν ἀπολώλειτε, *if it had depended on yourselves, you would long ago have been ruined.* Dem. xviii. 49. (So sometimes καθ᾽ ὑμᾶς.) Πάλαι γὰρ ἂν ἕνεκά γε ψηφισμάτων ἐδεδώκει δίκην, *for, if decrees were of any avail, he would long ago have suffered punishment.* Id. iii. 14. (Here the protasis is implied in ἕνεκα ψηφισμάτων.) Οὕτω γὰρ οὐκέτι τοῦ λοιποῦ πάσχοιμεν ἂν κακῶς, *for in that case we should no longer suffer.* Id. iv. 15. So ὡς οὕτω περιγενόμενος ἄν, Xen. An. i. 1, 10. Οὐδ᾽ ἂν δικαίως ἐς κακὸν πέσοιμί τι. Soph. Ant. 240.

In such cases the form of the apodosis generally shows what form of protasis is implied. When the apodosis is itself expressed by an infinitive or participle (479), as in Thuc. i. 10 (above), the form of the protasis is shown only by the general sense of the passage.

473. The future participle is not used to represent the future indicative in future conditions (447); it may, however, represent the future in *present* conditions (407), where it is equivalent to μέλλω and the infinitive; as in DEM. xxiv. 189, μὴ περὶ τούτων ὑμῶν οἰσόντων τὴν ψῆφον, τί δεῖ ταῦτα λέγοντα ἐνοχλεῖν με νυνί; *if you are not to give your vote about this*, μὴ οἰσόντων representing εἰ μὴ οἴσετε = εἰ μὴ μέλλετε φέρειν. The present and aorist participles, when they represent the present and aorist subjunctive, express future conditions, thus making the future participle unnecessary. The aorist participle in protasis can always represent an aorist subjunctive in the sense explained in 90.

474. The verb of the protasis is suppressed in the Homeric εἰ δ᾽ ἄγε, *come now!* This is commonly explained by an ellipsis of βούλει, *if you will, come now!* But it is probable that no definite verb was in the speaker's mind in such expressions, even when we find it necessary to supply one. *E.g.*

Εἰ δ᾽ ἄγε, τοι κεφαλῇ κατανεύσομαι, *come now! I will nod my assent to thee.* Il. i. 524. Εἰ δ᾽ ἄγε μὴν, πείρησαι, ἵνα γνώωσι καὶ οἴδε, *well! come now, try it.* Il. i. 302. Εἰ μὲν δὴ θεός ἐσσι θεοῖό τε ἔκλυες αὐδῆς, εἰ δ᾽ ἄγε μοι καὶ κεῖνον ὀϊζυρὸν κατάλεξον (the apodosis being introduced by εἰ δ᾽ ἄγε, *come now, tell me*). Od. iv. 831.

475. ('Ως εἰ.) There is a probably unconscious suppression of the verb of the protasis when ὡς εἰ or ὡς εἴ τε is used in comparisons (especially in Homer) with a noun or adjective or with a participle. *E.g.*

Τῶν νέες ὠκεῖαι ὡς εἰ πτερὸν ἠὲ νόημα, *their ships are swift as (if) a wing or thought.* Od. vii. 36. 'Ως μ᾽ ἀσύφηλον ἔρεξεν Ἀτρεΐδης ὡς εἴ τιν᾽ ἀτίμητον μετανάστην, *for the son of Atreus insulted me like* (i.e *as if he were insulting) some despised wanderer.* Il. ix. 648. Ἐπλέομεν Βορέῃ ἀνέμῳ ῥηϊδίως ὡς εἴ τε κατὰ ῥόον, *we sailed on with the north-east wind easily, as if (we were sailing) down stream.* Od. xiv. 253. In all these cases no definite verb was in mind after εἰ, but the addition of εἰ to ὡς shows that a conditional force was felt (at least originally) in addition to the comparison ; and this is the only difference between these examples and those with the simple ὡς or ὡς τε, as ἑστήκειν ὡς τίς τε λέων, *he stood like a lion.*[1] In Attic poetry we find μάτηρ ὡσεί τις πιστά, *like some faithful mother*, SOPH. El. 234 ; and πτύσας ὡσεί τε δυσμενῆ, *spurning her as an enemy*, Ant. 653. With Od. vii. 36 compare Hymn. Ap. Py. 8, πρὸς Ὄλυμπον ὥστε νόημα εἶσι, and 270, ἐπὶ νῆα νόημ᾽ ὡς ἆλτο πέτεσθαι.

---

[1] See Lange, *Partikel EI*, p. 234. Lange is at great pains to show that there is no ellipsis here, or indeed in any cases of εἰ without a verb like εἴ περ ἀνάγκη, *if necessary.* By "ellipsis" we often mean merely what one language finds it necessary to supply to translate an idiom of another. There are few ellipses of which a speaker is really conscious when he uses them. In this sense, it seems to me that, whenever we use *if* without a verb, there is at least a *suppression* (if not an *ellipsis*) of a verb.

'Ολοφυρόμενοι ὡς εἰ θανατόνδε κιόντα, *bewailing him as if going to
his death* (in full *as if they were bewailing him going*), for which we say
(changing the construction) *as if he were going.* Il. xxiv. 328. See also
Il. xvi. 192, v. 374. Ἀμφὶ δὲ καπνὸς γίγνεται ἐξ αὐτῆς ὡς εἰ πυρὸς
αἰθομένοιο, i.e. *the smoke rises from it* (the fountain) *as if (it rose) from a
blazing fire.* Il. xxii. 150. So Od. xix. 39. What seems like a more
natural construction with ὡς εἰ or ὡς εἴ τε is that of the optative with
the apodosis suppressed (485).

In all these cases there is also a suppression of the verb of the
apodosis (see 485).

For the participle in such expressions see 867-869.

476. (Εἰ μή.) Εἰ μή is used without a verb in various expressions to introduce an exception.

1. With nouns and adjectives. *E.g.*

Τίς γάρ τοι Ἀχαιῶν ἄλλος ὁμοῖος, εἰ μὴ Πάτροκλος; *who is like
to you, except (unless it be) Patroclus?* Il. xvii. 475. See Il. xviii. 192,
xxiii. 792 ; Od. xii. 325, xvii. 383. Such expressions are like the
simple εἰ τό γ᾽ ἄμεινον, *if this is better,* Il. i. 116 ; εἰ ἐτεόν περ, xiv.
125 ; εἴ περ ἀνάγκη, xxiv. 667.

2. With participles. *E.g.*

Εἰ μὴ κρεμάσας τὸ νόημα, i.e. *I could never have done it, except by
suspending thought.* Ar. Nub. 229. So οὐδέν ποτ᾽ εἰ μὴ ξυνθανουμένην,
Aesch. Ag. 1139 ; εἰ μὴ καταδύσαντες, Thuc. vii. 38 ; ἐὰν μὴ τῆς
ἀδείας δοθείσης, Dem. xxiv. 46.

3. In the expression εἰ μὴ διὰ τοῦτο (or τοῦτον). *E.g.*

Καὶ εἰ μὴ διὰ τὸν πρύτανιν, ἐνέπεσεν ἄν, *and, had it not been for the
Prytanis, he would have been thrown in.* Plat. Gorg. 516 E. (Compare
διά γε ὑμᾶς, Dem. xviii. 49, quoted in 472.) Οὐ γὰρ ὡς εἰ μὴ διὰ
Λακεδαιμονίους, οὐδ᾽ ὡς εἰ μὴ Πρόξενον οὐχ ὑπεδέξαντο, οὐδ᾽ ὡς εἰ μὴ
δι᾽ Ἡγήσιππον, οὐδ᾽ ὡς εἰ μὴ διὰ τὸ καὶ τὸ, ἐσώθησαν ἂν οἱ Φωκεῖς,
οὐχ οὕτω τότε ἀπήγγειλεν, *for he did not then report that if it had not
been for the Lacedaemonians, or if they had not refused to receive Proxenus,
or if it had not been for Hegesippus, or if it had not been for this and that,
the Phocians would have been saved.* Dem. xix. 74.

4. In the rare expression εἰ μὴ εἰ, *except if, except in case that.*
E.g.

Ὁ χρηματιστικὸς τὴν τοῦ τιμᾶσθαι ἡδονὴν ἢ τὴν τοῦ μανθάνειν
οὐδενὸς ἀξίαν φήσει εἶναι, εἰ μὴ εἴ τι αὐτῶν ἀργύριον ποιεῖ, *the
money-maker will say that the pleasure of receiving honour or that of
learning is not worth anything, unless* (it is worth something) *in case either
of them produces money.* Plat. Rep. 581 D. In Prot. 351 C, ἐγὼ γὰρ
λέγω, καθ᾽ ὃ ἡδέα ἐστίν, ἆρα κατὰ τοῦτο οὐκ ἀγαθὰ, μὴ εἴ τι ἀπ᾽
αὐτῶν ἀποβήσεται ἄλλο ;—*for I ask this : so far as they are pleasant, are
they not just so far good, without taking into account any other result* (i.e.
other than their pleasantness) *which may come from them?*—μή is not
a mistake for εἰ μή, but it seems to imply a conditional participle like

ὑπολογιζόμενος (though no precise word can be supplied), very much
as μὴ ὅτι and μὴ ὅπως imply a verb of *saying* (707). The meaning
clearly is, *Are not things good just so far as they are pleasant, if we take
no account of any other* (i.e. *unpleasant*) *element in them?* This sense
would hardly be found in the emended reading εἰ μή τι. In Thuc.
i. 17 the Cod. Vat. reads εἰ μή τι, although εἰ μὴ εἴ τι can be understood as in Plat. Rep. 581 D (above).

477. Equivalent to εἰ μὴ εἰ (476, 4) is πλὴν εἰ, *except if* or
unless, in which πλήν represents the apodosis. *E.g.*

Οὐδὲ τὰ ὀνόματα οἷόν τε αὐτῶν εἰδέναι, πλὴν εἴ τις κωμῳδιοποιὸς
τυγχάνει ὤν, *it is not possible to know even their names, except in case one
happens to be a comedian.* Plat. Ap. 18 C.

478. In *alternatives*, εἰ δὲ μή, *otherwise*, regularly introduces
the latter clause, even when the former clause is negative. Εἰ
δὲ μή is much more common here than ἐὰν δὲ μή, even when ἐὰν
μέν with the subjunctive precedes. The formula εἰ δὲ μή was
fixed in the sense of *otherwise, in the other case,* and no definite
form of the verb was in mind.

Πρὸς ταῦτα μὴ τύπτ᾽· εἰ δὲ μή, σαυτόν ποτ᾽ αἰτιάσει, *therefore do
not beat me; but if you do, you will have yourself to blame for it.* Ar.
Nub. 1433. Εἰ μὴ θανοῦμαί γ᾽· εἰ δὲ μή, οὐ λείψω ποτέ, *if I do
not die (I will leave the place); otherwise (if I die) I shall never leave it.*
Eur. And. 254. See Soph. Tr. 587. Πόλεμον οὐκ εἴων ποιεῖν· εἰ
δὲ μή, καὶ αὐτοὶ ἀναγκασθήσεσθαι ἔφασαν φίλους ποιεῖσθαι οὓς οὐ
βούλονται, *they said that otherwise* (εἰ δὲ μή) *they should be obliged,* etc.
Thuc. i. 28. Εἶπον (Παυσανίᾳ) τοῦ κήρυκος μὴ λείπεσθαι· εἰ δὲ
μή, πόλεμον αὐτῷ Σπαρτιάτας προαγορεύειν, *they ordered him not to be
left behind by the herald: and if he should be* (εἰ δὲ μή), *(they told him)
that the Spartans declared war against him.* Id. i. 131. Μὴ ποιήσῃς
ταῦτα· εἰ δὲ μή, αἰτίαν ἕξεις. Xen. An. vii. 1, 8. Ἐὰν μέν τι ὑμῖν
δοκῶ ἀληθὲς λέγειν, ξυνομολογήσατε· εἰ δὲ μή, παντὶ λόγῳ ἀντι-
τείνετε. Plat. Phaed. 91 C. So ἐὰν μὲν πείσητε, . . . εἰ δὲ μή,
κ.τ.λ., Dem. ix. 71.

Εἰ δέ alone is sometimes used for εἰ δὲ μή; as in Plat. Symp. 212
C, εἰ μὲν βούλει, . . . εἰ δέ. So εἰ δ᾽ οὖν (sc. μή), Soph. Ant. 722,
Eur. Hipp. 508.

The potential optative and indicative with ἄν, so far as they are
apodoses, might be classed here; but these have higher claims to be
treated as independent sentences. See Chapter IV., Section I.

Substitution and Ellipsis in Apodosis.

479. The apodosis, in any of its forms, may be expressed by
an infinitive or participle, if the structure of the sentence requires it.

1. It may be expressed by the infinitive or participle in indirect discourse, each tense representing its own tenses of the indicative or optative, the present including the imperfect, and the perfect the pluperfect. If the finite verb in the apodosis would have taken ἄν, this particle is used with the infinitive or participle. *E.g.*

Ἡγοῦμαι, εἰ τοῦτο ποιεῖτε, πάντα καλῶς ἔχειν, *I believe that, if you are doing this, all is well.* Ἡγοῦμαι, ἐὰν τοῦτο ποιῆτε, πάντα καλῶς ἕξειν, *I believe that, if you (shall) do this, all will be well.* Ἡγοῦμαι, εἰ τοῦτο ποιοῖτε, πάντα καλῶς ἂν ἔχειν, *I believe that, if you should do this, all would be well.* Ἡγοῦμαι, εἰ τοῦτο ἐποιήσατε, πάντα καλῶς ἂν ἔχειν, *I believe that, if you had done this, all would now be* (or *would have been*) *well.* Οἶδα ὑμᾶς, ἐὰν τοῦτο ποιῆτε, εὖ πράξοντας, *I know that, if you do this, you will prosper.*

Πῶς γὰρ οἴεσθε δυσχερῶς ἀκούειν Ὀλυνθίους, εἴ τίς τι λέγοι κατὰ Φιλίππου κατ᾽ ἐκείνους τοὺς χρόνους; *how unwillingly do you think the O. heard it, if any one said anything against Philip in those times?* Dem. vi. 20. (Here ἀκούειν represents the imperfect ἤκουον, and εἰ λέγοι is a general supposition, 462.)

For examples of each tense of the infinitive and participle, see 689. For the use of each tense of the infinitive or participle with ἄν and examples, see 204-208 ; 213-216.

2. It may be expressed by the infinitive in any of its various constructions out of indirect discourse, especially by one depending on a verb of *wishing, commanding, advising, preparing*, etc., from which the infinitive receives a future meaning. Such an infinitive is a common form of future apodosis with a protasis in the subjunctive or indicative. *E.g.*

Βούλεται ἐλθεῖν ἐὰν τοῦτο γένηται, *he wishes to go if this shall be done.* Παρασκευαζόμεθα ἀπελθεῖν ἢν δυνώμεθα, *we are preparing to depart if we shall be able.* Κελεύει σε ἀπελθεῖν εἰ βούλει, *he bids you depart if you please.* (See 403 and 445.)

3. The apodosis may be expressed in an attributive or circumstantial participle. *E.g.*

Ῥᾳδίως ἂν ἀφεθεὶς εἰ καὶ μετρίως τι τούτων ἐποίησε, προείλετο ἀποθανεῖν, *whereas he might easily have been acquitted* (ἀφείθη ἄν), *if he had done any of these things even in a moderate degree, he chose to die.* Xen. Mem. iv. 4, 4. Σκέμματα τῶν ῥᾳδίως ἀποκτιννύντων καὶ ἀναβιωσκομένων γ᾽ ἄν, εἰ οἷοί τε ἦσαν, *considerations for those who readily put men to death, and who would bring them to life again too if they could.* Plat. Crit. 48 C. (Ἀναβιωσκομένων ἄν = ἀνεβιώσκοντο ἄν.) Ὡς οἷός τ᾽ ὢν σε σῴζειν εἰ ἤθελον ἀναλίσκειν χρήματα, *whereas I might have saved you if I had been willing to spend money.* Ib. 44 B.

480. A verbal noun may take the place of an apodosis. *E.g.*

Ὡς ὄντ᾽ ἀναστητῆρα Καδμείων χθονὸς εἰ μὴ θεῶν τις ἐμποδὼν

ἔστη δορί, as one who would have laid waste (= ἀνέστησεν ἄν) the
Cadmeans' land, if some one of the Gods had not stood in the way of his
spear. AESCH. Sept. 1015.

481. Other forms in which an apodosis may appear, as a final
clause, need no discussion. (See 445.)

In indirect discourse, after past tenses, an optative in the apodosis
often represents an original indicative or subjunctive. (See 15 and
457.)

482. The apodosis is sometimes omitted, when some such
expression as *it is well* or *it will be done* can be supplied, or when
some other apodosis is at once suggested by the context. *E.g.*

Ἀλλ' εἰ μὲν δώσουσι γέρας μεγάθυμοι Ἀχαιοί, ἄρσαντες κατὰ
θυμὸν, ὅπως ἀντάξιον ἔσται, — εἰ δέ κε μὴ δώωσιν, ἐγὼ δέ κεν
αὐτὸς ἕλωμαι, *if they give me a prize,—well ; but if they do not, I shall
take one for myself.* Il. i. 135. (Here we must understand something
like εὖ ἕξει, *it will be well,* after ἔσται.) Εἴ περ γάρ κ' ἐθέλῃσιν
Ὀλύμπιος ἀστεροπητὴς ἐξ ἑδέων στυφελίξαι·—ὁ γὰρ πολὺ φέρτατός
ἐστιν. Il. i. 580. (Here we must understand *he can do it* after the
protasis. The following γάρ refers to this suppressed apodosis.) Εἰ
μὲν ἐγὼ ὑμᾶς ἱκανῶς διδάσκω οἵους δεῖ πρὸς ἀλλήλους εἶναι·—εἰ δὲ
μὴ, καὶ παρὰ τῶν προγεγενημένων μανθάνετε. XEN. Cyr. viii. 7, 24.

Ξεῖνοι πατρώϊοι εὐχόμεθ' εἶναι, εἴ πέρ τε γέροντ' εἴρηαι ἐπελθὼν
Λαέρτην, *we boast that we are friends by inheritance, (as you may know)
if you go and ask Laertes.* Od. i. 187. Προσηγορεύθης ἡ Διὸς κλεινὴ
δάμαρ μέλλουσ' ἔσεσθ', εἰ τῶνδε προσσαίνει σέ τι. AESCH. Prom. 834.

483. Sometimes the adverb ἄν, without a verb expressed, represents an apodosis in the indicative or optative, when the verb
can easily be supplied. *E.g.*

Οἱ οἰκέται ῥέγκουσιν· ἀλλ' οὐκ ἂν πρὸ τοῦ (sc. οὕτως ἔρρεγκον),
but they would not have been snoring at this late hour in old times. AR.
Nub. 5. (See 227.) So πῶς γὰρ ἄν ; (sc. εἴη), *how could it be ?*

484. In ὥσπερ ἂν εἰ with a noun, as ὥσπερ ἂν εἰ παῖς, *like a child,*
there is originally a suppression of the verbs of both protasis and
apodosis (227 ; 485) ; but in use the expression hardly differs from
ὥσπερ. (See 868-870.)

485. (Ὡς εἰ and ὥσπερ εἰ.) There is an unconscious suppression of the verb of the apodosis when ὡς εἰ, ὡς εἴ τε, and
ὥσπερ εἰ are used in similes and comparisons. *E.g.*

Λαοὶ ἕποντ', ὡς εἴ τε μετὰ κτίλον ἕσπετο μῆλα, *the hosts followed
as if sheep followed a ram.* Il. xiii. 492. (No definite verb is understood here, either with ὡς in Greek or with *as* in English, but the
origin of the expression is the same in both.) Φιάλαν ὡς εἴ τις δωρή-
σεται. PIND. Ol. vii. 1. Καί με φίλησ' ὡς εἴ τε πατὴρ ὃν παῖδα
φιλήσῃ. Il. ix. 481. Οἱ δ' ἄρ' ἴσαν ὡς εἴ τε πυρὶ χθὼν πᾶσα νέμοιτο,
i.e. *their march was as if the whole land should flame with fire* (originally

as it would be if, etc.) Il. ii. 780. Βῆ δ' ἴμεν, πάντοσε χεῖρ' ὀρέγων ὡς εἰ πτωχὸς πάλαι εἴη, *holding out his hand as if he had long been a beggar* (438). Od. xvii. 366. For other optatives with ὡς εἰ, see Il. xi. 467, xxii. 410; Od. ix. 314, x. 416, 420. Ὥσπερ εἰ παρεστάτεις, *as if you had dwelt near by.* AESCH. Ag. 1201. Ὅμοια ὥσπερ εἴ τις πολλὰ ἐσθίων μηδέποτε ἐμπίπλαιτο, *just as if one should eat much and never be filled.* XEN. Symp. iv. 37.

There is the same suppression of the apodosis in the examples in 475, where the protasis also is wanting with ὡς εἰ and similar expressions.

Apodosis contained in the Protasis.

486. A protasis may depend on a verb which is not its apodosis, the real apodosis being so distinctly implied in the form of expression that it need not be stated separately.

487. 1. This is found especially in Homer, where εἴ κε (αἴ κε) or ἤν (without an expressed apodosis) often seems to have the force of *in the hope that;* as in πατρὸς ἐμοῦ κλέος μετέρχομαι, ἤν που ἀκούσω, *I am going to seek tidings of my father, if I shall chance to hear of him,* i.e. *that I may hear of him if perchance I shall,* or *in the hope that I shall hear of him* (Od. iii. 83). Here the protasis carries with it its own apodosis, which consists of an implied idea of *purpose.*[1] The whole sentence (both protasis and apodosis) is thus condensed into the protasis; but the apodosis is always felt in the implied idea of purpose or desire which is inherent in the idiom. As we have seen (312, 2) that final clauses with ἄν or κέ and the subjunctive originally included both a conditional relative clause and a final sentence, so here we have both a conditional and a final force included under a single conditional form; and this double force is felt also in the English translation, *if haply, in the hope that, in case that,* etc. E.g.

Αὐτὰρ σοὶ πυκινῶς ὑποθήσομεθ', αἴ κε πίθηαι, *but we will make you a wise suggestion, for you to obey it if you will.* Il. xxi. 293. (Here the protasis αἴ κε πίθηαι with its implied apodosis seems like πείθοι ἂν εἰ πείθοι, *you can obey if you please,* AESCH. Ag. 1049, and χαίροιτ' ἂν εἰ χαίροιτ', Ib. 1394.) So Il. i. 207, 420, xi. 791, xxiii. 82; Od. i. 279. Πέμψω δ' ἐς Σπάρτην . . . νόστον πευσόμενον πατρὸς φίλου, ἤν που ἀκούσῃ, ἠδ' ἵνα μιν κλέος ἔχῃσιν, *I will send him to Sparta, to ask about his father's return, in hope that he may hear of it, and in order that glory may possess him.* Od. i. 93. (Here the

---

[1] The English translation of certain conditional clauses in the New Testament which have this peculiar construction preserves the sense of purpose or desire with the original form of protasis. Thus, *that they should seek the Lord, if haply they might feel after him and find him,* Acts xvii. 27; and *he came* (to the fig tree), *if haply he might find anything thereon,* MARK xi. 13.

added final clause shows the distinction between this and the protasis ἥν που ἀκούσῃ.) So Od. i. 281, ii. 216, 360, iii. 83. Εἰπέ μοι, αἴ κέ ποθι γνώω τοιοῦτον ἐόντα, *if haply I may recognise him.* Od. xiv. 118. Βάλλ᾽ οὕτως, αἴ κέν τι φόως Δαναοῖσι γένηαι, *if haply you may become* (i.e. *in hope that you may become*), etc. Il. viii. 282. So Il. xi. 797, 799, xiii. 236, xiv. 78, xvi. 39, 41 (cf. 84), xvii. 121, 692, xviii. 199. Καί οἱ ὑποσχέσθαι δυοκαίδεκα βοῦς ἱερευσέμεν, αἴ κ᾽ ἐλεήσῃ ἄστυ, . . . αἴ κεν Τυδέος υἱὸν ἀπόσχῃ Ἰλίου ἱρῆς, *let her promise to sacrifice twelve oxen* (to Athena), *in hope that she may pity the city,* . . . *if haply she may keep the son of Tydeus from sacred Ilios,* etc. Il. vi. 93. (For αἴ κεν ἀπόσχῃ Aristarchus read ὥς κεν.) Εὐφημῆσαί τε κέλεσθε, ὄφρα Διὶ Κρονίδῃ ἀρήσομεθ᾽, αἴ κ᾽ ἐλεήσῃ, *in order that we may pray to Zeus to pity us if he will* (*if haply he shall pity us*). Il. ix. 171. So Il. vi. 281, 309, xvii. 245, xxii. 419, xxiv. 116, 301, 357; Od. xiii. 182. See also εἴ κέν πως βούλεται λοιγὸν ἀμῦναι, Il. i. 66. Πατρόκλῳ ἔφεπε κρατερώνυχας ἵππους, αἴ κέν πώς μιν ἕλῃς, δώῃ δέ τοι εὖχος Ἀπόλλων. Il. xvi. 724. So Il. xv. 297; Od. xxii. 76. Δεῦρ᾽ ἱκόμεθ᾽, αἴ κε ποθι Ζεὺς ἐξοπίσω περ παύσῃ ὀϊζύος. Od. iv. 34. So Od. i. 379, ii. 144, xii. 215, xvii. 51, 60, xxii. 252. Εκτορος ὄρσωμεν κρατερὸν μένος, ἥν τινά που Δαναῶν προκαλέσσεται. Il. vii. 39. Ὑψόσε δ᾽ αὐγὴ γίγνεται ἀΐσσουσα περικτιόνεσσι ἰδέσθαι, αἴ κέν πως σὺν νηυσὶν ἀρῆς ἀλκτῆρες ἵκωνται. Il. xviii. 211. Εἰ δέ κ᾽ ἔτι προτέρω παρανήξομαι, ἥν που ἐφεύρω ἠιόνας, δείδω, κ.τ.λ., *but if I shall swim on still farther, to find a shore if haply I may, I fear,* etc. Od. v. 417. (Here ἥν που ἐφεύρω depends on an ordinary protasis, which, however, is not its apodosis.) Ἀλλ᾽ ἄγετ᾽, αἴ κέν πως θωρήξομεν υἷας Ἀχαιῶν, i.e. *let us arm them if we can.* Il. ii. 72 (so 83). Σκέπτεο νῦν, αἴ κε ἴδηαι ζωὸν ἔτ᾽ Ἀντίλοχον, *if haply you may see.* Il. xvii. 652. Σῷ οἴκῳ δῶρον ποτιδέγμενος, αἴ κε πόρῃσιν, *expecting a gift, if haply he shall give one* (i.e. *in hope that he will give one*). Od. ii. 186. So Od. xv. 312. Ἀλλ᾽ οὐ γάρ σ᾽ ἐθέλω βαλέειν τοιοῦτον ἐόντα λάθρῃ ὀπιπεύσας, ἀλλ᾽ ἀμφαδὸν, εἴ κε τύχωμι, *if haply I may hit you.* Il. vii. 242. Νῦν αὖτ᾽ ἐγχείῃ πειρήσομαι, αἴ κε τύχωμι, *I will try with my spear, if haply I may hit you.* Il. v. 279. Ὡς ὅτε τις τροχὸν κεραμεὺς πειρήσεται, αἴ κε θέῃσιν, i.e. *tries a wheel, in case it will run* (i.e. *to let it run if it will*). Il. xviii. 600. (The analogy of the two preceding examples shows that there is no indirect question.)

Παρέζεο καὶ λαβὲ γούνων, αἴ κέν πως ἐθέλῃσιν ἐπὶ Τρώεσσιν ἀρῆξαι, i.e. *clasp his knees in the hope that he will aid the Trojans* (*that he may aid them in case he will*). Il. i. 407. So Il. vii. 394, x. 55, xiii. 743, xviii. 457; Od. iii. 92, iv. 322. For these last examples, see 490, 2.

For αἴ κε in the common text of Homer, here as elsewhere, Bekker and Delbrück write εἴ κε (see footnote to 379).

2. In alternatives with two opposite suppositions, this construction implies that the subject is ready for either result, though the former is hoped for or expected. *E.g.*

Ἰθὺς φέρεται μένει, ἤν τινα πέφνῃ ἀνδρῶν ἢ αὐτὸς φθίεται πρώτῳ ἐν ὁμίλῳ, i.e. *he* (a lion) *rushes on, ready to slay or to perish.* Il. xx. 172. In Od. xxiv. 216, the common text has πατρὸς πειρήσομαι, αἴ κε (or εἴ κε) μ᾽ ἐπιγνώῃ . . . ἦέ κεν ἀγνοιῇσι, *I will try my father* (ready for either result), *in case he shall recognise me or shall not know me* (where κέν alone in the second clause is very strange). But La Roche reads ἤ κέ μ᾽ ἐπιγνώῃ, as an indirect question, one Ms. having ἦ κε : see also Od. xviii. 265. Ἐπιγνώῃ is Hermann's conjecture for ἐπιγνοίη or γνοίη.

488. The optative with εἰ (rarely εἴ κε) is sometimes used in Homer like the subjunctive after primary tenses in sentences of this class. It is also very common after past tenses, representing a subjunctive of the original form, though occasionally the subjunctive is retained in indirect discourse (696). *E.g.*

Ἀλλ᾽ ἔτι τὸν δύστηνον ὀΐομαι, εἴ ποθεν ἐλθὼν ἀνδρῶν μνηστήρων σκέδασιν κατὰ δώματα θείη, *but I am still expecting the poor man, if haply he should come and scatter the suitors.* Od. xx. 224. So Od. ii. 351. Ἀλλά τις εἴη Ἀγαμέμνονι, εἰ πλείονας παρὰ ναῦφιν ἐποτρύνειε νέεσθαι, *let some one go to A., in hope that he may exhort,* etc. Od. xiv. 496. See also 491, below.

Βούλευον ὅπως ὄχ᾽ ἄριστα γένοιτο, εἴ τιν᾽ ἑταίροισιν θανάτου λύσιν εὑροίμην, i.e. *if haply I might find some escape.* Od. ix. 420. Ἀλλ᾽ ἐγὼ οὐ πιθόμην, ὄφρ᾽ αὐτόν τε ἴδοιμι καὶ εἴ μοι ξείνια δοίη, *but I disobeyed them, in order that I might see him* (the Cyclops) *and in hope that he would show me hospitality.* Od. ix. 228. (The final clause and the protasis are here again clearly distinguished : see Od. i. 93 under 487, 1.) Πολλὰ δέ τ᾽ ἄγκε᾽ ἐπῆλθε μετ᾽ ἀνέρος ἴχνι᾽ ἐρευνῶν, εἴ ποθεν ἐξεύροι. Il. xviii. 321. Πειρήθη δὲ εὖ αὐτοῦ ἐν ἔντεσι, εἰ οἱ ἐφαρμόσσειε καὶ ἐντρέχοι ἄγλαα γυῖα, i.e. *he tried himself in his armour, eager for it to fit him and for his limbs to play freely in it* (*if haply it should fit him,* etc.). Il. xix. 384. (See the cases of the subjunctive after πειρῶμαι in 487, 1. Here there is no indirect question, for Achilles can have no *real* doubt about the fit.) Ἐν δὲ πίθοι οἴνοιο ἔστασαν, εἴ ποτ᾽ Ὀδυσσεὺς οἴκαδε νοστήσειε, i.e. *the casks of wine were waiting for the return of Ulysses.* Od. ii. 340. Ἧστο κάτω ὁρόων, ποτιδέγμενος εἴ τί μιν εἴποι, i.e. *he sat looking down, waiting for Penelope to speak.* Od. xxiii. 91. Τόδ᾽ ἠνώγει εἰπεῖν ἔπος, εἴ κ᾽ ἐθέλητε παύσασθαι πολέμου, *he bade me say this word, if haply you might be willing to stop the war.* Il. vii. 394. (This appears in vs. 387 as εἴ κε γένοιτο, and the direct form of the command in vs. 375 is εἴ κ᾽ ἐθέλωσιν.) In Il. xiv. 163-165 we have εἴ πως ἱμείραιτο . . . τῷ δὲ χεύῃ after a past tense. Νῆχε παρὲξ, εἴ που ἐφεύροι ἠιόνας. Od. v. 439. (Compare vs. 417, εἰ δέ κε παρανήξομαι, ἤν που ἐφεύρω, under 487, 1.)

See also Il. ii. 97, iii. 450, iv. 88, x. 19, xii. 122, 333, xiii. 807, xx. 464, xxiii. 40; Od. i. 115, iv. 317, iv. 267, 317, 418, x. 147, xi. 479, 628, xii. 334, xiv. 460, xxii. 91, 381.

489. This construction (487 ; 488) with both subjunctive and

optative is found also in Attic Greek and in Herodotus, but with
less variety of expression, and at the same time with some extension of the usage. Especially to be noticed are the protases
depending on verbs like βούλομαι and θέλω in Herodotus. *E.g.*

Θήβας ἡμᾶς πέμψον, ἐάν πως διακωλύσωμεν ἰόντα φόνον τοῖσιν
ὁμαίμοις, *send us to Thebes, to prevent, if haply we may*, etc. SOPH. O. C.
1769. Τῆς ἐμῆς γνώμης ἄκουσον, ἤν τί σοι δοκῶ λέγειν, *hear my
judgment, in the hope that you may think there is something in what I
say.* EUR. H. F. 278. Ἐδέοντο τοῦ Ἀρισταγόρεω, εἴ κως αὐτοῖσι
παράσχοι δύναμίν τινα καὶ κατέλθοιεν ἐς τὴν ἑωυτῶν, *they besought A.,
if in any way he might supply them with an armed force and they might
be restored to their own land (to do this).* HDT. v. 30.   Φρονήσαντες εἴ
κως ἓν γένοιτο τὸ Ἑλληνικόν, *having it at heart that, if it were in any
way possible, the Hellenic race should be made one.* Id. vii. 145.   Βουλο-
μένην εἴ κως ἀμφότεροι γενοίατο βασιλέες, i.e. *wishing that both might
be made kings, if in any way this could be done.* Id. vi. 52.   Ἐβουλεύετο
θέλων εἴ κως τούτους πρώτους ἕλοι. Id. ix. 14.   Πρόθυμοι ἦσαν ἐπι-
χειρέειν (sc. τῆσι νηυσί), εἴ κως ἕλοιεν αὐτάς. Id. viii. 6.   Πέμψαντες
παρ᾽ Ἀθηναίους πρέσβεις, εἴ πως πείσειαν μὴ σφῶν πέρι νεωτερίζειν
μηδέν, *to persuade them if they might*, etc. THUC. i. 58.   Πορευόμενοι ἐς
τὴν Ἀσίαν ὡς βασιλέα, εἴ πως πείσειαν αὐτόν, followed by βουλόμενοι
πεῖσαι αὐτὸν, εἰ δύναιντο, στρατεῦσαι, in nearly the same sense. Id.
ii. 67.   Πυνθανόμενοι τοὺς Ἀθηναίους ἐς τὴν Καμάριναν πρεσβεύ-
εσθαι, εἴ πως προσαγάγοιντο αὐτούς, *that they went on an embassy to
C., to bring the town over if they could.* Id. vi. 75. (Compare ἐς Ἀκρά-
γαντα Σικανὸν ἀπέστειλαν, ὅπως ὑπαγάγοιτο τὴν πόλιν εἰ δύναιτο,
vii. 46. This might have been εἴ πως ὑπαγάγοιτο τὴν πόλιν, and in
vi. 75 we might have had ὅπως προσαγάγοιντο αὐτοὺς εἰ δύναιντο,
with nearly the same force, but with different constructions.) See v.
4, εἴ πως . . . διασώσειαν. Ἱκέται πρὸς σὲ δεῦρ᾽ ἀφίγμεθα, εἴ τινα
πόλιν φράσειας ἡμῖν εὔερον, *we have come hither to you as suppliants,
in the hope that you might tell us of some city soft as a fleece (to have you
tell us, if perchance you might do so).* AR. Av. 120.   Ἄκουσον καὶ
ἐμοῦ, ἐάν σοι ταὐτὰ δοκῇ, *listen to me too, in the hope that you may think
the same (in case the same shall seem true to you).* PLAT. Rep. 358 B :
so 434 A.   Ὅρα οὖν καὶ προθυμοῦ κατιδεῖν, ἐάν πως πρότερος ἐμοῦ
ἴδῃς καὶ ἐμοὶ φράσῃς, i.e. *for the chance that you may see it first and
tell me.* Ib. 432 C : so 618 C, Theaet. 192 C, Soph. 226 C.   See also
XEN. An. ii. 1, 8, ἄν τι δύνωνται, and AR. Nub. 535.   On this principle
we must explain AR. Ran. 339, οὔκουν ἀτρέμ᾽ ἕξεις, ἤν τι καὶ χορδῆς
λάβῃς, *will you not keep quiet then, in the hope of getting some sausage
too (i.e. to have some sausage if you chance to get any)?*

490. 1. The apodosis may, further, be suggested by the
context, even by the protasis itself, without implying that the
protasis expresses a purpose or desire of the leading subject.
This gives rise to a variety of constructions. *E.g.*

Κτανεῖν ἐμοί νιν ἔδοσαν, εἴτε μὴ κτανὼν θέλοιμ᾽ ἄγεσθαι πάλιν ἐς

'Αργείαν χθόνα, *they gave her (Helen) to me to slay, or, in case I should prefer not to slay her but to carry her back to the land of Argos (for me to do this).* EUR. TRO. 874. Ἦν (τὴν ξυμμαχίαν) γε οὐκ ἐπὶ τοῖς φίλοις ἐποιήσασθε, τῶν δὲ ἐχθρῶν ἤν τις ἐφ' ὑμᾶς ἴῃ, i.e. *you made it (to use) in case any of your enemies should come against you.* THUC. vi. 79. Πρὸς τὴν πόλιν, εἰ ἐπιβοηθοῖεν, ἐχώρουν, *they marched towards the city, (to be ready) in case the citizens should rush out.* Id. vi. 100. Τἄλλα, ἢν ἔτι ναυμαχεῖν οἱ Ἀθηναῖοι τολμήσωσι, παρεσκευάζοντο, *they made other preparations, (to be ready) in case the Athenians should venture on further sea-fights.* Id. vii. 59. Κήρυγμα ποιοῦνται . . . τῶν νησιωτῶν εἴ τις βούλεται ἐπ' ἐλευθερίᾳ ὡς σφᾶς ἀπιέναι, *they make proclamation, in case any of the islanders wishes to come over to them with promise of freedom (for him to do so).* Id. vii. 82. Οὐδεμία βλάβη τῶν πρὸς τὰς πόλεις διαπομπῶν ἔς τε κατασκοπὴν καὶ ἤν τι ἄλλο φαίνηται ἐπιτήδειον, *there is no harm in the envoys whom we have sent to the various cities, partly for inquiry, and also in case any other advantage may appear (to secure this),* i.e. *to secure any other advantage that may appear.* Id. vi. 41. So καὶ εἴ τινα πρὸς ἄλλον δέοι, Id. v. 37. Ἀρὰς ποιοῦνται, εἴ τις ἐπικηρυκεύεται Πέρσαις, *they invoke curses, if any one* (i.e. *to fall on any one who) sends heralds to the Persians.* ISOC. iv. 157. Φιλοτιμεῖσθαι μηδ' ἐνὶ ἐφ' ἄλλῳ ἢ ἐπὶ χρημάτων κτήσει καὶ ἐάν τι ἄλλο εἰς τοῦτο φέρῃ, i.e. *for anything else that may lead to this.* PLAT. Rep. 553 D. See ARISTOT. Eth. x. 9, 2 : ἔχειν (τὴν ἀρετὴν) καὶ χρῆσθαι πειρατέον, ἢ εἴ πως ἄλλως ἀγαθοὶ γινόμεθα, *we must try to possess and employ virtue, or if there is any other means of becoming virtuous (to use this).*

2. In the Homeric examples in which the protasis consists of an infinitive depending on ἐθέλω (487, 1, end), the apodosis is suggested by the infinitive rather than by ἐθέλω. This shows that αἴ κ ἐθέλησι *in itself* has no final force. See also Od. xxii. 381, πάπτηνεν δ' Ὀδυσεὺς καθ' ἑὸν δόμον, εἴ τις ἔτ' ἀνδρῶν ζωὸς ὑποκλοπέοιτο ἀλύσκων κῆρα μέλαιναν, *he peered through his house, in case any man might still be alive and hiding himself* (i.e. *to find any such man),* where no desire or hope is implied, and the construction is like that of THUC. vi. 100 (above).

In PLAT. Rep. 327 C, οὐκοῦν ἔτι ἐλλείπεται τὸ ἢν πείσωμεν ὑμᾶς ὡς χρὴ ἡμᾶς ἀφεῖναι; the subject of ἐλλείπεται is a protasis introduced by τό, into which the apodosis has been wholly absorbed. The construction is, *is there not still left the supposition of our persuading you that you must let us go ?* But the meaning is, *is it not left for us to persuade you that you must let us go, if we can* (i.e. πεῖσαι ἢν πείσωμεν)? This is an important example for explaining this whole class of sentences (486–490). The cases in 490 make it plain that the final force often ascribed to εἰ or ἤν comes from the suppression of an apodosis containing the idea of purpose or desire, since the same form of protasis which is sometimes called final has no final force when a slightly different apodosis is implied (as in THUC. vi. 79, 100, vii. 59).

491. Sometimes a clause with εἴ κε or ἤν (rarely εἰ) and the subjunctive, or with εἴ κε or εἰ and the optative, in Homer is the object of οἶδα, εἶδον, or a verb of *saying*, expressing in a conditional form a result which is hoped for or desired. These clauses have the appearance of indirect questions; but the analogy of the preceding examples (487-490) shows that all are based on the same idiom,—a protasis which involves its own apodosis so that it would be useless to express the latter separately. The examples are these :—

Τίς οἶδ᾽ εἴ κε καὶ αὐτὸς ἰὼν κοίλης ἐπὶ νηὸς τῆλε φίλων ἀπόλη-ται, *who knows the chances that he too may perish*, etc. ? or *who knows the chances of his perishing*, etc., *if haply he may?* Od. ii. 332. (We may translate colloquially : *who knows? supposing he too shall perish?*) Τίς οἶδ᾽ εἴ κ᾽ Ἀχιλεὺς φθήῃ ἐμῷ ὑπὸ δουρὶ τυπεὶς ἀπὸ θυμὸν ὀλέσσαι; *who knows the chances that Achilles may first be struck (the chances of his being first struck, if haply he shall be)?* Il. xvi. 860. (We should naturally express this by a different construction, *whether he may not be first struck.*) Τίς οἶδ᾽ εἴ κέν οἱ σὺν δαίμονι θυμὸν ὀρίνω παρειπών; *who knows the chances of my rousing his spirit by persuasion, if haply I shall do so?* Il. xv. 403. In Il. xi. 792 we have Nestor's advice to Patroclus, τίς οἶδ᾽ εἴ κέν οἱ σὺν δαίμονι θυμὸν ὀρίναις παρειπών; *who knows the chances that you could rouse his spirit by persuasion?* (ὀρίναις κε being potential). Οὐ μὴν οἶδ᾽ εἰ αὖτε κακορραφίης ἀλεγεινῆς πρώτη ἐπαύρηαι καί σε πληγῇσιν ἱμάσσω, *I am not sure of the chances of your being the first to enjoy your own device*, etc., i.e. *I am not so sure that you may not be the first to enjoy it, if it shall so chance.* Il. xv. 16. Ζεὺς γάρ που τό γε οἶδε καὶ ἀθάνατοι θεοὶ ἄλλοι, εἴ κέ μιν ἀγγείλαιμι ἰδών· ἐπὶ πολλὰ δ᾽ ἀλήθην, *Zeus and the other immortals (alone) know this, the chance of my bringing news of him, if haply I have seen him and so might do this.* Od. xiv. 119. Εἰ δ᾽ ἄγε δή μοι τοῦτο, θεά, νημερτὲς ἐνίσπες, εἴ πως τὴν ὀλοὴν μὲν ὑπεκπροφύγοιμι Χάρυβδιν, τὴν δέ κ᾽ ἀμυναίμην ὅτε μοι σίνοιτό γ᾽ ἑταίρους, i.e. *tell me this without fault, the chance of my escaping Charybdis if haply I should do this, and of my then keeping Scylla off if I could* (lit. *tell me this, supposing I should escape Charybdis and could then keep Scylla off*). Od. xii. 112 (this translation supposes κ᾽ to be potential, affecting only ἀμυναίμην).

Ἦ μένετε Τρῶας σχεδὸν ἐλθέμεν, ὄφρα ἴδητ᾽ αἴ κ᾽ ὕμμιν ὑπέρσχῃ χεῖρα Κρονίων; *are you waiting for the Trojans to come near, that you may see the chances of the son of Cronos holding his hand over you?*—or *that you may see him hold his hand over you, if haply he may do this?* Il. iv. 247. (We might say, *is it that you may see it,—supposing the son of Cronos to hold his hand over you?*) Τῶν σ᾽ αὖτις μνήσω, ἵν᾽ ἀπολλήξῃς ἀπατάων, ὄφρ᾽ ἴδῃς ἤν τοι χραίσμῃ φιλότης τε καὶ εὐνή, i.e. *that you may see the chances of your device availing you, or that you may see it if perchance your device shall avail you.* Il. xv. 31.

See also Il. xx. 435, ἀλλ᾽ ἦ τοι μὲν ταῦτα θεῶν ἐν γούνασι κεῖται, αἴ κέ σε χειρότερός περ ἐὼν ἀπὸ θυμὸν ἕλωμαι, i.e. *this rests with the Gods, for me to take your life away, weaker though I am, if perchance I may.* The conditional construction is more obvious here than in Il. iv. 247 and xv. 31; but in all three we naturally fall into an indirect question when we attempt to express the thought in English.

492. A comparison of these peculiar conditional constructions (491) expressing hope or desire with clauses with μή expressing anxiety and desire to prevent a result, both depending on οἶδα or εἶδον, is suggestive. With Od. ii. 332 and Il. xvi. 860 (in 491) compare Il. x. 100, οὐδέ τι ἴδμεν, μή πως καὶ διὰ νύκτα μενοινήσωσι μάχεσθαι, *nor do we know any way to prevent their being impelled*, etc., and Plat. Phaed. 91 D (quoted in 366); and with Il. iv. 247 and xv. 31 (491) compare Od. xxiv. 491, ἴδοι μὴ δὴ σχεδὸν ὦσι κιόντες (366). This comparison shows that εἰδέναι (or ἰδεῖν) εἴ κε τοῦτο γένηται means *to know (or see) the chances of gaining this* (object of desire); while εἰδέναι (or ἰδεῖν) μὴ τοῦτο γένηται means *to know (or see) some way to prevent this* (object of fear). The idea of desire or anxiety belongs to the dependent clause, and not at all to the leading verb.

493. These Homeric expressions (491), in which nearly all the force is in the protasis, so that the apodosis is not only suppressed but hardly felt at all, helps to show how the particle εἰ came to be an indirect interrogative, in the sense of *whether*. But in Attic Greek, where the interrogative use is fully established, only the simple εἰ (never ἤν or ἐάν) can mean *whether*, even when the verb is subjunctive (680).

Εἰ AFTER EXPRESSIONS OF WONDER, INDIGNATION, ETC.

494. After many expressions of *wonder, delight, contentment, indignation, disappointment, pity,* and similar emotions, a protasis with εἰ may be used to express the object of the emotion. When the supposition of the protasis is present or past, a causal sentence would generally seem more natural. Such expressions are especially θαυμάζω, αἰσχύνομαι, ἀγαπῶ, ἀγανακτῶ, and δεινόν ἐστιν. *E.g.*

Θαυμάζω δ' ἔγωγε εἰ μηδεὶς ὑμῶν μήτ' ἐνθυμεῖται μήτ' ὀργίζεται, ὁρῶν, κ.τ.λ., *I wonder that no one of you is either concerned or angry, when he sees,* etc. (lit. *if no one is either concerned or angry, I wonder*). Dem. iv. 43. 'Αλλ' ἐκεῖνο θαυμάζω, εἰ Λακεδαιμονίοις μέν ποτε ἀντήρατε, νυνὶ δ' ὀκνεῖτε ἐξιέναι καὶ μέλλετε εἰσφέρειν, *but I wonder at this, that you once opposed the Lacedaemonians, but now are unwilling,* etc. Id. ii. 24. (The literal meaning is, *if (it is true that) you once opposed,* etc., *then I wonder.*) Οὐκ ἀγαπᾷ εἰ μὴ δίκην δέδωκεν, ἀλλ' εἰ μὴ καὶ χρυσῷ στεφάνῳ στεφανωθήσεται ἀγανακτεῖ, *he is not content if he has not been punished; but if he is not also to be crowned with a*

golden crown, he is indignant. AESCHIN. iii. 147. Καὶ ὡς ἀληθῶς
ἀγανακτῶ, εἰ οὑτωσὶ ἃ νοῶ μὴ οἷός τ᾽ εἰμὶ εἰπεῖν, *I am indignant that*
(*or if*) *I am not able, etc.* PLAT. Lach. 194 A. Οὐ δὴ θαυμαστόν
ἐστιν, εἰ στρατευόμενος καὶ πονῶν ἐκεῖνος αὐτὸς ὑμῶν μελλόντων
καὶ ψηφιζομένων καὶ πυνθανομένων περιγίγνεται, *it is no wonder that*
he gets the advantage of you, etc. DEM. ii. 23. Μηδὲ μέντοι τοῦτο μεῖον
δόξητε ἔχειν, εἰ οἱ Κυρεῖοι πρόσθεν σὺν ἡμῖν ταττόμενοι νῦν ἀφε-
στήκασιν, i.e. *do not be discontented, if* (*or that*) *the Cyraeans have now*
withdrawn. XEN. An. iii. 2, 17. Αἰνῶ σε, εἰ κτενεῖς δάμαρτα σήν.
EUR. Tro. 890.
    Δεινὸν ἂν εἴη πρῆγμα, εἰ Σάκας μὲν δούλους ἔχομεν, Ἕλληνας δὲ
οὐ τιμωρησόμεθα. HDT. vii. 9. Αἰσχρόν ἐστιν, εἰ ἐγὼ μὲν τὰ ἔργα
ὑπέμεινα, ὑμεῖς δὲ μηδὲ τοὺς λόγους ἀνέξεσθε. DEM. xviii. 160. Δεινὸν
ἂν εἴη, εἰ οἱ μὲν ἐκείνων ξύμμαχοι οὐκ ἀπεροῦσιν, ἡμεῖς δὲ οὐκ ἄρα
δαπανήσομεν. THUC. i. 121. Τέρας λέγεις, εἰ . . . οὐκ ἂν δύναιντο
λαθεῖν. PLAT. Men. 91 D (see 506). Δεινὸν εἰ οἱ αὐτοὶ μάρτυρες
τούτοις μὲν ἂν μαρτυροῦντες πιστοὶ ἦσαν, ἐμοὶ δὲ μαρτυροῦντες ἄπιστοι
ἔσονται, *it is hard that the same witnesses testifying for them would have*
been trustworthy, and testifying for me are to be untrustworthy. ANT. vi.
29. See AESCHIN. i. 85.

    In all the preceding examples the protasis belongs under 402, the
futures expressing present suppositions (407). For εἰ οὐ see 386 and
387, with examples.

495. The same construction is sometimes used when the
leading verb is past. *E.g.*

    Κατεμέμφετο αἰτὸν καὶ τοὺς σὺν αὐτῷ, εἰ οἱ ἄλλοι ἀκμάζειν μᾶλ-
λον ἑαυτῶν ἐδόκουν. XEN. Cyr. iv. 3, 3. But generally such sentences
are affected by the principle of indirect discourse, and have either the
optative or the form of the direct discourse : see XEN. Cyr. ii. 2, 3,
ἠχθέσθην εἴ τι μεῖον δοκοῖεν ἔχειν (where δοκοῦσι might have been
used). See EUR. Med. 931, εἰσῆλθέ μ᾽ οἶκτος, εἰ γενήσεται, and XEN.
An. i. 4, 7, ᾤκτειρον εἰ ἁλώσοιντο. For such sentences see 697.

496. These expressions may also be followed by ὅτι and a causal
sentence, as in PLAT. Theaet. 142 A, ἐθαύμαζον ὅτι οὐχ οἷός τ᾽ ἦ
εὑρεῖν. The construction with εἰ gives a milder or more polite form
of expression, putting the object of the *wonder* etc. into the form of a
supposition, instead of stating it as a fact as we should do in English.
They may also be followed by protases expressing ordinary conditions,
which have nothing peculiar : see ISOC. xv. 17, ἀγαπητὸν (sc. ἐστίν)
ἦν ἐκλαβεῖν δυνηθῶσι τὸ δίκαιον, *they must be content if they are able*
(cf. xix. 20); and PLAT. Prot. 315 E, DEM. ii. 23 (εἰ περιῆμεν).

497. This construction must not be mistaken for that in which εἰ
is used in the sense of *whether*, to introduce an indirect question ; as
ἠρώτων εἰ ἦλθεν, *I asked whether he had come.*

MIXED CONSTRUCTIONS.

498. The forms of protasis and apodosis which are contained in the classification above (388-397) include by far the greater number of the examples found in the classic authors. Many cases remain, however, in which the protasis and apodosis do not belong to the same form. Especially, the great wealth of conditional expressions which the Homeric language exhibits in both protasis and apodosis (399) allowed great variety of combination ; and the early poets used much greater freedom in these sentences than suited the more exact style of Attic prose.

I. *Optative in Protasis, with Future or Present Indicative or an equivalent form in Apodosis.*

499. (*a*) In the earlier language a protasis with the optative is not infrequently followed by an apodosis with the future indicative or imperative or (in Homer) with the subjunctive. The subjunctive or future indicative in Homer may also take κέ or ἄν (452). *E.g.*

Εἴ τίς μοι ἀνὴρ ἅμ᾽ ἕποιτο καὶ ἄλλος, μᾶλλον θαλπωρὴ καὶ θαρσαλεώτερον ἔσται, *if any other man should follow with me, there will be more comfort and greater courage.* Il. x. 222. (The want of symmetry in the Greek is here precisely what it is in the English; and εἴη ἄν is no more required in the apodosis than *would be* is, though both are the conventional forms.) See Il. ix. 388, and xxiii. 893, πόρωμεν, εἰ ἐθέλοις. Τόν γ᾽ εἴ πως σὺ δύναιο λοχησάμενος λελαβέσθαι, ὅς κέν τοι εἴπῃσι ὁδόν, *he will tell you,* etc. Od. iv. 388. See Il. xi. 386, εἰ πειρηθείης, οὐκ ἄν τοι χραίσμῃσι βιός; and Il. ii. 488, xx. 100, Od. xvii. 539. Εἰ δὲ δαίμων γενέθλιος ἕρποι, Δὶ τοῦτ᾽ Ἐνναλίῳ τ᾽ ἐκδώσομεν πράσσειν. PIND. Ol. xiii. 105.[1] So in an old curse, εἴ τις τάδε παραβαίνοι, ἐναγὴς ἔστω, AESCHIN. iii. 110. See SOPH. O. T. 851, εἴ τι κἀκτρέποιτο, οὗτοι τόν γε Λαΐου φόνον φανεῖ δικαίως ὀρθόν.

500. (*b*) A present indicative in the apodosis with an optative in the protasis is sometimes merely an emphatic future expression. *E.g.*

Πάντ᾽ ἔχεις, εἴ σε τούτων μοῖρ᾽ ἐφίκοιτο καλῶν, *you have the whole, should a share of these glories fall to your lot.* PIND. Isth. iv. (v.) 14. So καιρὸν εἰ φθέγξαιο, μείων ἕπεται μῶμος ἀνθρώπων, i.e. *should you speak seasonably, you are sure to be followed by less censure of men,* Py. i. 81. In THUC. ii. 39 we have καίτοι εἰ ῥαθυμίᾳ μᾶλλον ἢ πόνων μελέτῃ ἐθέλοιμεν κινδυνεύειν, περιγίγνεται ἡμῖν, κ.τ.λ.,

[1] For the cases in Pindar here and in 500 and 501, see *Am. Jour. Phil.* iii. p. 444.

and now supposing that we should choose to meet dangers with a light heart rather than with laborious training, we secure the advantage, etc. This sentence is loosely jointed, like the others which have this combination; the condition is stated as a remotely supposed case, in the vague future form, but the apodosis, *we at once gain this advantage,* etc., is adapted to a present supposition. The optative is generally emended to ἐθέλομεν, although it is one of the best attested words in Thucydides, being in the best Mss. and also being quoted by Dion. Hal. as a faulty expression. The criticism of Dionysius (*de Thuc. Idiom.* 12, 1) is instructive : ἐνταῦθα γὰρ τὸ μὲν ἐθέλοιμεν ῥῆμα τοῦ μέλλοντός ἐστι χρόνου δηλωτικὸν, τὸ δὲ περιγίγνεται τοῦ παρόντος· ἀκόλουθον δ' ἂν ἦν εἰ συνέζευξε τῷ ἐθέλοιμεν τὸ περιέσται, i.e. the future expression εἰ ἐθέλοιμεν should have a future form like περιέσται to correspond to it.

In DEM. xviii. 21, εἰ γὰρ εἶναί τι δοκοίη τὰ μάλιστα ἐν τούτοις ἀδίκημα, οὐδέν ἐστι δήπου πρὸς ἐμέ, the apodosis refers to the real protasis *if there is any apparent fault.*

501. (*c*) In most cases, however, the present indicative in the apodosis precedes, containing a general statement, and the optative adds a remote future condition where we should expect a general present supposition. *E.g.*

Οὔ μοι θέμις ἔστ', οὐδ' εἰ κακίων σέθεν ἔλθοι, ξεῖνον ἀτιμῆσαι, *it is not right for me—even supposing a more wretched man than you should come—to dishonour a stranger.* Od. xiv. 56. Θαρσαλέος γὰρ ἀνὴρ ἐν πᾶσιν ἀμείνων ἔργοισιν τελέθει, εἰ καί ποθεν ἄλλοθεν ἔλθοι. Od. vii. 51. So v. 484, viii. 138 ; Il. ix. 318. Οὔτ' οὖν ἀγγελίῃ ἔτι πείθομαι, εἴ ποθεν ἔλθοι, οὔτε θεοπροπίης ἐμπάζομαι, ἥν τινα μήτηρ ἐξερέηται, *neither do I any longer put trust in reports—should any one come—nor do I regard any divination which my mother may ask.* Od. i. 414. (Here the remoteness of the supposition in εἰ ἔλθοι is contrasted with the greater vividness of that expressed in ἐξερέηται). Δεινόν τ', εἴ κ' ἐφ' ἅμαξαν ὑπέρβιον ἄχθος ἀείρας ἄξονα καυκάξαις τὰ δὲ φόρτι' ἀμαυρωθείη, *it is hard, . . . supposing you should break your axle and your load should perish.* HES. Op. 692. Κέρδος δὲ φίλτατον, ἑκόντος εἴ τις ἐκ δόμων φέροι, *it is the dearest gain, if one should bring it from the house of a willing giver.* PIND. Py. viii. 13. See Isth. ii. 33. So SOPH. Ant. 1032.

In most of these examples a general supposition with the subjunctive (or present indicative) in the protasis would have agreed more closely with the thought. If the protasis had preceded, so as to determine the character of the sentence, the apodosis would naturally have had the optative with κέ or ἄν, or some future form (as in the cases under *a*).

502. (*d*) The optative in protasis sometimes depends on the present of a verb of *obligation, propriety,* or *possibility* with an infinitive, the two forming an expression that is nearly equivalent in sense to an optative with ἄν. *E.g.*

Εἰ γὰρ εἴησαν δύο τινὲς ἐναντίοι νόμοι, οὐκ ἀμφοτέροις ἔνι δήπου ψηφίσασθαι, *for if there should be two laws opposed to each other, you could not surely vote for both.* DEM. xxiv. 35. This is analogous to the apodosis formed by ἔδει, χρῆν, ἐνῆν, etc., with the infinitive (415). There, for example, ἐνῆν αὐτῷ ἐλθεῖν, *he could have gone,* is nearly equivalent to ἦλθεν ἄν, and here ἔνεστιν αὐτῷ ἐλθεῖν, *he could go,* is nearly equivalent to ἔλθοι ἄν. This use of the optative is more common in the corresponding relative conditional sentences (555).

II. *Indicative or Subjunctive in Protasis, with Potential Optative or Indicative in Apodosis.*

503. (*a*) A present or past tense of the indicative in the protasis with a potential optative or indicative (with ἄν) in the apodosis is a perfectly natural combination, each clause having its proper force. *E.g.*

Εἰ δέ τις ἀθανάτων γε κατ' οὐρανοῦ εἰλήλουθας, οὐκ ἂν ἔγωγε θεοῖσιν ἐπουρανίοισι μαχοίμην, *but if thou art one of the immortals come from heaven, I would not fight against the Gods of heaven.* Il. vi. 128. Πολλὴ γὰρ ἂν εὐδαιμονία εἴη περὶ τοὺς νέους, εἰ εἷς μὲν μόνος αὐτοὺς διαφθείρει, οἱ δ' ἄλλοι ὠφελοῦσιν, *for there would (naturally) be great happiness,* etc. PLAT. Ap. 25 B. Εἴ τι θέσφατον πατρὶ χρησμοῖσιν ἱκνεῖθ', ὥστε πρὸς παίδων θανεῖν, πῶς ἂν δικαίως τοῦτ' ὀνειδίζοις ἐμοί; *if a divine decree came to my father through oracles that he was to die by his sons' hands, how can you justly reproach me with this?* SOPH. O. C. 969 ; so 974-977. Ὥστ' εἴ μοι καὶ μέσως ἡγούμενοι μᾶλλον ἑτέρων προσεῖναι αὐτὰ πολεμεῖν ἐπείσθητε, οὐκ ἂν εἰκότως νῦν τοῦ γε ἀδικεῖν αἰτίαν φεροίμην, *if you were persuaded to make war by thinking,* etc., *I should not now justly be charged with injustice.* THUC. ii. 60. Εἰ γὰρ οὗτοι ὀρθῶς ἀπέστησαν, ὑμεῖς ἂν οὐ χρεὼν ἄρχοιτε, *for if these had a right to secede, it would follow that your dominion is unjust.* Id. iii. 40 : see vi. 92, and DEM. xxi. 37. Καίτοι τότε τὸν Ὑπερείδην, εἴπερ ἀληθῆ μου νῦν κατηγορεῖ, μᾶλλον ἂν εἰκότως ἢ τόνδ' ἐδίωκεν, *and yet, if he is now making true charges against me, he would then have prosecuted Hypereides with much more reason than (he now has for prosecuting) this man.* DEM. xviii. 223. Εἰ γὰρ γυναῖκες εἰς τόδ' ἥξουσιν θράσους, . . . παρ' οὐδὲν αὐταῖς ἦν ἂν ὀλλύναι πόσεις, *for if women are to come to this height of audacity (407) it would be as nothing for them to slay their husbands.* EUR. Or. 566. Τοῦτο, εἰ καὶ τἆλλα πάντα ἀποστεροῦσιν, ἀποδοῦναι προσῆκεν, *even if they steal all the rest, they ought to have restored this (415).* DEM. xxvii. 37.

504. (*b*) An unreal condition in the indicative followed by a potential optative seldom occurs and is not a strictly logical combination. *E.g.*

Εἰ τοῦτ' ἐπεχείρουν λέγειν, οὐκ ἔσθ' ὅστις οὐκ ἂν εἰκότως

ἐπιτιμήσειέ μοι, *if I were undertaking to say this, (the result would be that) every one would censure me with reason.* DEM. xviii. 206. (Here many Mss. and Dion. Hal. p. 1054 read ἐπετίμησε, the ordinary form in such an apodosis.) See [LYS.] xv. 8.

505. (*c*) When a subjunctive or a future indicative in protasis has a potential optative in the apodosis, there is sometimes a distinct potential force in the apodosis (as in 503), and sometimes is the optative with ἄν is merely a softened expression for the future indicative (235). *E.g.*

Εἰ μέν κεν πατρὸς βίοτον καὶ νόστον ἀκούσω, ἤ τ' ἂν τρυχόμενός περ ἔτι τλαίην ἐνιαυτόν, *if I hear of my father's life and return, wasted as I am, I can still endure it for a year.* Od. ii. 218. (See the next verses, 220-223, εἰ δέ κε τεθνεῶτος ἀκούσω, with future forms in the apodosis. See also the corresponding verses, Od. i. 287-292.) 'Αλλ' ἔτι μέν κε καὶ ὡς κακά περ πάσχοντες ἵκοισθε, αἴ κ' ἐθέλῃς σὸν θυμὸν ἐρυκακέειν, *but still even so, though suffering evils, you may come home, if you will curb your passion.* Od. xi. 104 ; so xi. 110 and xii. 137. See Il. xxi. 556. Εἰ δέ κεν ὄψ' ἀρόσῃς, τόδε κέν τοι φάρμακον εἴη, *but if you plough late, this may be your remedy.* HES. Op. 485 ; so 665. 'Αλλ' ἦν ἐφῆς μοι, . . . λέξαιμ' ἂν ὀρθῶς, i.e. *I would fain speak.* SOPH. El. 554. So O. T. 216, Phil. 1259 ; EUR. Hel. 1085. Οὐδὲ γὰρ ἂν πολλαὶ γέφυραι ὦσιν, ἔχοιμεν ἂν ὅποι φυγόντες ἡμεῖς σωθῶμεν, *for not even if there are (shall be) many bridges, could we (in the case supposed) find a place to fly to and be safe.* XEN. An. ii. 4, 19.

Εἰ γάρ τι λέξεις ᾧ χολώσεται στρατός, οὔτ' ἂν ταφείη παῖς ὅδ' οὔτ' οἴκτου τύχοι, *for if you say anything by which the army shall be made angry, this child cannot be buried or find pity.* EUR. Tro. 730 ; see Suppl. 603, Cycl. 474. Φρούριον εἰ ποιήσονται, τῆς μὲν γῆς βλάπτοιεν ἄν τι μέρος, οὐ μέντοι ἱκανόν γε ἔσται κωλύειν ἡμᾶς, κ.τ.λ., *if they (shall) build a fort, they might perhaps injure some part of our land ; but it will not be sufficient to prevent us,* etc. THUC. i. 142.

In the following examples the optative with ἄν seems to form a future apodosis to the future protasis ; though in some of them it may be thought to be potential :—

Εἰ δέ κεν εὐπλοίην δώῃ κλυτὸς εἰνοσίγαιος, ἤματί κεν τριτάτῳ Φθίην ἐρίβωλον ἱκοίμην, i.e. *on the third day I shall arrive.* Il. ix. 362. (The reference to this in PLAT. Crit. 44 B shows that ἱκοίμην ἄν is a mere future.) See Il. xiii. 377, xvii. 38 ; Od. xxi. 114. 'Αδικοίημεν ἂν εἰ μὴ ἀποδώσω, *I should be guilty of wrong, should I (shall I) not restore her.* EUR. Hel. 1010. See Ion. 374, Suppl. 520, I. A. 1189, Cycl. 198. Ἢν οὖν μάθῃς μοι τὸν ἄδικον τοῦτον λόγον, οὐκ ἂν ἀποδοίην οὐδ' ἂν ὀβολὸν οὐδενί, *if you (shall) learn this cheating reason for me, I will not (or I would not) pay even an obol to any one.* AR. Nub. 116. Καὶ οὕτως ἂν δεινότατα πάντων πάθοιεν, εἰ οὗτοι ὁμόψηφοι κατ' ἐκείνων τῶν ἀνδρῶν τοῖς τριάκοντα γενήσονται. LYS. xiii. 94. (Here we should expect εἰ γένοιντο.) Τῶν ἀτοπωτάτων μέντ᾽ ἂν εἴη, εἰ, ἃ νῦν ἄνοιαν ὀφλισκάνων ὅμως ἐκλαλεῖ, ταῦτα δυνηθεὶς μὴ πράξει. DEM. i. 26.

III. *Potential Optative or Indicative (with ἄν) in the Protasis.*

506. A potential optative (with ἄν) in the protasis may express a present condition, and a potential indicative (with ἄν) a present or past condition. *E.g.*

Εἰ μηδὲ δοῦλον ἀκρατῆ δεξαίμεθ᾽ ἄν, πῶς οὐκ ἄξιον αὐτόν γε φυλάξασθαι τοιοῦτον γενέσθαι; *if we would not take even a slave who was intemperate, how can it be other than fitting to guard oneself against becoming so?* XEN. Mem. i. 5, 3.   Καὶ ἐγώ, εἴπερ ἄλλῳ τῳ ἀνθρώπων πειθοίμην ἄν, καὶ σοὶ πείθομαι, *and I, if I would trust any man, trust you.* PLAT. Prot. 329 B.   Οὗτοι παντελῶς, οὐδ᾽ εἰ μὴ ποιήσαιτ᾽ ἂν τοῦτο ὡς ἔγωγέ φημι δεῖν, εὐκαταφρόνητόν ἐστιν, *this (preparation) is not wholly to be despised, even if you would not do this as I say you ought.* DEM. iv. 18.   Notice the difference between this supposition that *you would not do this if you could* (i.e. οὐκ ἂν ποιήσαιτε τοῦτο) and the ordinary εἰ μὴ ποιήσαιτε τοῦτο, *supposing you not to do this.*

Εἰ τοίνυν τοῦτο ἰσχυρὸν ἦν ἂν τούτῳ τεκμήριον, κἀμοὶ γενέσθω τεκμήριον, κ.τ.λ., *if then this would have been a strong proof for him* (sc. had he had it), *so let it be also a proof for me,* etc. DEM. xlix. 58.   Εἰ μὴ διὰ τὸ τούτους βούλεσθαι σῶσαι, ἐξώλης ἀπολοίμην καὶ προώλης εἰ προσλαβών γ᾽ ἂν ἀργύριον πάνυ πολὺ μετὰ τούτων ἐπρέσβευσα, *had it not been for my wish to save these* (captives), *may I perish utterly and before my day if I would have gone on an embassy with these men even for very high pay.* DEM. xix. 172.   (Here the protasis to which the apodosis ἀπολοίμην refers is really the whole expression εἰ . . . ἐπρέσβευσα ἄν εἰ μὴ . . . σῶσαι, *if I would have gone except to save these,* ἐπρέσβευσα ἄν in the protasis being itself the apodosis to εἰ μὴ . . . σῶσαι.)   In DEM. xviii. 101, καὶ τίς οὐκ ἂν ἀπέκτεινέ με δικαίως, εἴ τι τῶν ὑπαρχόντων τῇ πόλει καλῶν λόγῳ μόνον καταισχύνειν ἐπεχείρησ᾽ ἄν;—if we retain the final ἄν (strongly supported by Mss.), we must translate *if (it is true that) I would (under any circumstances) have undertaken,* etc., and not simply *if I had undertaken* (εἰ ἐπεχείρησα).   (See 557.)

507. It is obvious that such forms (506) express simple present or past conditions, the real protasis always being *if it* IS (or WAS) *the case that something would now be* (or *would have been*), or *if it* IS *the case that something would hereafter be under certain circumstances.*   (See 409.)

IV. *Irregular Combinations.—Present or Past with Future in one Protasis.*

508. In a few irregular constructions, which are only cases

of *anacoluthon*, the speaker adapts his apodosis to a form of
protasis different from that which he has actually used. *E.g.*

'Εγὼ μὲν ἄν, εἰ ἔχοιμι, ὡς τάχιστα ὅπλα ἐποιούμην πᾶσι Πέρσαις. ΧΕΝ. Cyr. ii. 1, 9. (Here ἐποιούμην ἄν is used as if εἰ εἶχον,
if I were able, had preceded. We should expect ποιοίμην ἄν, which
is found in one Ms.) Εἰ οὖν εἰδεῖεν ὅτι θεᾶται αὐτοὺς, ἵεντο ἂν
ἐπὶ τοὺς πόνους . . . καὶ κατεργάζοιντο ἂν αὐτήν, *if then they
knew that she* (virtue) *sees them, they would rush into labours and would
secure her.* ΧΕΝ. Cyn. xii. 22. Εἰ μὲν γὰρ εἰς γυναῖκα σωφρονεστέραν
ξίφος μεθεῖμεν, δυσκλεὴς ἂν ἦν φόνος. ΕUR. Or. 1132. (Here we
should expect εἴη ; or μεθεῖμεν may be indicative.)

509. The same protasis may have one verb in the indicative referring to present or past time, and another in the optative referring
to the future. *E.g.*

'Εγὼ οὖν δεινὰ ἂν εἴην εἰργασμένος, εἰ, ὅτε μέν με οἱ ἄρχοντες
ἔταττον, τότε μὲν ἔμενον, τοῦ δὲ θεοῦ τάττοντος λίποιμι τὴν τάξιν,
*I should therefore (prove to) have behaved outrageously, if when the state
authorities stationed me I stood my ground, but (if) now when God stations
me I should desert my post.* ΡLAT. Ap. 28 Ε. (Here the supposed combination of the two acts is the future condition to which the future
apodosis refers.) 'Επεύχομαι πᾶσι τούτοις, εἰ ἀληθῆ πρὸς ὑμᾶς
εἴποιμι καὶ εἶπον καὶ τότ᾽ εὐθὺς ἐν τῷ δήμῳ, εὐτυχίαν μοι δοῦναι,
i.e. *if I should speak the truth and if I did speak it then,* etc. DΕΜ. xviii.
141. Εἰ δὲ μήτ᾽ ἔστι μήτε ἦν μήτε ἂν εἰπεῖν ἔχοι μηδεὶς μηδέπω
καὶ τήμερον, τί τὸν σύμβουλον ἐχρῆν ποιεῖν; *but if there neither is
nor was (any such thing), and if no man yet even at this day could possibly
tell of any, what ought the statesman to have done?* Ib. 190.

V. Several Protases in one Sentence.

510. Two or more protases, not co-ordinate, may belong to
the same sentence ; but one always contains the leading condition, to which the rest of the sentence (including the other
conditions) is the conclusion. Here several protases may belong
to one apodosis ; or the leading condition may be followed by
two subordinate conditions, each with its own apodosis. *E.g.*

Καὶ γὰρ ἂν οὗτός τι πάθῃ, ταχέως ὑμεῖς ἕτερον Φίλιππον ποιήσετε, ἄνπερ οὕτω προσέχητε τοῖς πράγμασι τὸν νοῦν, *for if anything shall happen to this Philip, you will soon create another if this is
your way of attending to the business.* DΕΜ. iv. 11. So xviii. 195, 217
(two cases in each). Εἰ δ᾽ ἦμεν νέοι δὶς καὶ γέροντες, εἴ τις ἐξη-
μάρτανε, διπλοῦ βίου λαχόντες ἐξωρθούμεθ᾽ ἄν, *if we were twice
young and twice old, in case any one of us was in fault we should secure
a double life and set ourselves right.* ΕUR. Supp. 1084. See AR. Ran.
1449. Εἰ ξένος ἐτύγχανον ὤν, ξυνεγιγνώσκετε δήπου ἄν μοι εἰ ἐν
ἐκείνῃ τῇ φωνῇ τε καὶ τῷ τρόπῳ ἔλεγον ἐν οἷσπερ ἐτεθράμμην, i.e.

if I were a foreigner, you would pardon me if I spoke in· my own dialect,
etc. PLAT. Ap. 17 D. Εἰ τίς σε ἀνέροιτο τοῦτο, τί ἐστι σχῆμα;
εἰ αὐτῷ εἶπες ὅτι στρογγυλότης, εἰ σοι εἶπεν ἅπερ ἐγώ, εἶπες
δήπου ἂν ὅτι σχῆμά τι. Id. Men. 74 B.

Εἰ μὲν περὶ καινοῦ τινος πράγματος προυτίθετο λέγειν, ἐπισχὼν
ἂν ἕως οἱ πλεῖστοι τῶν εἰωθότων γνώμην ἀπεφήναντο, εἰ μὲν ἤρεσκέ
τί μοι τῶν ὑπὸ τούτων ῥηθέντων, ἡσυχίαν ἂν ἦγον, εἰ δὲ μή, τότ᾿ ἂν
αὐτὸς ἐπειρώμην ἃ γιγνώσκω λέγειν, i.e. *if the subject of debate were
new, I should have waited for others to speak; and then, if I liked anything that was said, I should keep quiet, and if not, I should try to say
something myself.* DEM. iv. 1 ;. see also xxxiii. 25.

511. It will be noticed that when the leading condition is unreal
(as in EUR. Supp. 1084, PLAT. Ap. 17 D, and DEM. iv. 1, above), this
makes all subordinate past or present conditions also unreal, so far as
the supposed case is concerned, without regard to their own nature.
Thus, in DEM. iv. 1 and xxxiii. 25 we have two directly opposite suppositions both stated as contrary to fact, which could not be unless
the leading supposition had made the whole state of things supposed
in the sentence unreal like itself. It is obvious, therefore, that such a
subordinate condition may refer to a case which is not *in itself* unreal,
although it is part of a supposition which *as a whole* is unreal. This
can be seen more easily in English. We can say, *if he had been an
Athenian, he would have been laughed at if he had talked as he did;* but
we are far from implying that the latter supposition (the subordinate
one) is contrary to fact, although it would be expressed in Greek by
εἰ ἔλεγεν. Still it is part of a supposed unreal state of things. This
explains an apparent inconsistency in respect to sentences like εἰκὸς
ἦν σε τοῦτο παθεῖν, *you ought properly to have suffered this,* when the
opposite of the infinitive is implied (415), the expression being practically equivalent (as a conditional form) to τοῦτο ἔπαθες ἂν εἰ τὸ εἰκὸς
ἔπαθες. As τοῦτο and τὸ εἰκός are here identical, the apodosis is
denied in the denial of the protasis. But if a new unreal protasis is
added, the opposite of the infinitive is not necessarily implied (see 422,
1) ; and if we add a concessive protasis and say καὶ εἰ μηδὲν ἠδίκησας,
εἰκὸς ἦν σε τοῦτο παθεῖν, *even if you had done nothing unjust, you
ought (still) to have suffered this,* τοῦτο generally represents what actually
took place (see 422, 2). Here a new chief protasis has come in and
changed the whole relation of the apodosis to the sentence. This offers
a satisfactory explanation of the apparent anomaly in SOPH. O. T. 221,
οὐ γὰρ ἂν μακρὰν ἴχνευον αὐτός, μὴ οὐκ ἔχων τι σύμβολον, where
μὴ οὐκ ἔχων is obviously equivalent to the condition εἰ μὴ εἶχον, while
there is yet no such opposite implied as *but I have a clue.* The chief
condition lies in the emphatic αὐτός, which is especially forcible after
ξένος μέν and ξένος δέ, and involves εἰ μόνος ἴχνευον. The meaning
is, *for I should not be very far on the track, if I were attempting to trace
it alone without a clue.* Thus *without a clue* becomes part of the unreal
supposition without being itself contrary to fact, while μή in μὴ οὐκ

ἔχων shows that ἔχων is conditional, and not merely descriptive (as if
it were οὐκ ἔχων). For μὴ οὐ with the participle, see 818.

Δέ, ἀλλά, AND αὐτάρ IN APODOSIS.

512. The apodosis is sometimes introduced by δέ, ἀλλά, or
αὐτάρ, *but*, as if the apodosis were co-ordinate with the protasis,
and were not the leading sentence. This occurs when the
apodosis is to be emphatically opposed to the protasis. It is
especially common in Homer and Herodotus. *E.g.*

Εἰ δέ κε μὴ δώωσιν, ἐγὼ δέ κεν αὐτὸς ἔλωμαι, *but if they do not
give it to me, (then) I will take one myself.* Il. i. 137. Εἴ περ γάρ τ᾽
ἄλλοι γε περικτεινώμεθα πάντες νηυσὶν ἐπ᾽ Ἀργείων, σοὶ δ᾽ οὐ δέος
ἔστ᾽ ἀπολέσθαι. Il. xii. 245. Εἴ περ . . . καταπέψῃ, ἀλλά τε καὶ
μετόπισθεν ἔχει κότον. Il. i. 81. Εἰ δὲ θανόντων περ καταλήθοντ᾽ εἰν
Ἀΐδαο, αὐτὰρ ἐγὼ καὶ κεῖθι φίλου μεμνήσομ᾽ ἑταίρου. Il. xxii. 389.
Εἰ ὑμῖν ἐστι τοῦτο μὴ δυνατὸν ποιῆσαι, ὑμεῖς δὲ ἔτι καὶ νῦν ἐκ τοῦ
μέσου ἡμῖν ἕζεσθε. Hdt. viii. 22. Ἀλλ᾽ εἰ μηδὲ τοῦτο βούλει ἀπο-
κρίνασθαι, σὺ δὲ τοὐντεῦθεν λέγε. Xen. Cyr. v. 5, 21.

513. This *apodotic* δέ cannot be expressed in English ; as our
adverbs *then, yet, still,* etc., necessarily fail to give the force of the
Greek δέ, which is always a conjunction.

The expression ἀλλὰ νῦν, *now at least,* is elliptical for εἰ μὴ πρότερον ἀλλὰ νῦν (with apodotic ἀλλά) ; as ἐὰν τὸ δίκαιον ἀλλὰ νῦν
ἐθέλητε δρᾶν, *if even now (though not before) you will do what is right,*
Ar. Av. 1598. See Dem. iii. 33. Sometimes ἀλλά alone seems to
imply εἰ μή τι ἄλλο ; as in Ar. Nub. 1364, ἐκέλευσ᾽ αὐτὸν ἀλλὰ
μυρρίνην λαβόντα τῶν Αἰσχύλου λέξαι τί μοι, *I bade him at least
(if nothing more) take a myrtle branch and give me a bit of Aeschylus.*
So 1369. In Plat. Rep. 509 C, εἰ μή τι ἀλλὰ . . . διεξιών, *if for
nothing (else), that you may at least describe,* etc., ἀλλά introduces an
apodosis after εἰ μή τι (sc. ἄλλο).

For δέ used in the same way to introduce the sentence upon which
a relative clause depends, see 564.

SECTION VII.

Relative and Temporal Sentences.

514. Relative sentences may be introduced by relative
pronouns and pronominal adjectives, or by relative adverbs
of *time, place,* or *manner.* They include therefore all
temporal sentences.

Clauses introduced by ἕως, πρίν, and other particles meaning *until* have many peculiarities, and are treated separately (611-661).

515. Relative sentences may be divided into two classes :—

First, those in which the antecedent of the relative is *definite*; that is, in which the relative pronouns refer to definite persons or things, and the relative adverbs to definite points of time, place, etc. Secondly, those in which the antecedent is *indefinite*; that is, in which no such definite persons, things, times, or places are referred to.

516. Both the definite and the indefinite antecedent may be either expressed or understood. *E.g.*

(*Definite.*) Ταῦτα ἃ ἔχω ὁρᾷς, *you see these things which I have*; or ἃ ἔχω ὁρᾷς. Ὅτε ἐβούλετο ἦλθεν, (*once*) *when he wished, he came.*

(*Indefinite.*) Πάντα ἃ ἂν βούλωνται ἕξουσιν, *they will have everything which they may want*; or ἃ ἂν βούλωνται ἕξουσιν, *they will have whatever they may want.* Ὅταν ἔλθῃ, τότε τοῦτο πράξω, *when he shall come* (or *when he comes*), *then I will do this.* Ὅτε βούλοιτο, τοῦτο ἔπρασσεν, *whenever he wished, he (always) did this.* Ὡς ἂν εἴπω, οὕτως ποιῶμεν, *as I shall direct, so let us act.*

517. The relative may be used to express a *purpose* (565), or in a *causal* sense (580). The antecedent may then be either definite or indefinite.

518. When the antecedent is indefinite, the negative of the relative clause is μή; when it is definite, οὐ is used unless the general construction requires μή (as in prohibitions, wishes, final expressions, etc.).

A. RELATIVE WITH DEFINITE ANTECEDENT.

519. A relative with a *definite* antecedent has no effect upon the mood of the following verb; and it therefore may take the indicative (with οὐ for its negative) or any other construction that can occur in an independent sentence. *E.g.*

Λέγω ἃ οἶδα, *I say what I know.* Λέγω ἃ ἤκουσα. Λέξω ἃ ἀκήκοα. Ἔλεξαν ἃ ἤκουσαν. Πάντα λέγει ἃ γενήσεται. Πράσσουσιν ἃ βούλονται (or ὡς βούλονται), *they are doing what* (or *as*) *they please.* (On the other hand, πράξουσιν ἃ ἂν βούλωνται, or ὡς ἂν βούλωνται, *they will do what they please,* or *as they please*; the antecedent being indefinite.) Λέγω ἃ οὐκ ἀγνοῶ, *I am saying that of which I am not ignorant.*

'Αλλ' ὅτε δή ῥ' ἐκ τοῖο δυωδεκάτη γένετ' ἠώς, καὶ τότε δὴ πρὸς 'Ολυμπον ἴσαν θεοὶ αἰὲν ἐόντες, *but when now the twelfth day from that came,* etc. Il. i. 493. Τίς ἔσθ' ὁ χῶρος δῆτ', ἐν ᾧ βεβήκαμεν. SOPH. O. C. 52. Ἕως ἐστὶ καιρός, ἀντιλάβεσθε τῶν πραγμάτων, i.e. *now, while there is an opportunity,* etc. DEM. i. 20. (If the exhortation were future, he would say ἕως ἂν ᾖ καιρός, *so long as there shall be an opportunity.*) Ὁ δὲ ἀναβὰς, ἕως μὲν βάσιμα ἦν, ἐπὶ τοῦ ἵππου ἦγεν· ἐπεὶ δὲ ἄβατα ἦν, καταλιπὼν τὸν ἵππον ἔσπευδε πεζῇ. XEN. An. iii. 4, 49. So Il. i. 193, εἷος ὥρμαινε. Οἵπερ δὲ καὶ τῶν ἀποβαινόντων τὸ πλέον τῆς αἰτίας ἕξομεν, οὗτοι καὶ καθ' ἡσυχίαν τι αὐτῶν προΐδωμεν, *we who are to bear the greater part of the blame,* etc. THUC. i. 83. Ὅθεν δ' οὖν ῥᾷστα μαθήσεσθε περὶ αὐτῶν, ἐντεῦθεν ὑμᾶς καὶ ἐγὼ πρῶτον πειράσομαι διδάσκειν. DEM. xxvii. 3. (Here ἐντεῦθεν refers to the point at which he intends to begin.) Ἢ δὴ λοίγια ἔργ', ὅτε μ' ἐχθοδοπῆσαι ἐφήσεις Ἥρῃ, ὅτ' ἂν μ' ἐρέθῃσιν ὀνειδείοις ἐπέεσσιν, *surely there will be sad work, when you shall impel me,* etc. Il. i. 518. (Here ὅτε refers to some time conceived as definite ; whereas ὅτ' ἂν ἐρέθῃσιν, *when (if ever) she shall provoke me,* is indefinite ; see 530.) Νὺξ δ' ἔσται ὅτε δὴ στυγερὸς γάμος ἀντιβολήσει οὐλομένης ἐμέθεν, τῆς τε Ζεὺς ὄλβον ἀπηύρα. Od. xviii. 272. (The time is conceived as definite.) Τηνικαῦτα, ὅτε οὐδ' ὅ τι χρὴ ποιεῖν ἕξετε, *then, when you will not even be able to do what you ought.* DEM. xix. 262.

Ἄρξομαι δ' ἐντεῦθεν ὅθεν καὶ ὑμεῖς ῥᾷστ' ἂν μάθοιτε κἀγὼ τάχιστ' ἂν διδάξαιμι. DEM. xxix. 5. (With the potential optative compare the future indicative in DEM. xxvii. 3, above.) Νῦν δὲ τοῦτο οὐκ ἐποίησεν, ἐν ᾧ τὸν δῆμον ἐτίμησεν ἄν, *but he did not do this, in which he might have honoured the people.* Id. xxi. 69. Εἰς καλὸν ὑμῖν Ἄνυτος ὅδε παρεκαθέζετο, ᾧ μεταδῶμεν τῆς ζητήσεως. PLAT. Men. 89 E (subjunctive in exhortation). Οὔκουν ἄξιον τοῖς τῶν κατηγόρων λόγοις πιστεῦσαι μᾶλλον ἢ τοῖς ἔργοις καὶ τῷ χρόνῳ, ὃν ὑμεῖς σαφέστατον ἔλεγχον τοῦ ἀληθοῦς νομίσατε. LYS. xix. 61. (Here the imperative νομίσατε is used in a sort of exclamation after ὅν, where ordinarily δεῖ νομίσαι would be used. See 253.) Ἂν γὰρ ἀποφύγῃ με οὗτος, ὃ μὴ γένοιτο, τὴν ἐπωβελίαν ὀφλήσω. DEM. xxvii. 67 (optative in wish).

So in μέμνημαι ὅτε and similar expressions. *E.g.*

Οὐ μέμνῃ ὅτε τ' ἐκρέμω ὑψόθεν; *do you not remember* (the time) *when you hung aloft?* Il. xv. 18. Εἰ μέμνησαι ὅτ' ἐγώ σοι ἀπεκρινάμην. PLAT. Men. 79 D. Οἶσθ' ὅτε ἐφάνη. EUR. Hec. 112. (See 913.)

B. RELATIVE WITH INDEFINITE ANTECEDENT.—CONDITIONAL RELATIVE.

520. A relative with an *indefinite* antecedent gives a

conditional force to the clause in which it stands, and is called a *conditional relative*. The conditional relative clause stands in the relation of a protasis to the antecedent clause, which is its apodosis (380). The negative particle is μή.

Thus, when we say ἃ νομίζει ταῦτα λέγει, *he is saying what he (actually) thinks*, or ἃ ἐνόμιζε ταῦτα ἔλεγεν, *he was saying what he thought*, the actions of νομίζει and ἐνόμιζε are stated as actual facts, occurring at definite times ; but when we say ἃ ἂν νομίζῃ (ταῦτα) λέγει, *he (always) says whatever he thinks*, or ἃ νομίζοι (ταῦτα) ἔλεγεν, *he (always) said whatever he happened to be thinking*, νομίζῃ and νομίζοι do not state any such definite facts, but rather what some one *may think* (or *may have thought*) on *any* occasion on which he may speak or may have spoken. So, when we say ἃ νομίζει ταῦτα λέξει, *he will say what he (now) thinks*, νομίζει denotes a fact ; but when we say ἃ ἂν νομίζῃ λέξει, *he will say whatever he happens to be (then) thinking*, νομίζῃ denotes a supposed future case. Again,—to take the case in which the distinction is most liable to be overlooked,—when we say ἃ οὐκ οἶδα οὐκ οἴομαι εἰδέναι, *what I do not know, I do not think that I know*, οὐκ οἶδα, as before, denotes a simple fact, and its object ἅ has a definite antecedent ; but when Socrates says ἃ μὴ οἶδα οὐδὲ οἴομαι εἰδέναι, the meaning is *whatever I do not know* (i.e. *if there is anything which I do not know*), *I do not even think that I know it*. In sentences like this, unless a negative is used (518), it is often difficult to decide whether the antecedent is definite or indefinite : thus ἃ οἶδα οἴομαι εἰδέναι may mean either *what I (actually) know, I think that I know*, or *whatever I know* (*if there is anything which I know*), *I think that I know it*.

521. The analogy of these indefinite relative clauses to conditional sentences will be seen at once. The following examples will make this clearer :—

Ὅ τι βούλεται δώσω, *I will give him whatever he (now) wishes.*
Εἴ τι βούλεται, δώσω, *if he wishes anything, I will give it.* (402.)

Ὅ τι ἐβούλετο ἔδωκα ἄν, *I should have given him whatever he had wished.* Ὅ τι μὴ ἐγένετο οὐκ ἂν εἶπον, *I should not have told what had not happened.* Εἴ τι ἐβούλετο, ἔδωκα ἄν, *if he had wished anything, I should have given it.* Εἴ τι μὴ ἐγένετο, οὐκ ἂν εἶπον, *I should not have told anything if it had not happened.* (410.)

Ὅ τι ἂν βούληται, δώσω, *I will give him whatever he shall wish.*
Ἐάν τι βούληται, δώσω, *if he shall wish anything, I will give it.* (444.)

Ὅ τι βούλοιτο δοίην ἄν, *I should give him whatever he might wish.* Εἴ τι βούλοιτο, δοίην ἄν, *if he should wish anything, I should give it.* (455.)

Ὅ τι ἂν βούληται δίδωμι, I (always) give him whatever he wishes.
Ὅ τι βούλοιτο ἐδίδουν, I always gave him whatever he wished. Ἐάν
τι βούληται, δίδωμι, if he ever wishes anything, I (always) give it.
Εἴ τι βούλοιτο, ἐδίδουν, if he ever wished anything, I (always) gave it.
(462.)

522. The particle ἄν (Epic κέ) is regularly joined with
all relative words when they are followed by the subjunctive.
With ὅτε, ὁπότε, ἐπεί, and ἐπειδή, ἄν forms ὅταν, ὁπόταν, ἐπάν or
ἐπήν (Ionic ἐπεάν), and ἐπειδάν. In Homer, where κέ is generally
used for ἄν, we have ὅτε κε, ἐπεί κε, etc. (like εἴ κε), also ὅτ’ ἄν, where
in Attic we have ὅταν, ὁπόταν, ἐπειδάν. Ἐπήν, however, occurs often,
and ἐπεὶ ἄν once, in Homer. Both ἐπήν and ἐπάν are rare in Attic.

523. The classification of common conditional sentences, with
four classes of ordinary conditions and two of general conditions,
given in 388-395, applies equally to conditional relative sentences.

I. FOUR FORMS OF ORDINARY CONDITIONAL RELATIVE SENTENCES.

524. The conditional relative sentence has *four* forms,
two of *present* and *past* (525 and 528) and two of *future*
conditions (529 and 531), which correspond to the four forms
of ordinary protasis.

(a) PRESENT AND PAST CONDITIONS.

525. When the relative clause simply states a present
or past supposition, implying nothing as to the fulfilment of
the condition, the verb is in one of the present or past tenses
of the indicative. The antecedent clause can have any
form of the verb, like an ordinary apodosis. (See 402.)
E.g.

Ἃ μὴ οἶδα, οὐδὲ οἴομαι εἰδέναι (like εἴ τινα μὴ οἶδα). PLAT. Ap. 21 D.
(See 520.) Χρήσθων ὅ τι βούλονται, let them deal with me as they please
(i.e. εἴ τι βούλονται). AR. Nub. 439. Ἐπίσταμαι ὁρᾶν θ’ ἅ δεῖ με,
κοὐχ ὁρᾶν ἃ μὴ πρέπει, I know how to see anything which I ought to see,
and not to see anything which I ought not. EUR. Ino, Fr. 417. (Ἃ δεῖ
is nearly equivalent to εἴ τινα δεῖ, and ἃ μὴ πρέπει to εἴ τινα μὴ
πρέπει.) Τοὺς πλείστους ἔνθαπερ ἔπεσον ἑκάστους ἔθαψαν· οὓς δὲ μὴ
εὕρισκον, κενοτάφιον αὐτοῖς ἐποίησαν, i.e. they raised a cenotaph for
any of them whom they did not find (like εἴ τινας μὴ εὕρισκον). XEN.
An. vi. 4, 9. Τί γάρ; ὅστις δαπανηρὸς ὢν μὴ αὐτάρκης ἐστὶν, ἀλλ’
ἀεὶ τῶν πλησίον δεῖται, καὶ λαμβάνων μὴ δύναται ἀποδιδόναι, μὴ

λαμβάνων δὲ τὸν μὴ διδόντα μισεῖ, οὐ δοκεῖ σοι καὶ οὗτος χαλεπὸς φίλος εἶναι; (i.e. *supposing a case*, εἴ τις . . . μὴ αὐτάρκης ἐστὶν, κ.τ.λ.). Id. Mem. ii. 6, 2. So ἥτις μηδαμοῦ ξυμμαχεῖ, THUC. i. 35. Ἃ γάρ τις μὴ προσεδόκησεν, οὐδὲ φυλάξασθαι ἐγχωρεῖ, *for there is no opportunity even to guard against what we did not expect* (like εἴ τινα μὴ προσεδόκησέ τις). ANT. v. 19. Εἰς τὰ πλοῖα τούς τε ἀσθενοῦντας ἐνεβίβασαν καὶ τῶν σκευῶν ὅσα μὴ ἀνάγκη ἦν ἔχειν (like εἴ τινα τῶν σκευῶν μὴ ἀνάγκη ἦν ἔχειν), i.e. *any which they did not need.* XEN. An. v. 3, 1. Ἀνθρώπους διέφθειρεν (ἡ θάλασσα) ὅσοι μὴ ἐδύναντο φθῆναι πρὸς τὰ μετέωρα ἀναδραμόντες, i.e. *if any were unable to escape soon enough to the high land, so many the sea destroyed.* THUC. iii. 89. Οἷς μὲν αἵρεσις γεγένηται τἆλλα εὐτυχοῦσι, πολλὴ ἄνοια πολεμῆσαι· εἰ δ᾽ ἀναγκαῖον ἦν, κ.τ.λ., *for any who have had the choice given them, while they are prosperous in other respects, it is great folly to go to war* (i.e. εἴ τισιν αἵρεσις γεγένηται). Id. ii. 61. Πάντες ἴσμεν Χαβρίαν οὔτε τύπτοντα οὔθ᾽ ἁρπάζοντα τὸν στέφανον οὔθ᾽ ὅλως προσιόντ᾽ ὅποι μὴ προσῆκεν αὐτῷ, *nor going anywhere at all where it was not lawful for him* (i.e. εἴ ποι μὴ προσῆκεν). DEM. xxi. 64. Πῶς οὖν οἱ ἀγαθοὶ τοῖς ἀγαθοῖς φίλοι ἔσονται, οἳ μήτε ἀπόντες ποθεινοὶ ἀλλήλοις μήτε παρόντες χρείαν αὐτῶν ἔχουσι; (i.e. εἰ μὴ ἔχουσι). PLAT. Lys. 215 B. Νικῴη δ᾽ ὅ τι πᾶσιν ὑμῖν μέλλει συνοίσειν (i.e. εἴ τι μέλλει), *may any plan prevail which will benefit you all.* DEM. iv. 51.

526. Care must be taken here (as in conditional sentences) not to include in this class general suppositions which require the subjunctive or optative (532). On the other hand, the examples falling under 534, in which the indicative is allowed, might properly be placed here, as they state a general supposition as if it were a particular one.

527. A conditional relative clause (like a clause with εἰ, 407) may take the future indicative to express a *present* intention or necessity. *E.g.*

Ἐν τούτῳ κεκωλῦσθαι ἐδόκει ἑκάστῳ τὰ πράγματα ᾧ μή τις αὐτὸς παρέσται, *each man felt that all progress was at an end in any affair in which he was not personally to take part.* THUC. ii. 8. The direct form was ἐν τούτῳ κεκώλυται (51 ; 122) ᾧ μὴ παρέσομαι. Οὗ δὲ ἀληθείας τις ἀτυχήσει, ποτὲ τούτου ἐπιστήμων ἔσται; *but if one is to miss the truth of anything, will he ever understand it?* PLAT. Theaet. 186 C. So probably XEN. Cyr. i. 5, 13, ὅ τι γὰρ μὴ τοιοῦτον ἀποβήσεται παρ᾽ ὑμῶν, εἰς ἐμὲ τὸ ἐλλεῖπον ἔσται, i.e. *if there is to be any failure on your part to come up to my expectations, the loss will fall on me.*

This is the only form of conditional relative sentence that regularly takes the future indicative. (See 530.)

528. When a relative clause expresses a present or past condition, implying that it *is not* or *was not* fulfilled (like a protasis of the form 410), the verb is in a past tense of the indicative.

Tho antocedont clauso gonorally has a past tonso of tho indicative with ἄν; but it may have a past tense of the indicative in an unreal condition, in an unaccomplished wish, or in a final clause. *E.g.*

Ἃ μὴ ἐβούλετο δοῦναι, οὐκ ἂν ἔδωκεν, *he would not have given what he had not wished to give* (i.e. εἴ τινα μὴ ἐβούλετο δοῦναι, οὐκ ἂν ἔδωκεν). Ὁπότερον τούτων ἐποίησεν, οὐδενὸς ἂν ἧττον Ἀθηναίων πλούσιοι ἦσαν, *whichever of these he had done* (he did neither), *they would be as rich as any of the Athenians.* Lys. xxxii. 23. Οὔτε γὰρ ἂν αὐτοὶ ἐπεχειροῦμεν πράττειν ἃ μὴ ἠπιστάμεθα, οὔτε τοῖς ἄλλοις ἐπετρέπομεν ὧν ἤρχομεν ἄλλο τι πράττειν ἢ ὅ τι πράττοντες ὀρθῶς ἔμελλον πράξειν· τοῦτο δ᾽ ἦν ἂν οὗ ἐπιστήμην εἶχον, *for* (*if that were so*) *we should not be undertaking* (*as we are*) *to do things which we did not understand, nor should we permit any others whom we were ruling to do anything else than what they were likely to do properly; and this would be whatever they had knowledge of.* Plat. Charm. 171 E. (Here ἃ μὴ ἠπιστάμεθα = εἴ τινα μὴ ἠπιστάμεθα, *if there were any things which we did not know,*—ὧν ἤρχομεν = εἴ τινων ἤρχομεν,—ὅ τι ἔμελλον = εἴ τι ἔμελλον,—and οὗ ἐπιστήμην εἶχον = εἴ τινος εἶχον. It is implied that none of the cases here supposed ever actually arose. Ὥσπερ τοίνυν ἄλλων τινῶν τεττάρων, εἰ ἕν τι ἐζητοῦμεν αὐτῶν ἐν ὁτῳοῦν, ὁπότε πρῶτον ἐκεῖνο ἔγνωμεν, ἱκανῶς ἂν εἶχεν ἡμῖν, εἰ δὲ τὰ τρία πρότερον ἐγνωρίσαμεν, αὐτῷ ἂν τούτῳ ἐγνώριστο τὸ ζητούμενον. Plat. Rep. 428 A. (Here the antithesis of ὁπότε πρῶτον ἐκεῖνο ἔγνωμεν, *in* (*whatever*) *case we had recognised this first,* and εἰ τὰ τρία πρότερον ἐγνωρίσαμεν, *if we had recognised the three sooner,* makes the force of the relative especially clear.) Ἐβασάνιζον ἂν μέχρι οὗ αὐτοῖς ἐδόκει, *they would have questioned them* (*under torture*) *so long as they pleased.* Dem. liii. 25. Εἰ δὲ οἴκοι εἶχον ἕκαστοι τὰς δίκας, τούτους ἂν ἀπώλλυσαν οἵτινες φίλοι μάλιστα ἦσαν Ἀθηναίων τῷ δήμῳ, *if each had their trials at home, they would ruin any who were especially friendly,* etc. Xen. Rep. Ath. i. 16. (Here οἵτινες ἦσαν, = εἴ τινες ἦσαν, forms a second protasis to the apodosis ἀπώλλυσαν ἄν. See 511.) Καὶ ὁπηνίκα ἐφαίνετο ταῦτα πεποιηκὼς, ὡμολογεῖτ᾽ ἂν ἡ κατηγορία τοῖς ἔργοις αὐτοῦ, *and if he ever appeared to have done this, his form of accusation would agree with his acts.* Dem. xviii. 14.

Εἰ ξένος ἐτύγχανον ὤν, ξυνεγιγνώσκετε δήπου ἄν μοι εἰ ἐν ἐκείνῃ τῇ φωνῇ τε καὶ τῷ τρόπῳ ἔλεγον ἐν οἷσπερ ἐτεθράμμην, *if I happened to be a foreigner, you would surely pardon me, if I were* (*now*) *addressing you in both the language and the manner in which I had been brought up.* Plat. Ap. 17 D. Ὡς δὴ ἐγώ γ᾽ ὄφελον μάκαρός νύ τευ ἔμμεναι υἱὸς ἀνέρος, ὃν κτεάτεσσιν ἑοῖς ἔπι γῆρας ἔτετμεν, *O that I were the son of some fortunate man, whom old age had found upon his own estate* (i.e. *if old age had found any such man, would that I had been his son*). Od. i. 217. So Il. vi. 348 and 351.

So when the relative sentence depends on a past indicative in a final clause (333); as in Dem. xxiii. 48, ταῦτά γε δήπου προσῆκε

γράψαι, ἵνα ὅτῳ ποτὲ τοὔργον ἐπράχθη, τούτῳ τὰ ἐκ τῶν νόμων
ὑπῆρχε δίκαια, *he ought to have written it in this way, in order that
any one by whom the deed had been done might have his rights according
to the laws.* (This implies that the law was not so written, so that the
case supposed in ὅτῳ ἐπράχθη never arose.) So DEM. liii. 24, ἵν᾽ ἀκούσαντες ἐκ τούτων ἐψηφίσασθε ὁποῖόν τι ὑμῖν ἐδόκει, *that you might
have voted whatever seemed good to you.*

All examples of this form fall equally well under the general rule
for *assimilation* (559).

(b) FUTURE CONDITIONS.

529. (*Subjunctive.*) When the relative clause expresses
a future condition of the more vivid form (like a protasis
of the form 444), and the verb of the antecedent clause
also refers to the future, the relative is joined with ἄν (or
κέ) and takes the subjunctive. *E.g.*

Τάων ἥν κ᾽ ἐθέλωμι φίλην ποιήσομ᾽ ἄκοιτιν (like εἴ κέ τινα ἐθέλωμι), *whomsoever of these I may wish I shall make my wife.* Il. ix. 397.
Ἐκ γὰρ Ὀρέσταο τίσις ἔσσεται Ἀτρεΐδαο, ὁππότ᾽ ἄν ἡβήσῃ τε καὶ
ἧς ἱμείρεται αἴης, i.e. *vengeance will come from Orestes, when he shall
grow up,* etc. (like ἐάν ποτε ἡβήσῃ). Od. i. 40. Τότε δ᾽ αὖτε μαχήσεται, ὁππότε κέν μιν θυμὸς ἐνὶ στήθεσσιν ἀνώγῃ καὶ θεὸς ὄρσῃ.
Il. ix. 702. Ἀλλ᾽ ἄγεθ᾽, ὡς ἄν ἐγὼν εἴπω, πειθώμεθα πάντες, *let us
obey as I may direct,* i.e. *if I give any direction* (ἐάν πως εἴπω), *let us
obey it.* Il. ii. 139. Ἡμεῖς αὖτ᾽ ἀλόχους τε φίλας καὶ νήπια τέκνα
ἄξομεν ἐν νήεσσιν, ἐπὴν πτολίεθρον ἕλωμεν, *when we shall have taken
the city.* Il. iv. 238. So εὖτ᾽ ἄν πίπτωσιν, Il. i. 242. Οὐκοῦν, ὅταν
δὴ μὴ σθένω, πεπαύσομαι, *therefore, when I shall have no more strength,
I will cease.* SOPH. ANT. 91. Ταῦτα, ἐπειδὰν περὶ τοῦ γένους εἴπω,
τότε ἐρῶ, *I will speak of this, when I shall have spoken about my birth.*
DEM. lvii. 16. (See 90.) Ἐπειδὰν διαπράξωμαι ἃ δέομαι, ἥξω.
XEN. AN. ii. 3, 29. Τίνα οἴεσθε αὐτὴν ψυχὴν ἕξειν, ὅταν ἐμὲ ἴδῃ
τῶν πατρῴων ἀπεστερημένον; *what feelings do you think she will have,
when* (or *if at any time*) *she shall see me,* etc. ? DEM. xxviii. 21. Τούτων
δὲ Ἀθηναίους φημὶ δεῖν εἶναι πεντακοσίους, ἐξ ἧς ἄν τινος ὑμῖν ἡλικίας
καλῶς ἔχειν δοκῇ, *from whatever age it shall seem good to you to take
them* (i.e. *if from any particular age,* etc.). Id. iv. 21. Τῶν πραγμάτων
τοὺς βουλευομένους (ἡγεῖσθαι δεῖ), ἵνα ἃ ἄν ἐκείνοις δοκῇ ταῦτα
πράττηται, *in order that whatever shall seem good to them shall be done.*
Ib. 39. Οὔ μοι φόβου μέλαθρον ἐλπὶς ἐμπατεῖν, ἕως ἄν αἴθῃ πῦρ
ἐφ᾽ ἑστίας ἐμῆς Αἴγισθος, *so long as Aegisthus shall kindle fire upon my
hearth.* AESCH. AG. 1434.

530. The future indicative is very rarely used in conditional relative
clauses, as it is in common protasis (447), in the place of the subjunctive; as it would generally be ambiguous, appearing as if the ante-

cedent were definite. Some cases of ὅσος with the future, as ὅτοι βουλήσονται, THUC. i. 22, are perhaps exceptions. (See 527.)

531. (*Optative.*) When the relative clause expresses a future condition of the less vivid form (like a protasis of the form 455), and the antecedent clause contains an optative referring to the future, the relative takes the optative (without ἄν).

The optative in the antecedent clause may be in an apodosis with ἄν, in a protasis, in an expression of a wish, or in a final clause. *E.g.*

Μάλα κεν θρασυκάρδιος εἴη, ὃς τότε γηθήσειεν ἰδὼν πόνον οὐδ' ἀκάχοιτο (i.e. εἴ τις γηθήσειε, μάλα κεν θρασυκάρδιος εἴη), *any one who should then rejoice would be very stout-hearted.* Il. xiii. 343. Βουλοίμην κ' ἐπάρουρος ἐὼν θητευέμεν ἄλλῳ . . . ᾧ μὴ βίοτος πολὺς εἴη, *I should wish to be a serf attached to the soil, serving another man who had not much to live on.* Od. xi. 489. Ζηνὸς οὐκ ἂν ἄσσον ἱκοίμην, ὅτε μὴ αὐτός γε κελεύοι, *unless he should himself bid me.* Il. xiv. 247. So Il. vi. 329 and 521; and ὅστις καλέσειε, AR. Nub. 1250. Οὐκ ἂν οὖν θρέψαις ἄνδρα, ὅστις τε καὶ δύναιτο σοῦ ἀπερύκειν τοὺς ἐπιχειροῦντας ἀδικεῖν σε; *would you not support any man who should be both willing and able, etc.?* XEN. Mem. ii. 9, 2. Πεινῶν φάγοι ἂν ὁπότε βούλοιτο, *when he is hungry, he would eat whenever he might wish* (like εἴ ποτε βούλοιτο). Ib. ii. 1, 18. So i. 5, 4; i. 7, 3; iv. 2, 20. Πῶς οὖν ἂν εἰδείης περὶ τούτου τοῦ πράγματος οὗ παντάπασιν ἄπειρος εἴης; *how then could you know about that thing of which you had no experience at all?* PLAT. Men. 92 C. Ἆρ' ἂν ἡγοῖο ταῦτα σὰ εἶναι, ἅ σοι ἐξείη καὶ ἀποδόσθαι καὶ δοῦναι καὶ θῦσαι ὅτῳ βούλοιο θεῶν; Id. Euthyd. 302 A. Τί ἂν παθεῖν (δύναιτο), ὃ μὴ καὶ ὑφ' αὐτοῦ πάθοι; *what could he suffer, unless he should suffer it also from himself?* (i.e. εἰ μὴ πάθοι). Id. Lys. 214 E. Ὃ δὲ μὴ ἀγαπῴη, οὐδ' ἂν φιλοῖ (i.e εἴ τι μὴ ἀγαπῴη, οὐδ' ἂν φιλοῖ τοῦτο). Ib. 215 B. Ἰδίαν ἕκαστος ἂν κατασκευὴν κατασκευάζοιτο, ἥτις ἕκαστον ἀρέσκοι. Id. Rep. 557 B. Ὅσῳ δὲ πρεσβύτερος γίγνοιτο, μᾶλλον ἀεὶ ἀσπάζοιτο ἂν (χρήματα), *the older he should grow, the more he would always cling to it* (i.e. εἴ τι πρεσβύτερος γίγνοιτο, τοσούτῳ μᾶλλον ἀσπάζοιτο ἄν). Ib. 549 B. So 412 D. Φήσομεν μηδέποτε μηδὲν ἂν μεῖζον μηδὲ ἔλαττον γενέσθαι, ἕως ἴσον εἴη αὐτὸ ἑαυτῷ, *so long as it should remain equal to itself.* Id. Theaet. 155 A.

Εἰ δὲ βούλοιο τῶν φίλων τινὰ προτρέψασθαι ὁπότε ἀποδημοίης ἐπιμελεῖσθαι τῶν σῶν, τί ἂν ποιοίης; XEN. Mem. ii. 3, 12. Εἰκότως ἂν καὶ παρὰ θεῶν πρακτικώτερος εἴη, ὅστις μὴ ὁπότε ἐν ἀπόροις εἴη τότε κολακεύοι, ἀλλ' ὅτε τὰ ἄριστα πράττοι τότε μάλιστα τῶν θεῶν μεμνῷτο. Id. Cyr. i. 6, 3. Ὡς ἀπόλοιτο καὶ ἄλλος, ὅ τις τοιαῦτά γε ῥέζοι, *O that any other man might likewise perish who should do the like* (i.e. εἴ τις τοιαῦτα ῥέζοι). Od. i. 47. Εἰ γάρ μιν θανάτοιο

δυσηχέος ὧδε δυναίμην νόσφιν ἀποκρύψαι, ὅτε μιν μόρος αἰνὸς
ἱκάνοι. Il. xviii. 464. Δῶρα θεῶν ἔχοι, ὅττι διδοῖεν, may he have
gifts of the Gods, whatever they may give. Od. xviii. 142. Ἐγίγνωσκε
δεῖν τοὺς ὑπηρέτας τοῦτο ἀσκεῖν, ὡς πάντα νομίζοιεν πρέπειν αὐτοῖς
πράττειν ὅσα ὁ ἄρχων προστάττοι. ΧΕΝ. Cyr. ii. 1, 31.
For κέ or ἄν in these relative sentences in Homer, see 542. All
these examples fall also under the general rule for assimilation (558).

II. GENERAL CONDITIONAL RELATIVE SENTENCES.

532. A conditional relative sentence may express a
general supposition, when the verb of the antecedent clause
denotes a customary or repeated action or a general truth,
while the relative clause refers in a general way to any act
or acts of a given class. Here the subjunctive with ὅς ἄν,
ὅταν, etc., follows primary tenses, and the optative (without
ἄν) follows secondary tenses. (See 462.) E.g.

Ἐχθρὸς γάρ μοι κεῖνος ὁμῶς ᾿Αΐδαο πύλῃσιν, ὅς χ᾽ ἕτερον μὲν
κεύθῃ ἐνὶ φρεσὶν, ἄλλο δὲ εἴπῃ, for that man (i.e. any man) is hated by
me like the very gates of Hades, who conceals one thing in his mind and
speaks another. Il. ix. 312. Νεμεσσῶμαί γε μὲν οὐδὲν κλαίειν ὅς κε
θάνῃσι βροτῶν καὶ πότμον ἐνίσπῃ, I am never at all indignant at
weeping for any mortal who may die, etc. Od. iv. 195. Οἶνος, ὅς τε καὶ
ἄλλους βλάπτει, ὃς ἄν μιν χάνδον ἕλῃ μηδ᾽ αἴσιμα πίνῃ. Od. xxi.
293. Καὶ γὰρ συμμαχεῖν τούτοις ἐθέλουσιν ἅπαντες, οὓς ἂν ὁρῶσι
παρεσκευασμένους, for all men are (always) willing to be allies to those
whom they see prepared. DEM. iv. 6. Καίπερ τῶν ἀνθρώπων, ἐν ᾧ μὲν
ἂν πολεμῶσι, τὸν παρόντα (πόλεμον) ἀεὶ μέγιστον κρινόντων, although
men always consider the present war the greatest, so long as they are engaged
in it. THUC. i. 21. Πορεύονταί τε γὰρ αἱ ἀγέλαι ᾗ ἂν αὐτὰς εὐθύνω-
σιν οἱ νομεῖς, νέμονταί τε χωρία ἐφ᾽ ὁποῖα ἂν αὐτὰς ἐφιῶσιν,
ἀπέχονταί τε ὧν ἂν αὐτὰς ἀπείργωσι· καὶ τοῖς καρποῖς ἐῶσι τοὺς
νομέας χρῆσθαι οὕτως ὅπως ἂν αὐτοὶ βούλωνται· ἄνθρωποι δὲ ἐπ᾽
οὐδένας μᾶλλον συνίστανται ἢ ἐπὶ τούτους οὓς ἂν αἴσθωνται ἄρχειν
αὐτῶν ἐπιχειροῦντας. ΧΕΝ. Cyr. i. 1, 2. Νομίζω προστάτου ἔργον
εἶναι οἷον δεῖ, ὃς ἂν ὁρῶν τοὺς φίλους ἐξαπατωμένους μὴ ἐπιτρέπῃ,
i.e. such as one ought always to be, who, etc. Id. Hell. ii. 3, 51. Κατα-
φρόνησις δὲ (ἐγγίγνεται), ὃς ἂν καὶ γνώμῃ πιστεύῃ τῶν ἐναντίων
προέχειν, ὃ ἡμῖν ὑπάρχει. THUC. ii. 62. (Here the ὃ refers to all that
precedes, as a definite antecedent.)

Οὐ μὲν γὰρ μεῖζον κλέος ἀνέρος, ὄφρα κ᾽ ἔῃσιν, ἢ ὅ τι ποσσίν τε
ῥέξῃ καὶ χερσίν. Od. viii. 147. (Ὄφρα κ᾽ ἔῃσιν, so long as he lives.)
(Θεοὺς) παρατρωπῶσ᾽ ἄνθρωποι λισσόμενοι, ὅτε κέν τις ὑπερβήῃ καὶ
ἁμάρτῃ. Il. ix. 500. Ἥμισυ γάρ τ᾽ ἀρετῆς ἀποαίνυται εὐρύοπα
Ζεὺς ἀνέρος, εὖτ᾽ ἄν μιν κατὰ δούλιον ἦμαρ ἕλῃσιν. Od. xvii. 322.
Φιλέει δέ κως προσημαίνειν, εὖτ᾽ ἂν μέλλῃ μεγάλα κακὰ ἢ πόλι ἢ

ἔθνεἴ ἔπεσθαι. HDT. vi. 27. Φεύγουσι γάρ τοι χοὶ θρασεῖς, ὅταν πέλας
ἤδη τὸν Ἀιδην εἰσορῶσι τοῦ βίου. SOPH. Ant. 580. 'Ηνίκ' ἂν δ'
οἴκοι γένωνται, δρῶσιν οὐκ ἀνασχετά. AR. Pac. 1179. Ἐπειδὰν δὲ
ἡ ἐκφορὰ ᾖ, λάρνακας ἄγουσιν ἅμαξαι. THUC. ii. 34. Ἐπειδὰν δὲ
κρύψωσι γῇ, ἀνὴρ ᾑρημένος ὑπὸ τῆς πόλεως, ὃς ἂν γνώμῃ τε δοκῇ
μὴ ἀξύνετος εἶναι, λέγει ἐπ' αὐτοῖς ἔπαινον τὸν πρέποντα. Ibid. Ἕως
ἂν σῴζηται τὸ σκάφος, τότε χρὴ προθύμους εἶναι· ἐπειδὰν δὲ ἡ
θάλαττα ὑπέρσχῃ, μάταιος ἡ σπουδή. DEM. ix. 69. So ἔστ' ἂν
δείσωσιν, XEN. Mem. iii. 5, 6.

Ὃν δ' αὖ δήμου ἄνδρα ἴδοι βόωντά τ' ἐφεύροι, τὸν σκήπτρῳ
ἐλάσασκεν, whatever man of the people he saw and found brawling, he
drove him with his sceptre. Il. ii. 198; see ii. 188. Οὔ τινα γὰρ τίεσκον
ἐπιχθονίων ἀνθρώπων, οὐ κακὸν οὐδὲ μὲν ἐσθλὸν, ὅ τίς σφεας εἰσαφί-
κοιτο, i.e. they were never in the habit of honouring any one who came
to them. Od. xxii. 414. Ὅτε μὲν σκιρτῷεν, . . . θέον. Il. xx. 226;
so 228. See Od. xx. 138. Καὶ οὓς μὲν ἴδοι εὐτάκτως καὶ σιωπῇ
ἰόντας, προσελαύνων αὐτοῖς τίνες τε εἶεν ἠρώτα, καὶ ἐπεὶ πύθοιτο
ἐπῄνει. XEN. Cyr. v. 3, 55. (Here ἠρώτα and ἐπῄνει denote the habit
of Cyrus.) Καὶ τοῖς μὲν Ἀθηναίοις ηὔξετο τὸ ναυτικὸν ἀπὸ τῆς δαπάνης
ἣν ἐκεῖνοι ξυμφέροιεν, αὐτοὶ δὲ, ὁπότε ἀποσταῖεν, ἀπαράσκευοι
καὶ ἄπειροι ἐς τὸν πόλεμον καθίσταντο, and the Athenian navy continued
to increase from the money which these contributed (pres.), and they, whenever they revolted (aor.), always found themselves unprepared and inex-
perienced for war. THUC. i. 99.

Ἐπὶ Μοίριος βασιλέος, ὅκως ἔλθοι ὁ ποταμὸς ἐπ' ὀκτὼ πήχεας,
ἄρδεσκε Αἴγυπτον τὴν ἔνερθε Μέμφιος, i.e. whenever the river rose. HDT.
ii. 13. Τὸν δὲ χοῦν τὸν ἐκφορεόμενον, ὅκως γένοιτο νὺξ, ἐς τὸν
Τίγριν ἐξεφόρεον, i.e. they carried it away every night. Id. ii. 150. Οἱ
δὲ (Κᾶρες), ὅκως Μίνως δέοιτο, ἐπλήρουν οἱ τὰς νέας. Id. i. 171.
Ἐπειδὴ δὲ ἀνοιχθείη, εἰσῄειμεν παρὰ τὸν Σωκράτη, i.e. each morning, when the prison was opened, etc. PLAT. Phaed. 59 D. Ὅτε ἔξω
τοῦ δεινοῦ γένοιντο, πολλοὶ αὐτὸν ἀπέλειπον, many used to leave him
when they were out of danger. XEN. An. ii. 6, 12. (If ἐγένοντο had
been used, the whole sentence would refer to a particular case.)

533. The gnomic aorist and the other gnomic and iterative
tenses (154-164) can be used in the antecedent clause of these
general propositions. The gnomic aorist, as usual, is a primary
tense, and is followed by the subjunctive (171). *E.g.*

Ὅς κε θεοῖς ἐπιπείθηται, μάλα τ' ἔκλυον αὐτοῦ, *whoever obeys
the Gods, to him they are ready to listen* (ἔκλυον is aoristic). Il. i. 218.
Ὅταν τις ὥσπερ οὗτος ἰσχύσῃ, ἡ πρώτη πρόφασις ἅπαντα ἀνεχαίτισε καὶ διέλυσεν. DEM. ii. 9. Ὁπότε προσβλέψειέ τινας τῶν ἐν
ταῖς τάξεσι, εἶπεν ἄν, ὦ ἄνδρες, κ.τ.λ., i.c. he used to say, etc. XEN.
Cyr. vii. 1, 10. Οὔτ' ἄλλοτε πώποτε πρὸς χάριν εἱλόμην λέγειν, ὅ
τι ἂν μὴ καὶ συνοίσειν πεπεισμένος ὦ, *I have never on other occasions
preferred to say anything to please which I have not been convinced would
also be for your advantage.* DEM. iv. 51. (Here εἱλόμην has a sense

approaching that of the gnomic aorist, and is followed by a subjunctive. See 156.

) Homeric examples of relatives with κέ or ἄν and the subjunctive in general conditions are here included with the others, because this construction is fixed in the Homeric usage. In the greater number of general relative conditions which have the subjunctive, however, Homer uses the relative without κέ or ἄν, as he prefers the simple εἰ in the corresponding conditional sentences (468). See examples in 538.

534. (*Indicative.*) The indicative is sometimes used instead of the subjunctive and optative in relative sentences of this class. (See 467.) Here one of the cases in which the event may occur is referred to as if it were the only one. This use of the indicative occurs especially after the indefinite relative ὅστις; as the idea of indefiniteness, which is usually expressed by the subjunctive or optative, is here sufficiently expressed by the relative itself. *E.g.*

Ἐχθρὸς γάρ μοι κεῖνος ὁμῶς Ἀίδαο πύλῃσιν
Γίγνεται, ὃς πενίῃ εἴκων ἀπατήλια βάζει. Od. xiv. 156.
Compare this with Il. ix. 312, the first example under 532.

Ἐμοὶ γὰρ ὅστις πᾶσαν εὐθύνων πόλιν
Μὴ τῶν ἀρίστων ἅπτεται βουλευμάτων,
Ἀλλ' ἐκ φόβου του γλῶσσαν ἐγκλείσας ἔχει,
Κάκιστος εἶναι νῦν τε καὶ πάλαι δοκεῖ·
Καὶ μείζον' ὅστις ἀντὶ τῆς αὑτοῦ πάτρας
Φίλον νομίζει, τοῦτον οὐδαμοῦ λέγω. SOPH. Ant. 178.

(Here we might have had ὃς ἄν . . . μὴ ἅπτηται, ἀλλ' . . . ἔχῃ, and ὃς ἂν νομίζῃ, without any essential difference in meaning.)

Οἵτινες πρὸς τὰς ξυμφορὰς γνώμῃ μὲν ἥκιστα λυποῦνται, ἔργῳ δὲ μάλιστα ἀντέχουσιν, οὗτοι καὶ πόλεων καὶ ἰδιωτῶν κράτιστοί εἰσιν. THUC. ii. 64. So in the same chapter, ὅστις λαμβάνει. Ὅστις δ' ἀφικνεῖτο τῶν παρὰ βασιλέως πρὸς αὐτὸν, πάντας οὕτω διατιθεὶς ἀπεπέμπετο, *whoever came to him, he always sent away*, etc. XEN. An. i. 1, 5. Ὅπου δὲ χιλὸς σπάνιος πάνυ εἴη, αὐτὸς δ' ἐδύνατο παρασκευάσασθαι, διαπέμπων ἐκέλευε τοὺς φίλους ἵπποις ἐμβάλλειν τοῦτον. Ib. i. 9, 27. (In the last two examples there is some Ms. authority for the more regular ἀφικνοῖτο and δύναιτο.)

535. This use of the indicative (534) is rare in temporal sentences. See, however, the following :—

Περὶ τῶν ἄλλων τῶν ἀδικούντων, ὅτε δικάζονται, δεῖ παρὰ τῶν κατηγόρων πυθέσθαι. LYS. xxii. 22. Εἶχον μαχαίριον, ᾧ ἔσφαττον ὧν κρατεῖν δύναιντο, καὶ ἀποτέμνοντες ἂν τὰς κεφαλὰς ἔχοντες ἐπορεύοντο, ὁπότε οἱ πολέμιοι αὐτοὺς ὄψεσθαι ἔμελλον. XEN. An. iv. 7, 16. So ὁπότε ἀφίστατο, ii. 6, 27.

All these examples fall under the first class of conditional relative sentences (525).

536. The Greek generally uses the indicative in relative clauses

depending on general negative sentences, where in Latin a subjunctive
is more common. A general negation is really particular. *E.g.*

Παρ' ἐμοὶ δὲ οὐδεὶς μισθοφορεῖ, ὅστις μὴ ἱκανός ἐστιν ἴσα πονεῖν
ἐμοί, i.e. *no one who is not able (no one unless he is able)*, nemo qui non
possit. XEN. Hell. vi. 1, 5. Οὐδεὶς γὰρ οὐδενὶ ὠργίζετο ὅστις μὴ
ᾤετο ἀπολεῖσθαι, *for no one was angry with any one who did not think that
he was about to perish* (i.e. εἰ μὴ ᾤετο). Ib. vii. 4, 37. Οὐδαμοῦ πώποθ',
ὅποι πρεσβευτὴς ἐπέμφθην ὑφ' ὑμῶν ἐγώ, ἡττηθεὶς ἀπῆλθον τῶν
παρὰ Φιλίππου πρέσβεων, *nowhere, whither I was sent as ambassador,
did I ever come off worsted by Philip's ambassadors.* DEM. xviii. 244. Here
the leading sentence is particular, *on no single occasion was I worsted*, so
that ἐπέμφθην is regular; if the nearly equivalent universal affirmative
on every occasion I proved superior had been intended, we should have
had πεμφθείην. See xviii. 45, προύλεγον καὶ διεμαρτυρόμην καὶ
παρ' ὑμῖν ἀεὶ καὶ ὅποι πεμφθείην; and the following in 244,
ἐν οἷς κρατηθεῖεν οἱ πρέσβεις αὐτοῦ τῷ λόγῳ, ταῦτα τοῖς ὅπλοις
ἐπιὼν κατεστρέφετο. Notice the imperfects in the two affirmative
examples, and the aorist in the preceding negative example.

537. 1. The indicative is generally used in Greek (as in Latin)
in pa·enthetical relative clauses, like ὅ τι ποτ' ἐστίν, *whatever it is*
(quidquid est), ὅστις ποτ' ἐστίν (or ἔσται), etc. *E.g.*

Ζεὺς, ὅστις ποτ' ἐστὶν, εἰ τόδ' αὐτῷ φίλον κεκλημένῳ, τοῦτό νιν
προσεννέπω, *Zeus, whoever he may be*, etc. AESCH. Ag. 160. Δουλεύο-
μεν θεοῖς, ὅ τι ποτ' εἰσὶν θεοί. EUR. Or. 418. Ἡμῖν γε κρέσσον
. . . δουληίην ὑπομεῖναι ἥτις ἔσται, *but it is better for us to submit
to slavery, whatever it may be.* HDT. vi. 12. So ὅ τι δή κοτέ ἐστι, vii.
16.

2. But ὅστις in such expressions can have the construction of
an ordinary conditional relative, so that in future and general
conditions it may take the subjunctive. *E.g.*

Ἀλλ' ὁ προσαψάμενος αὐτῶν, ὅστις ἂν ᾖ, λόγον παρέχει, *but each
one who has to do with them, whoever he may be, gives his own account of
them.* AESCHIN. i. 127. Ἀλλ' ὑφ' ὑμῶν ἔδει κεχειροτονημένον εἶναι
τοῦτον, ὅστις ἂν ᾖ, *but this officer ought always to be elected by you, whoever he may be.* DEM. iv. 27. See THEOG. 964.

*Homeric and other Poetic Peculiarities in Conditional
Relative Sentences.*

SUBJUNCTIVE WITHOUT κέ OR ἄν.

538. In general conditions which take the subjunctive, Homer
commonly uses the relatives without κέ or ἄν. This corresponds
to his preference for the simple εἰ in general conditions (468);
but relative clauses of this class are much more frequent with
him than the clauses with εἰ. *E.g.*

Ὅττι μάλ' οὐ δηναιὸς ὃς ἀθανάτοισι μάχηται. Il. v. 407.
Ἀνθρώπους ἐφορᾷ, καὶ τίννται ὅς τις ἁμάρτῃ. Od. xiii. 214.
Ζεὺς
δ' αὐτὸς νέμει ὄλβον Ὀλύμπιος ἀνθρώποισιν, ἐσθλοῖς ἠδὲ κακοῖσιν,
ὅπως ἐθέλῃσιν, ἑκάστῳ. Od. vi. 188. Οὐ μὴν σοί ποτε ἶσον ἔχω
γέρας, ὁππότ' Ἀχαιοὶ Τρώων ἐκπέρσωσ' εὐναιόμενον πτολίεθρον.
Il. i. 163. So also Il. i. 554, iii. 109, xiv. 81; Od. viii. 546, xviii. 134.
Here the meaning is essentially the same as when κέ or ἄν is added,
as in the examples under 532. The greater development of the general
relative condition in Homer, especially in the use of the optative,
compared with the less developed general condition with εἰ, has already
been noticed (17 ; 400 ; 468).

539. The relative (like εἰ) is sometimes found in Homer
without κέ or ἄν in future conditions. *E.g.*

Γήμασθ' ὅς τις ἄριστος ἀνὴρ καὶ πλεῖστα πόρῃσιν, (tell her) to
marry whoever may be the best man and may offer the most. Od. xx. 335.
But in vs. 342, referring to the same thing, we have γήμασθ' ᾧ κ'
ἐθέλῃ, to marry whom she may please. Πείθεο δ' ὡς . . . ἐν φρεσὶ θείω.
Il. xvi. 83 ; so Od. vi. 189. Οὐ μὴν γάρ ποτέ φησι κακὸν πείσεσθαι
ὀπίσσω, ὄφρ' ἀρετὴν παρέχωσι θεοὶ καὶ γούνατ' ὀρώρῃ, *he says he
shall never suffer evil hereafter, so long as the Gods shall supply valour,* etc.
Od. xviii. 132. So Il. xiii. 234.

540. Ἄν is sometimes omitted in relative conditions with the
subjunctive in lyric, elegiac, and dramatic poetry, as in Homer ;
chiefly in general conditions. A few examples occur in Herodotus ;
and even in Attic prose exceptional cases are occasionally found
in the manuscripts. (See 469-471.) *E.g.*

Μέγα τοι κλέος αἰεί, ᾧτινι σὸν γέρας ἔσπητ' ἀγλαόν, *great always
is his glory, whom thy illustrious honour* (Olympia) *follows.* PIND. Ol.
viii. 10. So Ol. iii. 11, Nem. ix. 44. Πάντας ἐπαίνημι καὶ φιλέω
ἑκὼν ὅστις ἔρδῃ μηδὲν αἰσχρόν. SIMON. v. 20 (but ὃς ἂν μὴ κακὸς ᾖ
in the same ode). See TYRT. xii. 34 ; SOL. xiii. 9 and 55, xxvii. 3 ;
SIMON. lviii. 5, lxxxv. 7 (ὄφρα . . . ἔχῃ, but ὅταν ᾖ in vs. 10).
Γέροντα δ' ὀρθοῦν φλαῦρον, ὃς νέος πέσῃ. SOPH. O. C. 395. Τῶν
δὲ πημονῶν μάλιστα λυποῦσ' αἳ φανῶσ' αὐθαίρετοι. Id. O. T. 1231.
So AESCH. Sept. 257, Eum. 211, 661, and probably 618 (ὃ μὴ κελεύσῃ,
for MSS. κελεύσει, after εἶπον denoting a habit). Τοῖσι γὰρ μήτε
ἄστεα μήτε τείχεα ᾖ ἐκτισμένα, . . . κῶς οὐκ ἂν εἴησαν οὗτοι ἄμαχοι;
HDT. iv. 46. So i. 216, ii. 85, iv. 66. Ἐπιχώριον ὂν ἡμῖν οὗ μὲν
βραχεῖς ἀρκέῃ μὴ πολλοῖς χρῆσθαι, *it being our national habit not
to use many words where few suffice.* THUC. iv. 17. (Here οὗ μὲν . . .
πολλοῖς make five feet of an iambic trimeter, and the words are probably quoted from some poet. See Classen's note. The sentence continues, πλείοσι δὲ ἐν ᾧ ἂν καιρὸς ᾖ, κ.τ.λ.) See also PLAT. Leg. 737
B, οἷς ᾖ and ὅσοις μετῇ. In SOPH. El. 225, ὄφρα ἔχῃ is particular.

541. In the lyric and elegiac poets, as in Homer, the form with ἄν
or κέ was in good use in these sentences. See PIND. Py. i. 100 (ὃς ἂν

ἐγκύρσῃ, v. 65 (οἷς ἂν ἐθέλῃ) ; Μιμν. ii, 9, iii. 1 (ἐπὴν παραμείψεται);
Sol. xiii. 75 ; Theogn. 405, 406 (ἃ μὲν ᾗ κακὰ, . . . ἃ δ' ἂν ᾗ
χρήσιμα). (For ordinary protasis see 469 and 470.) In the dramatists
the relative with ἄν is completely established with the subjunctive as
the regular form (like ἐάν, etc.) in both general and particular conditions.
(See 471.)

Relative with κέ or ἄν and the Optative in Conditions.

542. In Homer the conditional relative (like εἰ) sometimes
takes κέ or ἄν with the optative, the particle apparently not
affecting the sense. *E.g.*

Ἡ δέ κ' ἔπειτα γήμαιθ' ὅς κεν πλεῖστα πόροι καὶ μόρσιμος ἔλθοι,
and she then would marry whoever might give the most gifts, etc. Od.
xxi. 161. Ὣς κε . . . δοίη ᾧ κ' ἐθέλοι, *that he might give her to
whomsoever he pleased.* Od. ii. 54. In these two cases ὃς πόροι and ᾧ
ἐθέλοι would be the common expressions. In Od. iv. 600, however,
δῶρον δ' ὅττι κέ μοι δοίης, κειμήλιον ἔστω, *whatever gift you might
choose to give me*, etc., may be potential. Νῦν γάρ χ' Ἕκτορ' ἕλοις,
ἐπεὶ ἂν μάλα τοι σχέδον ἔλθοι. Il. ix. 304. Ὃς τὸ καταβρόξειεν
ἐπὴν κρητῆρι μιγείη, οὔ κεν ἐφημέριός γε βάλοι κατὰ δάκρυ παρειῶν,
*whoever should drink this when it was mingled in the bowl, would let no
tear fall down his cheeks on that day.* Od. iv. 222. So ἐπὴν . . . εἴην,
Il. xxiv. 227.

One case occurs of ὅτε κε with the optative in a general relative
sentence of past time : ἐπευθόμεθα . . . ὅτε κέν τιν' ἐπιζάφελος
χόλος ἵκοι, Il. ix. 525.

Homeric Similes with Ὡς etc.

543. In Homer similes and comparisons may be expressed by
the subjunctive with ὡς ὅτε (rarely ὡς ὁπότε), *as when*, sometimes
by ὡς or ὥς τε, *as*. Except in a few cases of ὡς ὅτ' ἄν, neither ἄν
nor κέ is found in these expressions.

544. With ὡς ὅτε or ὡς ὁπότε the subjunctive clearly expresses a general condition, and the meaning is *as happens when,*
etc. *E.g.*

Ὡς δ' ὅτε κινήσῃ Ζέφυρος βαθὺ λήιον ἐλθὼν,
λάβρος ἐπαιγίζων, ἐπί τ' ἠμύει ἀσταχύεσσιν,
ὣς τῶν πᾶσ' ἀγορὴ κινήθη,

*and as (happens) when the west wind comes and moves a deep grain field,
and it bows with its ears, so was their whole assembly moved.* Il. ii. 147.

Ὡς δ' ὅτ' ὀπωρινὸς Βορέης φορέῃσιν ἀκάνθας
ἂμ πεδίον, πυκιναὶ δὲ πρὸς ἀλλήλῃσιν ἔχονται,
ὣς τὴν ἂμ πέλαγος ἄνεμοι φέρον ἔνθα καὶ ἔνθα. Od. v. 328.

See Il. v. 597, vi. 506, viii. 338 ; Od. ix. 391, xix. 518 ; for ὡς
ὁπότε, Od. iv. 335, xvii. 126.

'Ως δ' ὅτ' ἂν ἀστράπτῃ πόσις Ἥρης ἠυκόμοιο, ὡς πυκίν' ἐν
στήθεσσιν ἀνεστενάχιζ' Ἀγαμέμνων. Il. x. 5. So Il. xi. 269, xv. 170;
Od. v. 394, xxii. 468.

545. With ὡς or ὥς τε the conditional force of the subjunctive is
not so obvious, especially as it depends directly on the verb of the
antecedent clause, which is always particular and generally past.
Here we should expect the present indicative, which sometimes occurs
(548). We may suppose that the analogy of the far more frequent
clauses with ὡς ὅτε (544)[1] caused the same construction to be used
also in these, in which the meaning is clearly the same. *E.g.*

'Ως δὲ γυνὴ κλαίῃσι φίλον πόσιν ἀμφιπεσοῦσα,
ὅς τε ἑῆς πρόσθεν πόλιος λαῶν τε πέσῃσιν,
ὡς Ὀδυσεὺς ἐλεεινὸν ὑπ' ὀφρύσι δάκρυον εἶβεν,

i.e. *Ulysses wept as a wife weeps*, etc. Od. viii. 523.

'Ως δὲ λέων ἐν βουσὶ θορὼν ἐξ αὐχένα ἄξῃ πόρτιος ἠὲ βοὸς, . . .
ὡς τοὺς ἀμφοτέρους ἐξ ἵππων Τυδέος υἱὸς βῆσε, and as a lion leaps
among the cattle and breaks the neck of a heifer or an ox, so did the son of
Tydeus dismount them both from their chariot. Il. v. 161. So Il. ix. 323,
x. 183, 485 ; Od. v. 368.

546. In all the cases of ὥς τε the pronominal article οἱ or τούς
precedes, referring to the subject or object of the antecedent clause.
E.g.

Οἱ δ', ὥς τ' ἀμητῆρες ἐναντίοι ἀλλήλοισιν ὄγμον ἐλαύνωσιν, ὡς
Τρῶες καὶ Ἀχαιοὶ ἐπ' ἀλλήλοισι θορόντες δῄουν, and they,—as reapers
against each other drive their swaths,—so did Trojans and Achaeans leap
upon each other and destroy. Il. xi. 67. So Il. xii. 167, xv. 323 ; Od.
xxii. 302.

547. When a simile has been introduced by the subjunctive
with ὡς or ὡς ὅτε, it may be continued by verbs in the present
indicative, which seem to be independent of the original construction. Even the aorist indicative may be used to add vividness to the description. *E.g.*

'Ως δ' ὅτε τίς τ' ἐλέφαντα γυνὴ φοίνικι μιήνῃ
Μῃονὶς ἠὲ Κάειρα, παρήιον ἔμμεναι ἵππῳ·
κεῖται δ' ἐν θαλάμῳ, πολέες τέ μιν ἠρήσαντο
ἱππῆες φορέειν· βασιλῆι δὲ κεῖται ἄγαλμα·
τοῖοί τοι, Μενέλαε, μιάνθην αἵματι μηροί. Il. iv. 141.

'Ως δ' ὅτ' ἀφ' ὑψηλῆς κορυφῆς ὄρεος μεγάλοιο
κινήσῃ πυκινὴν νεφέλην στεροπηγερέτα Ζεύς·
ἔκ τ' ἔφανεν πᾶσαι σκοπιαὶ καὶ πρώονες ἄκροι
καὶ νάπαι, οὐρανόθεν δ' ὑπερράγη ἄσπετος αἰθήρ·
ὣς Δαναοὶ νηῶν μὲν ἀπωσάμενοι δήιον πῦρ
τυτθὸν ἀνέπνευσαν πολέμου δ' οὐ γίγνετ' ἐρωή. Il. xvi. 296.

---

[1] Delbrück, *Conj. u. Opt.* pp. 161, 162, cites 63 cases of this construction
(49 in the Iliad, 14 in the Odyssey), of which 35 have ὡς ὅτε, 10 ὡς ὅτ' ἂν, 3
ὡς ὁπότε, 8 ὡς, and 7 ὥς τε.

'Ὡς δ' ὅτε καπνὸς ἰὼν εἰς οὐρανὸν εὐρὺν ἵκηται
ἄστεος αἰθομένοιο, θεῶν δέ ἑ μῆνις ἀνῆκεν,
πᾶσι δ' ἔθηκε πόνον, πολλοῖσι δὲ κήδε' ἐφῆκεν,
ὡς Ἀχιλεὺς Τρώεσσι πόνον καὶ κήδε' ἔθηκεν. Il. xxi. 522.

548. Sometimes the first clause of the simile has the present
or aorist indicative. *E.g.*

'Ὡς δ' ἀναμαιμάει βαθέ' ἄγκεα θεσπιδαὲς πῦρ, ὡς ὅ γε πάντη
θῦνε. Il. xx. 490. 'Ὡς δ' ὁπότε πλήθων ποταμὸς πεδίονδε κάτεισιν,
πολλὰς δὲ δρῦς ἐσφέρεται, ὡς ἔφεπεν. Il. xi. 492. Ἤριπε δ' ὡς ὅτε
τις δρῦς ἤριπεν, *and he fell as when an oak falls (once fell)*. Il. xiii. 389.
'Ὡς δ' ὅτε τίς τε δράκοντα ἰδὼν παλίνορσος ἀπέστη. Il. iii. 33 : so
ὥς τε λέων ἐχάρη, iii. 23.

549. Another form of Homeric simile consists of ὡς with a
noun, followed by a relative with the subjunctive, which may be
followed by an indicative as in 547. *E.g.*

Ὁ δ' ἐν κονίῃσι χαμαὶ πέσεν, αἴγειρος ὥς,
ἥ ῥά τ' ἐν εἰαμενῇ ἕλεος μεγάλοιο πεφύκῃ
λείη, ἀτάρ τέ οἱ ὄζοι ἐπ' ἀκροτάτῃ πεφύασιν·
τὴν μέν θ' ἁρματοπηγὸς ἀνὴρ αἴθωνι σιδήρῳ
ἐξέταμ', ὄφρα ἴτυν κάμψῃ περικαλλέι δίφρῳ·
ἡ μέν τ' ἀζομένη κεῖται ποταμοῖο παρ' ὄχθας·
τοῖον ἄρ' Ἀνθεμίδην Σιμοείσιον ἐξενάριξεν
Αἴας διογενής. Il. iv. 482.

For ὡς εἰ or ὡς εἴ τε with the optative in Homeric similes, see 485.

Ὅ τι μή and ὅσον μή without a Verb.

550. Ὅ τι μή and ὅσον μή, like εἰ μή (476), are used in the
sense of *except, unless*, with no verb expressed. *E.g.*

Ὅ τι γὰρ μὴ Ἀθῆναι, ἦν οὐδὲν ἄλλο πόλισμα λόγιμον, *for except
Athens (what was not Athens) there was no (Ionic) city of any account.*
Hdt. i. 143. So i. 18, οὐδαμοὶ ὅ τι μὴ Χῖοι μοῦνοι. Οὐ γὰρ ἦν
κρήνη, ὅ τι μὴ μία ἐν αὐτῇ τῇ ἀκροπόλει, *for there was no spring, except
one on the very citadel.* Thuc. iv. 26 : so iv. 94, vii. 42. Οὔτ' ἐπὶ
θεωρίαν ἐξῆλθες ὅ τι μὴ ἅπαξ εἰς Ἰσθμὸν, οὔτε ἄλλοσε οὐδαμόσε εἰ
μή ποι στρατευσόμενος. Plat. Crit. 52 B. So Phaed. 67 A, Rep.
405 C.

Ἴσθι γὰρ δοκῶν ἐμοὶ καὶ ξυμφυτεῦσαι τοὔργον εἰργάσθαι θ', ὅσον
μὴ χερσὶ καίνων, i.e. *and to have done the deed too, except so far as you
did not slay with your own hands.* Soph. O. T. 346.

551. Homer once has ὅ τι μή or ὅτε μή in the same sense : οὔ τέ
τεῳ σπένδεσκε θεῶν ὅ τι μὴ Διὶ πατρί, i.e. *except to Zeus (ὅ τι μή
= εἰ μή)*, Il. xvi. 227. Here Lange (p. 161) reads ὅτε μή.

Special Forms of Antecedent Clause.

552. A conditional relative clause (like a protasis with εἰ) may depend on an infinitive or participle (with or without ἄν), on a final clause, on a protasis, or on a verbal noun representing the antecedent clause (or apodosis). *E.g.*

See DEM. xxi. 64 (quoted in 525); PLAT. Ap. 17 D, DEM. xxiii. 48 (quoted in 528); AESCH. Ag. 1434, DEM. iv. 21 and 39, xxviii. 21 (quoted in 529); PLAT. Euthyd. 302 A, Theaet. 155 A, XEN. Mem. ii. 3, 12, Cyr. i. 6, 3, ii. 1, 31 (quoted in 531). Ὁρῶ σοι τούτων δεῆσον ὅταν ἐπιθυμήσῃς φιλίαν πρός τινας ποιεῖσθαι. XEN. Mem. ii. 6, 29.

Καὶ ἐμὲ δεῖ ἀπηλλάχθαι κατὰ τὰς συνθήκας, ἐπειδὴ τὸ περὶ τοῦ Πρωταγόρου λόγου τέλος σχοίη, i.e. *I ought to be released according to what we agreed to do when the discussion of the doctrine of Protagoras should come to an end.* PLAT. Theaet. 183 C.

553. After past verbs of *waiting* or *expecting* in Homer ὁπότε with the optative sometimes has the meaning of *until*, like ἕως. *E.g.*

Οἱ δ' ἔατ' . . . ποτιδέγμενοι ὁππότ' ἄρ' ἔλθοι Ἰδαῖος, *and they sat waiting until (for the time when) Idaeus should come.* Il. vii. 414. So iv. 334, ix. 191, xviii. 524. (See 698.)

Mixed Conditional Constructions.

554. The relative with the optative sometimes depends on a present or future tense. This occurs chiefly in Homer, and arises from the slight distinction between the subjunctive and optative in such sentences. *E.g.*

Αἰπύ οἱ ἐσσεῖται νῆας ἐνιπρῆσαι, ὅτε μὴ αὐτός γε Κρονίων ἐμβάλοι αἰθόμενον δαλὸν νήεσσι, *it will be a hard task for him to fire the ships, unless the son of Kronos should himself hurl a flaming brand upon the ships.* Il. xiii. 317. (Regularly ὅτε κε μὴ ἐμβάλῃ, *unless he shall hurl.*) So Od. xix. 510. Καὶ δ' ἄλλῃ νεμεσῶ ἥ τις τοιαῦτα γε ῥέζοι, *and I am angry with any other woman who says (should say) the like.* Od. vi. 286. (This resembles the loosely jointed examples in 500.)

Τοιούτῳ δὲ ἔοικας, ἐπεὶ λούσαιτο φάγοι τε, εὐδέμεναι μαλακῶς, *and you seem like such a man as would sleep comfortably (like one likely to sleep comfortably) after he had washed and eaten.* Od. xxiv. 254. (This resembles the examples in 555.)

The optative regularly follows an optative in a wish (177).

555. In Attic Greek an optative in the relative clause sometimes depends on a verb of *obligation, propriety, possibility,* etc., with an infinitive, the two forming an expression nearly equivalent to an optative with ἄν, which would be expected in their place. (See 502.) *E.g.*

Ἀλλ' ὃν πόλις στήσειε, τοῦδε χρὴ κλύειν, *we should obey any one whom the state might appoint* (*if the state should appoint any one, we ought to obey him*). Soph. Ant. 666. (Χρὴ κλύειν is followed by the optative from its nearness to δικαίως ἂν κλύοι τις.) Ἀλλὰ τοῦ μὲν αὐτὸν λέγειν ἃ μὴ σαφῶς εἰδείη φείδεσθαι δεῖ, i.e. *we ought to abstain*, etc.; like φείδοιτο ἄν τις. Xen. Cyr. i. 6, 19. Οὓς δὲ ποιήσασθαί τις βούλοιτο συνεργοὺς προθύμους, τούτους παντάπασιν ἔμοιγε δοκεῖ ἀγαθοῖς θηρατέον εἶναι (θηρατέον εἶναι = θηρᾶν δεῖν). Ib. ii. 4, 10. Ὑπερορᾶν οὐ δυνατὸν ὑμῶν ἀνδρὶ ὃς εἰδείη κυρίους ὄντας ὅ τι βούλεσθε αὐτῷ χρῆσθαι. Id. Hell. vii. 3, 7. So Ib. iii. 4, 18. Σωφρόνων ἐστὶ μηδὲ εἰ μικρὰ τὰ διαφέροντα εἴη πόλεμον ἀναιρεῖσθαι. Ib. vi. 3, 5. So after πολὺ ῥᾷόν (ἐστι), Ib. vi. 5, 52. Σωφρόνων ἐστίν, εἰ μὴ ἀδικοῖντο, ἡσυχάζειν, i.e. *it is proper for prudent men*, etc. Thuc. i. 120. Ἀποδοτέον οὐδ' ὁπωστιοῦν τότε, ὁπότε τις μὴ σωφρόνως ἀπαιτοῖ. Plat. Rep. 332 A. So Aesch. Eum. 726.

556. An indicative or subjunctive in the relative clause may depend on a potential optative (with ἄν), sometimes when the potential force is felt in the apodosis, and sometimes when the optative with ἄν is treated as a primary tense from its nearness to the future indicative. *E.g.*

Οὐκοῦν καὶ τὸ ὑγιαίνειν καὶ τὸ νοσεῖν, ὅταν ἀγαθοῦ τινος αἴτια γίγνηται, ἀγαθὰ ἂν εἴη, *therefore, both health and disease, when they prove to be the causes of any good, would naturally be good things.* Xen. Mem. iv. 2, 32; so ii. 2, 3. Ὅταν δέ τις θεῶν βλάπτῃ, δύναιτ' ἂν οὐδ' ἂν ἰσχύων φυγεῖν, *when one of the Gods does mischief, not even a strong man could escape.* Soph. El. 696. Ὥστ' ἀποφύγοις ἂν ἥντιν' ἂν βούλῃ δίκην, *so that you can (could) get off in any suit you please.* Ar. Nub. 1151. Οἵτινες τοῖς μὲν ἴσοις μὴ εἴκουσι, τοῖς δὲ κρείσσοσι καλῶς προσφέρονται, πρὸς δὲ τοὺς ἥσσους μέτριοί εἰσι, πλεῖστ' ἂν ὀρθοῖντο. Thuc. v. 111. Ὁ δὲ μηδὲν κακὸν ποιεῖ, οὐδ' ἄν τινος εἴη κακοῦ αἴτιον; *and what does no harm could not be the cause of any harm at all, could it?* Plat. Rep. 379 B. Ἐγὼ δὲ ταύτην μὲν τὴν εἰρήνην, ἕως ἂν εἷς Ἀθηναίων λείπηται, οὐδέποτ' ἂν συμβουλεύσαιμι ποιήσασθαι τῇ πόλει, *I would never advise the city to make this peace, so long as a single Athenian shall be left.* Dem. xix. 14. (Here ἕως λείποιτο, *so long as one should be left*, would be more regular.) Ὅταν δ' ἀφανίσας τις τἀκριβὲς λόγῳ ἐξαπατᾶν πειρᾶται, πῶς ἂν δικαίως πιστεύοιτο; Id. xxxiii. 36. (See 178.)

557. A conditional relative clause may contain a potential optative or indicative (with ἄν), which has its proper meaning. *E.g.*

Ἐξ ὧν ἄν τις εὖ λέγων διαβάλλοι, ἐκ τούτων αὐτοὺς πείσεσθαι (ἔφη), *he said that they would form their opinion upon any slanders which any good speaker might chance to utter.* Thuc. vii. 48. Ὅντιν' ἂν ὑμεῖς εἰς ταύτην τὴν τάξιν κατεστήσατε, οὗτος τῶν ἴσων αἴτιος ἦν ἂν κακῶν ὅσωνπερ καὶ οὗτος, *any one soever whom you might have appointed to this post would have been the cause of as great calamities as this man has been.* DEM. xix. 29. (Without ἄν, ὅντινα κατεστήσατε would be equivalent to εἴ τινα ἄλλον κατεστήσατε, *if you had appointed any one else (which you did not do).* With ἄν, it is a potential indicative.)

See 506, and for the optative with κέ in conditional relative sentences in Homer (probably not potential), see 542.

Assimilation in Conditional Relative Clauses.

558. When a conditional relative clause *referring to the future* depends on a subjunctive or optative referring to the future, it regularly takes by assimilation the same mood with its leading verb. The leading verb may be in a protasis or apodosis, in another conditional relative clause, in an expression of a wish, or in a final clause. *E.g.*

Ἐάν τινες οἳ ἂν δύνωνται τοῦτο ποιῶσι, καλῶς ἕξει, *if any who shall be able do this, it will be well.* Εἴ τινες οἳ δύναιντο τοῦτο ποιοῖεν, καλῶς ἂν ἔχοι, *if any who should be able should do this, it would be well.* Εἴθε πάντες οἳ δύναιντο τοῦτο ποιοῖεν, *O that all who may be able would do this.* (Here the principle of assimilation makes οἳ δύναιντο after an optative preferable to οἳ ἂν δύνωνται, which would express the same idea.) Τεθναίην ὅτε μοι μηκέτι ταῦτα μέλοι, *may I die when these are no longer my delight.* MIMN. i. 2. So in Latin: Si absurde canat is qui se haberi *velit* musicum, turpior sit.—Sic injurias fortunae quas ferre *nequeas* defugiendo relinquas.

For examples see 529 and 531.

559. When a conditional relative clause depends on a past tense of the indicative implying the non-fulfilment of a condition, it regularly takes a past tense of the indicative by *assimilation.* The leading verb may be in a protasis or apodosis, in another conditional relative clause, in an expression of a wish, or in a final clause. *E.g.*

Εἴ τινες οἳ ἐδύναντο τοῦτο ἔπραξαν, καλῶς ἂν ἔσχεν, *if any who had been able had done this, it would have been well.* Εἴθε πάντες οἳ ἐδύναντο τοῦτο ἔπραξαν, *O that all who had been able had done this.* So in Latin: Nam si solos eos diceres miseros quibus moriendum *esset*, neminem tu quidem eorum qui *viverent* exciperes.

For examples see 528.

560. It will be seen that this principle of assimilation accounts for the unreal indicative and the optative in conditional relative sentences, which have been already explained by the analogy of the forms of protasis. (See 528 and 531.) In fact, wherever this assimilation occurs, the relative clause stands as a protasis to its antecedent clause.

Occasionally this principle is disregarded, so that a subjunctive depends on an optative (178).

For the influence of assimilation in determining the mood of a dependent sentence, see 176.

561. The indicative in the construction of 525, referring simply to the present or past, cannot be affected by assimilation, as this would change its time. *E.g.*

῾Υμεῖς δ᾽ ἕλοισθε ὅ τι καὶ τῇ πόλει καὶ ἅπασι συνοίσειν ὑμῖν μέλλει, *and may you choose what is likely to benefit the state and all of you.* DEM. iii. 36. Compare this with DEM. ix. 76, ὅ τι δ᾽ ὑμῖν δόξειε (so Σ originally), τοῦτ᾽, ὦ πάντες θεοὶ, συνενέγκοι, *whatever you may decide, may this be for our good.*

In SOPH. Ant. 373, ὃς τάδ᾽ ἔρδει would belong here ; but ὃς τάδ᾽ ἔρδοι (Laur.), = εἴ τις τάδ᾽ ἔρδοι, falls under 558.

562. The principle of 558 and 559 applies only to *conditional* relative clauses. If the relative refers to a definite antecedent, there can be no assimilation, and the indicative or any other construction required by the sense is used. *E.g.*

Εἰ τῶν πολιτῶν οἷσι νῦν πιστεύομεν, τούτοις ἀπιστήσαιμεν, οἷς δ᾽ οὐ χρώμεθα, τούτοισι χρησαίμεσθ᾽, ἴσως σωθεῖμεν ἄν. AR. Ran. 1446. Εἴθ᾽ ἦσθα δυνατὸς δρᾶν ὅσον πρόθυμος εἶ, *O that thou couldst do as much as thou art eager to do.* EUR. Her. 731. (With ἦσθα for εἶ, the meaning would be *as much as thou wert (or mightest be) eager to do.*)

563. Conditional relative clauses depending on a subjunctive or optative in a general supposition (462 ; 532) are generally assimilated to the subjunctive or optative ; but sometimes they take the indicative (534). *E.g.*

Οὐδ᾽, ἐπειδὰν ὧν ἂν πρίηται κύριος γέγηται, τῷ προδότῃ συμβούλῳ περὶ τῶν λοιπῶν ἔτι χρῆται. DEM. xviii. 47. See PLAT. Rep. 508 C and D (reading ὧν ὁ ἥλιος καταλάμπει) ; Charm. 164 B. Ὁ δὲ τότε μάλιστα ἔχαιρεν, ὁπότε τάχιστα τυχόντας ὧν δέοιντο ἀποπέμποι. XEN. Ag. ix. 2.

Αἰτία μὲν γάρ ἐστιν, ὅταν τις ψιλῷ χρησάμενος λόγῳ μὴ παράσχηται πίστιν ὧν λέγει, ἔλεγχος δέ, ὅταν ὧν ἂν εἴπῃ τις καὶ τἀληθὲς ὁμοῦ δείξῃ. DEM. xxii. 22. (Here ὧν λέγει and ὧν ἂν εἴπῃ are nearly equivalent.) Ἐκάλει δὲ καὶ ἐτίμα ὁπότε τινὰς ἴδοι τοιοῦτον ποιήσαντας ὃ πάντας ἐβούλετο ποιεῖν. XEN. Cyr. ii. 1, 30. (Here βούλοιτο for ἐβούλετο would correspond to δέοιντο in Ag. ix. 2, above.)

Δέ *in the Antecedent Clause.*

564. The conjunction δέ sometimes introduces the clause on which a relative depends. Its force here is the same as in apodosis (512). *E.g.*

Οἵη περ φύλλων γενεή, τοίη δὲ καὶ ἀνδρῶν. Il. vi. 146. Ἐπεί

τε ὁ πόλεμος κατέστη, ὁ δὲ φαίνεται καὶ ἐν τούτῳ προγνοὺς τὴν δύναμιν, *and when the war broke out, (then) he appears, etc.* THUC. ii. 65. Μέχρι μὲν οὖν οἱ τοξόται εἶχον τε τὰ βέλη αὐτοῖς καὶ οἷοί τε ἦσαν χρῆσθαι, οἱ δὲ ἀντεῖχον, *so long as their archers both had their arrows and were able to use them, they held out.* Id. iii. 98. Ἐπειδὴ δὲ ἀφικόμενοι μάχῃ ἐκράτησαν . . . φαίνονται δὲ οὐδ᾿ ἐνταῦθα πάσῃ τῇ δυνάμει χρησάμενοι. Id. i. 11. Ὥσπερ οἱ ὁπλῖται, οὕτω δὲ καὶ οἱ πελτασταί. XEN. Cyr. viii. 5, 12.

FINAL RELATIVE CLAUSES EXPRESSING PURPOSE.

565. (*Future Indicative.*) In Attic Greek a relative with the future indicative often expresses a purpose, like a final clause. Its negative is μή. *E.g.*

Πρεσβείαν δὲ πέμπειν, ἥτις ταῦτ᾿ ἐρεῖ καὶ παρέσται τοῖς πράγμασιν, *and to send an embassy to say these things, and to be present at the transaction.* DEM. i. 2. Φημὶ δὴ δεῖν ἡμᾶς πρὸς Θετταλοὺς πρεσβείαν πέμπειν, ἢ τοὺς μὲν διδάξει ταῦτα, τοὺς δὲ παροξυνεῖ. Id. ii. 11. Ἔδοξε τῷ δήμῳ τριάκοντα ἄνδρας ἑλέσθαι, οἳ τοὺς πατρίους νόμους ξυγγράψουσι, καθ᾿ οὓς πολιτεύσουσι, *the people voted to choose thirty men, to compile the ancestral laws by which they were to govern.* XEN. Hell. ii. 3, 2. Εἴσω δὲ πέμψαι (ἐκέλευσε) τινὰς, οἵτινες αὐτῷ τὰ ἔνδον ἰδόντες ἀπαγγελοῦσιν. XEN. Cyr. v. 2, 3. Ναυτικὸν παρεσκεύαζον ὅ τι πέμψουσιν ἐς τὴν Λέσβον, καὶ ναύαρχον προσέταξαν Ἀλκίδαν, ὃς ἔμελλεν ἐπιπλεύσεσθαι. THUC. iii. 16. See DEM. xxi. 109. Οὐ γὰρ ἔστι μοι χρήματα, ὁπόθεν ἐκτίσω, *for I have no money to pay the fine with.* PLAT. Ap. 37 C.

Ῥῖψόν με γῆς ἐκ τῆσδε, ὅπου θνητῶν φανοῦμαι μηδενὸς προσήγορος. SOPH. O. T. 1437 ; so 1412. Μέλλουσι γάρ σ᾿ ἐνταῦθα πέμψειν, ἔνθα μή ποθ᾿ ἡλίου φέγγος προσόψει, ζῶσα δ᾿ ὑμνήσεις κακά, *they are to send you where you shall never behold the sun's light (to some place, that there you may never behold, etc.).* Id. El. 379. So Aj. 659 ; Tr. 800.

566. The antecedent of the relative in this construction may be either definite or indefinite ; but the negative is always μή because of the final force. The future indicative is regularly retained after past tenses, as in object clauses with ὅπως (340) ; but see 573 and 574.

567. A past purpose may be expressed by the imperfect of μέλλω. See 76 ; and THUC. iii. 16, quoted in 565.

568. (*Subjunctive and Optative in Homer.*) In these final relative clauses have the subjunctive (generally with κέ) after primary tenses, and the present or aorist optative (without κέ) after secondary tenses. *E.g.*

Καὶ ἅμ᾿ ἡγεμόν᾿ ἐσθλὸν ὄπασσον, ὅς κέ με κεῖσ᾿ ἀγάγῃ, *and also send a good guide, who shall lead me thither (to lead me thither).* Od. xv. 310.

Αὐτὸς νῦν ὄνομ' εὕρεο, ὅ τι κε θῆαι παιδὸς παιδὶ φίλῳ, *find a name to give the child.* Od. xix. 403. Τεὸν οὔνομα εἰπέ, ἵνα τοι δῶ ξείνιον, ᾧ κε σὺ χαίρῃς. Od. ix. 355. Αὐτίκα μάντις ἐλεύσεται, ὅς κέν τοι εἴπῃσιν ὁδόν. Od. x. 538. Ἕλκος δ' ἰητὴρ ἐπιμάσσεται, ἠδ' ἐπιθήσει φάρμαχ', ἅ κεν παύσῃσι μελαινάων ὀδυνάων. Il. iv. 191. Ἀλλ' ἄγετε, κλητοὺς ὀτρύνομεν, οἵ κε τάχιστα ἔλθωσ' ἐς κλισίην Πηληϊάδεω Ἀχιλῆος. Il. ix. 165. Ἔκδοτε, καὶ τιμὴν ἀποτινέμεν ἥν τιν' ἔοικεν, ἥ τε καὶ ἐσσομένοισι μετ' ἀνθρώποισι πέληται. Il. iii. 459. The last verse (found also iii. 287) and Od. xviii. 336 are the only cases in Homer of the subjunctive without κέ in these sentences. Ἄγγελον ἧκαν, ὃς ἀγγείλεҍε γυναικί, *they sent a messenger to tell the woman.* Od. xv. 458. Πάπτηνεν δ' ἀνὰ πύργον Ἀχαιῶν, εἴ τιν' ἴδοιτο ἡγεμόνων, ὅς τίς οἱ ἀρὴν ἑτάροισιν ἀμύναι. Il. xii. 333. This optative is rare.

569. The earlier Greek here agrees with the Latin in using the subjunctive and optative, while the Attic adopts a new construction with the future indicative.

570. The future indicative occurs in Od. xiv. 333, ὤμοσε νῆα κατειρύσθαι καὶ ἐπαρτέας ἔμμεν ἑταίρους, οἵ δή μιν πέμψουσι φίλην ἐς πατρίδα γαῖαν. The potential optative with κέ may take the place of a future form ; as οὐδέ οἱ ἄλλοι εἴσ', οἵ κεν κατὰ δῆμον ἀλάλκοιεν κακότητα, Od. iv. 166. So τῶν κ' ἐπιβαίην, Il. v. 192 (cf. xxii. 348). In none of the Homeric examples of this construction is the relative clause negative.

571. A final force is seen in a few Homeric temporal clauses with ὅτε (ὅτ' ἄν, ὅτε κε) or ὁπότε with the subjunctive, which are chiefly expressions of emphatic prediction :—

Ἔσσεται ἧμαρ ὅτ' ἄν ποτ' ὀλώλῃ Ἴλιος ἱρή, Ζεὺς δέ σφιν αὐτὸς ἐπισσείῃσιν ἐρεμνὴν αἰγίδα πᾶσιν, *a day shall come when sacred Ilios shall fall* (i.e. *a day for the fall of Ilios*) *and when Zeus shall shake his terrible aegis before them all.* Il. iv. 164 ; so vi. 448. See Il. viii. 373, xxi. 111. See Monro, *Hom. Gr.* p. 209.

572. 1. In Attic Greek the subjunctive is not used in final relative sentences as it is in Homer (568). A few expressions like ἔχει ὅ τι εἴπῃ, *he has something to say,* follow the analogy of οὐκ ἔχει ὅ τι εἴπῃ, *he knows not what to say,* which contains an indirect question (667). E.g.

Τοιοῦτον ἔθος παρέδοσαν, ὥστε ἑκατέρους ἔχειν ἐφ' οἷς φιλοτιμῶσιν, *that both may have things in which they may glory.* Isoc. iv. 44. (Here there is really no indirect question, for the meaning is not *that they may know in what they are to glory.*) Οὐδὲν ἔτι διοίσει αὐτῷ, ἐὰν μόνον ἔχῃ ὅτῳ διαλέγηται, *if only he shall have some one to talk with.* PLAT. Symp. 194 D. Τοῖς μέλλουσιν ἕξειν ὅ τι εἰσφέρωσιν. XEN. Oec. vii. 20. Compare ἀπορεῖς ὅ τι λέγῃς and εὐπορεῖς ὅ τι λέγῃς in the same sentence, PLAT. Ion 536 B.

2. The subjunctive and optative may be used with a deliberative force, even when the relative has an antecedent, provided the leading clause expresses doubt or perplexity. E.g.

Οὐ γὰρ ἄλλον οἶδ' ὅτῳ λέγω. SOPH. Ph. 938. Οὐκ ἔχω
σόφισμ' ὅτῳ πημονῆς ἀπαλλαγῶ. AESCH. Pr. 470. Οὐδένα εἶχον
ὅστις ἐπιστολὰς πέμψειε. EUR. I. T. 588. So ἱκανοὺς οἷς δῶ,
XEN. An. i. 7, 7 (cf. 677). See SOPH. Ph. 281.

573. The present or aorist optative occurs rarely in Attic with a
final sense, where there is no deliberative force. *E.g.*

Κρύψασ' ἑαυτὴν ἔνθα μή τις εἰσίδοι, βρυχᾶτο. SOPH. Tr. 903.
So ὅστις λάκοι, AR. Ran. 97. See PLAT. Rep. 398 B and 578 E.

For the construction of 572 and 573 see Appendix VI (p. 411).

574. The future optative also occasionally occurs, as the natural
correlative of the regular future indicative, which is generally retained
after past tenses (566). *E.g.*

Ἔφευγον ἔνθα μήποτ' ὀψοίμην ὀνείδη τελούμενα, *I fled to (some
place) where I might never see the disgrace accomplished.* SOPH. O. T. 796.
Ἐσκόπει ὅπως ἔσοιτο αὐτῷ ὅστις ζῶντα γηροτροφήσοι καὶ τελευτήσαντα θάψοι αὐτὸν καὶ τὰ νομιζόμενα αὐτῷ ποιήσοι. ISAE. ii. 10.
Αἱρεθέντες ἐφ' ᾧτε ξυγγράψαι νόμους, καθ' οὕστινας πολιτεύσοιντο,
*having been chosen with the condition that they should compile laws, by
which they were to govern.* XEN. Hell. ii. 3, 11. (See Ib. ii. 3, 2, quoted
in 565, where καθ' οὓς πολιτεύσουσι is used in the same sense.)

CONSECUTIVE RELATIVE CLAUSES EXPRESSING RESULT.—
CAUSAL RELATIVE.

575. (*Indicative, with negative* οὐ.) The relative with any tense
of the indicative can be used to denote a *result*, in the sense of
ὥστε with the indicative (582). The negative here is οὐ. This
occurs chiefly after negative clauses, or interrogatives implying a
negative. *E.g.*

Τίς οὕτω μαίνεται ὅστις οὐ βούλεταί σοι φίλος εἶναι; *who is so
mad that he does not wish to be your friend?* XEN. An. ii. 5, 12. (Here
ὥστε οὐ βούλεται might be used.) Ἀκούσας τοιαῦθ' ἃ τὸν τοῦδ' οὔ
ποτ' εὐφρανεῖ βίον. SOPH. O. C. 1352. So HDT. vii. 46. Τίς οὕτως
εὐήθης ἐστὶν ὑμῶν, ὅστις ἀγνοεῖ τὸν ἐκεῖθεν πόλεμον δεῦρο ἥξοντα,
ἂν ἀμελήσωμεν; i.e. *who of you is so simple that he does not know,* etc.?
DEM. i. 15. (Here ὥστε ἀγνοεῖ might be used.) Τίς οὕτω πόρρω
τῶν πολιτικῶν ἦν πραγμάτων, ὅστις οὐκ ἐγγὺς ἠναγκάσθη γενέσθαι
τῶν συμφορῶν; ISOC. iv. 113. Τίς οὕτως ῥάθυμός ἐστιν, ὅστις
οὐ μετασχεῖν βουλήσεται ταύτης τῆς στρατείας; Id. iv. 185.

So also with the potential optative; as οὐδεὶς ἂν γένοιτο οὕτως
ἀδαμάντινος, ὃς ἂν μείνειεν ἐν τῇ δικαιοσύνῃ, *no one would ever become
so adamantine that he would remain firm in justice.* PLAT. Rep. 360 B.

576. (*Future or Present Indicative, with negative* μή.)   The
relative with the future (sometimes the present) indicative may
denote a result which is *aimed at*, in the same general sense as
ὥστε with present or aorist infinitive (582), but with more exactness (577). The negative is μή. *E.g.*

Εὔχετο μηδεμίαν οἱ συντυχίην τοιαύτην γενέσθαι, ἥ μιν παύσει κατατρέψασθαι τὴν Εὐρώπην, i.e. *no such occurrence as to prevent him from subjugating Europe.* HDT. vii. 54. (We might have ὥστε μιν παῦσαι. Compare εἰς τοσαύτην ἦλθε μεταβολὴν ὥσθ᾽ ἁπάσης τῆς Ἀσίας γενέσθαι δεσπότης, ISOC. v. 66.) Ἀνόητον ἐπὶ τοιούτους ἰέναι ὧν κρατήσας μὴ κατασχήσει τις, *it is absurd to attack men of such a kind that if we overcome them we shall not hold them.* THUC. vi. 11. (Here ὥστε μὴ κατασχεῖν, *so as not to hold them,* could express only the general sense of the construction.) Ὁ γράφων ἰδίᾳ τι Χαριδήμῳ τοιοῦτον ὃ μὴ πᾶσι καὶ ὑμῖν ἔσται. DEM. xxiii. 86. Τοιαῦτ᾽ ἀπαγγελοῦσι ἐξ ὧν μηδ᾽ ἂν ὁτιοῦν ᾖ κινηθήσονται. Id. xix. 324. Τίς οὐκ ἂν δέξαιτο τοιαύτης πολιτείας μετέχειν, ἐν ᾗ μὴ διαλήσει χρηστὸς ὤν; ISOC. iii. 16. Οὐδὲ τοιαῦτα λέγειν (πρέπει) ἐξ ὧν ὁ βίος μηδὲν ἐπιδώσει τῶν πεισθέντων. Id. iv. 189. Τοιαῦτα ζητήσεις λέγειν ἐξ ὧν μήτε αὐτὸς χείρων εἶναι δόξεις μήτε τοὺς μιμουμένους λυμανεῖ. Id. xi. 49. Βουληθεὶς τοιοῦτον μνημεῖον καταλιπεῖν, ὃ μὴ τῆς ἀνθρωπίνης φύσεώς ἐστιν (= ὥστε μὴ εἶναι). Id. iv. 89.

577. The construction of ὥστε after τοιοῦτος (584), which best corresponds to this relative expression, is not common, as οὕτως is the natural antecedent of ὥστε, while τοιοῦτος is naturally followed by οἷος or ὅς. The relative clause with the future is a much more definite expression, with its power of designating time, number, and person, than the infinitive. (See THUC. vi. 11, under 576.) Τοιοῦτος may also be followed by οἷος and the infinitive (759).

578. Ὅπως as a relative is sometimes used in this construction in a way which illustrates its use as a final particle. (See 313.) *E.g.*
Ποίεε δὲ οὕτω ὅκως τῶν σῶν ἐνδεήσει μηδέν, *and act so that there shall be nothing wanting on your part;* lit. *act in that way by which,* etc. HDT. vii. 18. Τὸ οὕτως ἐπίστασθαι ἀνθρώπων ἄλλων προστατεύειν ὅπως ἔξουσι πάντα τὰ ἐπιτήδεια, . . . τοῦτο θαυμαστὸν ἐφαίνετο, i.e. *in such a way that they should have,* etc. XEN. Cyr. i. 6, 7. So Cyr. ii. 4, 31.

579. *(Optative.)* The relative in this consecutive construction does not take the subjunctive. The optative occurs occasionally depending upon another optative. We find the future optative in PLAT. Rep. 416 C, φαίη ἄν τις δεῖν καὶ τὰς οἰκήσεις καὶ τὴν ἄλλην οὐσίαν τοιαύτην αὐτοῖς παρασκευάσασθαι, ἥτις μήτε τοὺς φύλακας ὡς ἀρίστους εἶναι παύσοι αὐτούς, κακουργεῖν τε μὴ ἐπαροῖ περὶ τοὺς ἄλλους πολίτας, with which compare 415 E, τοιαύτας οἵας χειμῶνός τε στέγειν καὶ θέρους ἱκανὰς εἶναι. The aorist occurs in DEM. vi. 8, τῇ ἡμετέρᾳ πόλει οὐδὲν ἂν ἐνδείξαιτο τοσοῦτον οὐδὲ ποιήσειεν, ὑφ᾽ οὗ πεισθέντες τινὰς Ἑλλήνων ἐκείνῳ προεῖσθε, i.e. *nothing so great as to persuade you to sacrifice any of the Greeks to him* (= ὥστε ὑμᾶς πεισθέντας προέσθαι). The practical difference between the pure optative here and the potential προεῖσθε ἄν, like ὃς ἂν μείνειεν in PLAT. Rep. 360 B (quoted in 575), is slight; but it would be seen if we had ὥστε προέσθαι here (*so great as to make you sacrifice*) and ὥστε μείνειεν ἄν there (*so firm that he would remain*).

580. The relative may have a causal signification, being equivalent to ὅτι, *because*, and a personal pronoun or demonstrative word. The verb is generally in the indicative, as in ordinary causal sentences (713); but it may be in the potential optative or potential indicative. The negative is οὐ; but when the relative clause is conditional as well as causal, the negative is μή. *E.g.*

Θαυμαστὸν ποιεῖς, ὃς ἡμῖν οὐδὲν δίδως, *you do a strange thing in giving us nothing* (like ὅτι σὺ οὐδὲν δίδως). XEN. Mem. ii. 7, 13. Δόξας ἀμαθέα εἶναι, ὃς . . . ἐκέλευε, *believing him to be unlearned, because he commanded*, etc. HDT. i. 33. Τὴν μητέρα (ἐμακάριζον), οἵων τέκνων ἐκύρησε (like ὅτι τοίων). Id. i. 31. Εὐδαίμων ἐφαίνετο, ὡς ἀδεῶς καὶ γενναίως ἐτελεύτα, i.e. *because he died so fearlessly and nobly* (ὡς being equivalent to ὅτι οὕτως). PLAT. Phaed. 58 E.

Ταλαίπωρος εἶ, ᾧ μήτε θεοὶ πατρῷοί εἰσι μήθ᾽ ἱερά, *you are wretched, since you have no ancestral Gods (if you really have none)*, etc. Id. Euthyd. 302 B. Πῶς ἂν ὀρθῶς ἐμοῦ καταγιγνώσκοιτε, ᾧ τὸ παράπαν πρὸς τουτονὶ μηδὲν συμβόλαιόν ἐστιν; i.e. *since I have no contract at all with this man* (or *if I have no contract*). DEM. xxxiii. 34. Ὅπου τοίνυν μηδεὶς τετόλμηκε τῶν οἰκείων τούτῳ μαρτυρῆσαι, πῶς οὐκ εἰκός ἐστιν ὑμᾶς ἡγεῖσθαί με τἀληθῆ λέγειν; *whereas then* (or *if then*) *no one has dared*, etc. Id. xlix. 38. So lv. 26. Ὁπότε αἱ μὲν ἐξ ἀρχῆς συνθῆκαι ἠφανίσθησαν ἕτεραι δὲ μὴ ἐγράφησαν, πῶς ὀρθῶς ἂν ἐμοὶ δικάζοιτο, καθ᾽ οὗ μὴ ἔχει παρασχέσθαι συνθήκας; *whereas the original agreement disappeared and the other was never written, how can he justly go to law with me, when* (or *if*) *he cannot bring forward any agreement against me?* Id. xxxiii. 30. So SOPH. O. T. 817, 1335, O. C. 1680, Ant. 696, Ph. 178, 255; AR. Ran. 1459; HDT. i. 71 (τοῖσί γε μή ἐστι μηδέν); THUC. iv. 126 (οἵ γε μηδὲ . . . ἥκετε). The potential imperfect occurs in ANT. v. 66, μὴ τοίνυν ἐμοὶ νείμητε τὸ ἄπορον τοῦτο, ἐν ᾧ μηδ᾽ ἂν αὐτοὶ εὐπορεῖτε, *do not then bring upon me this perplexity, in which you yourselves would not know what to do* (half causal, half conditional).

581. In the last examples with μή, the causal and the conditional forces are united, but in English we can express only one of them. Thus ᾧ μήτε θεοὶ πατρῷοί εἰσι, besides its causal force, implies a condition; so that we might translate equally well *if (as it appears) you have no ancestral Gods, you are wretched.* The same combination of cause and condition is seen in the Latin *siquidem.*

CONSECUTIVE CLAUSES WITH ὥστε OR ὡς AND WITH ἐφ᾽ ᾧ OR ἐφ᾽ ᾧτε.[1]

582. A consecutive clause expresses a consequence, that

---

[1] See Gildersleeve in *Am. Jour. Phil.* vii. pp. 161-175; and Seume, *De Sententiis Consecutivis Graecis*, Göttingen, 1883.

is, the effect or result (actual or potential) of something that
is stated in the leading clause.   Such a clause is introduced
by some relative word, generally by ὥστε, *so as, so that*.
(See 575.)   The consequence may be either one which the
action of the leading verb aims at and *tends* to produce, or
one which that action actually *does* produce.   This is the
fundamental distinction between ὥστε with the infinitive
(with μή for its negative) and ὥστε with the indicative
(with οὐ for its negative).   *E.g.*

Πᾶν ποιοῦσιν ὥστε δίκην μὴ διδόναι, *they do everything in such
a way as* (i.e. *so as*) *not to suffer punishment*, i.e. *they aim, in all they do,
at not being punished;* it is not, however, implied that they actually
escape. PLAT. Gorg. 479 C.   On the other hand, πᾶν ποιοῦσιν ὥστε
δίκην οὐ διδόασιν would mean *they do everything in such a way
that* (i.e. *so that*) *they are not punished.*

583. Though this illustrates the fundamental distinction in
thought on which the distinction in form is based, there are
many examples in which ὥστε with the infinitive and ὥστε with
the indicative seem to amount to essentially the same thing,
although the processes by which the meaning is expressed in
the two constructions are essentially different.   Thus we can
say οὕτως ἐστὶ δεινὸς ὥστε δίκην μὴ διδόναι, *he is so skilful as not
to be punished*, and also οὕτως ἐστὶ δεινὸς ὥστε δίκην οὐ δίδωσιν,
he is so skilful that he is not punished; and though we should
receive the same impression from both statements, so that both
might be made of the same man under the same circumstances,
yet the two constructions (one stating a *tendency* and the other
a *fact*) are very different, and they seemed far more so to a
Greek than they do to us.

584. Ὥστε is properly a relative particle of comparison, meaning *as*.   Its correlative *so* may be expressed in a demonstrative
like οὕτως, or implied ; as οὕτως ἐστὶ δεινὸς ὥστε σε πεῖσαι, *he is so
skilful as to persuade you*, or ἡ πόλις τετείχισται ὥστε ἱκανὴ εἶναι
σώζειν τοὺς ἐνοικοῦντας, *the city is walled so as to be able to keep its
inhabitants safe*.   (See τοιούτους καὶ οὕτω τρέφειν κύνας ὥστε ἐπιχειρῆσαι, PLAT. Rep. 416 A ; and compare τοιοῦτος οἷος with the
infinitive in 759.)   These expressions in Greek *state* no more than
he has the skill to persuade you and *the city has walls enough to be
able*, etc. ; the further ideas that *he does persuade* and *the city is
able* are inferences, which are strongly suggested and generally
felt when the expressions are used, but they do not lie in the
words.   When the Greek wishes to express these facts definitely
and not to leave them to inference, it uses the indicative with

ὥστε ; as οὕτως ἐστὶ δεινὸς ὥστε σε πείθει, *he is so skilful that he persuades you*, or ἡ πόλις τετείχισται ὥστε ἱκανή ἐστιν. But here the use of a finite verb compels the writer to make his expression more definite than it was before ; for, whereas ὥστε πεῖσαι and ὥστε ἱκανὴ εἶναι meant only (*so*) *as to persuade* and (*so*) *as to be able*, without limiting the expressions to past, present, or future time, he cannot use a tense of the indicative without fixing its time, that is, without making a definite statement. So long as the infinitive has no subject and can be translated by our simple infinitive (as above), we can generally express its force without putting into our translation more than we find in the Greek ; the formal distinction between *so skilful as to persuade* and *so skilful that he persuades* being apparent even when we mean substantially the same by both. When the clause with ὥστε is negative, a marked distinction appears in Greek to show the different point of view taken in the two expressions, and we have ὥστε μὴ πεῖσαι and ὥστε οὐ πείθει. This is of course lost in English with our single negative. But when the infinitive has a subject, it must be translated by a finite verb in some definite tense, number, and person, that is, by a statement and not by a mere expression of tendency, although the force of the infinitive in Greek is the same as before. Thus we generally translate σχολάζεις, ὥστε θαυμάζειν ἐμέ (EUR. Hec. 730), *you delay, so that I am astonished*, as if it were ὥστε θαυμάζω ἐγώ, simply because we cannot use our infinitive with a subject expressed. If, however, we substitute an equivalent form which avoids this difficulty, like *so as to astonish me*, we see that there is really no such definite character in ὥστε θαυμάζειν ἐμέ as we impose upon it, and that it no more expresses a statement than ὥστε σε πεῖσαι (above) does. The same difficulty of translating the Greek infinitive with its subject has done much to obscure the force of the tenses of the articular infinitive and of the infinitive with ἄν. (See also 603.)

In many uses of the infinitive with ὥστε it is not even inferred that the result towards which the infinitive expresses a tendency is actually reached. Thus, in clauses with ὥστε expressing a purpose or a condition, and where the infinitive is generally used without ὥστε, we cannot substitute the indicative for the infinitive (see the examples under 587, 2 and 3, and 588).[1]

---

[1] Shilleto (in the Appendix to his edition of Demosthenes *de Falsa Legatione*) thus illustrates the distinction between ὥστε οὐκ ἐβούλετο and ὥστε μὴ βούλεσθαι. "The difference seems simply to be this : οὕτως ἄφρων ἦν ὥστε οὐκ ἐβούλετο, *he was so foolish that he did not wish* (expressive of the *real* result or consequence) ; οὕτως ἄφρων ἦν ὥστε μὴ βούλεσθαι, *he was so foolish as not to wish* (expressive of the *natural* consequence). . . . Now it is obvious that an energetic speaker, wishing to express that the result (was not only of a

585. In Homer ὥστε (or rather ὥς τε) is found, with two exceptions (589), only in the sense of *as*, like ὥσπερ. See its use in similes, as ὥς τε λέων ἐχάρη, Il. iii. 23. The τε here is like that commonly added to relatives in Homer (as in ὅς τε) and to ἐπεί in Herodotus. The Attic poets are the first to use ὥστε freely with the infinitive. In Sophocles we first find ὥστε with the finite moods; this seems to have arisen from a desire to express definitely the accomplishment of the result, which the infinitive expressed only by inference.

586. Ὡς, originally of the same meaning with ὥς τε, was seldom used in consecutive sentences except in certain authors. (See 608.)

῟Ωστε WITH THE INFINITIVE.

587. ῟Ωστε with the infinitive, with a demonstrative expressed or implied, means *so as;* but when the infinitive has a subject which must be expressed in English, we are generally obliged to translate the particle with its antecedent by *so that.* The expression properly means only that one action or state is of such a nature as to be followed by another as a consequence; but it is often implied also, apart from the words, that the second action or state actually does follow.

1. The consequence may be simply a result which a previous act tends to produce. *E.g.*

Ἀμφὶ δὲ κυκλοῦντο πᾶσαν νῆσον, ὥστ᾽ ἀμηχανεῖν ὅποι τράποιντο, *and they encircled the whole island, so that they* (the Persians) *knew not whither to turn* (i.e. *so as to perplex the Persians*, etc.) AESCH. Pers. 457. Τόσονδε μισεῖν ὥστε τὴν δίκην πατεῖν, *to hate so violently as to trample on justice.* SOPH. Aj. 1335 ; so 1325. Σὺ δὲ σχολάζεις, ὥστε θαυμάζειν ἐμέ, *but you delay, so that I am astonished* (see 584). EUR. Hec. 730. Πάντας οὕτω διατιθεὶς ἀπεπέμπετο ὥστε αὐτῷ μᾶλλον φίλους εἶναι ἢ τῷ βασιλεῖ. XEN. An. i. 1, 5. Δυσκολία καὶ μανία πολλάκις εἰς τὴν διάνοιαν ἐμπίπτουσιν οὕτως ὥστε καὶ τὰς ἐπιστήμας ἐκβάλλειν. Id. Mem. iii. 12, 6. Ἦν πεπαιδευμένος οὕτως ὥστε πάνυ μικρὰ κεκτημένος πάνυ ῥᾳδίως ἔχειν ἀρκοῦντα, *he had been so educated as very easily to have enough, although he possessed very little.* Ib. i. 2, 1. Φῦναι δὲ ὁ Κῦρος λέγεται φιλοτιμότατος, ὥστε πάντα μὲν πόνον ἀνατλῆναι πάντα δὲ κίνδυνον ὑπομεῖναι. Id. Cyr. i. 2, 1. Ἀπέχρη γὰρ ἂν τοῖς γνωσθεῖσιν ἐμμένειν, ὥστε μηδεμίαν ἡμῖν εἶναι πρὸς τοῦτον

nature to follow, but) actually did follow, would employ the *indicative :* whereas in ordinary and unimpassioned language the *infinitive* would imply all that was necessary, *the natural* consequence supposing *the real.*"

διαφοράν, for we should be content to abide by the decision so as to have no difference with him. DEM. xxvii. 1. Πολλὰς ἐλπίδας ἔχω ἀρκούντως ἐρεῖν, ὥστε ὑμᾶς μήτ᾽ ἀπολειφθῆναι τῶν πραγμάτων μήτ᾽ ἀγνοῆσαι, κ.τ.λ. Id. xxvii. 2. Τοιοῦτον ἔθος ἡμῖν παρέδοσαν, ὥστε σπεισαμένους συνελθεῖν ἐς ταὐτόν. ISOC. iv. 43. So iv. 42. Εἰ τοιοῦτον εἴη ἡ σοφία, ὥστ᾽ ἐκ τοῦ πληρεστέρου εἰς τὸν κενώτερον ῥεῖν ἡμῶν, of such a nature as to flow. PLAT. Symp. 175 D.

Πείσομαι γὰρ οὐ τοσοῦτον οὐδὲν ὥστε μὴ οὐ καλῶς θανεῖν, for I shall suffer nothing so terrible as to prevent me from dying gloriously. SOPH. Ant. 96. (For μὴ οὐ see 815, 2.)

2. The consequence may have the form of a stipulation, condition, or limitation. E.g.

Ποιοῦνται ὁμολογίαν πρὸς Πάχητα, ὥστε Ἀθηναίοις ἐξεῖναι βουλεῦσαι περὶ τῶν Μυτιληναίων, they make a treaty with Paches, to the effect that the Athenians shall be permitted, etc. THUC. iii. 28. Ἀναστήσας αὐτοὺς ὥστε μὴ ἀδικῆσαι, having removed them on condition of doing them no harm. Ibid. So i. 29, vii. 83. So Id. iii. 114, ξυμμαχίαν ἐποιήσαντο ἐπὶ τοῖσδε, ὥστε μὴ στρατεύειν. Ἐξὸν αὐτοῖς τῶν λοιπῶν ἄρχειν Ἑλλήνων, ὥστ᾽ αὐτοὺς ὑπακούειν βασιλεῖ, it being in their power to rule the rest of the Greeks, on condition that they should themselves serve the King. DEM. vi. 11.

3. The consequence may be aimed at as a *purpose*, the consecutive clause becoming also final. E.g.

Πᾶν ποιοῦσιν, ὥστε δίκην μὴ διδόναι, they do everything in such a way as not to suffer punishment, i.e. that they may not suffer. PLAT. Gorg. 479 C. (Here ἵνα μή with the subjunctive might be used, but it would express only the *final* element.) Ἐβουλήθησαν Ἐλευσῖνα ἐξιδιώσασθαι, ὥστε εἶναι σφίσι καταφυγὴν εἰ δεήσειε, they wished to appropriate Eleusis, so that they might have a refuge if they should need it. XEN. Hell. ii. 4, 8. Μηχαναὶ πολλαί εἰσιν, ὥστε διαφεύγειν θάνατον, there are many devices for escaping death. PLAT. Ap. 39 A. (Here we might have ὅπως διαφευξεῖταί τις.) Μηχανὰς εὑρήσομεν, ὥστ᾽ ἐς τὸ πᾶν σε τῶνδ᾽ ἀπαλλάξαι πόνων, we will find devices to free you, etc. (= ὅπως σε ἀπαλλάξομεν). AESCH. Eum. 82.

588. The infinitive with ὥστε sometimes follows verbs of *wishing, commanding*, etc., which regularly take a simple infinitive of the object (746), less frequently verbs which take an infinitive of the subject (745); and sometimes adjectives and nouns which regularly take the simple infinitive (758). E.g.

Κύπρις γὰρ ἤθελ᾽ ὥστε γίγνεσθαι τάδε, for the Cyprian Goddess wished this to be done, i.e. had (such) a wish (as) that this should be done. EUR. Hipp. 1327. Δικαιῶν ὥστ᾽ ἐμοῦ κλύειν λόγους, asking that he (Polynices) should hear my words (to the effect that he should hear). SOPH. O. C. 1350. Τοὺς στρατηγοὺς τῶν πόλεων ἐδίδασκεν ὥστε δόντα χρήματα αὐτὸν πεῖσαι, he instructed him to give money and persuade the generals. THUC. viii. 45. Τὸ μὲν δύνασθαι, ὦ Φαῖδρε, ὥστε ἀγωνιστὴν τέλεον γενέσθαι, the ability to become a finished disputer (i.e. having such power as to become). PLAT. Phaedr. 269 D. Ἐλθόντες πρὸς αὐτοὺς πείθουσιν ὥστε μετὰ σφῶν Ἄργει ἐπιχειρῆσαι. THUC. iii. 102. (In the same chapter, πείθει Ἀκαρνᾶνας βοηθῆσαι Ναυπάκτῳ.) Ἔπεισαν τοὺς Ἀθηναίους ὥστε ἐξαγαγεῖν ἐκ Πύλου Μεσσηνίους. Id. v. 35. Ψηφισάμενοι αὐτοὶ πρῶτοι ὥστε πάσῃ προθυμίᾳ ἀμύνειν, having voted to defend them, etc. Id. vi. 88. Εἰς ἀνάγκην καθέσταμεν ὥστε κινδυνεύειν. ISOC. vi. 51. (See 749.) So δύναμιν ὥστε ἐγγενέσθαι, power to grow up in it, PLAT. Rep. 433 B. Εἴ τι θέσφατον πατρὶ χρησμοῖσιν ἱκνεῖθ᾽, ὥστε πρὸς παίδων θανεῖν, i.e. if my father was warned by oracles that he should perish by his children's hands. SOPH. O. C. 969.

Πάνυ μοι ἐμέλησεν ὥστε εἰδέναι, it concerned me very much to know. XEN. Cyr. vi. 3, 19. Ἀδύνατον ὑμῖν ὥστε Πρωταγόρου τοῦδε σοφώτερόν τινα ἑλέσθαι, it is impossible for you to choose any one wiser than Protagoras here (you have not such power as to choose). PLAT. Prot. 338 C. So XEN. Mem. i. 3, 6. Ξυνέβη εὐθὺς μετὰ τὴν μάχην ὥστε πολέμου μὲν μηδὲν ἔτι ἅψασθαι μηδετέρους, πρὸς δὲ τὴν εἰρήνην μᾶλλον τὴν γνώμην εἶχον. THUC. v. 14. (Here the construction changes suddenly to the indicative in εἶχον.) Ἆρ᾽ ἔστιν ὥστε κἀγγύθεν θέαν λαβεῖν; is it possible for me to have a sight of it near by? SOPH. Ph. 656.

Πῶς γάρ τις ἱκανὸς γένοιτ᾽ ἂν ὥστε ἀεὶ προστάττειν τὸ προσῆκον; for how could one become capable of always giving the proper command (so capable as)? PLAT. Polit. 295 A. Πότερα παῖδές εἰσι φρονιμώτεροι ὥστε μαθεῖν τὰ φραζόμενα ἢ ἄνδρες; i.e. are they wiser than men in learning, etc.? XEN. Cyr. iv. 3, 11. Νέοι ὥστε τοσοῦτο πρᾶγμα διελέσθαι, too young to decide. PLAT. Prot. 314 B. So γέρων ὥστε σ᾽ ὠφελεῖν, EUR. Andr. 80. Ψυχρόν (ἐστι τὸ ὕδωρ) ὥστε λούσασθαι, the water is too cold to bathe in. XEN. Mem. iii. 13, 3. (Cf. λούσασθαι ψυχρότερον and θερμότερον πιεῖν, in the same section.)

In many of these cases it seems impossible to believe that ὥστε added anything to the sense, even as it was felt by the Greeks. The expressions were probably stereotyped in usage, and their origin was forgotten. Indeed, ὥστε and ὡς (608) sometimes seem to have no more meaning than our to with the infinitive, which in some cases we can use or omit at pleasure, though with some change of sense, as in I dare say and I dare to say. Compare I command you to go and I bid you go. The examples show that there is hardly a construction in which the simple infinitive was used where ὥστε is not occasionally prefixed to it. It is important here to remember that ὥστε means only as (or, including the antecedent, so as); never so that, except in the construction with the finite moods, although this is often a necessary makeshift in our translation.

For ὥστε or ὡς with the infinitive after the comparative and ἤ, see 764 (b).

589. (Ὥς τε in Homer.) The only two Homeric examples of ὥστε (ὥς τε) with the infinitive are Il. ix. 42, εἰ δὲ σοὶ αὐτῷ θυμὸς ἐπέσσυται ὥς τε νέεσθαι, ἔρχεο, but *if your own mind is eagerly set upon returning, go;* and Od. xvii. 20, οὐ γὰρ ἐπὶ σταθμοῖσι μένειν ἔτι τηλίκος εἰμὶ, ὥς τ᾽ ἐπιτειλαμένῳ σημάντορι πάντα πιθέσθαι, for *I am no longer of a fit age to abide at the sheepfolds, (and there) to obey in everything a master's command* (this comes under 587, 2, above). These cases seem to show that the usage was already established; although Lehrs (*de Aristarchi Stud. Hom.* p. 157) proposes to expunge ὥς τε in both. In HES. Op. 43 we have ῥηιδίως γάρ κεν καὶ ἐπ᾽ ἤματι ἐργάσσαιο, ὥς τέ σε κεῖς (= καὶ εἰς) ἐνιαυτὸν ἔχειν καὶ ἀεργὸν ἐόντα, i.e. *so as to have enough for a year, even without working.*

590. (*Tenses.*) The tenses of the infinitive most frequently used with ὥστε are the present and aorist, with their usual distinction (87). See the examples above.

The perfect is sometimes used to express completion or decisiveness of the action (109; 110). *E.g.*

Νεωστὶ ἀπὸ νόσου βραχύ τι λελωφήκαμεν, ὥστε καὶ χρήμασι καὶ τοῖς σώμασιν ηὐξῆσθαι, i.e. *we have recovered a little, so as to have increased.* THUC. vi. 12. Λόγων καὶ βουλευμάτων κοινωνὸν ἄν σε ποιοῖντο, ὥστε μηδὲ ἕν σε λεληθέναι ὧν βουλόμεθα εἰδέναι, *so that not a single one of the things we wish to know should have escaped you.* XEN. Cyr. vi. 1, 40. Τοιαῦτα πολιτεύματα ἐλέσθαι (ἐμοὶ ὑπῆρξεν) ὥστε πολλάκις ἐστεφανῶσθαι, καὶ μηδὲ τοὺς ἐχθροὺς ἐπιχειρεῖν λέγειν, κ.τ.λ., *so as often to have been crowned* (perfect), *and so as not even to have my enemies undertake* (present) *to say,* etc. DEM. xviii. 257. See Id. xxiii. 68; LYS. xxxii. 27; ISOC. iii. 32, iv. 45; ISAE. x. 1; and the examples quoted in 109 and 110.

591. 1. The future infinitive with ὥστε is common only when it depends on an infinitive in indirect discourse and represents a future indicative of the direct form; so εἰς τοῦτ᾽ ἀναιδείας αὐτὸν ἥξειν ἀκούω, ὥστε Λακεδαιμονίων κατηγορήσειν, DEM. xix. 72. So LYS. v. 2. See other examples under 594.

2. Elsewhere it is rare and perhaps doubtful. In DEM. xxix. 5 and xxx. 5, ὥσθ᾽ ὑμᾶς ἅπαντας εἴσεσθαι is found in all MSS., and it is no more objectionable than other exceptional uses of the future, as that after βούλομαι and δέομαι (see 113), or than ὥστε with the infinitive with ἄν not in indirect discourse (211; 592). In DEM. xvi. 4 we have, ἔστι τοίνυν ἔν τινι τοιούτῳ καιρῷ τὰ πράγματα νῦν, . . . ὥστε Θηβαίοις μὲν ἀσθενεῖς γενέσθαι, Λακεδαιμονίους δ᾽, εἰ ποιήσονται τὴν Ἀρκαδίαν ὑφ᾽ ἑαυτοῖς, πάλιν ἰσχυροὺς γενήσεσθαι, the change of time making the change of tense natural.

In THUC. iii. 34 we have, προκαλεσάμενος ἐς λόγους Ἱππίαν, ὥστε, ἢν μηδὲν ἀρέσκον λέγῃ, πάλιν αὐτὸν καταστήσειν ἐς τὸ τεῖχος σῶν καὶ ὑγιᾶ, *on the condition that, if his proposals should not be satisfactory, he would restore H. to the fort safe and sound.* Here καταστήσειν represents καταστήσω in the words of Paches; but the future is still exceptional in its use (see 113). In THUC. i. 29, iii. 28 (two passages) and 114,

vii. 83, where there was the same ground for the future, we find the present or aorist infinitive with ὥστε.

592. The infinitive with ἄν (not in indirect discourse) can follow ὥστε to express a consequence in a potential form, corresponding to the potential optative or indicative. *E.g.*

Ἀποτετειχισμένοι ἂν ἦσαν, ὥστε μηδ᾽ εἰ μετέπεμψαν ἔτι ὁμοίως ἂν αὐτοὺς ὠφελεῖν, *they would have been already walled in, so that, even if they had sent for them, it would not any longer have been of as much use to them.* THUC. vii. 42. Τῶν οἰκείων μοι πραγμάτων τοιούτων συμβεβηκότων ὥστε ὑμᾶς ἂν ἀκούσαντας ἐλεῆσαι, *such as would make you pity me if you should hear them.* DEM. l. 59. Ἀποληφθέντος, ὥστε μὴ ἂν δύνασθαι ἐπανελθεῖν οἴκαδε, *so that he would not be able to return.* Id. viii. 35. See also the examples under 211, and the cases of indirect discourse with ὥστε ἄν under 594. (The translation of the infinitive here is necessarily inexact. See 584.)

593. Herodotus often writes οὕτω ὥστε together, οὕτω referring to the whole leading sentence, and not (as it generally does) to a single word or expression. *E.g.*

Ἀπέδρη ἐς Τεγέην, τὰς μὲν νύκτας πορευόμενος, τὰς δὲ ἡμέρας καταδύνων ἐς ὕλην, οὕτω ὥστε τρίτῃ εὐφρόνῃ γενέσθαι ἐν Τεγέῃ, *he escaped to Tegea, travelling by night and hiding in the woods by day, (in such wise) as on the third night to arrive at Tegea.* HDT. ix. 37. So iii. 105, viii. 27, ix. 61, 73.

For the same usage before a finite verb, see 601 (end).

594. (*Ὥστε with Infinitive in Indirect Discourse.* Ὥστε οὐ.) When a clause with ὥστε depends on an infinitive in indirect discourse, and is itself a part of the quotation, its verb representing a finite mood of the direct form, it regularly has the infinitive, in the tense of the direct discourse, even when on other grounds a finite verb would seem more natural. Here the future infinitive and the infinitive with ἄν may be used, as in other indirect discourse (135; 204). The negative οὐ of the direct form is generally retained with such an infinitive. *E.g.*

Ἔφασαν τοὺς στρατιώτας εἰς τοῦτο τρυφῆς ἐλθεῖν ὥστ᾽ οὐκ ἐθέλειν πίνειν εἰ μὴ ἀνθοσμίας εἴη (*they said εἰς τοῦτο τρυφῆς ἦλθον ὥστε οὐκ ἤθελον πίνειν), they said that the soldiers became so fastidious that they would not drink any wine unless it had a strong bouquet.* XEN. Hell. vi. 2, 6. Ὑμᾶς εἰδέναι ἡγοῦμαι τοῦτον οὕτω σκαιὸν εἶναι ὥστε οὐ δύνασθαι μαθεῖν τὰ λεγόμενα. LYS. x. 15. Οὕτω δὲ ἀτόπους τινὰς ἐν τῇ πόλει εἶναι ὥστε οὐκ αἰσχύνεσθαι λοιδορουμένους αὐτῷ (i.e. οὕτως ἄτοποι ὥστε οὐκ αἰσχύνονται). DEM. xix. 308. So xviii. 283, xix. 152. Εἶναι δὲ πολλοὺς ἄλλους (sc. ἔφη), οὓς βούλεσθαι κοινωνεῖν τῆς συντάξεως, ὥστε οὔτε χρημάτων οὔτε στρατιωτῶν ἔσεσθαι ἀπορίαν (i.e. ἄλλοι εἰσίν, οὓς βούλομαι (see 755) κοινωνεῖν, ὥστε οὐκ ἔσται ἀπορία). AESCHIN. iii. 96 : so i. 174. Τοσοῦτον φρονῆσαι φῇς αὐτοὺς ὥστε οὐχ ἡγήσασθαι σφᾶς αὐτοὺς ἀξίους εἶναι ζῆν, κ.τ.λ.

(i.e. τοσοῦτον ἐφρόνησαν ὥστε οὐχ ἡγήσαντο). Isoc. xii. 255. Εἶναι
δὲ (sc. λέγεται) ταχυτῆτα οὐδενὶ ἑτέρῳ ὅμοιον, οὕτω ὥστε, εἰ μὴ προλαμβάνειν τοὺς Ἰνδοὺς τῆς ὁδοῦ ἐν ᾧ τοὺς μύρμηκας συλλέγεσθαι,
οὐδένα ἂν σφεων ἀποσῴζεσθαι (i.e. εἰ μὴ προλαμβάνοιεν τῆς ὁδοῦ
ἐν ᾧ συλλέγοιντο, οὐδεὶς ἂν ἀποσῴζοιτο). HDT. iii. 105 (see 755): so
i. 189. Τοιαῦτα ἐνομίζετο τὰ ὑπάρχοντα αὐτῷ εἶναι, ὥστε οὐκ ἄν
ποθ' ἑτέρας ἐπιθυμῆσαι πολιτείας (i.e. οὐκ ἂν ἐπιθυμήσειε). LYS.
xviii. 6: so xxi. 18. See also THUC. v. 40, viii. 76 ; ISAE. iii. 39,
xi. 27 ; PLAT. Ap. 26 D, Euthyd. 305 C, Leg. 806 A, Alcib. ii. 143 D.

595. Ὥστε μή, however, as the ordinary form with the infinitive,
may be used in indirect discourse (594), even with the future infinitive
or the infinitive with ἄν. *E.g.*

Τηλικαύτην ἡγεῖσθαι πόλιν οἰκεῖν τὸ μέγεθος, ὥστε μηδ' ἂν ὁτιοῦν
ᾖ δεινὸν πείσεσθαι. DEM. ix. 67. Ὤιμην οὕτως ἐμφανὴς εἶναι τοῖς
ἀλαζονευομένοις πολεμῶν, ὥστε μηδέν' ἄν ποτε γενέσθαι πιστὸν τῶν
λεγόντων. Isoc. xii. 20 : so xii. 144. In ISAE. iii. 51, ὥστε μηδὲ
ἐκδοῦναι would have been the same in the direct form.

596. Cases of ὥστε with a finite verb in indirect discourse are rare,
but sometimes occur ; as οἴομαί σ' ἀναπείσειν, ὥστε γε οὐδὲν ἀντερεῖς,
AR. Nub. 1342. So EUR. Tro. 973; PLAT. Leg. 692 D.

597. 1. Occasionally ὥστε οὐ with the infinitive represents a finite
mood with οὐ of direct discourse, even when there is no preceding
infinitive to assimilate it (as there is in all the cases in 594). *E.g.*

Ἐννοησάτω ὅτι οὕτως ἤδη τότε πόρρω τῆς ἡλικίας ἦν ὥστ', εἰ καὶ
μὴ τότε, οὐκ ἂν πολλῷ ὕστερον τελευτῆσαι τὸν βίον, *let him reflect
that he* (Socrates) *was then already so far advanced in life that he would
have ended his days not much later,* etc. (i.e. οὐκ ἂν πολλῷ ὕστερον
ἐτελεύτησεν). XEN. Mem. iv. 8, 1. (Seume classes this with the cases
in 597, 2 because of οὐ πολλῷ. But the infinitive depends directly
on a clause with ὅτι in indirect discourse.) So in ARISTOT. Pol. ii. 9,
17 : λέγουσι ὡς μετεδίδοσαν τῆς πολιτείας, ὥστ' οὐ γίνεσθαι τότε
τὴν ὀλιγανθρωπίαν.

2. Sometimes οὐ is found with ὥστε and the infinitive when the
negative belongs to a single word, as in οὐ πολλοί for ὀλίγοι. See
Isoc. viii. 107 : οὕτω κακῶς προύστησαν τῶν πραγμάτων ὥσθ' ἡμᾶς
οὐ πολλοῖς ἔτεσιν ὕστερον πάλιν ἐπιπολάσαι. So ISAE. ix. 17.

598. In a few cases, however, ὥστε οὐ is found with the infinitive
where none of the preceding explanations (594; 597) will apply.
Such are the following :—

Ὥστ' οὔτε νυκτὸς ὕπνον οὔτ' ἐξ ἡμέρας ἐμὲ στεγάζειν ἡδὺν, ἀλλ' ὁ
προστατῶν χρόνος διῆγέ μ' αἰὲν ὡς θανουμένην, *so that neither by night
nor by day did sweet sleep spread her wings over me.* SOPH. El. 780.
(Here there is an easy transition from the infinitive to the following
indicative.) Οὐ μακρὰν γὰρ τειχέων περιπτυχαὶ, ὥστ' οὐχ ἅπαντά
σ' εἰδέναι τὰ δρώμενα, *not so large that you do not know all* (i.e. *the city
is so small, that you know all*) *that is done.* EUR. Ph. 1357. Ὥστ' οὐδ'

ἴχνος γε τειχέων εἶναι σαφές, yes ; so that not even a trace of the walls
is to be seen. Id. Hel. 107. Νῦν δὲ περιέστηκεν εἰς τοῦτο, ὥστε τὸν
ἰδίᾳ κινδυνεύοντα οὐ φιλόπολιν ἀλλὰ φιλοπράγμονα δοκεῖν εἶναι.
LYCURG. 3. Οὐδ' αὖ οὕτως ἄπορος ἦν οὐδ' ἄφιλος ὥστ' οὐκ ἂν ἐξευ-
ρεῖν τὸν ἀπογράψοντα, nor, moreover, was I so helpless or friendless that
I could not find one to bring an ἀπογραφή (οὐκ ἂν ἐξεύροιμι). DEM. liii.
1. Οὕτω δ' ἀρχαίως εἶχον, μᾶλλον δὲ πολιτικῶς, ὥστε οὐδὲ χρημάτων ὠνεῖσθαι παρ' οὐδενὸς οὐδέν. Id. ix. 48. (This may be explained
as oratio obliqua, on the ground of ἀκούω and the infinitive in the
preceding clause. But I agree with Seume in thinking this connection
too remote to account for ὥστε οὐ. Here there is neither an assimilat-
ing infinitive, as in the examples in 594, nor a leading clause with ὅτι
or ὡς, as in those in 597, 1. In fact, ὥστε οὐ gives the only ground
for calling the clause with εἶχον indirect discourse.)

599. The examples in 598 have one common character : in all of
them the thought could be expressed equally well by ὥστε with the
infinitive or ὥστε with a finite verb, for even in EUR. Ph. 1357 and
DEM. liii. 1 a fact rather than a mere tendency is expressed. We
can, therefore, easily suppose a mixture of two constructions by which,
for example in EUR. Hel. 107, instead of ὥστε μὴ εἶναι or ὥστε
οὐκ ἔστιν, either of which would express the sense, we have ὥστε
οὐκ εἶναι.[1] This occasional confusion would be made easier by
familiarity with ὥστε οὐ and the infinitive in indirect discourse.

600. In a few cases ὥστε seems to be omitted, even when its
antecedent is expressed ; as in AESCH. Ag. 478, τίς ὧδε παιδνὸς ἢ
φρενῶν κεκομμένος, φλογὸς παραγγέλμασιν νέοις πυρωθέντα καρδίαν
ἔπειτ' ἀλλαγᾷ λόγου καμεῖν; who is so childish, etc., (as) to be inflamed in heart, etc., and then to suffer from a change of report? See
also HDT. iii. 12, οὕτω ἰσχυραί, μόγις ἂν λίθῳ παίσας διαρρήξειας,
so strong, you could hardly break them with a stone.

Ὥστε WITH THE FINITE MOODS.

601. Ὥστε with the indicative means properly so that,
and expresses the actual result of the action of the leading
verb. E.g.

---

[1] The explanation of ὥστε οὐ with the infinitive on the ground of oratio
obliqua was first made, I believe, by Shilleto in the Appendix to his Demosthenes de Falsa Legatione (1844). It is also given by Madvig (Synt. § 205,
Anm. 3), who confines ὥστε οὐ to clauses depending on the infinitive of oratio
obliqua after verbs like φημί, οἶμαι, etc. (i.e. like the examples in 594).
Shilleto's faith in his own explanation was somewhat shaken by finding that
four of the passages quoted in 598 could not be brought under his canon.
Under the influence of Shilleto's essay, I originally suggested the mixture of
two equivalent constructions given above, as applicable to all cases of ὥστε οὐ,
not appreciating the wide influence of the principle of oratio obliqua upon the
construction.

Οὕτως ἀγνωμόνως ἔχετε, ὥστε ἐλπίζετε αὐτὰ χρηστὰ γενήσεσθαι, κ.τ.λ.; are you so senseless that you expect, etc.? DEM. ii. 26. (Here ὥστε ἐλπίζειν, so senseless as to expect, would express the senselessness of expecting, without necessarily implying that you do expect.) Βέβηκεν, ὥστε πᾶν ἐν ἡσύχῳ, πάτερ, ἔξεστι φωνεῖν, he has gone, so that we can say everything in quiet. SOPH. O. C. 82. So Ph. 75, El. 1204. Οὕτως ἡμῖν δοκεῖ παντὸς ἄξια εἶναι, ὥστε πάντες τὸ καταλιπεῖν αὐτὰ μάλιστα φεύγομεν, so that we all especially avoid, etc. XEN. Mem. ii. 2, 3. Οὐχ ἧκεν· ὥσθ' οἱ Ἕλληνες ἐφρόντιζον. Id. An. ii. 3, 25. Εἰς τοῦτ' ἀπληστίας ἦλθον, ὥστ' οὐκ ἐξήρκεσεν αὐτοῖς ἔχειν τὴν κατὰ γῆν ἀρχήν, ἀλλὰ καὶ τὴν κατὰ θάλατταν δύναμιν οὕτως ἐπεθύμησαν λαβεῖν, ὥστε τοὺς συμμάχους τοὺς ἡμετέρους ἀφίστασαν. ISOC. xii. 103. Ταῦτα πεποίηκα ἀκόντων Ἀθηναίων, ὥστ', εἴπερ εὖ φρονεῖτε, τούτους μὲν ἐχθροὺς ὑπολήψεσθε, ἐμοὶ δὲ πιστεύσετε. DEM. xviii. 40. Οὕτως ἐναργές ἐστι, ὥσθ' εὑρήσετε. AESCHIN. i. 128. Ὥστ' ἐὰν τέτταρας μόνον πόλεις πείσῃς, καὶ τὰς ἄλλας πολλῶν κακῶν ἀπαλλάξεις. ISOC. v. 31. (Examples like ὥστ' . . . πιστεύσετε in DEM. xviii. 40 might be punctuated in this way.)

So οὕτω ὥστε in Herodotus (see 593); as ἐς πᾶν κακοῦ ἀπίκατο, οὕτω ὥστε ἀνάστατοι ἐγίνοντο, vii. 118.

602. As ὥστε in this construction has no effect upon the mood of its verb, it may have any construction that would be allowed in an independent sentence. It may thus take a potential optative or indicative with ἄν, a prohibitory subjunctive, an imperative, or an interrogative. E.g.

Ὥστ' οὐκ ἂν αὐτὸν γνωρίσαιμ' ἂν εἰσιδών. EUR. Or. 379. Παθὼν μὲν ἀντέδρων, ὥστ', εἰ φρονῶν ἔπρασσον, οὐδ' ἂν ὧδ' ἐγιγνόμην κακός. SOPH. O. C. 271. Ὥστ', εἰ μακρὰ ἡ περίοδος, μὴ θαυμάσῃς. PLAT. Phaedr. 274 A. Θνητὸς δ' Ὀρέστης· ὥστε μὴ λίαν στένε. SOPH. El. 1172. Ὥστε πόθεν ἴσασιν; so how do they know? DEM. xxix. 47. So οὐ μή and the subjunctive (296); οὕτως ἐπιτεθύμηκα ἀκοῦσαι, ὥστε . . . οὐ μή σου ἀπολειφθῶ, PLAT. Phaedr. 227 D (see 296, above).

603. Occasionally there is a change from the infinitive to a finite verb in a sentence after ὥστε, with a corresponding change in meaning; as in THUC. iii. 21, ὥστε πάροδον μὴ εἶναι παρὰ πύργον, ἀλλὰ δι' αὐτῶν μέσων διῄεσαν, i.e. the towers were built so as to allow no passage by a tower outside, but so THAT the men passed through the inside of them. (See 584.)

604. A few cases occur of a peculiar assimilation of a clause with ὥστε to a preceding optative in protasis, ὥστε having apparently the force of a conditional relative. E.g.

Εἴ τις τὴν γυναῖκα τὴν σὴν οὕτω θεραπεύσειεν ὥστε φιλεῖν αὐτὴν μᾶλλον ποιήσειεν ἑαυτὸν ἢ σέ, ἆρ' ἄν σε εὐφράναι; if one should court your wife so as to make her more fond of himself than of you, etc. XEN. Cyr. v. 5, 30 (two MSS. have ποιήσειν). So v. 3, 47 (εἴσοιτο). Εἴ τις χρῷτο τῷ ἀργυρίῳ ὥστε πριάμενος οἷον ἑταίραν διὰ ταύτην κάκιον

μὲν τὸ σῶμα ἔχοι, κάκιον δὲ τὴν ψυχήν, πῶς ἂν ὠφέλιμόν εἴη; Id.
Oec. i. 13. Καταγελαστότερον εἰ . . . ἡμεῖς εἰς τοσοῦτον μικροψυχίας
ἔλθοιμεν, ὥστε τὰ προστάγματα τούτων ὑπομείναιμεν (so Cod.
Urb. ; other Mss. ὑπομεῖναι). Isoc. vi. 84.

605. A few cases occur of ὥστε with the optative in indirect discourse. *E.g.*

Ἐλογίζοντο δὲ καὶ τὸ ἱππικόν, ὡς τὸ μὲν ἀντίπαλον πολύ, τὸ δὲ
αὐτῶν ὀλίγον εἴη, τὸ δὲ μέγιστον, ὅτι οἱ νεκροὶ ὑπὸ τῷ τείχει ἔκειντο,
ὥστε οὐδὲ κρείττοσιν οὖσι ῥᾴδιον εἴη ἀνελέσθαι. XEN. Hell. iii. 5,
23. See also Isoc. xvii. 11.

606. As the regular negative of the infinitive after ὥστε is μή, so
that of the indicative and potential optative is οὐ. In DEM. xix. 218
we have ὥστε μήτε . . . μήτε . . . μήτε . . . ἀλλὰ καὶ . . . εἶτα
τὴν εἰρήνην ἐποιήσασθε ἀγαπητῶς, where the force of a preceding
εἰ seems really to govern the verb, that of ὥστε being wasted in the
eight lines which separate the verb from it. In DEM. liv. 15, μηδ᾿
ὁτιοῦν ἔσται can be taken with εἰ. In SOPH. Tr. 575, ἔσται τοῦτο
κηλητήριον, ὥστε μήτιν᾿ εἰσιδὼν στέρξει γυναῖκα κεῖνος ἀντὶ σοῦ
πλέον, i.e. *a charm to prevent him from loving more than you any other
woman whom he may see*, ὥστε μή seems to have a final sense with the
future, like a final relative. Compare ὥστε μή with the infinitive in
PLAT. Gorg. 479 C (quoted in 587, 3).

῞Ωστε WITH THE PARTICIPLE.

607. (*a*) As a clause with ὥστε depending on an infinitive
in indirect discourse is generally assimilated to that infinitive,
so one depending on a participle in indirect discourse may be
assimilated to the participle. *E.g.*

Οὐδ᾿ οὕτως ἀγνώμονα οὐδ᾿ ἄτοπον οὐδένα (sc. ὁρῶ ὄντα) ὥστε, εἰ
μὴ ποιήσουσιν ἅπαντες ὅσ᾿ ἂν αὐτός, οὐ φάσκοντα ποιήσειν οὐδὲν
οὐδ᾿ αὐτόν, *nor do I see that any one is so unwise or absurd, that, if all
will not do whatever he does, he too refuses to do anything* (i.e. οὐδεὶς
οὕτως ἀγνώμων ἐστὶν ὥστε οὐ φάσκει). DEM. x. 40. Τὰ δὲ πράγματα
(ὁρῶ) εἰς τοῦτο προήκοντα, ὥστε ὅπως μὴ πεισόμεθα αὐτοὶ πρότερον
κακῶς σκέψασθαι δέον, *but I see things have come to this, that we must
(ὥστε δεῖ) consider how we may not ourselves suffer harm first.* Id. iii.
1. Ἐπιδείξω Ἀστύφιλον οὕτω σφόδρα μισοῦντα τοῦτον, ὥστε πολὺ
ἂν θᾶττον διαθέμενον μηδένα ποτὲ τῶν ἑαυτοῦ οἰκείων διαλεχθῆναι
Κλέωνι, μᾶλλον ἢ τὸν τούτου υἱὸν ποιησάμενον, *I will show that
Astyphilus so hates him, that he would much sooner have ordered in his
will that no one of his relatives should ever speak to Cleon, than have
adopted his son as his own* (πολὺ ἂν θᾶττον διέθετο). ISAE. ix. 16.
Other examples are [DEM.] Erot. 3 ; ISOC. iv. 64 ; PLAT. Rep. 519 A.

(*b*) In two cases there is a like assimilation to a participle
not in indirect discourse :—

Τῶν θεατῶν συμφιλονεικούντων ἐκείνῳ καὶ μισούντων τοῦτον, ὥστε τῶν χορῶν τὸν μὲν ἐπαινούντων, τοῦ δ' ἀκροάσασθαι οὐκ ἐθελόντων. AND. iv. 20. Συγγνώμην ἔχειν εἰ, προεληλυθὼς εἰς τοῦτο ὥστε ὑπὸ τῶν ἐμαυτοῦ δούλων ὑβρισθεὶς, οὐ δύναμαι κατασχεῖν, κ.τ.λ. DEM. xlv. 83.

The last examples seem to show that clauses with ὥστε can be assimilated to a preceding participle as we have seen them assimilated to an optative (604). Compare with this construction Isoc. iv. 21, οὐδεὶς γὰρ ἂν ἑτέραν πόλιν ἐπιδείξειε τοσοῦτον ἐν τῷ πολέμῳ τῷ κατὰ γῆν ὑπερέχουσαν, ὅσον τὴν ἡμετέραν ἐν τοῖς κινδύνοις τοῖς κατὰ θάλατταν διαφέρουσαν.

Ὡς USED LIKE ὥστε.

608. In their original use ὡς and ὥς τε are related precisely as ὅς and ὅς τε in Homer. But in consecutive sentences ὥστε gradually gained almost exclusive control, so that ὡς here became very rare. Ὡς occurs chiefly in Aeschylus, Sophocles, Herodotus, and Xenophon, where it is used in the same constructions and in the same sense as ὥστε. *E.g.*

(With Infin.) Ἥκουσιν ἐκφυγόντες· ὡς στένειν πόλιν Περσῶν. AESCH. Pers. 510. Πεπωκώς γ', ὡς θρασύνεσθαι μᾶλλον, βρότειον αἷμα, κῶμος ἐν δόμοις μένει, *having drunk of mortals' blood so as to be more emboldened, a band of revellers abides in the house.* Id. Ag. 1188. So Pers. 437, Ag. 546, Eum. 36, 427, 799, 895. Σύμμετρος γὰρ ὡς κλύειν, *for he is near enough for us to hear.* SOPH. O. T. 84. Οὐδ' ὑπὸ ζυγῷ λόφον δικαίως εἶχον, ὡς· στέργειν ἐμέ. Id. Ant. 292. So Tr. 1125. Οὐκ ἐς τοῦτο ἀφροσύνης ἀπικόμενος ὡς δόξαι τὴν ἑωυτοῦ δύναμιν περιέσεσθαι τῆς βασιλέος. HDT. iii. 146. Ὑψηλὸν δὲ οὕτω δή τι λέγεται, ὡς τὰς κορυφὰς αὐτοῦ οὐχ οἷά τε εἶναι ἰδέσθαι, *and it (the mountain) is said to be so high, that it is not possible to see its summits.* Id. iv. 184. Ὁ ποταμὸς τοσοῦτος τὸ βάθος, ὡς μηδὲ τὰ δόρατα ὑπερέχειν τοῦ βάθους. XEN. An. iii. 5, 7. So ii. 3, 10. Φέρονται κώθωνα, ὡς ἀπὸ τοῦ ποταμοῦ ἀρύσασθαι. Id. Cyr. i. 2, 8. Ἐν τῷ ἀσφαλεῖ ἤδη ἔσομαι, ὡς μηδὲν ἂν ἔτι κακὸν παθεῖν. Ib. viii. 7, 27. See iv. 2, 8. Οὕτω γὰρ δοκοῦμεν παρεσκευάσθαι ὡς, ἢν μὲν ἀληθεύητε, ἱκανοὶ εἶναι ὑμᾶς εὖ ποιεῖν· ἢν δὲ ἐξαπατᾶτε, οὕτω νομίζομεν ἔχειν ὡς οὐχ ἡμᾶς ἐφ' ὑμῖν ἔσεσθαι, ἀλλὰ μᾶλλον ὑμᾶς ἐφ' ἡμῖν γενήσεσθαι. Ib. iv. 2, 13. (In the last clauses we have ὡς in indirect discourse, like ὥστε in 594, the direct form being οὐχ ἡμεῖς ἐσόμεθα, ἀλλὰ μᾶλλον ὑμεῖς γενήσεσθε. Most Mss., however, have γενέσθαι.)

(With Indic.) Πρὸς τάδ' ὡς Σούσων μὲν ἄστυ πᾶν κενανδρίαν στένει. AESCH. Pers. 730. Οὕτως ἔχει γ' ἡ πίστις, ὡς τὸ μὲν δοκεῖν ἔνεστι, πείρᾳ δ' οὐ προσωμίλησά πω, *so stands my confidence, that belief is in it, while I have had nothing to do yet with testing it.* SOPH.

Tr. 590. Οὕτω δή τι κλεινὴ ἐγένετο ὡς καὶ οἱ πάντες Ἕλληνες Ῥοδώπιος τὸ οὔνομα ἐξέμαθον, i.e. *so that all the Greeks came to know well the name of Rhodopis.* HDT. ii. 135. Τούτῳ προσφιλέες οὕτω δή τι ἐγένοντο ὡς σφέας ἐκέλευε τῆς ἑαυτοῦ χώρης οἰκῆσαι. HDT. i. 163. So iii. 130. Οὕτω μοι προθύμως ἐβοήθησας ὡς νῦν τὸ μὲν ἐπ᾽ ἐμοὶ οἴχομαι, τὸ δ᾽ ἐπὶ σοὶ σέσωσμαι. XEN. Cyr. v. 4, 11. Τοσούτῳ πλεονεκτήσει ὡς πεινήσας τῶν ἡδίστων σιτίων τεύξεται. Ib. vii. 5, 81. So Hell. iv. 4, 16.

609. Besides the authors above mentioned, Euripides has one example of ὡς with the infinitive like ὥστε, Cycl. 647 ; Thucydides one, vii. 34 ; and Plato one, Rep. 365 D. We have ὡς with the indicative in PLAT. Men. 71 A ; and with the participle in XEN. Cyr. vii. 5, 46, and PLAT. Tim. 56 C (ὡς here having both the participle and the infinitive).

For ὡς with the infinitive after the comparative and ἤ, see 764.

Ἐφ᾽ ᾧ AND ἐφ᾽ ᾧτε WITH THE INFINITIVE AND THE FUTURE INDICATIVE.

610. 1. Ἐφ᾽ ᾧ and ἐφ᾽ ᾧτε, *on condition that, for the purpose of,* take the infinitive, like ὥστε in some of its senses. *E.g.*

Εἶπεν ὅτι σπείσασθαι βούλοιτο, ἐφ᾽ ᾧ μήτε αὐτὸς τοὺς Ἕλληνας ἀδικεῖν μήτε ἐκείνους καίειν τὰς οἰκίας, λαμβάνειν τε τἀπιτήδεια ὅσων δέοιντο. XEN. An. iv. 4, 6. Πῶς ἂν οὗτος ἐθέλοι τὰ ἀλλότρια ἀποστερεῖν ἐφ᾽ ᾧ κακόδοξος εἶναι ; Id. Ag. iv. 1. Ἀφίεμέν σε, ἐπὶ τούτῳ μέντοι, ἐφ᾽ ᾧτε μηκέτι φιλοσοφεῖν, *on condition that you will no longer be a philosopher.* PLAT. Ap. 29 C. Αἱρεθέντες ἐφ᾽ ᾧτε ξυγγράψαι νόμους, καθ᾽ οὕστινας πολιτεύσοιντο, *for the purpose of compiling laws.* XEN. Hell. ii. 3, 11. (For πολιτεύσοιντο, see 574.) Διωμολογήθη αὐτῷ ἀποσταλήσεσθαι Ἀθήναζε τοῦ ἐνιαυτοῦ ἑκάστου μνᾶς εἴκοσι, ἐφ᾽ ᾧτε βοηθήσειν τοῖς Ἀμφισσεῦσιν. AESCHIN. iii. 114. (For the future infinitive, see 113.)

2. Herodotus and Thucydides sometimes have ἐφ᾽ ᾧ or ἐφ᾽ ᾧτε, *on condition that,* with the future indicative. *E.g.*

Ἐπὶ τούτῳ δὲ ὑπεξίσταμαι τῆς ἀρχῆς, ἐφ᾽ ᾧτε ὑπ᾽ οὐδενὸς ὑμέων ἄρξομαι, *I withdraw upon this condition, that I shall be ruled by none of you.* HDT. iii. 83. Τούτοισι δ᾽ ὦν πίσυνος ἐὼν κατήγαγε, ἐφ᾽ ᾧτε οἱ ἀπόγονοι αὐτοῦ ἱροφάνται τῶν θεῶν ἔσονται. Id. vii. 153. Καὶ τὴν Βοιωτίαν ἐξέλιπον Ἀθηναῖοι πᾶσαν, σπονδὰς ποιησάμενοι ἐφ᾽ ᾧ τοὺς ἄνδρας κομιοῦνται. THUC. i. 113. Ξυνέβησαν ἐφ᾽ ᾧτε ἐξίασιν ἐκ Πελοποννήσου ὑπόσπονδοι καὶ μηδέποτε ἐπιβήσονται αὐτῆς, *they made an agreement with the condition that they should depart from Peloponnesus under truce, and never again set foot in it.* Id. i. 103.

Temporal Particles signifying Until and Before.

A. Ἕως,[1] ὄφρα, εἰς ὅ OR εἰσόκε, ἔστε, ἄχρι, μέχρι, UNTIL.

611. All of these words are used also in the sense of *while*, *so long as*, and have the constructions of ordinary relative clauses (514). In common with *dum*, *donec*, and *quoad* in Latin, and *while* or *whiles* in Elizabethan English,[2] they mean not only *during the time when*, but also *up to the time when*. As relatives, in the former sense they can have an antecedent like τέως, *so long*, ἕως etc. meaning *as ;* in the latter sense they can have one like μέχρι τούτου, *down to that time*, ἕως etc. supplementing this by *at which* or *when*. The idea of a clause with *until* is that the action (or negation) of the leading clause continues to a time *at which* that of the dependent clause takes place. That the former action then *ceases* is an inference generally made, but not positively implied in the language, and not necessary. Our word *until* thus includes what the Greek may express by μέχρι τούτου ἕως or (omitting the antecedent) by ἕως alone.

Τέως is occasionally used like ἕως, as in DEM. xxi. 16.

612. A clause with *until* referring to an actual past occurrence (613) is simply a temporal clause of this peculiar character, with the construction of a relative clause with a definite antecedent (519). But when it refers to the future, it becomes a conditional relative clause, and μαχοῦμαι ἕως ἂν τὴν πόλιν ἕλω, *I shall (continue to) fight to the time at which I shall take the city*, has the conditional force which comes from the indefinite antecedent ; for even if μέχρι τούτου were inserted here, it would denote no definite period, but only one limited or *conditioned* by the future capture of the city. The actual apodosis to the condition is not μαχοῦμαι alone, but rather the whole implied idea, *I shall go on fighting* to the future time, the limit of which is set by ἕως ἂν ἕλω. It has been seen (486 ; 490) that ordinary conditional clauses may condition not their expressed leading clause, but one which the context implies ; as ξυμμαχίαν ποιοῦμεν, ἤν τις ἐφ' ἡμᾶς ἴῃ, *we are making an alliance*, (to be ready) *in case any one shall attack us*. Again, a conditional clause may refer to an object which is aimed at in the action of the leading verb ; as Πάτροκλον ἔφεπε ἵππους, εἴ κέν μιν ἕλῃς, *turn your horses on P., if haply you may take him*, i.e. *that you may take him, if haply you may* (487, 1). In like manner a conditional relative clause with *until* is

---

[1] In Homer, where the form ἕως would seldom suit the verse, εἵως or εἷος is commonly written.

[2] "He shall conceal it *whiles* (= *until*) you are willing it shall come to note." Shakespeare. *Twelfth Night*, iv. 3.

very apt to refer to an object aimed at, and thus to become at
once final, relative, and conditional : thus in Il. iii. 291 (see 613,
3), it is distinctly implied that the *end of the war* (τέλος πολέμοιο)
is a condition which is to limit the time of fighting, and also an
object at which the fighting aims. The same is true in general
of the other forms of conditional relative sentence which the
clause with *until* may take. It will be seen (614, 2) that in the
Odyssey ἕως develops a peculiar force in this direction, which
makes it almost a final particle.

613. ("Εως.) 1. When ἕως, *until*, refers to a definite
past action, it takes the indicative, usually the aorist. *E.g.*

Νῆχον πάλιν, εἷος ἐπῆλθον εἰς ποταμόν, *I swam on again until I
came into a river.* Od. vii. 280. Αὐτὰρ ὁ πεζὸς θῦνε διὰ προμάχων,
εἵως φίλον ὤλεσε θυμόν. Il. xi. 341. So Od. v. 123. Οἰμωγὴ
κατεῖχε πελαγίαν ἅλα, ἕως κελαινῆς νυκτὸς ὄμμ' ἀφείλετο, *until the
eye of dark night interrupted.* Aesch. Pers. 426. Πίνει ἕως ἐθέρμην'
αὐτὸν ἀμφιβᾶσα φλὸξ οἴνου. Eur. Alc. 758. Ἔμειναν ἕως ἀφίκοντο
οἱ στρατηγοί. Xen. Hell. i. 1, 29. Καὶ τοῦτ' ἐποίουν ἕως ἐκ τῆς
χώρας ἀπῆν. Id. Cyr. iii. 3, 4. Οὐ πρότερον ἐπαύσαντο, ἕως τὴν
πόλιν εἰς στάσεις κατέστησαν. Lys. xxv. 26. Μέχρι τούτου φίλος
ὠνομάζετο, ἕως προὔδωκεν Ὄλυνθον. Dem. xviii. 48.

In the last two examples πρότερον and μέχρι τούτου are antecedents
of ἕως, *until*, as τέως often corresponds to ἕως, *while*.

2. When a clause with ἕως, *until*, refers to a result
which was *not attained* in past time in consequence of the
non-fulfilment of a condition, it takes a past tense of the
indicative, like a conditional relative clause in a similar
case (528). *E.g.*

Ἡδέως ἂν τούτῳ ἔτι διελεγόμην, ἕως αὐτῷ τὴν τοῦ Ἀμφίονος ἀπέ-
δωκα ῥῆσιν ἀντὶ τῆς τοῦ Ζήθου, *I should gladly have continued to talk
with him, until I had paid him back Amphion's speech in return for
Zethus's.* Plat. Gorg. 506 B. Οὐκ ἂν ἐπαυόμην, ἕως ἀπεπειράθην
τῆς σοφίας ταυτησί. Id. Crat. 396 C. Ἐπισχὼν ἄν, ἕως οἱ πλεῖστοι
τῶν εἰωθότων γνώμην ἀπεφήναντο, . . . ἡσυχίαν ἂν ἦγον, i.e. *I
should have waited until most of the regular speakers had declared their
opinion, etc.* Dem. iv. 1. (For ἄν here, see 223.) So Ar. Pac. 71.
In Lys. xxii. 12 we have ἕως ἐπέλιπε after ἐχρῆν φαίνεσθαι.

The leading verb must be an indicative with ἄν, or some other
form implying the non-fulfilment of a condition. (See 559.)

3. When a clause with ἕως refers to the future, and
depends on a verb of future time (not an optative), ἕως has
ἄν or κέ and the subjunctive, like a conditional relative
clause (529). *E.g.*

Μαχήσομαι αὖθι μένων, εἴως κε τέλος πολέμοιο κιχείω, *I shall remain here and fight, until I (shall) find an end of the war.* Il. iii. 291. So xxiv. 183. Ἔως δ᾽ ἂν οὖν πρὸς τοῦ παρόντος ἐκμάθῃς, ἔχ᾽ ἐλπίδα, *until you learn the whole from him who was present, continue to hope.* SOPH. O. T. 834. So AR. Nub. 1489. Μέχρι γὰρ τούτου νομίζω χρῆναι κατηγορεῖν, ἕως ἂν θανάτου δόξῃ τῷ φεύγοντι ἄξια εἰργάσθαι, *for so far do I think I ought to proceed in my accusation, until it shall appear that deeds deserving death have been done by the defendant.* LYS. xii. 37. Δεῖ μὴ περιμένειν ἕως ἂν ἐπιστῶσιν, *we must not wait until they are upon us.* ISOC. iv. 165. Οὐκ ἀναμένομεν ἕως ἂν ἡ ἡμετέρα χώρα κακῶται, *we are not waiting until our land shall be ravaged* (i.e. *until the ravaging shall be going on*). XEN. Cyr. iii. 3, 18. The present subjunctive is rare ; but when it is needed, it is unobjectionable : see THUC. i. 90 (quoted in 614, 1).

4. When a clause with ἕως refers to the future and depends on an optative with ἄν, it generally has the optative (without ἄν) by assimilation, like a conditional relative clause (531). *E.g.*

Εἰ δὲ πάνυ σπουδάζοι φαγεῖν, εἴποιμ᾽ ἂν ὅτι παρὰ ταῖς γυναιξίν ἐστιν, ἕως παρατείναιμι τοῦτον, *but if he should be very eager to eat, I should tell him that his dinner is with the women, until I put him to torture.* XEN. Cyr. i. 3, 11. Καὶ τὸ μὲν ἂν ἐξαλείφοιεν, τὸ δὲ πάλιν ἐγγράφοιεν, ἕως ὅτι μάλιστα ἀνθρώπεια ἤθη θεοφιλῆ ποιήσειαν, *and they would blot out one thing and again put in another, until they made human characters as pleasing as possible to God.* PLAT. Rep. 501 B. Ὡσαύτως ἂν διδοίης (λόγον), ἕως ἐπί τι ἱκανὸν ἔλθοις. Id. Phaed. 101 D. So after an infinitive depending on an optative ; as δέοιτό γ᾽ ἂν αὐτοῦ μένειν ἕως ἀπέλθοις, *he would ask him to remain until you departed (should depart).* XEN. Cyr. v. 3, 13. In Od. ii. 77 we have ἕως κε with the optative (542) : τόφρα γὰρ ἂν κατὰ ἄστυ ποτιπτυσσοίμεθα μύθῳ χρήματ᾽ ἀπαιτίζοντες, ἕως κ᾽ ἀπὸ πάντα δοθείη. In PLAT. Phaed. 101 D, ἕως ἂν σκέψαιο represents ἕως ἂν σκέψωμαι of direct discourse (see 702).

The optative with ἕως is most common after past tenses, in the construction of 614.

5. When the clause introduced by ἕως, *until,* depends upon a verb denoting a *customary* or *repeated action* or a *general truth,* and refers in a general way to any act or acts of a given class, it takes ἄν and the subjunctive after primary tenses, and the simple optative after secondary tenses. (See 532.) *E.g.*

Ἃ δ᾽ ἂν ἀσύντακτα ᾖ, ἀνάγκη ταῦτα ἀεὶ πράγματα παρέχειν, ἕως ἂν χώραν λάβῃ, *they must always make trouble until they are put in order.* XEN. Cyr. iv. 5, 37. Ποιοῦμεν ταῦθ᾽ ἑκάστοθ᾽, ἕως ἂν αὐτὸν ἐμβάλωμεν ἐς κακόν, *we always treat him thus, until we cast him into trouble.* Aʀ. Nub. 1458. Περιεμένομεν οὖν ἑκάστοτε, ἕως ἀνοιχθείη τὸ δεσμωτήριον, *we waited every day until the prison was opened.* Pʟᴀᴛ. Phaed. 59 D.

614. (*Final use of* ἕως.) 1. It will be seen by the examples under 613 (see the first under 3 and the first three under 4) that the clause with ἕως very often implies a *purpose*, the attainment of which is aimed at or expected. When such a clause, implying a purpose which would originally be expressed by a subjunctive, depends on a past tense, it generally takes the optative; but the subjunctive also may be used, to retain the mood in which the purpose would be originally conceived, as in final clauses (318). *E.g.*

Οὐδ᾽ ἔτλη πόσιος εἰρύσθαι μέγα δῶμα διαμπερές, εἷος ἵκοιτο, *nor did she dare to guard her husband's great house constantly until he should come.* Od. xxiii. 150. Ἡσύχαζε τῷ στράτῳ, ἕως τοῖς Ἀμπρακιώταις δέοι βοηθεῖν, *he kept quiet until it should be necessary to help the Ambraciots.* Tʜᴜᴄ. iii. 102. (The present optative is rare.) So Lʏs. xiii. 25. Σπονδὰς ἐποιήσαντο, ἕως ἀπαγγελθείη τὰ λεχθέντα εἰς Λακεδαίμονα, *they made a truce, (to continue) until what had been said should be announced at Sparta.* Xᴇɴ. Hell. iii. 2, 20. (Here ἕως ἂν ἀπαγγελθῇ might have been used, as in the following examples.) Ἕως δ᾽ ἂν ταῦτα διαπράξωνται, φυλακὴν καὶ μισθὸν τοῖς φρουροῖς ἐξ μηνῶν κατέλιπε. Ib. v. 3, 25. Ἀλλ᾽ ἐπισχεῖν (τοὺς πρέσβεις ἐκέλευεν) μέχρι τοσούτου, ἕως ἂν τὸ τεῖχος ἱκανὸν αἴρωσιν ὥστε ἀπομάχεσθαι, *but he bade them detain the ambassadors until they* (the Athenians) *should be getting their wall high enough to defend.* Tʜᴜᴄ. i. 90. (Most editors emend αἴρωσιν to the aorist ἄρωσιν, which with ἕως would mean *until they should get the wall high enough,* the former being less definite and exact in its time, and therefore more appropriate here.)

For the intermediate form of ἕως ἄν with the optative in such sentences, see Sᴏᴘʜ. Tr. 687, Aɴᴅ. i. 81, Isᴏᴄ. xvii. 15 (in 702).

2. In five passages in the Odyssey ἕως with the optative after a past tense has an unusually strong final force, so that it appears almost like a final particle.

Πέμπε δέ μιν πρὸς δώματ᾽ Ὀδυσσῆος, εἵως Πηνελόπειαν ὀδυρομένην γοόωσαν παύσειε κλαυθμοῖο, *she sent her to the house of Ulysses, (to the end) that she might cause Penelope to cease her lamenting.* iv. 799. Ὦρσε δ᾽ ἐπὶ κραιπνὸν Βορέην πρὸ δὲ κύματ᾽ ἔαξεν, ἕως ὅ γε Φαιήκεσσι φιληρέτμοισι μιγείη, *and she roused swift Boreas and broke the waves before him, that Ulysses might come to the oar-loving Phaeacians.* v. 385. Μοχλὸν ὑπὸ σποδοῦ ἤλασα πολλῆς, εἵως θερμαίνοιτο, *I pushed the club under the deep ashes, that it might be heated (to remain until it should be heated).* ix. 375. So δῶκεν ἔλαιον, εἵως χυτλώσαιτο, vi. 79; and ἀρώμενος εἷος ἵκοιτο, xix. 367.

In none of these cases will *until* express the final force of the clause with ἕως. It appears as if ἕως here began the same course by which ὄφρα, ὡς, and ὅπως became final particles (312-314), but did not complete the change.

615. (Ὄφρα.) In epic poetry ὄφρα, *until*, is used like ἕως. *E.g.*

Ὡς μὲν Θρήικας ἄνδρας ἐπῴχετο Τυδέος υἱός, ὄφρα δυώδεκ᾽ ἔπεφνεν, *until he had slain twelve.* Il. x. 488. Ἡρχ᾽ ἴμεν, ὄφρ᾽ ἀφίκοντο κατὰ στρατόν, ᾗ μιν ἀνώγει. Il. xiii. 329. Ἧιεν, ὄφρα μέγα σπέος ἵκετο. Od. v. 57. (See 613, 1.)

Ἀλλὰ μέν᾽, ὄφρα κέ τοι μελιηδέα οἶνον ἐνείκω, *but wait, until I shall bring you honey-sweet wine.* Il. vi. 258. Τόφρα δ᾽ ἐπὶ Τρώεσσι τίθει κράτος, ὄφρ᾽ ἂν Ἀχαιοὶ υἱὸν ἐμὸν τίσωσιν, ὀφέλλωσίν τέ ἑ τιμῇ. Il. i. 509. So Il. xv. 232. (See 613, 3.)

Νωλεμέως δ᾽ ἐχόμην, ὄφρ᾽ ἐξεμέσειεν ὀπίσσω ἱστὸν καὶ τρόπιν αὖτις, *I clung steadfastly, until she* (Charybdis) *should vomit forth again the mast and keel.* Od. xii. 437. (See 614, 1.)

616. (Εἰς ὅ κε and ἐς ὅ.) Homer uses εἰς ὅ κε (or εἰσόκε), *until*, like ἕως κε, with the subjunctive, and once with the optative. Herodotus uses ἐς ὅ and ἐς οὗ, *until*, like ἕως, with the indicative, and ἐς ὅ ἄν with the subjunctive. *E.g.*

Μίμνετε εἰς ὅ κε ἄστυ μέγα Πριάμοιο ἕλωμεν, *wait until we capture Priam's great city.* Il. ii. 331. Ὕψι δ᾽ ἐπ᾽ εὐνάων ὁρμίσσομεν, εἰς ὅ κεν ἔλθῃ νὺξ ἀμβρότη, *and we will moor them far out by stones, until divine night shall come.* Il. xiv. 77. In Il. xv. 70 we have εἰς ὅ κ᾽ Ἀχαιοὶ Ἴλιον ἕλοιεν, depending on an optative with ἄν (613, 4 ; 542).

Οὗτος δὲ ἀνηκούστεέ τε καὶ λόγον εἶχε οὐδένα, ἐς ὃ ἔλαβε τὴν δίκην, *but he disobeyed and paid no attention to me, until he got his punishment.* HDT. i. 115. Ὁ Δηιόκης ἦν πολλὸς αἰνεόμενος, ἐς ὃ τοῦτον καταινέουσι βασιλέα σφίσι εἶναι. Id. i. 98. So i. 158, 202 ; v. 92 ; vi. 75. Ἀπεῖχον τῆς ἐξευρέσιος οὐδὲν ἔλασσον, ἐς οὗ δὴ Λίχης ἀνεῦρε. Id. i. 67. (Many editors change ἐς οὗ to ἐς ὅ.) In ii. 143, ἕως οὗ ἀπέδεξαν ἁπάσας αὐτάς, *until they had shown them all,* ἕως οὗ of the Mss. is generally emended to ἐς ὅ. Ἀλλ᾽ αὐτὰ ἐγὼ τῷ Ἕλληνι ξείνῳ φυλάξω, ἐς ὃ ἄν αὐτὸς ἐλθὼν ἐκεῖνος ἀπαγαγέσθαι ἐθέλῃ, *I shall keep them until he comes himself and wishes to take them away.* Id. ii. 115.

A singular case of ἐς ὅ occurs in THUC. v. 66, ἐς ὃ ἐμέμνηντο, *as far back as they remembered* (Schol. μετὰ τὴν τῶν ἀνθρώπων μνήμην).

617. (Ἔστε.) Ἔστε, *until*, is not found in Homer, but is used like ἕως in tragedy, in Attic prose (especially in Xenophon), and in Herodotus. *E.g.*

Χρόνον τάδ᾽ ἦν τοσοῦτον, ἔστ᾽ ἐν αἰθέρι μέσῳ κατέστη λαμπρὸς ἡλίου κύκλος καὶ καῦμ᾽ ἔθαλπε. SOPH. Ant. 415 : so El. 753 ; AESCH. Prom. 457. Ξυνεῖρον ἀπιόντες, ἔστε ἐπὶ ταῖς σκηναῖς ἐγένοντο, *they marched away without stopping, until they came to the tents.* XEN. Cyr. vii. 5, 6 ; so An. iii. 4, 49.

Τὴν παροῦσαν ἀντλήσω τύχην, ἔστ᾽ ἂν Διὸς φρόνημα λωφήσῃ

χόλου. AESCH. Prom. 375; so 697. Ἄφθογγον εἶναι τὸν παλαμναῖον νόμος, ἔστ᾽ ἂν σφαγαὶ καθαιμάξωσι, *it is the law that the murderer shall be speechless until streams of blood have been poured upon him.* Id. Eum. 448. Αὐτοῦ τῇδε μενέομεν ἔστ᾽ ἂν καὶ τελευτήσωμεν. HDT. vii. 141. Περιμένετε ἔστ᾽ ἂν ἐγὼ ἔλθω. XEN. An. v. 1, 4. Ἐπιμεῖναι κελεύσαντες ἔστε βουλεύσαιντο, ἐθύοντο, *bidding them wait until they had consulted, they made sacrifice.* Id. An. v. 5, 2. (Ἔστ᾽ ἂν βουλεύσωνται might have been retained from the direct form, as in the next example.) Ἀπεκρίνατο φυλάττειν αὐτά, ἔστ᾽ ἂν αὐτὸς ἐλθὼν λάβῃ τὰ δῶρα, *until he should come and take the gifts.* Id. Hell. iii. 1, 15. So An. vii. 1, 33; HDT. viii. 4.

Ὁπότε ὥρα εἴη ἀρίστου, ἀνέμενεν αὐτοὺς ἔστε ἐμφάγοιέν τι, ὡς μὴ βουλιμιῷεν, *he always waited until they had eaten something.* XEN. Cyr. viii. 1, 44.

618. (Ἄχρι and μέχρι.) Ἄχρι and μέχρι, *until,* are used like ἕως, but chiefly in prose and in later Greek. *E.g.*

Καὶ ταῦτα ἐποίουν μέχρι σκότος ἐγένετο, *until darkness came on.* XEN. An. iv. 2, 4; so iii. 4, 8. Εἱστήκει μέχρι ἕως ἐγένετο. PLAT. Symp. 220 D.

Μέχρι δ᾽ ἂν ἐγὼ ἥκω, αἱ σπονδαὶ μενόντων, *but until I come, let the truce remain.* XEN. An. ii. 3, 24; so i. 4, 13. Εἶπε τοῖς προφύλαξι κελεύειν τοὺς κήρυκας περιμένειν ἄχρι ἂν σχολάσῃ, *to wait until he should find leisure.* Ib. ii. 3, 2. Μέχρι δὲ τοῦτο ἴδωμεν, μενέομεν παρ᾽ ἡμῖν αὐτοῖσι, *but until we see this, we shall remain by ourselves.* HDT. iv. 119 (for the omission of ἄν see 620). Herodotus prefers the form with οὗ (619).

Ἄχρι is much less common in this sense than μέχρι. The forms ἄχρις and μέχρις are not used by the best writers.

619. Ἄχρι οὗ and μέχρι οὗ are used like ἄχρι and μέχρι. *E.g.*

Τῶν δὲ ταῦτα πραξάντων, ἄχρι οὗ ὅδε ὁ λόγος ἐγράφετο, Τισίφονος πρεσβύτατος ὢν τῶν ἀδελφῶν τὴν ἀρχὴν εἶχε. XEN. Hell. vi. 4, 37. So Cyr. v. 4, 16; THUC. v. 26; HDT. i. 187, vii. 60. Τοὺς Ἕλληνας ἀπελύσατο δουλείας, ὥστ᾽ ἐλευθέρους εἶναι μέχρι οὗ πάλιν αὐτοὶ αὑτοὺς κατεδουλώσαντο. PLAT. Menex. 245 A.

Παραδίδωμι ἐντειλάμενος θεῖναί μιν ἐς ἔρημον ὄρος καὶ φυλάσσειν ἄχρι οὗ τελευτήσῃ, *to watch him until he dies.* HDT. i. 117 (see 614). Κατατίθεται ἐς Τένεδον μέχρι οὗ τοῖς Ἀθηναίοις τι δόξῃ, *until the Athenians shall pass some vote about them* (see 620). THUC. iii. 28.

620. (Omission of ἄν.) Ἄν is sometimes omitted after ἕως and the other particles meaning *until* (including πρίν), when they take the subjunctive. This is most frequent in tragic poetry, but it occurs sometimes with ἐς ὅ or ἐς οὗ in Herodotus, and with μέχρι and μέχρι (or ἄχρι) οὗ in Herodotus and Thucydides. *E.g.*

Ἕως τὸ χαίρειν καὶ τὸ λυπεῖσθαι μάθῃς. SOPH. Aj. 555. Ἀρήγετ᾽ ἔστ᾽ ἐγὼ μελnθῶ. Ib. 1183. So O. C. 77, Tr. 148, Ph. 764. Ἐς οὗ ἀποθάνωσι ἢ σφι παρευρεθῇ τι ἄδικον, μέχρι τούτου. HDT. iii. 31. Μηδένα ἐκβῆναι μέχρι πλοῦς γένηται, *that nobody should leave the ship before she sailed.* Thuc. i. 137. Αὐτοὺς ἐς φυλακὴν διεκόμισαν, μέχρι οὗ Ἀθήναζε πεμφθῶσιν. Id. iv. 46 ; see iv. 16 and 41, and iii. 28 (quoted in 619). See also μέχρι δὲ τοῦτο ἴδωμεν, Hdt. iv. 119, and ἄχρι οὗ τελευτήσῃ, Id. i. 117.

The only case in Homer of this omission of κέ or ἄν is the doubtful one, ἔχει κότον ὄφρα τελέσσῃ, Il. i. 82, where ὄφρα may perhaps be final. (See 468.)

For πρίν without ἄν with the subjunctive, even in Attic prose, see 648.

B. Πρίν, *BEFORE, UNTIL.*[1]

Meaning and General Use of πρίν.

621. Πρίν was originally a comparative adverb (= πρότερον and πάρος), formed from πρό and meaning *before.* It appears in the usual adverbial relations ; as πρίν μοι ὑπέσχετο, *he once promised me ;* πρὶν ὤν, *having been of old ;* ἐν τῷ πρὶν χρόνῳ, *in the former time ;* and it once takes the genitive like a preposition in Pind. Py. iv. 43, πρὶν ὥρας, *before its time.* With the infinitive it originally expressed a simple temporal relation, πρὶν ἐλθεῖν being the equivalent of the later πρὸ τοῦ ἐλθεῖν, *before going.* With the finite moods πρίν always expresses a *limit* of time and means *until*, like ἕως, having become a conjunction, not losing, however, its original meaning of *before.* From this original comparative meaning, πρίν has a negative force, implying that something does or does not happen *before* (i.e. *in the absence of*) another event ; so that οὔπω or μήπω with a temporal participle may generally be substituted for πρίν and the infinitive. Thus, in ναῖε δὲ Πήδαιον πρὶν ἐλθεῖν υἷας Ἀχαιῶν, Il. xiii. 172, for πρὶν ἐλθεῖν, *before they came,* we could substitute οὔπω ἐλθόντων, etc. So πρὶν ἄν with the subjunctive is often interchangeable with ἢν μή, and always implies it ; thus μὴ ἀπέλθῃς πρὶν ἂν ἀκούσῃς, *do not depart until you hear,* implies ἢν μὴ ἀκούσῃς, *without hearing.* One result of this negative character of πρίν is its strong affinity for the aorist, the tense which denotes simple *occurrence.* (See *Am. Jour. Phil.* ii. pp. 466 ff.)

622. In Homeric Greek πρίν generally takes the primitive construction with the infinitive without regard to the nature of the leading verb. In lyric poetry, Herodotus, and Attic Greek, πρίν takes the infinitive chiefly when the leading clause is affirmative ; otherwise, it takes one of the finite moods, like ἕως, having the sense of *until.* But, while the indicative may sometimes follow πρίν, meaning *until*, when the leading clause is affirmative, the

[1] *Geschichtliche Entwickelung der Constructionen mit* Πρίν, von Josef Sturm : Heft 3 of Schanz's *Beiträge.*

subjunctive and optative are never used unless the leading clause
is negative or involves a negative idea.

Development of the Constructions with πρίν.

623. The Attic uses of πρίν with the indicative, subjunctive,
and optative, are seen in a primitive stage of development in
Homer. The construction of πρίν itself with the indicative was
yet unknown ; but four cases of πρίν γ' ὅτε with the indicative
show a tendency in this direction. Six cases of πρίν (without ἄν
or κέ) with the subjunctive and one with the optative (in indirect
discourse) mark the beginning of the later usage with these moods.
On the other hand, 81 cases of πρίν with the infinitive show the
prevailing Homeric construction. Here, as in all periods of the
language, when πρίν takes the infinitive, we have simply a statement of fact, that one thing precedes another ; in ναῖε δὲ Πήδαιον
πρὶν ἐλθεῖν υἶας Ἀχαιῶν, and he dwelt in Pedaeum before the coming
of the sons of the Greeks, πρὶν ἐλθεῖν implies no more than πρὸ
ἀφίξεως or the later πρὸ τοῦ ἐλθεῖν. Any further idea that may
be implied comes from the context, and is not found in the
words. This use of πρίν has little analogy in Greek syntax, its
nearest parallel being the later use of ὥστε or ὡς with the infinitive.
The simplest theory, which best suits the Homeric usage, seems
to be that πρίν has a " quasi-prepositional" relation to the infinitive, which is a verbal noun, a relation the same in effect as
that of πρό in πρὸ τοῦ ἐλθεῖν in the later Attic construction.
(See XEN. Mem. ii. 6, 6, and DEM. xix. 73.)   A similar use of
ἀντί with the infinitive in a few cases in Herodotus (see 803)
shows a tendency to go further in the same direction.

624. The Homeric language was generally contented with
the simple πρίν and the infinitive, even when it was implied that
the clause with πρίν set a limit to the action (or negation) of the
leading clause, i.e. when πρίν could be expressed by until. So in
Il. xxi. 100, πρὶν Πάτροκλον ἐπισπεῖν αἴσιμον ἦμαρ, τόφρα τί μοι
πεφιδέσθαι φίλτερον ἦεν Τρώων, i.e. until the death of Patroclus I
preferred to spare the Trojans (which he will no longer do); and
xix. 312, οὐδέ τι θυμῷ τέρπετο πρὶν πολέμου στόμα δύμεναι, i.e. he
felt no pleasure until he entered the battle ; in both cases the Attic
Greek might have used πρίν with the indicative.   So also when
the clause with πρίν is future and conditional ; as in Il. xix. 423,
οὐ λήξω πρὶν Τρῶας ἄδην ἐλάσαι πολέμοιο, I will not stop until I have
given the Trojans enough of war.   It was in cases like the last,
where the mere temporal πρὶν ἐλάσαι expresses the future condition very imperfectly, that the need of a more exact form was

first felt. The need existed only after negative sentences, as here only could such a future condition be expressed by πρίν consistently with its original meaning *before*. *I shall not cease fighting until (before) I see the end of the war* contains a future condition (= ἢν μή) which πρίν can properly express ; but the equivalent affirmative, *I shall go on fighting until I see the end of the war*, could not be expressed by πρίν, as we cannot substitute *before* for *until*, but it would require ἕως, which is *until* with no sense of *before*. The forms of parataxis suggested a simple and natural way of meeting this want, through the adverbial use of πρίν. In a sentence like οὐδέ μιν ἀνστήσεις· πρὶν καὶ κακὸν ἄλλο πάθῃσθα, *nor will you recall him to life :—sooner than this will you suffer some new affliction*, Il. xxiv. 551, we have only to remove the colon and make πρίν a conjunction to obtain the regular construction of πρίν with the subjunctive, *nor will you recall him to life before (until) you suffer some new affliction.* This result could not have been attained with an affirmative leading clause; for while οὐ τοῦτο ποιήσω· πρίν με κελεύσῃς, *I shall not do this :—you shall command me first*, gives the meaning *I shall not do this before you command me*, the paratactic affirmative, τοῦτο ποιήσω· πρίν με κελεύσῃς, would give only *you will command me before I do this.* *I shall do this before you command me* would be τοῦτο ποιήσω πρίν σε κελεῦσαι, which is not the result of any form of parataxis. The six cases of πρίν with the subjunctive in Homer are all without ἄν or κέ, and all follow negatives. The primitive character and the rarity of this construction seem to show that we are nearer the original parataxis here than in any other form ; while the change of the subjunctive to the optative after a past tense in Il. xxi. 580 (see 639) shows that the dependence of the clause with πρίν is thoroughly established (cf. 307). An attempt to arrive at the same result in a more awkward way appears in two cases of πρίν γ᾽ ὅτ᾽ ἄν with the subjunctive in the Odyssey (641), where πρίν introduces the subjunctive with ὅτ᾽ ἄν very much as it introduces the infinitive.

625. No case of πρίν with the indicative occurs in Homer ; but the want was supplied by πρίν γ᾽ ὅτε δή with the indicative, which resembles πρίν γ᾽ ὅτ᾽ ἄν with the subjunctive just mentioned. As this construction is not the result of parataxis, and there is no such obstacle to combining the ideas of *until* and *before* in statements of past fact after affirmative clauses as was felt in future conditions (624), we find πρίν γ᾽ ὅτε with the indicative after both affirmative and negative sentences (see the examples in 636). It thus appears that πρίν was not sufficiently established as a conjunction in Homer to take the indicative without the intervention of ὅτε, although πρίν with the subjunctive had become a fixed construction.

The history of the uses of πρίν after Homer will be found below. (See 627; 632-634; 637; 642; 643; 645.)

Πρίν WITH THE INFINITIVE.

626. (*In Homer.*) In Homer the infinitive regularly follows πρίν after both affirmative and negative sentences, often where the Attic Greek would have the finite moods. *E.g.*

Ναῖε δὲ Πήδαιον πρὶν ἐλθεῖν υἷας ᾿Αχαιῶν. Il. xiii. 172. Τοῦ δ᾿ ἔφθη ὀρεξάμενος πρὶν οὐτάσαι, οὐδ᾿ ἀφάμαρτεν. Il. xvi. 322. Σφῶιν δὲ πρίν περ τρόμος ἔλλαβε φαίδιμα γυῖα, πρὶν πόλεμόν τ᾿ ἰδέειν πολέμοιό τε μέρμερα ἔργα, *before they saw the war*, etc. Il. viii. 452. (See 657.) Φεύγει πρίν περ ὅμιλον ἀ ο λ λ ι σ θ ή μ ε ν α ι ἀνδρῶν. Il. xv. 588. ῍Η κ᾿ ἔτι πολλοὶ γαῖαν ὀδὰξ εἷλον πρὶν ῎Ιλιον εἰσαφι- κέσθαι. Il. xxii. 17. ᾿Αλλά οἱ αὐτῷ Ζεὺς ὀλέσειε βίην πρὶν ἡμῖν πῆμα φυτεῦσαι. Od. iv. 668. Αἴθ᾿ ὤφελλ᾿ ἄλλοθ᾿ ὀλέσθαι πρὶν ἐλθεῖν. Od. xviii. 402. Οὐδ᾿ ἀπολήγει πρὶν χροὸς ἀνδρομέοιο δι ε λ- θεῖν. Il. xx. 100. Οὐ λήξω πρὶν Τρῶας ἅδην ἐλάσαι πολέμοιο. Il. xix. 423. Οὔ μ᾿ ἀποτρέψεις πρὶν χαλκῷ μαχέσασθαι. Il. xx. 257. Οὐδ᾿ ὅ γε λοιγὸν ἀπώσει πρίν γ᾿ ἀπὸ πατρὶ φίλῳ δόμεναι κούρην. Il. i. 97.

In the last three examples the subjunctive would be regular in Attic, and even Homer uses it in a few such cases (639). In Il. xx. 100 πρὶν διῆλθεν would have been the common Attic form. In the other examples, in which a mere temporal relation is expressed, the infinitive would be required in Attic Greek.

Hesiod has one example (Scut. 40) and the Homeric Hymns one (Ven. 151) of πρίν with the infinitive, both after negative sentences.

627. (*After Homer.*) The lyric poets, Herodotus, and the Attic writers use the infinitive after πρίν chiefly when the leading sentence is *affirmative*. But the infinitive is always required when πρίν means simply *before*, not *until*. *E.g.*

Πρὶν ἐκτελέσαι κατέβη δόμον ῞Αιδος. THEOG. 917. ῞Ισταμαι ἀμπνέων πρίν τι φάμεν, *I stand taking breath before I speak.* PIND. Nem. viii. 19; so Py. ix. 113. Πρὶν ὦν παρεῖναι ἐκεῖνον ἐς τὴν ᾿Αττικήν, ὑμέας καιρός ἐστι προβοηθῆσαι ἐς τὴν Βοιωτίαν, *before he comes into Attica*, etc. HDT. viii. 144. Πρὶν νῦν τὰ πλείον᾿ ἱστο- ρεῖν, ἐκ τῆσδ᾿ ἕδρας ἔξελθ᾿, *before seeking further*, etc. SOPH. O. C. 36. ᾿Αποπέμποισιν οὖν αὐτὸν πρὶν ἀκοῦσαι. THUC. ii. 12. So ii. 13, πρὶν ἐσβαλεῖν εἰς τὴν ᾿Αττικήν. ᾿Αφίεσαν τὰ βέλη πολὺ πρὶν ἐξικνεῖ- σθαι. XEN.Cyr.iii. 3, 60. ῾Ημεῖς τοίνυν Μεσσήνην εἵλομεν πρὶν Πέρσας λαβεῖν τὴν βασιλείαν καὶ κρατῆσαι τῆς ἠπείρου, καὶ πρὶν οἰκισθῆναί τινας τῶν πόλεων τῶν Ἑλληνίδων. Isoc. vi. 26. Καὶ πρὶν ἒξ μῆνας γεγονέναι, ἀπέδωκε. Plat. Prot. 320 A. Ἀπωλόμεσθ᾽ ἄρ᾽, εἰ κακὸν προσοίσομεν νέον παλαιῷ, πρὶν τόδ᾽ ἐξηντληκέναι, *we are ruined, then, if we shall add a new calamity to the former one, before we shall have exhausted this* (109). Eur. Med. 78.

In the following cases the infinitive is necessary, even after negatives. Πρὶν ὡς Ἄφοβον ἐλθεῖν μίαν ἡμέραν οὐκ ἐχήρευσεν, *she was not a widow a single day before she went to Aphobus* (where *until* would be absurd). Dem. xxx. 33. Οὐδὲ γὰρ πρὶν ἡττηθῆναι τὴν δίκην εἶχεν ὧν δικαζόμεθα, i.e. *he did not have it even before he lost the suit* (much less afterwards). Isae. v. 21. So Ar. Av. 964 ; Thuc. i. 39, 68. See also Isoc. v. 70, ὅταν δεδίωσι μὴ πρότερόν τι πάθῃς πρὶν τέλος ἐπιθεῖναι τοῖς πραττομένοις, *when they fear lest you may meet with some disaster before you finish what you are doing* (not *until you finish*). Indeed, μή after a verb of fearing does not make a negative sentence so far as the sense is concerned, what affects the dependent clause being the positive idea in πάθῃς : see Soph. Tr. 632.

628. An infinitive with πρίν sometimes depends on a negative clause, where a finite mood might be allowed, because the temporal relation is still so prominent as to determine the construction. This may happen when the clause with πρίν precedes, so that the dependence which *until* expresses is obscured by the position. *E.g.*

Ὅπως μὴ πρότερον νὺξ ἔσται πρὶν πυθέσθαι ἅπαντας, i.e. *lest night should come before they had heard them all.* And. i. 43. Πρὶν τὴν ναυμαχίαν νικῆσαι ἡμᾶς, γῆ οὐκ ἦν ἀλλ᾽ ἢ χωρίδιον μικρόν, *before we gained the naval victory, he had only a little piece of land* (the argument tries to prove that he died poor). Lys. xix. 28. Καί μοι μὴ θορυβήσῃ μηδεὶς πρὶν ἀκοῦσαι, *and let no one interrupt me before he hears* (where πρὶν ἂν ἀκούσῃ, *until he hears,* would suggest the wrong idea). Dem. v. 15. Πρὶν δὲ ταῦτα πρᾶξαι, μὴ σκοπεῖτε τίς εἰπὼν τὰ βέλτιστα ἀπολέσθαι βουλήσεται (where the irony of the question would make *until* absurd). Id. iii. 12 : so 13. Πρὶν μὲν γὰρ τοῦτο πρᾶξαι Λεωκράτην ἄδηλον ἦν ὁποῖοί τινες ὄντες ἐτύγχανον· νῦν δὲ πᾶσι φανερόν (where the temporal relation in πρὶν μέν and νῦν δέ is the only important one). Lycurg. 135. See also Aesch. Sept. 1048, Ag. 1067 ; Soph. Aj. 1419 ; Xen. Cyr. iv. 3, 10.

629. The infinitive sometimes follows πρίν after negative sentences where we might have the optative, which for some reason was not common after πρίν. *E.g.*

Οὐκ ἂν μεθεῖτο πρὶν καθ᾽ ἡδονὴν κλύειν, *he would not give it up until he should hear (before hearing) what he desired.* Soph. Tr. 197. (We might have πρὶν κλύοι : cf. Tr. 2, οὐκ ἂν αἰῶν᾽ ἐκμάθοις βροτῶν, πρὶν ἂν θάνῃ τις, where πρὶν θάνοι might have been used.) So Aesch. Supp. 772. Οὐδ᾽ ἂν διαβουλεύσασθαι ἔτι ἔφη, πρὶν τρὶς ἐννέα ἡμέρας μεῖναι, *until he should wait,* etc. Thuc. vii. 50. Ἱκέτευον μηδαμῶς ἀποτρέπεσθαι, πρὶν ἐμβαλεῖν εἰς τὴν χώραν, *until they should invade the country.* XEN. Hell. vi. 5, 23. Οὔτε αὐτός ποτε πρὶν ἱδρῶσαι δεῖπνον ᾑρεῖτο. Id. Cyr. viii. 1, 38. (Here πρὶν ἱδρώσειε in the generic sense would be the natural expression ; but it is doubtful whether this construction was ever used with πρίν. For An. iv. 5, 30, see 646.)

630. There remain some cases of πρίν with the infinitive after negative clauses where the older usage seems to be retained in place of the more exact later use of the indicative or subjunctive. *E.g.*

Οὐδὲ πρὸς δικαστηρίῳ οὐδὲ βουλευτηρίῳ ὤφθην οὐδεπώποτε, πρὶν ταύτην τὴν συμφορὰν γενέσθαι, i.e. *never, until this calamity befell me.* LYS. xix. 55. Ἐπειδὴ δ᾽ οὐκ οἷόν τ᾽ ἐστὶν αἰσθέσθαι (τοὺς πονηροὺς) πρὶν κακῶς τινα παθεῖν ὑπ᾽ αὐτῶν, *but since it is not possible to recognise them until somebody is hurt by them* (for πρὶν ἂν πάθῃ τις). ISOC. xx. 14. In such cases the temporal relation seems to exclude the other in the writer's mind.

631. (῍Η πρίν.) We sometimes find ἢ πρίν, *than before,* with the infinitive, a past verb being understood after ἤ. *E.g.*

Οἱ πολέμιοι πολὺ μὲν ἐλάττονές εἰσιν νῦν ἢ πρὶν ἡττηθῆναι, πολὺ δ᾽ ἐλάττονες ἢ ὅτε ἀπέδρασαν ἡμᾶς, *they are much fewer now than (they were) before they were beaten,* etc. XEN. Cyr. v. 2, 36. So vii. 5, 77. Παραλαβὼν τὴν πόλιν χεῖρον μὲν φρονοῦσαν ἤ (sc. ἐφρόνει) πρὶν κατασχεῖν τὴν ἀρχήν. ISOC. viii. 126. This ellipsis occurs first in Xenophon.

Πρίν WITH THE INDICATIVE.

632. (*Early Poets.*) Πρίν with the indicative does not occur in the Iliad or Odyssey, except in πρίν γ᾽ ὅτε (see 636). The first case of simple πρίν with the indicative is Hymn. Ap. Py. 178, ὃς τῇ γ᾽ ἀντιάσειε, φέρεσκέ γέ μιν αἴσιμον ἦμαρ, πρίν γέ οἱ ἰὸν ἐφῆκεν Ἀπόλλων, i.e. *every one was slain, until Apollo sent an arrow at the monster.* Three cases occur in Pindar : Ol. ix. 57, xiii. 65 ; Nem. iv. 28. The last is the first case of πρίν with the indicative after a negative sentence. These are the only cases before the Attic writers.

633. (*Attic Poets.*) Aeschylus has one example, after a negative : οὐκ ἦν ἀλέξημ᾽ οὐδέν, ἀλλὰ φαρμάκων χρείᾳ κατεσκέλλοντο, πρίν γ᾽ ἐγώ σφισιν ἔδειξα κράσεις ἠπίων ἀκεσμάτων, *until I showed them,* etc., Prom. 479. So likewise Aristophanes : πρότερον δ᾽ οὐκ ἦν γένος ἀθανάτων, πρὶν ἔρως ξυνέμιξεν ἅπαντα, Av. 700. Sophocles has one, after an affirmative : ἡγόμην δ᾽ ἀνὴρ ἀστῶν μέγιστος, πρίν μοι τύχη τοιάδ᾽ ἐπέστη, *until this fortune befell me,* O. T. 775. Euripides has seven examples, all (according to Sturm) after affirmatives, as follows :—

Ἐν εὐδίᾳ δέ πως ἔστη, πρὶν δή τις ἐφθέγξατο. And. 1145. ῍Αφρων νεός τ᾽ ἦν, πρὶν ἐσεῖδον οἷον ἦν, *I was a witless youth, until I saw,* etc. I. A. 489 (where there is a negative force in ἄφρων). Ἀνωλόλυξε, πρίν γ᾽ ὁρᾷ, *she shouted, until she saw*, etc. Med. 1173. (Here the contrast of εἶτ᾽ ἧκεν μέγαν κώκυτον in 1176 gives the idea that she did *not* begin the loud wailing *until* she saw the foam.) Σπονδαὶ ἦσαν ἴσαι, πρὶν Λαερτιάδης πείθει στρατιάν. Hec. 132. The others are Alc. 128; Rhes. 294, 568.

These are all the cases of πρίν with the indicative which precede those in prose. It will be seen that the idea of *until* is always conspicuous, even when the leading verb is affirmative; and in the earlier stages of the construction little regard was paid to the character of the leading sentence. With prose a new and stricter usage begins (634).

634. (*Prose.*) In Attic prose and in Herodotus, πρίν, *until*, referring to a definite past action, regularly takes the indicative after negative sentences or those implying a negative, very rarely after affirmative sentences. *E.g.*

Οὔτι κω συμβολὴν ἐποιέετο πρίν γε δὴ αὐτοῦ πρυτανηίη ἐγένετο, *he did not yet make an attack until his own day of command came.* Hdt. vi. 110. So vi. 79, vii. 239, ix. 22; all with πρίν γε δή. Τούτου τοῦ ἔπεος λόγον οὐδένα ἐποιεῦντο πρὶν δὴ ἐπετελέσθη. Id. i. 13. For πρὶν ἤ in Herodotus see 651; and for πρότερον ἤ in Herodotus and Thucydides, see 653.

Οὐ πρότερον ἐπαύσαντο ἐν ὀργῇ ἔχοντες αὐτὸν, πρὶν ἐζημίωσαν χρήμασιν, *they did not cease to regard him with wrath until they fined him.* Thuc. ii. 65. Οὐδ᾽ ἠξίωσαν νεώτερόν τι ποιεῖν ἐς αὐτὸν, πρίν γε δὴ αὐτοῖς ἀνὴρ Ἀργίλιος μηνυτὴς γίγνεται, i.e. *until he becomes*, etc. Id. i. 132. Οὔτε τότε ἰέναι ἤθελε, πρὶν ἡ γυνὴ αὐτὸν ἔπεισε. Xen. An. i. 2, 26. Οὐ πρότερον ἠθέλησεν ἀπελθεῖν, πρὶν αὐτὸν ἐξήλασαν βίᾳ. Lys. iii. 7. Μεσσηνίους πολιορκοῦντες οὐ πρότερον ἐπαύσαντο, πρὶν ἐξέβαλον ἐκ τῆς χώρας. Isoc. xii. 91. (Isocrates has the formula οὐ πρότερον ἐπαύσαντο πρίν with the indicative nine times.) Οὐκ ἦν ἐν Θήβαις ἀσφαλὲς, πρὶν τὴν Βοιωτίαν ἀπέδωκε καὶ τοὺς Φωκέας ἀνεῖλεν. Dem. viii. 65. Πάλιν τοῦτο τέμνων οὐκ ἐπανῆκε, πρὶν ἐφευρὼν σκαιόν τιν᾽ ἔρωτα ἐλοιδόρησε μάλ᾽ ἐν δίκῃ. Plat. Phaedr. 266 A. (This is the only case in Plato; but he has three indicatives in unfulfilled conditions. See 637.)

635. The only examples in prose of πρίν with the indicative after strictly affirmative sentences are these three:—

Ἐπὶ πολὺ διῆγον τῆς ἡμέρας πειρώμενοι ἀλλήλων, πρὶν δὴ Ἀρίστων πείθει τοὺς ἄρχοντας. Thuc. vii. 39. Παραπλήσια ἔπασχον, πρίν γε δὴ οἱ Συρακόσιοι ἔτρεψάν τε τοὺς Ἀθηναίους καὶ κατεδίωκον ἐς τὴν γῆν. Id. vii. 71. Προσεπολέμει Ἀριστοφῶντι, πρὶν αὐτῷ τὴν αὐτὴν ταύτην ἠπείλησεν ἐπαγγελίαν ἐν τῷ δήμῳ ἥνπερ ἐγὼ Τιμάρχῳ ἐπήγγειλα, *he continued to attack Aristophon, until A. threatened him before the people with this same kind of summons* (to δοκιμασία) *which I served on Timarchus.* Aeschin. i. 64. In these cases the force of *until* in πρίν is made especially emphatic by the continuation of the state of things described by the leading imperfects. There seems to be a feeling implied like that in οὐ πρότερον ἐπαύσαντο πρίν (see Sturm, p. 333).

Sturm cites also THUC. i. 51 and 118, iii. 29 and 104, as examples. But the first two have actual negatives in the leading sentence ; in iii. 29, τοὺς Ἀθηναίους λανθάνουσι, πρὶν δὴ τῇ Δήλῳ ἔσχον, the idea is that *the Athenians did not see them until*, etc. ; in iii. 104, τὰ περὶ τοὺς ἀγῶνας κατελύθη ὑπὸ ξυμφορῶν, πρὶν δὴ οἱ Ἀθηναῖοι τότε τὸν ἀγῶνα ἐποίησαν, the meaning is, *the games were broken up* (i.e. *were no longer held) until the Athenians renewed them at this time.* (See *Am. Jour. Phil.* ii. p. 469.)

636. Πρίν γ' ὅτε, *until*, has the indicative in Homer, after affirmative as well as negative sentences. These cases occur :—

Ἐπὶ ἶσα μάχη τέτατο, πρίν γ' ὅτε δὴ Ζεὺς κῦδος ὑπέρτερον Ἕκτορι δῶκεν, *the battle hung equally balanced, until (when) Zeus gave higher glory to Hector.* Il. xii. 436. Ἦμεθ' ἀτυζόμεναι, πρίν γ' ὅτε δή με σὸς υἱὸς ἀπὸ μεγάροιο κάλεσσεν, *until your son called me.* Od. xxiii. 42. Οὐδ' ὡς τοῦ θυμὸν ἔπειθον, πρίν γ' ὅτε δὴ θάλαμος πύκ' ἐβάλλετο, i.e. *until the battering began.* Il. ix. 587. So in the suspected verses, πρίν γ' ὅτε . . . θάρσυνας, Od. xiii. 322. For Od. iv. 178, see 637.

Four cases of πρίν γ' ὅτε δή with the indicative are found in the Homeric Hymns : Ap. Del. 49 ; Cer. 96, 195, 202 ; after which this strange construction disappears.

637. (*Indicative with πρίν in unfulfilled conditions.*) When the clause introduced by πρίν, *until*, refers to a result *not attained* in past time in consequence of the non-fulfilment of some condition, it takes a past tense of the indicative like the corresponding clause with ἕως (613, 2). We find examples only of the aorist indicative after negative sentences :—

Ἐχρῆν τοὺς ἄλλους μὴ πρότερον περὶ τῶν ὁμολογουμένων συμβουλεύειν, πρὶν περὶ τῶν ἀμφισβητουμένων ἡμᾶς ἐδίδαξαν, *they ought not to have given advice about undisputed matters, until they had instructed us about what is in dispute.* ISOC. iv. 19. Χρῆν τοίνυν Λεπτίνην μὴ πρότερον τιθέναι τὸν ἑαυτοῦ νόμον, πρὶν τοῦτον ἔλυσε, *before he had repealed this one.* DEM. xx. 96. Οὐκ ἂν ἐπεσκεψάμεθα πρότερον εἴτε διδακτὸν εἴτε οὐ διδακτὸν ἡ ἀρετή, πρὶν ὅ τι ἔστι πρῶτον ἐζητήσαμεν αὐτό, *we should not have inquired whether virtue was teachable or not, until we had first asked what it is in itself.* PLAT. Men. 86 D ; so 84 C, and Theaet. 165 D.

Besides these five cases in prose, we have the same construction with πρίν γ' ὅτε δή in Od. iv. 178 : οὐδέ κεν ἡμέας ἄλλο διέκρινεν, πρίν γ' ὅτε δὴ θανάτοιο μέλαν νέφος ἀμφεκάλυψεν, *nor would aught else have separated us until the black cloud of death had covered us.*

For the same construction with πρότερον ἤ in HDT. viii. 93, see 653.

Πρίν WITH THE SUBJUNCTIVE AND OPTATIVE.

SUBJUNCTIVE.

638. When a clause with πρίν, *until*, refers to the future, and depends on a *negative* clause of future time (not containing an optative), πρίν takes the subjunctive, like ἕως in a similar case (613, 3).

639. In Homer πρίν does not take κέ or ἄν with the subjunctive, the form of the original parataxis being still retained (624). The examples of the subjunctive are these :—

Οὐ γάρ πω καταδύσομεθ' εἰς Ἀίδαο δόμους, πρὶν μόρσιμον ἦμαρ ἐπέλθῃ, *we shall not yet descend to the house of Hades, until the fated day shall come.* Od. x. 174. (Here, if we insert a colon after δόμους and take πρίν as an adverb, *sooner than this,* we have the paratactic form.) So Il. xviii. 135 ; Od. xiii. 335, xvii. 7. In Il. xviii. 190, οὔ με πρίν γ' εἴα θωρήσσεσθαι, πρὶν γ' αὐτὴν ἴδωμαι, *she did not permit me to arm myself until I should see her,* the subjunctive of direct discourse (seen in xviii. 135) is retained after a past tense. So Il. xxiv. 781. In Il. xxi. 580 a similar subjunctive has been changed to the optative (644).

640. Hesiod has two cases of πρίν with the subjunctive, Th. 222, Op. 738, still without κέ or ἄν as in Homer. Πρὶν ἄν first occurs in THEOGN. 963 (see 642).

641. Two cases of πρίν γ' ὅτ' ἄν (used like πρίν) with the subjunctive occur in the Odyssey. The first is especially instructive, ii. 373 : ἀλλ' ὄμοσον μὴ μητρὶ φίλῃ τάδε μυθήσασθαι, πρίν γ' ὅτ' ἄν ἑνδεκάτη τε δυωδεκάτη τε γένηται, ἢ αὐτὴν ποθέσαι καὶ ἀφορμηθέντος ἀκοῦσαι, *but swear not to tell this to my mother until the eleventh or twelfth day shall come, or (until) she shall miss me and hear of my departure.* Here πρίν first introduces ὅτ' ἄν γένηται and then the two infinitives, having the same prepositional force with both. But in iv. 746, where the same scene is described, we have ἐμεῦ δ' ἕλετο μέγαν ὅρκον, μὴ πρὶν σοὶ ἐρέειν πρὶν δωδεκάτην γε γενέσθαι ἢ σ' αὐτὴν ποθέσαι καὶ ἀφορμηθέντος ἀκοῦσαι, the simpler and more common πρὶν γενέσθαι taking the place of the unwieldy πρίν γ' ὅτ' ἄν γένηται. The other case is iv. 475 : οὐ πρὶν μοῖρα φίλους ἰδέειν, πρίν γ' ὅτ' ἄν Αἰγύπτοιο ὕδωρ ἔλθῃς.

642. After Homer and Hesiod πρίν ἄν is established as the regular form with the subjunctive. *E.g.*

Μή ποτ' ἐπαινήσῃς πρὶν ἄν εἰδῇς ἄνδρα σαφηνέως. THEOG. 963 (the earliest case of πρὶν ἄν). Οὐδὲ λήξει πρὶν ἄν ἢ κορέσῃ κέαρ ἢ ἔλῃ τις ἀρχάν. AESCH. Prom. 165. Οὐ γάρ ποτ' ἔξει πρὶν ἄν κείνας ἐναργεῖς δεῦρό μοι στήσῃς ἄγων, *you shall not depart until you bring those girls and place them before my eyes.* SOPH. O. C. 909. Οὐ μὴ

ναῦς ἀφορμίσῃ χθονὸς, πρὶν ἂν κόρην σὴν Ἰφιγένειαν Ἄρτεμις λάβῃ
σφαγεῖσαν. EUR. I. T. 19. Μὴ προκαταγίγνωσκ᾽, ὦ πάτερ, πρὶν ἂν γ᾽
ἀκούσῃς ἀμφοτέρων. AR. Vesp. 919. Οὔ κώ σε ἐγὼ λέγω (εὐδαί-
μονα), πρὶν ἂν τελευτήσαντα καλῶς τὸν αἰῶνα πύθωμαι, until I
shall hear that you have ended your life happily. HDT. i. 32. Οὐ χρή
μ᾽ ἐνθένδε ἀπελθεῖν, πρὶν ἂν δῶ δίκην. XEN. An. v. 7, 5. Οὐκ οἷόν
τε ὑμᾶς πρότερον εἰδέναι, πρὶν ἂν καὶ ἐμοῦ ἀκούσητε ἀπολογουμένου.
AND. i. 7. Τοὺς δ᾽ οὐ πρότερον παύσονται πρὶν ἂν οὕτως ὥσπερ
ἡμᾶς διαθῶσιν. ISOC. xiv. 18. Μήπω γε, πρὶν ἂν τὸ καῦμα παρέλ-
θῃ, not yet,—until the heat of the day is past. PLAT. Phaedr. 242 A.

OPTATIVE.

643. When a clause with πρίν, until, referring to the future,
depends on a negative clause containing an optative in protasis
or apodosis, in a wish, or in a final clause, it may have the
optative (without ἄν) by assimilation, like a conditional relative
clause (613, 4), or it may take the infinitive. These cases of
the optative occur:—

Οὐ γὰρ ἂν εἰδείης ἀνδρὸς νόον οὐδὲ γυναικὸς, πρὶν πειρηθείης, for
you cannot know the mind of a man or a woman until you have tested it.
THEOG. 125 (the earliest example). Οὔποτ᾽ ἔγωγ᾽ ἄν, πρὶν ἴδοιμ᾽ ὀρθὸν
ἔπος, μεμφομένων ἂν καταφαίην, never would I assent when men blame
him, until I should see the word proved true. SOPH. O. T. 505. Μὴ
σταίη πολύκωπον ὄχημα ναὸς αὐτῷ, πρὶν τάνδε πρὸς πόλιν ἀνύσειε,
may his ship of many oars not stop until it makes its way to this city.
Id. Tr. 655 ; so Phil. 961 (both after optative of wish). Παρανίσχον
φρυκτοὺς, ὅπως μὴ βοηθοῖεν πρὶν σφῶν οἱ ἄνδρες οἱ ἐξιόντες διαφύ-
γοιεν, they raised signal torches, that the enemy might not come to the
rescue until their own men who had gone forth had escaped. THUC. iii. 22.
Νομίσαντες οὐκ ἂν ἔτι τὸν Βρασίδαν σφῶν προσαποστῆσαι οὐδὲν πρὶν
παρασκευάσαιντο, thinking that B. would not cause any further
secessions of their allies until they had made preparations. Id. iv. 117.
So XEN. Hell. ii. 3, 48 (two examples). Οὐκ ἂν πρότερον ὁρμήσειε,
πρίν πῃ βεβαιώσαιτο τὴν σκέψιν τῆς πορείας. PLAT. Leg. 799 D.
Εἰ ἕλκοι τις αὐτὸν, καὶ μὴ ἀνείη πρὶν ἐξελκύσειεν εἰς τὸ τοῦ ἡλίου
φῶς, if one should drag him, and not let him go until he had dragged him
out into the sunlight. Id. Rep. 515 E.

These are all the cases of this use of the optative with πρίν cited
by Sturm. In many cases where the optative could have been used,
the infinitive appears (see 629).

644. The optative with πρίν is more frequent in indirect
discourse after a negative verb of past time, representing a
subjunctive of the direct form, which is often retained. (See
the corresponding use of ἕως, 614.) E.g.

Οὐκ ἔθελεν φεύγειν πρὶν πειρήσαιτ᾽ Ἀχιλῆος, he would not fly

until he should try Achilles. Il. xxi. 580. (The direct form was πρὶν
πειρήσωμαι, and πειρήσηται might have been used here. See Il.
xviii. 190, in 639.) So Hymn. Cer. 334 ; Hes. Scut. 18. Ἔδοξέ
μοι μὴ σῖγα, πρὶν φράσαιμί σοι, τὸν πλοῦν ποιεῖσθαι. Soph. Ph.
551. (In Aj. 742 we have πρὶν τύχῃ in a similar sentence.) Ἐδέοντο
μὴ ἀπελθεῖν πρὶν ἀπαγάγοι τὸ στράτευμα (v. l. πρὶν ἂν ἀπαγάγῃ).
Xen. An. vii. 7, 57. (See εἶπον μηδένα τῶν ὄπισθεν κινεῖσθαι πρὶν
ἂν ὁ πρόσθεν ἡγῆται, Cyr. ii. 2, 8.) Ἀπηγόρευε μηδένα βάλλειν,
πρὶν Κῦρος ἐμπλησθείη θηρῶν, *until Cyrus should be satisfied.* Id.
Cyr. i. 4, 14. Ἡγοῦνθ' οὐδὲν οἷοί τ' εἶναι κινεῖν, πρὶν ἐκποδὼν
ἐκεῖνος αὐτοῖς γένοιτο. Isoc. xvi. 5. So Plat. Ap. 36 C, Rep. 402
B, Leg. 678 D.

For the infinitive, often preferred to the optative in such sentences,
see 629.

Πρίν with Subjunctive in General Suppositions.

645. When the clause introduced by πρίν, *until,* is
generic, and depends on a negative clause of present time
expressing customary or repeated action or a general truth,
we have πρὶν ἄν with the sᵕʰjunctive (613, 5). *E.g.*

Ὁρῶσι τοὺς πρεσβυτέρους οὐ πρόσθεν ἀπιόντας γαστρὸς ἕνεκα,
πρὶν ἂν ἀφῶσιν οἱ ἄρχοντες. Xen. Cyr. i. 2, 8. Οὐ γὰρ πρότερον
κατήγορος παρὰ τοῖς ἀκούουσιν ἰσχύει, πρὶν ἂν ὁ φεύγων ἀδυνατήσῃ
τὰς προειρημένας αἰτίας ἀπολύσασθαι. Aeschin. ii. 2. Οὐδεὶς πώποτε
ἐπέθετο (gnomic) πρότερον τῇ τοῦ δήμου καταλύσει, πρὶν ἂν μεῖζον
τῶν δικαστηρίων ἰσχύσῃ. Id. iii. 235. Οὐ πρότερον παύονται, πρὶν
ἂν πείσωσιν οὓς ἠδίκησαν. Plat. Phaed. 114 B. So Leg. 968 C.

646. It is doubtful whether the optative was ever used with πρίν
in the corresponding generic sense. In Xen. An. iv. 5, 30, for πρὶν
παραθεῖεν the weight of Mss. authority seems to favour πρὶν παραθεῖναι.
In Il. ix. 488 πρίν γ' ὅτε δή σ' ἄσαιμι is of this class.

---

647. The principle by which πρίν takes the subjunctive and
optative only after negative sentences, or sentences which were felt as
negative, seems to have allowed of no exceptions. The two following
cases have been cited :—

Αἰσχρὸν δ' ἡγοῦμαι πρότερον παύσασθαι, πρὶν ἂν ὑμεῖς ὅ τι ἂν
βούλησθε ψηφίσησθε, which is practically equivalent to *I refuse to
stop until you have voted what you wish,* αἰσχρόν having elsewhere a
negative force (see 817). Lys. xxii. 4. Ὅστις οὖν οἴεται τοὺς ἄλλους
κοινῇ τι πράξειν ἀγαθὸν, πρὶν ἂν τοὺς προεστῶτας αὐτῶν διαλλάξῃ,
λίαν ἁπλῶς ἔχει καὶ πόρρω τῶν πραγμάτων ἐστίν, which amounts to
this : *nobody but a simpleton thinks that the others will do anything in
common until their leaders are united.* Isoc. iv. 16. In Simon. Am.

i. 12, πρὶν ἵκηται cannot be correct, as πρίν here does not mean *until*, but merely *before*.

648. Πρίν, like ἕως, etc. (620), sometimes takes the subjunctive without ἄν, even in Attic Greek. *E.g.*

Μὴ στέναζε πρὶν μάθῃς. Soph. Ph. 917. So Ant. 619, Aj. 742, 965, Tr. 608, 946. Οὐκ ἔστιν ὅστις αὐτὸν ἐξαιρήσεται, πρὶν γυναῖκ' ἐμοὶ μεθῇ. Eur. Alc. 848. So Or. 1218, 1357. Μὴ, πρίν γ' ἀκούσῃς χἀτέραν στάσιν μελῶν. Ar. Ran. 1281. So Eccl. 629. See Hdt. i. 32, iv. 157, vi. 82. Even in Attic prose the Mss. omit ἄν in some places; as Thuc. vi. 10, 29, 38, viii. 9; Xen. Oec. xii. 1, Cyn. iii. 6; Aeschin. iii. 60; Hyper. Eux. xx. 10 (§ 4); Plat. Theaet. 169 B, Tim. 57 B; but many editors insert ἄν in all these places on their own responsibility.

649. A few cases of πρὶν ἄν with the optative, if the text is sound, are to be explained (like those of ἕως ἄν, 613, 4, end) as indirect discourse in which the direct form had πρίν ἄν with the subjunctive. See Xen. Hell. ii. 4, 18 (quoted in 702).

650. In sentences with πρίν we sometimes have a subjunctive depending on an optative with ἄν, as in conditional relative sentences (556). *E.g.*

Οὐκ ἂν αἰῶν' ἐκμάθοις βροτῶν, πρὶν ἂν θάνῃ τις, *you cannot fully understand the life of mortals, until one dies.* Soph. Tr. 2. Οὐκ ἂν ἀπέλθοιμι πρὶν παντάπασιν ἡ ἀγορὰ λυθῇ. Xen. Oec. xii. 1. Ἡ λέγοιμεν ἄν τι ἀληθὲς, οὐ μὴν σαφές γε οὐδὲ τέλεον πρὶν αὖ (?) καὶ ταύτας αὐτῆς πάσας περιέλωμεν; Plat. Polit. 281 D. The leading verb here has merely the effect of a future form on the clause with πρίν.

Πρὶν ἤ, πρότερον ἤ, AND πάρος, IN THE SENSE OF πρίν.

651. Πρὶν ἤ, *sooner than*, which is a more developed form of πρίν, is found twice in the Iliad with the infinitive; and very frequently in Herodotus with the infinitive (only after past tenses), the indicative, and the subjunctive (without ἄν). *E.g.*

Οὐ μὴν σφῶϊ γ' ὀΐω πρίν γ' ἀποπαύσασθαι πρὶν ἢ ἕτερόν γε πεσόντα αἵματος ἆσαι Ἄρηα. Il. v. 287. The same words occur after πρὶν ἤ in xxii. 266. Οἱ δὲ Αἰγύπτιοι, πρὶν μὲν ἢ Ψαμμήτιχον σφέων βασιλεῦσαι, ἐνόμιζον ἑωυτοὺς πρώτους γενέσθαι πάντων ἀνθρώπων. Hdt. ii. 2. Πρὶν γὰρ ἢ ὀπίσω σφέας ἀναπλῶσαι ἐς τὰς Σάρδις ἥλω ὁ Κροῖσος. Id. i. 78. Οὐ γὰρ δὴ πρότερον ἀπανέστη, πρὶν ἢ σφεας ὑποχειρίους ἐποιήσατο. Id. vi. 45. Ἀδικέει ἀναπειθόμενος πρὶν ἢ ἀτρεκέως ἐκμάθῃ. Id. vii. 10. Οὐ πρότερον παύσομαι πρὶν ἢ ἕλω τε καὶ πυρώσω τὰς Ἀθήνας. Id. vii. 8.

652. A few cases of πρὶν ἤ occur in the Mss. in Attic prose, as in

THUC. v. 61, and XEN. Cyr. i. 4, 23, Ag. ii. 4, An. iv. 5, 1; but many editors omit ἤ.

653. Πρότερον ἤ is sometimes used like πρὶν ἤ, in the sense of πρίν. This occurs chiefly with the infinitive in Herodotus and Thucydides, and with the subjunctive in Herodotus. Πρότερον ἤ with the indicative is sometimes used like πρίν, but it more frequently expresses a looser relation between two sentences which are independent in their construction (654). *E.g.*

(Infin., only after past tenses.) Ταῦτα ἐξαγγέλθη πρότερον ἢ τὸν Δαυρίσην ἀπικέσθαι, *this was announced before D. arrived.* HDT. v. 118. Ἦσαν οὗτοι τὸ μὲν πρότερον ἢ Πέρσας ἄρξαι Μήδων κατήκοοι, τότε δὲ Κύρου. Id. i. 72. (Πρότερα as adj. for πρότερον) : ταῦτα καὶ πέντε γενεῇσι ἀνδρῶν πρότερά ἐστι ἢ Ἡρακλέα ἐν τῇ Ἑλλάδι γενέσθαι. Id. ii. 44. Ἐπὶ τοὺς πομπέας πρότερον ἢ αἰσθέσθαι αὐτοὺς εὐθὺς ἐχώρησεν, *before they perceived them.* THUC. vi. 58. So i. 69. Besides the cases in Herodotus and Thucydides, a few occur in the orators: see DEM. xxxi. 14, and lv. 14 (πρότερον ἤ and πρίν together).

(Subj., without ἄν.) Μὴ ἀπανίστασθαι ἀπὸ τῆς πόλιος πρότερον ἢ ἐξέλωσι. HDT. ix. 86 ; so ix. 87. In iv. 196 we have οὔτε πρὶν ἂν ἀπισωθῇ οὔτε πρότερον ἢ λάβωσι. Besides five cases in Herodotus, we have only THUC. vii. 63, μὴ πρότερον ἀξιοῦν ἀπολύεσθαι ἢ ἀπαράξητε, and ANT. Tetr. A. α. 2, οὐ πρότερον ἐπιχειροῦσιν ἢ ποιήσωνται.

(Indic.) Οὐδὲ ᾔδεσαν ἐοῦσαν (τὴν ἄτραπον) πρότερον ἢ περ ἐπύθοντο Τρηχινίων, *until they learned of it.* HDT. vii. 175. Οὐ πρότερον ἐνέδοσαν ἢ αὐτοὶ ἐν σφίσι περιπεσόντες ἐσφάλησαν. THUC. ii. 65. Οὐδ' αὐτὴν τὴν ἀπόστασιν πρότερον ἐτόλμησαν ποιήσασθαι ἢ μετὰ πολλῶν ξυμμάχων ἔμελλον ξυνκινδυνεύσειν. Id. viii. 24 (see the following example). Οὐκ ἐν νόῳ ἔχοντες ταύτης τῆς ἡμέρης ἐπιθήσεσθαι, οὐδὲ πρότερον ἢ τὸ σύνθημά σφι ἔμελλε φανήσεσθαι, i.e. *nor did they mean to make an attack until the signal was ready to appear to them.* HDT. viii. 7. (With πρίν we should probably have had πρὶν ἂν μέλλῃ.) Εἰ ἔμαθε, οὐκ ἂν ἐπαύσατο πρότερον ἢ εἷλέ μιν ἢ καὶ αὐτὸς ἥλω, *if he had known it, he would not have stopped until he had either captured her or had been captured himself* (indicative in unfulfilled condition). Id. viii. 93.

654. In other cases of πρότερον ἤ with the finite moods or the infinitive, there is no meaning of *until,* and ἤ merely connects two verbs as when it follows μᾶλλον. *E.g.*

Ἐκέλευε τὸν ἄγγελον ἀπαγγέλλειν ὅτι πρότερον ἥξοι ἢ αὐτὸς βουλήσεται, *he bade the messenger announce that he should come sooner than he wanted him* (the direct form being ἥξω πρότερον ἢ βουλήσει). HDT. i. 127. Πολὺ πλεῖον πλῆθος περιεστήκει βουλομένων προσιέναι, καὶ πολὺ πρότερον ἢ οἱ φίλοι παρῆσαν, i.e. *much sooner than his friends arrived.* XEN. Cyr. vii. 5, 41. Πρότερον ἄν τίς μοι δοκεῖ ἐν τῇ ὁδῷ εὑρεῖν ἢ δανειζόμενος λαβεῖν (i.e. πρότερον εὕροι ἂν ἢ

λάβοι). Id. Mem. ii. 7, 2 : see i. 2, 17. Πρότερον ἐπεθύμησαν ἢ τὸν
τρόπον ἔγνωσαν. PLAT. Phaedr. 232 E. Compare μᾶλλον ἢ ζῆν,
XEN. Mem. iv. 4, 4.

So with πρόσθεν ἤ, which is not used like πρίν; as πρόσθεν ἢ σὺ
ἐφαίνου, τοῦτ' ἐκηρύχθη. SOPH. O. T. 736. See also XEN. An. ii. 1,
10, ἀπεκρίνετο ὅτι πρόσθεν ἂν ἀποθάνοιεν ἢ τὰ ὅπλα παραδοίησαν,
they answered, that they would die before they would give up their arms.

655. Thucydides once uses ὕστερον ἤ with the infinitive, after the
analogy of πρότερον ἤ : πρὶν δὲ ἀναστῆναι, ἔτεσιν ὕστερον ἑκατὸν ἢ
αὐτοὺς οἰκῆσαι, Πάμμιλον πέμψαντες Σελινοῦντα κτίζουσιν, *before
they were removed, and a hundred years after their own settlement,* vi. 4.

656. Πάρος, *before*, which is originally an adverb like πρίν,
is used in Homer with the infinitive, but never with the other
moods. *E.g.*

Τέκνα ἀγρόται ἐξείλοντο πάρος πετεηνὰ γενέσθαι. Od. xvi. 218.
Ἔνθα με κῦμ' ἀπόερσε, πάρος τάδε ἔργα γενέσθαι. Il. vi. 348.
Οὐδέ οἱ ὕπνος πῖπτεν ἐπὶ βλεφάροισι πάρος καταλέξαι ἅπαντα.
Od. xxiii. 309.

Πάρος with the infinitive occurs twelve times in Homer, always
after affirmative sentences (except in Od. xxiii. 309).

Πρίν (AS ADVERB), πάρος, πρότερον, πρόσθεν, ETC., BEFORE
πρίν, IN THE LEADING SENTENCE.

657. Homer very frequently has the adverb πρίν, and occasionally other adverbs of the same meaning, in the clause on
which πρίν with the infinitive or subjunctive depends. *E.g.*

Μὴ πρὶν ἐπ' ἠέλιον δῦναι, πρίν με κατὰ πρηνὲς βαλέειν Πριάμοιο
μέλαθρον, *may the sun not (sooner) go down before I have thrown to the
ground Priam's palace* (the first πρίν emphasising in advance the idea
of the second). Il. ii. 413. So Il. i. 97, ii. 348, 354, iv. 114 ; Od.
iv. 747 ; Il. ix. 403 (τὸ πρίν). Οὐ γάρ μιν πρόσθεν παύσεσθαι
ὀίω, πρίν γ' αὐτόν με ἴδηται. Od. xvii. 7. So with οὐ γάρ πω, Od.
x. 174.[1]

658. In Attic Greek πρότερον or πρόσθεν frequently stands in
the clause on which πρίν depends, like the adverb πρίν in Homer
(657). *E.g.*

Ἀποθνήσκουσι πρότερον πρὶν δῆλοι γίγνεσθαι οἷοι ἦσαν. XEN.
Cyr. v. 2, 9. Καὶ ἔτι πρότερον, πρὶν ἐς τὴν Ῥόδον αὐτοὺς ἀναστῆ-

---

[1] See Sturm, pp. 239, 261-263, who calls attention to the decrease of the
double πρίν in the Odyssey. Of 43 cases of πρίν with the infinitive in the
Iliad, 20 have a preceding πρίν or other adverb ; of 30 cases in the Odyssey,
only 10 have such an adverb. Besides πρίν or τὸ πρίν in the leading clause in
Homer, πάρος occurs three times, and πρόσθεν and πρότερος each once. Before
πρίν with the subjunctive in Homer such an adverb is always found, πρίν twice,
οὔπω or μήπω three times, and πρόσθεν once.

ναι, τάδε ἐπράσσετο. Thuc. viii. 45. Πρότερον οὐκ ἦν γένος ἀθανά
των, πρὶν ἔρως ξυνέμιξεν ἅπαντα. Ar. Av. 700. Οὐ πρότερον πρὸς
ἡμᾶς τὸν πόλεμον ἐξέφηναν, πρὶν ἐνόμισαν, κ.τ.λ. Xen. An. iii. 1,
16. Οὐ τοίνυν ἀποκρινοῦμαι πρότερον, πρὶν ἂν πύθωμαι. Plat.
Euthyd. 295 C. Καὶ οὐ πρόσθεν ἔστησαν, πρὶν (ἢ) πρὸς τοῖς πεζοῖς
τῶν Ἀσσυρίων ἐγένοντο. Xen. Cyr. i. 4, 23. Δεῖται αὐτοῦ μὴ πρό
σθεν καταλῦσαι πρὶν ἂν αὐτῷ συμβουλεύσηται. Xen. An. i. 1, 10.
The formula οὐ πρότερον παύσασθαι πρίν with the indicative in the
orators is familiar (see 634).

659. Other adverbs of time sometimes occur in the leading clause :
thus πάροιθεν . . . πρίν, Soph. El. 1131; οὔπω . . . πρίν, Thuc.
vi. 71, viii. 9. Πρίν (used as in Homer) occurs twice in Euripides,
and before πρὶν ἤ in Hdt. i. 165. Even πρό in composition may
refer to a following πρίν, as προϋφαιρῶν τὰς ἐκκλησίας πρὶν ἐπιδη
μῆσαι τοὺς πρέσβεις, Aeschin. ii. 61. See Dem. iv. 41, οὐδὲ πρὸ τῶν
πραγμάτων προορᾶτε οὐδέν, πρὶν ἂν πύθησθε.

660. Φθάνω in the leading sentence may emphasise a following πρίν. E.g.

Ἔφθην αἰνήσας πρίν σου κατὰ πάντα δαῆναι ἤθεα. Theog.
969 (see 887). So Il. xvi. 322, ἔφθη ὀρεξάμενος πρὶν οὐτάσαι.
Ἔφθησαν ἀπικόμενοι πρὶν ἢ τοὺς βαρβάρους ἥκειν, they arrived
before the barbarians came. Hdt. vi. 116 : so ix. 70. Φθήσονται
πλεύσαντες πρὶν Χίους αἰσθέσθαι. Thuc. viii. 12. Φθῆναι συμβα
λόντες πρὶν ἐλθεῖν τοὺς βοηθήσοντας, to join battle before the auxiliaries
should come up. Isoc. iv. 87.

661. In Hdt. vi. 108 we find the infinitive depending on φθάνω
. . . ἤ, the verb implying πρότερον or πρίν : φθαίητε ἂν πολλάκις
ἐξανδραποδισθέντες ἤ τινα πυθέσθαι ἡμέων, you would often be
reduced to slavery before any of us heard of it.

SECTION VIII.

Indirect Discourse or Oratio Obliqua, including Indirect Quotations and Questions.

662. The words or thoughts of any person may be
quoted either *directly* or *indirectly*. A direct quotation is
one which gives the exact words of the original speaker or
writer. An indirect quotation is one in which the original
words conform to the construction of the sentence in which
they are quoted. Thus the expression ταῦτα βούλομαι may
be quoted either directly (in *oratio recta*), as λέγει τις
"ταῦτα βούλομαι"; or indirectly (in *oratio obliqua*), as

λέγει τις ὅτι ταῦτα βούλεται or φησί τις ταῦτα βούλεσθαι, *some one says that he wishes for these.*

663. Indirect quotations may be introduced by ὅτι or ὡς and occasionally by other particles (negatively ὅτι οὐ, ὡς οὐ, etc.) with a finite verb; sometimes by the infinitive without a particle; sometimes also by the participle.

1. ῞Οτι, *that,* was originally the neuter relative ὅ τι, used as a limiting accusative, *in respect to which* (or *what*), *as to which, how far,* etc. In Homer ὅ, neuter of the relative ὅς, is used like ὅτι (709, 1). Thus οἶδα ὅ τι (or ὅ) κακὰ μήδεται at first meant *I know as to what he plans evil,* or *I know about his planning evil,* and afterwards came to mean *I know that he plans evil.*

2. ῾Ως, the relative adverb of manner (312, 1), in this construction originally meant *in what manner, how;* and afterwards became established in the same sense as ὅτι, *that.* Compare the German use of *wie (how)* in narration. *How* for *that* is heard in vulgar English (as *I told him how I saw this*), and *how that* was once in good use in this sense for *that.* ῞Οπως is sometimes used like ὡς in indirect discourse (706).

3. By a use similar to that of ὡς (2), οὕνεκα and ὁθούνεκα are sometimes weakened from their meaning *for which purpose, wherefore,* to the same sense as ὅτι and ὡς, *that* (710, 1). These words are also used in a causal sense, *because,* like ὅτι, ὅ, and ὡς (712).

On the other hand, διότι, *because,* sometimes has the sense of ὅτι, *that* (710, 2).

4. ῞Οτε, *when,* in Homer sometimes loses its temporal force, and approaches ὅτι in meaning (709, 3).

664. 1. Indirect quotations with ὅτι, ὡς, etc., form the chief part of the class of *substantive* sentences, in which an assertion introduced by one of these particles is the subject or the object of a verb. But these sentences have no peculiar construction, except after verbs implying thought or the expression of thought (*verba sentiendi et declarandi*), as they elsewhere have the simple indicative or any other form which would be used in the corresponding independent assertions. See οὐχ ἅλις ὡς ἐκείρετε κτήματ᾽ ἐμά, *is it not enough that you wasted my property?* Od. ii. 312 ; πολὺ κέρδιον ἔπλετο ὅττι ὑπόειξεν, Il. xv. 227 ; τοῦτο ἄξιον ἐπαινεῖν, ὅτι τὸν φόβον διέλυσαν τῶν ῾Ελλήνων (668), Plat. Menex. 241 B ; τοῦτ᾽ ἀδικεῖ, ὅτι ἀχρεῖον τὴν ἐπιείκειαν καθίστησιν, Dem. xx. 155.

2. The infinitive of indirect discourse belongs to the large class of subject and object infinitives (745 ; 746 ; 751), being distinguished from the others of this class by preserving the time of its tense from the finite verb which it represents (85 ; 667, 3).[1]

---

[1] See Schmitt, *Ueber den Ursprung des Substantivsatzes mit Relativpartikeln im Griechischen,* in Schanz's *Beiträge,* Heft 8.

665. 1. Indirect questions may be introduced by εἰ, *whether* (rarely by ἆρα), and also by interrogative pronouns, pronominal adjectives, and adverbs, and by most relatives. Alternative indirect questions may be introduced by πότερον (πότερα) . . . ἤ, εἴτε . . . εἴτε, εἰ . . . ἤ, εἰ . . . εἴτε, *whether* . . . *or*.

'Εάν or ἤν never means *whether* (see 493).

2. In Homer single indirect questions (when they are not introduced by interrogatives) generally have ἤ or εἰ, *whether;* and alternative questions have ἤ (ἠέ) . . . ἤ (ἠε), sometimes εἴ τε . . . εἴ τε, *whether* . . . *or*.

Bekker never allows εἰ or εἴ τε in indirect questions in Homer, always writing ἤ or ἤ τε, without regard to the Mss.

3. Indirect questions follow the same principles as indirect quotations with ὅτι or ὡς, in regard to their moods and tenses. (For examples, see 669.)

666. The term *indirect discourse* or *oratio obliqua* includes all clauses which express indirectly the words or thoughts of any person (including those of the speaker himself), after verbs which imply thought or the expression of thought (*verba sentiendi et declarandi*), and after such expressions as φαίνεται, *it appears,* δοκεῖ, *it seems,* δῆλόν ἐστιν, *it is evident,* σαφές ἐστιν, etc.

The term may be further applied to any single dependent clause, in any sentence, which indirectly expresses the thought of any other person than the speaker (or past thoughts of the speaker himself), even when the preceding or following clauses are not in indirect discourse. (See 694 and 684.)

GENERAL PRINCIPLES OF INDIRECT DISCOURSE.

667. The following are the general principles of indirect discourse, the particular applications of which are shown in 669-710.

1. In indirect quotations after ὅτι or ὡς and in indirect questions,

(a) after primary tenses, each verb retains both the mood and the tense of the direct discourse, no change being made except (when necessary) in the person of the verb;

(b) after secondary tenses, each primary tense of the indicative and each subjunctive of the direct discourse may be either changed to the same tense of the optative or retained in its original mood and tense. The imperfect and pluperfect, having no tenses in the optative, are generally retained in the indicative (but see 673). An aorist indicative belonging to a *dependent* clause of the direct discourse remains unchanged, but one belonging to the leading clause may be changed to the optative like a primary tense.

2. Secondary tenses of the indicative expressing an unreal condition, indicatives with ἄν, and all optatives (with or without ἄν), are retained, with no change in either mood or tense, after both primary and secondary tenses.

3. When the quotation depends on a verb which takes the infinitive or participle, the leading verb of the quotation is changed to the *corresponding tense* of the infinitive or participle, after both primary and secondary tenses, ἄν being retained if it is in the direct form; and the dependent verbs follow the preceding rules.

4. The adverb ἄν is never joined with a verb in indirect discourse unless it stood also in the direct form. On the other hand, ἄν is never omitted in indirect discourse if it was used in the direct form; except that, when it is joined to a relative word or a particle before a subjunctive in direct discourse, it is regularly dropped when the subjunctive is changed to the optative after a past tense in indirect discourse.

5. The indirect discourse regularly retains the same negative particle which would be used in the direct form. But the infinitive and participle sometimes take μή in indirect discourse where οὐ would be used in the direct form. (See examples under 685 and 688.) In indirect questions introduced by εἰ, *whether,* and in the second part of alternative indirect questions (665), μή can be used as well as οὐ.

668. As an indirect quotation or question is generally the object or subject of its leading verb, it may stand in apposition with a pronoun like τοῦτο which represents such an object or subject ; as τοῦτο λέγομεν, ὅτι σοφός ἐστιν, *we say this, that he is wise;* τοῦτο δῆλόν ἐστιν, ὅτι σοφός ἐστιν, *this is plain, that he is wise;* τοῦτο σκεψόμεθα, εἰ ἀληθῆ λέγεις, *we shall inquire into this, whether you tell the truth.*

SIMPLE SENTENCES IN INDIRECT DISCOURSE.

Indicative and Optative after ὅτι and ὡς. and in Indirect Questions.

669. When the direct form is an indicative (without ἄν) in a simple sentence, we have (667, 1) the following rules for indirect quotations after ὅτι or ὡς and for indirect questions :—

1. After *primary* tenses the verb stands in the indicative, in the tense of the direct discourse. *E.g.*

Λέγει ὅτι γράφει, *he says that he is writing;* λέγει ὅτι ἔγραφεν, *he says that he was writing;* λέγει ὅτι γέγραφεν, *he says that he has written;* λέγει ὅτι ἐγεγράφει, *he says that he had written;* λέγει ὅτι ἔγραψεν, *he says that he wrote;* λέγει ὅτι γράψει, *he says that he shall write.*

Εἴφ᾽ ὅτι οἱ σῶς εἰμι καὶ ἐκ Πύλου εἰλήλουθα, *say that I am safe and have come from Pylos.* Od. xvi. 131. Ὄτρυνον δ᾽ Ἀχιλῆι εἰπεῖν ὅττι ῥά οἱ πολὺ φίλτατος ὤλεθ᾽ ἑταῖρος, *urge him to tell Achilles that his dearest friend perished.* Il. xvii. 654. (See 663, 1.) Γνωτὸν δὲ ὡς ἤδη Τρώεσσιν ὀλέθρου πείρατ᾽ ἐφῆπται. Il. vii. 401.

Λέγει γὰρ ὡς οὐδέν ἐστιν ἀδικώτερον φήμης. AESCHIN. i. 125. Οὐ γὰρ ἂν τοῦτό γ᾽ εἴποις, ὡς ἔλαθεν. Id. ii. 151. Εὖ δ᾽ ἴστε, ὅτι πλεῖστον διαφέρει φήμη καὶ συκοφαντία. Ib. 145. Ἀλλ᾽ ἐννοεῖν χρὴ τοῦτο μὲν, γυναῖχ᾽ ὅτι ἔφυμεν. SOPH. Ant. 61. Καὶ ταῦθ᾽ ὡς ἀληθῆ λέγω, καὶ ὅτι οὔτε ἐδόθη ἡ ψῆφος ἐν ἅπασι πλείους τ᾽ ἐγένοντο τῶν ψηφισαμένων, μάρτυρας ὑμῖν παρέξομαι, *I shall bring witnesses to show that I speak the truth,* etc. DEM. lvii. 14.

(Indirect Questions.) Ἐρωτᾷ τί βούλονται, *he asks what they want;* ἐρωτᾷ τί ποιήσουσιν, *he asks what they will do.*

Σὺ δὲ φράσαι εἴ με σαώσεις (Bekker ἤ με), *and do you consider whether you will save me.* Il. i. 83. Σάφα δ᾽ οὐκ οἶδ᾽ εἰ θεός ἐστιν. Il. v. 183. Ὄφρα καὶ Ἕκτωρ εἴσεται ἢ καὶ ἐμὸν δόρυ μαίνεται ἐν παλάμῃσιν (v. l. εἰ καὶ). Il. viii. 111. Ὄφρα δαῶμεν ἢ ἐτεὸν Κάλχας μαντεύεται ἦε καὶ οὐκί. Il. ii. 299 ; so Od. iv. 487, 712. Ὃς εἴπῃ ὅ τι τόσσον ἐχώσατο Φοῖβος Ἀπόλλων, εἴ τ᾽ ἄρ ὅ γ᾽ εὐχωλῆς ἐπιμέμφεται εἴ θ᾽ ἑκατόμβης (Bekker ἤ τ᾽ . . . ἤ θ᾽). Il. i. 64 ; see ii. 349. Πύστεις ἐρωτῶντες εἰ λῃσταί εἰσιν, *asking whether they are pirates.* THUC. i. 5. Εἰ ξυμπονήσεις καὶ ξυνεργάσει σκόπει. SOPH. Ant. 41. See EUR. Alc. 784. Εὐβοιίς᾽ ὧν δ᾽ ἔβλαστεν οὐκ ἔχω λέγειν. SOPH. Tr. 401. Ἐρωτᾷς εἰ οὐ καλή μοι δοκεῖ εἶναι, *you ask whether it does not seem to me to be fine.* PLAT. Gorg. 462 D. Βουλόμενος ἐρέσθαι εἰ μαθών τίς τι μεμνημένος μὴ οἶδεν. Id. Theaet. 163 D. Σκοπῶμεν εἰ ἡμῖν πρέπει ἢ οὔ. Id. Rep. 451 D. Τοῦτ᾽ αὐτό, εἰ χαίρεις ἢ μὴ χαίρεις, ἀνάγκη δή πού σε ἀγνοεῖν. Id. Phil. 21 B. (For οὐ and μή in the last four examples, representing οὐ of the direct question, see 667, 5.) Θαυμάζω πότερα ὡς κρατῶν αἰτεῖ τὰ ὅπλα ἢ ὡς διὰ φιλίαν δῶρα. XEN. An. ii. 1, 10. Σήμαιν᾽ εἴτ᾽ ἔχει χῶρον πρὸς αὐτὸν τόνδε γ᾽ εἴτ᾽ ἄλλῃ κυρεῖ. SOPH. Ph. 22. Εἴτε κατὰ τρόπον κεῖται εἴτε μή, οὕτω θεᾶσθαι. PLAT. Crat. 425 B (667, 5). See also XEN. Cyr. ii. 1, 7 (εἰ . . . εἴτε μή) ; EUR. Alc. 139 (εἰ . . . εἴτε). Περὶ πάντων ἴδωμεν, ἆρ᾽ οὑτωσὶ γίγνεται πάντα. PLAT. Phaed. 70 D. (Ἆρα regularly introduces only direct questions.)

It is to be noticed that indirect *questions* after primary tenses retain an indicative of the direct question in Greek, where the subjunctive is used in Latin. Thus, nescio quis sit, *I know not who he is*, in Greek is simply ἀγνοῶ τίς ἐστιν. This does not apply to indirect questions which would require the subjunctive in the direct form (677).

2. After *secondary* tenses the verb may be either changed to the optative or retained in the indicative, the *tense* of the direct discourse being retained in either case. The optative is the more common form. *E.g.*

Ἔλεξεν ὅτι γράφοι (or ὅτι γράφει), he said that he was writing ; i.e. he said γράφω. Ἔλεξεν ὅτι γεγραφὼς εἴη (or ὅτι γέγραφεν), he said that he had written ; i.e. he said γέγραφα. Ἔλεξεν ὅτι γράψοι (or ὅτι γράψει), he said that he should write ; i.e. he said γράψω. Ἔλεξεν ὅτι γράψειεν (or ὅτι ἔγραψεν), he said that he had written ; i.e. he said ἔγραψα. (For the imperfect and pluperfect, see 672.)

(Optative.) Ἐνέπλησε φρονήματος τοὺς Ἀρκάδας, λέγων ὡς μόνοις μὲν αὐτοῖς πατρὶς Πελοπόννησος εἴη, πλεῖστον δὲ τῶν Ἑλληνικῶν φῦλον τὸ Ἀρκαδικὸν εἴη, καὶ σώματα ἐγκρατέστατα ἔχοι. XEN. Hell. vii. 1, 23. (He said μόνοις μὲν ὑμῖν ἐστι, πλεῖστον δέ ἐστι, καὶ σώματα ἔχει : these indicatives might have been used in the place of εἴη, εἴη, and ἔχοι.) Ἔλεγε δὲ ὁ Πελοπίδας ὅτι Ἀργεῖοι καὶ Ἀρκάδες μάχῃ ἡττημένοι εἶεν ὑπὸ Λακεδαιμονίων, i.e. he said that they had been defeated (he said ἥττηνται). Ib. vii. 1, 35. So HDT. i. 83 (perf. and pres.) Ὑπειπὼν τἄλλα ὅτι αὐτὸς τἀκεῖ πράξοι, ᾤχετο, having hinted that he would himself attend to affairs there. THUC. i. 90. (He said τἀκεῖ πράξω, and πράξει might have been retained. See 128.) Ὁ δὲ εἶπεν ὅτι ἔσοιντο (he said ἔσονται). XEN. Cyr. vii. 2, 19. Ἔλεξαν ὅτι πέμψειε σφᾶς ὁ Ἰνδῶν βασιλεύς, κελεύων ἐρωτᾶν ἐξ ὅτου ὁ πόλεμος εἴη, they said that the king of the Indians had sent them, commanding them to ask on what account there was war. Ib. ii. 4, 7. (They said ἔπεμψεν ἡμᾶς, and the question to be asked was ἐκ τίνος ἐστὶν ὁ πόλεμος ;) Ἔλεγον ὅτι οὐ πώποθ᾽ οὗτος ὁ ποταμὸς διαβατὸς γένοιτο πεζῇ εἰ μὴ τότε, they said that this river had never been (ἐγένετο) fordable except then. Id. An. i. 4, 18. Περικλῆς προηγόρευε τοῖς Ἀθηναίοις, ὅτι Ἀρχίδαμος μέν οἱ ξένος εἴη, οὐ μέντοι ἐπὶ κακῷ γε τῆς πόλεως γένοιτο, he announced that A. was his friend, but that he had not been made his friend to the injury of the state. THUC. ii.

13. (He said ξένος μοί ἐστιν, οὐ μέντοι ἐγένετο. See 116, 1 ; 124, 1.) Ἔγνωσαν ὅτι κενὸς ὁ φόβος εἴη. XEN. An. ii. 2, 21. Προϊδόντες ὅτι ἔσοιτο ὁ πόλεμος, ἐβούλοντο τὴν Πλάταιαν προ-καταλαβεῖν. THUC. ii. 2. Ἐπειρώμην αὐτῷ δεικνύναι, ὅτι οἴοιτο μὲν εἶναι σοφὸς, εἴη δ᾽ οὔ. PLAT. Ap. 21 C. (Indicative.) Ἔλεγον ὡς ἐλπίζουσιν σὲ καὶ τὴν πόλιν ἕξειν μοι χάριν, they said that they hoped, etc. ISOC. v. 23. (They said ἐλπίζομεν, which might have been changed to ἐλπίζοιεν.) Ἧκε δ᾽ ἀγγέλλων τις ὡς τοὺς πρυτάνεις ὡς Ἐλάτεια κατείληπται, some one had come with the report that Elatea had been taken. DEM. xviii. 169. (Here the perf. opt. might have been used.) Δεινοὺς λόγους ἐτόλμα περὶ ἐμοῦ λέγειν, ὡς ἐγὼ τὸ πρᾶγμ᾽ εἰμὶ τοῦτο δεδρακώς. Id. xxi. 104. Αἰτιασά-μενος γάρ με ἃ καὶ λέγειν ἂν ὀκνήσειέ τις, τὸν πατέρα ὡς ἀπέκτονα ἐγὼ τὸν ἐμαυτοῦ, κ.τ.λ. Id. xxii. 2. Φανερῶς εἶπεν ὅτι ἡ μὲν πόλις σφῶν τετείχισται ἤδη, he said that their city had already been fortified. THUC. i. 91. Ἀποκρινάμενοι ὅτι πέμψουσιν πρέσβεις, εὐθὺς ἀπήλλαξαν. Id. i. 90. (Cf. ὅτι πράξοι, quoted above from the same chapter.) Ἤιδεσαν ὅτι τοὺς ἀπενεγκόντας οἰκέτας ἐξαιτή-σομεν. DEM. xxx. 23. (Ἐξαιτήσοιμεν might have been used.) Ἐτόλμα λέγειν ὡς ὑπὲρ ὑμῶν ἐχθροὺς ἐφ᾽ ἑαυτὸν εἵλκυσε καὶ νῦν ἐν τοῖς ἐσχάτοις ἐστὶ κινδύνοις. Id. xxii. 59.

(Indirect Questions.) Ἠρώτησεν αὐτὸν τί ποιοίη (or τί ποιεῖ), he asked him what he was doing ; i.e. he asked τί ποιεῖς; Ἠρώτησεν αὐτὸν τί πεποιηκὼς εἴη (or τί πεποίηκεν), he asked him what he had done ; i.e. he asked τί πεποίηκας; Ἠρώτησεν αὐτὸν τί ποιήσοι (or τί ποιήσει), he asked him what he should do; i.e. he asked τί ποιήσεις; Ἠρώτησεν αὐτὸν τί ποιήσειεν (or τί ἐποίησεν), he asked him what he had done ; i.e. he asked τί ἐποίησας;

Ὤιχετο πευσόμενος μετὰ σὸν κλέος, ἤ που ἔτ᾽ εἴης, i.e. he went to inquire whether you were still living. Od. xiii. 415. Ἀλλήλους τ᾽ εἴροντο τίς εἴη καὶ πόθεν ἔλθοι (i.e. τίς ἐστιν καὶ πόθεν ἦλθεν;). Od. xvii. 368. Ἤρετο, εἴ τις ἐμοῦ εἴη σοφώτερος, he asked whether any one was wiser than I. PLAT. Ap. 21 A. (The direct question was ἔστι τις σοφώτερος;) Ὅ τι δὲ ποιήσοι οὐ διεσήμηνε, but he did not indicate what he would do. XEN. An. ii. 1, 23. (The direct question was τί ποιήσω;) Ἐπειρώτα, τίνα δεύτερον μετ᾽ ἐκεῖνον ἴδοι, he asked whom he had seen (who came) next to him. HDT. i. 31. (The direct question was τίνα εἶδες;) Εἴρετο κόθεν λάβοι τὸν παῖδα, he asked whence he had received the boy. Id. i. 116. Ἠρώτων αὐτὸν εἰ ἀνα-πλεύσειεν ἔχων ἀργύριον, I asked him whether he had set sail with the money. DEM. l. 55. (The direct question was ἀνέπλευσας; See 125 and 670, b.)

Εἴρετο ὅττευ χρηίζων ἱκόμην, he asked what I wanted that I came. Od. xvii. 120. Ἠπόρουν τί ποτε λέγει, I was uncertain what he meant. PLAT. Ap. 21 B. (Here λέγοι might have been used.) Ἐβου-λεύονθ᾽ οὗτοι τίν᾽ αὐτοῦ καταλείψουσιν, they were considering whom they should leave here. DEM. xix. 122. Ἐρωτώντων τινῶν διὰ τί ἀπέ-θανεν, παραγγέλλειν ἐκέλευεν, κ.τ.λ. XEN. Hell. ii. 1, 4.

670. (*a*) After past tenses the indicative and optative are in equally good use ; the optative being used when the writer incorporates the quotation entirely into his own sentence, and the indicative when he quotes it in the original words as far as his own construction allows. The indicative here, like the subjunctive in final clauses after past tenses (318), is merely a more vivid form of expression than the optative, with no difference in meaning. We even find both moods in the same sentence. *E.g.*

Οὗτοι ἔλεγον ὅτι Κῦρος μὲν τέθνηκεν, Ἀριαῖος δὲ πεφευγὼς ἐν τῷ σταθμῷ εἴη καὶ λέγοι, κ.τ.λ. ΧΕΝ. An. ii. 1, 3. (Here τέθνηκεν contains the most important part of the message.) Ἐκ δὲ τούτου ἐπυνθάνετο ἤδη αὐτῶν καὶ ὁπόσην ὁδὸν διήλασαν, καὶ εἰ οἰκοῖτο ἡ χώρα. Id. Cyr. iv. 4, 4. Ἐτόλμα λέγειν, ὡς χρέα τε πάμπολλα ἐκτέτικεν ὑπὲρ ἐμοῦ καὶ ὡς πολλὰ τῶν ἐμῶν λάβοιεν. DEM. xxvii. 49. Ὅμοιοι ἦσαν θαυμάζειν ὅποι ποτὲ τρέψονται οἱ Ἕλληνες καὶ τί ἐν νῷ ἔχοιεν. ΧΕΝ. An. iii. 5, 13.

(*b*) The perfect and future were less familiar than the other tenses of the optative, so that these tenses were sometimes retained in the indicative even when the present or the aorist was changed to the optative. See the last two examples under (*a*). In indirect *questions* the aorist indicative was generally retained (see 125). Some writers (as Thucydides) preferred the more direct forms in all indirect discourse (320).

671. In Homer this construction (669) is fully developed in indirect questions : see examples of both indicative and optative in 669, 1 and 2. But in indirect quotations, while the indicative is freely used after both present and past tenses, the change of the indicative to the optative after past tenses had not yet been introduced. In the single case of εἰπεῖν ὡς with the optative, μερμήριξε .. ἕκαστα εἰπεῖν, ὡς ἔλθοι καὶ ἵκοιτ᾽ ἐς πατρίδα γαῖαν, *he hesitated about telling him each event, how he had returned,* etc., Od. xxiv. 237, ὡς appears only on its way from its meaning *how* (663, 2) to its later use with the optative as *that*. We first find the optative in genuine oratio obliqua (with ὡς) Hymn. Ven. 214, εἶπεν ὡς ἔοι. Further, the later principle by which the indicative after past tenses (when it is not changed to the optative) retains the *tense* of the direct form is almost unknown in the Homeric language. Here a present or perfect indicative of the direct discourse after a past tense is changed to an imperfect or pluperfect ; so that *I knew that he was planning evil,* which in Attic would be ἐγίγνωσκον ὅτι κακὰ μήδοιτο (or μήδεται), in Homer is γίγνωσκον ὅ (= ὅτι) κακὰ μήδετο, Od. iii. 166. (For examples, see 674.) The aorist indicative, which has no corresponding tense to express its own time referred to the past, was always retained after past tenses ; as in γνῶ ὅ οἱ οὔτι ἦλθεν, Il. xi. 439 ; so i. 537, xxii. 445. Likewise the future indicative is once retained, in Od. xiii. 340, ἥδε ὃ νοστήσεις, *I knew that you would return ;* but elsewhere the past future with ἔμελλον is used, as in Il. xx. 466, οὐδὲ τὸ ἤδη ὃ οὐ πείσεσθαι ἔμελλεν, and Od. xix. 94, Il. xi. 22. These examples show the need of the later future optative (129). In Il. xxii. 10, οὐδέ νύ πώ με ἔγνως ὡς θεός εἰμι, and xx. 265 the present expresses a present truth rather than a past fact.

It thus appears that the peculiar constructions with ὅτι and ὡς in oratio obliqua (667, 1, b), which gave such grace and variety to the later language, were not yet developed in Homer; but clauses with ὅτι, ὡς, etc., were still connected with the leading verb by the same looser construction which we use in English (as *I knew that he was planning evil*), the dependent verb expressing its own absolute time (see 22), as it did in the relative clauses in which these clauses originated, or in the more primitive parataxis. Thus γίγνωσκον ὃ κακὰ μήδετο (above) meant originally *I knew as to what he was planning evil;* and without ὃ, in a still earlier stage, *I knew: he was planning evil* (which we can say in English). Even after the more thorough incorporation of the dependent clause was established, by which either μήδεται or μήδοιτο became the regular form, the more primitive imperfect is occasionally found, even in Attic prose (see 674, 2).

The most common Homeric construction in indirect discourse is that of φημί with the infinitive, of which 130 examples occur.[1]

672. An imperfect or pluperfect of the direct discourse is regularly retained in the indicative, after past tenses, for want of an imperfect or pluperfect optative. *E.g.*

Ἀκούσας δὲ Ξενοφῶν ἔλεγεν ὅτι ὀρθῶς ᾐτιῶντο καὶ αὐτὸ τὸ ἔργον αὐτοῖς μαρτυροίη, *he said that they had accused him rightly, and that the fact itself bore witness to them;* i.e. *he said* ὀρθῶς ᾐτιᾶσθε καὶ τὸ ἔργον ὑμῖν μαρτυρεῖ. XEN. An. iii. 3, 12. Εἶχε γὰρ λέγειν, καὶ ὅτι μόνοι τῶν Ἑλλήνων βασιλεῖ συνεμάχοντο ἐν Πλαταιαῖς, καὶ ὅτι ὕστερον οὐδέποτε στρατεύσαιντο ἐπὶ βασιλέα (*he said μόνοι συνεμαχόμεθα, καὶ οὐδέποτε ἐστρατευσάμεθα*). Id. Hell. vii. 1, 34. Τούτων ἔκαστον ἠρόμην εἴ τινες εἶεν μάρτυρες ὧν ἐναντίον τὴν προῖκ' ἀπέδοσαν, αὐτὸν δ' Ἄφοβον, εἴ τινες παρῆσαν ὅτ' ἀπελάμβανεν, *I asked each of these men whether there were any witnesses before whom they had paid the dowry; and Aphobus, whether there had been any present when he received it.* DEM. xxx. 19. (The two questions were εἰσὶ μάρτυρές τινες; and παρῆσάν τινες;)

---

[1] See Schmitt, *Ursprung des Substantivsatzes,* p. 70. The following statistics are based on Schmitt's collection of Homeric examples. Homer has 40 cases of ὅτι, ὅττι, or ὅ with the indicative after verbs of *knowing, hearing, perceiving,* or *remembering* (23 of ὅ, 17 of ὅτι or ὅττι); and 4 after verbs of *saying* (3 of ὅτι, 1 of ὅ).

18 of ὡς after verbs of *knowing,* etc.; 8 after verbs of *saying.*

5 of ὅ τ' (for ὅ τε = ὅ) after γιγνώσκω, εἴδομαι, and δῆλον.

2 of οὕνεκα after verbs of *knowing,* etc.; 4 after verbs of *saying* (omitting Od. vii. 299 as causal).

Only 3 of the 16 cases of these particles after verbs of *saying* are in the Iliad; while of the 65 cases after verbs of *knowing,* etc., 42 are in the Iliad (29 with ὅτι, etc., 9 with ὡς, 3 with ὅ τ', 1 with οὕνεκα).

673. (*Imperfect Optative.*) In a few cases, the present optative is used after past tenses to represent the imperfect indicative. The present optative thus supplies the want of an imperfect, like the present infinitive and participle (119 and 140). This can be done only when the context makes it perfectly clear that the optative represents an imperfect, and not a present. *E.g.*

Τὸν Τιμαγόραν ἀπέκτειναν, κατηγοροῦντος τοῦ Λέοντος ὡς οὔτε συσκηνοῦν ἐθέλοι ἑαυτῷ μετά τε Πελοπίδου πάντα βουλεύοιτο. XEN. Hell. vii. 1, 38. (The words of Leon were οὔτε συσκηνοῦν ἤθελέ μοι, μετά τε Πελ. πάντα ἐβουλεύετο.) Τὰ πεπραγμένα διηγοῦντο, ὅτι αὐτοὶ μὲν ἐπὶ τοὺς πολεμίους πλέοιεν, τὴν δὲ ἀναίρεσιν τῶν ναυαγῶν προστάξαιεν ἀνδράσιν ἱκανοῖς. Ib. i. 7, 5. (The direct discourse was αὐτοὶ μὲν ἐπλέομεν, τὴν δὲ ἀναίρεσιν προσετάξαμεν.) Καί μοι πάντες ἀπεκρίναντο, ὅτι οὐδεὶς μάρτυς παρείη, κομίζοιτο δὲ λαμβάνων καθ' ὁποσονοῦν δέοιτο Ἄφοβος παρ' αὐτῶν, *they all replied, that no witness had been present, and that Aphobus had received the money from them, taking it in such sums as he happened to want.* DEM. xxx. 20. (The direct discourse was οὐδεὶς μάρτυς παρῆν, ἐκομίζετο δὲ λαμβάνων καθ' ὁποσονοῦν δέοιτο. Παρείη contains the answer to the question εἴ τινες παρῆσαν in the preceding sentence, quoted in 672. The imperfect in that sentence prevents the optatives in the reply from being ambiguous.) Ἀκούσας πιστεύω τούτῳ, ὡς ἄρα Λεόντιος, αἰσθόμενος νεκροὺς παρὰ τῷ δημίῳ κειμένους, ἅμα μὲν ἰδεῖν ἐπιθυμοῖ, ἅμα δ' αὖ δυσχεραίνοι καὶ ἀποτρέποι ἑαυτὸν, καὶ τέως μάχοιτό τε καὶ παρακαλύπτοιτο. PLAT. Rep. 439 E. (All the optatives represent imperfects.)   See also HDT. ix. 16 (end).

674. 1. In Homer, where clauses with ὅτι, ὡς, etc. are not yet constructed on the principles of indirect discourse (see 671), a present or perfect of the direct form appears as an imperfect or pluperfect in these clauses after past tenses. *E.g.*

Οὐδέ τι ᾔδη ὅττι δηιόωντο λαοί. Il. xiii. 674 (here the present optative or indicative would be regular in Attic Greek). Ἐπόρουσε, γιγνώσκων ὅ οἱ αὐτὸς ὑπείρεχε χεῖρας Ἀπόλλων (later ὑπερέχοι or ὑπερέχει). Il. v. 433. Οὐ γάρ οἵ τις ἤγγειλ' ὅττι ῥά οἱ πόσις ἔκτοθι μίμνε πυλάων. Il. xxii. 438. See Od. xxiv. 182 ; and iii. 166, discussed in 671.

2. We sometimes find the imperfect and pluperfect with ὅτι or ὡς representing the present or perfect of the direct form after past tenses, even in Attic Greek. In such cases the context always makes it clear that the tense represented is not an imperfect or pluperfect (672). *E.g.*

Ἐν πολλῇ ἀπορίᾳ ἦσαν οἱ Ἕλληνες, ἐννοούμενοι μὲν ὅτι ἐπὶ ταῖς βασιλέως θύραις ἦσαν, κύκλῳ δὲ αὐτοῖς πόλεις πολέμιαι ἦσαν, ἀγορὰν δὲ οὐδεὶς ἔτι παρέξειν ἔμελλεν, ἀπεῖχον δὲ τῆς Ἑλλάδος οὐ μεῖον ἢ μύρια στάδια, προυδεδώκεσαν δὲ αὐτοὺς καὶ οἱ βάρβαροι, μόνοι δὲ καταλελειμμένοι ἦσαν οὐδὲ ἱππέα οὐδένα σύμμαχον ἔχοντες, the Greeks thought : *We are at the king's gates ; hostile cities surround us ; no one will supply us a market ; we are not less than ten thousand stades from Greece ; the barbarians have betrayed us, and we have been left alone.* XEN. An. iii. 1, 2. (The direct forms would be the present and perfect indicative.) Διὰ τὸν χθιζινὸν ἄνθρωπον, ὃς ἡμᾶς διεδύετ᾽, ἐξαπατῶν καὶ λέγων ὡς φιλαθήναιος ἦν καὶ τὰν Σάμῳ πρῶτος κατείποι, i.e. *saying* φιλαθήναιός εἰμι καὶ τὰν Σάμῳ πρῶτος κατεῖπον. AR. Vesp. 283. (Here εἰμί is changed to ἦν, not to εἴη or ἐστί: κατεῖπον could be changed only to κατείποι.)

3. In such cases the more thorough incorporation of the dependent clause which is required to make the oratio obliqua complete is wanting, and the clause stands in the loose relation in which, for example, causal sentences usually stand to their leading verb (see 715). For the same incomplete oratio obliqua in dependent clauses of a quotation, see 691 and 701.

675. 1. An indirect quotation with ὅτι or ὡς and the optative is sometimes followed by an independent optative, generally introduced by γάρ, which continues the quotation as if it were itself dependent on the ὅτι or ὡς. *E.g.*

Ἤκουον δ᾽ ἔγωγέ τινων ὡς οὐδὲ τοὺς λιμένας καὶ τὰς ἀγορὰς ἔτι δώσοιεν αὐτῷ καρποῦσθαι· τὰ γὰρ κοινὰ τὰ Θετταλῶν ἀπὸ τούτων δέοι διοικεῖν, *for (as they said) they must administer*, etc. DEM. i. 22. Ἀπεκρίναντο αὐτῷ ὅτι ἀδύνατα σφίσιν εἴη ποιεῖν ἃ προκαλεῖται ἄνευ Ἀθηναίων· παῖδες γὰρ σφῶν καὶ γυναῖκες παρ᾽ ἐκείνοις εἴησαν. THUC. ii. 72. Ἔλεγον ὅτι παντὸς ἄξια λέγοι Σεύθης· χειμὼν γὰρ εἴη, κ.τ.λ. XEN. An. vii. 3, 13.

2. Such independent optatives are sometimes found even when no optative precedes ; but the context always contains some allusion to another's thought or expression. *E.g.*

Ὑπέσχετο τὸν ἄνδρ᾽ Ἀχαιοῖς τόνδε δηλώσειν ἄγων· οἴοιτο μὲν μάλισθ᾽ ἑκούσιον λαβὼν, εἰ μὴ θέλοι δ᾽, ἄκοντα, i.e. *he thought (as he said)*, etc. SOPH. Ph. 617. Ἀλλὰ γὰρ οὐδέν τι μᾶλλον ἦν ἀθάνατον, ἀλλὰ καὶ αὐτὸ τὸ εἰς ἀνθρώπου σῶμα ἐλθεῖν ἀρχὴ ἦν αὐτῇ ὀλέθρου, ὥσπερ νόσος· καὶ ταλαιπωρουμένη τε δὴ τοῦτον τὸν βίον ζῴη, καὶ τελευτῶσά γε ἐν τῷ καλουμένῳ θανάτῳ ἀπολλύοιτο, *and (according to the theory) it lives in misery*, etc., *and finally perishes in what is called death.* PLAT. Phaed. 95 D. (Plato is here stating the views of others.)

676. We may even have ὅτι or ὡς with the optative when the leading verb is not past, if there is an implied reference to some former expression of the thought quoted. *E.g.*

Ἆρ᾽ οὖν δὴ οὐ μετρίως ἀπολογησόμεθα, ὅτι πρὸς τὸ ὂν πεφυκὼς εἴη ἁμιλλᾶσθαι, καὶ οὐκ ἐπιμένοι, . . . ἀλλ᾽ ἴοι καὶ οὐκ ἀμβλύνοιτο οὐδ᾽ ἀπολήγοι τοῦ ἔρωτος, κ.τ.λ., i.e. *shall we not defend him very properly by stating (what we once said) that it is (was) his nature to press on towards pure Being*, etc. (the optatives representing indicatives). PLAT. Rep. 490 A.

Subjunctive or Optative representing the Interrogative Subjunctive.

677. In indirect questions, after a primary tense, an *interrogative subjunctive* (287) retains its mood and tense; after a secondary tense, it may be either changed to the same tense of the optative or retained in the subjunctive. *E.g.*

Φραζώμεθ᾽ ... ἤ ῥ᾽ αὖτις πόλεμον ὄρσομεν (subj.) ἦ φιλότητα μετ᾽ ἀμφοτέροισι βάλωμεν, *let us consider whether we shall again rouse war or cast friendship upon both armies.* Il. iv. 14. Σὺ δέ μοι νημερτὲς ἐνίσπες, ἤ μιν ἀποκτείνω ἦε σοὶ ἐνθάδ᾽ ἄγω, *and do you tell me truly whether I shall slay him or bring him hither to you.* Od. xxii. 166. See Od. xvi. 73, xix. 524. Πρὸς ἀμφότερα ἀπορῶ, ταύτην θ᾽ ὅπως ἐκδῶ καὶ τἄλλ᾽ ὁπόθεν διοικῶ, *I am at a loss on both questions, how I shall give her a dowry* (πῶς ταύτην ἐκδῶ;), *and how (whence) I shall pay my other expenses* (πόθεν τἄλλα διοικῶ;). DEM. xxvii. 66. Βουλεύομαι ὅπως σε ἀποδρῶ, *I am trying to think how I shall escape you* (πῶς σε ἀποδρῶ;). XEN. Cyr. i. 4, 13. Οὐκ ἔχω τί λέγω, *I know not what I shall say.* DEM. ix. 54. So in Latin, *non habeo quid* (or *quod*) *dicam.* Οὐκ ἔχω σόφισμ᾽ ὅτῳ ἀπαλλαγῶ, *I have no device* (i.e. *I know not*) *how I shall escape.* AESCH. Prom. 470. Οὐ γὰρ δὴ δι᾽ ἀπειρίαν γε οὐ φήσεις ἔχειν ὅ τι εἴπῃς, *for it is not surely through inexperience that you will declare that you know not what to say* (i.e. τί εἴπω;). DEM. xix. 120. So ὅ τι δῶ and οἷς δῶ, XEN. An. i. 7, 7. (See 572.) Τὰ δὲ ἐκπώματα οὐκ οἶδ᾽ εἰ Χρυσάντᾳ τούτῳ δῶ, *I do not know whether I shall give them,* etc. Id. Cyr. viii. 4, 16. Ἐπανερομένου Κτησιφῶντος εἰ καλέσῃ Δημοσθένην, *when Ctesiphon asks whether he shall call Demosthenes.* AESCHIN. iii. 202. (For εἰ see 680.)

Ἐν δέ οἱ ἦτορ μερμήριξεν, ἦ ὅ γε τοὺς μὲν ἀναστήσειεν, ὁ δ᾽ Ἀτρείδην ἐναρίξοι, ἦε χόλον παύσειεν ἐρητύσειέ τε θυμόν. Il. i. 188. (The direct questions were τοὺς μὲν ἀναστήσω; Ἀτρείδην δ᾽ ἐναρίζω; παύσω ἐρητύσω τε;) Κλήρους πάλλον, ὁππότερος δὴ πρόσθεν ἀφείη χάλκεον ἔγχος, i.e. *they shook the lots (to decide) which should first throw his spear,* the question being πότερος πρόσθεν ἀφῇ; Il. iii. 316. Ἐχρηστηριάζετο εἰ ἐκβάλοι τὸν Ἄδρηστον. HDT. v. 67. Ἐπήροντο εἰ παραδοῖεν Κορινθίοις τὴν πόλιν, *they asked whether they should give up their city,* the question being παραδῶμεν τὴν πόλιν; THUC. i. 25. Ἐβουλεύοντο εἰ τὰ σκευοφόρα ἐνταῦθα ἄγοιντο ἢ ἀπίοιεν ἐπὶ τὸ στρατόπεδον. XEN. An. i. 10, 17: so i. 10, 5. Ἠπόρει ὅ τι χρήσαιτο τῷ πράγματι, *he was at a loss how to act in the matter,* i.e. τί χρήσωμαι; Id. Hell. vii. 4, 39. Οὐ γὰρ εἴχομεν ὅπως δρῶντες καλῶς πράξαιμεν, *for we could not see how we should fare well if we did it.* SOPH. Ant. 270.

Ἀπορέοντος δὲ βασιλέος ὅ τι χρήσηται τῷ παρεόντι πρήγματι, Ἐπιάλτης ἦλθέ οἱ ἐς λόγους. HDT. vii. 213. Ἠπόρησε μὲν ὁποτέ-

ρωσε διακινδυνεύσῃ χωρήσας. Thuc. i. 63. Οἱ Πλαταιῆς ἐβουλεύοντο εἴτε κατακαύσωσιν ὥσπερ ἔχουσιν, ἐμπρήσαντες το οἴκημα,
εἴτε τι ἄλλο χρήσωνται, whether they should set the house on fire and
burn them as they were, or should dispose of them in some other way. Id.
ii. 4. Ἀπορήσαντες ὅπῃ καθορμίσωνται, ἐς Πρώτην τὴν νῆσον
ἔπλευσαν. Id. iv. 13.

678. The context must decide whether the optative in an indirect
question represents a subjunctive (as here) or an indicative (669). The
distinction is especially important with the aorist optative (see 125).

679. When the leading verb is an optative referring to the future,
the optative can be used, by assimilation, to represent the subjunctive
in these indirect questions. *E.g.*

Χαρίεντα γοῦν πάθοιμ' ἄν, εἰ μὴ 'χοιμ' ὅποι ταῦτα καταθείην, *if
I should not have anywhere to put these down (know where to put them).*
Ar. Eccl. 794. (See other examples under 186.)

680. Εἰ, *whether,* can introduce the subjunctive here, as well as the
indicative or optative : see Xen. Cyr. viii. 4, 16, and Aeschin. iii.
202, quoted in 677. Ἐάν cannot mean *whether,* and wherever this
introduces a subjunctive the expression is conditional. (See 493.)

Indicative or Optative with ἄν.

681. An indicative or optative with ἄν retains its mood
and tense (with ἄν) unchanged in indirect discourse with
ὅτι or ὡς and in indirect questions, after both primary and
secondary tenses. *E.g.*

Λέγει ὅτι τοῦτο ἂν ἐγένετο, *he says that this would have happened :*
ἔλεγεν ὅτι τοῦτο ἂν ἐγένετο, *he said that this would have happened.*
Λέγει (or ἔλεγεν) ὅτι οὗτος δικαίως ἂν θάνοι, *he says (or said) that
this man would justly be put to death.*

(Θεμιστοκλῆς) ἀπεκρίνατο, ὅτι οὔτ' ἂν αὐτὸς Σερίφιος ὢν ὀνομαστὸς
ἐγένετο οὔτ' ἐκεῖνος Ἀθηναῖος, *he replied that he should not have become
famous himself if he had been a Seriphian, nor would the other if he had
been an Athenian.* Plat. Rep. 330 A. Ἐννοεῖτε, ὅτι ἧττον ἂν στάσις
εἴη ἑνὸς ἄρχοντος ἢ πολλῶν. Xen. An. vi. i. 29. Ἀπεκρίνατο, ὅτι
πρόσθεν ἂν ἀποθάνοιεν ἢ τὰ ὅπλα παραδοίησαν. Ib. ii. 1, 10.
(The direct discourse was πρόσθεν ἂν ἀποθάνοιμεν.) Οὐκ ἂν ἐλπί-
σαντας ὡς ἂν ἐπεξέλθοι τις αὐτοῖς ἐς μάχην, *when they would never
have expected that any one would come out to fight with them.* Thuc. v. 9.
Παρελθών τις δειξάτω, ὡς οἱ Θετταλοὶ νῦν οὐκ ἂν ἐλεύθεροι γένοιντο
ἄσμενοι. Dem. ii. 8. Οὐδ' εἰδέναι φησὶ τί ἂν ποιῶν ὑμῖν χαρίσαιτο,
he says he does not even know what he could do to gratify you. Id. xix. 48.
Οὐκ ἔχω τίς ἂν γενοίμαν. Aesch. Prom. 905 ; so 907. Ἠρώτων
εἰ δοῖεν ἂν τούτων τὰ πιστά. Xen. An. iv. 8, 7.

682. The same principle applies when a secondary tense of the indicative without ἄν in the construction of 415 is quoted. *E.g.*

(Ἔλεγεν) ὅτι κρεῖττον ἦν αὐτῷ τότε ἀποθανεῖν, *he said that he had
better have died at once.* LYS. x. 25.   (The direct discourse was κρεῖττον
ἦν μοι ἀποθανεῖν.)

Infinitive in Indirect Discourse.

683. When the infinitive stands in indirect discourse,
its tense represents the corresponding tense of the finite
verb in the direct form, the present and perfect including
the imperfect and pluperfect. If ἄν was used in the direct
form, it must be retained in the quotation, each tense with
ἄν representing the corresponding tenses of either indicative
or optative with ἄν. *E.g.*

Φησὶ γράφειν, *he says that he is writing;* ἔφη γράφειν, *he said that
he was writing;* φήσει γράφειν, *he will say that he is (then) writing.*
(He says γράφω.)   Φησὶ (ἔφη) γράφειν ἄν, εἰ ἐδύνατο, *he says (or
said) that he should now be writing, if he were able.* (He says ἔγραφον
ἄν.)   Φησὶ (ἔφη) γράφειν ἄν, εἰ δύναιτο, *he says (or said) that he should
write, if he should (ever) be able.* (He says γράφοιμι ἄν.)

Φησὶ γράψαι, *he says that he wrote;* ἔφη γράψαι, *he said that he had
written;* φήσει γράψαι, *he will say that he wrote.* (He says ἔγραψα.)
Φησὶ (ἔφη) γράψαι ἄν, εἰ ἐδυνήθη, *he says (or said) that he should have
written, if he had been able.* (He says ἔγραψα ἄν.)   Φησὶ (ἔφη) γράψαι
ἄν, εἰ δυνηθείη, *he says (or said) that he should write, if he should (ever)
be able.* (He says γράψαιμι ἄν.)

Φησὶ (φήσει) γεγραφέναι, *he says (or will say) that he has written;*
ἔφη γεγραφέναι, *he said that he had written.* (He says γέγραφα.)
For the perfect with ἄν, see below and 206.

Φησὶ (φήσει) γράψειν, *he says (or will say) that he will write;* ἔφη
γράψειν, *he said that he would write.* (He says γράψω.)

(Present.) Καί τέ μέ φησι μάχῃ Τρώεσσιν ἀρήγειν. Il. i. 521.
Πῶς δὴ φῂς πολέμοιο μεθιέμεν; Il. iv. 351.   So Il. xvii. 338.   Σκύ-
ζεσθαί οἱ εἰπὲ θεούς, ἐμὲ δ' ἔξοχα πάντων ἀθανάτων κεχολῶσθαι,
*tell him that the Gods are angry with him and that I am enraged with him
beyond all the immortals.* Il. xxiv. 113. Ἀρρωστεῖν προφασίζεται,
he pretends that he is sick: ἐξώμοσεν ἀρρωστεῖν τουτονί, *he took his
oath that this man was sick.* DEM. xix. 124.   Οὐκ ἔφη αὐτὸς ἀλλ' ἐκεῖνον
στρατηγεῖν, i.e. *Cleon said that not he himself, but Nicias, was general;*
i.e. *he said,* οὐκ ἐγὼ αὐτὸς ἀλλ' ἐκεῖνος στρατηγεῖ. THUC. iv. 28.
Τίνας οὖν εὐχὰς ὑπολαμβάνετ' εὔχεσθαι τὸν Φίλιππον ὅτ' ἔσπενδεν;
what prayers do you suppose Philip made, etc.? DEM. xix. 130.   (Εὔχεσθαι represents ηὔχετο: see 119.)   Οἶμαι γὰρ ἂν οὐκ ἀχαρίστως μοι
ἔχειν, *for I think it would not be a thankless labour;* i.e. οὐκ ἂν ἔχοι.
XEN. An. ii. 3, 18.   Οἴεσθε γὰρ τὸν πατέρα οὐκ ἂν φυλάττειν καὶ
τὴν τιμὴν λαμβάνειν τῶν πωλουμένων ξύλων; *do you think that my
father would not have taken care and have received the pay for the timber*

sold? i.e. οὐκ ἂν ἐφύλαττεν καὶ ἐλάμβανεν; DEM. xlix. 35. (See 205.)

(Aorist.) Οὐδέ κε φαίης ἀνδρὶ μαχησάμενον τόν γ' ἐλθέμεν, *nor would you say that he came after a battle with a man.* Il. iii. 393. Κατασχεῖν φησι τούτους, *he says that he detained them.* Τοὺς δ' αἰχμαλώτους οὐδ' ἐνθυμηθῆναί φησι λύσασθαι, *but he says that he did not even think of ransoming the prisoners.* DEM. xix. 39. (He says κατέσχον and οὐδ' ἐνεθυμήθην.) Ὁ Κῦρος λέγεται γενέσθαι Καμβύσεω, *Cyrus is said to have been the son of Cambyses.* XEN. Cyr. i. 2, 1. Τοὺς Ἀθηναίους ἤλπιζεν ἴσως ἂν ἐπεξελθεῖν καὶ τὴν γῆν οὐκ ἂν περιιδεῖν τμηθῆναι, *he hoped that the Athenians would perhaps march out and not allow their land to be laid waste;* i.e. ἴσως ἂν ἐπεξέλθοιεν καὶ οὐκ ἂν περιίδοιεν. THUC. ii. 20. Ἀπῄεσαν νομίσαντες μὴ ἂν ἔτι ἱκανοὶ γενέσθαι κωλῦσαι τὸν τειχισμόν. Id. vi. 102. (Here οὐκ ἂν γενοίμεθα would be the direct form : see 685.) So i. 139. Οὐκ ἂν ἡγεῖσθ' αὐτὸν κἂν ἐπιδραμεῖν, *do you not believe that (in that case) he would have run thither?* i.e. ἐπέδραμεν ἄν. DEM. xxvii. 56. (See 223.) A single infinitive with ἄν occurs in Homer : καὶ δ' ἂν τοῖς ἄλλοισιν ἔφη παραμυθήσασθαι, Il. ix. 684. (The direct discourse is given in the words of Achilles in vs. 417, καὶ δ' ἂν παραμυθησαίμην.) (See 207.)

(Perfect.) Φρονέω τετιμῆσθαι Διὸς αἴσῃ, *I feel that I have been honoured.* Il. ix. 608. Φησὶν αὐτὸς αἴτιος γεγενῆσθαι, *he says αἴτιος γεγένημαι.* DEM. xix. 37. Εἴκαζον ἢ διώκοντα οἴχεσθαι ἢ καταληψόμενόν τι προελ ηλακέναι. XEN. An. i. 10, 16. (Their thought was ἢ διώκων οἴχεται, ἢ προελήλακεν.) Ἔφη χρήμαθ' ἑαυτῷ τοὺς Θηβαίους ἐπικεκηρυχέναι, *he said that the Thebans had offered a reward for him.* DEM. xix. 21. Ἀντέλεγον μὴ δικαίως σφῶν καταδεδικάσθαι, λέγοντες μὴ ἐπηγγέλθαι πω ἐς Λακεδαίμονα τὰς σπονδὰς ὅτ' ἐσέπεμψαν τοὺς ὁπλίτας, *they rejoined that they (the Eleans) had not justly condemned them, saying that the truce had not yet been announced at Sparta when they sent in the soldiers* (they said οὐ καταδεδίκασθε, and οὐκ ἐπηγγελμέναι ἦσάν πω αἱ σπονδαὶ ὅτ' ἐσεπέμψαμεν). THUC. v. 49. So ἐκπεπλῆχθαι, representing ἐξεπέπληκτο, XEN. Cyr. i. 4, 27. (See 123, above.)

(For examples of the perfect infinitive with ἄν, representing the pluperfect indicative and the perfect optative, see 206.)

(Future.) Ἔφης σῶς ἔσσεσθαι. Il. xxii. 331. So Od. iv. 664. Καί μοι ἔειπεν Μυρμιδόνων τὸν ἄριστον λείψειν φάος ἠελίοιο, *he told me ὁ ἄριστος . . . λείψει.* Il. xviii. 9. Καὶ δή μοι γέρας αὐτὸς ἀφαιρήσεσθαι ἀπειλεῖς. Il. i. 161. Ἐπαγγέλλεται τὰ δίκαια ποιήσειν, *he promises to do what is right.* DEM. xix. 48. Ἔφη ἐντὸς ἡμερῶν εἴκοσιν ἢ ἄξειν Λακεδαιμονίους ζῶντας ἢ αὐτοῦ ἀποκτενεῖν, *he said that within twenty days he would either bring them alive or kill them where they were.* THUC. iv. 28. (Cleon said ἢ ἄξω ἢ ἀποκτενῶ.) Ταῦτα (φησὶ) πεπράξεσθαι δυοῖν ἢ τριῶν ἡμερῶν, *he says that this will have been accomplished within two or three days* (137). DEM. xix. 74. (For the rare future infinitive with ἄν, see 208.)

684. The infinitive is said *to stand in indirect discourse* and its tenses correspond to those of the indicative or optative, when it depends on a verb implying thought or the expression of thought (one of the class of *verba sentiendi et declarandi*), and when *also* the thought, as originally conceived, would have been expressed by some tense of the indicative (with or without ἄν) or optative (with ἄν), so that it can be transferred without change of tense to the infinitive. Thus in βούλεται ἐλθεῖν, *he wishes to go*, ἐλθεῖν represents no form of either aorist indicative or aorist optative, and is therefore said to be not in indirect discourse. But in φησὶν ἐλθεῖν, *he says that he went*, ἐλθεῖν represents ἦλθον of the direct discourse. The distinction in the time of the infinitive (especially of the aorist infinitive) in these two uses is obvious.

It may be asked why the infinitive after certain other verbs should not be said to stand in indirect discourse ; for example, why in κελεύει σε ἐλθεῖν or μὴ ἐλθεῖν we should not say that ἐλθεῖν represents ἐλθέ or μὴ ἔλθῃς of direct discourse. This might perhaps be done ; and we might possibly make ἐλθεῖν in βούλομαι ἐλθεῖν represent ἔλθοιμι, *may I go*. But with other verbs of the same class, as those of *advising, teaching, striving, choosing,* no form of direct discourse can even be imagined. It is much harder to draw a line between these last verbs and verbs like κελεύω and βούλομαι, or even between these two, than where it is drawn above. It is impossible to say where a Greek would have drawn the line, or to be sure that he would have drawn any line at all ; for our own use, the usual definition of the infinitive in oratio obliqua (as given above) is certainly the most convenient.

685. (Μή *with Infinitive.*) The negative particle of the infinitive in indirect discourse is regularly οὐ, which is retained from the direct form (667, 5). But, after certain verbs which belong to the intermediate class between those which take the infinitive in indirect discourse and those which do not (see 136), the infinitive regularly takes μή for its negative. Such are verbs of *hoping, promising,* and *swearing ;* with those signifying *to agree* or *consent* (ὁμολογῶ), *to trust* (πιστεύω), *to be persuaded* (πέπεισμαι), *to testify* (μαρτυρῶ).[1] The infinitive occasionally has μή even after the verbs which most regularly take the infinitive with οὐ in indirect discourse, as φημί, λέγω, νομίζω, ἡγοῦμαι, etc. *E.g.*

Χρῆν ὀμόσαι μὴ ἑκόντα ἐλθεῖν, *he had to swear that he did not come intentionally.* HDT. ii. 179 ; so i. 165. Ὄμνυσιν μὴ πώποτ᾽ ἀμεινον᾽ ἔπη μηδέν᾽ ἀκοῦσαι, *he swears that nobody ever heard better verses.* AR. Vesp. 1047. Ὤμνυε μηδὲν εἰρηκέναι. DEM. xxi. 119. Ὅταν ἐλπίσωσιν οὗτοι μὴ ἄλλως τὸν νέον καθέξειν. PLAT. Rep. 572 E. Οὐδεμίαν ὑμέων ἔχω ἐλπίδα μὴ οὐ δώσειν ὑμέας δίκην. HDT. vi. 11. (For μὴ οὐ see 815, 2.) Μαιάδος υἱὸς ὑποσχόμενος κατένευσε μή ποτ᾽ ἀποκλέψειν ὅσ᾽ Ἑκηβόλος ἐκτεάτισται. Hymn. Merc. 521 ; so μή τινα ἔσεσθαι. Ibid. 525.

---

[1] See Liddell and Scott, ed. 7, under μή, B. 5, C ; also Gildersleeve in *Am. Jour. Phil.* i. p. 51.

Ὡμολογήσαμεν μήποτ' ἂν αὐτὴν ἐναντία ᾄδειν. Plat. Phaed. 94 C.
Μεμαρτυρήκασιν οἱ πρότερον ἐργαζόμενοι μὴ εἶναι σηκὸν ἐν τῷ χωρίῳ.
Lys. vii. 11. So Dem. xlv. 15. Σωκράτη γε ἐγὼ ἐγγυῶμαι μὴ ἐπι-
λήσεσθαι. Plat. Prot. 336 D. Πιστεύω μὴ ψεύσειν με ταύτας τὰς
ἀγαθὰς ἐλπίδας. Xen. Cyr. i. 5, 13. Πέπεισμαι ἐγὼ μηδένα ἀδικεῖν
ἀνθρώπων. Plat. Ap. 37 A : so 37 B.
Φαίην δ' ἂν ἔγωγε μηδενὶ μηδεμίαν εἶναι παίδευσιν παρὰ τοῦ μὴ
ἀρέσκοντος. Xen. Mem. i. 2, 39. So Plat. Theaet. 155 A. Πάντες
ἐροῦσι τὸ λοιπὸν μηδὲν εἶναι κερδαλεώτερον ἀρετῆς. Xen. Cyr. vii.
1, 18. Ἐνόμισε δὲ μὴ ἂν γενέσθαι ποτὲ πιστὸν ἄνθρωπον. Ib. vii. 5,
59. Καὶ ἄρτι ἔλεγον μηδένα ἐθέλειν ἑκόντα ἄρχειν. Plat. Rep. 346
E. Τίς ἂν θεῶν μὲν παῖδας ἡγοῖτο εἶναι, θεοὺς δὲ μή; Id. Ap.
27 D. Προύλεγον μὴ ἂν γίγνεσθαι πόλεμον (i.e. οὐκ ἂν γίγνοιτο
πόλεμος). Thuc. i. 139. See also Thuc. v. 49, vi. 102, quoted in 683.

The examples in the last paragraph are opposed to the regular
usage of the language, which would demand οὐ in all of them. We
must suppose that the use of μή with the infinitive was so fixed, before
the infinitive began to be used in indirect discourse, that μή always
seemed natural, even after οὐ had become the regular form after verbs
of *saying*, *thinking*, etc. We sometimes find strange uses of μή. In
Thuc. i. 118, ὄντες μὲν καὶ πρὸ τοῦ μὴ ταχεῖς ἰέναι ἐς τοὺς πολέμους, *having even before this been not hasty to go into wars*, it may be
difficult to find a better explanation of the anomalous μή than the
perhaps heretical one, that τοῦ μὴ ταχεῖς ἰέναι had a more natural
sound than τοῦ οὐ ταχεῖς ἰέναι, although neither τοῦ nor the negative
has anything to do with the infinitive. So some people say *between
you and I*, merely because *you and me* sounds vulgar.

686. With μή and the infinitive in indirect discourse we may
compare the rare ὅτι μή with the indicative, which occurs in Theog.
659, οὐδ' ὀμόσαι χρὴ τοῦθ', ὅτι μήποτε πρῆγμα τόδ' ἔσται, and
Ant. v. 21, ταῦτα σκοπεῖτε, ὅτι μὴ προνοίᾳ μᾶλλον ἐγίγνετο ἢ
τύχῃ : see also Soph. Ant. 685, ὅπως σὺ μὴ λέγεις ὀρθῶς τάδε.
Ὅτι μή with the indicative became a regular construction in later
Greek (as in Lucian). Ὀμόσαι ὅτι μή ἔσται in Theognis suggests the
still more puzzling cases of μή alone with the indicative after oaths
in Homer and Aristophanes : ἴστω Ζεὺς, μὴ μὲν τοῖς ἵπποισιν ἀνὴρ
ἐποιχήσεται ἄλλος, Il. x. 329 ; ἴστω νῦν τόδε γαῖα . . . μὴ δι'
ἐμὴν ἰότητα Ποσειδάων ἐνοσίχθων πημαίνει Τρῶας, Il. xv. 36 ; μὰ
τὸν Ἀπόλλω μή σ' ἐγὼ κατακλινῶ χαμαί, Ar. Lys. 917 ; so Eccl.
1000 ; μὰ γῆν, μὰ παγίδας, . . . μὴ 'γὼ νόημα κομψότερον ἤκουσά
πω, Av. 194. I have no explanation, even to suggest, of the strange
use of μή in these last examples.

Participle in Indirect Discourse.

687. When the participle stands in indirect discourse,

it follows the rules already given for the infinitive (683), in regard to its tense and the use of ἄν. *E.g.*

Ἀγγέλλει τούτους ἐρχομένους, *he announces that they are coming;* ἤγγειλε τούτους ἐρχομένους, *he announced that they were coming.* (The announcement is οὗτοι ἔρχονται.) Ἀγγέλλει τούτους ἐλθόντας, *he announces that they came;* ἤγγειλε τούτους ἐλθόντας, *he announced that they had come.* (He says ἦλθον.) Ἀγγέλλει τούτους ἐληλυθότας, *he announces that they have come;* ἤγγειλε τούτους ἐληλυθότας, *he announced that they had come.* (He says ἐληλύθασιν.) Ἀγγέλλει (ἤγγειλε) τοῦτο γενησόμενον, *he announces (or announced) that this is (or was) about to happen.* (He says τοῦτο γενήσεται.)

Οὐδ' ἄρα πώ τι ᾔδη Πάτροκλον τεθνηότα δῖος Ἀχιλλεύς, *nor yet did Achilles have any knowledge that Patroclus was dead.* Il. xvii. 402. Γίγνωσκε θεοῦ γόνον ἠΰν ἐόντα. Il. vi. 191. Τηλέμαχος δ' ἄρα μιν πάλαι ᾔδεεν ἔνδον ἐόντα. Od. xxiii. 29 : so xvii. 549, 556. Τοῖς τε γὰρ ἐπιχειρήμασιν ἑώρων οὐ κατορθοῦντες καὶ τοὺς στρατιώτας ἀχθομένους τῇ μονῇ, *for they saw that they were not succeeding in their attempts, and that the soldiers were distressed by the delay;* i.e. they saw οὐ κατορθοῦμεν καὶ οἱ στρατιῶται ἄχθονται. Thuc. vii. 47. Ἐμμένομεν οἷς ὡμολογήσαμεν δικαίοις οὖσιν; *do we abide by what we acknowledged to be just* (i.e. δίκαιά ἐστιν)? Plat. Crit. 50 A. Πάνθ' ἕνεκα ἑαυτοῦ ποιῶν ἐξελήλεγκται, *it has been proved that he is doing everything for his own interest.* Dem. ii. 8. Αὐτῷ Κῦρον ἐπιστρατεύοντα πρῶτος ἤγγειλα, *I first announced to him that Cyrus was on his march against him.* Xen. An. ii. 3, 19. See Soph. O. T. 395.

Ἢ σάφα οἶδε νοστήσαντά σε δεῦρο, *whether she is perfectly certain that you have returned hither.* Od. xxiv. 404. Ἐπιστάμενοι καὶ τὸν βάρβαρον αὐτὸν περὶ αὑτῷ τὰ πλείω σφαλέντα, καὶ πρὸς αὐτοὺς τοὺς Ἀθηναίους πολλὰ ἡμᾶς ἤδη τοῖς ἁμαρτήμασιν αὐτῶν μᾶλλον ἢ τῇ ἀφ' ὑμῶν τιμωρίᾳ περιγεγενημένους (i.e. ὁ βάρβαρος ἐσφάλη, καὶ ἡμεῖς περιγεγενήμεθα). Thuc. i. 69. So in the same chapter, τὸν Μῆδον αὐτοὶ ἴσμεν ἐκ περάτων γῆς ἐπὶ τὴν Πελοπόννησον ἐλθόντα, i.e. ὁ Μῆδος ἦλθεν. Ἐπειδὴ ἔγνωσαν οὐ μετ' Ἀθηναίων πραχθεῖσαν τὴν τῶν Βοιωτῶν ξυμμαχίαν, ἀλλ' ἐς διαφορὰν μεγάλην καθεστῶτας αὐτοὺς πρὸς τοὺς Λακεδαιμονίους (i.e. οὐκ ἐπράχθη and καθεστᾶσιν). Id. v. 44. Οὐ γὰρ ᾔδεσαν αὐτὸν τεθνηκότα, *for they did not know that he was dead* (i.e. τέθνηκεν). Xen. An. i. 10, 16. See And. i. 23 ; Soph. Tr. 739. Ἐπέδειξα οὐδὲν ἀληθὲς ἀπηγγελκότα ἀλλὰ φενακίσανθ' ὑμᾶς, *I have shown that he has reported nothing that is true, and that he deceived you* (ἀπήγγελκεν and ἐφενάκισεν). Dem. xix. 177.

Εἰ εὖ ᾔδειν καὶ τὴν συμμαχίαν μοι γενησομένην, *if I were sure that I should obtain an alliance also* (i.e. συμμαχία μοι γενήσεται). Ibid. 40. So Xen. Hell. iv. 7, 3. Ὁ δ' ἀντοφείλων ἀμβλύτερος, εἰδὼς οὐκ ἐς χάριν ἀλλ' ἐς ὀφείλημα τὴν ἀρετὴν ἀποδώσων, *knowing that*

he shall not return the benefit, etc. (i.e. οὐκ ἀποδώσω). THUC. ii. 40.
Γνόντες οὔτ᾽ ἀποκωλύσειν δυνατοὶ ὄντες, εἴ τ᾽ ἀπομονωθήσονται τῆς
ξυμβάσεως, κινδυνεύσοντες, ποιοῦνται ὁμολογίαν (i.e. οὔτε δυνατοί
ἐσμεν, εἴ τ᾽ ἀπομονωθησόμεθα, κινδυνεύσομεν). Id. iii. 28.
Εὖ δ᾽ ἴσθι μηδὲν ἄν με τούτων ἐπιχειρήσαντα σε πείθειν, εἰ
δυναστείαν μόνον ἢ πλοῦτον ἑώρων ἐξ αὐτῶν γενησόμενον. ISOC.
v. 133 (μηδὲν ἂν ἐπιχειρήσαντα represents οὐδὲν ἂν ἐπεχείρησα,
and γενησόμενον represents γενήσεται). Εὖ ἴσμεν μὴ ἂν ἧσσον ὑμᾶς
λυπηροὺς γενομένους (i.e. οὐκ ἂν ἐγένεσθε). THUC. i. 76. Σκοπού-
μενος οὖν εὕρισκον οὐδαμῶς ἂν ἄλλως τοῦτο διαπραξάμενος, *I
found that I could accomplish this* (διαπραξαίμην ἄν) *in no other way.*
ISOC. xv. 7.
Ὅπως δέ γε τοὺς πολεμίους δύναισθε κακῶς ποιεῖν, οὐκ οἶσθα
μανθάνοντας ὑμᾶς πολλὰς κακουργίας; *do you not know that you
learned*, etc.? XEN. Cyr. i. 6, 28. (Here δύναισθε and the whole context show that μανθάνοντας represents ἐμανθάνετε.) Μέμνημαι δὲ
ἔγωγε καὶ παῖς ὢν Κριτίᾳ τῷδε ξυνόντα σε, *I remember that you
were with* (ξυνῆσθα) *this Critias.* PLAT. Charm. 156 A. (See 140
and the examples.)

See other examples in 904.

688. (*Negative* μή.) The participle of indirect discourse, like the
infinitive, regularly retains the negative οὐ from the direct form. But,
as in the case of the infinitive (685), we find many exceptions. Compare ISOC. v. 133 and THUC. i. 76, which have μή after οἶδα, with
THUC. ii. 40 and ISOC. xv. 7, which have οἶδα οὐ (all quoted in 687).
See also SOPH. O. C. 656, 797 (οἶδα μή), Ph. 79 (ἔξοιδα μή), O. C.
1121 (ἐπίσταμαι μή); EUR. Tro. 970 (δείξω μή); THUC. ii. 17
(προῄδει μή). Here also the irregularity may be explained by the
fixed earlier use of μή in other constructions affecting the later construction of indirect discourse (685).

INDIRECT QUOTATION OF COMPLEX SENTENCES.

689. When a complex sentence is indirectly quoted, its
leading verb follows the principles already stated for simple
sentences (669-688).

1. If the quotation depends on a primary tense, all the
dependent verbs of the original sentence retain the mood
and tense of the direct discourse.

2. After a secondary tense, all dependent verbs of the
original sentence which there stood in the present, perfect,
or future indicative, or in any tense of the subjunctive, may
either be changed to the same tense of the optative or retain

both the mood and tense of the direct discourse, the optative being the more common form. When the subjunctive is changed to the optative, ἄν is dropped, ἐάν, ὅταν, etc., becoming εἰ, ὅτε, etc.

3. But dependent secondary tenses of the indicative and all dependent optatives remain unchanged after all tenses (see, however, 693). *E.g.*

1. (After primary tenses.) Ἂν δ᾽ ὑμεῖς λέγητε, ποιήσειν (φησὶ) ὃ μήτ᾽ αἰσχύνην μήτ᾽ ἀδοξίαν αὐτῷ φέρει. DEM. xix. 41 (i.e. ποιήσω, ὃ μήτ᾽ . . . ἐμοὶ φέρει). Νομίζω γὰρ, ἂν τοῦτ᾽ ἀκριβῶς μάθητε, μᾶλλον ὑμᾶς τούτοις μὲν ἀπιστήσειν ἐμοὶ δὲ βοηθήσειν. Id. xxx. 25. Ἐὰν ἐκεῖνο εἰδῶμεν, ὅτι ἄπανθ᾽ ὅσα πώποτ᾽ ἠλπίσαμέν τινα πράξειν ὑπὲρ ἡμῶν καθ᾽ ἡμῶν εὕρηται, κἂν μὴ νῦν ἐθέλωμεν ἐκεῖ πολεμεῖν αὐτῷ, ἐνθάδ᾽ ἴσως ἀναγκασθησόμεθα τοῦτο ποιεῖν, κ.τ.λ. Id. iv. 50. Προλέγω ὅτι, ὁπότερ᾽ ἂν ἀποκρίνηται, ἐξελεγχθήσεται. PLAT. Euthyd. 275 E. See DEM. xxi. 66, where two such conditional sentences depend on εἰ πρόδηλον γένοιτο, and Il. xiii. 741 (see 178 and 184, above).

Ὁρῶ σοὶ τούτων δεῆσον, ὅταν ἐπιθυμήσῃς φιλίαν πρός τινας ποιεῖσθαι. XEN. Mem. ii. 6, 29. Παράδειγμα σαφὲς καταστήσατε, ὃς ἂν ἀφιστῆται, θανάτῳ ζημιωσόμενον. THUC. iii. 40. See 687.

2. (Optative after secondary tenses.) Εἶπε ὅτι ἄνδρα ἄγοι ὃν εἶρξαι δέοι, *he said that he was bringing a man whom it was necessary to confine*, i.e. *he said* ἄνδρα ἄγω ὃν εἶρξαι δεῖ. XEN. Hell. v. 4, 8. Ἀπεκρίνατο ὅτι μανθάνοιεν οἱ μανθάνοντες ἃ οὐκ ἐπίσταιντο, i.e. *he replied*, μανθάνουσι ἃ οὐκ ἐπίστανται. PLAT. Euthyd. 276 E. (Here οὐκ shows that ἃ has a definite antecedent, and takes the optative only because it is in indirect discourse. So with ὅν in the preceding example.) Ἀγησίλαος ἔλεγεν ὅτι, εἰ βλαβερὰ πεπραχὼς εἴη, δίκαιος εἴη ζημιοῦσθαι, i.e. *he said* εἰ βλαβερὰ πέπραχε, δίκαιός ἐστι ζημιοῦσθαι. XEN. Hell. v. 2, 32. So An. ii. 1, 3, iii. 5, 15, vi. 6, 25. Εἰ δέ τινα φεύγοντα λήψοιτο, προηγόρευεν ὅτι ὡς πολεμίῳ χρήσοιτο. Id. Cyr. iii. 1, 3. (This is a quotation of εἴ τινα λήψομαι, χρήσομαι.) Γνόντες δὲ ὅτι, εἰ δώσοιεν εὐθύνας, κινδυνεύσοιεν ἀπολέσθαι, πέμπουσι καὶ διδάσκουσι τοὺς Θηβαίους ὡς, εἰ μὴ στρατεύσοιεν, κινδυνεύσοιεν οἱ Ἀρκάδες πάλιν λακωνίσαι. Id. Hell. vii. 4, 34. Ἤδει γὰρ ὅτι, εἰ μάχης ποτὲ δεήσοι, ἐκ τούτων αὐτῷ παραστάτας ληπτέον εἴη. Id. Cyr. viii. 1, 10. (The direct discourse was εἴ τι δεήσει, ληπτέον ἐστίν.) Ἐλογίζοντο ὡς, εἰ μὴ μάχοιντο, ἀποστήσοιντο αἱ περιοικίδες πόλεις. Id. Hell. vi. 4, 6. (Ἐὰν μὴ μαχώμεθα, ἀποστήσονται.) Χρήμαθ᾽ ὑπισχνεῖτο δώσειν, εἰ τοῦ πράγματος αἰτιῷντο ἐμέ. DEM. xxi. 104. (Δώσω, ἐὰν αἰτιᾶσθε.) Ἡγεῖτο γὰρ ἅπαν ποιήσειν αὐτὸν, εἴ τις ἀργύριον διδοίη. LYS. xii. 14. Εὔξαντο σωτήρια θύσειν, ἔνθα πρῶτον εἰς φιλίαν γῆν ἀφίκοιντο. XEN. An. v. 1, 1.

(The dependent clause is found in the direct form in iii. 2, 9 : δοκεῖ μοι εὔξασθαι τῷ θεῷ τούτῳ θύσειν σωτήρια ὅπου ἂν πρῶτον εἰς φιλίαν χώραν ἀφικώμεθα.) Τοῦτο ἐπραγματεύετο νομίζων, ὅσα τῆς πόλεως προλάβοι, πάντα ταῦτα βεβαίως ἕξειν (ὅσ᾽ ἂν προλάβω, βεβαίως ἕξω). DEM. xviii. 26. Ἤλπιζον ὑπὸ τῶν παίδων, ἐπειδὴ τελευτήσειαν τὸν βίον, ταφήσεσθαι (ἐπειδὰν τελευτήσωμεν, ταφησόμεθα). LYS. xiii. 45. Κόνων ἐδίδασκεν ὡς οὕτω μὲν ποιοῦντι πᾶσαι αὐτῷ αἱ πόλεις φιλίαι ἔσοιντο, εἰ δὲ δουλοῦσθαι βουλόμενος φανερὸς ἔσοιτο, ἔλεγεν ὡς μία ἑκάστη πολλὰ πράγματα ἱκανὴ εἴη παρέχειν, καὶ κίνδυνος εἴη μὴ καὶ οἱ Ἕλληνες, εἰ ταῦτα αἴσθοιντο, συσταῖεν. XEN. Hell. iv. 8, 2. Εἶπε τε ὅτι πᾶσα ἀνάγκη εἴη τοῦτον ἐλλόγιμον γενέσθαι, εἴπερ εἰς ἡλικίαν ἔλθοι (ἀνάγκη ἐστὶν, ἐὰν ἔλθῃ). PLAT. Theaet. 142 D. Ἐνόμισε μὴ ἂν γενέσθαι ποτὲ πιστὸν ἄνθρωπον ὅστις ἄλλον μᾶλλον φιλήσοι τοῦ τῆς φυλακῆς δεομένου, he believed that no man could ever be made faithful who was to love (see 527) any one more than the one needing his guardianship (οὐκ ἂν γένοιτο εἰ φιλήσει). XEN. Cyr. vii. 5, 59. Ὤμοσεν Ἀγεσιλάῳ, εἰ σπείσαιτο ἕως ἔλθοιεν οὓς πέμψειε πρὸς βασιλέα ἀγγέλους, διαπράξεσθαι, κ.τ.λ. Id. Ag. i. 10. (The oath was ἐὰν σπείσῃ ἕως ἂν ἔλθωσιν ἄγγελοι οὓς ἂν πέμψω, διαπράξομαι.) Even in Homer, Il. ii. 597, we find στεῦτο γὰρ εὐχόμενος νικησέμεν, εἴ περ ἂν αὐταὶ Μοῦσαι ἀείδοιεν, for he promised with a boast that he would be victor, even if the Muses themselves should sing. (For εἰ ἄν with the optative, see 460 ; or ἀείδοιεν may represent a subjunctive, 692.)

Ἔτι δὲ γιγνώσκειν ἔφασαν φθονοῦντας μὲν αὐτοὺς εἴ τι σφίσιν ἀγαθὸν γίγνοιτο, ἐφηδομένους δ᾽ εἴ τις συμφορὰ προσπίπτοι, they said they knew that they (the Mantineans) were envious if any good came to them, but pleased if any calamity befell them. XEN. Hell. v. 2, 2. (Φθονεῖτε μὲν ἐάν τι ἡμῖν ἀγαθὸν γίγνηται, ἐφήδεσθε δ᾽ ἐάν τις συμφορὰ προσπίπτῃ.) Τὴν αἰτίαν, ἣ πρόδηλος ἦν ἐπ᾽ ἐκείνους ἥξουσα εἴ τι πάθοι Χαρίδημος (ἥξει, ἐάν τι πάθῃ Χαρίδημος). DEM. xxiii. 12.

(Subjunctive and Indicative retained after secondary tenses.) Ἔλεγον ὅτι ἄκρα τέ ἐστιν ἔνδον καὶ οἱ πολέμιοι πολλοί, οἳ παίουσιν τοὺς ἔνδον ἀνθρώπους, they said that there was a height, etc. XEN. An. v. 2, 17. (Here εἶεν and παίοιεν might have been used.) Ἐδόκει μοι ταύτῃ πειρᾶσθαι σωθῆναι, ἐνθυμουμένῳ ὅτι, ἐὰν μὲν λάθω, σωθήσομαι, κ.τ.λ. LYS. xii. 15. (Here εἰ λάθοιμι, σωθησοίμην might have been used.) Φάσκων τε, ἢν σωθῇ οἴκαδε, κατά γε τὸ αὑτῷ δυνατὸν διαλλάξειν Ἀθηναίους καὶ Λακεδαιμονίους, ἀπέπλευσεν. XEN. Hell. i. 6, 7. (He said ἢν σωθῶ, which might have been changed to εἰ σωθείην.) Ταῦθ᾽ ὑμᾶς ἔπεισε πρᾶξαι, εὖ εἰδὼς ὅτι, εἰ μὴ πασῶν τῶν ἐλπίδων ἀποστερηθήσεσθε, ταχεῖαν παρ᾽ αὑτοῦ τὴν τιμωρίαν κομιεῖσθε. LYS. xii. 70. Ὑπέσχοντο αὐτοῖς, ἢν ἐπὶ Ποτίδαιαν ἴωσιν Ἀθηναῖοι, ἐς τὴν Ἀττικὴν ἐσβαλεῖν (ἢν ἴωσιν, ἐσβαλοῦμεν). THUC. i. 58. Καὶ οὐκ ἔφασαν ἰέναι, ἐὰν μή τις αὐτοῖς χρήματα διδῷ· ὁ δ᾽ ὑπέσχετο ἀνδρὶ ἑκάστῳ δώσειν πέντε μνᾶς, ἐπὰν εἰς Βαβυλῶνα ἥκωσι, καὶ τὸν μισθὸν ἐντελῆ, μέχρι ἂν καταστήσῃ

τοὺς Ἕλληνας εἰς Ἰωνίαν πάλιν. ΧΕΝ. An. i. 4, 12 and 13. Ἔφη
χρῆναι, οἳ ἂν ἐλεγχθῶσι διαβάλλοντες τῶν Ἑλλήνων, ὡς προδότας
ὄντας τιμωρηθῆναι. Ib. ii. 5, 27. See AESCHIN. iii. 145.

Εἰ δὲ μὴ, καὶ αὐτοὶ ἔφασαν αὐτῶν τοὺς ἄνδρας ἀποκτενεῖν οὓς
ἔχουσι ζῶντας, otherwise, they said, they should themselves kill their men
whom they had in their hands alive (ἔχοιεν might have been used).
THUC. ii. 5. Κατασχίσειν τὰς πύλας ἔφασαν, εἰ μὴ ἑκόντες
ἀνοίξουσιν. ΧΕΝ. An. vii. 1, 16. (Εἰ μὴ ἀνοίξοιεν might have
been used.) So THUC. i. 137. Αὐτοῖς τοιαύτη δόξα παρειστήκει, ὡς,
εἰ μὲν πρότερον ἐπ᾽ ἄλλην πόλιν ἴασιν, ἐκείνοις καὶ Ἀθηναίοις πο-
λεμήσουσιν· εἰ δ᾽ ἐνθάδε πρῶτον ἀφίξονται, οὐδένας ἄλλους
τολμήσειν, κ.τ.λ. LYS. ii. 22. Οὐδὲν ὄφελος ἔφη τῶν χθὲς εἰρημένων εἶναι λόγων, εἰ ταῦθ᾽ οἱ Φιλίππου μὴ συμπεισθήσονται
πρέσβεις. AESCHIN. iii. 71. Ὁ πρόδηλον ἦν ἐσόμενον, εἰ μὴ ὑμεῖς
κωλύσετε, it was manifest that this would be so unless you should prevent
it (i.e. ἔσται, εἰ μὴ κωλύσετε). Id. iii. 90. (Κωλύσοιτε might be used ;
and εἰ μὴ κωλύσαιτε representing ἐὰν μὴ κωλύσητε is in one Ms.)

3. (Past tenses of Indicative retained after secondary tenses.) Ἐπι-
στεῖλαι δὲ σφίσιν αὐτοῖς τοὺς ἐφόρους (ἔφασαν) εἰπεῖν, ὡς ὧν μὲν
πρόσθεν ἐποίουν μέμφοιντο αὐτοῖς, that the Ephors charged them to
say that they blamed them for what they had done before (i.e. ὧν πρόσθεν
ἐποιεῖτε μεμφόμεθα ὑμῖν). ΧΕΝ. Hell. iii. 2, 6.
Ἤλπιζον τοὺς Σικελοὺς ταύτῃ, οὓς μετέπεμψαν, ἀπαντήσεσθαι,
they hoped that the Sikels whom they had sent for would meet them here.
THUC. vii. 80. Λέγουσι δέ τινες καὶ ἑκούσιον φαρμάκῳ ἀποθανεῖν
αὐτὸν, ἀδύνατον νομίσαντα εἶναι ἐπιτελέσαι βασιλεῖ ἃ ὑπέσχετο,
and some say even that he (Themistocles) died a voluntary death by poison,
believing that it was impossible to perform for the King what he had
promised (ἀδύνατόν ἐστιν ἐπιτελέσαι ἃ ὑπεσχόμην). Id. i. 138. Ἀντέλεγον, λέγοντες μὴ ἐπηγγέλθαι πω τὰς σπονδὰς ὅτ᾽ ἐσέπεμψαν
τοὺς ὁπλίτας. Id. v. 49. Ἔλεγον ὡς Ξενοφῶν οἴχοιτο ὡς Σεύθην
οἰκήσων καὶ ἃ ὑπέσχετο αὐτῷ ἀποληψόμενος. ΧΕΝ. An. vii. 7, 55.
Ἕκαστον ἠρόμην, εἴ τινες εἶεν μάρτυρες ὧν ἐναντίον τὴν προῖκ᾽ ἀπέδοσαν (εἰσὶ μάρτυρες, ὧν ἐναντίον ἀπέδοτε ;). DEM. xxx. 19.

The aorist indicative is not changed to the aorist optative here, to
avoid confusion, as the latter tense in such dependent clauses generally
represents the aorist subjunctive of the direct form. Thus ἔφη ἃ εὕροι
δώσειν means he said that he would give whatever he might find (ἃ ἂν
εὕρω δώσω) ; but if ἃ εὕροι could also represent ἃ εὗρον, it might
also mean he said that he would give what he had found. In the leading
clause the ambiguity is confined to indirect questions, in which the
aorist indicative is generally retained for the same reason (see 125).

(Past tenses of the Indicative in unreal conditions retained.) Ἐδόκει,
εἰ μὴ ἔφθασαν ξυλλαβόντες τοὺς ἄνδρας, προδοθῆναι ἂν τὴν πόλιν.
THUC. vi. 61. (If ἔφθασαν were optative, it would represent an
optative of direct discourse.) Οἴεσθε τὸν πατέρα, εἰ μὴ Τιμοθέου ἦν
τὰ ξύλα καὶ ἐδεήθη οὗτος αὐτοῦ παρασχεῖν τὸ ναῦλον, ἐᾶσαι ἄν ποτε,

κ.τ.λ., ἀλλ' οὐκ ἂν φυλάττειν καὶ τὴν τιμὴν λαμβάνειν, ἕως ἐκομί-
σατο τὰ ἑαυτοῦ; DEM. xlix. 35. Τούτων εἴ τι ἦν ἀληθές, οἴεσθ'
οὐκ ἂν αὐτὴν λαβεῖν; Id. xxvii. 56. Ἡδέως ἂν ὑμῶν πυθοίμην, τίν'
ἄν ποτε γνώμην περὶ ἐμοῦ εἴχετε εἰ μὴ ἐπετριηράρχησα ἀλλὰ
πλέων ᾠχόμην. Id. L. 67. (Dependent Optatives retained.) Εἶπεν ὅτι ἔλθοι ἂν εἰς λόγους εἰ
ὁμήρους λάβοι (he said ἔλθοιμι ἂν εἰ ὁμήρους λάβοιμι). XEN. Hell.
iii. 1, 20. Ἧττον ἂν διὰ τοῦτο τυγχάνειν (δοκεῖ μοι), εἴ τι δέοισθε
παρ' αὐτῶν. Id. An. vi. 1, 26. Ἔλεγεν ὅτι οὐκ ἄν ποτε προοῖτο, ἐπεὶ
ἅπαξ φίλος αὐτοῖς ἐγένετο, οὐδ' εἰ ἔτι μὲν μείους γένοιντο ἔτι δὲ
κάκιον πράξειαν. Ib. i. 9, 10. Δεινὸν ἄν τι παθεῖν σαυτὸν ἤλπιζες,
εἰ πύθοινθ' οὗτοι τὰ πεπραγμένα σοι. DEM. xix. 240.

Sentences such as these are often translated like those which had a
future and a dependent subjunctive in the direct discourse. Thus
ἔλεγεν ὅτι χαίροι ἂν εἰ τοῦτο γένοιτο or ἔλεγε χαίρειν ἂν εἰ τοῦτο
γένοιτο, as well as ἔλεγεν ὅτι χαιρήσοι εἰ τοῦτο γένοιτο or ἔλεγε
χαιρήσειν εἰ τοῦτο γένοιτο, may all be translated he said that he should
rejoice if this should happen; although in the first two sentences the
direct discourse was χαίροιμι ἂν εἰ τοῦτο γένοιτο, I should rejoice if
this should happen, and in the last two, χαιρήσω ἐὰν τοῦτο γένηται, I
shall rejoice if this shall happen. (See 456.)

690. The dependent verbs of a quotation may be changed
to the optative in indirect discourse, even when the leading verb
retains the indicative; and sometimes (though rarely) a dependent
verb retains the subjunctive or indicative, when the leading verb
is changed to the optative. This may give rise to a great variety
of constructions in the same sentence. *E.g.*

Δηλώσας ὅτι ἕτοιμοί εἰσι μάχεσθαι εἴ τις ἐξέρχοιτο. XEN.
Cyr. iv. 1, 1. (Ἕτοιμοί εἰσιν ἐάν τις ἐξέρχηται.) Λύσανδρος εἶπε
ὅτι παρασπόνδους ὑμᾶς ἔχοι, καὶ ὅτι οὐ περὶ πολιτείας ὑμῖν ἔσται
ἀλλὰ περὶ σωτηρίας, εἰ μὴ ποιήσαιθ' ἃ Θηραμένης κελεύοι. LYS. xii.
74. (Ἔχω, καὶ οὐκ ἔσται ἐὰν μὴ ποιήσηθ' ἃ Θ. κελεύει.) There is
no need of the emendations ποιήσετ' and κελεύει.) Ἐδόκει δῆλον
εἶναι ὅτι αἱρήσονται αὐτὸν εἴ τις ἐπιψηφίζοι. XEN. An. vi. 1, 25.
Οὐκ ἠγνόει Εὐβουλίδης ὅτι, εἰ λόγος ἀποδοθήσοιτο καὶ παρα-
γένοιντό μοι πάντες οἱ δημόται καὶ ἡ ψῆφος δικαίως δοθείη, οὐδαμοῦ
γενήσονται οἱ μετὰ τούτου συνεστηκότες. DEM. lvii. 16. (Εἰ ἀπο-
δοθήσεται καὶ ἐὰν παραγένωνται καὶ ψῆφος δοθῇ, οὐδαμοῦ γενήσονται.)
Ἀγησίλαος γνοὺς ὅτι, εἰ μὲν μηδετέρῳ συλλήψοιτο, μισθὸν οὐδέτερος
λύσει τοῖς Ἕλλησιν, ἀγορὰν δὲ οὐδέτερος παρέξει, ὁπότερος τ' ἂν
κρατήσῃ, οὗτος ἐχθρὸς ἔσται· εἰ δὲ τῷ ἑτέρῳ συλλήψοιτο, οὗτός
γε φίλος ἔσοιτο, κ.τ.λ. XEN. Ag. ii. 31.
Ἔλεγον ὅτι εἰκότα δοκοῖεν λέγειν βασιλεῖ, καὶ ἥκοιεν ἡγεμόνας
ἔχοντες, οἳ αὐτοὺς, ἐὰν σπονδαὶ γένωνται, ἄξουσιν ἔνθεν ἕξουσι
τὰ ἐπιτήδεια. Id. An. ii. 3, 6. Ἐπηρώτα, ποῖα εἴη τῶν ὀρέων ὁπόθεν
οἱ Χαλδαῖοι καταθέοντες ληΐζονται. Id. Cyr. iii. 2, 1. Ἔλεξας ὅτι
μέγιστον εἴη μαθεῖν ὅπως δεῖ ἐξεργάζεσθαι ἕκαστα· εἰ δὲ μή, οὐδὲ

τῆς ἐπιμελείας ἔφησθα ὄφελος οὐδὲν γίγνεσθαι, εἰ μή τις ἐπίσταιτο
ἃ δεῖ καὶ ὡς δεῖ ποιεῖν. Id. Occ. xv. 2.

In DEM. xviii. 148, we have both constructions of 689, 2 in the
same sentence : εἰ μὲν τοῦτο τῶν ἐκείνου συμμάχων εἰσηγοῖτό τις,
ὑπόψεσθαι τὸ πρᾶγμα ἐνόμιζε πάντας· ἂν δ᾽ Ἀθηναῖος ᾖ ὁ τοῦτο
ποιῶν, εὐπόρως λήσειν. Here εἰ εἰσηγοῖτο represents ἄν (= ἐὰν)
εἰσηγῆται, corresponding to ἂν ᾖ. By keeping the subjunctive in
the latter case, the expression is made more vivid by contrast.

In PLAT. Rep. 337 A we have τούτοις προὔλεγον, ὅτι εἰρωνεύσοιο
καὶ πάντα μᾶλλον ποιήσοις ἢ ἀποκρινοῖο, εἴ τίς τί σε ἐρωτᾷ,
which must mean I warned them that you would dissemble and would do
anything rather than answer if any one should ask you anything. The
direct discourse must be εἰρωνεύσεται καὶ πάντα μᾶλλον ποιήσει ἢ
ἀποκρινεῖται ἐάν τίς τι αὐτὸν ἐρωτᾷ (subj.). Ἐὰν ἐρωτᾷ must have
been retained or changed to εἰ with the optative ; and ἐρωτᾷ in the
text is probably a copyist's mistake for ἐρωτῷ, a form of the optative
frequently found in the Cod. A Parisin. of Plato. See in the Republic
516 A (καθορῷ), 518 A (γελῷ), 559 A (μελετῷ), 598 C (ἐξαπατῷ).
There is, however, a various reading ἔροιτο in a few Mss. in 337 A.

691. The imperfect or pluperfect sometimes stands irregularly in
a dependent (as well as in the leading) clause of the indirect discourse
after a secondary tense, to represent a present or perfect indicative,
which would regularly be retained or changed to the present or perfect
optative.   Such clauses are really not included in the indirect discourse.
(See 674 ; 701.)   E.g.

Ἔλεγον οὐ καλῶς τὴν Ἑλλάδα ἐλευθεροῦν αὐτὸν, εἰ ἄνδρας διε-
φθειρεν οὔτε χεῖρας ἀνταιρομένους οὔτε πολεμίους (οὐ καλῶς ἐλευ-
θεροῖς, εἰ διαφθείρεις). THUC. iii. 32. Οὔτε γὰρ τοῖς θεοῖς ἔφη
καλῶς ἔχειν, εἰ ταῖς μεγάλαις θυσίαις μᾶλλον ἢ ταῖς μικραῖς ἔχαιρον
(εἰ χαίρουσιν). XEN. Mem. i. 3, 3. Καὶ ἔφη εἶναι παρ᾽ ἑαυτῷ ὅσον μὴ
ἦν ἀνηλωμένον (ὅσον μή ἐστιν ἀνηλωμένον). DEM. xlviii. 16. Ἃ
μὲν εἰλήφει τῆς πόλεως ἀποδώσειν (ἡγούμην), I thought that he would
give back what he had taken from the city; i.e. ἃ εἴληφεν ἀποδώσει.
Id. xix. 151.

692. In a few cases, a relative or particle which had ἄν with the
subjunctive in the direct form irregularly retains ἄν in indirect discourse
after a past tense, although the verb has been changed to the optative.
This must not be confounded with ἄν belonging to a potential optative
(506 ; 557). E.g.

Οὐκ ἔσθ᾽ ὅστις οὐχ ἡγεῖτο τῶν εἰδότων δίκην με λήψεσθαι παρ᾽ αὐτῶν, ἐπειδὰν τάχιστα ἀνὴρ εἶναι δοκιμασθείην (so the Mss.).
DEM. xxx. 6. (The direct discourse was ἐπειδὰν δοκιμασθῇ, and the
regular indirect form would be ἐπειδὴ δοκιμασθείην or ἐπειδὰν δοκιμα-
σθῶ.)   (See also 702.)

693. When no ambiguity can arise from the change of an aorist
indicative to the optative in a dependent clause of the indirect discourse,
this tense may follow the general principle. This occurs chiefly in

causal sentences after ὅτι, ἐπεί, etc., *because* (713), in which the sub-junctive can never be used. *E.g.*

Εἶχε γὰρ λέγειν ὡς Λακεδαιμόνιοι διὰ τοῦτο πολεμήσειαν αὐτοῖς, ὅτι οὐκ ἐθελήσαιεν μετ᾽ Ἀγησιλάου ἐλθεῖν ἐπ᾽ αὐτὸν οὐδὲ θῦσαι ἐάσειαν αὐτὸν ἐν Αὐλίδι. XEN. Hell. vii. 1, 34. (The direct discourse was ἐπολέμησαν ἡμῖν, ὅτι οὐκ ἠθελήσαμεν ἐλθεῖν οὐδὲ θῦσαι εἰάσαμεν αὐτόν.) Ἀπηγήσασθαί (φασι) ὡς ἀνοσιώτατον μὲν εἴη εἰργασμένος ὅτε τοῦ ἀδελφεοῦ ἀποτάμοι τὴν κεφαλὴν, σοφώτατον δὲ ὅτι τοὺς φυλάκους καταμεθύσας κ α τ α λ ύ σ ε ι ε τοῦ ἀδελφεοῦ κρεμά-μενον τὸν νέκυν. HDT. ii. 121. Here ὅτι καταλύσειε represents ὅτι κατέλυσα, *because I took down;* ὅτε ἀποτάμοι (so the Mss.) might also be understood in a causal sense, *since he had cut off,* although in the sense of *when he cut off* it could not be ambiguous here. Madvig, however, reads ὅτι in both clauses. See XEN. Mem. i. 4, 19 (quoted in 714). (See also 700, and the examples.)

SINGLE DEPENDENT CLAUSES IN INDIRECT DISCOURSE.

694. 1. The principles which govern dependent clauses of indirect discourse (689) apply also to all dependent clauses in sentences of every kind (even when what precedes is not in indirect discourse), if such clauses express *indirectly* the past thought of any person, even that of the speaker himself. This affects the construction only when the leading verb is past; then the dependent clause may either take the optative, in the *tense* in which the thought was originally conceived, or retain both the mood and the tense of the direct discourse. When a subjunctive is changed to an optative, ἄν is dropped.

2. Secondary tenses of the indicative here (as in 689, 3) regularly remain unchanged. But an aorist indicative sometimes becomes optative when no ambiguity can result from the change (see 693): this may occur in causal sentences (699 and 714) and in the relative sentences of 700.

The principle of 694 applies to the following constructions :—

695. I. Clauses depending on the infinitive which follows verbs of *wishing, commanding, advising,* and others which imply *thought* but do not take the infinitive in indirect discourse (684). *E.g.*

Ἐβούλοντο ἐλθεῖν εἰ τοῦτο γένοιτο, *they wished to go if this should happen.* (Here the original expression of the thought would be βουλό-μεθα ἐλθεῖν ἐὰν τοῦτο γένηται, and therefore ἐὰν γένηται might be

retained.) Γαδάταν δὲ καὶ Γωβρύαν ἐκέλευσεν ὅ τι δύναιντο λαβόν
τας μεταδιώκειν· καὶ ὅστις εἶχε τὰς ἑπομένας ἀγέλας, εἶπε τούτῳ καὶ
ἅμα πρόβατα πολλὰ ἐλαύνειν ὅπῃ ἂν αὐτὸν πυνθάνηται ὄντα, ὡς
ἐπισφαγείη. XEN. Cyr. vii. 3, 7. (Here ὅ τι δύναιντο represents ὅ τι
ἂν δύνησθε, while ὅπῃ ἂν πυνθάνηται represents ὅπῃ ἂν πυνθάνῃ.)
Ἐβούλοντο γὰρ σφίσιν, εἴ τινα λάβοιεν, ὑπάρχειν ἀντὶ τῶν ἔνδον,
ἢν ἄρα τύχωσί τινες ἐζωγρημένοι, for they wished that, if they should
capture any one, he might be a hostage for their friends within the city, in
case any should chance to have been taken prisoners (ἢν λάβωμεν, and ἢν
τύχωσι). THUC. ii. 5.   Οἱ δ' ἄλλοι Θηβαῖοι, οὓς ἔδει παραγενέσθαι εἴ
τι μὴ προχωροίη τοῖς ἐσεληλυθόσιν, ἐπεβοήθουν, who were to come
up if anything should go wrong with those who had entered the city (ἤν τι
μὴ προχωρῇ). Ibid.
Προεῖπον αὐτοῖς μὴ ναυμαχεῖν Κορινθίοις, ἢν μὴ ἐπὶ Κέρκυραν
πλέωσι καὶ μέλλωσιν ἀποβαίνειν. Id. i. 45.   Καὶ παρήγγειλαν
ἐπειδὴ δειπνήσειαν συνεσκευασμένους πάντας ἀναπαύεσθαι, καὶ
ἕπεσθαι ἡνίκ' ἄν τις παραγγέλλῃ. XEN. An. iii. 5, 18. (Ἐπειδὰν
δειπνήσητε, and ἡνίκ' ἄν τις παραγγέλλῃ.)   Περὶ αὐτῶν κρύφα πέμπει,
κελεύων μὴ ἀφεῖναι πρὶν ἂν αὐτοὶ πάλιν κομισθῶσιν, he sent bidding
the Athenians not to let them go until they should themselves have returned.
THUC. i. 91.   (Πρὶν κομισθεῖεν might be used.)   Καὶ πολλάκις τοῖς
Ἀθηναίοις παρῄνει, ἢν ἄρα ποτὲ κατὰ γῆν βιασθῶσι, καταβάντας
ἐς αὐτὸν ταῖς ναυσὶ πρὸς ἅπαντας ἀνθίστασθαι. Id. i. 93.   (Εἰ βια
σθεῖεν might be used.)   Ἠξίουν αὐτοὺς ἡγεμόνας σφῶν γενέσθαι, καὶ
Παυσανίᾳ μὴ ἐπιτρέπειν ἤν που βιάζηται. Id. i. 95.   (Εἴ που
βιάζοιτο might be used.)   Ἀφικνοῦνται ὡς Σιτάλκην, βουλόμενοι
πεῖσαι αὐτόν, εἰ δύναιντο, στρατεῦσαι ἐπὶ τὴν Ποτίδαιαν. Id. ii. 67.
Ἕτοιμος ἦν ἀποτίνειν, εἰ καταγνοῖεν αὐτοῦ. ISOC. xvii. 16.   Εἶπον
μηδένα τῶν ὄπισθεν κινεῖσθαι πρὶν ἂν ὁ πρόσθεν ἡγῆται, I commanded
that no one at the rear should move until the one before him should lead.
XEN. Cyr. ii. 2, 8.
Παρηγγέλλετο γὰρ αὐτοῖς δέκα μὲν οὓς Θηραμένης ἀπέδειξε
χειροτονῆσαι, δέκα δὲ οὓς οἱ ἔφοροι κελεύοιεν, they were bidden to
choose ten whom Theramenes had nominated, and ten whom the Ephors commanded (i.e. οὓς ἀπέδειξε and οὓς κελεύουσιν). LYS. xii. 76.   Ἐκέλευσέ
με τὴν ἐπιστολὴν ἣν ἔγραψα οἴκαδε δοῦναι, the letter which I had
written. XEN. Cyr. ii. 2, 9. (Ἣν γράψαιμι would mean whatever letter
I might write, representing ἣν ἂν γράψῃς.)   Διενοοῦντο αὐτοὺς πάλιν ὅθεν
ἦλθον ἐς Θρᾴκην ἀποπέμπειν, they planned to send them back to Thrace,
whence they had come. THUC. vii. 27. (See 689, 3.)

696.   II. Clauses containing a protasis, the apodosis of which
is implied in the past leading verb or its adjuncts. E.g.

Διδόντος δ' αὐτῷ πάμπολλα δῶρα Τιθραύστου, εἰ ἀπέλθοι,
ἀπεκρίνατο, when T. offered (to give) him many gifts, if he would go
away. XEN. Ag. iv. 6. (Ἐὰν ἀπέλθῃ might be used.)   Φύλακας
συμπέμπει, ὅπως φυλάττοιεν αὐτόν, καὶ εἰ τῶν ἀγρίων τι φανείη
θηρίων, and (to be ready) in case any wild beast should appear; his

thought being ἐάν τι φανῇ. Id. Cyr. i. 4, 7. Πρὸς τὴν πόλιν, εἰ ἐπιβοηθοῖεν, ἐχώρουν, *they marched towards the city, in case they* (the citizens) *should rush out* (*i.e.* so as to meet them, if they should rush out), the thought being ἦν ἐπιβοηθῶσιν (490, 1). Thuc. vi. 100. Οὐδ' ἦν τοῦ πολέμου πέρας οὐδ' ἀπαλλαγὴ Φιλίππῳ, εἰ μὴ Θηβαίους καὶ Θετταλοὺς ἐχθροὺς ποιήσειε τῇ πόλει, *i.e. Philip saw that he could neither end nor escape the war unless he should make the Thebans and Thessalians hostile to the city* (the original apodosis, *I cannot end or escape the war,* to which ἐὰν μὴ ποιήσω was the protasis, is implied in οὐδ' ἦν . . . Φιλίππῳ). Dem. xviii. 145.

Ἢν δέ τις εἴπῃ ἢ ἐπιψηφίσῃ κινεῖν τὰ χρήματα ταῦτα ἐς ἄλλο τι, θάνατον ζημίαν ἐπέθεντο, *they set death as the penalty* (*i.e. voted that death should be the penalty*) *if any one should move, or put to vote a motion, to divert this money to any other purpose.* Thuc. ii. 24. (Εἰ εἴποι ἢ ἐπιψηφίσειεν *might be used.*) Τἆλλα, ἦν ἔτι ναυμαχεῖν οἱ Ἀθηναῖοι τολμήσωσι, παρεσκευάζοντο, *i.e. they made their other preparations,* (to be ready) *in case the Athenians should still dare to risk a sea fight* (their thought being *we will be ready in case they shall dare,* ἦν τολμήσωσι). Id. vii. 59. So ἦν ἴωσιν, Id. iv. 42. Οὐ τὸ λοιπὸν ἔμελλον ἕξειν εἰ μὴ ναυκρατήσουσιν, *they were not likely to have them* (provisions) *for the future* (as they thought) *unless they should hold the sea.* Id. vii. 60. Ἢν οὐδὲν μᾶλλον μέγ' αὐτῷ καθ' ὑμῶν οὐδ' οὕτω πρᾶξαι, εἰ μὴ τοὺς Φωκέας ἀπολεῖ, *he was none the more able even then to do you any great harm* (he thought) *unless he should destroy the Phocians* (εἰ μὴ ἀπολῶ). Dem. xix. 317. See Il. v. 301. Καὶ ἐγὼ τὸν Εὐηνὸν ἐμακάρισα, εἰ ὡς ἀληθῶς ἔχει ταύτην τὴν τέχνην καὶ οὕτως ἐμμελῶς διδάσκει, *I congratulated him* (told him he was happy), *if he really had this art.* Plat. Ap. 20 B. (Here ἔχοι and διδάσκοι might be used.)

697. III. Clauses containing a protasis depending on a past verb of emotion, like θαυμάζω, αἰσχύνομαι, etc. (494). *E.g.*

Ἐθαύμαζε δ' εἴ τις ἀρετὴν ἐπαγγελλόμενος ἀργύριον πράττοιτο, *he wondered that any demanded money,* etc. Xen. Mem. i. 2, 7. (But in i. 1, 13, we find ἐθαύμαζε δ' εἰ μὴ φανερὸν αὐτοῖς ἐστιν, *he wondered that it was not plain.*) Ἔχαιρον ἀγαπῶν εἴ τις ἐάσοι, *I rejoiced, being content if any one would let it pass.* Plat. Rep. 450 A. Οὐκ ᾐσχύνθη εἰ τοιοῦτο κακὸν ἐπάγει τῳ, *he was not ashamed if* (or *that*) *he was bringing such a calamity on any one.* Dem. xxi. 105. Τῷ δὲ μηδὲν ἑαυτῷ συνειδότι δεινὸν εἰσῄει, εἰ πονηρῶν ἔργων δόξει κοινωνεῖν τῷ σιωπῆσαι, *it seemed hard, if he was to appear to be implicated,* etc. ; he thought, δεινόν ἐστιν εἰ δόξω (407). Id. xix. 33. (Here δόξοι might be used like ἐάσοι above.) Οἱ δ' ᾤκτειρον, εἰ ἁλώσοιντο, *and others pitied them if they were to be captured,* the direct thought being *we pity them if they are to be captured,* εἰ ἁλώσονται, which might be retained (see the next example). Xen. An. i. 4, 7. Οὐκ ἔφασαν ἐπιτρέψαι, οὐκ ἐλεοῦντες τὰ τείχη εἰ πεσεῖται, οὐδὲ κηδόμενοι τῶν νεῶν εἰ Λακεδαιμονίοις παραδοθήσονται, *i.e. they felt no pity for the*

*walls if they were to fall, nor care for the ships if they were to be sur-
rondorod.* LYS. xiii. 15.

698. IV. Temporal sentences expressing a past *intention*,
vurpose, or *expectation*, especially those introduced by ἕως or πρίν,
until, after past tenses. *E.g.*

Ὦρσε δ' ἐπὶ κραιπνὸν Βορέην, πρὸ δὲ κύματ' ἔαξεν, ἕως ὅ γε
Φαιήκεσσι φιληρέτμοισι μιγείη, i.e. *to the end that (until) Ulysses
should get to the Phaeacians;* originally ἕως ἂν μιγῇ (614, 2). Od. v.
385.   So εἴως θερμαίνοιτο, Od. ix. 376.   Σπονδὰς ἐποιήσαντο ἕως
ἀπαγγελθείη τὰ λεχθέντα εἰς Λακεδαίμονα, *they made a truce (to
continue) until what had been said should be announced at Sparta;* i.e.
ἕως ἂν ἀπαγγελθῇ, which might have been retained. XEN. Hell. iii.
2, 20.   Ἀπηγόρευε μηδένα βάλλειν πρὶν Κῦρος ἐμπλησθείη θηρῶν,
until Cyrus should be satisfied. Id. Cyr. i. 4, 14.   (His words were πρὶν
ἂν ἐμπλησθῇ.)   Οἱ δὲ μένοντες ἔστασαν ὁπότε πύργος Ἀχαιῶν
ἄλλος ἐπελθὼν Τρώων ὁρμήσειε καὶ ἄρξειαν πολέμοιο, i.e. *they
stood waiting for the time when,* etc. Il. iv. 334.   So Il. ii. 794.   Πρού-
κίνησαν τὸ στῖφος, ὡς παυσομένους τοῦ διωγμοῦ ἐπεὶ σφᾶς ἴδοιεν
προορμήσαντας, *when they should see them,* etc. XEN. Cyr. i. 4, 21.
Οὐ γὰρ δή σφεας ἀπίει ὁ θεὸς τῆς ἀποικίης πρὶν δὴ ἀπίκωνται
ἐς αὐτὴν Λιβύην. HDT. iv. 157.   (Ἀπίκοιντο might be used.)   Οἱ δὲ
Κορίνθιοι οὐ προεθυμήθησαν ξυμπλεῖν πρὶν τὰ Ἴσθμια, ἃ τότε ἦν,
διεορτάσωσιν, *until they had (should have) finished celebrating the
Isthmian games, which were then going on.* THUC. viii. 9.

699. V. Past causal sentences in which the cause is stated
as one assigned by another, so far as these allow the optative
(714). *E.g.*

Ἐκάκιζον ὅτι στρατηγὸς ὢν οὐκ ἐπεξάγοι, *they abused him because
(as they said) he did not lead them out.* THUC. ii. 21.   See other
examples under 714.

Though the optative is allowed here, on the principle of indirect
discourse, the indicative of the direct form (*e.g.* ἐπεξάγει in the above
example) seems not to have been allowed (see 715). Causal sentences
are usually constructed without reference to the principle of indirect
discourse (see 713).

700. VI. Even some ordinary relative sentences expressing
the previous thought of another, which allow the optative in
place of the ordinary indicative. *E.g.*

Καὶ ἤτεε σῆμα ἰδέσθαι, ὅττι ῥά οἱ γαμβροῖο πάρα Προίτοιο
φέροιτο, *he asked to see the token, which* (he said) *he was bringing from
Proetus,* i.e. he said φέρομαι. Il. vi. 176.   So Od. v. 240.   Εἴρετο
παῖδα τὸν Εὐάδνα τέκοι, *he asked for the child which Evadne had borne.*
PIND. Ol. vi. 49.   Κατηγόρεον τῶν Αἰγινητέων τὰ πεποιήκοιεν πρυ-
δόντες τὴν Ἑλλάδα, i.e. *they accused them for what* (as they said) *they
had done.* HDT. vi. 49.   So τὰ πεπονθὼς εἴη, i. 44.   Καλεῖ τὸν Λάιον,
μνήμην παλαιῶν σπερμάτων ἔχουσ', ὑφ' ὧν θάνοι μέν αὐτός, τὴν δὲ

τίκτουσαν λίποι, by which (as she said) *he had perished himself, and had left her the mother*, etc. SOPH. O. T. 1245. If the relative clause contained merely the idea of the speaker, ἔθανε and ἔλιπε would be used. Here no ambiguity can arise from the use of the aorist optative (see 693). Τὸ τοῦ κρείττονος ξυμφέρον ἔλεγεν ὃ ἡγοῖτο ὁ κρείττων αὐτῷ ξυμφέρειν, *he meant the superior's advantage which the superior believed to be his own advantage.* PLAT. Rep. 340 B. This construction is rare in Attic Greek, but is not uncommon in Herodotus.

701. The imperfect and pluperfect occasionally represent the present and perfect indicative in this construction. Such clauses are simply *not included* in the indirect discourse. (See 674 ; 691.) *E.g.*

Ἕτοιμος ἦν, εἰ μὲν τούτων τι εἴργαστο, δίκην δοῦναι, εἰ δ᾽ ἀπο-λυθείη, ἄρχειν, *he was ready, if he had done any of these things, to be punished ; but if he should be acquitted, to hold his command.* THUC. vi. 29. (Εἰ εἴργαστο represents εἰ εἴργασμαι, while εἰ ἀπολυθείη represents ἐὰν ἀπολυθῶ.)

702. Ἄν is occasionally retained with relatives and temporal particles in sentences of this kind, even when the subjunctive to which they belonged has been changed to the optative. (See 692.) *E.g.*

Τοὺς δὲ λαμβάνοντας τῆς ὁμιλίας μισθὸν ἀνδραποδιστὰς ἑαυτῶν ἀπεκάλει, διὰ τὸ ἀναγκαῖον αὐτοῖς εἶναι διαλέγεσθαι παρ᾽ ὧν ἂν λάβοιεν τὸν μισθόν, *because they were obliged* (as he said) *to converse with those from whom they received the pay.* XEN. Mem. i. 2, 6. (Here ὧν ἂν λάβοιεν represents ὧν ἂν λάβωσιν.) Καί μοι τάδ᾽ ἦν πρόρρητα, τὸ φάρμακον τοῦτο σῴζειν ἐμὲ ἕως ἂν ἀρτίχριστον ἁρμόσαιμί που. SOPH. Tr. 687 (see Schneidewin's note). Ἠξίουν αὐτοὺς μαστιγοῦν τὸν ἐκδοθέντα ἕως ἂν τἀληθῆ δόξειεν αὐτοῖς λέγειν. ISOC. xvii. 15. Χαίρειν ἐφῃς ἂν καὶ οὐκ ἀποκρίναιο ἕως ἂν τὰ ἀπ᾽ ἐκείνης ὁρμηθέντα σκέψαιο, *you would not answer* (you would say) *until you should have examined*, etc. (ἕως ἂν σκέψωμαι). PLAT. Phaed. 101 D. Here we must place ὅταν ἐκσῳζοίατο, AESCH. Pers. 450, if the text is sound. Παρ-ήγγειλεν αὐτοῖς μὴ πρότερον ἐπιτίθεσθαι πρὶν ἂν τῶν σφετέρων ἢ πέσοι τις ἢ τρωθείη. XEN. Hell. ii. 4, 18 ; so πρὶν ἂν μετέχοιεν, ii. 3, 48. See ἕως ἂν οἱ νόμοι τεθεῖεν. AND. i. 81. Many scholars repudiate this use of ἄν and emend the passages : see Dindorf on SOPH. Tr. 687.

It is doubtful whether ἐάν was ever thus used with the optative.

703. Upon this principle (694) final and object clauses with ἵνα, ὡς, ὅπως, ὄφρα, and μή, after past tenses, admit the double construction of indirect discourse, and allow the subjunctive or the future indicative instead of the optative, to retain the form in which the purpose would be originally conceived. (See 318 and 339.)

704. The principles of indirect discourse (689, 2) apply to future conditional and conditional relative clauses which depend upon final and object clauses or other expressions of purpose after past tenses. *E.g.*

Ἐλθόντες ἐς Λακεδαίμονα (ἔπρασσον) ὅπως ἑτοιμάσαιντο τιμωρίαν, ἣν δέῃ. Thuc. i. 58.   (Here εἰ δέοι might have been used.)
Ἐφοβεῖτο γὰρ μὴ οἱ Λακεδαιμόνιοι σφᾶς, ὁπότε σαφῶς ἀκούσειαν,
οὐκέτι ἀφῶσιν. Id. i. 91.   (Here ὁπόταν ἀκούσωσιν is changed to
ὁπότε ἀκούσειαν, although ἀφῶσιν is retained.)

ΟἾΔ' ὅτι without a Verb.

705. ΟἾΔ' ὅτι sometimes means *I am sure*, when the context
readily suggests a verb for ὅτι.   *E.g.*

Πάρειμι δ' ἄκων οὐχ ἑκοῦσιν, οἶδ' ὅτι, and here *I am, against my
will, and against your will, I am sure.* Soph. Ant. 276.   Μὰ τὸν Δί'
οὔκουν τῷ γε σῷ, σάφ' ἴσθ' ὅτι, i.e. *be assured.* Ar. Pl. 889.   Πάντων
οἶδ' ὅτι φησάντων γ' ἄν, *when all, I am sure, would say.* Dem. ix. 1.
Βούλομαι μνημονεύοντας ὑμῶν οἶδ' ὅτι τοὺς πολλοὺς ὑπομνῆσαι, i.e.
I wish to remind you, though I am sure most of you remember it. Id. xix. 9.
In such cases it would be useless or impossible to add the implied
verb.

Ὅπως, ὅ, οὕνεκα, and ὁθούνεκα in Indirect Quotations.

706. Ὅπως is sometimes (especially in poetry) used in
indirect quotations in the sense of ὡς.   *E.g.*

Τοῦτ' αὐτὸ μή μοι φράζ', ὅπως οὐκ εἶ κακός, *this very thing tell
me not, that you are not base.* Soph. O. T. 548.   Ἄναξ, ἐρῶ μὲν οὐχ
ὅπως τάχους ὕπο δύσπνους ἱκάνω, *I will not say exactly that I come
breathless with haste.* Id. Ant. 223.   Μὴ γὰρ ἐλπίσῃς ὅπως ἐμ'
ἐκβαλεῖς, *for do not hope that you will expel me.* Eur. Her. 1051.   So
Soph. El. 963.   Ἀνάπεισον ὅκως μοι ἀμείνω ἐστὶ ταῦτα οὕτω
ποιεόμενα. Hdt. i. 37.   Οὐ μὲν οὐδὲ φήσω ὅκως Αἰγύπτιοι παρ'
Ἑλλήνων ἔλαβον τοῦτο. Id. ii. 49.   So iii. 115, 116.   See also
ὅπως οὐ πάντα ἐπίσταμαι, Plat. Euthyd. 296 E.   In most of these,
the original modal force of ὅπως, *how*, can be seen.

In Soph. Ant. 685, we have ὅπως σὺ μὴ λέγεις ὀρθῶς τάδε,
where μή is a standing puzzle.   It probably must be classed with the
very rare ὅτι μή with the indicative, and with the irregular μή with
the infinitive after verbs of *saying* and *thinking* (for all these see 685
and 686, above).

707. (Οὐχ ὅπως, οὐχ ὅτι, etc.)   Οὐχ ὅπως or (rarely) μή
ὅπως, and οὐχ ὅτι or μὴ ὅτι, by the ellipsis of a verb of *saying*,
often mean *I do not speak of* or *not to speak of.* Ἀλλά, ἀλλὰ καί,
ἀλλ' οὐδέ, or ἀλλὰ μηδέ usually follows in a clause which expresses
a strong antithesis.   After οὐχ the implied verb of *saying* would
be an indicative, after μή it would be an imperative or subjunctive; but, like most elliptical idioms, this is often used
where the ellipsis cannot be precisely supplied.   What is men-

tioned in the former clause as *not to be spoken of* may be understood to be either affirmed or negatived by the expression, according to the context; so that the force of οὐχ ὅπως may sometimes be conveniently given by *not only*, sometimes by *so far from (not only not)*. *E.g.*

Οὐχ ὅπως τὰ σκεύη ἀπέδοσθε, ἀλλὰ καὶ αἱ θύραι ἀφηρπάσθησαν, *not to speak of your selling the furniture* (i.e. *not only did you sell the furniture, but), even the doors were carried off.* LYS. xix. 31. (With λέγω supplied with οὐχ ὅπως we have *I do not speak of your selling the furniture;* but this would be awkward, and probably no precise verb was thought of.) Εἰ κατώρθωσεν ἐκεῖνος, οὐχ ὅτι τῶν ὄντων ἂν ἀπεστερήμην, ἀλλ᾽ οὐδ᾽ ἂν ἔζην, *if he had succeeded, not to speak of being deprived of my property, (not only should I have been deprived of my property, but) I should not even be alive.* DEM. xxiv. 7. Οὐκ ἔστιν ἄξια μὴ ὅτι δυοῖν ταλάντοιν προσόδου, ἀλλ᾽ οὐδ᾽ εἴκοσι μνῶν, *it is not sufficient to represent an income even of twenty minas, not to speak of two talents.* Id. xxxvi. 39. Τῶνδε οὐχ ὅπως κωλυταὶ γενήσεσθε, ἀλλὰ καὶ ἀπὸ τῆς ὑμετέρας ἀρχῆς δύναμιν προσλαβεῖν περιόψεσθε, *not to speak of (so far from) your becoming a hindrance to them, you will even permit them to add to their power from your own dominions.* THUC. i. 35. Μὴ ὅπως ὀρχεῖσθαι ἐν ῥυθμῷ, ἀλλ᾽ οὐδ᾽ ὀρθοῦσθαι ἐδύνασθε, *not to speak of dancing in time, you could not even stand erect.* XEN. Cyr. i. 3, 10. Τοὺς Θηβαίους ἡγεῖτο ἐάσειν ὅπως βούλεται πράττειν ἑαυτόν, καὶ οὐχ ὅπως ἀντιπράξειν καὶ διακωλύσειν, ἀλλὰ καὶ συστρατεύσειν, *he thought the Thebans would let him do as he pleased, and—not to speak of opposing and hindering him—would even join forces with him.* DEM. vi. 9. (Here no definite verb can be supplied.) Ἐδίδασκον τὸν δῆμον ὡς οὐχ ὅπως τιμωρήσαιντο, ἀλλὰ καὶ ἐπαινέσαιεν τὸν Σφοδρίαν, *that, so far from having punished S., they had even praised him* (οὐχ ὅπως with an optative after ὡς in indirect discourse). XEN. Hell. v. 4, 34.

708. Occasionally one of these expressions stands in the second clause; as διὰ τὸν χειμῶνα οὐδὲ πλεῖν, μὴ ὅτι ἀναιρεῖσθαι τοὺς ἄνδρας, δυνατὸν ἦν, *on account of the storm it was not possible even to sail, much less to pick up the men (not to speak of picking up the men).* XEN. Hell. ii. 3, 35. So πεπαύμεθ᾽ ἡμεῖς, οὐχ ὅπως σε παύσομεν, *we have been stopped ourselves; there is no talk of our stopping you,* SOPH. El. 796.

Compare DEM. xix. 137 : ἐπύθετο αὐτὸν οὐδὲ τοῦ ζῆν ὄντα κύριον αὑτῷ βεβαιῶσαι, μήτι γ᾽ ἃ ἐκείνῳ ὑπέσχετο πρᾶξαι, i.e. *not at all (much less) to do what he had promised him.*

709. 1. In Homer ὅ, the neuter of ὅς, is used like ὅτι, *that.* *E.g.*

Γιγνώσκων ὅ οἱ αὐτὸς ὑπείρεχε χεῖρας Ἀπόλλων, *knowing that Apollo himself held over him his hands.* Il. v. 433. Εὖ νυ καὶ ἡμεῖς ἴδμεν ὅ τοι σθένος οὐκ ἐπιεικτόν. Il. viii. 32. Λεύσσετε γὰρ τό γε πάντες, ὅ μοι γέρας ἔρχεται ἄλλῃ, *that my prize goes elsewhere.* Il. i. 120. So Od. xii. 295. (See 663, 1, and 671.)

2. In the following cases ὅ τ' for ὅ τε (neuter of ὅς τε) is used in Homer like ὅ and ὅτι:—Γιγνώσκων ὅ τ' ἀναλκις ἔην θεός, *knowing that the Goddess was weak.* Il. v. 331 : so xvii. 623, Od. viii. 299. Ὡς εἴδονθ' ὅ τ' ἄρ ἐκ Διὸς ἤλυθεν ὄρνις. Il. viii. 251. Νῦν δ' ἤδη τόδε δῆλον, ὅ τ' οὐκέτι νόστιμός ἐστιν. Od. xx. 333.

Since ὅτι does not allow elision, it is now customary to write this form ὅ τ' (as above). But Schmitt (after Capelle) writes ὅτ' in all these cases, assuming the form to be an elided ὅτε (709, 3).

3. In a few cases ὅτε, *when*, is used in Homer in a sense which approaches very near that of ὅτι, *that. E.g.*

Οὐδ' ἔλαθ' Αἴαντα Ζεὺς, ὅτε δὴ Τρώεσσι δίδω νίκην, i.e. *nor was Ajax unaware that Zeus was giving victory to the Trojans* (lit. *when* Zeus was giving). Il. xvii. 626. Compare Il. xxiv. 563, οὐδέ με λήθεις, ὅττι θεῶν τίς σ' ἦγε. See Schmitt, pp. 40-50.

This occasional use of ὅτε seems hardly to justify the assumption that ὅ τ' in all the cases in 709, 2 stands for ὅτε.

710. 1. Οὕνεκα in Homer, and ὁθούνεκα and οὕνεκα in the tragedians, are sometimes used like ὅτι or ὡς, *that. E.g.*

Πεύθετο γὰρ Κύπρονδε μέγα κλέος, οὕνεκ' Ἀχαιοὶ ἐς Τροίην νήεσσιν ἀναπλεύσεσθαι ἔμελλον, *for in Cyprus he heard a mighty rumour, that the Achaeans were about to sail for Troy in ships.* Il. xi. 21. So Od. v. 216, xiii. 309. Ἄγγελλε ὁθούνεκα τέθνηκ' Ὀρέστης, *report that Orestes is dead.* Soph. El. 47 ; see El. 1478. Ἴσθι τοῦτο, οὕνεκα Ἕλληνές ἐσμεν, *know this,* that *we are Greeks.* Id. Ph. 232. Ἐκδιδαχθεὶς οὕνεκα ἄκουσα ἔρξειεν τάδε. Id. Tr. 934.

2. Διότι is sometimes used in the sense of ὅτι, *that,* by Aristotle, and occasionally by Herodotus and even by Isocrates. *E.g.*

Διότι μὲν τοίνυν οὐχ ἡ αὐτὴ (sc. ἐστί), φανερὸν ἐκ τούτων, i.e. *that it is not the same, is plain from this.* Aristot. Pol. iii. 4, 7. So Metaph. x. 5, 3. Διότι ἐκ τῶν βαρβάρων ἥκει, πυνθανόμενος οὕτω εὑρίσκω ἐόν. Hdt. ii. 50 : see ii. 43 (with Stein's note). See Isoc. iv. 48 : συνειδυῖα ὅτι τοῦτο . . . ἔφυμεν ἔχοντες, καὶ διότι . . . αὐτῶν διηνέγκαμεν.

"Οτι before Direct Quotations.

711. Even direct quotations are sometimes introduced by ὅτι, rarely by ὡς, without further change in the construction. "Οτι or ὡς here cannot be expressed in English. *E.g.*

Ὁ δὲ ἀπεκρίνατο ὅτι Οὐδ' εἰ γενοίμην, ὦ Κῦρε, σοί γ' ἄν ποτε ἔτι δόξαιμι. Xen. An. i. 6, 8. Ἀπεκρίνατο ὅτι Ὦ δέσποτα, οὐ ζῇ. Id. Cyr. vii. 3, 3. Εἶπε δ' ὅτι Εἰς καιρὸν ἥκεις, ἔφη, ὅπως τῆς δίκης ἀκούσῃς. Ib. iii. 1, 8. Ἢ ἐροῦμεν πρὸς αὐτούς, ὅτι Ἠδίκει γὰρ ἡμᾶς ἡ πόλις, καὶ οὐκ ὀρθῶς τὴν δίκην ἔκρινε,—ταῦτα ἢ τί ἐροῦμεν; Plat. Crit. 50 B; so Phaed. 60 A. Ἂν λέγῃ τις τἀληθῆ, ὅτι Ληρεῖτε, ὦ ἄνδρες Ἀθηναῖοι. Dem. viii. 31 : so xviii. 40, 174 ; xix. 22, 40, 253. See also

HDT. ii. 115 (the earliest example); THUC. i. 137, iv. 38 ; AND. i. 49 ;
LYS. i. 26 ; AESCHIN. iii. 22, 120 ; DIN. i. 12, 102 (both with ὡς).[1]

SECTION IX.

Causal Sentences.

712. Causal sentences express the cause of something
stated in the leading sentence. They may be introduced by
ὅτι, διότι or διόπερ, ὡς, οὕνεκα or ὁθούνεκα, *because;* by
ἐπεί, ἐπειδή, ὅτε, ὁπότε, εὖτε, and sometimes ὅπου, *since,
seeing that;* and in Homer by ὅ or ὅ τε (ὅ τ'), *because.*

713. (*Indicative.*) Causal sentences regularly take the
indicative, after both primary and secondary tenses ; past
causes being expressed by the past tenses of the indicative.
The negative particle is οὐ. *E.g.*

Κήδετο γὰρ Δαναῶν, ὅτι ῥα θνήσκοντας ὁρᾶτο, *for she pitied the
Danaans, because she saw them dying.* Il. i. 56. Χωόμενος, ὅ τ' ἄριστον
'Αχαιῶν οὐδὲν ἔτισας, *angry, because you did in no way honour the best
of the Achaeans.* Il. i. 244. Δημοβόρος βασιλεὺς, ἐπεὶ οὐτιδανοῖσιν
ἀνάσσεις. Il. i. 231. Μὴ δ' οὕτως κλέπτε νόῳ, ἐπεὶ οὐ παρελεύσεαι
οὐδέ με πείσεις. Il. i. 132. Νοῦσον ἀνὰ στρατὸν ὦρσε κακὴν, ὀλέ-
κοντο δὲ λαοὶ, οὕνεκα τὸν Χρύσην ἠτίμασεν ἀρητῆρα 'Ατρεΐδης. Il. i.
11. Τηλέμαχον θαύμαζον, ὃ θαρσαλέως ἀγόρευεν, *because he spoke
boldly.* Od. i. 382. Καὶ τριήρης δέ τοι ἡ σεσαγμένη ἀνθρώπων διὰ τί
ἄλλο φοβερόν ἐστι ἢ ὅτι ταχὺ πλεῖ; διὰ τί δὲ ἄλλο ἄλυποι ἀλλήλοις εἰσὶν οἱ ἐμπλέοντες ἢ διότι ἐν τάξει κάθηνται; XEN. Oec. viii. 8.
Οἱ ἐμοὶ φίλοι οὕτως ἔχοντες περὶ ἐμοῦ διατελοῦσιν, οὐ διὰ τὸ φιλεῖν
ἐμὲ, ἀλλὰ διόπερ καὶ αὐτοὶ ἂν οἴονται βέλτιστοι γίγνεσθαι. Id. Mem.
iv. 8, 7. Οἱ 'Αθηναῖοι ἐνόμιζον ἡσσᾶσθαι ὅτι οὐ πολὺ ἐνίκων, *the
Athenians thought they were defeated because they were not signally
victorious.* THUC. vii. 34. Μᾶλλόν τι ἐδεινολογεῖτο ὅτι μιν ἀπέκτεινε
τὸν αὑτὸς φόνου ἐκάθηρε. HDT. i. 44. Πρὸς ταῦτα κρύπτε μηδὲν, ὡς
ὁ πάνθ' ὁρῶν καὶ πάντ' ἀκούων πάντ' ἀναπτύσσει χρόνος, i.e. *since
time develops all things.* SOPH. Fr. 280. Μέγα δὲ τὸ ὁμοῦ τραφῆναι,
ἐπεὶ καὶ τοῖς θηρίοις πόθος τις ἐγγίγνεται τῶν συντρόφων. XEN.
Mem. ii. 3, 4. Ὅτ' οὖν παραινοῦσ' οὐδὲν ἐς πλέον ποιῶ, ἱκέτις
ἀφῖγμαι. SOPH. Ο. T. 918. Ὁπότε οὖν πόλις μὲν τὰς ἰδίας ξυμφορὰς
οἵα τε φέρειν, εἷς δὲ ἕκαστος τὰς ἐκείνης ἀδύνατος (sc. ἐστὶ), πῶς οὐ
χρὴ πάντας .ἀμύνειν αὐτῇ; THUC. ii. 60. Ὅτε τοίνυν τοῦθ' οὕτως
ἔχει, προσήκει προθύμως ἐθέλειν ἀκούειν τῶν βουλομένων συμβου-

---

[1] See Spieker in *Am. Jour. Phil.* v. pp. 221-227, who has traced the history
of this construction and collected examples, especially those in the Orators.

λεύειν. DEM. i. 1. For εὖτε, *since*, see SOPH. Aj. 715, O. C. 84 ; for ὅπου (ὅκου) see HDT. i. 68.

714. (*Optative.*) When, however, the speaker implies that a cause was assigned by some other person, the principle of indirect discourse (694), after past tenses, allows the verb to stand in the optative, in the tense originally used by the person who assigned the cause (699). *E.g.*

Τὸν Περικλέα ἐκάκιζον, ὅτι στρατηγὸς ὢν οὐκ ἐπεξάγοι, *they abused Pericles, because being general he did not lead them out.* THUC. ii. 21. (This states the reason of the Athenians for reproaching Pericles (ὅτι ἡμᾶς οὐκ ἐπεξάγει) ; if Thucydides had wished to assign the cause merely on his own authority, he would have used ὅτι οὐκ ἐπεξῆγεν. Cf. THUC. vii. 34 in 713.) Τοὺς συνόντας ἐδόκει ποιεῖν ἀπέχεσθαι τῶν ἀνοσίων, ἐπείπερ ἡγήσαιντο μηδὲν ἄν ποτε ὧν πράττοιεν θεοὺς διαλαθεῖν (see 693). XEN. Mem. i. 4, 19. Οἶσθα ἐπαινέσαντα αὐτὸν ("Ομηρον) τὸν Ἀγαμέμνονα, ὡς βασιλεὺς εἴη ἀγαθός, *because* (*as he said*) *he was a good king.* Id. Symp. iv. 6. Ἐκάλεε . . . τὸν μὲν ἐπίστιον (Δία), διότι φονέα τοῦ παιδὸς ἐλάνθανε (694, 2) βόσκων, τὸν δὲ ἑταιρήιον, ὡς φύλακα συμπέμψας αὐτὸν εὑρήκοι πολεμιώτατον. HDT. i. 44. (Croesus would have said διότι ἐλάνθανον and ὡς εὕρηκα.)

715. We should suppose that in causal sentences of the latter class (714) the mood and tense by which the cause would be originally stated might also be retained, as in ordinary indirect discourse ; so that in THUC. ii. 21, above, for example, we might have ὅτι οὐκ ἐπεξάγει in the same sense as ὅτι οὐκ ἐπεξάγοι. This, however, seems to have been avoided, to prevent the ambiguity which might arise from the three forms, ἐπεξῆγεν, ἐπεξάγοι, and ἐπεξάγει. It will be remembered that the form ἐπεξῆγεν, which is the most common in the expression of a past cause, is also the original form for expressing the corresponding time in indirect discourse, although it became exceptional here in the later usage (671 ; 674).

For causal relative sentences see 580. For the causal participle see 838.

716. The optative in causal sentences is not found in Homer.

717. A cause may be expressed by a potential indicative or optative with ἄν.

Δέομαι οὖν σου παραμεῖναι ἡμῖν· ὡς ἐγὼ οὐδ᾽ ἂν ἑνὸς ἥδιον ἀκούσαιμι ἢ σοῦ, *I beg you then to remain with us ; as there is not one whom I should hear more gladly than you.* PLAT. Prot. 335 D. Νῦν δὲ, ἐπειδὴ οὐκ ἐθέλεις καὶ ἐμοί τις ἀσχολία ἐστὶ καὶ οὐκ ἂν οἷός τ᾽ εἴην σοι παραμεῖναι ἀποτείνοντι μακροὺς λόγους, ἐλθεῖν γάρ ποί με δεῖ, εἶμι· ἐπεὶ καὶ ταῦτ᾽ ἂν ἴσως οὐκ ἀηδῶς σου ἤκουον (for ἐπεί see 719, 2). Ib. 335 C. Ὅτι τῶν ἀδικημάτων ἂν ἐμέμνητο τῶν αὑτοῦ, εἴ τι περὶ ἐμοῦ γ᾽ ἔγραφεν. DEM. xviii. 79 ; so xviii. 49.

718. A causal sentence may be interrogative, or its verb may express a wish or a command. *E.g.*

'Επεὶ, φέρ' εἰπὲ, ποῦ σὺ μάντις εἶ σαφής; *for—come tell me—where do you ever show yourself a prophet?* SOPH. O. T. 390. 'Επεὶ δίδαξον, ἢ μάθ' ἐξ ἐμοῦ, τί μοι κέρδος γένοιτ' ἄν. Id. El. 352: so O. C. 969. See PLAT. Gorg. 474 B: ἐπεὶ σὺ δέξαι' ἄν; 'Επεὶ ἄθεος ἄφιλος ὅτι πύματον ὀλοίμαν, *for—may I perish!* SOPH. O. T. 662.

719. 1. A causal sentence may give the cause of something that is implied, but not expressed, in the leading sentence. Especially it may give the reason for making a statement, rather than for the fact stated. In dialogues, a causal sentence may refer to an implied *yes* or *no*. *E.g.*

Οὔ νυ καὶ ὑμῖν οἴκοι ἔνεστι γόος, ὅτι μ' ἤλθετε κηδήσοντες; *have you now no mourning at home, that you have come to distress me?* (i.e. *I ask this, because you have come*). Il. xxiv. 239. (If the two clauses were reversed—*have you come because you have no mourning at home?*—the causal relation would be plainer.) Οὔ μ' ἔτ' ἐφάσκεθ' ὑπότροπον οἴκαδ' ἱκέσθαι, ὅτι μοι κατεκείρετε οἶκον, i.e. *you thought I should never return* (as is plain), *because you wasted my house.* Od. xxii. 35. See ἐπεί in Od. i. 231. 'Ὡς ἔστιν ἀνδρὸς τοῦδε τἄργα ταῦτά σοι, *yes* (answering the preceding question), *for here you have the deeds of this man.* SOPH. Aj. 39: so Ph. 812.

2. By a natural ellipsis, ἐπεί sometimes has virtually the force of *although* or *and yet*. *E.g.*

Αἰσχυνοίμην ἂν ἔγωγε τοῦτο ὁμολογεῖν, ἐπεὶ πολλοί γέ φασι τῶν ἀνθρώπων, *I should be ashamed for my part to admit this, and yet many men do say so* (in full, *I speak for myself alone, since many say this*). PLAT. Prot. 333 C. See ibid. 335 C (quoted in 717), where ἐπεὶ ἂν . . . ἤκουον refers to the implied idea *I am sorry after all to go.* In Od. i. 236, ἐπεὶ οὔ κε . . . ἀκαχοίμην, *and yet I should not be thus afflicted by his death,* refers to what ἄιστον suggests, *I am especially grieved by his death in obscurity* (cf. vss. 241, 242).

SECTION X.

Expression of a Wish.

720. Wishes may be divided into two classes: (*a*) those referring to a future object, and (*b*) those referring to a present or past object which (it is implied) is not or was not attained. To the former class belong such wishes as *O that he may come!* or *O that this may happen!*—Utinam veniat, Utinam fiat; and to the latter, such as *O that this had happened!* or *O that this were true!*—Utinam hoc factum esset, Utinam hoc verum esset.

From its use in wishes the *optative* mood (ἔγκλισις εὐκτική) received its name.

WISHES REFERRING TO THE FUTURE.

721. A wish referring to the future may be expressed in Greek in two ways :—

I. by the optative alone; as in γένοιτο τοῦτο, *may this happen*, μὴ γένοιτο τοῦτο, *may this not happen ;*

II. by the optative with εἴθε or εἰ γάρ (Homeric also αἴθε or αἰ γάρ), sometimes by the simple εἰ, negatively εἴθε μή, εἰ γὰρ μή, etc. ; as in εἴθε γένοιτο τοῦτο, *O that this may happen*, εἰ γὰρ μὴ γένοιτο, *O that it may not happen.*

722. I. The pure optative in a wish (with no introductory particle) is an independent verb. *E.g.*

Ὑμῖν μὲν θεοὶ δοῖεν ᾿Ολύμπια δώματ᾿ ἔχοντες ἐκπέρσαι Πριάμοιο πόλιν εὖ δ᾿ οἴκαδ᾿ ἱκέσθαι, *may the Gods grant you to destroy Priam's city*, etc. Il. i. 18.   Μὴ μὰν ἀσπουδί γε καὶ ἀκλειῶς ἀπολοίμην, *may I not perish*, etc. Il. xxii. 304.   Μηκέτ᾿ ἔπειτ᾿ ᾿Οδυσῆι κάρη ὤμοισιν ἐπείη, μηδ᾿ ἔτι Τηλεμάχοιο πατὴρ κεκλημένος εἴην, *then may the head of Ulysses no longer stand on his shoulders, and no longer may I be called the father of Telemachus.* Il. ii. 259.   Τεθναίην ὅτε μοι μηκέτι ταῦτα μέλοι, *may I die when these are no longer my care.* Μιμν. i. 2.   Τὸ μὲν νῦν ταῦτα πρήσσοις τάπερ ἐν χερσὶ ἔχεις, *may you for the present continue to do what you now have in hand.* Ηδτ. vii. 5.   ᾿Ω παῖ, γένοιο πατρὸς εὐτυχέστερος. Σοπη. Aj. 550.   Οὕτω νικήσαιμί τ᾿ ἐγὼ καὶ νομιζοίμην σοφός, *on this condition may I gain the prize (in this contest) and be (always) considered wise.* Αρ. Νub. 520.   Θήσω πρυτανεῖ᾿, ἢ μηκέτι ζῴην ἐγώ, *or. may I no longer live.* Ib. 1255.   Ξυνενέγκοι μὲν ταῦτα ὡς βουλόμεθα, *may this prosper as we desire.* Τηυc. vi. 20.   ᾿Αλλὰ βουληθείης, *but may you only be willing!* Πλατ. Euthyd. 296 D.   Πλούσιον δὲ νομίζοιμι τὸν σοφόν. Id. Phaedr. 279 C.   Νικῴη δ᾿ ὅ τι πᾶσιν ὑμῖν μέλλει συνοίσειν, *and may that opinion prevail which is to benefit you all.* Δεμ. iv. 51.   ῝Ο τι δ᾿ ὑμῖν δόξειε, τοῦτ᾿, ὦ πάντες θεοί, συνενέγκοι (see 561). Id. ix. 76.   So εἶεν, *well, be it so.*

For the relation of the optative in wishes to the optative in its most primitive meaning, see Appendix I.

723. II. The optative in a wish with εἴθε (αἴθε), εἰ γάρ (αἰ γάρ), or εἰ is probably in its origin a protasis with the apodosis suppressed. *E.g.*

Αἴθ᾿ οὕτως ἐπὶ πᾶσι χόλον τελέσει᾿ ᾿Αγαμέμνων, *O if Agamemnon would thus fulfil his wrath upon all.* Il. iv. 178.   Αἴθ᾿ οὕτως,

Εὔμαιε, φίλον Διὶ πατρὶ γένοιο ὡς ἐμοί, *mayest thou become in like*
manner a friend to father Zeus. Od. xiv. 440. Αἲ γὰρ δὴ οὕτως εἴη,
φίλος ὦ Μενέλαε, *O that this may be so.* Il. iv. 189. Αἲ γὰρ ἐμοὶ
τοσσήνδε θεοὶ δύναμιν περιθεῖεν, *O if the Gods would clothe me with*
so much strength! Od. iii. 205. Ἀλλ᾽ εἴ μιν ἀεικισσαίμεθ᾽ ἑλόντες,
τεύχεα τ᾽ ὤμοιιν ἀφελοίμεθα, καί τιν ἑταίρων αὐτοῦ ἀμυνομένων
δαμασαίμεθα νηλέι χαλκῷ, *but if we could only take him and insult*
him, and strip him of his armour, and subdue, etc. Il. xvi. 559.[1] Εἴθε
μήποτε γνοίης ὃς εἶ, *may you never learn who you are.* SOPH. O. T. 1068.
Εἴθ᾽ ὑμῖν ἀμφοῖν νοῦς γένοιτο σωφρονεῖν. Id. Aj. 1264. Εἴθε παῖς
ἐμὸς εὔθηρος εἴη. EUR. Bacch. 1252. Εἰ γὰρ γενοίμην, τέκνον, ἀντὶ
σοῦ νεκρός. Id. Hipp. 1410. Εἴθ᾽, ὦ λῷστε, σὺ τοιοῦτος ὢν φίλος
ἡμῖν γένοιο. XEN. Hell. iv. 1, 38. Εἰ γὰρ γένοιτο. Id. Cyr. vi.
1, 38. Εἰ γὰρ ἐν τούτῳ εἴη, *if it may only depend on this!* PLAT.
Prot. 310 D. Εἴθε γράψειεν ὡς χρή, κ.τ.λ. Id. Phaedr. 227 C.

The simple εἰ (without -θε or γάρ) with the optative in wishes is
poetic. Ἀλλ᾽ εἴ τις καὶ τούσδε μετοιχόμενος καλέσειεν. Il. x. 111.
See three other Homeric examples cited in the footnote.[2] Εἴ μοι
ξυνείη μοῖρα. SOPH. O. T. 863. Εἴ μοι γένοιτο φθόγγος ἐν βρα-
χίοσιν. EUR. Hec. 836.

The future optative was not used in wishes. The perfect was
probably not used, except in the signification of the present (see 48);
as in Il. ii. 259, quoted in 722.

724. In Homer, as the examples show, both present and
aorist optative are freely used in future wishes, as in the corresponding future conditions (455). But the present optative

---

[1] On this passage we have the note of Aristarchus in the Scholia : ἡ διπλῆ,
ὅτι ἔξωθεν προσυπακουστέον τὸ καλῶς ἂν ἔχοι· εἰ αὐτὸν ἀνελόντες ἀεικισσαίμεθα,
καλῶς ἂν ἔχοι. Schol. A. It does not follow *necessarily* from this that
Aristarchus explained all optatives with forms of εἰ in wishes by supplying
καλῶς ἂν ἔχοι as an apodosis (see Lange, p. 6, note 15); but if he explained
this passage as an elliptical protasis, he can hardly have objected to the
same explanation of other similar passages. It is surely no more necessary
or logical to insist on explaining both forms of wishes alike, than it would
be in English to insist that *may I see him again* and *O if I might see him*
again are originally of the same construction.

[2] The Homeric examples of the optative with various forms of εἰ or αἰ are
of the highest importance for the understanding of the construction generally.
The following is a list of the passages (according to Lange, *Partikel EI*, pp.
19-40) :—
Simple εἰ with optative: Il. x. 111, xv. 571, xvi. 559, xxiv. 74. (4.)
Αἲ γάρ or εἰ γάρ with optative: Il. iv. 189, x. 536, xvi. 97, xviii. 272, 464,
xxii. 346, 454 ; Od. iii. 205, iv. 697, vi. 244, viii. 339, ix. 523, xv. 156, xvii.
251, 513, xviii. 235, 366, xix. 22, xx. 169, xxi. 402. (20.)
Αἴθε or εἴθε with optative: Il. iv. 178 ; Od. ii. 33, xiv. 440, xv. 341, xvii.
494, xviii. 202, xx. 61. (7.)
Eight examples (five with εἴθε, two with εἰ γάρ, one with αἰ γάρ), in which
the present optative expresses an unattained present wish, are omitted here
and will be found under 739. The cases discussed in 730 are not included
here.
For the use of αἴθε, αἲ γάρ, and αἰ (for εἴθε, etc.) in Homer, see footnote to
379.

in Homer also expresses a *present* wish implying that it is not attained, as it may express a present unreal condition (438). For this use, see 739.

725. In the poets, especially Homer, the simple optative may express a command or exhortation, in a sense approaching that of the imperative. *E.g.*

Ταῦτ᾽ εἴποις ᾽Αχιλῆι, (*you may*) *say this to Achilles.* Il. xi. 791. Τεθναίης, ὦ Προῖτ᾽, ἢ κάκτανε Βελλεροφόντην, (*you may*) *either die, or kill Bellerophontes.* Il. vi. 164. ᾽Αλλά τις Δολίον καλέσειε, *let some one call Dolios.* Od. iv. 735. So in prohibitions with μή : μηδ᾽ ἔτι σοῖσι πόδεσσιν ὑποστρέψειας ᾽Ολυμπον, Il. iii. 407 (between two pairs of imperatives). See also Aesch. Prom. 1049 and 1051.

For Homeric optatives (without ἄν), which form a connecting link between the potential and the wishing optative (like Il. iv. 18, 19), see 13 and 233.

726. The poets, especially Homer, sometimes use ὡς before the optative in wishes. This ὡς cannot be expressed in English, and it is probably exclamatory. It must not be confounded with οὕτως used as in 727. *E.g.*

῾Ως ἀπόλοιτο καὶ ἄλλος ὅτις τοιαῦτά γε ῥέζοι, *O that any other may likewise perish,* etc. Od. i. 47. See Od. xxi. 201. ῾Ως ὁ τάδε πορὼν ὄλοιτ᾽, εἴ μοι θέμις τάδ᾽ αὐδᾶν. Soph. El. 126. Compare *ut pereat telum,* Hor. Sat. ii. 1, 43.

727. Οὕτως, *thus, on this condition,* may be prefixed to the optative in *protestations,* where a wish is expressed upon some condition ; the condition being usually added in another clause. *E.g.*

Οὕτως ὄναισθε τούτων, μὴ περιίδητέ με, *may you enjoy these on this condition,—do not neglect me.* Dem. xxviii. 20.

728. When the potential optative is used to express a wish, as in πῶς ἂν ὀλοίμην, *how gladly should I perish,* Eur. Supp. 796, it does not belong here, as ὀλοίμην ἄν and ὀλοίμην are, in use, wholly different constructions. If εἰ γάρ κεν μίμνοις, Od. xv. 545, is a wish, εἴ κεν may be used as it often is in protasis in Homer (460) in the same sense as εἰ, or the optative may be potential in the sense *O if you could remain.* In Il. vi. 281, ὥς κέ οἱ αὖθι γαῖα χάνοι, if κέ is correct, must mean *O that the earth could gape for him at once* (potential). But the exceptional character of these expressions makes both suspicious. Hermann and Bekker read εἰ γὰρ καί in Od. xv. 545; and Bekker reads ὡς δέ in Il. vi. 281.

729. The infinitive occurs twice in Homer in wishes with αἲ γάρ : see 786, and 739 (end). For the infinitive used like the simple optative in wishes, especially in poetry, see 785.

730. There are many passages in Homer in which it is open to doubt whether the poet intended to express a wish with some form of εἰ, followed by a potential optative in a new sentence, or to form a complete conditional sentence. Such are—

Εἰ γὰρ ἐπ᾽ ἀρῇσιν τέλος ἡμετέρῃσι γένοιτο·
οὐκ ἄν τις τούτων γε εὔθρονον Ἠῶ ἵκοιτο. Od. xvii. 496.

Αἲ γὰρ τοῦτο, ξεῖνε, ἔπος τετελεσμένον εἴη·
τῷ κε τάχα γνοίης φιλότητά τε πολλά τε δῶρα
ἐξ ἐμεῦ. Od. xv. 536.

If we keep the colon after γένοιτο in the former passage, we may translate, *O that fulfilment may be granted our prayers: not one of these would (then) see the fair-throned Dawn.* With a comma after γένοιτο, we may translate, *if fulfilment should be granted our prayers, not one of these would see the fair-throned Dawn.* So in the second passage we may translate, according to the punctuation, *O that this word may be accomplished: then would you quickly be made aware of kindness and many gifts from me;*—or *if this word should be accomplished, you would then quickly be made aware,* etc. These are probably rightly punctuated above, especially the second; and the wish is on the verge of independent existence, being almost ready to dispense with the apodosis. The half-independent half-dependent nature of such clauses is best seen in a case like the following, where εἰ ἐθέλοι is first stated as an independent wish, and is afterwards repeated as the protasis of a regular apodosis :—

Εἰ γάρ σ᾽ ὣς ἐθέλοι φιλέειν γλαυκῶπις Ἀθήνη
ὣς τότ᾽ Ὀδυσσῆος περικήδετο κυδαλίμοιο
δήμῳ ἔνι Τρώων, ὅθι πάσχομεν ἄλγε᾽ Ἀχαιοί· . . .
εἴ σ᾽ οὕτως ἐθέλοι φιλέειν κήδοιτό τε θυμῷ,
τῷ κέν τις κείνων γε καὶ ἐκλελάθοιτο γάμοιο. Od. iii. 217.

The meaning is, *if only Athena would love you as she then loved Ulysses; . . . if (I say) she would thus love you, then would many a one (of the suitors) cease to think of marriage.* Here, instead of leaving a simple apodosis like the καλῶς ἂν ἔχοι of Aristarchus to be mentally supplied, or to be felt without being actually supplied, the protasis is repeated (as if by afterthought) and a more precise form of conclusion is then actually expressed.

Such examples as the first two are sometimes adduced as evidence that εἰ with the optative in protasis was originally a form of wish, to which an apodosis was afterwards appended. For a discussion of this view, see Appendix I.

WISHES (NOT ATTAINED) IN PRESENT OR PAST TIME.

731. A wish referring to a present or past object, which (it is implied) is not or was not attained, may be expressed in Greek in two ways :—

I. by the past tenses of the indicative, used as in unreal conditions, with εἴθε or εἰ γάρ ; or

II. by ὤφελον, aorist of ὀφείλω, *owe*, with the infinitive.

732. I. The past tenses of the indicative with εἴθε or εἰ γάρ, in present and past wishes, correspond to the optative with these particles in future wishes. The construction was originally a protasis with its apodosis suppressed, εἰ γάρ με εἶδες meaning, *O if you had seen me!* This form of wish is common in the Attic writers, but is unknown to Homer (735).

The imperfect and aorist indicative are distinguished here as in the unreal condition (410). *E.g.*

Ἰὼ γᾶ γᾶ, εἴθ' ἔμ' ἐδέξω, *O Earth, Earth, would that thou hadst received me.* AESCH. Ag. 1537. Εἰ γάρ μ' ὑπὸ γῆν ἧκεν, *O if he had sent me beneath the earth.* Id. Prom. 152. Εἴθε σε εἴθε σε μήποτ' εἰδόμαν. SOPH. O. T. 1217. Εἴθ' εὕρομέν σ', Ἄδμητε, μὴ λυπούμενον. EUR. Alc. 536. Εἴθε σοι, ὦ Περίκλεις, τότε συνεγενόμην, *would that I had met you then.* XEN. Mem. i. 2, 46. Εἴθ' εἶχες, ὦ τεκοῦσα, βελτίους φρένας, *O mother, would that you had a better understanding.* EUR. El. 1061. Εἰ γὰρ τοσαύτην δύναμιν εἶχον, *would that I had so great power.* Id. Alc. 1072. Εἴθ' ἦσθα δυνατὸς δρᾶν ὅσον πρόθυμος εἶ. Id. Her. 731.

733. The indicative cannot be used in wishes without εἴθε or εἰ γάρ, as it would occasion ambiguity; this cannot arise in the case of the optative, which is not regularly used in independent sentences without ἄν, except in wishes. SOPH. O. C. 1713, ἰώ, μὴ γᾶς ἐπὶ ξένας θανεῖν ἐχρῇζες (so the Mss.) is often quoted to show that at least the indicative with μή alone can be used in negative wishes, with the translation, *O that thou hadst not chosen to die in a foreign land.* But the passage is probably corrupt, as the following words ἀλλ' ἔρημος ἔθανες show. See, however, Hermann's note on this passage, and on EUR. Iph. Aul. 575.

734. II. The aorist ὤφελον, *ought*, and sometimes (in Homer) the imperfect ὤφελλον, of ὀφείλω (Epic ὀφέλλω), *owe, debeo*, may be used with the infinitive to express a present or past unattained wish. The present infinitive is used when the wish refers to the present or to continued or repeated past action, and the aorist (rarely the perfect) when it refers to the past.

Ὤφελον or ὤφελλον may be preceded by the particles of wishing, εἴθε and εἰ γάρ, and in negative wishes by μή (not οὐ). *E.g.*

Ὤφελε τοῦτο ποιεῖν, *would that he were (now) doing this* (lit. *he ought to be doing it*), or *would that he had (habitually) done this* (lit. *he ought to have done this*). Ὤφελε τοῦτο ποιῆσαι, *would that he had done this*.

Ὤν ὄφελον τριτάτην περ ἔχων ἐν δώμασι μοῖραν ναίειν, οἱ δ' ἄνδρες σόοι ἔμμεναι οἳ τότ' ὄλοντο, *O that I were living with even a third part*, etc., *and that those men were safe who then perished*. Od. iv. 97. So Il. i. 415. Ἀνδρὸς ἔπειτ' ὤφελλον ἀμείνονος εἶναι ἄκοιτις, ὃς ᾔδη νέμεσίν τε καὶ αἴσχεα πόλλ' ἀνθρώπων, *O that I were the wife of a better man, who knew*, etc. Il. vi. 350. Τὴν ὄφελ' ἐν νήεσσι κατακτάμεν Ἄρτεμις ἰῷ, *O that Artemis had slain her*, etc. Il. xix. 59. Αἴθ' ὤφελλες στρατοῦ ἄλλου σημαίνειν. Il. xiv. 84. Αἴθ' ἅμα πάντες Ἕκτορος ὠφέλετ' ἀντὶ θοῆς ἐπὶ νηυσὶ πεφάσθαι, *would that ye all had been slain instead of Hector*. Il. xxiv. 253. Μηδ' ὄφελες λίσσεσθαι ἀμύμονα Πηλείωνα, *would that you had not besought the son of Peleus*. Il. ix. 698. (See 736, below.) So xviii. 86; Od. viii. 312. Μηκέτ' ἔπειτ' ὤφειλον (?) ἐγὼ πέμπτοισι μετεῖναι ἀνδράσιν, ἀλλ' ἢ πρόσθε θανεῖν ἢ ἔπειτα γενέσθαι, *would that I were no longer living with this fifth race of men, but had either died before it or been born after it*. HES. Op. 174. Ὀλέσθαι ὤφελον τῇδ' ἡμέρᾳ, *O that I had perished on that day*. SOPH. O. T. 1157. Μή ποτ' ὤφελον λιπεῖν τὴν Σκῦρον, *O that I never had left Scyros*. Id. Ph. 969. See El. 1021. Εἴθ' ὤφελ' Ἀργοῦς μὴ διαπτάσθαι σκάφος Κόλχων ἐς αἶαν κυανέας Συμπληγάδας. EUR. Med. 1. Εἰ γὰρ ὤφελον οἷοί τε εἶναι οἱ πολλοὶ τὰ μέγιστα κακὰ ἐξεργάζεσθαι, *O that the multitude were able*, etc. PLAT. Crit. 44 D. Εἰ γὰρ ὤφελον (sc. κατιδεῖν). Id. Rep. 432 C. Παθόντων ἃ μή ποτ' ὤφελον (sc. παθεῖν), *when they suffered what would they had never suffered*. DEM. xviii. 288; so 320. So ὡς μήποτε ὤφελεν, XEN. Cyr. iv. 6, 3 (see 737).

735. This form with ὤφελον or ὤφελλον is the only expression known to Homer for *past* wishes, the secondary tenses of the indicative being not yet used in this construction, although they were already in good use in past (though not in present) conditions (435). In present wishes, Homer has the present optative (739) as well as the construction with ὤφελον. (See 438.)

736. For an explanation of the origin of the use of ὤφελον in wishes, see 424. It is there seen to be analogous to ἔδει and χρῆν, with the infinitive, implying that what *ought to be* or *to have been* does not or did not happen. Only after its original meaning was obscured by familiar use could εἴθε or εἰ γάρ have been prefixed to it. Μὴ ὤφελον may be explained in the same way; or we may suppose that μή originally belonged to the infinitive, and afterwards came to negative the whole expression. See the examples in 734.

737. Ὡς, used as in 726, often precedes ὤφελον etc. in Homer, and rarely in the Attic poets. *E.g.*
Ἦλθες ἐκ πολέμου· ὡς ὤφελες αὐτόθ' ὀλέσθαι, *would you had perished there*. Il. iii. 428. Ὡς δὴ μὴ ὄφελον νικᾶν τοιῷδ' ἐπ' ἀέθλῳ, *O that I had not been victorious in such a contest*. Od. xi. 548.

Ὡς ὤφελλ' Ἑλένης ἀπὸ φῦλον ὀλέσθαι. Od. xiv. 68. So Il. iii.
173, xxii 481. Ὡς πρὶν διδάξαι γ' ὤφελες μέσος διαρραγῆναι,
would that you had split in two before you ever taught it. Ar. Ran. 955.

738. Neither the secondary tenses of the indicative nor the form
with ὤφελον in wishes can (like the optative) be preceded by the simple
εἰ (without -θε or γάρ).

739. (*Present Wishes in Homer.*) In Homer a present unattained wish may be expressed by the present optative, like a
present unfulfilled condition (438). Here εἴθε or εἰ γάρ generally
introduces the wish. *E.g.*

Εἰ γὰρ ἐγὼν οὕτω γε Διὸς πάις αἰγιόχοιο
εἴην ἤματα πάντα, τέκοι δέ με πότνια Ἥρη,
τιοίμην δ' ὡς τίετ' Ἀθηναίη καὶ Ἀπόλλων,
ὡς νῦν ἡμέρη ἥδε κακὸν φέρει Ἀργείοισιν,

*O that I were the son of Zeus, and that Hera were my mother, and that I
were honoured as Athena and Apollo are honoured,* etc. Il. xiii. 825.
(Here τέκοι is nearly equivalent to μήτηρ εἴη : cf. ὦ τεκοῦσα, *O mother,*
quoted under 732.) Almost the same wish occurs in Il. viii. 538.

Ὦ γέρον, εἴθ' ὡς θυμὸς ἐνὶ στήθεσσι φίλοισιν
ὥς τοι γούναθ' ἕποιτο, βίη δέ τοι ἔμπεδος εἴη ·
ἀλλά σε γῆρας τείρει ὁμοίιον · ὡς ὄφελέν τις
ἀνδρῶν ἄλλος ἔχειν, σὺ δὲ κουροτέροισι μετεῖναι,

*would that, even as thy spirit is in thy breast, so thy knees obeyed and thy
strength were firm.* Il. iv. 313. At the end we have the more common
form of a present wish, ὄφελέν τις ἄλλος ἔχειν, *would that some other
man had it* (γῆρας).

Εἴθ' ὡς ἡβώοιμι, βίη δέ μοι ἔμπεδος εἴη ·
τῷ κε τάχ' ἀντήσειε μάχης κορυθαίολος Ἕκτωρ,

O that I were again so young, and my strength were firm, etc. Il. vii. 157.
The same wish, in precisely the same words, occurs also in Il. xi. 670,
xxiii. 629, and Od. xiv. 468; also in Il. vii. 132 in the form αἶ γὰρ,
Ζεῦ τε πάτερ, . . . ἡβῷμ' ὡς ὅτ' . . . μάχοντο. See Od. xiv. 503,
ὡς νῦν ἡβώοιμι, repeating the idea of vs. 468. In Od. xviii. 79 we have
νῦν μὲν μήτ' εἴης, βουγάιε, μήτε γένοιο, *better that thou wert not now,
thou braggart, and hadst never been born,* where γένοιο looks like a past
wish ; but *not having been born* may be included in the present wish of
εἴης : compare τέκοι in Il. xiii. 826 (above). For αἶ γὰρ ἐλασαίατο,
Il. x. 536, see 93 (end).

For the infinitive with αἶ γάρ in a past unattained wish in Homer,
see 786.

---

740. It has been seen that the use of the moods and tenses
in both classes of wishes with εἰ γάρ and εἴθε is precisely the
same as in the corresponding forms of protasis (455 ; 410).
The analogy with the Latin is also the same as in protasis :—

εἰ γὰρ τοῦτο ποιοίη (or ποιήσειεν), O si hoc faciat, O that he may do this; εἰ γὰρ τοῦτο ἐποίει, O si hoc faceret, O that he were doing this; εἰ γὰρ τοῦτο ἐποίησεν, O si hoc fecisset, O that he had done this; εἰ γὰρ μὴ ἐγένετο, utinam ne factum esset, O that it had not happened.

It must be remembered that it is the *futurity* of the object of a wish, and not its probability or possibility, that requires the optative. No amount of absurdity or extravagance in a future wish can make anything but the optative proper in expressing it. As Aristotle says (Eth. iii. 2, 7), βούλησις δ' ἐστὶ τῶν ἀδυνάτων, οἷον ἀθανασίας, wish may refer to impossibilities, as that we may live for ever; but this very wish would require the optative. So no amount of reasonableness in a present or past wish can make the imperfect or aorist indicative improper; for we may wish that the most reasonable thing were or had been ours, only such wishing implies that we do not or did not have it.

CHAPTER V.

THE INFINITIVE.

741. The infinitive is originally a verbal noun, expressing the simple idea of the verb. As a verb, it has voices and tenses; it has a subject (expressed or understood), which may define its number and person; it may have an object and other adjuncts, and, further, it is qualified by adverbs, and not by adjectives. It may have ἄν in a potential sense. It thus expresses the verbal idea with much greater definiteness than the corresponding substantives; compare, for example, πράττειν and πρᾶξαι with πρᾶξις, as expressions of the idea of *doing*.

742. The origin of the infinitive in a verbal noun is beyond question. In the oldest Sanskrit certain verbal nouns in the dative express purpose, that is, the object *to* or *for* which something is done, and are almost identical in form with the equivalent infinitives in the older Greek. Thus *vidmáne*, dative of *vidman*, *knowledge* (from root *vid*), may mean *for knowing* or *in order to know* (old English *for to know*); and in Homer we have Ϝίδμεναι (= Attic ἰδεῖν) from the same root Ϝιδ. So Sanskrit *dávane*, dative of *dávan*, *giving* (from root *da*), is represented in Greek by the Cyprian δόϝεναι (= Attic δοῦναι) from root δο.[1] It is safe to assume, therefore, that the Greek infinitive was originally developed in a similar way, chiefly from the dative of a primitive verbal noun; that in the growth of the language this case-form became obscured, its origin as a dative was forgotten, and it

---

[1] Whitney (*Sanskrit Grammar*, p. 314) says of these primitive Sanskrit datives: "It is impossible to draw any fixed line between the uses classed as infinitive and the ordinary case-uses." See Delbrück, *Synt. Forsch.* iv. p. 121; and Monro, *Hom. Gr.* p. 163.

came to be used for other cases of the verbal noun, especially the accusative; that it was allowed to take an object, like the corresponding verb, and afterwards a subject (in the accusative) to make the agent more distinct; that in course of time, as its relation to the verb became closer, it developed tenses like those of the verb, so as to appear as a regular mood of the verb. The final step, taken when the use of the definite article was established, was to allow the half-noun and half-verb to have the article and so be declined like a noun in four cases, while it still retained its character as a verb. This last step was taken after Homer; but the earlier stages were already passed, more or less decidedly, before the Homeric period, so that they cannot be traced historically. Thus, although the infinitive in Homer retained some of its uses as a dative more distinctly than the later infinitive, it is hardly possible that those who used the Homeric language retained any consciousness of the original dative; for the infinitive was already established as an accusative and a nominative, it had formed its various tenses to express present, past, and future time, and it could even be used with ἄν (683). Indeed, the condition in which the infinitive appears in indirect discourse in Homer seems utterly inconsistent with any conscious survival of its force as a dative (see examples in 683).

743. The later addition of the article enlarged the uses of the infinitive and extended it to new constructions, especially to the use with prepositions. It thus gained a new power of taking adjuncts, not merely single words, but whole dependent clauses. (See examples in 806.) In all the constructions which were developed before the article came into use with the infinitive, as when it is the subject or the object of a verb, or follows adjectives or nouns, the infinitive continued to be used regularly without the article, although even in these constructions the article might be added to emphasise the infinitive more especially as a noun, or to enable it to carry adjuncts which would otherwise be cumbrous; in other words, all constructions in which the original force of the noun had become obscured or forgotten before the article began to be used generally remained in their original form. On the other hand, newer expressions, in which the infinitive was distinctly felt as a noun in the structure of the sentence, generally added the article to designate the case.

744. The subject of the infinitive, if expressed, is in the accusative. The most indefinite infinitive, so far as it is a verb, must at least have a subject implied; but as the infinitive has no person or number in itself, its subject can remain more obscure than that of a finite verb. Thus καλόν ἐστιν ἀποθανεῖν, *it is* *glorious to die*, may imply a subject in any number or person, according to the context, while ἀποθνῄσκεις or ἀπέθανε is restricted to *thou* or *he* as its subject. Still, in the former case, ἀποθανεῖν must have an implied subject in the accusative; and if this is not pointed out by the context, we can supply τινά or τινάς, as sometimes appears when a predicate word agrees with the omitted subject, as in φιλάνθρωπον εἶναι δεῖ (sc. τινά), *one must be humane*, ISOC. ii. 15, and δρῶντας ἥδιον θανεῖν (sc. τινάς), *it is sweeter to die acting*, EUR. Hel. 814. The infinitive of indirect discourse, which seems to have been developed originally by the Greek language, must always refer to a definite subject, as it represents a finite verb in a definite mood, tense, number, and person. Other infinitives, both with and without the article, may have a subject whenever the sense demands it, although sometimes the meaning of the leading verb makes it impossible to express an independent subject, as in πειρᾶται μανθάνειν, *he tries to learn*. In general, when the subject of the infinitive is the same as the subject or object of the leading verb, or when it has been clearly expressed elsewhere in the sentence, it is not repeated with the infinitive.[1]

A. INFINITIVE WITHOUT THE ARTICLE.

Infinitive as Subject, Predicate, or Appositive.

745. The infinitive may be the subject nominative of a finite verb, or the subject accusative of another infinitive. It is especially common as subject of an impersonal verb or of ἐστί. It may also be a predicate nominative or accusative, and it may stand in apposition to a noun in the nominative or accusative. *E.g.*

Συνέβη αὐτῷ ἐλθεῖν, *it happened to him to go.* Οὐκ ἔνεστι τοῦτο ποιῆσαι, *it is not possible to do this.* Ἀδύνατόν ἐστι τοῦτο ποιῆσαι. Ἐξῆν αὐτῷ μένειν, *he might have remained* (i.e. *to remain was possible for him*). Δεῖ μένειν. Οὐ μὴν γάρ τι κακὸν βασιλευέμεν, *for it*

---

[1] A few exceptional cases are quoted by Birklein (p. 93) in which the infinitive with the article appears to have a subjective genitive, like an ordinary verbal noun, instead of a subject accusative. These are γιγνώσκω τὰς τούτων ἀπειλὰς οὐχ ἧττον σωφρονιζούσας ἢ ἄλλων τὸ ἤδη κολάζειν, XEN. An. vii. 7, 24; τὸ εὖ φρονεῖν αὐτῶν μιμεῖσθε, DEM. xix. 269; and εἰ τῆς πόλεως τέθνηκε τὸ τοὺς ἀδικοῦντας μισεῖν, Ib. 289. In the first case the parallelism between τούτων and ἄλλων caused the anomaly; in the second, αὐτῶν has a partitive force, as if it were τοῦτο αὐτῶν μιμεῖσθε; and in the third, πόλεως is separated from the infinitive by the verb, and the idea is *whether the hatred of evil-doers has died out* (i.e. *disappeared from*) the state. In none of these cases would a subject accusative be the exact equivalent of the genitive. For undoubted examples in later Greek, see *Trans. of Am. Phil. Assoc. for* 1877, p. 7.

is no bad thing to be a king. Od. i. 392. Ἀεὶ γὰρ ἡβᾷ τοῖς γέρουσιν
εὖ μαθεῖν. AESCH. Ag. 584. Πολὺ γὰρ ῥᾷον ἔχοντας φυλάττειν
ἢ κτήσασθαι πάντα πέφυκεν. DEM. ii. 26. (Compare i. 23, quoted
in 790.) Ἡδὺ πολλοὺς ἐχθροὺς ἔχειν; Id. xix. 221. Δοκεῖ οἰκο-
νόμου ἀγαθοῦ εἶναι εὖ οἰκεῖν τὸν ἑαυτοῦ οἶκον. XEN. Oec. i. 2. Φησὶ
δεῖν τοῦτο ποιῆσαι, *he says that it is necessary to do this.* (Here
ποιῆσαι as accusative is subject of δεῖν.) Τὸ γνῶναι ἐπιστήμην που
λαβεῖν ἐστιν, *to learn is to acquire knowledge* (pred. nom.). PLAT. Theaet.
209 E. Ξυνέβη τοὺς Ἀθηναίους θορυβηθῆναι, *it chanced that the
Athenians fell into confusion.* THUC. v. 10. Οὐ φάσκων ἄνεκτον εἶναι
ξυγκεῖσθαι κρατεῖν βασιλέα τῶν πόλεων. Id. viii. 52. (Here κρατεῖν βασιλέα τῶν πόλεων is subject of ξυγκεῖσθαι, which is subject of
εἶναι, the whole being object of φάσκων.) Εἷς οἰωνὸς ἄριστος,
ἀμύνεσθαι περὶ πάτρης, *one omen is best, to fight for our country.* Il.
xii. 243.

For the subject infinitive in indirect discourse, see 751.

Infinitive as Object.

746. The infinitive may be the object of a verb, generally
appearing as the accusative of the direct object, sometimes
as the accusative of kindred meaning. Here belong (1) the
infinitive after verbs of *wishing, commanding,* and the like
(*not* in indirect discourse), and (2) the infinitive *in* indirect
discourse as the object of verbs of *saying* and *thinking.*

For the infinitive in indirect discourse, see 751.

Object Infinitive not in Indirect Discourse.

747. The verbs which take the ordinary object infinitive
are in general the same in Greek as in English. Any verb
whose action directly implies another action or state as its
object, if this object is to be expressed by a verb and not
by a noun, may take the infinitive.

Such are verbs signifying to *wish, ask, advise, entreat, exhort,
command, persuade, compel, teach, learn, accustom, cause, intend, begin,
attempt, effect, permit, decide, dare, prefer, choose ;* those expressing
*willingness, unwillingness, eagerness, caution, neglect, danger, postpone-
ment, forbidding, hindrance, escape,* etc.; and all implying *ability,
fitness, ·desert, qualification, sufficiency, necessity,* or their *opposites.*
E.g.

Διδάσκουσιν αὐτὸν βάλλειν, *they teach him to shoot.* Ἔμαθον τοῦτο
ποιῆσαι, *they learned to do this.* Βούλεται ἐλθεῖν. Παραινοῦμέν σοι

πείθεσθαι. Αἱροῦνται πολεμεῖν. Ἡ πόλις κινδυνεύει διαφθαρῆναι, *the city is in danger of being destroyed.* Δύναται ἀπελθεῖν. Τοῖς ξυμμάχοις ἔφραζον ἰέναι ἐς τὸν Ἰσθμόν, *they told the allies to go to the Isthmus.* Thuc. iii. 15. Δέομαι ὑμῶν συγγνώμην μοι ἔχειν. Εἶπε στρατηγοὺς ἑλέσθαι, *he proposed to choose generals.* Ἀπαγορεύουσιν αὐτοῖς μὴ τοῦτο ποιῆσαι, *they forbid them to do this* (815, 1). Τί κωλύσει αὐτὸν βαδίζειν ὅποι βούλεται; *what will prevent him from marching whither he pleases?* Ἀξιῶ λαμβάνειν τοῦτο, *I claim the right to take this.* Ἀξιοῦται θανεῖν, *he is thought to deserve death.* Οὐ πέφυκε δουλεύειν, *he is not born to be a slave.* Ἀναβάλλεται τοῦτο ποιεῖν, *he postpones doing this.*

Λαοὺς δ' Ἀτρεΐδης ἀπολυμαίνεσθαι ἄνωγεν, *and the son of Atreus ordered the hosts to purify themselves.* Il. i. 313. Βούλομ' ἐγὼ λαὸν σόον ἔμμεναι ἢ ἀπολέσθαι, *I wish that the people may be safe, rather than that they perish.* Il. i. 117. Ἔπειθεν αὐτὸν πορεύεσθαι. Xen. An. vi. 2, 13. Ἔδοξε πλεῖν τὸν Ἀλκιβιάδην, *it was decided that Alcibiades should sail.* Thuc. vi. 29. Φυλακὴν εἶχε μήτ' ἐκπλεῖν μηδένα μήτ' ἐσπλεῖν, *he kept guard against any one's sailing out or in* (815, 1). Id. ii. 69. Τί δῆτα μέλλεις μὴ οὐ γεγωνίσκειν τὸ πᾶν; *why do you hesitate to speak out the whole?* Aesch. Prom. 627.

This use of the infinitive is too familiar to need more illustration. The tenses commonly used are the present and aorist (87), for examples of which see 96; for the perfect see 109 and 110; for the exceptional future see 113; and for the infinitive with ἄν (seldom used in this construction) see 211. For μή and μὴ οὐ with the infinitive (as used above) see 815–817.

748. The poets, especially Homer, allow an infinitive after many verbs which commonly do not take this construction. The meaning of the verb, however, makes the sense clear. *E.g.*

Ὀδύρονται οἴκόνδε νέεσθαι, *they mourn* (i.e. *long*) *to go home.* Il. ii. 290. Ἐπευφήμησαν Ἀχαιοὶ αἰδεῖσθαι ἱερῆα, *the Achaeans shouted with applause,* (*commanding*) *that they should reverence the priest.* Il. i. 22. Ὄφρα τις ἐρρίγῃσι κακὰ ῥέξαι, *that one may shudder (dread) to do evil.* Il. iii. 353. Ἕκτορα μεῖναι μοῖρα πέδησεν, *Fate bound (fettered) Hector to remain.* Il. xxii. 5.

For the infinitive of direct object after verbs of *fearing* and *caution,* see 373. For the infinitive (not in indirect discourse) after χράω and other verbs meaning *to give an oracle,* see 98.

749. When a noun and a verb (especially ἐστί) form an expression which is equivalent to any of the verbs above mentioned (747), they may take the infinitive. Some other expressions with a similar force may have the infinitive. *E.g.*

Ἀνάγκη ἐστὶ πάντας ἀπελθεῖν. Κίνδυνος ἦν αὐτῷ παθεῖν τι. Ὄκνος ἐστί μοι τοῦτο ποιῆσαι. Φόβος ἐστὶν αὐτῷ ἐλθεῖν. Οὐ μάντις εἰμὶ τἀφανῆ γνῶναι, *I am not enough of a prophet to decide, etc.* Eur. Hipp. 346. (Here *ability* is implied in μάντις εἰμί.) Ἄμαξα ἐν αὐταῖς ἦν, κώλυμα οὖσα (τὰς πύλας) προσθεῖναι, *a wagon, which prevented them from shutting the gates.* THUC. iv. 67. So ἐπεγένετο δὲ ἄλλοις τε ἄλλοθι κωλύματα μὴ αὐξηθῆναι, *obstacles to their increase.* Id. i. 16. (See 815, 1.) Τοῖς στρατιώταις ὁρμὴ ἐνέπεσε ἐκτειχίσαι τὸ χωρίον. Id. iv. 4. Τὸ ἀσφαλὲς καὶ μένειν καὶ ἀπελθεῖν αἱ νῆες παρέξουσιν, *safety both to remain and to depart.* Id. vi. 18. Ἔχοντα τιθασεύεσθαι φύσιν, *capable by nature of being tamed* (= πεφυκότα τιθασεύεσθαι). PLAT. Polit. 264 A. Τίς μηχανὴ μὴ οὐχὶ πάντα καταναλωθῆναι εἰς τὸ τεθνάναι; i.e. *how can it be effected that all things shall not be destroyed in death?* Id. Phaed. 72 D. (See 815, 2.) Δέδοικα μὴ πολλὰ καὶ χαλεπὰ εἰς ἀνάγκην ἔλθωμεν ποιεῖν, *lest we may come to the necessity of doing.* DEM. i. 15. Ὥρα ἀπιέναι, *it is time to go away* (like χρὴ ἀπιέναι, *we must go away*). PLAT. Ap. 42 A. Ἐλπίδας ἔχει τοῦτο ποιῆσαι (= ἐλπίζει τοῦτο ποιῆσαι), *he hopes to do this.* But ἐλπὶς τοῦ ἑλεῖν, THUC. ii. 56 (798). Οἱ δὲ ζῶντες αἴτιοι θανεῖν, *and the living are those who caused them to die.* SOPH. Ant. 1173. We might also have αἴτιοι τοῦ τούτους θανεῖν or αἴτιοι τὸ τούτους θανεῖν. (See 101.) So in phrases like πολλοῦ (or μικροῦ) δέω ποιεῖν τι, *I want much (or little) of doing anything;* παρὰ μικρὸν ἦλθον ποιεῖν τι, *they came within a little of doing anything;* where the idea of *ability, inability,* or *sufficiency* appears: so in THUC. vii. 70, βραχὺ γὰρ ἀπέλιπον διακόσιαι γενέσθαι. So ἐμποδὼν τούτῳ ἐστὶν ἐλθεῖν (= κωλύει τοῦτον ἐλθεῖν), *it prevents him from going;* where τοῦ ἐλθεῖν may be used (807). The infinitive depending on a noun is generally an *adnominal* genitive with the article τοῦ. See the examples above, and 798.

750. In *laws, treaties, proclamations,* and *formal commands,* the infinitive is often used in the leading sentences, depending on some word like ἔδοξε, *it is enacted,* or κελεύεται, *it is commanded;* which may be either expressed in a preceding sentence or understood. *E.g.*

Ταμίας δὲ τῶν ἱερῶν χρημάτων αἱρεῖσθαι μὲν ἐκ τῶν μεγίστων τιμημάτων· τὴν δὲ αἵρεσιν τούτων καὶ τὴν δοκιμασίαν γίγνεσθαι καθάπερ ἡ τῶν στρατηγῶν ἐγίγνετο, and (*it is enacted*) *that treasurers of the sacred funds be chosen,* etc. PLAT. Leg. 759 E. So in most of the laws (genuine or spurious) standing as quotations in the text of the orators, as in DEM. xxiii. 22: δικάζειν δὲ τὴν ἐν Ἀρείῳ πάγῳ φόνου καὶ τραύματος ἐκ προνοίας, κ.τ.λ. See AR. Av. 1661. Ἔτη δὲ εἶναι τὰς σπονδὰς πεντήκοντα, and *that the treaty shall continue fifty years.* THUC. v. 18. Ἀκούετε λεῴ· τοὺς ὁπλίτας νυνμενὶ ἀνελομένους θὦπλ' ἀπιέναι πάλιν οἴκαδε. AR. Av. 448.

Infinitive in Indirect Discourse.

751. The infinitive in indirect discourse is generally the object of a verb of *saying* or *thinking* or some equivalent expression. It may also be the subject of a passive verb of this class (as λέγεται), or of such a verb as φαίνεται, *it appears*, or δοκεῖ, *it seems* (see 754). Here each tense of the infinitive represents the corresponding tense of the indicative (with or without ἄν) or the optative (with ἄν). (See 664, 2.) For examples see 683 and 689. For the various tenses of the infinitive with ἄν, representing the indicative or optative with ἄν, see 204-210.

752. Verbs of *hoping, expecting, promising, swearing*, and a few others of like meaning, form an intermediate class between this construction and that of 747. For examples of the infinitive (in both constructions) after these verbs, see 136.

753. 1. Of the three common verbs signifying *to say*, φημί is regularly followed by the infinitive in indirect discourse, εἶπον by ὅτι or ὡς and the indicative or optative, while λέγω allows either construction. The active voice of λέγω, however, generally has ὅτι or ὡς.

2. Exceptional cases of ὅτι or ὡς after φημί are very rare and strange : one occurs in LYS. vii. 19, ὅς φησιν ὡς ἐγὼ μὲν παρειστήκειν οἱ δ' οἰκέται ἐξέτεμνον τὰ πρέμνα. See also XEN. Hell. vi. 3, 7, and PLAT. Gorg. 487 D (where a clause with ὅτι precedes φῄς).

3. Cases of εἶπον with the infinitive of indirect discourse are less rare, but always exceptional. See Il. xxiv. 113, xviii. 9, quoted in 683 ; HDT. ii. 30 ; THUC. vii. 35 ; PLAT. Gorg. 473 A, εἶπον τὸ ἀδικεῖν τοῦ ἀδικεῖσθαι κάκιον εἶναι. A remarkable case of οὐ μή with the infinitive after εἶπε occurs in EUR. Phoen. 1590 (quoted in 296). Εἶπον and the active voice of λέγω take the infinitive chiefly as verbs of *commanding* (747).

754. After many verbs of this class in the passive both a personal and an impersonal construction are allowed : thus, we can say λέγεται ὁ Κῦρος ἐλθεῖν, *Cyrus is said to have gone*, or λέγεται τὸν Κῦρον ἐλθεῖν, *it is said that Cyrus went*. Δοκέω in the meaning *I seem* (videor) usually has the *personal* construction, as in English ; as οὗτος δοκεῖ εἶναι, *he seems to be*. When an infinitive with ἄν follows a personal verb like δοκέω, this must be translated by an impersonal construction, to suit the English idiom : thus, δοκεῖ τις ἂν ἔχειν τοῦτο must be translated *it seems that some one would have this*, although τις is the subject of δοκεῖ, since we cannot use *would* with our infinitive to translate ἔχειν ἄν.

755. When an indirect quotation has been introduced by an infinitive, a dependent relative or temporal clause sometimes takes the infinitive by assimilation, where we should expect an indicative or optative. The temporal particles ὡς, ὅτε, ἐπεί, ἐπειδή, as well as the relative pronouns, are used in this construction. Herodotus uses even εἰ, *if*, and διότι, *because*, in the same way. *E.g.*

Μετὰ δὲ, ὡς οὐ παύεσθαι, ἄκεα δίζησθαι (λέγουσι), *and afterwards,
when it did not cease, they say that they sought for remedies.* HDT. i. 94.
(Here we should expect ὡς οὐκ ἐπαύετο.) Ὥς δ' ἀκοῦσαι τοὺς παρόντας, θόρυβον γενέσθαι (φασίν), *they say that, when those present heard it,
there was a tumult.* DEM. xix. 195. Ἐπειδὴ δὲ γενέσθαι ἐπὶ τῇ οἰκίᾳ
τῇ Ἀγάθωνος, (ἔφη) ἀνεῳγμένην καταλαμβάνειν τὴν θύραν. PLAT.
Symp. 174 D. Ἔφη δὲ, ἐπειδὴ οὗ ἐκβῆναι τὴν ψυχὴν, πορεύεσθαι.
Id. Rep. 614 B. So ὡς φαίνεσθαι, *as it appeared,* 359 D. Λέγεται
Ἀλκμαίωνι, ὅτε δὴ ἀλᾶσθαι αὐτὸν, τὸν Ἀπόλλω ταύτην τὴν γῆν
χρῆσαι οἰκεῖν. THUC. ii. 102. Καὶ ὅσα αὖ μετ' ἐκείνων βουλεύεσθαι, οὐδενὸς ὕστερον γνώμῃ φανῆναι (ἔφασαν). Id. i. 91. (Here
ἐβουλεύοντο would be the common form.) Ἡγουμένης δὴ ἀληθείας
οὐκ ἄν ποτε φαῖμεν αὐτῇ χορὸν κακῶν ἀκολουθῆσαι, ἀλλ' ὑγιές
τε καὶ δίκαιον ἦθος, ᾧ καὶ σωφροσύνην ἕπεσθαι. PLAT. Rep. 490 C.
Εἰ γὰρ δὴ δεῖν πάντως περιθεῖναι ἄλλῳ τέῳ τὴν βασιληίην, (ἔφη)
δικαιότερον εἶναι Μήδων τέῳ περιβαλεῖν τοῦτο, *for if he was bound
(= εἰ ἔδει) to give the kingdom to any other,* etc. HDT. i. 129. Εἰ ὦν
εἶναι τῷ θεῷ τοῦτο μὴ φίλον, *if this were (= εἰ ἦν) not pleasing to
God.* Id. ii. 64. So iii. 108 (εἰ μὴ γίνεσθαι = εἰ μὴ ἐγίνετο, *had
there not occurred*) ; vii. 229 (εἰ ἀπονοστῆσαι, *if he had returned*) ; ii.
172 (εἰ εἶναι, *if he was*); iii. 105 (εἰ μὴ προλαμβάνειν = εἰ μὴ
προλαμβάνοιμεν). Τιμᾶν δὲ Σαμίους ἔφη, διότι ταφῆναί οἱ τὸν
πάππον δημοσίῃ ὑπὸ Σαμίων. Id. iii. 55.

756. In some cases, particularly when the provisions of a *law* are
quoted, a relative is used with the infinitive, even when no infinitive
precedes. *E.g.*

Ἔθηκεν ἐφ' οἷς ἐξεῖναι ἀποκτιννύναι, *he enacted on what conditions
it is allowed to kill.* DEM. xx. 158. Καὶ διὰ ταῦτα, ἄν τις ἀποκτείνῃ
τινὰ, τὴν βουλὴν δικάζειν ἔγραψε, καὶ οὐχ ἅπερ, ἂν ἁλῷ, εἶναι, *and
he did not enact what should be done if he should be convicted.* Id. xxiii.
26. (Here εἶναι, the reading of Cod. Σ, is amply defended by the preceding example, in which all allow ἐξεῖναι.) Δέκα γὰρ ἄνδρας προσείλοντο
αὐτῷ ξυμβούλους, ἄνευ ὧν μὴ κύριον εἶναι ἀπάγειν στρατιὰν ἐκ τῆς
πόλεως. THUC. v. 63.

757. In narration, the infinitive often appears to stand for the
indicative. It depends, however, on some word like λέγεται, *it
is said,* expressed (or at least implied) in something that precedes.
E.g.

Ἀπικομένους δὲ τοὺς Φοίνικας ἐς δὴ τὸ Ἄργος τοῦτο, διατίθεσθαι
τὸν φόρτον, *and (they say) that the Phoenicians, when now they had come
to this Argos, were setting out their cargo for sale.* HDT. i. 1. (Here
διατίθεσθαι is imperfect.) "Ἀλλ', ὦ παῖ," φάναι τὸν Ἀστυάγην,
"οὐκ ἀχθόμενοι ταῦτα περιπλανώμεθα." "Ἀλλὰ καὶ σὲ," φάναι
τὸν Κῦρον, "ὁρῶ," κ.τ.λ. Καὶ τὸν Ἀστυάγην ἐπερέσθαι, "καὶ τίνι
δὴ σὺ τεκμαιρόμενος λέγεις;" "Ὅτι σὲ," φάναι, "ὁρῶ," κ.τ.λ. Πρὸς
ταῦτα δὲ τὸν Ἀστυάγην εἰπεῖν, κ.τ.λ. Καὶ τὸν Κῦρον εἰπεῖν, κ.τ.λ.
XEN. Cyr. i. 3, 5 and 6. (Here all these infinitives, and twelve

others which follow, depend on λέγεται in § 4.) Καὶ τὸν κελεῦσαι δοῦναι, *and he commanded him to give it.* Id. i. 3, 9. So in HDT. i. 24 the story of Arion and the dolphin is told in this construction, the infinitives all depending on λέγουσι at the beginning.

Infinitive after Adjectives, Adverbs, and Nouns.

758. The infinitive may depend on adjectives denoting *ability, fitness, desert, qualification, sufficiency, readiness,* and their *opposites;* and, in general, those expressing the same relations as the verbs which govern the infinitive (747). The omitted subject of the infinitive is the same as the substantive to which the adjective belongs. *E.g.*

Δυνατὸς ποιεῖν, *able to do.* Δεινὸς λέγειν, *skilled in speaking.* Ἄξιός ἐστι ταῦτα λαβεῖν, *he deserves to receive this.* Ἄξιος τιμᾶσθαι, *worthy to be honoured.* Οὐχ οἷός τε ἦν τοῦτο ἰδεῖν, *he was not able to see this.* Πρόθυμος λέγειν, *eager to speak.* Ἕτοιμος κίνδυνον ὑπομένειν, *ready to endure danger.*

Θεμιστοκλέα, ἱκανώτατον εἰπεῖν καὶ γνῶναι καὶ πρᾶξαι. LYS. ii. 42. Αἱ γὰρ εὐπραξίαι δειναὶ συγκρύψαι τὰ τοιαῦτα ὀνείδη. DEM. ii. 20. Κυρίαν ἐποίησαν ἐπιμελεῖσθαι τῆς εὐταξίας, *they gave it* (the Areopagus) *power to superintend good order.* ISOC. vii. 39. Βίην δὲ ἀδύνατοι ἦσαν προσφέρειν. HDT. iii. 138. Μαλακοὶ καρτερεῖν, *too effeminate to endure.* PLAT. Rep. 556 B. Ταπεινὴ ὑμῶν ἡ διάνοια ἐγκαρτερεῖν ἃ ἔγνωτε, *your minds are too dejected to persevere,* etc. THUC. ii. 61. (In the last two examples, μαλακοί and ταπεινή govern the infinitive by the idea of *inability* implied in them.) Χρήματα πορίζειν εὐπορώτατον γυνή. AR. Eccl. 236. Σοφώτεροι δὴ συμφορὰς τὰς τῶν πέλας πάντες διαθρεῖν ἢ τύχας τὰς οἴκοθεν. EUR. Fr. 103. Ἐπιστήμων λέγειν τε καὶ σιγᾶν. PLAT. Phaedr. 276 A. Τἄλλα εὑρήσεις ὑπουργεῖν ὄντας ἡμᾶς οὐ κακούς. AR. Pac. 430.

For examples of nouns followed by the infinitive in a similar sense, see 749. (See also 766.)

759. The infinitive after τοιοῦτος οἷος and τοσοῦτος ὅσος depends on the idea of *ability, fitness,* or *sufficiency* which is expressed in these combinations. The antecedent may be omitted, leaving οἷος with the infinitive in the sense of *able, fit, likely,* and ὅσος in that of *sufficient.* *E.g.*

Τοιοῦτοι οἷοι πονηροῦ τινος ἔργου ἐφίεσθαι, *capable of aiming at any vicious act.* XEN. Cyr. i. 2, 3. Τοιαύτας οἵας χειμῶνός τε στέγειν καὶ θέρους ἱκανὰς εἶναι. PLAT. Rep. 415 E. Ἔφθασε τοσοῦτον ὅσον Πάχητα ἀνεγνωκέναι τὸ ψήφισμα, *it came enough in advance* (of the other ship) *for Paches to have already read the decree* (the fact that he *had read* it is inferred, but not expressed : see 584). THUC. iii. 49.

Εἶπεν ὡς ἐγώ εἰμι οἷος ἀεί ποτε μεταβάλλεσθαι, *that I am (such)*

a man (as) to be always changing. XEN. Hell. ii. 3, 45. Οὐ γὰρ ἦν ὥρα
οἷα τὸ πεδίον ἄρδειν, *for it was not the proper season to irrigate the land.*
Id. An. ii. 3, 13. Νεμόμενοι τὰ αὐτῶν ἕκαστοι ὅσον ἀποζῆν, *each
cultivating their own land enough (to an extent sufficient) to live upon it.*
THUC. i. 2. Ἐλείπετο τῆς νυκτὸς ὅσον σκοταίους διελθεῖν τὸ πεδίον,
there was left enough of the night for crossing the plain in the dark. XEN.
An. iv. 1, 5.

This construction suggests at once the analogous use of οὕτως ὥστε
or ὥστε alone, in the sense of *so as,* with the infinitive (see 593).
Here, as with ὥστε, the subject of the infinitive is not restricted as it
is in 758.

760. In Homer, the pronominal adjectives τοῖος, τοιόσδε, τοιοῦτος,
τόσος, τηλίκος, and ποῖος, without a relative, sometimes take an
infinitive in the same way (759) ; as ἡμεῖς δ' οὔ νύ τι τοῖοι ἀμυνέμεν,
but we are not able to keep it off, Od. ii. 60 ; ποῖοι κ' εἴτ' Ὀδυσσῆι
ἀμυνέμεν; Od. xxi. 195. See also Il. vi. 463 ; Od. iii. 205, vii. 309,
xvii. 20.

761. Certain impersonal verbs (like ἔνεστι, πρέπει, προσήκει),
which regularly take an infinitive as their subject (745), are used in the
participle in a *personal* sense with the infinitive, the participle having
the force of one of the adjectives of 758. Thus τὰ ἐνόντα εἰπεῖν is
equivalent to ἃ ἔνεστι εἰπεῖν, *what it is permitted to say;* τὰ προσήκοντα
ῥηθῆναι is equivalent to ἃ προσήκει ῥηθῆναι, *what is proper to be said,*
as if it represented a personal construction like ταῦτα προσήκει ῥηθῆναι,
these things are becoming to be said. E.g.

Κατιδὼν τὸ πλῆθος τῶν ἐνόντων εἰπεῖν, *seeing the number of
things that may be said.* ISOC. v. 110. Τὸν θεὸν καλεῖ οὐδὲν προσή-
κοντ' ἐν γόοις παραστατεῖν, *she is calling on the God who ought not
to be present at lamentations.* AESCH. Ag. 1079. (Προσήκοντα is used
like adjectives meaning *fit, proper.*) Φράζ', ἐπεὶ πρέπων ἔφυς πρὸ
τῶνδε φωνεῖν. SOPH. O. T. 9. So τὰ ἡμῖν παραγγελθέντα διεξελθεῖν (= ἃ παρηγγέλθη ἡμῖν διεξελθεῖν). PLAT. Tim. 90 E.

762. In the same way (761) certain adjectives, like δίκαιος,
ἐπικαίριος, ἐπιτήδειος, ἐπίδοξος, may be used personally with
the infinitive; as δίκαιός ἐστι τοῦτο ποιεῖν, *it is right for him to do
this* (equivalent to δίκαιόν ἐστιν αὐτὸν τοῦτο ποιεῖν). E.g.

Φημὶ πολλῷ μειζόνων ἔτι τούτων δωρεῶν δίκαιος εἶναι τυγχάνειν, *I say that I have a right to receive even far greater rewards
than these.* DEM. xviii. 53. Ἐδόκουν ἐπιτήδειοι εἶναι ὑπεξαιρεθῆ-
ναι, *they seemed to be convenient persons to be disposed of.* THUC. viii. 70.
Θεραπεύεσθαι ἐπικαίριοι, *important persons to be taken care of.*
XEN. Cyr. viii. 2, 25. Τάδε τοι ἐξ αὐτῶν ἐπίδοξα γενέσθαι, *it is to
be expected that this will result from it.* HDT. i. 89. Πολλοὶ ἐπίδοξοι
τωὐτὸ τοῦτο πείσεσθαί εἰσι, *it is to be expected that many will suffer
this same thing.* Id. vi. 12 (for the future infinitive see 113).

763. Any adjective may take an infinitive to limit its

meaning to a particular action ; as αἰσχρὸν ὁρᾶν, *disgraceful to look upon*. The infinitive is here regularly active or middle, even when the passive would seem more natural. The omitted subject of the infinitive (except when it is passive) is distinct from that of the adjective. *E.g.*

Αἰσχρὸν γὰρ τόδε γ᾽ ἐστὶ καὶ ἐσσομένοισι π υ θ έ σ θ α ι, *for this is disgraceful even for future men to hear*. Il. ii. 119. So Il. i. 107 and 589. Τοὺς γὰρ ὑπὲρ τούτων λόγους ἐμοὶ μὲν ἀναγκαιοτάτους π ρ ο ε ι-π ε ῖ ν ἡγοῦμαι, ὑμῖν δὲ χρησιμωτάτους ἀ κ ο ῦ σ α ι, i.e. *most necessary for me to speak, and most useful for you to hear*. DEM. xxi. 24. Φοβερὸν π ρ ο σ π ο λ ε μ ῆ σ α ι, *a terrible man to fight against*. Id. ii. 22. (Οἰκία) ἡδίστη ἐ ν δ ι α ι τ ᾶ σ θ α ι, *a house most pleasant to live in*. XEN. Mem. iii. 8, 8. Χαλεπώτατα ε ὑ ρ ε ῖ ν, *hardest to find:* ῥᾷστα ἐ ν τ υ γ χ ά ν ε ι ν, *easiest to obtain*. Ib. i. 6, 9. (Πολιτεία) χαλεπὴ σ υ ζ ῆ ν, *a form of government hard to live under:* ἄνομος δὲ (μοναρχία) χαλεπὴ καὶ βαρυτάτη ξ υ ν ο ι κ ῆ σ α ι. PLAT. Polit. 302 B and E. Λόγος δυνατὸς κ α τ α-ν ο ῆ σ α ι, *a speech capable of being understood (which it is possible to understand)*. Id. Phaed. 90 D. Ὁ χρόνος βραχὺς ἀξίως δ ι η γ ή σ α σ θ α ι, *the time is too short for narrating it properly*. Id. Menex. 239 B. Ἡ ὁδὸς ἐπιτηδεία πορευομένοις καὶ λ έ γ ε ι ν καὶ ἀ κ ο ύ ε ι ν, *convenient both for speaking and for hearing*. Id. Symp. 173 B. Πότερον δὲ λ ο ύ σ α σ θ α ι ψυχρότερον ; *which of the two (waters) is colder for bathing ?* XEN. Mem. iii. 13, 3.

(Passive.) (Κύνες) αἰσχραὶ ὁ ρ ᾶ σ θ α ι (instead of ὁρᾶν). Id. Cyn. iii. 3. Ἔστι δ᾽ ὁ λόγος φιλαπεχθήμων μὲν, ῥ η θ ῆ ν α ι δ᾽ οὐκ ἀσύμφορος. ISOC. xv. 115.

The infinitive with adjectives (here and in 758) shows distinct traces of its origin as a dative, though this origin was already forgotten. See 742 (end) and 767.

764. (*a*) The infinitive after the comparative with ἤ depends on the idea of *ability* or *inability* implied in the expression. *E.g.*

Τὸ γὰρ νόσημα μεῖζον ἢ φ έ ρ ε ι ν, *for the disease is too heavy to bear*. SOPH. O. T. 1293. (See 763, above.) Ἡ ἀνθρωπίνη φύσις ἀσθενεστέρα ἢ λ α β ε ῖ ν τέχνην ὧν ἂν ᾖ ἄπειρος, *human nature is too weak to acquire the art of those things of which it has no experience*. PLAT. Theaet. 149 C. (See 758.)

(*b*) Ὥστε or ὡς is sometimes expressed before this infinitive ; as in XEN. Hell. iv. 8, 23, ᾔσθοντο αὐτὸν ἐλάττω ἔχοντα δύναμιν ἢ ὥστε τοὺς φίλους ὠφελεῖν, and Cyr. vi. 4, 17, τὰς ἀσπίδας μείζους ἔχουσιν ἢ ὡς ποιεῖν τι καὶ ὁρᾶν. (See 588.)

765. The infinitive may be used after adverbs which correspond to the adjectives of 763. *E.g.*

Συνεβουλεύετο αὐτῷ πῶς ἂν τοῖς μὲν εὔνοις κάλλιστα ἰ δ ε ῖ ν ποιοῖτο τὴν ἐξέλασιν, τοῖς δὲ δυσμενέσι φοβερώτατα, *he took counsel with him how he might proceed forth in a manner most splendid for the friendly to behold, and most terrible for the indisposed*. XEN. Cyr. viii. 3, 5.

766. Certain nouns, which correspond in meaning to adjectives which take the infinitive as in 763, may themselves have the same construction. *E.g.*

Θαῦμα ἰδέσθαι, *a wonderful thing to behold* (like θαυμαστὸν ἰδέσθαι). Od. viii. 366. See the examples under 749.

767. In Homer, verbs expressing *excellence* or *fitness* sometimes take a limiting infinitive, like adjectives of similar meaning. *E.g.*

Ἕκτορος ἥδε γυνὴ, ὃς ἀριστεύεσκε μάχεσθαι, *this is the wife of Hector, who was the first* (= ἄριστος ἦν) *in fighting.* Il. vi. 460. Ὁμηλικίην ἐκέκαστο ὄρνιθας γνῶναι καὶ ἀναίσιμα μυθήσασθαι, *he excelled all of his age in knowledge of birds and in declaring fate.* Od. ii. 158. Οἳ περὶ μὲν βουλὴν Δαναῶν, περὶ δ᾽ ἐστὲ μάχεσθαι, *ye who excel the Danai in counsel and excel them in battle.* Il. i. 258. (Here βουλήν shows that μάχεσθαι was already felt as a limiting accusative, notwithstanding its primitive force as a dative. See 763, and 742, end.)

768. Even in Attic Greek a limiting infinitive, like the Homeric infinitive just mentioned (767), is sometimes found. Especially ἀκούειν, ἀκοῦσαι, *in sound,* and ὁρᾶν, ἰδεῖν, *in appearance,* are used in this way. *E.g.*

Δοκεῖς οὖν τι διαφέρειν αὐτοὺς ἰδεῖν χαλκέως φαλακροῦ καὶ σμικροῦ; *do you think that they differ at all in appearance from a bald little tinker?* PLAT. Rep. 495 E. Ἀκοῦσαι παγκάλως ἔχει, *it is very fine to hear.* DEM. xix. 47. Πράγματα παρέξουσιν (οἱ ἵπποι) ἐπιμέλεσθαι, *the horses will be troublesome to tend.* XEN. Cyr. iv. 5, 46.

769. The Homeric use of ὁμοῖος, *equal, like,* with the infinitive belongs here. *E.g.*

Λευκότεροι χιόνος, θείειν δ᾽ ἀνέμοισιν ὁμοῖοι, *(horses) whiter than snow, and like the winds in swiftness* (lit. *to run*). Il. x. 437. Οὐ γάρ οἵ τις ὁμοῖος ἐπισπέσθαι ποσὶν ἦεν, ἀνδρῶν τρεσσάντων, *for none was like him for following with his feet when men fled.* Il. xiv. 521.

Infinitive of Purpose.

770. The infinitive may express a *purpose.* *E.g.*

Τρώων ἄνδρα ἕκαστον (εἰ) ἑλοίμεθα οἰνοχοεύειν, *if we should choose every man of the Trojans to be our cup-bearers.* Il. ii. 127. Χέρνιβα δ᾽ ἀμφίπολος προχόῳ ἐπέχευε φέρουσα, νίψασθαι, i.e. *brought and poured water for washing.* Od. i. 136. So Il. i. 338, δὸς ἄγειν, and Il. 107, 108. Τὴν ἐξ Ἀρείου πάγου βουλὴν ἐπέστησαν ἐπιμελεῖσθαι τῆς εὐκοσμίας, i.e. *to guard good order.* ISOC. vii. 37. Οἱ ἄρχοντες, οὓς ὑμεῖς εἵλεσθε ἄρχειν μου, *the rulers, whom you chose to rule me.* PLAT. Ap. 28 E. Δέκα δὲ τῶν νεῶν προὔπεμψαν ἐς τὸν μέγαν λιμένα πλεῦσαί τε καὶ κατασκέψασθαι, καὶ κηρῦξαι, κ.τ.λ., i.e. *they sent them to sail and examine, and to proclaim,* etc. THUC. vi. 50. Τοὺς ἱππέας παρείχοντο Πελοποννησίοις ξυστρατεύειν. Id. ii. 12. Ξυνέβησαν τοῖς Πλαταιεῦσι παραδοῦναι σφᾶς αὐτοὺς καὶ τὰ ὅπλα, χρήσασθαι

ὅ τι ἂν βούλωνται, i.e. *to do with them whatever they pleased.*· Id. ii. 4.
Εἰ βουλοίμεθά τῳ ἐπιτρέψαι ἢ παῖδας παιδεῦσαι ἢ χρήματα διασῶσαι, *if we should wish to entrust to any one either children to instruct or money to keep.* Xen. Mem. i. 5, 2. Θεάσασθαι παρῆν τὰς γυναῖκας πιεῖν φερούσας, *women bringing (something) to drink.* Id. Hell. vii. 2, 9. Τὴν πόλιν καὶ τὴν ἄκραν φυλάττειν αὐτοῖς παρέδωκαν, *they delivered the city and the citadel to them to guard.* Ib. iv. 4, 15. Ὃς γὰρ ἂν ὑμᾶς λάθῃ, τοῦτον ἀφίετε τοῖς θεοῖς κολάζειν. Dem. xix. 71. Ἡ θύρα ἡ ἐμὴ ἀνέῳκτο εἰσιέναι τῷ δεομένῳ τι ἐμοῦ. Xen. Hell. v. 1, 14. Οὐκ εἶχον ἀργύριον ἐπισιτίζεσθαι, *they had no money to buy provisions.* Id. An. vii. 1, 7. Ἀριστάρχῳ ἔδοτε ἡμέραν ἀπολογήσασθαι, i.e. *a day to efend himself in.* Id. Hell. i. 7, 28. Ἐμαυτόν σοι ἐμμελετᾶν παρέχειν οὐ πάνυ δέδοκται, i.e. *to practise on.* Plat. Phaedr. 228 E. Οἷς ἐνευδαιμονῆσαί τε ὁ βίος ὁμοίως καὶ ἐντελευτῆσαι ξυνεμετρήθη, i.e. *for enjoyment as well as for death.* Thuc. ii. 44.

771. Here, as in 763, the infinitive is generally active or middle, even where the passive would seem more natural ; as κτανεῖν ἐμοί νιν ἔδοσαν, *they gave her to me to be killed.* Eur. Tro. 874.

772. (a) The infinitive is thus used in prose chiefly after verbs signifying *to choose* or *appoint, to give* or *take,* to express the purpose for which anything is given or taken ; and also after those signifying *to send* or *bring.* (See examples in 770.) With the last class the future participle is still more common (840). A final clause after ἵνα etc. may also be used in the same sense.

(b) In poetry, the same construction occurs after verbs of *motion,* like εἶμι, ἥκω, and βαίνω; and also after εἰμί, ἔπειμι, and πάρειμι (to be, to be at hand), expressed or understood. *E.g.*
Ἀλλά τις εἴη εἰπεῖν Ἀτρείδῃ Ἀγαμέμνονι, ποιμένι λαῶν, *but let some one go to tell Agamemnon.* Od. xiv. 496. Βῆ δὲ θέειν, *and he started to run.* Il. ii. 183. Οὐδέ τις ἔστιν ἀρὴν καὶ λοιγὸν ἀμῦναι, *nor is there any one to keep off curse and ruin.* Il. xxiv. 489. Πολλοὶ δ᾽ αὖ σοὶ Ἀχαιοὶ ἐναιρέμεν ὅν κε δύνηαι, i.e. *for you to slay whomsoever you can.* Il. vi. 229. Οὐ γὰρ ἔπ᾽ ἀνήρ οἷος Ὀδυσσεὺς ἔσκεν, ἀρὴν ἀπὸ οἴκου ἀμῦναι. Od. ii. 59. Μανθάνειν γὰρ ἥκομεν, *for we are come to learn.* Soph. O. C. 12.

(c) Even in prose, the infinitive occasionally occurs after εἰμί in this sense, as in Plat. Phaedr. 229 A, ἐκεῖ σκιά τ᾽ ἐστὶ, καὶ πόα καθίζεσθαι ἢ ἂν βουλώμεθα κατακλιθῆναι, *there is grass to sit upon,* etc. See also Xen. An. ii. 1, 6, πολλαὶ δὲ καὶ πέλται καὶ ἅμαξαι ἦσαν φέρεσθαι ἔρημοι, i.e. *they were left to be carried away.*

773. In Homer and Herodotus εἶναι is often introduced to denote a purpose, where in Attic Greek a simple noun, connected directly with the leading verb, would be sufficient. *E.g.*
Θώρηκα, τόν ποτέ οἱ Κινύρης δῶκε ξεινήιον εἶναι, i.e. *which they gave him as a present* (lit. *to be a present*). Il. xi. 20. Λίθον εἵλετο

χειρὶ παχείῃ, τόν ῥ᾽ ἄνδρες πρότεροι θέσαν ἔμμεναι οὖρον ἀρούρης, *which former men had placed (to be) as a boundary of the land.* Il. xxi. 405. Δαρεῖος καταστήσας 'Αρταφέρνεα ὕπαρχον εἶναι Σαρδίων. HDT. v. 25. So in the passive construction : Γέλων ἀπεδέχθη πάσης τῆς ἵππου εἶναι ἵππαρχος. Id. vii. 154.

774. Even in Attic prose, this use of εἶναι (773) sometimes occurs ; as in DEM. xxix. 25, μνημονεύουσιν ἀφεθέντα τοῦτον ἐλεύθερον εἶναι τότε, *they remember his having been then manumitted (so as) to be a freeman.* So ἀφίησιν αὐτὰ δημόσια εἶναι, *he gives them up to be public property,* THUC. ii. 13.

775. The simple infinitive in Homer may express a result as well as a purpose, as ὥστε is seldom used there in the sense of *so as* (589). It thus follows many expressions which would not allow it in Attic Greek. *E.g.*

Τίς τ᾽ ἄρ σφωε θεῶν ἔριδι ξυνέηκε μάχεσθαι; i.e. *who brought them into conflict, so as to contend?* Il. i. 8. So i. 151 ; and ἐριζέμεναι, ii. 214. 'Αλλ᾽ ὅτε δὴ κοίλη νηῦς ἤχθετο τοῖσι νέεσθαι, *when now their ship was loaded, so as* (to be ready) *to sail.* Od. xv. 457.

For the infinitive in consecutive sentences with ὥστε or ὡς, and ἐφ᾽ ᾧ or ἐφ᾽ ᾧτε, see 582-600 ; 608-610.

For the infinitive with πρίν, see 626-631.

Absolute Infinitive.[1]

776. The infinitive may stand absolutely in certain parenthetical phrases, expressing a limitation or qualification of some word or of the whole sentence.

777. 1. Most frequent are the simple ὡς ἔπος εἰπεῖν and ὡς εἰπεῖν, *so to speak ;* and ὡς εἰπεῖν or εἰπεῖν with an adverb or other adjunct, sometimes with an object. *E.g.*

Καὶ ἔργου, ὡς ἔπος εἰπεῖν, ἢ οὐδενὸς προσδέονται ἢ βραχέος πάνυ, *and of action, so to speak, they need either none or very little.* PLAT. Gorg. 450 D. Plato uses ὡς ἔπος εἰπεῖν 77 times. Ὡς εἰπεῖν ἔπος, *so to speak.* AESCH. Pers. 714 : so EUR. Hipp. 1162, Her. 167 (see Or. 1). Ὡς δὲ συντόμως εἰπεῖν, *to speak concisely.* ISOC. vii. 26 : so PLAT. Tim. 25 E. Ὡς συνελόντι εἰπεῖν. XEN. Mem. iii. 8, 10. Ὡς εἰπεῖν. PLAT. Phaedr. 258 E : so Rep. 619 D. Ὡς ἀπλῶς εἰπεῖν, *to speak simply.* ISOC. iv. 154. Ὡς ἐν κεφαλαίῳ εἰπεῖν. PLAT. Symp. 186 C. Ὡς τὸ ὅλον εἰπεῖν γένος. Id. Crat. 192 C. Ὡς ἐπὶ τὸ πᾶν εἰπεῖν. Id. Leg. 667 D. So ὡς περὶ ὅλης εἰπεῖν ψυχῆς, Rep. 577 E. Ὡς γε τὸ δικαιότατον εἰπεῖν. Id. Leg. 624 A. Ὡς πόλιν εἰπεῖν, *speaking of a state.* Id. Rep. 577 C. Without ὡς : τὸ σύμπαν εἰπεῖν, HDT. ii. 91 ; THUC. i. 138, vii. 49. Ἐς τὸ ἀκριβὲς εἰπεῖν. Id. vi. 82. Σὺν θεῷ

---

[1] See Grünewald, *Der freie formelhafte Infinitiv der Limitation im Griechischen,* in Schanz's *Beiträge,* Heft 6.

εἰπεῖν. PLAT. Prot. 317 B. Τὸ δ' ὀρθὸν εἰπεῖν, ἀνέπνευσα, SOPH.
O. T. 1220.

2. Other verbs of *saying* are used in the same way with ὡς.
E.g.

Ὡς τορῶς φράσαι. AESCH. Ag. 1584. Ὡς ἐκ τοῦ παραχρῆμα
λέγειν. PLAT. Crat. 399 D. Ὡς γε ἐν τῷ νῦν παρόντι λέγειν. Id. Leg.
857 C. Ὡς ἐν φράζειν. Id. Polit. 282 B. Ὡς πρὸς ὑμᾶς εἰρῆσθαι,
i.e. *between ourselves*. Id. Rep. 595 B. Ὡς γε πρὸς σὲ εἰρῆσθαι τἀληθῆ.
Id. Prot. 339 E. Ὡς ἐν τύπῳ, μὴ δι' ἀκριβείας, εἰρῆσθαι. Id. Rep.
414 A.

For ὡς λόγῳ εἰπεῖν in Herodotus, see 782.

778. Ἐμοὶ δοκεῖν or (less frequently) ὡς ἐμοὶ δοκεῖν means *in
my opinion, it seems to me*. Other similar expressions are (ὡς)
εἰκάσαι, *to make a guess;* (ὡς) συμβάλλειν, *to compare, if we may
compare;* (ὡς) ἀκοῦσαι, *to the ear;* ὡς ἰδεῖν or ὅσον ἰδεῖν, *to the eye,
in appearance;* ὅσον ἐμὲ εἰδέναι, *so far as my knowledge goes;* ὡς
τεκμήρασθαι, *so far as one can judge.* E.g.

Ἀλλ' ἐμοὶ δοκεῖν, τάχ' εἴσει, *but, methinks, you will soon know.*
AESCH. Pers. 246 : so SOPH. El. 410. Αὐτόχθονες δοκέειν ἐμοί εἰσι.
HDT. i. 172. Ἀπεπέμπετο ἡ στρατιή, ὡς ἐμοὶ δοκέειν, ἐπὶ Λιβύης
καταστροφῇ. Id. iv. 167. Δοκεῖν δ' ἐμοί. THUC. viii. 64 : so vii. 87.
Ἀληθῆ, ἔμοιγε δοκεῖν. PLAT. Men. 81 A. See Id. Rep. 432 B, ὥς
γε οὑτωσὶ δόξαι.
Χῶρος ὅδ' ἱρός, ὡς ἀπεικάσαι. SOPH. O. C. 16. Ὡς θύραθεν εἰκάσαι. EUR. H. F. 713. See HDT. i. 34. Ὡς μικρὸν μεγάλῳ εἰκάσαι. THUC. iv. 36. Once εἰκάσαι alone : SOPH. O. T. 82. Ὕδωρ γε
ἐν πρὸς ἐν συμβάλλειν, i.e. *to compare the waters one with the other.*
HDT. iv. 50 (cf. ἐν πρὸς ἔν, THUC. ii. 97). Ἔστι δὲ τοῦτο οὑτωσὶ μὲν
ἀκοῦσαι λόγον τιν' ἔχον, i.e. *on first hearing it.* DEM. xx. 18. Ἄτοπα,
ὡς οὕτω γ' ἀκοῦσαι. PLAT. Euthyph. 3 B. Ὡς ἐντεῦθεν ἰδεῖν,
as it looks from this point. Id. Rep. 430 E. Ὅσσον ἴδην. SAPPH. Fr.
101. Ὅσα γ' ὧδ' ἰδεῖν. AR. Pac. 856. Οὐχ, ὅσον γέ μ' εἰδέναι,
no, as far as I know. Id. Nub. 1252. See also Eccl. 350, ὅ τι κἄμ'
εἰδέναι, and Thesm. 34, ὥστε (ὥς τε) κἀμέ γ' εἰδέναι, in the same
sense. Ὡς γε τῷ ποδὶ τεκμήρασθαι. PLAT. Phaedr. 230 B.
See also ὥς γ' ἐμοὶ χρῆσθαι κριτῇ, EUR. Alc. 801 ; ὥς γε κατὰ
τὴν ἐμὴν δόξαν ἀποφήνασθαι, PLAT. Polit. 272 D. See further, for
Herodotus, 782.

779. (a) Here belong ὀλίγου δεῖν and μικροῦ δεῖν, *wanting little,
almost*, and the rare πολλοῦ δεῖν, *far from*. E.g.

Πολλῶν λόγων γιγνομένων ὀλίγου δεῖν καθ' ἑκάστην ἐκκλη-
σίαν, *when many speeches are made almost in every assembly.* DEM. ix. 1.
Μικροῦ δεῖν ὅμοιόν ἐστι τῷ ὀνειδίζειν. Id. xviii. 269 : so ISOC. iv.
144, viii. 44, 89. Ἵν' εἰδῆτε πολλοῦ δεῖν ἄξιον ὄντα, *that you may
know that he is far from deserving*, etc. DEM. xxiii. 7 (the only case of
πολλοῦ δεῖν).

(*b*) Here δεῖν is often omitted, leaving ὀλίγου or μικροῦ in the sense of *almost*. *E.g.*

Ὀλίγου φροῦδος γεγένημαι, *I am almost gone myself*, Ar. Nub. 722, and μικροῦ κατηκόντισαν ἅπαντας, *they came near shooting them all.* Dem. xviii. 151.

780. In many expressions εἶναι is used absolutely, and it often seems to us superfluous. The most common case is that of ἑκὼν εἶναι, so *far as being willing goes*, or *willingly*, used almost exclusively in negative sentences. *E.g.*

Οὔτε αὐτὸς ἔφη ἑκὼν εἶναι δουλεύσειν. Hdt. viii. 116. See Thuc. ii. 89, vi. 14. Ἑκὼν γὰρ εἶναι οὐδὲν ψεύσομαι, *willingly I will tell no falsehood.* Plat. Symp. 215 A. Οὐκ ᾤμην γε κατ᾽ ἀρχὰς ὑπὸ σοῦ ἑκόντος εἶναι ἐξαπατηθήσεσθαι. Id. Gorg. 499 C. (Ἀνάγκη ἔχειν) τὴν ἀψεύδειαν καὶ τὸ ἑκόντας εἶναι μηδαμῇ προσδέχεσθαι τὸ ψεῦδος. Id. Rep. 485 C: see 336 E. One positive sentence occurs, Hdt. vii. 164.

781. Other cases of absolute εἶναι are τὸ ἐπὶ σφᾶς (ἐπὶ ἐκείνοις, ἐπὶ τούτοις, κατὰ τοῦτον) εἶναι, *so far as they were concerned,* etc. Thuc. iv. 28, viii. 48 ; Xen. An. i. 6, 9, Hell. iii. 5, 9 ;—κατὰ (εἰς) δύναμιν εἶναι, Isae. ii. 32 ; Plat. Polit. 300 C ;—κατὰ τοῦτο εἶναι, *so far as concerns this.* Id. Prot. 317 A ;—τὴν πρώτην εἶναι, *at first*, Hdt. i. 153. So especially τὸ νῦν εἶναι, *at present* (τό belonging to νῦν) : see Isoc. xv. 270 ; Plat. Lach. 201 C, Rep. 506 E ; Xen. Cyr. v. 3, 42 ; also τὸ τήμερον εἶναι, *to-day*, Plat. Crat. 396 E. In Aristotle's τὸ τί ἦν εἶναι, the εἶναι is probably absolute, and τί ἦν may be a "philosophic" imperfect (40), the expression meaning *the original essence* (*the "what was it ?"*).

Two expressions have ὡς : ὡς πάλαια εἶναι, *considering their antiquity,* Thuc. i. 21 ; and ὥς γε διακόνους εἶναι πόλεως, *considering that they were servants of a state,* i.e. *for servants*, Plat. Gorg. 517 B.

782. Herodotus has a remarkable variety of expressions of this kind. Besides those already quoted, see the following :—

Τὸ Δέλτα ἐστὶ κατάρρυτόν τε καὶ νεωστὶ, ὡς λόγῳ εἰπεῖν, ἀναπεφηνός, *and recently, so to speak, has appeared above water.* ii. 15. (Ὡς λόγῳ εἰπεῖν is peculiar to Herodotus.) Καὶ ὡς ἐμὲ εὖ μεμνῆσθαι τὰ ὁ ἑρμηνεύς μοι ἔφη, *so far as I remember rightly what the interpreter told me*, etc. ii. 125. Ὡς ἐμὲ κατανοέειν, *as I understand it.* ii. 28. Ὡς μέν νυν ἐν ἐλαχίστῳ δηλῶσαι, *πᾶν* εἴρηται· ὡς δὲ ἐν πλέονι λόγῳ δηλῶσαι, ὧδε ἔχει. ii. 24 and 25. Μετὰ δὲ, οὐ πολλῷ λόγῳ εἰπεῖν, χρόνος διέφυ. i. 61. Ὡς ἐμὲ συμβαλλόμενον εὑρίσκειν, *so far as I find by conjecture.* vii. 24. Ὡς ἐμοὶ δοκέειν συμβαλλομένῳ. iv. 87. Ὡς εἶναι ταῦτα σμικρὰ μεγάλοισι συμβάλλειν, *so far as I may* (εἶναι) *compare these small things with great ones.* iv. 99 : see ii. 10. Ὡς Σκύθας εἶναι, *for Scythians, considering that they are Scythians.* iv. 81. Ὡς εἶναι Αἰγύπτου, *for Egypt,* i.e. *for a land like Egypt.* ii. 8. Μεγάλα ἐκτήσατο χρήματα ὡς ἂν εἶναι Ῥοδῶπιν, *she gained great sums of money for a Rhodopis.* ii. 135. (The force of ἄν is very doubtful here ; and ʿΡοδῶπιν is often emended to ʿΡοδῶπιος or ʿΡοδῶπι, neither of which is satisfactory.)

783. The absolute infinitive was probably felt as a limiting accusative ; and in AR. Pac. 232, ἐξιέναι γνώμην ἐμὴν μέλλει, we might substitute ἐμοὶ δοκεῖν for γνώμην ἐμήν.[1] Ὡς as used here can hardly be expressed in English ; but it resembles some uses of ὥστε and ὡς with the infinitive after adjectives in 588. It cannot be demonstrative, as might be supposed from our inadequate translation of ὡς εἰπεῖν, *so to speak.*

Infinitive in Commands and Prohibitions for the Imperative.
Infinitive in Wishes and Exclamations.

784. 1. The infinitive is sometimes used in the sense of the second person of the imperative, especially in Homer. *E.g.*

Τῷ νῦν μή ποτε καὶ σὺ γυναικί περ ἤπιος εἶναι· μή οἱ μῦθον ἅπαντα πιφαυσκέμεν, ὅν κ᾿ ἐὺ εἰδῇς, ἀλλὰ τὸ μὲν φάσθαι, τὸ δὲ καὶ κεκρυμμένον εἶναι, *now therefore be thou never indulgent to thy wife,* etc. Od. xi. 441. So Il. i. 20, 582, ii. 10, xvii. 501 ; Od. x. 297, xi. 72, xvii. 278, xviii 106, xxii. 287. Οἷς μὴ πελάζειν, *do not approach these* (= μὴ πέλαζε). AESCH. Prom. 712. Πρὶν δ᾿ ἂν τελευτήσῃ, ἐπισχεῖν μηδὲ καλέειν κω ὄλβιον, *wait, and do not yet call him happy.* HDT. i. 32. Σὺ δὲ τὰς πύλας ἀνοίξας ὑπεκθεῖν καὶ ἐπείγεσθαι, *and do you open the gates, and rush out and press on.* THUC. v. 9. Ἐὰν οἱοί τε γενώμεθα εὑρεῖν, φάναι ἡμᾶς ἐξευρηκέναι, *say that we have found it.* PLAT. Rep. 473 A. Τοῦτο παρ᾿ ὑμῖν αὐτοῖς βεβαίως γνῶναι, *understand this in your own minds.* DEM. viii. 39.

2. In the cases of the second person just given (1), the subject is in the nominative. But when the infinitive is equivalent to the third person of the imperative, its subject is in the accusative, as if some word like δός, *grant,* were understood. *E.g.*

Εἰ μέν κεν Μενέλαον Ἀλέξανδρος κατακτέφνῃ, αὐτὸς Ἑλένην ἐχέτω· εἰ δέ κ᾿ Ἀλέξανδρον κτείνῃ Μενέλαος, Τρῶας ἔπειθ᾿ Ἑλένην ἀποδοῦναι, i.e. *let him keep Helen himself,—and let the Trojans surrender Helen.* Il. iii. 281-285. Τεύχεα συλήσας φερέτω, σῶμα δὲ οἴκαδ᾿ ἐμὸν δόμεναι πάλιν (sc. αὐτόν). Il. vii. 78. These examples follow the construction of the infinitive in wishes (785).

785. The infinitive with a subject accusative is sometimes used for the optative in the expression of a wish referring to the future. This occurs chiefly in poetry. *E.g.*

Ζεῦ πάτερ, ἢ Αἴαντα λαχεῖν ἢ Τυδέος υἱόν, *Father Zeus, may the lot fall on Ajax or on the son of Tydeus* (= Αἴας λάχοι). Il. vii. 179. Ζεῦ ἄνα, Τηλέμαχόν μοι ἐν ἀνδράσιν ὄλβιον εἶναι, καί οἱ πάντα γένοιθ᾿

---

[1] See Grünewald, page 17.

ὄσσα φρεσὶν ἦσι μενοινᾷ (εἶναι = εἴη is followed by γένοιτο). Od. xvii.
354. Μὴ πρὶν ἐπ᾽ ἠέλιον δῦναι καὶ ἐπὶ κνέφας ἐλθεῖν. Il. ii. 413.
Αἰεὶ δὲ τοιαύταν αἶσαν διακρίνειν ἔτυμον λόγον ἀνθρώπων. PIND.
Py. i. 67. Θεοὶ πολῖται, μή με δουλείας τυχεῖν (= μὴ τύχοιμι).
AESCH. Sept. 253. Δήμητερ, εὐδαιμονεῖν με Θησέα τε παῖδ᾽ ἐμόν.
EUR. Supp. 3. Ἑρμᾶ ᾽μπολαῖε, τὰν γυναῖκα τὰν ἐμὰν οὕτω μ᾽
ἀποδόσθαι τάν τ᾽ ἐμαυτοῦ ματέρα, O that I could sell my wife and my
mother at this rate! AR. Ach. 816. Ὦ Ζεῦ, ἐκγενέσθαι μοι ᾽Αθη-
ναίους τίσασθαι, may it be permitted me to punish the Athenians. HDT.
v. 105. Ὁκότεροι δ᾽ ἂν ἡμέων νικήσωσι, τούτους τῷ ἅπαντι στρατο-
πέδῳ νικᾶν, i.e. let their victory count for the whole army. Id. ix. 48.
   This construction, like the preceding (784, 2), is often explained
by an ellipsis of δός, grant; see Il. iii. 351, δὸς τίσασθαι. Aristarchus
supplied γένοιτο or εἴη.

786. In two passages of the Odyssey, we find the infinitive in a wish
introduced by αἲ γάρ, once in the sense of the optative and once in
that of a past tense of the indicative, with the subject (understood) in
the nominative :—
   Αἲ γάρ, τοῖος ἐὼν οἷός ἐσσι, . . . παῖδά τ᾽ ἐμὴν ἐχέμεν καὶ ἐμὸς
γαμβρὸς καλέεσθαι, O that, being such as you now are, you might have
(= ἔχοις) my daughter and be called my son-in-law. Od. vii. 311. Αἲ
γάρ, οἷος Νήρικον εἷλον, . . . τοῖος ἐών τοι χθιζὸς ἐφεστάμεναι καὶ
ἀμύνειν ἄνδρας μνηστῆρας· τῷ κε σφέων γούνατ᾽ ἔλυσα, O that I had
stood by you yesterday and had punished the suitors; then would I have
loosened their knees. Od. xxiv. 376. So also AESCH. Cho. 362-366, and 368.
These passages agree in construction with the second person of the
infinitive in commands (784, 1).

787. The infinitive, with its subject accusative, may be used
in exclamations of surprise or indignation. E.g.
   Ἐμὲ παθεῖν τάδε, φεῦ, ἐμὲ παλαιόφρονα, κατά τε γᾶν οἰκεῖν,
ἀτίετον, φεῦ, μύσος, that I should suffer this, alas! I, with my thoughts of
old; and that I should dwell in this land, alas! an unhonoured plague!
AESCH. Eum. 837. Ἀλλὰ τούσδ᾽ ἐμοὶ ματαίαν γλῶσσαν ὧδ᾽ ἀπαν-
θίσαι κἀκβαλεῖν ἔπη τοιαῦτα, that these should thus cast at me the
flowers of their idle tongues, etc. Id. Ag. 1662. Ὦ δυστάλαινα, τοιάδ᾽
ἄνδρα χρησιμὸν φωνεῖν. SOPH. Aj. 410. Τοιουτονὶ τρέφειν κύνα,
to keep a dog like that! AR. Vesp. 835. Τοῦτον δὲ ὑβρίζειν· ἀνα-
πνεῖν δέ, and that he should be thus insulting, and should draw his
breath! DEM. xxi. 209.
   Compare Mene incepto desistere victam! VERG. Aen. i. 37. This
infinitive often has the article τό (805).

B. INFINITIVE WITH THE ARTICLE.[1]

788. It has been seen that the infinitive without the article

[1] See Gildersleeve, *Contributions to the History of the Articular Infinitive*,

was already established in the Homeric language, in nearly all
the constructions in which it was most frequently used in later
times. In this simple form it developed its various tenses, and
their uses became fixed, especially in indirect discourse ; so that
the infinitive gradually came to be more of a verb and less of a
noun. When the definite article had become common with nouns,
it was soon prefixed to the infinitive, which thus, with all its
attributes as a verb unimpaired, was restored to new life as a
neuter verbal noun.[1] As a nominative and accusative, it could
be used with τό in all the constructions in which the simple
infinitive was already familiar as subject or object, although here
the older form was preferred except when it was desired to
emphasise the infinitive especially as a nominative or accusative.
But in other constructions (especially in the genitive, dative, and
accusative with prepositions), and in its wonderful capacity for
carrying dependent clauses and adjuncts of every kind, the
articular infinitive appears as a new power in the language, of
which the older simple infinitive gave hardly an intimation.

As might be expected, the articular infinitive found its chief
use in the rhetorical language, as in Demosthenes and in the
speeches of Thucydides. It appears first in Pindar (for τό in
Od. xx. 52 and HES. Frag. clxxi. can hardly be the article), but
always as a subject nominative, with one doubtful exception. In
the dramatists and Herodotus it is not uncommon, being generally
a nominative or accusative with τό, although it occurs also as a
genitive or dative with τοῦ or τῷ; and it is found even with
prepositions. In Thucydides (especially in the speeches), we find
the nominative, accusative, genitive, and dative all used with the
greatest freedom (in 135 cases), besides the accusative, genitive,
and dative with prepositions (in 163 cases). Its fully developed
power of taking dependent clauses must be seen in the Orators,
especially in Demosthenes.[2]

in *Trans. of Am. Phil. Assoc. for* 1878, pp. 5-19 ; and *The Articular Infinitive
in Xenophon and Plato*, in *Am. Jour. Phil.*, iii. pp. 193-202 ; Birklein,
Entwickelungsgeschichte des substantivirten Infinitivs, in Schanz's *Beiträge*,
Heft 7.

[1] "By the substantial loss of its dative force the infinitive became ver-
balized ; by the assumption of the article it was substantivized again with a
decided increment of its power." *Am. Jour. Phil.* iii. p. 195.

[2] See the statistics given by Gildersleeve in the *Am. Jour. Phil.* viii. p.
332. It appears that the average number of articular infinitives in a Teubner
page of Demosthenes is 1.25 ; of the *speeches* of Thucydides, 1.00 ; of Xenophon
(whole), 1.02 ; of Isocrates, .60 ; of Antiphon, .50 ; of Aeschines, .30 ; of
Andocides, .20 ; of Isaeus, .25 ; of Lysias, .12. Hypereides even exceeds
Demosthenes. For the actual number of articular infinitives in each author
before Aristotle, see Birklein's table, p. 91.

Articular Infinitive as Subject or Object.

789. Although the infinitive, as subject or object of a verb, generally stands without the article, the article may be prefixed to make the infinitive more prominent as a noun in the structure of the sentence.

790. The infinitive with τό may stand as a subject, especially of ἐστίν. *E.g.*

Τὸ γνῶναι ἐπιστήμην που λαβεῖν ἐστιν, *to learn is to acquire knowledge.* PLAT. Theaet. 209 E. Τὸ δίκην διδόναι πότερον πά- σχειν τί ἐστιν ἢ ποιεῖν; Id. Gorg. 476 D. (In the last two examples the *subject* infinitive has the article to emphasise it, while the *predicate* infinitive stands alone.) Τὸ δὲ παθεῖν εὖ πρῶτον ἀέθλων. PIND. Py. i. 99. Οὗτοι ἡδύ ἐστι τὸ ἔχειν χρήματα οὕτως ὡς ἀνιαρὸν τὸ ἀποβάλλειν. XEN. Cyr. viii. 3, 42. Πολλάκις δοκεῖ τὸ φυλάξαι τἀγαθὰ τοῦ κτήσασθαι χαλεπώτερον εἶναι, *to keep advantages often seems to be harder than gaining them.* DEM. i. 23 (cf. ii. 26, quoted in 745, for both construction and sense). Τοῦτό ἐστι τὸ ἀδικεῖν, τὸ πλέον τῶν ἄλλων ζητεῖν ἔχειν. PLAT. Gorg. 483 C. 'Αλλ' οἶμαι, νῦν μὲν ἐπισκοτεῖ τούτοις τὸ κατορθοῦν. DEM. ii. 20. Τὸ γὰρ θάνατον δεδιέναι οὐδὲν ἄλλο ἐστὶν ἢ δοκεῖν σοφὸν εἶναι μὴ ὄντα· δοκεῖν γὰρ εἰδέναι ἐστὶν ἃ οὐκ οἶδεν. PLAT. Ap. 29 A. See also 29 C.

It will be seen by comparison that most of these examples would admit the construction without the article by making the infinitive less prominent as a subject nominative. Compare οὔτε κλαίειν οὔτ' ὀδύρεσθαι πρέπει, AESCH Sept. 656, with τοῖς δ' ὀλβίοις γε καὶ τὸ νικᾶσθαι πρέπει, Ag. 941.

791. The infinitive with τό can stand as an accusative of the direct object, sometimes as an accusative of kindred meaning. The relation of such an infinitive with τό to the verb is often less close than that of the simple infinitive in a similar case (see 811). *E.g.*

Τλήσομαι τὸ κατθανεῖν, *I shall dare to die.* AESCH. Ag. 1290. Ἔστιν τις, ἔστιν, ὅς σε κωλύσει τὸ δρᾶν, *who will prevent you from acting.* SOPH. Ph. 1241. So ἐπισπεύδειν τὸ δρᾶν, El. 467. Τὸ σπεύδειν δέ σοι παραινῶ. Id. Ph. 620. Τὸ δρᾶν οὐκ ἠθέλησαν, *they were unwilling to act (would not act).* Id. O. C. 442. Τὸ δ' αὖ ξυνοικεῖν τῇδ' ὁμοῦ τίς ἂν γυνὴ δύναιτο, *what woman would be able to live with her?* (*to live with her—what woman could do it?*). Id. Tr. 545. Τὸ ὑπὸ οἴνου μὴ σφάλλεσθαι ἐπιμελεῖσθαι, *to take care not to be upset by wine.* XEN. Rep. Lac. v. 7. Αἰσχύνονται τὸ τολμᾶν. PLAT. Soph. 247 C. Συνεθίζεσθαι ταῖς ψυχαῖς τὸ τὴν πατρίδα φιλεῖν. LYCURG. 100. Καὶ πῶς δὴ τὸ ἀρχιχοὺς εἶναι ἀνθρώπων παιδεύεις; XEN. Oec. xiii. 4 : see also ix. 12. (So παιδεύω τινά τι.) Ἐπέσχον τὸ εὐθέως τοῖς Ἀθηναίοις ἐπιχειρεῖν. THUC. vii. 33 (cf.

τοῦτο ἐπέσχον, ii. 76). Οὐδέ τοι τῇ χειρὶ πείθομαι τὸ δρᾶν, *nor am I persuaded by your violence to act* (as you bid me). SOPH. Ph. 1253 (cf. οὐ πείθομαί σοι ταῦτα). Καρδίας ἐξίσταμαι τὸ δρᾶν, *I withdraw from my resolution* (i.e. I consent) *to do it.* Id. Ant. 1105 : cf. φρονεῖν μετέγνω, i.e. *changed his purpose* (and resolved) *to contemplate,* AESCH. Ag. 221.

For τὸ μὴ οὐ with the infinitive after negatived verbs in this construction (*e.g.* AR. Ran. 68), see 815, 2, and 814.

792. The infinitive with τό as an object accusative may follow verbs which would not allow the simple infinitive in its place. *E.g.*

Τὸ τελευτῆσαι πάντων ἡ πεπρωμένη κατέκρινε, τὸ δὲ καλῶς ἀποθανεῖν ἴδιον τοῖς σπουδαίοις ἀπένειμεν, *Fate condemned all mankind to death; but a glorious death she reserved for the virtuous.* ISOC. i. 43. Μόνον ὁρῶν τὸ παίειν τὸν ἁλισκόμενον, *seeing only the beating of the captive.* XEN. Cyr. i. 4, 21. Τὸ μὲν εὐνοέειν τε καὶ προορᾶν ἄγαμαί σευ. HDT. ix. 79.

The double character of the articular infinitive, as noun and verb, permits it to stand as an object wherever the object accusative of a noun would be allowed.

793. A few of the verbs included in 747, which govern the genitive of a noun, allow also the genitive of the infinitive with τοῦ (798), as well as the simple infinitive. This applies chiefly to ἀμελέω, ἐπιμελέομαι, and to the verbs of *hindrance* etc. included in 807. *E.g.*

Ἀμελήσας τοῦ ὀργίζεσθαι. XEN. Mem. ii. 3, 9. (But ἀμελήσας λέγειν, PLAT. Phaed. 98 D.) Most verbs of *desiring* and *neglecting* take only the simple infinitive. Ἐπιμελέομαι, which usually takes ὅπως with the future indicative (339), allows also the simple infinitive (THUC. vi. 54), the infinitive with τό (XEN. Rep. Lac. v. 7), and the infinitive with τοῦ (Id. Mem. iii. 3, 11). (See 361, 791, and 798.)

794. The infinitive of indirect discourse after verbs of *saying* and *thinking* sometimes takes τό. Here each tense of the infinitive preserves its time, and even the infinitive with ἄν occurs. *E.g.*

Ἦμεν δ' ἕτοιμοι θεοὺς ὀρκωμοτεῖν τὸ μήτε δρᾶσαι μήτε τῳ ξυνειδέναι τὸ πρᾶγμα βουλεύσαντι, *to swear that we neither had done it* (ἐδράσαμεν) *nor were in the secret* (ξύνισμεν) *of any one who had plotted the deed.* SOPH. Ant. 264. Ἐξομεῖ τὸ μὴ εἰδέναι; *will you swear that you have no knowledge?* Ib. 535. Καὶ τὸ προειδέναι γε τὸν θεὸν τὸ μέλλον καὶ τὸ προσημαίνειν ᾧ βούλεται, τοῦτο πάντες καὶ λέγουσι καὶ νομίζουσιν. XEN. Ap. 13. See also Hell. v. 2, 36 (814).

(With ἄν.) Τῆς ἐλπίδος γὰρ ἔρχομαι δεδραγμένος, τὸ μὴ παθεῖν ἄν ἄλλο πλὴν τὸ μόρσιμον, *for I come clinging to the hope that I could suffer nothing except what is fated.* SOPH. Ant. 235. For the articular infinitive with ἄν in other constructions, see 212.

Infinitive with τό after Adjectives and Nouns.

795. In some constructions in which the simple infinitive
appears to preserve most distinct traces of its origin as a dative,
especially after adjectives or nouns (758 ; 763 ; 766), the articular
infinitive takes τό as an accusative. *E.g.*

Τὸ δὲ βίᾳ πολιτῶν δρᾶν ἔφυν ἀμήχανος, *but I am helpless to act
in defiance of the citizens.* SOPH. Ant. 79.   Μακρὸς τὸ κρῖναι ταῦτα
χὼ λοιπὸς χρόνος, *a long time to settle this.* Id. El. 1030 (cf. χρόνος
βραχὺς διηγήσασθαι, *a time short for narrating,* under 763).   Τὸ μὴ
βλέπειν ἑτοίμα, *ready to cease beholding the light.* Ib. 1079 (see 758).
Τὸ προσταλαιπωρεῖν οὐδεὶς πρόθυμος ἦν. THUC. ii. 53.   Τὸ μὲν
ἐς τὴν γῆν ἡμῶν ἐσβάλλειν, κἂν μὴ ἐκπλεύσωμεν, ἱκανοί εἰσι. Id.
vi. 17.   Ἐς δέον πάρεσθ' ὅδε Κρέων τὸ πράσσειν καὶ τὸ βουλεύειν,
he is here at the right moment to act and advise. SOPH. O. T. 1416.
Αἴτιος τὸ σὲ ἀποκρίνεσθαι μὴ τοῦτο. PLAT. Lach. 190 E.   (This
is rare, but see DEM. viii. 56, ix. 63.   Αἴτιος generally has the infinitive with τοῦ, 798, or the simple infinitive, 749.)

Ἡ ναυμαχία οὐχὶ δικαίαν ἔχει τέκμαρσιν τὸ ἐκφοβῆσαι, *the sea-
fight offers no just ground for alarm.* THUC. ii. 87.   Οὐδὲ τοὐξανι-
στάναι ἐστὶ θάρσος, *nor have I courage to remove you.* SOPH. O. C. 47.

The exact force given to these accusatives by those who used them
is not always clear ; but they come nearest to the accusative of *respect*
or *limitation* (as εἶδος κάλλιστος, *most beautiful in form*).   Sometimes
the infinitive with τό has this force, where the simple infinitive could
not be used ; as in LYCURG. 91, ἐπεί γε τὸ ἐλθεῖν τοῦτον, οἶμαι
θεόν τινα αὐτὸν ἐπ' αὐτὴν ἀγαγεῖν τὴν τιμωρίαν, *for, as to his departure,
I think that some God led him directly to punishment.*

796. We occasionally find τό with the infinitive in the Mss. in a
similar loose construction, where we should expect the infinitive with
τοῦ or τῷ in apposition with a preceding genitive or dative.   See
THUC. vii. 36, τῇ πρότερον ἀμαθίᾳ δοκούσῃ εἶναι, τὸ ἀντίπρῳρον
ξυγκροῦσαι, and viii. 87, καταβοῆς ἕνεκα τῆς ἐς Λακεδαίμονα, τὸ
λέγεσθαι ὡς οὐκ ἀδικεῖ, where most editors now read τῷ and τοῦ
against the Mss.   But Birklein defends the Mss. readings by HYPER.
Epitaph. 2, ἄξιον δέ ἐστιν ἐπαινεῖν τὴν μὲν πόλιν ἡμῶν τῆς προαιρέσεως ἕνεκεν, τὸ προελέσθαι ὅμοια, . . . τοὺς δὲ τετελευτηκότας
τῆς ἀνδρείας, τὸ μὴ καταισχῦναι τὰς τῶν προγόνων ἀρετάς, where
the two infinitives with τό explain προαιρέσεως and ἀνδρείας. (See 804.)

797. The infinitive with τό appears in its greatest variety of meanings in the construction of τὸ μή or τὸ μὴ οὐ after verbs implying a
negative (811).   See also 813 and 814.

Infinitive with τοῦ, τῷ, and τό, as a Noun, in various Constructions.

798. The infinitive with τοῦ appears as an adnominal genitive, a genitive after verbs and adjectives and with comparatives, a partitive genitive, a genitive absolute, and a genitive expressing cause, purpose, or motive. *E.g.*

Τοῦ πιεῖν ἐπιθυμία, *the desire to drink.* THUC. vii. 84. Πόνους δὲ τοῦ ζῆν ἡδέως ἡγεμόνας νομίζετε. XEN. Cyr. i. 5, 12. Πρὸς τὴν πόλιν προσβαλόντες ἐς ἐλπίδα ἦλθον τοῦ ἑλεῖν, i.e. *hope of taking the city.* THUC. ii. 56 (see 749). Τὸ γὰρ εὖ πράττειν παρὰ τὴν ἀξίαν ἀφορμὴ τοῦ κακῶς φρονεῖν τοῖς ἀνοήτοις γίγνεται, *for doing well beyond their deserts sets fools to thinking ill.* DEM. i. 23. Ἡ δὲ διαγνώμη αὕτη τῆς ἐκκλησίας τοῦ τὰς σπονδὰς λελύσθαι, *this vote of the assembly that the treaty had been broken.* THUC. i. 87. See XEN. Cyr. i. 4, 4. Δόξετε αἴτιοι εἶναι, ἄρξαντες τοῦ διαβαίνειν, *by having begun the passage of the river.* XEN. An. i. 4, 15. Ὀρεγόμενοι τοῦ πρῶτος ἕκαστος γίγνεσθαι, *being eager each to be first.* THUC. ii. 65. Παρεκάλει ἐπιμελεῖσθαι τοῦ ὡς φρονιμώτατον εἶναι. XEN. Mem. i. 2, 55 ; so iii. 3, 11. (See 793.) Ἐπέσχομεν τοῦ δακρύειν, *we ceased to weep.* PLAT. Phaed. 117 E. (See below, 807.) Καὶ γὰρ ἀήθεις τοῦ κατακούειν τινός εἰσιν, *for they are unused to obeying any one.* DEM. i. 23. See xxix. 17. Ἄξιος αὐτοῖς ἐδόκεις εἶναι τοῦ τοιαῦτ᾽ ἀκούειν. Id. xxi. 134. Τοὺς καρποὺς, οἳ τοῦ μὴ θηριωδῶς ζῆν ἡμᾶς αἴτιοι γεγόνασι, *the fruits of the earth, which are the cause of our not living like beasts.* ISOC. iv. 28. Κατηράσατο τῷ αἰτίῳ τοῦ μὴ πάλαι ἀποδεδόσθαι τὸν μισθόν, *he cursed him who was responsible for the wages not having been paid long before.* XEN. An. vii. 7, 48. (Αἴτιος may take the simple infinitive and even the infinitive with τό. See 749 and 795.) Πολλάκις δοκεῖ τὸ φυλάξαι τἀγαθὰ τοῦ κτήσασθαι χαλεπώτερον εἶναι. DEM. i. 23. So XEN. Cyr. i. 5, 13. Νέοις τὸ σιγᾶν κρεῖττόν ἐστι τοῦ λαλεῖν. MEN. Mon. 387. Τοῦ θαρσεῖν τὸ πλεῖστον εἰληφότες, i.e. *having become most emboldened.* THUC. iv. 34. Οὐδὲν οὔτε ἀναιδείας οὔτε τοῦ ψεύδεσθαι παραλείψει. DEM. xxxvii. 45. Εἰς τοῦτ᾽ ἐλήλυθε τοῦ νομίζειν. Id. xxii. 16. Τὸ μεγάλου ἔργου ὄντος τοῦ ἑαυτῷ τὰ δέοντα παρασκευάζειν μὴ ἀρκεῖν τοῦτο. XEN. Mem. ii. 1, 8 (see 806).

Ζηλῶ σε μᾶλλον ἢ 'μὲ τοῦ μηδὲν φρονεῖν, *for want of knowledge.* EUR. I. A. 677. (Μίνως) τὸ λῃστικὸν καθῄρει, τοῦ τὰς προσόδους μᾶλλον ἰέναι αὐτῷ, *in order that revenues might come in to him more abundantly.* THUC. i. 4. So ii. 22, 32, 75, 93 ; XEN. Cyr. i. 3, 9. Τοῦ μὴ τὰ δίκαια ποιεῖν, *to escape doing what was just.* DEM. xviii. 107. Πρὸς τὸ πρᾶγμα φιλονεικοῦντα λέγειν τοῦ καταφανὲς γενέσθαι. PLAT. Gorg. 457 E. This final use appears first and chiefly in Thucydides.

799. The infinitive with τῷ may express *cause, manner,* or *means;* or it may follow verbs, adjectives, and adverbs which take the dative. *E.g.*

Οὐδὲ τῷ δύνασθαι καὶ εἰωθέναι λέγειν ἐπαρθείς. LYS. xxxi. 2. Οὐδενὶ τῶν πάντων πλέον κεκράτηκε Φίλιππος ἢ τῷ πρότερος πρὸς τοῖς πράγμασι γίγνεσθαι. DEM. viii. 11. See xxiii. 9, τῷ μὲν ἀκοῦσαι, τῷ δ᾽ ἔργῳ. Ἀλλὰ τῷ φανερὸς εἶναι τοιοῦτος ὤν, *by making it plain that he was such a man.* XEN. Mem. i. 2, 3. So Cyr. iv. 5, 9. Οὐ γὰρ δὴ τῷ γε κοσμίως ζῆν ἄξιον πιστεύειν, *to trust in an orderly life.* ISOC. xv. 24. Ἵνα ἀπιστῶσι τῷ ἐμὲ τετιμῆσθαι ὑπὸ δαιμόνων, *that they may distrust my having been honoured by divine powers.* XEN. Ap. 14. Μεῖζον μέρος νέμοντες τῷ μὴ βούλεσθαι ἀληθῆ εἶναι. THUC. iii. 3. Ἴσον δὲ τῷ προστένειν. AESCH. Ag. 253. Τῷ ζῆν ἔστι τι ἐναντίον, ὥσπερ τῷ ἐγρηγορέναι τὸ καθεύδειν. PLAT. Phaed. 71 C. Ὅμοιόν ἐστι τῷ ὀνειδίζειν. DEM. xviii. 269. Τῷ πλουτεῖν ὑπήκοα, *obedient to wealth.* AR. Pl. 146. Ἅμα τῷ τιμᾶσθαι. PLAT. Rep. 468 D ; so ἅμα τῷ τιμᾶν, 468 E.

800. The infinitive with the article, as genitive, dative, or accusative, very often follows prepositions, or adverbs used as prepositions. *E.g.*

Τοὺς γὰρ λόγους περὶ τοῦ τιμωρήσασθαι Φίλιππον ὁρῶ γιγνομένους, *for I see that the speeches are made about punishing Philip.* DEM. iii. 1. Πρὸ τοῦ τοὺς ὅρκους ἀποδοῦναι, *before taking the oaths.* Id. xviii. 26. Ἐκ τοῦ πρὸς χάριν δημηγορεῖν ἐνίους. Id. iii. 3. Ἀντὶ τοῦ πόλις εἶναι φρούριον κατέστη. THUC. vii. 28 ; so i. 69. Ἀπὸ τοῦ πεῖραν διδοὺς ξυνετὸς φαίνεσθαι. Id. i. 138. Ἕνεκα τοῦ πλείω ποιῆσαι τὴν ὑπάρχουσαν οὐσίαν. ISOC. i. 19. Πρὸς τῷ μηδὲν ἐκ τῆς πρεσβείας λαβεῖν, *besides receiving nothing from the embassy.* DEM. xix. 229. Ἐν τῷ πολίτην ποιεῖσθαι (Χαρίδημον), *in making Charidemus a citizen.* Id. xxiii. 188. Ἐθαυμάζετο ἐπὶ τῷ εὐθύμως ζῆν. XEN. Mem. iv. 8, 2. Ὅμως διὰ τὸ ξένος εἶναι οὐκ ἂν οἴει ἀδικηθῆναι, *on account of being a stranger.* Ib. ii. 1, 15. Πάντων διαφέρων ἐφαίνετο καὶ εἰς τὸ ταχὺ μανθάνειν ἃ δέοι καὶ εἰς τὸ καλῶς ἕκαστα ποιεῖν. Id. Cyr. i. 3, 1. Πρὸς τὸ μετρίων δεῖσθαι πεπαιδευμένος. Id. Mem. i. 2, 1 ; so DEM. i. 4. Παρὰ τὸ αἰσχρόν τι ὑπομεῖναι. PLAT. Ap. 28 C.

801. The infinitive is not found with ἀνά in any case, with ἀμφί in accusative or dative, with κατά in genitive, with παρά in genitive or dative, with περί in dative, with πρός in genitive, with ὑπέρ in accusative, or with ὑπό in accusative or dative.

802. The genitive of the infinitive with ὑπέρ is often equivalent to a final clause. *E.g.*

Τὰς δεήσεις αἷς κέχρηνταί τινες ὑπὲρ τοῦ τὰ μέτρια καὶ τὰ συνήθη μὴ γίγνεσθαι ἐν τῇ πόλει (= ἵνα μὴ γίγνηται), *the solicitations which some have employed in order that moderate counsels and the ordinary principles may not prevail in the state.* AESCHIN. iii. 1. Εἰς τὰς τριήρεις ἐμβάντες ὑπὲρ τοῦ μὴ τὸ κελευόμενον ποιῆσαι (= ἵνα μὴ ποιήσωσιν),

embarking on shipboard that they might avoid doing what was bid. DEM.
xviii. 204.

803. The article cannot ordinarily be omitted when the infinitive
follows a preposition.

(a) A singular exception occurs in a few cases of ἀντί with the
simple infinitive in Herodotus. See ὃς ἀντὶ μὲν δούλων ἐποίησας
ἐλευθέρους Πέρσας εἶναι, ἀντὶ δὲ ἄρχεσθαι ὑπ᾽ ἄλλων ἄρχειν
ἁπάντων, i. 210, where the antithesis of ἀντὶ μὲν δούλων makes ἀντὶ
δὲ ἄρχεσθαι more natural ; also vi. 32 (with no antithesis). So vii.
170 (but with a various reading ἀντὶ τοῦ).

(b) Πλήν, *except*, as an adverb, may have the simple infinitive ; as
τί ἄλλο πλὴν ψευδῆ λέγειν, SOPH. Ph. 100.   So πλὴν γάμου
τυχεῖν, AESCH. Eum. 737.

804. An infinitive, with the article in any case, may stand in
apposition to a noun in the same case. *E.g.*

Ἡ τῶν παίδων ἀρχὴ, τὸ μὴ ἐᾶν ἐλευθέρους εἶναι, ἕως, κ.τ.λ., *the
government of children,—not permitting them to be free, until,* etc. PLAT.
Rep. 590 E.   Τοῦτό ἐστι τὸ ἀδικεῖν, τὸ πλέον τῶν ἄλλων ζητεῖν
ἔχειν. Id. Gorg. 483 C.   Τοῦτο προσόμοιον ἔχουσι τοῖς τυράννοις,
τὸ πολλῶν ἄρχειν. Id. Rep. 578 D.   Τί τούτου μακαριώτερον, τοῦ
γῇ μιχθῆναι; XEN. Cyr. viii. 7, 25.   Δοκεῖ τούτῳ διαφέρειν ἀνὴρ
τῶν ἄλλων ζώων, τῷ τιμῆς ὀρέγεσθαι. Id. Hier. vii. 3 ; so Oec.
xiv. 10.

For a few doubtful cases of the infinitive with τό, in apparent
apposition with a genitive or dative, see 796.

805. The infinitive with τό is used in exclamations of surprise
or indignation. *E.g.*

Τὸ δὲ μηδὲ κυνῆν οἴκοθεν ἐλθεῖν ἐμὲ τὸν κακοδαίμον᾽ ἔχοντα, *but
to think that I, wretched fellow, should come from home without even my
cap!* AR. Nub. 268.   Τῆς μωρίας· τὸ Δία νομίζειν, ὄντα τηλικου-
τονί, *what folly!* *to believe in Zeus, now you are so big!* Ib. 819.

For the simple infinitive in these exclamations, see 787.

806. The infinitive with its subject, object, or other adjuncts
(sometimes including dependent clauses) may be preceded by the
article τό, the whole sentence standing as a single noun, either as
the subject or object of a verb, as the object of a preposition, or
in apposition with a pronoun like τοῦτο. *E.g.*

Τὸ μὲν γὰρ πολλὰ ἀπολωλεκέναι κατὰ τὸν πόλεμον τῆς ἡμετέρας
ἀμελείας ἄν τις θείη δικαίως· τὸ δὲ μήτε πάλαι τοῦτο πεπονθέναι,
πεφηνέναι τέ τινα ἡμῖν συμμαχίαν τούτων ἀντίρροπον, ἂν βουλώμεθα
χρῆσθαι, τῆς παρ᾽ ἐκείνων εὐνοίας εὐεργέτημ᾽ ἂν ἔγωγε θείην. DEM. i. 10.
Τὸ γὰρ πρὸς ἄνδρα θνητὸν καὶ διὰ καιρούς τινας ἰσχύοντα γράφον-
τας εἰρήνην ἀθάνατον συνθέσθαι τὴν κατὰ τῆς πόλεως αἰσχύνην,
καὶ ἀποστερῆσαι μὴ μόνον τῶν ἄλλων ἀλλὰ καὶ τῶν παρὰ τῆς

τύχης εὐεργεσιῶν τὴν πόλιν, καὶ τοσαύτῃ περιουσίᾳ χρῆσθαι πονηρίας ὥστε μὴ μόνον τοὺς ὄντας Ἀθηναίους ἀλλὰ καὶ τοὺς ὕστερόν ποτε μέλλοντας ἔσεσθαι πάντας ἠδικηκέναι, πῶς οὐχὶ πάνδεινον ἐστίν; Id. xix. 55.

Simple Infinitive and Infinitive with τοῦ after Verbs of Hindrance, etc.[1]

807. After verbs and other expressions which denote *hindrance* or *freedom* from anything, two forms are allowed, the simple infinitive, and the genitive of the infinitive with τοῦ.

Thus we can say (a) εἴργει σε τοῦτο ποιεῖν (747) and (b) εἴργει σε τοῦ τοῦτο ποιεῖν (798), both with the same meaning, *he prevents you from doing this.* As the infinitive, after verbs implying a negation, can take μή to strengthen the previous negation without otherwise affecting the sense (815, 1), we have a third and a fourth form, still with the same meaning: (c) εἴργει σε μὴ τοῦτο ποιεῖν, and (d) εἴργει σε τοῦ μὴ τοῦτο ποιεῖν, *he prevents you from doing this.* (For a fifth form, εἴργει σε τὸ μὴ τοῦτο ποιεῖν, with the same meaning, see 811.)

If the leading verb is itself *negatived* (or is interrogative with a negative implied), the double negative μὴ οὐ is generally used instead of μή in the form (c) with the simple infinitive, but probably never in the form (d) with the genitive of the infinitive; as οὐκ εἴργει σε μὴ οὐ τοῦτο ποιεῖν, *he does not prevent you from doing this* (815, 2), but *not* τοῦ μὴ οὐ τοῦτο ποιεῖν. (See also 811, for τὸ μὴ οὐ.) *E.g.*

(a) Κακὸν δὲ ποῖον εἶργε τοῦτ᾽ ἐξειδέναι; SOPH. O. T. 129. Παιδὸς Φέρητος, ὃν θανεῖν ἐρρυσάμην. EUR. Alc. 11. Ἐπὶ Ὀλύνθου ἀποπέμπουσιν, ὅπως εἴργωσι τοὺς ἐκεῖθεν ἐπιβοηθεῖν. THUC. i. 62. Ἄλλως δέ πως πορίζεσθαι τὰ ἐπιτήδεια ὅρκους ἤδη κατέχοντας ἡμᾶς (ᾔδειν). XEN. An. iii. 1, 20. Εὐδοκιμεῖν ἐμποδὼν σφίσιν εἶναι. PLAT. Euthyd. 305 D. Εἰ τοῦτό τις εἴργει δρᾶν ὄκνος, *if any hesitation prevents you from doing this.* Id. Soph. 242 A. Τὴν ἰδέαν τῆς γῆς οὐδέν με κωλύει λέγειν. Id. Phaed. 108 D. Τὸν Φίλιππον παρελθεῖν οὐκ ἐδύναντο κωλῦσαι. DEM. v. 20.

(b) Τοῦ δὲ δραπετεύειν δεσμοῖς ἀπείργουσι; XEN. Mem. ii. 1, 16. Τὸ γὰρ ψευδόμενον φαίνεσθαι καὶ τοῦ συγγνώμης τινὸς τυγχάνειν ἐμποδὼν μάλιστα ἀνθρώποις γίγνεται. Id. Cyr. iii. 1, 9. Εἶπεν ὅτι κωλύσειε (ἂν) τοῦ καίειν ἐπιόντας. Id. An. i. 6, 2. Ἐπέσχομεν τοῦ δακρύειν. PLAT. Phaed. 117 E (cf. 117 C, quoted in 811). Ἀπεσχόμην τοῦ λαβεῖν τοῦ δικαίου ἕνεκα. DEM. xix. 223.

(c) Θνητούς γ᾽ ἔπαυσα μὴ προσδέρκεσθαι μόρον. AESCH. Prom.

[1] See Madvig's *Bemerkungen über einige Puncte der griechischen Wortfügungslehre*, pp. 47-66.

248. Τοὐμὸν φυλάξει σ' ὄνομα μὴ πάσχειν κακῶς. SOPH. O. C.
667. Ὅπερ ἔσχε μὴ τὴν Πελοπόννησον πορθεῖν, which prevented
him from ravaging the Peloponnesus. THUC. i. 73. Διεκώλυσε μὴ δια-
φθεῖραι. Id. iii. 49. Ἐπεγένετο κωλύματα μὴ αὐξηθῆναι. Id. i.
16. Πέμπουσι κήρυκα, ὑποδεξάμενοι σχήσειν τὸν Σπαρτιήτην μὴ
ἐξιέναι. HDT. ix. 12. Εἶργε μὴ βλαστάνειν. PLAT. Phaedr.
251 B.
Οὐ γὰρ ἔστι Ἕλλησι οὐδεμία ἔκδυσις μὴ οὐ δόντας λόγον εἶναι
σοὺς δούλους. HDT. viii. 100. (See 815, 2 ; 816.) Οὐ δυνατοὶ αὐτὴν
ἴσχειν εἰσὶ Ἀργεῖοι μὴ οὐκ ἐξιέναι. Id. ix. 12. Ὥστε ξένον γ' ἂν
οὐδέν' ὄνθ', ὥσπερ σὺ νῦν, ὑπεκτραποίμην μὴ οὐ συνεκσῴζειν.
SOPH. O. C. 565. Τί ἐμποδὼν μὴ οὐχὶ ὑβριζομένους ἀποθανεῖν;
XEN. An. iii. 1, 13. (Τί ἐμποδών implies οὐδὲν ἐμποδών.) Τίνος ἂν
δέοιο μὴ οὐχὶ πάμπαν εὐδαίμων εἶναι; what would hinder you from
being perfectly happy? Id. Hell. iv. 1, 36.

(d) Πᾶς γὰρ ἀσκὸς δύο ἄνδρας ἕξει τοῦ μὴ καταδῦναι, i.e. will
keep two men from sinking. XEN. An. iii. 5, 11. Ὃν οὐδείς πω προθεὶς
τοῦ μὴ πλέον ἔχειν ἀπετράπετο. THUC. i. 76. Εἰ δ' ἄρ' ἐμποδών
τι αὐτῷ ἐγένετο τοῦ μὴ εὐθὺς τότε δικάσασθαι. DEM. xxxiii. 25.
Ἠπίστατο τὴν πόλιν μικρὸν ἀπολιποῦσαν τοῦ μὴ ταῖς ἐσχάταις
συμφοραῖς περιπεσεῖν. ISOC. xv. 122. Ἀποσοβοῦντες ἂν ἐμποδὼν
γίγνοιντο τοῦ μὴ ὁρᾶν αὐτοὺς τὸ ὅλον στράτευμα. XEN. Cyr. ii. 4,
23. Εἰδότες ὅτι ἐν ἀσφαλεῖ εἰσι τοῦ μηδὲν παθεῖν. Ib. iii. 3, 31
(cf. THUC. vi. 18, quoted in 749). Τοῦ δὲ μὴ (κακῶς) πάσχειν
αὐτοὶ πᾶσαν ἄδειαν ἤγετε, you were entirely free from fear of suffering
harm. DEM. xix. 149. Ἐνούσης οὐδεμιᾶς ἔτ' ἀποστροφῆς τοῦ μὴ τὰ
χρήματ' ἔχειν ὑμᾶς, there being no longer any escape from the conclusion
that you have taken bribes (from your having bribes). Id. xxiv. 9.

The last two examples show that the genitive of the infinitive can
take μή, even after nouns implying hindrance or freedom. In the two
following, the addition of μή is more peculiar :—

Ἡ ἀπορία τοῦ μὴ ἡσυχάζειν, the inability to rest. THUC. ii. 49.
Τῇ τοῦ μὴ ξυμπλεῖν ἀπιστίᾳ, through distrust of sailing with them ; i.e.
through unwillingness to sail, caused by distrust. Id. iii. 75.

808. The infinitive with τοῦ μή can be used as a genitive in its
ordinary negative sense ; as οὔτε ἔστιν οὐδεμία πρόφασις ἡμῖν τοῦ μὴ
δρᾶν ταῦτα, no ground for not doing this. PLAT. Tim. 20 C. See also
examples in 798.

809. Although μὴ οὐ is more common than μή after negatives in
the form (c), the simple μή sometimes occurs. E.g.

Οὐ πολὺν χρόνον μ' ἐπέσχον μή με ναυστολεῖν ταχύ. SOPH. Ph.
349. Οὐδέ μ' ὄμματος φρουρὰν παρῆλθε, τόνδε μὴ λεύσσειν στόλον.
Id. Tr. 226.

810. The infinitive in the forms (a), (c), and (d), (but, according to
Madvig, not in the form (b), with τοῦ without μή) may follow negatives
in the construction of 807. See the examples.

Infinitive with τὸ μή *or* τὸ μὴ οὐ.

811. The infinitive with τὸ μή is used after many verbs and expressions which denote or even imply *hindrance, prevention, omission,* or *denial,* the μή merely strengthening the negative idea of the leading verb. If the leading verb is itself negatived, or is interrogative with a negative implied, τὸ μὴ οὐ is generally used with the infinitive instead of τὸ μή (compare 807).

This infinitive with τὸ μή or τὸ μὴ οὐ is often less closely connected with the leading verb than the simple infinitive (see 791), and it sometimes denotes merely the *result* of a prevention or omission. It is sometimes an object accusative, as after expressions of denial; but it oftener resembles the accusative of respect or limitation. It adds a fifth expression, εἴργει σε τὸ μὴ τοῦτο ποιεῖν, to the four already given in 807 as equivalents of *he prevents you from doing this;* and a corresponding form, οὐκ εἴργει σε τὸ μὴ οὐ τοῦτο ποιεῖν, for *he does not prevent you from doing this.* E.g.

Τὸν πλεῖστον ὅμιλον εἶργον τὸ μὴ προεξιόντας τῶν ὅπλων τὰ ἐγγὺς τῆς πόλεως κακουργεῖν, *they prevented them from injuring,* etc. Thuc. iii. 1.   Τὸ δὲ μὴ λεηλατῆσαι ἐλόντας σφέας τὴν πόλιν ἔσχε τόδε, *this prevented them from plundering the city.* Hdt. v. 101.   Οἷοί τε ἦσαν κατέχειν τὸ μὴ δακρύειν, *to restrain their tears.* Plat. Phaed. 117 C (cf. 117 E, quoted in 807).   Φόβος τε ξυγγενὴς τὸ μὴ ἀδικεῖν σχήσει, *will check injustice.* Aesch. Eum. 691.   Οὗτοί εἰσιν μόνοι ἔτι ἡμῖν ἐμποδὼν τὸ μὴ ἤδη εἶναι ἔνθα πάλαι ἐσπεύδομεν. Xen. An. iv. 8, 14.   Κίμωνα παρὰ τρεῖς ἀφεῖσαν ψήφους τὸ μὴ θανάτῳ ζημιῶσαι, *i.e. by three votes they allowed Cimon to escape the punishment of death.* Dem. xxiii. 205.   Τρεῖς δὲ μόναι ψῆφοι διήνεγκαν τὸ μὴ θανάτου τιμῆσαι, *and only three votes prevented you from condemning him to death* (lit. *made the difference about condemning,* etc.). Ib. 167. See Xen. Cyr. v. 1, 25, and Ag. v. 4.   Φόβος γὰρ ἀνθ᾽ ὕπνου παραστατεῖ τὸ μὴ βεβαίως βλέφαρα συμβαλεῖν ὕπνῳ, *i.e. stands by to prevent my closing my eyes in sleep.* Aesch. Ag. 15.

Οὐκ ἐναντιώσομαι τὸ μὴ οὐ γεγωνεῖν πᾶν ὅσον προσχρῄζετε. Id. Prom. 786.   Οὐδὲν γὰρ αὐτῷ ταῦτ᾽ ἐπαρκέσει τὸ μὴ οὐ πεσεῖν ἀτίμως πτώματ᾽ οὐκ ἀνασχετά, *this will not suffice to prevent him from falling,* etc. Ib. 918.   Λείπει μὲν οὐδ᾽ ἃ πρόσθεν ᾔδεμεν τὸ μὴ οὐ βαρύστον᾽ εἶναι, *they have no lack of being heavily grievous.* Soph. O. T. 1232.   Μήτοι, κασιγνήτη, μ᾽ ἀτιμάσῃς τὸ μὴ οὐ θανεῖν τε σὺν σοὶ τὸν θανόντα θ᾽ ἁγνίσαι, *do not think me too unworthy to die with thee,* etc. Id. Ant. 544.   (Compare Ant. 22, and O. C. 49.)   Οὐκ ἀπεσχόμην τὸ μὴ οὐκ ἐπὶ τοῦτο ἐλθεῖν, *I did not refrain from proceeding to this subject.* Plat. Rep. 354 B; see Crit. 43 C.   Οὐκ ἀπέσχοντο οὐδ᾽ ἀπὸ τῶν φίλων τὸ μὴ οὐχὶ πλεονεκτεῖν αὐτῶν πειρᾶσθαι. Xen. Cyr. i. 6, 32.   Αὐτὴν μὲν οὐ μισοῦντ᾽ ἐκείνην τὴν πόλιν τὸ μὴ οὐ

μεγάλην εἶναι κεὐδαίμονα, not grudging that city its right to be great,
etc. AR. Av. 36.   (Compare μίσησέν μιν κυσὶ κύρμα γενέσθαι, Il.
xvii. 272.) Οὐδεὶς ἀντιλέγει τὸ μὴ οὐ λέξειν ὅ τι ἕκαστος
ἡγεῖται πλείστου ἄξιον ἐπίστασθαι, no one objects to saying, etc. XEN.
Symp. iii. 3.   Μὴ παρῇς τὸ μὴ οὐ φράσαι, do not omit to speak of it.
SOPH. O. T. 283.   Οὐδένα δύνασθαι κρύπτειν τὸ μὴ οὐχ ἡδέως ἂν
καὶ ὠμῶν ἐσθίειν αὐτῶν, that no one is able to prevent people from
knowing that he would gladly even eat some of them raw. XEN. Hell. iii.
3, 6.

812. The form τὸ μή is more common here when the leading verb
is negative, where regularly τὸ μὴ οὐ would be used, than μή for μὴ
οὐ in the corresponding case (809).   E.g.
  Οὐκ ἂν ἐσχόμην τὸ μὴ ἀποκλῇσαι τοὐμὸν ἄθλιον δέμας. SOPH.
O. T. 1387.   Τίς σοῦ ἀπελείφθη τὸ μή σοι ἀκολουθεῖν; i.e. who
failed to follow you ? XEN. Cyr. v. 1, 25.   Ἄκος δ᾽ οὐδὲν ἐπήρκεσαν τὸ
μὴ πόλιν μὲν ὥσπερ οὖν ἔχει παθεῖν. AESCH. Ag. 1170.   Καὶ φημὶ
δρᾶσαι κοὐκ ἀπαρνοῦμαι τὸ μή. SOPH. Ant. 443.   Οὐδ᾽ ἄρνησις ἔστιν
αὐτοῖς τὸ μὴ ταῦθ᾽ ὑπὲρ Φιλίππου πράττειν, it is not even possible
for them to deny that they did these things in the interest of Philip. DEM.
xix. 163 ; so xx. 135.   So perhaps we may explain τὸ μὴ ἐπιβουλεύειν
in HDT. i. 209 (see § 814).

813. Although the infinitive with τὸ μή is most frequently used
(as in 811) after verbs containing a negative idea, it can also have a
negative sense as the ooject of other verbs or with adjectives. See τὸ
μὴ σφάλλεσθαι ἐπιμελεῖσθαι (quoted in 791), and τὸ μὴ βλέπειν
ἑτοίμα (quoted in 795), in both of which the infinitive is really negatived by μή.   We must distinguish also the use of τοῦ μή with the
infinitive as an ordinary negative expression (see examples in 798)
from that which is explained in 807. Compare, likewise, τὸ μὴ οὐ
with the infinitive in 814 and in 811.   The nature of the leading
verb will always make the force of the negative plain.   We have the
same distinction, with the simple infinitive, between ἀναγκάζει σε μὴ
ἐλθεῖν, he compels you not to go (747), and εἴργει σε μὴ ἐλθεῖν, he
prevents you from going (807).

814. The infinitive with τὸ μὴ οὐ may be used in a negative
sense in various constructions with verbs and expressions
which do not have a negative meaning, provided these are themselves negatived or are interrogative implying a negative.   Though
τὸ μὴ οὐ is more common here, τὸ μή is also allowed.   E.g.
  Κουδείς γέ μ᾽ ἂν πείσειεν ἀνθρώπων τὸ μὴ οὐκ ἐλθεῖν ἐπ᾽ αὐτόν,
and no man can persuade me not to go after him. AR. Ran. 68.   Οὐ
μέντοι ἔπειθέ γε τὸ μὴ οὐ μεγαλοπράγμων τε καὶ κακοπράγμων εἶναι,
but he did not persuade them that he was not full of great and evil under-
takings. XEN. Hell. v. 2, 36.   (For similar expressions with μὴ οὐ
without τό, see 749 and 815, 2.)   Τοῖς θεοῖς οὐδὲν ἂν ἔχοιμεν μέμψασθαι τὸ μὴ οὐχὶ πάντα πεπραχέναι, we cannot blame the Gods for not

having done everything. Id. Cyr. vii. 5, 42 (cf. ταῦτ᾽ οὖν ὑμῖν μέμφο-μαι, Ar. Nub. 525). Οὐδὲ ὅσιον ἔμοιγε εἶναι φαίνεται τὸ μὴ οὐ βοη-θεῖν τούτοις τοῖς λόγοις πάντα ἄνδρα. Plat. Leg. 891 A. Ἄλογον τὸ μὴ οὐ τέμνειν. Id. Soph. 219 E (see 817). Τοῖς δὲ οὐδὲ λόγος λείπεται τὸ μὴ οὐ πονηροῖς εἶναι. Dem. xxiv. 69.[1]
Οὔκων ἐστὶ μηχανὴ οὐδεμία τὸ μὴ ἐκεῖνον ἐπιβουλεύειν ἐμοί, *there is then no way by which I can believe that he is not plotting against me.* Hdt. i. 209 (cf. Plat. Phaed. 72 D). Ἕξει τίνα γνώμην λέγειν τὸ μὴ εὐρύπρωκτος εἶναι; Ar. Nub. 1084. Ἔφη οὐχ οἷόν τε εἶναι τὸ μὴ ἀποκτεῖναί με, *he said it was not possible not to condemn me to death.* Plat. Ap. 29 C.

Μὴ οὐ with Infinitive and Participle, and (rarely) with Nouns.

815. 1. The use of μή with the infinitive in the forms (*c*) and (*d*) in 807 is to be referred to the general principle, by which the infinitive after all verbs expressing a *negative* idea (as those of *denying, distrusting, concealing, forbidding, preventing,* etc.) can always take μή, to strengthen the negation implied in the leading verb. Thus we say ἀρνεῖται μὴ ἀληθὲς εἶναι τοῦτο, *he denies that this is true;* ἀπηγόρευε μηδένα τοῦτο ποιεῖν, *he forbade any one to do this.* This μή can, however, be omitted without affecting the sense.

2. An infinitive which *for any reason* would take μή (either affecting the infinitive itself, as an ordinary negative, or strengthening a preceding negation, as in the case just mentioned) generally takes the double negative μὴ οὐ, if the verb on which it depends is *itself negatived* or is interrogative with a negation implied. Thus the example given above, ἀρνεῖται μὴ ἀληθὲς εἶναι τοῦτο, if we negative the leading verb, generally becomes οὐκ ἀρνεῖται μὴ οὐκ ἀληθὲς εἶναι τοῦτο, *he does not deny that this is true.* So, when the original μή really negatives the infinitive, as in δίκαιόν ἐστι μὴ τοῦτον ἀφιέναι, *it is just not to acquit him,* if we negative the leading verb, we commonly have οὐ δίκαιόν ἐστι μὴ οὐ τοῦτον ἀφιέναι, *it is not just not to acquit him.* E.g.

Ὡς οὐχ ὅσιόν σοι ὂν μὴ οὐ βοηθεῖν δικαιοσύνῃ, *because* (you said) *it would be impious for you not to bring aid to Justice.* Plat. Rep. 427 E. Οὐκ ἂν πιθοίμην μὴ οὐ τάδ᾽ ἐκμαθεῖν σαφῶς, *I cannot consent not to learn the whole.* Soph. O. T. 1065. Ἄνδρα δ᾽ οὐκ ἔστι μὴ οὐ κακὸν ἔμμεναι, *it is not possible for a man not to be base.* Simon. v. 10. See also Plat. Phaed. 72 D (in 749). For examples in which μὴ οὐ strengthens the negation of the leading verb, see 807.

---

[1] This is cited by Birklein (p. 67) as the only case of the article with μὴ οὐ in the Orators; and no case occurs in either Herodotus or Thucydides.

This applies also to the infinitive with τὸ μή. See 811 and 814.

816. When μή or μὴ οὐ with the infinitive follows a verb of *hindrance*, etc. (807), neither μή nor μὴ οὐ can be translated. When μή really negatives the infinitive (as in the examples last given), μὴ οὐ must be translated by one negative. In PLAT. Rep. 368 B, the passage quoted in 427 E (815, 2, above), Socrates had said δέδοικα μὴ οὐδ᾽ ὅσιον ᾖ . . . ἀπαγορεύειν καὶ μὴ βοηθεῖν, being prevented from saying μὴ οὐ βοηθεῖν by the previous μὴ οὐδ᾽. In XEN. Ap. 34 we have οὔτε μὴ μεμνῆσθαι δύναμαι αὐτοῦ οὔτε μεμνημένος μὴ οὐκ ἐπαινεῖν.

817. Verbs and expressions which contain such negative ideas as *impossibility*, *difficulty*, *unwillingness*, or *impropriety* sometimes take μὴ οὐ (instead of the simple μή) with the infinitive, to express a real negation, even when the leading verb is not negatived. *E.g.*

Δήμου ἄρχοντος ἀδύνατα μὴ οὐ κακότητα ἐγγίνεσθαι, *it is impossible that vice should not come in* (as if it were οὐ δυνατά). HDT. iii. 82. Δεινὸν ἐδόκεε εἶναι μὴ οὐ λαβεῖν αὐτά. Id. i. 187. Ὥστε πᾶσιν αἰσχύνην εἶναι μὴ οὐ συσπουδάζειν, *so that all were ashamed not to join heartily in the work.* XEN. An. ii. 3, 11. So ᾐσχύνετο μὴ οὐ φαίνεσθαι, Cyr. viii. 4, 5. Αἰσχρόν ἐστι μὴ οὐχὶ φάναι. PLAT. Prot. 352 D. Πολλὴ ἄνοια μὴ οὐχ ἡγεῖσθαι. Id. Symp. 210 B. So after ἀνόητον, ib. 218 C ; after ἄλογον, id. Soph. 219 E (see 814). For χαλεπός followed by μὴ οὐ, see example under 819.

818. Μὴ οὐ is occasionally used with participles in negative sentences, in place of the simple μή, to express a negative condition. The following cases are quoted :—

Οὔκων δίκαιον εἶναι (Δαρεῖον ἀνδριάντα) ἱστάναι μὴ οὐκ ὑπερβαλλόμενον τοῖσι ἔργοισι, i.e. *he said that Darius had no right to set up his statue* (in front of that of Sesostris), *unless he surpassed him in his exploits* (= εἰ μὴ ὑπερβάλλεται). HDT. ii. 110. Καταρρωδῆσαν μὴ οὐ . . . τὴν Μίλητον οἷοί τε ἔωσι ἐξελεῖν μὴ οὐ ἐόντες ναυκράτορες *they feared that they might not be able to capture Miletus without being masters of the sea* (their thought was εἰ μὴ ναυκράτορές ἐσμεν). Id. vi. 9. Εἰνάτῃ δὲ οὐκ ἐξελεύσεσθαι ἔφασαν μὴ οὐ πλήρεος ἐόντος τοῦ κύκλου, *they refused to march out on the ninth of the month* (and thereafter) *until the moon should be full* (ἐὰν μὴ πλήρης ᾖ). Id. vi. 106. Δυσάλγητος γὰρ ἂν εἴην τοιάνδε μὴ οὐ κατοικτείρων ἕδραν, *for I should be hard of heart* (817) *should I feel no pity for such a band of suppliants* (εἰ μὴ κατοικτείροιμι). SOPH. O. T. 12. Οὐ γὰρ ἂν μακρὰν ἴχνευον αὐτός, μὴ οὐκ ἔχων τι σύμβολον, *for I should not have traced it far, if I had attempted it by myself without any clue.* Ib. 220. (For the force of the subordinate condition of μὴ οὐκ ἔχων in relation to the real protasis in αὐτός, see 511.) Ἥκεις γὰρ οὐ κενή γε, τοῦτ᾽ ἐγὼ σαφῶς ἔξοιδα, μὴ οὐχὶ δεῖμ᾽ ἐμοὶ φέρουσά τι, i.e. *you have not come empty-handed,—* (not at least) *without bringing me some cause for alarm* (i.e. οὐκ εἰ μὴ φέρεις). Id. O. C. 359. (Μὴ οὐχὶ φέρουσα adds a condition as a qualification to κενή.) Οὐκ ἄρα ἐστὶ φιλὸν τῷ φιλοῦντι οὐδὲν μὴ οὐκ ἀντιφιλοῦν, *unless it loves in return.* PLAT. Lys. 212 D. (Cf. φίλοι δέ γε οὐκ ἂν εἶεν μὴ περὶ πολλοῦ ποιούμενοι ἑαυτούς, 215 B.) Τίς γὰρ ἂν ἠβουλήθη μικρὰ κερδᾶναι, κ.τ.λ.; οὐδ' ἂν εἷς μὴ οὐ συνειδὼς ἑαυτῷ συκοφαντοῦντι, *not a man (would have wished for this) if he had not been conscious that he was a sycophant* (= εἰ μὴ συνῄδει). DEM. lviii. 13. Οὔτε γὰρ ναυαγὸς, ἂν μὴ γῆς λάβηται φερόμενος, οὔποτ' ἂν σώσειεν αὑτόν· οὔτ' ἀνὴρ πένης γεγὼς μὴ οὐ τέχνην μαθὼν δύναιτ' ἂν ἀσφαλῶς ζῆν τὸν βίον (i.e. εἰ μὴ μάθοι, corresponding to ἂν μὴ λάβηται). PHILEM. Fr. 213.

819. Μὴ οὐ occasionally occurs with nouns, in the same general sense as with participles, to express a negative condition to a negative statement. *E.g.*

Αἵ τε πόλεις πολλαὶ καὶ χαλεπαὶ λαβεῖν, μὴ οὐ χρόνῳ καὶ πολιορκίᾳ, *the cities were many, and difficult* (= *not easy,* 817) *to capture except by time and siege.* DEM. xix. 123. Τοιαύτης δὲ τιμῆς τυχεῖν οὐχ οἷόν τε μὴ οὐ τὸν πολὺ τῇ γνώμῃ διαφέροντα, *to attain such honour is not possible except for one who is of far transcendent wisdom.* ISOC. x. 47. (If τόν is omitted, διαφέροντα as a participle belongs under 818.)

820. It may be noted that μὴ οὐ in poetry always forms one syllable.

CHAPTER VI.

THE PARTICIPLE.

821. As the infinitive is a verbal noun, so the participle is a verbal adjective; both retaining all the attributes of a verb which are consistent with their nature.

822. The participle has three uses :—first, it may express an *attribute*, qualifying a noun like an ordinary adjective (824-831); secondly, it may define the *circumstances* under which the action of the sentence takes place (832-876); thirdly, it may be joined to a verb to *supplement* its meaning, often having a force resembling that of the infinitive (877-919).

823. The distinction between the second and third of these classes is less clearly marked than that between the first and the two others : thus in ἥδεται τιμώμενος, *he delights in being honoured*, the participle is generally classed as supplementary (881), although it expresses cause (838). Even an attributive participle may also be circumstantial ; as ὁ μὴ δαρεὶς ἄνθρωπος, *the unflogged man* (824), involves a condition. The three classes are, nevertheless, sufficiently distinct for convenience, though the lines (like many others in syntax) must not be drawn so strictly as to defeat their object.

A. ATTRIBUTIVE PARTICIPLE.

824. The participle may qualify a noun, like an attributive adjective. Here it may often be translated by a finite verb and a relative, especially when it is preceded by the article. *E.g.*

Πόλις κάλλει διαφέρουσα, *a city excelling in beauty.* Ἀνὴρ καλῶς πεπαιδευμένος, *a man (who has been) well educated.* Οἱ πρέ-

σβεις οἱ παρὰ Φιλίππου πεμφθέντες, *the ambassadors (who had been)*
sent from Philip. Ἄνδρες οἱ τοῦτο ποιήσοντες, *men who will do this.*
Ἐν τῇ Μεσσηνίᾳ ποτὲ οὔσῃ γῇ, *in the land which was once*
Messenia. THUC. iv. 3. Στρατεύουσιν ἐπὶ τὰς Αἰόλου νήσους καλου-
μένας, *they sail against the so-called Aeolian islands,* lit. *the islands called*
those of Aeolus. Id. iii. 88. Αἱ ἄρισται δοκοῦσαι εἶναι φύσεις,
the natures which seem to be best. XEN. Mem. iv. 1, 3. Αἱ πρὸ τοῦ
στόματος νῆες ναυμαχοῦσαι. THUC. vii. 23. Ἐπεπείσμην μέγαν
εἶναι τὸν κατειληφότα κίνδυνον τὴν πόλιν, *the danger which had*
overtaken the city. DEM. xviii. 220. Ὁ μὴ δαρεὶς ἄνθρωπος οὐ παι-
δεύεται. MEN. Mon. 422.

825. The participle with the article may be used *sub-*
stantively, like any adjective. Here it may generally be
translated by a finite verb and a relative, the verb expressing
the tense of the participle. *E.g.*

Οἱ κρατοῦντες, *the conquerors.* Οἱ πεπεισμένοι, *those who have been*
convinced. Οὗτός ἐστι ὁ τοῦτο ποιήσας, *this is the one who did it.*
Οὗτοί εἰσιν οἱ ὑμᾶς πάντας ἀδικήσοντες, *these are the men who will*
wrong you all. Πάντες οἱ παρόντες τοῦτο ἑώρων, *all who were present*
saw this. Τὸ κρατοῦν τῆς πόλεως, *the ruling part of the state.*
Ὁ μὴ λαβὼν καὶ διαφθαρεὶς νενίκηκε τὸν ὠνούμενον, *he who*
did not take (the bribe) and become corrupt has defeated the one who would
buy him. DEM. xviii. 247 (see 841). Τῶν ἐργασομένων ἐνόντων,
there being in the country those who would cultivate it (i.e. *men to cultivate*
it). XEN. An. ii. 4, 22. (See 826 and 840.) Παρὰ τοῖς ἀρίστοις
δοκοῦσιν εἶναι, *among those who seem to be best.* Id. Mem. iv. 2, 6.
Ἦν δὲ ὁ μὲν τὴν γνώμην ταύτην εἰπὼν Πείσανδρος, *and Peisander*
was the one who gave this opinion. THUC. viii. 68. Τοῖς Ἀρκάδων
σφετέροις οὖσι ξυμμάχοις προεῖπον, *they proclaimed to those of the*
Arcadians who were their allies. Id. v. 64. Ἀφεκτέον ἐγώ φημι εἶναι
τῷ σωφρονεῖν δυνησομένῳ, i.e. *one who is to be able to be discreet.* XEN.
Symp. iv. 26.

826. When the participle, in either of these constructions,
refers to a purpose, intention, or expectation, it is generally
future, though sometimes present. *E.g.*

Νόμον δημοσίᾳ τὸν ταῦτα κωλύσοντα τέθεινται τουτονί, *they*
have publicly enacted this law, which is to prevent these things. DEM. xxi.
49. See XEN. An. ii. 4, 22 in 825. Ὁ ἡγησόμενος οὐδεὶς ἔσται,
there will be nobody who will lead us. Ib. ii. 4, 5. Πολλοὺς ἕξομεν
τοὺς ἑτοίμως συναγωνιζομένους ἡμῖν. ISOC. viii. 139.

See the more common use of the circumstantial future participle to
express a purpose, in 840.

827. (*a*) Participles, like adjectives, are occasionally used
substantively even without the article, in an indefinite sense;
generally in the plural. *E.g.*

Ἔπλει δώδεκα τριήρεις ἔχων ἐπὶ πολλὰς ναῦς κεκτημένους, *he sailed with twelve triremes against men who had many ships.* XEN. Hell. v. 1, 19. Ὅταν πολεμούντων πόλις ἁλῷ, *whenever a city of belligerents is taken.* Id. Cyr. vii. 5, 73. Μετὰ ταῦτα ἀφικνοῦνταί μοι ἀπαγγέλλοντες ὅτι ὁ πατὴρ ἀφεῖται, *there come messengers announcing,* etc. ISOC. xvii. 11. Δύναιτ' ἂν οὐδ' ἂν ἰσχύων φυγεῖν, *not even a strong man could escape.* SOPH. El. 697. Οὐκ ἔστι φιλοῦντα (*a lover*) μὴ ἀντιφιλεῖσθαι; PLAT. Lys. 212 B.

(b) This use in the singular appears especially in θνητὸν ὄντα, *one who is a mortal.* This indefinite expression, though masculine, may refer to both sexes. *E.g.*

Ἐν ποικίλοις δὲ θνητὸν ὄντα κάλλεσιν βαίνειν ἐμοὶ μὲν οὐδαμῶς ἄνευ φόβου, i.e. *for a mortal (like myself) to walk on these rich embroideries,* etc. AESCH. Ag. 923. Κούφως φέρειν χρὴ θνητὸν ὄντα συμφοράς, (*one who is*) *a mortal (like yourself) must bear calamities lightly* (addressed to Medea). EUR. Med. 1018. So in SOPH. Ant. 455 θνητὸν ὄνθ' means *a mortal (like myself),* and refers to Antigone, not to Creon ; she means that Creon's proclamations could not justify her in violating the edicts of the Gods.

828. In the poets, the participle with the article sometimes becomes so completely a substantive, that it takes an adnominal genitive rather than the case which its verbal force would require. A few expressions like οἱ προσήκοντες, *relatives,* τὸ συμφέρον or τὰ συμφέροντα, *gain, advantage,* τὰ ὑπάρχοντα, *resources,* are thus used even in prose. *E.g.*

Ὁ ἐκείνου τεκών, *his father* (for ὁ ἐκεῖνον τεκών). EUR. El. 335. Τὰ μικρὰ συμφέροντα τῆς πόλεως, *the small advantages of the state.* DEM. xviii. 28. Βασιλέως προσήκοντές τινες, *certain relatives of the king.* THUC. i. 128.

829. (a) The neuter singular of the present participle with the article is sometimes used as an abstract noun, where we should expect the infinitive with the article. This occurs chiefly in Thucydides and in the poets. *E.g.*

Ἐν τῷ μὴ μελετῶντι ἀξυνετώτεροι ἔσονται, *in the want of practice they will be less skilful.* THUC. i. 142. (Here we should expect ἐν τῷ μὴ μελετᾶν.) Γνώτω τὸ μὲν δεδιὸς αὐτοῦ τοὺς ἐναντίους μᾶλλον φοβῆσον, τὸ δὲ θαρσοῦν ἀδεέστερον ἐσόμενον. Id. i. 36. (Here τὸ δεδιός, *fear,* is used like τὸ δεδιέναι, and τὸ θαρσοῦν, *courage,* like τὸ θαρσεῖν or τὸ θάρσος.) Μετὰ τοῦ δρωμένου, *with action* (like μετὰ τοῦ δρᾶσθαι). Id. v. 102. Τοῦ ὑπαπιέναι πλέον ἢ τοῦ μένοντος τὴν διάνοιαν ἔχουσιν (infin. and partic. combined). Id. v. 9. Καὶ σέ γ' εἰσάξω· τὸ γὰρ νοσοῦν ποθεῖ σε ξυμπαραστάτην λαβεῖν. SOPH. Ph. 674 (τὸ νοσοῦν = ἡ νόσος). Τὸ γὰρ ποθοῦν ἕκαστος ἐκμαθεῖν θέλων οὐκ ἂν μεθεῖτο, πρὶν καθ' ἡδονὴν κλύειν. Id. Tr. 196.

This is really the same use of the neuter singular of an adjective for the corresponding abstract noun, which is common in ordinary adjectives ; as τὸ καλόν, *beauty,* for τὸ κάλλος ; τὸ δίκαιον and τὸ ἄδικον for ἡ δικαιοσύνη and ἡ ἀδικία.

(*b*) A similar construction sometimes occurs when a participle and a noun are used like an articular infinitive with its subject, where in English we generally use a finite verb. *E.g.*

Μετὰ δὲ Σόλωνα οἰχόμενον ἔλαβε νέμεσις μεγάλη Κροῖσον, i.e. *after Solon was gone* (like μετὰ τὸ Σόλωνα οἴχεσθαι). HDT. i. 34. Ἐπὶ τούτου τυραννεύοντος, *in his reign.* Id. i. 15 : so viii. 44. Ἔτει πέμπτῳ μετὰ Συρακούσας οἰκισθείσας, *in the fifth year after the foundation of Syracuse.* THUC. vi. 3.   Compare *post urbem conditam* in Latin.   Μετὰ καλὸν οὕτω καὶ παντοδαπὸν λόγον ῥηθέντα (like μετὰ τὸ . . . ῥηθῆναι). PLAT. Symp. 198 B.   Τῇ πόλει οὔτε πολέμου κακῶς συμβάντος οὔτε στάσεως πώποτε αἴτιος ἐγένετο, i.e. *the cause of a disastrous result of any war* (like τοῦ πόλεμόν τινα κακῶς συμβῆναι). XEN. Mem. i. 2, 63.

(*c*) The same construction occurs in Homer ; as ἐς ἠέλιον καταδύντα, *to the going down of the sun,* Il. i. 601 ; ἅμ᾽ ἠοῖ φαινομένηφιν, Il. ix. 682.

For the peculiar use of the aorist participle here, see 149.

830. The participle is sometimes used like a predicate adjective, with εἰμί or γίγνομαι. *E.g.*

Τί ποτ᾽ ἐστὶν οὗτος ἐκείνου διαφέρων; *in what is this man different from that one* (another form for διαφέρει)? PLAT. Gorg. 500 C. Συμφέρον ἦν τῇ πόλει, *it was advantageous to the state* (= συνέφερεν). DEM. xix. 75.   Οὔτε γὰρ θρασὺς οὔτ᾽ οὖν προδείσας εἰμὶ τῷ γε νῦν λόγῳ. SOPH. O. T. 90.   Ἀπαρνεόμενός ἐστι (= ἀπαρνέεται). HDT. iii. 99.   Ἡ δὲ ἐστὶ δέκα σταδίους ἀπέχουσα, *and it* (the island) *is ten stades distant.* Id. ix. 51.

Ἂν ᾖ θέλουσα, πάντ᾽ ἐμοῦ κομίζεται, *whatever she wants, she always obtains from me* (for ἂν θέλῃ). SOPH. O. T. 580.   Ἦν γὰρ ὁ Θεμιστοκλῆς βεβαιότατα δὴ φύσεως ἰσχὺν δηλώσας, καὶ ἄξιος θαυμάσαι, *Themistocles was one who manifested,* etc. THUC. i. 138.   Τοῦτο οὐκ ἔστι γιγνόμενον παρ᾽ ἡμῖν; *is not this something that goes on in our minds?* PLAT. Phil. 39 C.   Τοῦτο κινδυνεύει τρόπον τινὰ γιγνόμενον ἡ δικαιοσύνη εἶναι, *justice seems somehow to be proving to be* (lit. *becoming*) *this.* Id. Rep. 433 B.

So with ὑπάρχω and the poetic πέλομαι; as τοῦτο ὑπάρχειν ὑμᾶς εἰδότας ἡγοῦμαι, *I think you may be presumed to know this,* DEM. xviii. 95 ; ἐμεῖο λελασμένος ἔπλευ, Il. xxiii. 69.

831. On the same principle, the participle is used in all periphrastic forms with εἰμί and ἔχω for the perfect, pluperfect, and future perfect. In the future perfect active, the periphrastic form is generally the only one in use ; in the third person plural of the perfect and pluperfect middle and passive of most verbs, it is the only form possible. Examples of the perfect participle with εἰμί or ἦν as peculiar forms of the perfect and pluperfect, in other persons, are given in 45 ; of ἔχω and εἶχον with the aorist and perfect participle for the perfect and pluperfect, in 47 and 48 ; of ἔσομαι with the perfect and aorist participle for the future perfect, in 80 and 81.

B. CIRCUMSTANTIAL PARTICIPLE.

832. The participle may define the *circumstances* under which an action takes place, agreeing with the noun or pronoun to which it relates. The negative of such a participle is οὐ, unless it has a conditional force. The relations expressed by the participle in this use are the following :—

833. I. *Time*, the tenses of the participle denoting various points of time, which is relative to that of the leading verb. *E.g.*

Ταῦτα εἰπὼν ἀπῄει, *when he had said this, he departed.* Ἀπήντησα Φιλίππῳ ἀπιόντι, *I met Philip as he was departing.* Τοῦτο πεποιη-κότες χαιρήσουσιν. *Ταῦτα ἔπραττε στρατηγῶν, he did these things while he was general.* Ταῦτα πράξει στρατηγῶν, *he will do these things when he is general.* Τυραννεύσας δὲ ἔτη τρία Ἱππίας ἐχώρει ὑπόσπονδος ἐς Σίγειον, *after a rule of three years.* THUC. vi. 59. Νῦν μὲν δειπνεῖτε· δειπνήσαντες δὲ ἀπελαύνετε, i.e. *after supping.* XEN. Cyr. iii. 1, 37. So vii. 5, 78 ; An. vii. 1, 13.

834. Certain temporal participles, agreeing with the subject of a sentence, have almost the force of adverbs. Such are ἀρχόμενος, *at first;* τελευτῶν, *at last, finally;* διαλιπὼν (or ἐπισχὼν) χρόνον, *after a while,* or διαλείπων χρόνον, *at intervals;* χρονίζων, *for a long time. E.g.*

Ἅπερ καὶ ἀρχόμενος εἶπον, *as I said also at first.* THUC. iv. 64. Τελευτῶν οὖν ἐπὶ τοὺς χειροτέχνας ᾖα, *finally then I went to the artisans.* PLAT. Ap. 22 C. Ὀλίγον χρόνον διαλιπὼν ἐκινήθη, *after a little while he moved.* Id. Phaed. 118. Οὐ πολὺν χρόνον ἐπισχὼν ἧκε, *after (waiting) no long time he came.* Ib. 59 E. Διαλείπουσαν χρόνον, *at intervals* (of Clotho's regular movements). Id. Rep. 617 C. Ὅπως χρονίζον εὖ μενεῖ βουλευτέον. AESCH. Ag. 847 : cf. χρονι-σθείς, Ib. 727.

835. II. *Means. E.g.*

Ληζόμενοι ζῶσιν, *they live by plunder.* XEN. Cyr. iii. 2, 25. Τοὺς Ἕλληνας ἐδίδαξαν, ὃν τρόπον διοικοῦντες τὰς αὐτῶν πατρίδας καὶ πρὸς οὓς πολεμοῦντες μεγάλην ἂν τὴν Ἑλλάδα ποιήσειαν. ISOC. xii. 44. Οὐ γὰρ ἀλλοτρίοις ὑμῖν χρωμένοις παραδείγμασιν ἀλλ' οἰκείοις, εὐδαίμοσιν ἔξεστι γενέσθαι, *for it is by using not foreign but domestic examples that you can become prosperous.* DEM. iii. 23. Τῶν νόμων ἄπειροι γίγνονται καὶ τῶν λόγων, οἷς δεῖ χρώμενον ὁμιλεῖν τοῖς ἀνθρώποις, *which we (τινά) must use in our intercourse with men.* PLAT. Gorg. 484 D. So often χρώμενος in the sense of *with* (cf. 843).

836. III. *Manner* and similar relations, including manner of employment, etc. *E.g.*

Προείλετο μᾶλλον τοῖς νόμοις ἐμμένων ἀποθανεῖν ἢ παρανομῶν ζῆν, *he preferred to die abiding by the laws, rather than to live disobeying them.* XEN. Mem. iv. 4, 4. Προαιροῦνται μᾶλλον οὕτω κερδαίνειν ἀπ᾽ ἀλλήλων ἢ συνωφελοῦντες αὑτούς, *they prefer to get gain by this means from each other, rather than by uniting to aid themselves.* Ib. iii. 5, 16. Καὶ ἣ γελάσασα ἔφη, *and she said with a laugh.* PLAT. Symp. 202 B. ῾Αρπάσαντας τὰ ὅπλα πορεύεσθαι, *to march having snatched up their arms* (i.e. *eagerly*). DEM. iii. 20 : cf. οἷον ῥίψαντας τὰ ἱμάτια, PLAT. Rep. 474 A.

837. The following participles of manner are used in peculiar senses : φέρων, *hastily ;* φερόμενος, *with a rush ;* ἀνύσας, *quickly ;* κατατείνας, *earnestly ;* διατεινάμενος and διατεταμένος, *with all one's might ;* φθάσας, *before (anticipating) ;* λαθών, *secretly ;* ἔχων, *continually ;* κλαίων, *to one's sorrow ;* χαίρων, *with impunity (to one's joy). E.g.*

Εἰς τοῦτο φέρων περιέστησε τὰ πράγματα, *he rapidly brought things to such a pass.* AESCHIN. iii. 82. ῾Ως ἐσέπεσον φερόμενοι ἐς τοὺς Ἕλληνας οἱ Μῆδοι, *when the Persians fell upon the Greeks with a rush.* HDT. vii. 210. So οἰχήσεσθαι φερομένην κατὰ ῥοῦν, PLAT. Rep. 492 C. ᾿Ανοιγ᾽ ἀνύσας τὸ φροντιστήριον, *make haste and open the thinking-shop.* AR. Nub. 181. Κατατείνας ἐρῶ τὸν ἄδικον βίον ἐπαινῶν, *I will speak earnestly in praise of the unjust life.* PLAT. Rep. 358 D : so 367 B. See Rep. 474 A, and XEN. Mem. iv. 2, 23. Εἶτ᾽ ἀνέῳξάς με φθάσας, *then you opened it* (the door) *before I could knock.* AR. Plut. 1102 : so ὅς μ᾽ ἔβαλε φθάμενος, Il. v. 119 ; but in such expressions ἔφθη βαλών etc. (887) is more common. ᾿Απὸ τείχεος ἄλτο λαθών, *he leaped from the wall secretly.* Il. xii. 390 : cf. λήθουσά μ᾽ ἐξέπινες, SOPH. Ant. 532 ; here again ἔλαθον with the participle is more common (see 893). Τί κυπτάζεις ἔχων ; *why do you keep poking about?* AR. Nub. 509. Κλαίων ἄψει τῶνδε, *you will lay hands on them to your sorrow.* EUR. Her. 270 : so SOPH. Ant. 754. Οὔ τι χαίρων ἐρεῖς, *you shall not speak with impunity.* Id. O. T. 363 ; so Ant. 759. Τοῦτον οὐδεὶς χαίρων ἀδικήσει. PLAT. Gorg. 510 D. Compare ταξαμένους, *according to agreement,* Id. Rep. 416 E.

838. IV. *Cause* or *ground of action.* *E.g.*

Λέγω δὲ τοῦδ᾽ ἕνεκα, βουλόμενος δόξαι σοὶ ὅπερ ἐμοί, *and I speak for this reason, because I wish,* etc. PLAT. Phaed. 102 D. ᾿Απείχοντο κερδῶν, αἰσχρὰ νομίζοντες εἶναι, *because they believed them to be base.* XEN. Mem. i. 2, 22. Τί γὰρ ἂν βουλόμενοι ἄνδρες σοφοὶ ὡς ἀληθῶς δεσπότας ἀμείνους αὑτῶν φεύγοιεν, *with what object in view,* etc. (i.e. *wishing what*)? PLAT. Phaed. 63 A. Τί γὰρ δεδιότες σφόδρα οὕτως ἐπείγεσθε ; *what do you fear, that you are in such great haste?* XEN. Hell. i. 7, 26.

For the participle with ὡς, used to express a cause assigned by the subject of the sentence, see 864.

839. (a) Here belong τί μαθών; and τί παθών; both of which have the general force of *wherefore?* Τί μαθὼν τοῦτο ποιεῖ; however, properly means *what put it into his head to do this?* or *with what idea does he do this?* and τί παθὼν τοῦτο ποιεῖ; means *what has happened to him that he does this?* *E.g.*

Τί τοῦτο μαθὼν προσέγραψεν; *with what idea did he add this to the law?* DEM. xx. 127. Τί παθοῦσαι, εἴπερ Νεφέλαι γ᾽ εἰσὶν ἀληθῶς, θνηταῖς εἴξασι γυναιξίν; *what has happened to them that they resemble mortal women?* AR. Nub. 340.

(b) These phrases may be used even in dependent sentences, τί becoming ὅ τι, and the whole phrase meaning *because.* *E.g.*

Τί ἄξιός εἰμι παθεῖν ἢ ἀποτῖσαι, ὅ τι μαθὼν ἐν τῷ βίῳ οὐχ ἡσυχίαν ἦγον; *what do I deserve to suffer or pay because I did not keep quiet?* i.e. *for taking it into my head not to keep quiet?* PLAT. Ap. 36 B. Ὅμως ἂν κακὰ ἦν, ὅ τι μάθοντα χαίρειν ποιεῖ καὶ ὁπηοῦν; *would they still be evil because they give us joy in any conceivable manner?* Id. Prot. 353 D. (In cases like this, the original meaning of the participle is forgotten.) So Euthyd. 283 E and 299 A.

840. V. *Purpose, object,* or *intention,* expressed by the future participle, rarely by the present. *E.g.*

Ἦλθε λυσόμενος θύγατρα, *he came to ransom his daughter.* Il. i. 13. Παρελήλυθα συμβουλεύσων, *I have risen to give my advice.* Isoc. vi. 1. Ἐβουλεύσαντο πέμπειν ἐς Λακεδαίμονα πρέσβεις ταῦτά τε ἐροῦντας καὶ Λύσανδρον αἰτήσοντας ἐπὶ τὰς ναῦς, *in order to say this, and to ask for Lysander as admiral.* XEN. Hell. ii. 1, 6. Ἐὰν εἰς πόλεμον (ἡ πατρὶς) ἄγῃ τρωθησόμενον ἢ ἀποθανούμενον, ποιητέον ταῦτα, *even if it lead any one into war to be wounded or to perish.* PLAT. Crit. 51 B. Αὖθις δὲ ὁ ἡγησόμενος οὐδεὶς ἔσται, *there will be nobody to lead us* (= ὃς ἡγήσεται). XEN. An. ii. 4, 5. (This participle is also attributive: see 826.) Προσβολὰς παρεσκευάζοντο τῷ τείχει ποιησόμενοι, *they prepared (themselves) to make attacks on the wall.* THUC. ii. 18.

Ἔτυχον γὰρ (νῆες) οἰχόμεναι, περιαγγέλλουσαι βοηθεῖν, *for some ships happened to be gone, to give notice to send aid.* Id. i. 116. So ἀρνύμενοι, Il. i. 159. The present here expresses an *attendant circumstance* (843) as well as a *purpose.* See also φθείροντε, AESCH. Ag. 652.

841. VI. *Condition,* the participle standing for a protasis, and its tenses representing the various forms of condition expressed by the indicative, subjunctive, or optative (472). *E.g.*

Οἴει σὺ Ἄλκηστιν ὑπὲρ Ἀδμήτου ἀποθανεῖν ἄν, ἢ Ἀχιλλέα Πατρόκλῳ ἐπαποθανεῖν, μὴ οἰομένους ἀθάνατον μνήμην ἀρετῆς πέρι ἑαυτῶν ἔσεσθαι, do you think that Alcestis would have died for Admetus, etc., if they had not believed, etc. PLAT. Symp. 208 D. (Here μὴ οἰομένους is equivalent to εἰ μὴ ᾤοντο.) Οὐ γὰρ ἂν αὐτοῖς ἔμελεν μὴ τοῦθ' ὑπολαμβάνουσιν, for it would not have concerned them, unless they had had this idea. DEM. ix. 45. (Μὴ ὑπολαμβάνουσιν = εἰ μὴ τοῦτο ὑπελάμβανον.) Ἄστρων ἂν ἔλθοιμ' ἡλίου πρὸς ἀντολὰς καὶ γῆς ἔνερθε, δυνατὸς ὢν δρᾶσαι τάδε, if I should be able to do this (εἰ δυνατὸς εἴην). EUR. Ph. 504. So the attributive participles ὁ μὴ δαρείς (824) and ὁ μὴ λαβών (825).

In SOPH. O. T. 289, πάλαι δὲ μὴ παρὼν θαυμάζεται, the construction represents θαυμάζομεν εἰ μὴ πάρεστιν, we wonder that he is not here (494).

For μὴ οὐ with the participle in negative conditions, where μή is more common, see 818.

See other examples under 472.

842. VII. *Opposition, limitation*, or *concession*, where the participle may often be translated by *although*. *E.g.*

Οὗτος δὲ καὶ μεταπεμφθῆναι φάσκων ὑπὸ τοῦ πατρὸς, καὶ ἐλθὼν εἰς τὴν οἰκίαν, εἰσελθεῖν μὲν οὔ φησιν, Δημοφῶντος δ' ἀκοῦσαι γραμματεῖον ἀναγιγνώσκοντος, καὶ προεισεληλυθὼς καὶ ἅπαντα διωμολογημένος πρὸς τὸν πατέρα, and this man, although he admits that he was summoned, and although he did go to the house, yet denies that he went in, etc., although he had previously gone in and arranged everything with my father. DEM. xxviii. 14. Ὀλίγα δυνάμενοι προορᾶν περὶ τοῦ μέλλοντος πολλὰ ἐπιχειροῦμεν πράττειν, although we are able to foresee few things, etc. XEN. Cyr. iii. 2, 15. Ἐλὼν καὶ δυνηθεὶς ἂν αὐτὸς ἔχειν, παρέδωκε, i.e. when he had captured it (Olynthus) and might have kept it himself, he surrendered it. DEM. xxiii. 107.

The participle in this sense is very often accompanied by καίπερ and other particles. (See 859.) This construction is the most common equivalent of a clause with *although*.

843. VIII. Any *attendant circumstance*, the participle being merely *descriptive*. *E.g.*

Παραλαβόντες Βοιωτοὺς καὶ Φωκέας ἐστράτευσαν ἐπὶ Φάρσαλον, they took Boeotians and Phocians with them and marched against Pharsalus. THUC. i. 111. Παραγγέλλει τῷ Κλεάρχῳ λαβόντι ἥκειν ὅσον ἦν αὐτῷ στράτευμα, he sends orders to Cl. to come with all the army that he has. XEN. An. i. 2, 1. Ἔρχεται Μανδάνη τὸν Κῦρον τὸν υἱὸν ἔχουσα, Mandane comes with her son Cyrus. Id. Cyr. i. 3, 1. Καταδιώξαντες καὶ ναῦς δώδεκα λαβόντες τούς τε ἄνδρας ἀνελόμενοι ἀπέπλεον, καὶ τρόπαιον στήσαντες ἀνεχώρησαν. THUC. ii. 84. Μία ἐς Πελοπόννησον ᾤχετο πρέσβεις ἄγουσα, one (ship) was gone to Peloponnesus with ambassadors. Id. vii. 25. Δὸς τῷ ξείνῳ ταῦτα φέρων, take these and give them to the stranger. Od. xvii. 345. Βοῇ χρώμενοι, with a shout. THUC. ii. 84.

844. The participles ἔχων, ἄγων, λαβών, φέρων, and χρώμενος may often be translated by *with :* see examples in 843. (For another use of φέρων see 837.)

845. IX. That *in which* the action of the verb *consists.* *E.g.*

Τόδ' εἶπε φωνῶν, *thus he spake saying.* AESCH. Ag. 205. Ὅσ' ἡμᾶς ἀγαθὰ δέδρακας εἰρήνην ποιήσας, *what blessings you have done us in making peace !* AR. Pac. 1199. Εὖ γ' ἐποίησας ἀναμνήσας με, *you did well in reminding me.* PLAT. Phaed. 60 C.

See other examples under 150, where the peculiar force of the aorist participle in such cases, denoting the same time with the verb, is illustrated.

846. The examples show that no exact distinctions of all circumstantial participles are possible, as many express various relations at the same time. See 823.

Genitive Absolute.

847. When a circumstantial participle (832-846) belongs to a substantive which is not grammatically connected with the main construction of the sentence, both the substantive and the participle generally stand in the genitive, in the construction called the *genitive absolute. E.g.*

Οὔ τις ἐμεῦ ζῶντος σοὶ βαρείας χεῖρας ἐποίσει, *no one while I live shall lay heavy hands upon you.* Il. i. 88. Ταῦτ' ἐπράχθη Κόνωνος μὲν στρατηγοῦντος, Εὐαγόρου δὲ τοῦτο παρασχόντος καὶ τῆς δυνάμεως τὴν πλείστην παρασκευάσαντος, *these were accomplished while Conon was general, and after Evagoras had thus supplied him,* etc. ISOC. ix. 56. Φοβοῦμαι μὴ, προσδεξαμένων τῶν νῦν ἀνθεστηκότων αὐτῷ καὶ μιᾷ γνώμῃ πάντων φιλιππισάντων, εἰς τὴν Ἀττικὴν ἔλθωσιν ἀμφότεροι. DEM. xviii. 176 : see xix. 50 (pres. and perf.). Ἀφίκετο δεῦρο τὸ πλοῖον, γνόντων τῶν Κεφαλλήνων ἀντιπράττοντος τούτου . . . καταπλεῖν, *the Cephallenians having determined to sail in, although this man opposed it.* Id. xxxii. 14. Ἀθηναίων δὲ τὸ αὐτὸ τοῦτο παθόντων, διπλασίαν ἂν τὴν δύναμιν εἰκάζεσθαι (οἶμαι), i.e. *if the Athenians should ever suffer this same thing,* etc. THUC. i. 10. Ὅλης γὰρ τῆς πόλεως ἐπιτρεπομένης τῷ στρατηγῷ, μεγάλα τά τε ἀγαθὰ κατορθοῦντος αὐτοῦ καὶ τὰ κακὰ διαμαρτάνοντος εἰκὸς γίγνεσθαι. XEN. Mem. iii. 1, 3.

The genitive absolute was probably used at first to express time (present or past according to the tense), and afterwards the other circumstantial relations, cause, condition, concession, etc. The construction is most fully developed in Attic prose, especially in the Orators.[1]

[1] See Spieker in *Am. Jour. Phil.* vi. pp. 310-343, on *The Genitive Absolute in the Attic Orators.*

848. A participle sometimes stands alone in the genitive absolute, when a noun or pronoun can easily be supplied from the context, or when some general word like ἀνθρώπων or πραγμάτων is understood. *E.g.*

Οἱ δὲ πολέμιοι, προσιόντων, τέως μὲν ἡσύχαζον, but the enemy, as they (men before mentioned) came on, for a time kept quiet. XEN. An. v. 4, 16. So ἐπαγομένων αὐτούς, when they were called in (when people called them in), THUC. i. 3. Οὕτω δ᾽ ἐχόντων, εἰκὸς, κ.τ.λ., and things being so (sc. πραγμάτων), etc. XEN. An. iii. 2. 10. Οὐκ ἐξαιτούμενος, οὐκ Ἀμφικτυονικὰς δίκας ἐπαγόντων, οὐκ ἐπαγγελλομένων, οὐδαμῶς ἐγὼ προδέδωκα τὴν εἰς ὑμᾶς εὔνοιαν. DEM. xviii. 322. (Here the vague idea *they* is understood with ἐπαγόντων and ἐπαγγελλομένων.) So πολεμούντων, PLAT. Rep. 557 E.

So when the participle denotes a state of the weather·; as ὕοντος πολλῷ, when it was raining heavily, XEN. Hell. i. 1, 16. In such cases the participle is masculine, Διός being understood. See AR. Nub. 370, ὕοντα ; and Il. xii. 25, ὗε δ᾽ ἄρα Ζεύς.

849. A passive participle may stand in the genitive absolute with a clause introduced by ὅτι. If the subject of such a clause is plural, or if there are several subjects, the participle itself may be plural, by a kind of attraction. *E.g*

Σαφῶς δηλωθέντος ὅτι ἐν ταῖς ναυσὶ τῶν Ἑλλήνων τὰ πράγματα ἐγένετο, it having been clearly shown, that, etc. THUC. i. 74. Ἐσαγγελθέντων ὅτι Φοίνισσαι νῆες ἐπ᾽ αὐτοὺς πλέουσιν, it having been announced, that, etc. Id. i. 116. So XEN. Cyr. i. 4, 18 ; vi. 2, 19.

850. The genitive absolute is regularly used only when a new subject is introduced into the sentence (847) and not when the participle can be joined with any substantive already belonging to the construction. Yet this principle is sometimes violated, in order to make the participial clause more prominent and to express its relation (time, cause, etc.) with greater emphasis. *E.g.*

Διαβεβηκότος ἤδη Περικλέους, ἠγγέλθη αὐτῷ ὅτι Μέγαρα ἀφέστηκε, when Pericles had already crossed over, it was announced to him that Megara had revolted. THUC. i. 114.

So sometimes in Latin, but generally with difference in meaning : as Galliam Italiamque tentari *se absente* nolebat, CAES. Bell. Civ. i. 29.

Accusative Absolute.

851. The participle of an *impersonal* verb stands in the *accusative* absolute, in the neuter singular, with or without an infinitive, when other participles with their subjects would stand in the genitive absolute.

Such are ἐξόν, δέον, παρόν, προσῆκον, πρέπον, παρέχον, μέλον, μεταμέλον, δοκοῦν, δόξαν, and the like ; also passive participles used impersonally (as προσταχθέν, εἰρημένον, δεδογμένον) ; and such expressions as ἀδύνατον ὄν, *it being impossible*, composed of an adjective and ὄν ; also τυχόν, *perchance. E.g.*

Οἱ δ' οὐ βοηθήσαντες δέον ὑγιεῖς ἀπῆλθον; *and did those who brought no aid when it was necessary escape safe and sound?* PLAT. Alcib. i. 115 B. Ἁπλᾶς δὲ λύπας ἐξὸν (sc. φέρειν), οὐκ οἴσω διπλᾶς. EUR. I. T. 688. Παρέχον δὲ τῆς Ἀσίης πάσης ἄρχειν εὐπετέως, ἄλλο τι αἱρήσεσθε; HDT. v. 49. Εὖ δὲ παρασχόν, *and when an opportunity offers.* THUC. i. 120. Οὐ προσῆκον, *improperly.* Id. iv. 95. Συνδόξαν τῷ πατρὶ καὶ τῇ μητρὶ, γαμεῖ τὴν Κυαξάρου θυγατέρα. ΧΕΝ. Cyr. viii. 5, 28. Εἰρημένον κύριον εἶναι ὅ τι ἂν τὸ πλῆθος τῶν ξυμμάχων ψηφίσηται. THUC. v. 30. So δεδογμένον, id. i. 125 ; γεγραμμένον, v. 56 ; and προστεταγμένον, PLAT. Leg. 902 D. Καὶ ἐνθένδε πάλιν, προσταχθέν μοι ὑπὸ τοῦ δήμου Μένωνα ἄγειν εἰς Ἑλλήσποντον, ᾠχόμην. DEM. L. 12. Παρεκελεύοντό τε, ἀδύνατον ὂν ἐν νυκτὶ ἄλλῳ τῳ σημῆναι. THUC. vii. 44. Ἔγωγ', ἔφη ὁ Κῦρος, οἶμαι, ἅμα μὲν συναγορευόντων ἡμῶν, ἅμα δὲ καὶ αἰσχρὸν ὂν τὸ ἀντιλέγειν, κ.τ.λ. ΧΕΝ. Cyr. ii. 2, 20. (See 876.) Ἀντιπαρεσκευά-ζετο ἐρρωμένως, ὡς μάχης ἔτι δεῆσον, *on the ground that there would still be need of a battle.* Ib. vi. 1, 26. Οἱ δὲ τριάκοντα, ὡς ἐξὸν ἤδη αὐτοῖς τυραννεῖν ἀδεῶς, προεῖπον, κ.τ.λ., i.e. *thinking that it was now in their power*, etc. Id. Hell. ii. 4, 1.

852. Rarely the infinitive in the accusative absolute has τό ; as αἰσχρὸν ὂν τὸ ἀντιλέγειν, ΧΕΝ. Cyr. ii. 2, 20 (above) : so v. 1, 13 ; PLAT. Rep. 521 A, 604 C.

853. Even the participles of *personal* verbs sometimes stand with their nouns in the accusative absolute, in all genders and numbers, if they are preceded by ὡς or ὥσπερ (864 ; 867). *E.g.*

Διὸ καὶ τοὺς υἱεῖς οἱ πατέρες ἀπὸ τῶν πονηρῶν ἀνθρώπων εἴργουσιν, ὡς τὴν μὲν τῶν χρηστῶν ὁμιλίαν ἄσκησιν οὖσαν τῆς ἀρετῆς, τὴν δὲ τῶν πονηρῶν κατάλυσιν (sc. οὖσαν). ΧΕΝ. Mem. i. 2, 20. Φίλους κτῶνται ὡς βοηθῶν δεόμενοι, τῶν δ' ἀδελφῶν ἀμελοῦσιν, ὥσπερ ἐκ πολιτῶν μὲν γιγνομένους φίλους, ἐξ ἀδελφῶν δὲ οὐ γιγνομένους, *as if friends were made from fellow-citizens, and were not made from brothers.* Ib. ii. 3, 3. Ὡς τοὺς Βοιωτοὺς τὴν τῶν ὀνομάτων σύνθεσιν τῶν Δημοσθένους ἀγαπήσοντας. AESCHIN. iii. 142. Ὥσπερ ὑμᾶς ἀγνοοῦντας. Ib. 189. Μέγιστον οὕτω διακεῖσθαι τὰς γνώμας ὑμῶν, ὡς ἕκαστον ἑκόντα προθύμως ὅ τι ἂν δέῃ ποιήσοντα. DEM. xiv. 14.

854. The accusative absolute used personally without ὡς or ὥσπερ is very rare. It occurs chiefly with neuter participles which are regularly impersonal. *E.g.*

Προσῆκον αὐτῷ τοῦ κλήρου μέρος ὅσον περ ἐμοί. ISAE. v. 12. Ταῦτα δὲ γινόμενα, πένθεα μεγάλα τοὺς Αἰγυπτίους καταλαμβάνει. HDT. ii. 66. Ἤδη ἀμφοτέροις μὲν δοκοῦν ἀναχωρεῖν, κυρωθὲν δὲ οὐδέν, νυκτός τε ἐπιγενομένης, οἱ μὲν Μακεδόνες ἐχώρουν ἐπ' οἴκου. THUC. iv. 125. Δόξαντα δὲ ταῦτα καὶ περανθέντα τὰ στρα-

τεύματα ἀπῆλθε. XEN. Hell. iii. 2, 19. Δόξαν ἡμῖν ταῦτα occurs in
PLAT. Prot. 314 C, where we may supply ποιεῖν, or δόξαν ταῦτα may
represent ἔδοξε ταῦτα. So XEN. An. iv. 1, 13.

Adverbs connected with the Circumstantial Participle.

855. The adverbs τότε, ἤδη (τότε ἤδη), ἐνταῦθα, εἶτα, ἔπειτα,
and οὕτως are often joined to the verb of the sentence in which
the *temporal* participle stands, to give greater emphasis to the
temporal relation. *E.g.*

Ἐκέλευεν αὐτὸν συνδιαβάντα, ἔπειτα οὕτως ἀπαλλάττεσθαι, *he
commanded that, after he had joined them in crossing, he should then
retire as he proposed* XEN. An. vii. 1, 4. Πειθομένων δὲ τῶν Σαμίων
καὶ σχόντων τὴν Ζάγκλην, ἐνθαῦτα οἱ Ζαγκλαῖοι ἐβοήθεον αὐτῇ.
HDT. vi. 23. Ἀποφυγὼν δε καὶ τούτους, στρατηγὸς οὕτω Ἀθηναίων
ἀπεδέχθη, *and having escaped these also, he was then (under these circumstances) chosen general of the Athenians.* Id. vi. 104.

856. Εἶτα, ἔπειτα, and οὕτως sometimes refer in the same way
to a participle expressing *opposition* or *limitation;* in which case
they may be translated by *nevertheless, after all. E.g.*

Πάντων δ᾽ ἀτοπώτατόν ἐστι, τηλικαύτην ἀνελόντας μαρτυρίαν
οὕτως οἴεσθαι δεῖν εἰκῇ πιστεύεσθαι παρ᾽ ὑμῖν, *it is most absurd of
all that, although they have destroyed so important a piece of evidence, they
should after all think,* etc. DEM. xxviii. 5. Δεινὰ μέντ᾽ ἂν πάθοις, εἰ
Ἀθήναζε ἀφικόμενος, οὗ τῆς Ἑλλάδος πλείστη ἐστὶν ἐξουσία τοῦ
λέγειν, ἔπειτα σὺ ἐνταῦθα τούτου μόνος ἀτυχήσαις, *if, although you
are come to Athens, you should after all be the only one to fail in obtaining this.* PLAT. Gorg. 461 E.

857. Οὕτως, διὰ τοῦτο, and διὰ ταῦτα sometimes refer in the
same way to a participle denoting a cause. *E.g.*

Νομίζων ἀμείνονας καὶ κρείττους πολλῶν βαρβάρων ὑμᾶς εἶναι,
διὰ τοῦτο προσέλαβον, *because I believed,* etc. XEN. An. i. 7, 3. Ὑμᾶς
δὲ ἡμεῖς ἡγησάμενοι ἱκανοὺς γνῶναι, οὕτω παρελάβομεν. PLAT.
Lach. 178 B.

858. The adverbs ἅμα, μεταξύ, εὐθύς (Ionic ἰθέως), αὐτίκα,
ἄρτι, and ἐξαίφνης are often connected (in position and in sense)
with the *temporal* participle, although grammatically they qualify
the verb of the sentence. *E.g.*

Ἅμα προιὼν ἐπεσκοπεῖτο εἴ τι δυνατὸν εἴη τοὺς πολεμίους ἀσθε-
νεστέρους ποιεῖν, *as he advanced, he looked at the same time to see whether
it was possible,* etc. XEN. Cyr. v. 2, 22. Ἅμα καταλαβόντες προσ-
εκέατό σφι, *as soon as they had overtaken them, they pressed hard upon
them.* HDT. ix. 57. Νεκὼς μεταξὺ ὀρύσσων ἐπαύσατο, μαντηίου
ἐμποδίου γενομένου, *Necho stopped while digging (the canal),* etc. Id. ii.
158. Πολλαχοῦ δή με ἐπέσχε λέγοντα μεταξύ, *it often checked me*

while speaking. PLAT. Ap. 40 B. Ἐπιπόνῳ ἀσκήσει εὐθὺς νέοι ὄντες τὸ ἀνδρεῖον μετέρχονται, *by toilsome discipline, even while they are still young,* etc. THUC. ii. 39. Τῷ δεξιῷ κέρᾳ εὐθὺς ἀποβεβηκότι οἱ Κορίνθιοι ἐπέκειντο, *the Corinthians pressed upon the right wing, as soon as it was disembarked.* Id. iv. 43. Ἀρξάμενος εὐθὺς καθισταμένου, *beginning as soon as it (the war) broke out.* Id. i. 1. Διόνυσον λέγουσι ὡς αὐτίκα γενόμενον ἐς τὸν μηρὸν ἐνερράψατο Ζεύς, *they say of Dionysus that, as soon as he was born, Zeus sewed him into his thigh.* HDT. ii. 146. Τὴν ψυχὴν θεωροῦντα ἐξαίφνης ἀποθανόντος ἑκάστου, *viewing the soul of each one the moment that he is dead.* PLAT. Gorg. 523 E. Καὶ αὐτοῦ μεταξὺ ταῦτα λέγοντος ὁ Κλεινίας ἔτυχεν ἀποκρινάμενος. Id. Euthyd. 275 E.

859. The participle expressing *opposition, limitation,* or *concession* is often strengthened by καίπερ or καί (after a negative, by οὐδέ or μηδέ, with or without πέρ), or by καὶ ταῦτα, *and that too.* Ὅμως, *nevertheless,* may be connected with the participle (like ἅμα, etc. in 858), belonging, however, grammatically to the leading verb. *E.g.*

Ἕκτορα καὶ μεμαῶτα μάχης σχήσεσθαι ὀίω. Il. ix. 655. Ἐποικτείρω δέ νιν δύστηνον ἔμπας, καίπερ ὄντα δυσμενῆ, *although he is my enemy.* SOPH. Aj. 122. Οὐκ ἂν προδοίην, οὐδέ περ πράσσων κακῶς. EUR. Ph. 1624. Γυναικὶ πείθου μηδὲ τἀληθῆ κλύων (= μηδὲ ἢν τἀληθῆ κλύῃς). Id. Fr. 443. Πείθου γυναιξί, καίπερ οὐ στέργων ὅμως, *although you are not fond of them.* AESCH. Sept. 712. (Here ὅμως qualifies πείθου; although, as usual, it is joined with the participle for emphasis.) Ἀδικεῖς ὅτι ἄνδρα ἡμῖν τὸν σπουδαιότατον διαφθείρεις γελᾶν ἀναπείθων, καὶ ταῦτα οὕτω πολέμιον ὄντα τῷ γέλωτι. XEN. Cyr. ii. 2, 16.

860. In Homer, the two parts of καί . . . περ are generally separated by the participle, or by some emphatic word connected with it. Καί is here very often omitted, so that πέρ stands alone in the sense of *although.* Both of these uses are found also in tragedy. *E.g.*

Τὸν μὲν ἔπειτ' εἴασε, καὶ ἀχνύμενός περ ἑταίρου, κεῖσθαι. Il. viii. 125. Καὶ κρατερός περ ἐών, μενέτω τριτάτῃ ἐνὶ μοίρῃ. Il. xv. 195. Τέτλαθι, μῆτερ ἐμή, καὶ ἀνάσχεο κηδομένη περ, μή σε φίλην περ ἐοῦσαν ἐν ὀφθαλμοῖσιν ἴδωμαι θεινομένην· τότε δ' οὔ τι δυνήσομαι ἀχνύμενός περ χραισμεῖν. Il. i. 586. Κἀγώ σ' ἱκνοῦμαι, καὶ γυνή περ οὖσ' ὅμως. EUR. Or. 680. Τάφον γὰρ αὐτὴ καὶ κατασκαφὰς ἐγώ, γυνή περ οὖσα, τῷδε μηχανήσομαι. AESCH. Sept. 1037. So πέρ alone in Herodotus, as ἀσκευής περ ἐών, iii. 131.

861. Καίτοι was very seldom used like καίπερ with the participle, its only regular use being with finite verbs. *E.g.*

Οὐδέ μοι ἐμμελέως τὸ Πιττάκειον νέμεται, καίτοι σοφοῦ παρὰ

φωτὸς εἰρημένον. Simon. Fr. 5, 8 (ap. Plat. Prot. 339 C). Ἱκανά μοι νομίζω εἰρῆσθαι, καίτοι πολλά γε παραλιπών. Lys. xxxi. 34.

862. Ἅτε, and οἷα or οἷον, as, inasmuch as, are used to emphasise a participle denoting the *cause* or *ground* of an action. Here the cause assigned is stated merely on the authority of the speaker or writer. (See 864.) *E.g.*

Ὁ δὲ Κῦρος, ἅτε παῖς ὢν καὶ φιλόκαλος καὶ φιλότιμος, ἤδετο τῇ στολῇ, but *Cyrus, inasmuch as he was a child (as being a child),* etc. Xen. Cyr. i. 3, 3. Ἅτε χρόνου ἐγγινομένου συχνοῦ, as a long *time intervened.* Hdt. i. 190 : in the same chapter, οἷα δὲ ἐξεπιστά-μενοι. So ἅτε ληφθέντων, Thuc. vii. 85. Μάλα δὲ χαλεπῶς πορευό-μενοι, οἷα δὴ ἐν νυκτί τε καὶ φόβῳ ἀπιόντες, εἰς Αἰγόσθενα ἀφι-κνοῦνται, *inasmuch as they were departing by night,* etc. Xen. Hell. vi. 4, 26. Οἷον δὲ διὰ χρόνου ἀφιγμένος, ἀσμένως ᾖα ἐπὶ τὰς συνήθεις διατριβάς. Plat. Charm. 153 A.

863. In Herodotus, ὥστε is used in the sense of ἅτε ; as in i. 8, ὥστε ταῦτα νομίζων, *inasmuch as he believed this.* So vi. 136, ἦν γὰρ ἀδύνατος, ὥστε σηπομένου τοῦ μηροῦ. In Thuc. vii. 24, ὥστε (so the Mss.) γὰρ ταμιείῳ χρωμένων τῶν Ἀθηναίων τοῖς τείχεσιν, Bekker wrote ἅτε for ὥστε, and Stahl reads ὥσπερ.

864. Ὡς may be prefixed to participles denoting a *cause* or *ground* or a *purpose,* sometimes to other circumstantial participles. It shows that what is stated in the participle is stated as the thought or assertion of the subject of the leading verb, or as that of some other person prominent in the sentence, without implying that it is also the thought of the speaker or writer. *E.g.*

Οἱ μὲν διώκοντες τοὺς καθ᾽ αὑτοὺς ὡς πάντας νικῶντες, οἱ δ᾽ ἁρπάζοντες ὡς ἤδη πάντες νικῶντες, *one side pursuing those opposed to them, thinking that they were victorious over all; and the other side proceeding to plunder, thinking that they were all victorious.* Xen. An. i. 10, 4. Τὴν πρόφασιν ἐποιεῖτο ὡς Πισίδας βουλόμενος ἐκβαλεῖν, *he made his pretence as if he wished to drive out the Pisidians.* Ib. i. 2, 1. Συλλαμβάνει Κῦρον ὡς ἀποκτενῶν, *he seizes Cyrus with the (avowed) object of putting him to death.* Ib. i. 1, 3. Διαβαίνει ὡς ἀμήσων τὸν σῖτον. Hdt. vi. 28. Οἱ Ἀθηναῖοι παρεσκευάζοντο ὡς πολεμήσοντες, *the Athenians prepared with the (avowed) intention of going to war.* Thuc. ii. 7. Τὸν Περικλέα ἐν αἰτίᾳ εἶχον ὡς πείσαντα σφᾶς πολεμεῖν καὶ δι᾽ ἐκεῖνον ταῖς ξυμφοραῖς περιπεπτωκότες, *they found fault with Pericles, on the ground that he had persuaded them to engage in the war, and that through him they had become involved in the calamities.* Id. ii. 59. (Here Thucydides himself is not responsible for the statements in the participles, as he would be if ὡς were omitted.) Ἀγανακτοῦσιν ὡς μεγάλων τινῶν ἀπεστερημένοι, *they are indignant, because (as they allege) they have been deprived,* etc. Plat. Rep. 329 A. Βασιλεῖ χάριν ἴσασιν, ὡς δι᾽ ἐκεῖνον τυχοῦσαι τῆς αὐτονομίας ταύτης, i.e. *they thank him because (they believe) they have obtained this independence through him.*

Isoc. iv. 175. 'Ὡς γὰρ εἰδότων περὶ ὧν ἐπέμφθησαν ἀκούετε, *for you hear them as men who (you believe) know about what they were sent for.* Dem. xix. 5.

'Ἔλεγε θαρρεῖν ὡς καταστησομένων τούτων εἰς τὸ δέον, *he bade them take courage, on the ground that these matters were about to be settled as they should be.* Xen. An. i. 3, 8. 'Εκ δὲ τούτων εὐθὺς ἐκήρυττον ἐξιέναι πάντας Θηβαίους, ὡς τῶν τυράννων τεθνεώτων, *because (as they said) the tyrants were dead.* Id. Hell. v. 4, 9. 'Ἀπελογήσατο ὅτι οὐχ ὡς τοῖς "Ελλησι πολεμησόντων σφῶν εἴποι, *that he said what he did, not because they intended to be at war with the Greeks.* Id. An. v. 6, 3. So ὡς ἐπιβουλεύοντος Τισσαφέρνους ταῖς πόλεσι, *on the ground that T. was plotting,* ib. i. 1, 6. 'Ὡς οὐ προσοίσοντος (sc. ἐμοῦ) τὰς χεῖρας, . . . δίδασκε, *since (as you may feel sure) I will not lay hands on you, teach me.* Id. Mem. ii. 6, 32. 'Ὡς ἀναμενοῦντος καὶ οὐκ ἀποθανουμένου (sc. ἐμοῦ), οὕτω παρασκευάζου, *make your preparations in the idea that I shall remain and shall not die.* Id. Cyr. viii. 4, 27. Νῦν δέ, ὡς οὕτω ἐχόντων, στρατιὴν ὡς τάχιστα ἐκπέμπετε. Hdt. viii. 144. So ὡς βέβαιον ὄν, Thuc. i. 2 ; Dem. xviii. 207.

865. It is a mistake to suppose that ὡς implies that the participle *does not* express the idea of the speaker or writer. It implies *nothing whatever* on this point, which is determined (if at all) by the context. The question whether the clause with ὡς gives the real or the pretended opinion of the leading subject is also determined (if at all) by the context.

866. 'Ὡς may also be used before participles standing in indirect discourse with verbs of *knowing,* etc. (see 916).

867. "Ωσπερ, *as, as it were,* with the participle denotes a comparison of the action of the verb with an assumed case. The expression may generally be translated by *as if* with a verb; but the participle is not felt to be conditional in Greek, as is shown by the negative οὐ (not μή). *E.g.*

'Ὠρχοῦντο ὥσπερ ἄλλοις ἐπιδεικνύμενοι, *they danced as if they were showing off to others* (i.e. *they danced,* not *really* but *in appearance showing off*). Xen. An. v. 4, 34. Τί ἐμοὶ τοῦτο λέγεις, ὥσπερ οὐκ ἐπὶ σοὶ ὄν ὅ τι ἂν βούλῃ περὶ ἐμοῦ λέγειν ; *why do you say this to me, as if it were not in your power to say what you please about me ?* Id. Mem. ii. 6, 36. In both these cases, there is a comparison between the action stated in the verb and dancing or speaking under circumstances stated in the participial clause. The *if* in our translation is a make-shift, which we find convenient in expressing the supposed case in a conditional form, which, however, is not the Greek form. The construction is the same as when ὥσπερ takes a noun, as τὸν κίνδυνον παρελθεῖν ἐποίησεν ὥσπερ νέφος, *it caused the danger to pass by like a cloud,* Dem. xviii. 188 ; only we can translate ὥσπερ νέφος, but we could not translate ὥσπερ νέφος ὄντα.

"Ωσπερ ἤδη σαφῶς εἰδότες ὃ πρακτέον ἐστίν, οὐκ ἐθέλετ' ἀκούειν,

you are unwilling to hear, as if you already knew well what should be done.
Isoc. viii. 9. Ἀπήντων ὀλίγοι πρὸς πολλὰς μυριάδας, ὥσπερ ἐν ἀλλοτρίαις ψυχαῖς μέλλοντες κινδυνεύσειν, *as if they had been about to incur the risk with others' lives.* Id. iv. 86. Τὴν ἡμίσειαν εἴληφεν, ὥσπερ πρὸς τὸν Δία τὴν χώραν νεμόμενος, ἀλλ᾽ οὐ πρὸς τοὺς ἀνθρώπους τὰς συνθήκας ποιούμενος, *he has taken half (of the land) as if he were dividing the country with Zeus, and not making a treaty with men.* Ib. 179. Πρὸς τοῖς ἄλλοις, ὥσπερ αὐτὸς ἁπλῶς καὶ μετ᾽ εὐνοίας πάντας εἰρηκὼς τοὺς λόγους, φυλάττειν ἐμὲ ἐκέλευεν, *as if he had himself spoken,* etc. Dem. xviii. 276. Οἱ Ἕλληνες οὕτως ἠγανάκτησαν, ὥσπερ ὅλης τῆς Ἑλλάδος πεπορθημένης, *as if the whole of Greece had been laid waste.* Isoc. x. 49. See Id. iv. 53, ὥσπερ οὐ τοὺς λόγους ὄντας, and Xen. An. iii. 1, 14, v. 7, 24 ; Mem. ii. 3, 3 ; Oec. ii. 7. In Plat. Ap. 35 A, we have ὥσπερ ἀθανάτων ἐσομένων ἐὰν ὑμεῖς αὐτοὺς μὴ ἀποκτείνητε, i.e. *as if they will be (like men who will be) immortal if you do not put them to death,* where the future participle indicates that there is no condition (473).

The participle with ὥσπερ generally denotes attendant circumstances (843), sometimes manner (836).

868. Ὥσπερ, like any particle meaning *as,* can be followed by εἰ and an actual condition, the apodosis of which it represents ; as in ὥσπερ εἰ παρεστάτεις, *as (you would do) if you had lived near by,* Aesch. Ag. 1201. A participle with ὥσπερ εἰ seems to have hardly more conditional force than one with the simple ὥσπερ; as ἐμὲ ᾤχου καταλιποῦσ᾽ ὡσπερεὶ προκείμενον, *you went off and left me as if I had been laid out,* Ar. Eccl. 537. See ὥσπερ εἰ νομίζων, Dem. xxx. 7.

When a real condition is expressed, we generally have ὥσπερ ἂν εἰ, as in ὥσπερ ἂν εἴ τις αἰτῷτο, Dem. xviii. 194. But when ὥσπερ ἂν εἰ (or ὡσπερανεί) is followed by a participle or a noun without a verb, it is hardly possible that either of the verbs which were originally understood with ἂν and εἰ (227) was felt as implied in the language as we find it : indeed, it would seldom be possible to supply an actual verb. Thus in ὁμοίως διεπορεύθησαν ὡσπερανεὶ προπεμπόμενοι, *they proceeded as if they were under escort,* Isoc. iv. 148, and in ὡσπερανεὶ ἡγούμενοι, *as if they believed,* Dem. xviii. 214, ὥσπερ alone would have given essentially the same sense. So in ἐφοβήθη ὡσπερανεὶ παῖς, Plat. Gorg. 479 A, ὥσπερ παῖς, *like a child,* would probably have expressed the whole idea with less emphasis.

REMARKS ON ὥσπερ AND ὡς WITH THE PARTICIPLE.

869. 1. In Homer ὥς τε, ὡς εἰ, and ὡς εἴ τε are used in a sense approaching that of ὥσπερ in Attic Greek. Ὡς here always expresses a comparison, and when εἰ is added the form must originally have included a condition ; but, even in Homer, the force of εἰ had become so weakened that it is hardly possible that any actual verb was felt to be implied in the expression. *E.g.*

'Αχαιῶν οἶτον ἀείδεις, ὥς τέ που ἢ αὐτὸς παρεὼν ἢ ἄλλου ἀκούσας, *you sing as if you had been present yourself or had heard from another.*
Od. viii. 490. Κίρκη ἐπήιξα ὥς τε κτάμεναι μενεαίνων, *I rushed
upon Circe as if I were eager to kill her.* Od. x. 322 : so x. 295. Τὸν δ᾽
ὁ γέρων ἐὺ ἔτρεφεν, ἀμφαγαπάζομενος ὡς εἴ θ᾽ ἑὸν υἱὸν ἐόντα,
welcoming him as (if he had been) his own son. Il. xvi. 191. Πόλλ᾽
ὀλοφυρόμενοι ὡς εἰ θανατόνδε κιόντα, *as (if he were) going to death.* Il.
xxiv. 327. Τίς νύ σε τοιάδ᾽ ἔρεξεν, ὡς εἴ τι κακὸν ῥέζουσαν ἐνωπῇ,
as if you were doing any evil openly. Il. v. 373. Καπνὸς γίγνεται ἐξ
αὐτῆς, ὡς εἰ πυρὸς αἰθομένοιο, *as (if) when a fire is burning.* Il. xxii.
149 ; so Od. xix. 39.

2. In Homer ὡς εἰ may have a noun without a participle. Here
the comparative force is specially clear, as the difficulty of supplying a
verb with εἰ is specially great : see μ᾽ ἀσύφηλον ἔρεξεν ὡς εἴ τιν᾽ ἀτίμητον μετανάστην, *he made me of no account, like some dishonoured stranger,*
Il. ix. 648, xvi. 59. So ὡς εἴ τε κατὰ ῥόον, *as if down stream,* Od.
xiv. 254 ; ὥς τε περὶ ψυχῆς, *as it were for my life,* Od. ix. 423.[1]

870. The weak conditional force that appears in the Homeric ὡς
εἰ with a participle or a noun (869) helps to explain the perhaps still
weaker condition of ὥσπερ εἰ or ὥσπερ ἂν εἰ in Attic Greek (868).

871. The very few cases of ὡς with the participle in Homer do not
indicate that ὡς had yet begun to develop its later force (864). See
Od. xvi. 21, πάντα κύσεν περιφὺς, ὡς ἐκ θανάτοιο φυγόντα, *he kissed
him all over, like one escaped from death,* though we might translate *since
he felt that T. had escaped from death.* No such force is possible, however, in Il. xxiii. 430, ὡς οὐκ ἀίοντι ἐοικώς, *appearing like one who
heard not.*

872. Herodotus uses ὥστε with the participle in the sense of ἅτε,
although he has ὡς with the participle in the Attic sense (864)ː See
examples under 863.

873. Ὡς εἰ (or ὡσεί) and ὡς εἴ τε appear occasionally in Attic
poetry with nouns or adjectives in their Homeric sense. So μάτηρ
ὡσεί τις πιστά, *like some faithful mother,* SOPH. El. 234 ; πτύσας
ὡσεί τε δυσμενῆ, *spurning her as an enemy,* Ant. 653.

874. Ὥσπερ with the participle occasionally seems to have the
same force as ἅτε or οἷον; as in EUR. Hipp. 1307, ὁ δ᾽ ὥσπερ ὢν
δίκαιος οὐκ ἐφέσπετο λόγοις, *inasmuch as he was just,* etc. Or is the
meaning here *he, like a just man?*

In PLAT. Rep. 330 E, ἤτοι ὑπὸ τῆς τοῦ γήρως ἀσθενείας ἢ καὶ
ὥσπερ ἤδη ἐγγυτέρω ὢν τῶν ἐκεῖ μᾶλλόν τι καθορᾷ αὐτά, the same
force is generally given to ὥσπερ. But it may have the comparative
force : *either because of the feebleness of old age, or perhaps (feeling) like
one who is nearer the other world, he takes a more careful view of it,—a*

---

[1] See Lange, *Partikel EI,* pp. 235-243. I cannot follow Lange (p. 241), in
making the Attic ὡς with the participle the natural successor of the Homeric
ὡς εἰ with the participle.

genitive of cause with ὑπό and a participle of circumstance being
united under ἤτοι and ἤ.

Omission of ὤν.

875. The participle ὤν is sometimes omitted, leaving a predicate adjective or noun standing by itself.

1. This occurs chiefly after ἅτε, οἷα, ὡς, or καίπερ, and much
more frequently with predicate adjectives than with nouns. *E.g.*

Ἀλλὰ γιγνώσκω σαφῶς, καίπερ σκοτεινὸς (sc. ὤν), τήν γε σὴν
αὐδὴν ὅμως, *although my sight is darkened.* SOPH. O. T. 1325. Ἔφη
κηρύξειν μηδεμίαν πόλιν δέχεσθαι αὐτούς, ὡς πολεμίους (sc. ὄντας),
that no city should receive them, on the ground that they were enemies.
XEN. An. vi. 6, 9. So ὡς φίλους ἤδη, Cyr. iii. 2, 25. Αὐτὸ ἐπιτη-
δεύουσιν ὡς ἀναγκαῖον ἀλλ᾿ οὐχ ὡς ἀγαθόν (sc. ὄν), *they practise it
on the ground that it is necessary, and not on the ground that it is good.*
PLAT. Rep. 358 C. Ἦ μὴν ἔτι Ζεὺς, καίπερ αὐθάδης (sc. ὤν) φρενῶν,
ἔσται ταπεινός. AESCH. Prom. 907.

So in the genitive and accusative absolute. Ὡς ἑτοίμων δὴ χρημάτων (sc. ὄντων). XEN. An. vii. 8, 11. Ὡς ἐμοῦ μόνης πέλας (sc.
οὔσης), *since I alone am near you.* SOPH. O. C. 83. Ὡς καλὸν (sc. ὄν)
ἀγορεύεσθαι αὐτόν, *on the ground that it is good for it* (the speech) *to
be spoken.* THUC. ii. 35. Σὺ πρῶτος, ὡς οὐκ ἀναγκαῖον (sc. ὄν) τὸ
κλέπτειν, αἰτιᾷ τὸν κλέπτοντα. XEN. Cyr. v. 1, 13. Ὡς ἄρα παντὶ
δῆλον (sc. ὄν) ὅτι κοινὰ τὰ φίλων ἔσται. PLAT. Rep. 449 C.

(With nouns.) Εὐθὺς, οἷα δὴ παῖς (sc. ὤν) φύσει φιλόστοργος,
ἠσπάζετο αὐτόν, *as he was by nature an affectionate child.* XEN. Cyr. i.
3, 2. Αὐτοὺς εἰς τὴν πολιτείαν οὐ παραδεξόμεθα, ἅτε τυραννίδος
ὑμνητάς (sc. ὄντας), *since they sing the praises of tyranny.* PLAT. Rep.
568 B.

2. Without the above mentioned particles (875, 1), ὤν is
rarely omitted, and probably only in poetry. *E.g.*

Τοὺς ὄρνις, ὧν ὑφηγητῶν (sc. ὄντων) ἐγὼ κτανεῖν ἔμελλον πατέρα
τὸν ἐμόν, *the birds, by whose guidance,* etc. SOPH. O. T. 966. So 1260,
and O. C. 1588. Νοεῖς θάπτειν σφ᾿, ἀπόρρητον πόλει (sc. ὄν); *do you
think of burying him, when it is forbidden to the city?* Id. Ant. 44.

3. The adjectives ἑκών, *willing,* and ἄκων, *unwilling,* omit ὤν
like participles. *E.g.*

Ἐμοῦ μὲν οὐχ ἑκόντος, *against my will.* SOPH. Aj. 455. Ἀέκον-
τος ἐμεῖο. Il. i. 301. Νικίαν καὶ Δημοσθένην ἄκοντος τοῦ Γυλίππου
ἀπέσφαξαν. THUC. vii. 86. So AESCH. Prom. 771. Παρὰ τούτων οὐκ
ἂν ποτε λάβοις λόγον οὔτε ἑκόντων οὔτε ἀκόντων. PLAT. Theaet.
180 C.

4. A predicate adjective or noun sometimes stands without ὤν,
when it is connected by a conjunction to a participle in the same
construction. *E.g.*

Τί με οὐκ ὀλομέναν ὑβρίζεις, ἀλλ᾽ ἐπίφαντον; *why do you insult me when I am not yet dead, but am before your eyes?* Soph. Ant. 839. Λόγοις δὲ συμβὰς καὶ θεῶν ἀνώμοτος. Eur. Mcd. 737 ι so Or. 457. Λύτρα φέρων καὶ ἱκέτης (sc. ὤν) τῶν Ἀχαιῶν. Plat. Rep. 393 D. So Hdt. i. 60 (ἀπολείπουσα . . . καὶ εὐειδής), and 65 (ἀδελφιδέου μὲν . . . βασιλεύοντος δέ); Thuc. iii. 82 (οὐκ ἂν ἐχόντων πρόφασιν οὐδ᾽ ἑτοίμων). See other examples in Kühner, vol. ii. § 491.

Combinations of Circumstantial Participles.

876. As the participle in the genitive or accusative absolute denotes the same relations (*time, cause,* etc.) as the circumstantial participle in its ordinary construction (833-845), both may be used in the same sentence and be connected by conjunctions. When several participles denoting these relations occur in any sentence, those which belong to substantives already connected with the main construction agree with these in case, while those which refer to some new subjects stand with these in the genitive absolute ; any which are impersonal standing in the accusative absolute. *E.g.*

Οἱ μὲν Ἕλληνες στραφέντες παρεσκευάζοντο ὡς ταύτῃ προσιόντος (sc. τοῦ βασιλέως) καὶ δεξόμενοι, *they prepared themselves with a view to his (the King's) coming up and to receiving him.* Xen. An. i. 10, 6. Καὶ πάντα διαπραξάμενος ἐν τῇ ἐκκλησίᾳ (Κλέων), καὶ ψηφισαμένων Ἀθηναίων αὐτῷ τὸν πλοῦν, τῶν τε ἐν Πύλῳ στρατηγῶν ἕνα προσελόμενος, τὴν ἀναγωγὴν διὰ τάχους ἐποιεῖτο. Thuc. iv. 29. Ἀλκιβιάδης τοῖς Πελοποννησίοις ὕποπτος ὤν, καὶ ἀπ᾽ αὐτῶν ἀφικομένης ἐπιστολῆς ὥστ᾽ ἀποκτεῖναι, ὑποχωρεῖ παρὰ Τισσαφέρνην. Id. viii. 45. Τῆς γὰρ ἐμπορίας οὐκ οὔσης οὐδ᾽ ἐπιμιγνύντες ἀδεῶς ἀλλήλοις οὔτε κατὰ γῆν οὔτε διὰ θαλάσσης, νεμόμενοί τε τὰ ἑαυτῶν ἕκαστοι ὅσον ἀποζῆν καὶ περιουσίαν χρημάτων οὐκ ἔχοντες οὐδὲ γῆν φυτεύοντες, ἄδηλον ὂν ὁπότε τις ἐπελθὼν καὶ ἀτειχίστων ἅμα ὄντων ἄλλος ἀφαιρήσεται, τῆς τε καθ᾽ ἡμέραν ἀναγκαίου τροφῆς πανταχοῦ ἂν ἡγούμενοι ἐπικρατεῖν, οὐ χαλεπῶς ἀπανίσταντο. Id. i. 2. Here οὔσης and ἐπιμιγνύντες belong to the leading clause; νεμόμενοι, ἔχοντες, and φυτεύοντες—corresponding to ἡγούμενοι—are in the second line; ἄδηλον ὄν depends on νεμόμενοι, etc., and introduces the indirect question ὁπότε . . . ἀφαιρήσεται, which contains ἐπελθών and ἀτειχίστων ὄντων as circumstantial participles.

C. SUPPLEMENTARY PARTICIPLE.

877. The supplementary participle completes the idea expressed by a verb, by stating that to which its action relates.   It often approaches very near the use of the object infinitive. It may belong to either the subject or the object of the verb and agree with it in case. *E.g.*

Παύομέν σε λέγοντα, *we stop you from speaking*; παυόμεθα λέγοντες, *we cease speaking.*

878. The supplementary participle has two uses. In one of these it corresponds to the infinitive in indirect discourse, with its tenses representing the same tenses of the direct form; and in the other it corresponds to the object infinitive in other constructions, so far as it approaches the infinitive at all in meaning. (See 746.)

Compare παύομέν σε λέγοντα, *we stop you from speaking*, with δείκνυσί σε λέγοντα τἀληθῆ, *he shows that you speak the truth*; and compare both with κωλύομέν σε λέγειν, *we prevent you from speaking*, and φησί σε λέγειν τἀληθῆ, *he says that you speak the truth.*

I. Not in Indirect Discourse.

879. I. The participle may be used with verbs signifying *to begin, to continue, to endure, to persevere, to cease, to stop* (i.e. *cause to cease*), and *to permit* or *put up with. E.g.*

'Εγὼ δ' ἦρχον χαλεπαίνων, *and I was the first to be angry.* Il. ii. 378. Ἄρξομαι ἀπὸ τῆς ἰατρικῆς λέγων, *I will begin my speech with the art of medicine.* PLAT. Symp. 186 B. Αὕτη ἡ οἰκίη διατελέει μούνη ἐλευθέρη ἐοῦσα Περσέων, *this house continues to be the only free one among the Persians.* HDT. iii. 83. So XEN. An. iv. 3, 2; DEM. xviii. 1. Οὐκ ἀνέξομαι ζῶσα, *I shall not endure life.* EUR. Hipp. 354. Ἀνέχεσθαί τινων ἐν ταῖς ἐκκλησίας λεγόντων, *to endure certain men saying.* DEM. ix. 6. So ἀνέξει λέγοντος ἐμοῦ περὶ τούτων; *will you allow me to say?* PLAT. Rep. 613 C. With the accusative: καὶ ταῦτ' Ἰάσων παῖδας ἐξανέξεται πάσχοντας; *and will Jason endure to have his children suffer this?* EUR. Med. 74. Λιπαρέετε μένοντες, *persevere and hold your ground.* HDT. ix. 45. Οἱ δ' ἐκαρτέρουν πρὸς κῦμα λακτίζοντες. EUR. I. T. 1395. Τρῶας δ' οὐ λήξω ἐναρίζων, *I will not stop slaying Trojans.* Il. xxi. 224. Παῦσαι λέγουσα, *stop talking.* EUR. Hipp. 706; so 474. Τὴν φιλοσοφίαν παῦσον ταῦτα λέγουσαν, *stop Philosophy from talking in this style.* PLAT. Gorg. 482 A. Ἐκείνοισι ταῦτα ποιεῦσι οὐκ ἐπιτρεπτέα ἐστί, *we must not allow them to act in this way.* HDT. ix. 58. Ἡ πόλις αὐτοῖς οὐκ ἐπιτρέψει παραβαίνουσι τὸν νόμον, *the city will not put up with their transgression of the law.* ISOC. xii. 170.

880. The poets sometimes have the participle with τολμάω and τλάω, *to endure, to have courage*, and with μένω, *to await*, which usually take the infinitive. *E.g.*

Ἐτόλμα βαλλόμενος. Od. xxiv. 162. Τόλμα δ᾽ ἐρῶσα, have
the courage to love. EUR. Hipp. 476. Τλῆναί σε δρῶσαν ἂν ἐγὼ
παραινέσω, that you take courage to do what I shall advise. SOPH. El.
943. So πραθέντα τλῆναι, endured to be sold, AESCH. Ag.
1041; σπείρας ἔτλα, was bold enough to plant, Sept. 754. Ὄφρα μένοιεν
νοστήσαντα ἄνακτα, that they might await the king's return. Il. xiii.
38 (compare iv. 247, μένετε Τρῶας ἐλθέμεν;).
For the aorist participle in the last three examples, see 148.

881. II. The participle may be used with many verbs which
denote a state of the feelings, as those signifying *to repent, to be
weary, to be pleased, displeased, satisfied, angry, troubled,* or *ashamed.*
E.g.

Μετεμέλοντο τὰς σπονδὰς οὐ δεξάμενοι, *they repented that they
had not accepted the peace.* THUC. iv. 27. Τοὺς δεσμώτας μετεμέλοντο
ἀποδεδωκότες, *they repented of having returned the prisoners.* Id. v.
35. Εἰ μετεμέλησέ οἱ τὸν Ἑλλήσποντον μαστιγώσαντι, *whether he
repented that he had scourged the Hellespont.* HDT. vii. 54. Ἐάν τις μὴ
ἀποκάμνῃ ζητῶν, *provided one is not weary of seeking.* PLAT. Men. 81
D. Τῷ μέν ῥα χαῖρον νοστήσαντι, *they rejoiced in his return.* Od.
xix. 463 : so Il. xviii. 259. Τιμώμενοι χαίρουσιν, *they delight to be
honoured.* EUR. Hipp. 8. Χαίρουσιν ἐξεταζομένοις τοῖς οἰομένοις
μὲν εἶναι σοφοῖς οὖσι δ᾽ οὔ, i.e. *they delight in having them examined.*
PLAT. Ap. 33 C. In poetry χαίρω may have the accusative : τοὺς
γὰρ εὐσεβεῖς θεοὶ θνήσκοντας οὐ χαίρουσι, *for the Gods do not rejoice
in the death of the pious.* EUR. Hipp. 1340. Σὲ μὲν εὖ πράσσοντ᾽
ἐπιχαίρω. SOPH. Aj. 136. Φιλέω with nominative : φιλεῖς δὲ δρῶσ᾽
αὐτὸ σφόδρα, *and you are very fond of doing it.* AR. Pl. 645. Οὐ γάρ
τίς τοι ἀνιᾶται παρεόντι. Od. xv. 335. Τῆς Αἰολίδος χαλεπῶς
ἔφερεν ἀπεστερημένος, *he took it hard that he was deprived of Aeolis.*
XEN. Hell. iii. 2, 13. Ὑπὸ σμικροτέρων τιμώμενοι ἀγαπῶσιν, *they
are content to be honoured by smaller men.* PLAT. Rep. 475 B. Ἐλεγ-
χόμενοι ἤχθοντο, *they were vexed at being exposed.* XEN. Mem. i. 2,
47. Τοὺς φρονίμους ἀγανακτεῖν ἀποθνήσκοντας πρέπει, *it is
right to be indignant when the wise die.* PLAT. Phaed. 62 E. Ὡς μισῶ
σ᾽ ἔχων. EUR. Supp. 1108. Οὐ νεμεσῶ Ἀγαμέμνονι ὀτρύνοντι
μάχεσθαι Ἀχαιούς. Il. iv. 413. Ἀδικούμενοι μᾶλλον ὀργίζονται
ἢ βιαζόμενοι. THUC. i. 77. Τοῦτο οὐκ αἰσχύνομαι λέγων, *I say
this without shame* (see 903, 1). XEN. Cyr. v. 1, 21. Αἴδεσαι πατέρα
προλείπων. SOPH. Aj. 506. Νικώμενος λόγοισιν οὐκ ἀναίνομαι,
I am not sorry (non piget) *to be overcome by your words.* AESCH. Ag. 583.
Εὖ δράσας δέ σ᾽ οὐκ ἀναίνομαι, *I do not regret that I helped you.* EUR.
H. F. 1235. Θανοῦσα οὐκ ἀναίνομαι, *I do not regret my death* (about
to come). Id. I. A. 1503. Ἀναίνομαι τὸ γῆρας ὑμῶν εἰσορῶν, *I am
troubled at the sight,* etc. Id. Bacch. 251. (Ἀναίνομαι, *refuse,* takes
the infinitive : see AESCH. Ag. 1652.)

882. Most of the participles of 881 denote a cause or ground of
action, and might be placed under 838. (See 823.)

883. III. The participle with verbs signifying *to find, to detect,* or *to represent,* denotes an act or state in which a person or thing is found, detected, or represented. *E.g.*

Εὗρεν δ᾽ εὐρύοπα Κρονίδην ἄτερ ἥμενον ἄλλων, *she found the son of Kronos sitting apart.* Il. i. 498. So i. 27. Ὁ δὲ κῆρυξ ἀφικόμενος εὗρε τοὺς ἄνδρας διεφθαρμένους, *the herald, when he came, found the men already put to death.* THUC. ii. 6. Ἦν γὰρ εὑρεθῇ λέγων σοὶ ταῦτ᾽, ἔγωγ᾽ ἂν ἐκπεφευγοίην πάθος, *if he shall be found to tell the same story as you,* etc. SOPH. O. T. 839. Καταλαμβάνουσι τὴν Ποτίδαιαν καὶ τἆλλα ἀφεστηκότα, *they find Potidaea and the other towns in revolt.* THUC. i. 59. Κακός γ᾽ ὢν ἐς φίλους ἁλίσκεται, *he is detected in baseness.* EUR. Med. 84. Ἐὰν ἁλῷς ἔτι τοῦτο πράττων, ἀποθανεῖ, *if you are ever caught doing this again, you shall die.* PLAT. Ap. 29 C. So Rep. 389 D. Βασιλέας πεποίηκε τοὺς ἐν Ἅιδου τὸν ἀεὶ χρόνον τιμωρουμένους, *he has represented kings in Hades as suffering punishment without ceasing.* Id. Gorg. 525 D. Ἄκλητον ἐποίησεν (Ὅμηρος) ἐλθόντα τὸν Μενέλεων ἐπὶ τὴν θοίνην. Id. Symp. 174 C.

It is sometimes difficult to distinguish this use of the participle from that of indirect discourse, especially with εὑρίσκω. (See 904.)

884. IV. The participle (not in indirect discourse) with verbs signifying *to hear, learn (hear of), see,* or *perceive* denotes the act which is perceived or heard of (not, as in indirect discourse, the fact that the act occurs). Here the participle approaches very nearly the ordinary object infinitive in its use, and the tenses of the participle differ only as the same tenses of the infinitive differ in such constructions, the aorist not denoting past time (148). *E.g.*

Βαρὺ δὲ στενάχοντος ἄκουσεν, *and he heard him groaning heavily.* Od. viii. 95. Εἰ δὲ φθεγξαμένου τευ ἢ αὐδήσαντος ἄκουσεν, *but if he had heard any one call or speak.* Od. ix. 497. (The aorist participles denote the occurrence of the act, as the present denotes its progress.) Ἤκουσα δέ ποτε αὐτοῦ καὶ περὶ φίλων διαλεγομένου, *I once heard him discourse,* etc. (see 886). XEN. Mem. ii. 4, 1. Τοσαῦτα φωνήσαντος (sc. αὐτοῦ) εἰσηκούσαμεν, *so much we heard him say.* SOPH. O. C. 1645. Ἤδη πώποτέ του ἤκουσας αὐτῶν λόγον διδόντος οὐ καταγέλαστον; PLAT. Rep. 493 D. Μεγάλ᾽ ἔκλυεν αὐδήσαντος. Od. iv. 505. Οὔ πω πεπύσθην Πατρόκλοιο θανόντος, *they had not yet heard of the death of Patroclus.* Il. xvii. 377; so 427. Ὡς ἐπύθοντο τῆς Πύλου κατειλημμένης, *when they heard of the capture of Pylus.* THUC. iv. 6. (But with the accusative, in ὅτι πύθοιτο τὸ Πλημμύριον ἑαλωκός, *that he had heard that P. was captured,* vii. 31, as indirect discourse. See Classen's note on iv. 6.) Οἱ τούτους ὁρῶντες πάσχοντας, *those who see these suffer.* PLAT. Gorg. 525 C. Μή σε ἴδωμαι θεινομένην. Il. i. 587. So Od. x. 99. Τῷ κέ μ᾽ ἴδοις πρώτοισιν ἐνὶ προμάχοισιν μιγέντα, *then would you see me mingle with the foremost champions.* Od. xviii. 379; so 176, ὃν ἡρῶ γενειήσαντα ἰδέσθαι, to see with a beard. Τῷ πώποτ᾽ εἶδες ἤδη ἀγαθόν τι γενόμενον; to whom did you ever yet see any good come? Ar. Nub. 1061. Ὅταν αὐτὸν ἴδῃ ἐξαίφνης πταίσαντα πρὸς τῇ πόλει καὶ ἐκχέαντα τά τε αὑτοῦ καὶ ἑαυτόν, when he sees him suddenly come into collision with the state and fall overboard with all his belongings. Plat. Rep. 553 A. Εἰ μὴ ὤφθησαν ἐλθόντες. Thuc. iv. 73. (The aorist participle with a verb of seeing is not common in prose.) Αἰσθόμενος Λαμπροκλέα πρὸς τὴν μητέρα χαλεπαίνοντα, perceiving Lamprocles angry with his mother. Xen. Mem. ii. 2, 1. Οὐδεμίαν πώποτε ἀγέλην ᾐσθήμεθα συστᾶσαν ἐπὶ τὸν νομέα. Id. Cyr. i. 1, 2. So also αἰσθάνομαι with the genitive: ᾔσθησαί μου ἢ ψευδομαρτυροῦντος ἢ συκοφαντοῦντος; Id. Mem. iv. 4, 11. Οἶμαί σε οὐκ ἂν φάναι γενομένου ποτὲ ἐν σαυτῷ τοῦ τοιούτου αἰσθέσθαι, I think you would not say that you ever knew such a thing to happen within yourself. Plat. Rep. 440 B. Τὸν δὲ νόησεν ἑστεῶτ᾽, and he perceived him standing. Il. iv. 200.

885. The participle may be used in a similar way, having the same distinction of present and aorist (884), with περιορῶ (περιεῖδον), and sometimes with ἐφορῶ, εἰσορῶ (ἐπεῖδον, εἰσεῖδον), and even the simple ὁρῶ (εἶδον), in the sense of overlook, allow, or not to prevent. E.g.

Τοὺς ξυμμάχους οὐ περιοψόμεθα ἀδικουμένους, we shall not let our allies be wronged. Thuc. i. 86. Μείζω γιγνόμενον τὸν ἄνθρωπον περιορῶμεν, we allow the man to grow greater. Dem. ix. 29. Ὑμῖν ἐπισκήπτω . . . μὴ περιιδεῖν τὴν ἡγεμονίην αὖτις ἐς Μήδους περιελθοῦσαν, I adjure you not to see the leadership come round again into the hands of the Medes. Hdt. iii. 65. Μὴ περιίδωμεν ὑβρισθεῖσαν τὴν Λακεδαίμονα καὶ καταφρονηθεῖσαν, let us not allow Lacedaemon to be insulted and despised. Isoc. vi. 108. Περιεῖδε τὸν αὑτοῦ πατέρα καὶ ζῶντα τῶν ἀναγκαίων σπανίζοντα καὶ τελευτήσαντα οὐ τυχόντα τῶν νομίμων, he allowed his own father to remain in want (pres.) of the necessaries of life while he lived, and not to receive (aor.) a decent burial when he died. Din. ii. 8. Καὶ μή μ᾽ ἔρημον ἐκπεσοῦσαν εἰσίδῃς, do not see me driven out without a friend. Eur. Med. 712. Μή μ᾽ ἰδεῖν θανόνθ᾽ ὑπ᾽ ἀστῶν; not to see me killed by citizens. Id. Or. 746. See other examples of the aorist participle with these verbs in 148. For the infinitive, often in nearly the same sense, see 903, 6.

886. The verbs of perception included in 884 may take the participle also in indirect discourse, with the natural force of each tense preserved (see 904). With some of these verbs, the construction of the participle is generally shown by its case: thus ἀκούω and πυνθάνομαι in Attic Greek regularly take the genitive in the construction of 884, and the accusative in indirect discourse. See Ellendt, Lex. Sophocl. s.v. ἀκούω, who does not allow an exception in Soph. Ph. 615. For the less fixed usage of Homer with ἀκούω and πεύθομαι, see Schmitt in Schanz's Beiträge, p. 9. Other verbs, as ὁρῶ, have the accusative regularly in both constructions, but the context generally makes the meaning plain : see, however, EUR. Hec. 342. Αἰσθάνομαι sometimes has the genitive, as in some examples in 884, but not in indirect discourse.

887. V. With λανθάνω, *to escape the notice of*, τυγχάνω, *to happen*, and φθάνω, *to anticipate* or *get the start of*, the participle contains the leading idea of the expression and is usually translated by a verb in English. Here the aorist participle does not denote time past relatively to the leading verb (unless the latter is a present or imperfect), but coincides with it in time (144). Other tenses of the participle express their usual relations of time to the verb (147). *E.g.*

Φονέα τοῦ παιδὸς ἐλάνθανε βόσκων, *he was unconsciously supporting the slayer of his son.* HDT. i. 44. Ἦ σε λανθάνει πρὸς τοὺς φίλους στείχοντα τῶν ἐχθρῶν κακά; *are you unaware that our enemies' evils are advancing upon our friends?* SOPH. Ant. 9. Τοὺς δ᾽ ἔλαθ᾽ εἰσελθὼν Πρίαμος, *and Priam entered unnoticed by them.* Il. xxiv. 477 ; so xvii. 1. Μή σε λάθῃσιν κεῖσ᾽ ἐξορμήσασα, *lest the ship be driven thither before you know it.* Od. xii. 220. Φύλασσε δ᾽ ὅ γ᾽ εἰς ἐνιαυτὸν, μή ἑ λάθοι παριών. Od. iv. 526. Ῥᾷον ἔλαθον ἐσελθόντες, *they entered more easily without being noticed.* THUC. ii. 2. Ἐλάθομεν ἡμᾶς αὐτοὺς παίδων οὐδὲν διαφέροντες; *did we never find out that all the time we were no better than children?* PLAT. Crit. 49 B. (See 147, 2.)

Ἀρχίδαμος αὐτῷ ξένος ὢν ἐτύγχανε. THUC. ii. 13. Ὁ ἡγεμὼν ἐτύγχανε τεθνηκώς, *it happened that the guide had died (was dead).* Id. iii. 98. Ἔτυχον ἔφοροι ἕτεροι ἄρχοντες ἤδη, *there happened to be other Ephors already in office.* Id. v. 36. Ἔτυχεν ἡμῶν ἡ φυλὴ πρυτανεύουσα, *our tribe happened to hold the prytany.* PLAT. Ap. 32 B. Ἔτυχον καθήμενος ἐνταῦθα. Id. Euthyd. 272 E. Ἐν τῷ σκότῳ γὰρ τοῦτ᾽ ἔτυχον ἔνδον λαβών. AR. Eccl. 375. Ἔτυχον παραγενόμενος ἵππον ἔχων, *I came, as it happened, with a horse.* PLAT. Symp. 221 A. Ἐς Ναύπακτον, ἣν ἔτυχον ἡρηκότες νεωστί, *in Naupactus, which it happened they had lately captured.* THUC. i. 103. (See 147, 1.) Ἐὰν μή τις αὐτῇ βοηθήσας θεῶν τύχῃ, *unless some God by chance comes to its aid.* PLAT. Rep. 492 A ; so 495 B. Κἂν εἰ τύχοιεν ἐν τῷ παραχρῆμα κυκεῶνα πιόντες, *even if they should happen to drink a κυκεών on the spot.* Ib. 408 B.

Φθάνουσιν ἐπ᾽ αὐτὰ καταφεύγοντες, *they are the first to run to them.* AESCHIN. iii. 248. Αὐτοὶ φθήσονται τοῦτο δράσαντες, *they will do this for themselves first.* PLAT. Rep. 375 C. Ἔφθησαν πολλῷ τοὺς Πέρσας ἀπικόμενοι, *they arrived long before the Persians.* HDT. iv. 136. Βουλόμενοι φθῆναι τοὺς Ἀθηναίους ἀπικόμενοι ἐς τὸ ἄστυ. Id. vi. 115. Φθάνει πᾶσαν ἐπ᾽ αἶαν βλάπτουσ᾽ ἀνθρώπους, i.e. *she (Ate) harms men over the whole earth before Prayers can avail.* Il. ix. 506. Ἔφθη ὀρεξάμενος, *he hit him first.* Il. xvi. 322. Ὁππότερός κε φθῇσιν ὀρεξάμενος χρόα καλόν, *whichever shall first hit.* Il. xxiii. 805. Οὐκ ἔφθασαν πυθόμενοι τὸν πόλεμον καὶ ἧκον, *no sooner did they hear of the war than they came.* ISOC. iv. 86. Φθάνουσιν (hist. pres.) ἐπὶ τῷ ἄκρῳ γενόμενοι τοὺς πολεμίους. XEN. An. iii. 4, 49.

888. So sometimes with διαλανθάνω and the poetic λήθω. *E.g.*
Τοιαύτης πολιτείας μετέχειν, ἐν ᾗ μὴ διαλήσει χρηστὸς ὤν. Isoc.
iii. 10. Οὐδέ σε λήθω κινύμενος, *nor do I ever move without your*
knowledge. Il. x. 279.

889. Κυρέω in poetry takes the participle like τυγχάνω. *E.g.*
Τοῦτον οἶσθ᾽ εἰ ζῶν κυρεῖ; *do you know whether perchance he is*
alive? Soph. Ph. 444. Σεσωσμένος κυρεῖ. Aesch. Pers. 503.
Ταῦτ᾽ εἰρηκὼς κυρεῖ; Id. O. C. 414. Ἐχθρὸς ὤν κυρεῖ. Eur. Alc.
954. So συγκυρέω in Hdt. viii. 87, with the aorist participle (144): εἰ
συνεκύρησε ἡ τῶν Καλυνδέων παραπεσοῦσα νηῦς.

890. Συμπίπτω (chiefly in Herodotus) and συμβαίνω may take
the participle like τυγχάνω. *E.g.*
Καὶ τόδε ἕτερον συνέπεσε γενόμενον, *and this other event occurred,*
as it chanced. Hdt. ix. 101. Συνεπεπτώκεε ἔρις ἐοῦσα, *it had happened*
that there was a quarrel. Id. i. 82. Οὕτω γὰρ συμβαίνει ἅμα καὶ ἡ
τῶνδε εὐγένεια κοσμουμένη. Plat. Menex. 237 C. Πάντα ξυμβαίνει
γιγνόμενα. Id. Phil. 42 C. Ὅπου ἂν ξυμπίπτῃ ἐν τῇ ψυχῇ καλὰ
ἤθη ἐνόντα. Id. Rep. 402 D.

891. Θαμίζω, *to be wont* or *frequent*, may take the participle.
E.g.
Οὔ τι κομιζόμενός γε θάμιζεν, *he was not used to being thus cared*
for. Od. viii. 451. Οὐ θαμίζεις καταβαίνων εἰς τὸν Πειραιά, *you*
do not come down to the Piraeus very often. Plat. Rep. 328 C.

For examples of the aorist participle with the present or imperfect
of some of the above verbs (887-890), retaining its own reference to
past time, see 146.

892. As λανθάνω is active and means *to escape the notice of*, it must
have an object expressed or understood. When none is expressed,
sometimes πάντας is understood, and sometimes a reflexive referring to
the subject. Thus ἔλαθε τοῦτο ποιήσας may mean either *he did this*
without any one's knowing it (sc. πάντας), or *he did this unconsciously*
(sc. ἑαυτόν).

893. The usual construction of λανθάνω and φθάνω (and rarely
that of τυγχάνω and κυρέω) with the participle may be reversed,
these verbs appearing in the participle, and what is generally the
participle becoming the verb. *E.g.*
Ἄψ ἀπὸ τείχεος ἆλτο λαθών, *back from the wall he leaped secretly*
(for ἔλαθεν ἁλόμενος). Il. xii. 390. Ὅπως μὴ ποιῶνται ἔκπλους αὐτό-
θεν λανθάνοντες. Thuc. iii. 51. Ὅς μ᾽ ἔβαλε φθάμενος, *who took*
advantage of me and hit me. Il. v. 119. Φθάνοντες ἤδη δῃοῦμεν τὴν
ἐκείνων γῆν. Xen. Cyr. iii. 3, 18. Τὴν ἐσβολὴν φθάσαντες προκατέ-
λαβον. Thuc. iv. 127 ; so ii. 52. Ὀλίγ᾽ ἀληθῆ πολλὰ δὲ ψευδῆ
λέγει τυχών, i.e. *speaks at random.* Eur. I. A. 957. Πλησίον γὰρ ἦν
κυρῶν, *for he happened to be near.* Soph. Ph. 371. See Aesch. Supp. 805.

894. The phrase οὐκ ἂν φθάνοις (or οὐκ ἂν φθάνοιτε), *you could not be too soon*, is used with the participle as an exhortation, meaning *the sooner the better.* The first and third persons are less common in this sense. *E.g.*

Ἀποτρέχων οὐκ ἂν φθάνοις, *the sooner you run off the better.* AR. Pl. 1133. So HDT. vii. 162 ; XEN. Mem. iii. 11, 1. Οὐκ ἂν φθάνοις λέγων, *the sooner you speak the better.* PLAT. Symp. 185 E. Οὐκ ἂν φθάνοιμι (λέγων), *I might as well speak at once.* Ib. 214 E. Εἰ μὴ τιμωρήσεσθε τούτους, οὐκ ἂν φθάνοι τὸ πλῆθος τούτοις τοῖς θηρίοις δουλεῦον, *the people might as well be slaves to these beasts at once.* DEM. xxiv. 143.

895. VI. The participle, with many verbs signifying *to come* or *to go*, contains the leading idea of the expression. Such verbs are οἴχομαι, *to be gone,* ἥκω, *to have come,* ἔρχομαι, εἶμι, with the Homeric βῆ, and ἔβαν or βάν, from βαίνω. Some of these uses are very peculiar. *E.g.*

Ὤιχετ᾽ ἀποπτάμενος, *it flew away and was gone.* Il. ii. 71. Οἴχεται φεύγων ὃν εἶχες μάρτυρα, *the witness whom you had has run away.* AR. Pl. 933. Ἵν᾽ εἰδῇς οὓς φέρων ἥκω λόγους, *that you may know the words I bring with me.* EUR. Or. 1628. Ἔρχομαι ἐπιχειρῶν σοι ἐπιδείξασθαι τῆς αἰτίας τὸ εἶδος, *I am going to undertake to show you the nature of the cause.* PLAT. Phaed. 100 B. Οὐκ ἔρχομαι ἐρέων ὡς οὕτω ἢ ἄλλως πως ταῦτα ἐγένετο, *I am not going to say that these things occurred so, or in some other way* (cf. French *je vais dire*). HDT. i. 5. Ἥιε ταύτην αἰνέων διὰ παντός, *he always praised her (he went on praising her,* French *il allait la louant toujours*: see Baehr's note). Id. i. 122. Καὶ ἐγὼ μὲν ᾖα τὰς ἐφεξῆς ἐρῶν, *and I was going to speak of them in order.* PLAT. Rep. 449 A; so 562 C. Βῆ φεύγων, *he took flight.* Il. ii. 665 ; so βῆ ἀΐξασα, ii. 167. Οὓς μὴ κῆρες ἔβαν θανάτοιο φέρουσαι, Il. ii. 302 ; so xix. 279.

896. VII. Herodotus uses the participle with πειρῶμαι, *to try,* and with πολλός εἰμι or γίνομαι, πολλὸς ἔγκειμαι, and παντοῖος γίνομαι, *to be urgent;* rarely with ἐπείγομαι, *to press on. E.g.*

Οὐκ ἐπειρᾶτο ἐπιὼν ὁ Κῦρος, *Cyrus did not attempt to approach.* i. 77 ; so i. 84, vi. 50, vii. 9. Πολλὸς ἦν λισσόμενος ὁ ξεῖνος, *the stranger entreated urgently.* ix. 91. Γέλων δὲ πολλὸς ἐνέκειτο λέγων τοιάδε, *and Gelon spoke urgently as follows.* vii. 158. Τότε παντοῖοι ἐγένοντο Σκύθαι δεόμενοι Ἰώνων λῦσαι τὸν πόρον, *they begged them in every way* (lit. *they took every form in begging them*), etc. vii. 10. Ἢν μὴ ἐπειχθῇς ναυμαχίην ποιεύμενος, *if you do not press on and fight a naval battle.* viii. 68 (but just below, ἢν ἐπειχθῇς ναυμαχῆσαι).

897. The participle with πειρῶμαι, πολὺς ἔγκειμαι, and ἔγκειμαι alone, occurs occasionally in Attic Greek. So also with πάντα ποιῶ and rarely with σπουδάζω. *E.g.*

Οὐκ ἐρῶ σοι πρὶν ἂν πανταχῇ πειραθῶ σκοπῶν. PLAT. Theaet.

190 E. So ANT. Tetr. A. γ. 1. Πολὺς ἐνέκειτο λέγων. THUC. iv.
22. Ἐνέκειντο φεύγοντες. Id. ii. 81. Πάντα ποιοῦσι καὶ λέγουσι
φεύγοντες τὴν δίκην. PLAT. Euthyph. 8 C. Τὰ πλούτου καὶ δυνά-
μεων διώγματα τί καί τις ἂν ὡς ἄξια λόγου σπουδάζοι μεμφό-
μενος; *why should any one seriously censure them as if they were worth
noticing?* Id. Polit. 310 B ; so XEN. Oec. ix. 1.

898. VIII. Ἀποδείκνυμι, καθίζω, and παρασκευάζω, in the meaning
to put into a certain condition, to render, may take the participle. *E.g.*

Ἅμα καὶ τἀπιτήδεια μάλιστα ἔχοντας ἀποδείξειν καὶ τὰ σώματα
ἄριστα ἔχοντας παρασκευάσειν, (*I undertake to say) that he will at the
same time make them (show them forth) best supplied with provisions, and
cause them to have their bodies in the best condition.* XEN. Cyr. i. 6, 18.
Βλέποντ' ἀποδείξω σ' ὀξύτερον τοῦ Λυγκέως, *I will make you see
sharper than Lynceus.* AR. Pl. 210. Ἐὰν κλαίοντας αὐτοὺς καθίσω.
PLAT. Ion. 535 E. So XEN. Cyr. ii. 2, 14. See these verbs in Liddell
and Scott.

899. IX. Ἀρκέω (and ἅλις εἰμί in poetry), *to be sufficient,* and
ἱκανός, ἡδίων, κρείσσων, ἀμείνων, or βελτίων with εἰμί, are sometimes
used in a personal construction with the participle (like δῆλός εἰμι,
etc. 907), where we should expect an impersonal construction with the
infinitive. *E.g.*

Ἀρκέσω θνῄσκουσ' ἐγώ, *it will be enough for me to die.* SOPH.
Ant. 547. (We might expect ἀρκέσει ἐμὲ θνῄσκειν.) So ἀρκείτω
δεδηλωμένον, THUC. v. 9. Ἱκανὸς ἔφη αὐτὸς ἀτυχῶν εἶναι, *he
said that it was enough for himself to be in misfortune.* ISAE. ii. 7.
Κρείσσων γὰρ ἦσθα μηκέτ' ὢν ἢ ζῶν τυφλός. SOPH. O. T. 1368.
Ἡδίους ἔσεσθε ἀκούσαντες, *you will be more pleased to hear.* DEM.
xxiii. 64. So ἅλις νοσοῦσ' ἐγώ (sc. εἰμί), *it is enough for me to be
afflicted.* SOPH. O. T. 1061.

900. X. The participles βουλόμενος, ἐθέλων (poetic), ἡδόμενος,
ἄσμενος, ἀχθόμενος, προσδεχόμενος, ἐλπόμενος, ἐλδόμενος (Ionic),
and occasionally others, may agree in case with a dative which
depends on εἰμί, γίγνομαι, or some verb signifying *to come, to
appear,* or *to happen.* *E.g.*

Ὡς ἄρα τὼ Τρώεσσιν ἐελδομένοισι φανήτην, *thus then did they
appear to the delight of the Trojans.* Il. vii. 7. Ἐμοὶ δέ κεν ἀσμένῳ
εἴη, *and I should be pleased with it.* Il. xiv. 108. Ἡδομένοισιν ἡμῖν
οἱ λόγοι γεγόνασι, *we are pleased with the proposals made to us.* HDT.
ix. 46. Θέλοντι κἀμοὶ τοῦτ' ἂν ἦν. SOPH. O. T. 1356. Τῷ πλήθει
οὐ βουλομένῳ ἦν, *it was not the wish of the majority.* THUC. ii. 3 ;
so vii. 35. Προσδεχομένῳ μοι τὰ τῆς ὀργῆς ὑμῶν ἐς ἐμὲ γεγένηται,
I have been expecting the manifestations of your wrath against me. Id. ii.
60 ; so vi. 46. Ὅτῳ ὑμῶν μὴ ἀχθομένῳ εἴη. XEN. Cyr. iv. 5, 21.
Ἂν βουλομένοις ἀκούειν ᾖ τουτοισί, μνημονεύσομαι, *if these shall
want to hear it.* DEM. xviii. 11. Ὅρα, εἴ σοι βουλομένῳ (sc. ἐστὶν)
ἃ λέγω. PLAT. Rep. 358 D.

See also τούτων πεπειραμένοις ἄν τι γένοιτο καὶ ὑμῖν, Thuc. v. 111 ; and ἀσμένῳ δέ σοι ἡ ποικιλείμων νὺξ ἀποκρύψει φάος, *you will be glad when spangled-robed night shall hide the light,* Aesch. Prom. 23. Compare Tac. Agric. 18 : Quibus bellum *volentibus* erat.

901. XI. In a similar way, the dative of any participle may be used with certain impersonal expressions which take the dative, especially those signifying *it is fitting, good, pleasant, profitable,* or their opposites, and those implying *fear* or *confidence. E.g.*

Εἰ τόδ' αὐτῷ φίλον κεκλημένῳ (sc. ἐστίν), *if it pleases him to be thus called.* Aesch. Ag. 161. Οὐκ ἄξιον τούτοις πολλάκις χρῆσθαι συμβούλοις, οἷς οὐδὲ ἅπαξ ἐλυσιτέλησε πειθομένοις (sc. ὑμῖν), *whom it did not profit you to obey even once.* Lys. xxv. 27. Φρονεῖν ὡς δεινὸν ἔνθα μὴ τέλη λύῃ φρονοῦντι, *where it does not profit one to be wise.* Soph. O. T. 316. Ἐπήρετο τὸν θεὸν εἰ λῷον καὶ ἄμεινον εἴη τῇ Σπάρτῃ πειθομένῃ οἷς οὗτος ἔθηκε νόμοις, *whether it was better for Sparta to obey.* Xen. Rep. Lac. viii. 5. Ἀντιπαραβάλλοντι (sc. ἐμοὶ) τὰ ἐμαυτοῦ πάθη πρὸς τὰ ἐκείνων οὐκ ἂν ἀηδὲς εἴη, *it would not be unpleasant for me to compare,* etc. Plat. Ap. 41 B. Αἲ δοκοῦσι κάλλισται τῶν ἐπιστημῶν καὶ ἐμοὶ πρέποι ἂν μάλιστα ἐπιμελομένῳ, *those which seem to be the noblest of the sciences, and which it would be most fitting for me to study.* Xen. Oec. iv. 1. Τοῦτο καὶ πρέπειν ἐμοὶ δοκεῖ καὶ ἄξιον κινδυνεῦσαι οἰομένῳ οὕτως ἔχειν (*i.e.* πρέπει μοι οἰομένῳ τοῦτο οὕτως ἔχειν), *it seems fitting and worth the risk for me to believe that this is so.* Plat. Phaed. 114 D. Ὧι μή 'στι δρῶντι τάρβος, οὐκ ἔπος φοβεῖ, *one who has no dread of a deed, a word does not frighten.* Soph. O. T. 296.

So εἴ μοι ξυνείη φέροντι μοῖρα τὰν εὔσεπτον ἁγνείαν, *may it continue to be my fate to bear,* etc. Id. O. T. 863.

With the expressions of 901 the infinitive is more common (903, 7).

Omission of ὤν.

902. Occasionally the participle ὤν is omitted in the constructions of the supplementary participle that have been enumerated (879-901). *E.g.*

Καταλαμβάνομεν Φιλίππου παρόντας πρέσβεις, καὶ τοὺς μὲν ἡμετέρους φίλους ἐν φόβῳ (sc. ὄντας) τοὺς δ' ἐκείνου θρασεῖς. Dem. xviii. 211. Ἀλλ' οὐ περιόψεταί μ' ὁ θεῖος ἄνιππον (sc. ὄντα), *but my uncle will not let me go without a horse.* Ar. Nub. 124. Εἰ δέ τι τυγχάνει ἀηδές (sc. ὄν). Plat. Gorg. 502 B. Τυγχάνει ἡμῶν ἕκαστος οὐκ αὐτάρκης (sc. ὤν). Id. Rep. 369 B.

Infinitive with Verbs which may also have the Supplementary Participle.

903. Some verbs which take the supplementary participle allow also the infinitive in a similar construction, but with some difference in the meaning or at least in the point of view.

1. Αἰσχύνομαι and αἰδοῦμαι with the participle (881) mean *I am ashamed of doing* (something which I am doing or have done); with the infinitive, *I am ashamed to do* (something which I have not yet done). *E.g.*

Τοῦτο μὲν οὐκ αἰσχύνομαι λέγων· τὸ δ᾽ "Ἐὰν μένητε παρ᾽ ἐμοὶ ἀποδώσω" αἰσχυνοίμην ἂν λέγειν, this (something just said) *I am not ashamed of saying; but I should be ashamed to say the following*, etc. XEN. Cyr. v. 1, 21.   Αἰσχύνομαι ὑμῖν εἰπεῖν τἀληθῆ, *I am ashamed to tell you the truth* (but still I must tell it). PLAT. Ap. 22 B.   Αἰδοῦνται τοὺς παρόντας ἀπολείπειν, i.e. *they are ashamed to leave them* (and do not). XEN. Symp. viii. 35.   But αἰδέσαι πατέρα προλείπων, *be ashamed of leaving your father* (as you threaten to do), SOPH. Aj. 506. A comparison of the last example with PLAT. Ap. 22 B (above) shows that the choice of the infinitive or participle may depend on the point of view of the speaker in a special case.   In Aj. 506, the threat is viewed as the inception of the act.

2. Ἀνέχομαι, ὑπομένω, τλάω, and τολμῶ with the participle (879 ; 880) mean *to endure* something now going on or already done ; with the infinitive, *to have the courage* or *to venture* to do something not yet done. *E.g.*

Καταμείναντες ἀνέσχοντο τὸν ἐπιόντα ἐπὶ τὴν χώρην δέξασθαι, *they remained and had the courage to receive the invader of their country.* HDT. vii. 139.   (Cf. οὐκ ἀνέξομαι ζῶσα under 879.)   So ὑπομείναντα τὰ πάντα πάσχειν, *taking courage to suffer everything.* PLAT. Leg. 869 C.   (Cf. μὴ ὑπομένειν Ξέρξην ἐπιόντα, *not to await the coming of Xerxes*, i.e. *not to wait to see his coming*, HDT. vii. 120.)   Ἔτλα οὐράνιον φῶς ἀλλάξαι. SOPH. Ant. 944.   Τόλμησόν ποτε ὀρθῶς φρονεῖν. AESCH. Prom. 999.

Ἀνέχομαι with the infinitive, and τλάω and τολμῶ with the participle, are rare.

3. Ἀποκάμνω τοῦτο ποιῶν (881) is *I am weary of doing this;* ἀποκάμνω τοῦτο ποιεῖν is *I cease to do this through weariness. E.g.*

Μήτε ταῦτα φοβούμενος ἀποκάμῃς σαυτὸν σῶσαι, *do not, through fear of this, despair of saving yourself.* PLAT. Crit. 45 B.   (Cf. οὐκ ἀποκάμνεις μηχανώμενος, *you are not tired of contriving*, XEN. Mem. ii. 6, 35.)

4. Ἄρχομαι (Homeric ἄρχω) with the participle (879) means *to be first in something, to begin with something*, or *to be at the*

beginning (not *at the end*); with the infinitive, *to begin to do something. E.g.*

Ἤρξαντο τὰ μακρὰ τείχη Ἀθηναῖοι οἰκοδομεῖν, *the Athenians began to build the long walls.* THUC. i. 107. Δεῖ ἐμὲ ἐπιδεικνύναι, ὡς οὔτ᾽ ἤρξατο λέγειν τὰ βέλτιστα οὔτε νῦν διατελεῖ πράττων τὰ συμφέροντα τῷ δήμῳ. AESCHIN. iii. 50.

5. Παύω with the participle (879) means *to stop* what is going on ; with the infinitive, *to prevent* a future act. *E.g.*

Ἐμ᾽ ἔπαυσας μάχεσθαι, *you prevented me from fighting.* Il. xi. 442. (But ἔμ᾽ ἔπαυσας μαχόμενον would be *you stopped me while fighting.*) Ῥαψῳδοὺς ἔπαυσε ἀγωνίζεσθαι. HDT. v. 67.

6. Περιορῶ and the other verbs signifying *to overlook* or *see* (in the sense of *permit*) with the participle (885) mean *to see an act done without interfering to stop it;* with the less frequent infinitive, *to permit* an act *to be done without interfering to prevent it.* Strictly speaking, the infinitive here expresses time future to that of the verb, while the time of the participle coincides with that of the verb. Still, both forms may sometimes be used to express practically the same sense, and may even refer to the same event, though the point of view is different. *E.g.*

Περιδεῖν αὐτὸν ἐν τῇ σκευῇ πάσῃ ἀεῖσαι, *to let him sing in full dress.* HDT. i. 24. Θάλασσαν πνεύματά φασι οὐ περιόψεσθαι φύσι τῇ ἑωυτῆς χρᾶσθαι, *they say that the winds will not permit the sea to follow its own nature.* Id. vii. 16. Τοὺς γὰρ Ἀθηναίους ἤλπιζεν ἴσως ἂν ἐπεξελθεῖν καὶ τὴν γῆν οὐκ ἂν περιδεῖν τμηθῆναι, *for he hoped that the Athenians would perhaps come forth and not let their land be ravaged.* THUC. ii. 20. But in ii. 18 he has said, προσδεχόμενος τοὺς Ἀθηναίους τῆς γῆς ἔτι ἀκεραίου οὔσης ἐνδώσειν τι καὶ κατοκνήσειν περιδεῖν αὐτὴν τμηθεῖσαν, ἀνεῖχεν, *that they would be unwilling to see it* (the land) *ravaged* (referring to the same thing with περιδεῖν τμηθῆναι, *to let it be ravaged*, in 20) ; and again in 20, οἱ Ἀχαρνῆς οὐ περιόψεσθαι ἐδόκουν τὰ σφέτερα διαφθαρέντα, *it did not seem likely that the Acharnians would see their property destroyed.*

7. The impersonal expressions of 901 take the infinitive more frequently than the participle, the distinction being similar to that in the last case (6). *E.g.*

Οὐ τοῦτο πρῶτον ἠρώτα πότερον λῷον εἴη αὐτῷ πορεύεσθαι ἢ μένειν, *whether it was better for him to go or stay.* XEN. An. iii. 1, 7. But in XEN. Vect. vi. 2 we have ἐπερέσθαι τοὺς θεοὺς εἰ λῷον καὶ ἄμεινον εἴη ἂν τῇ πόλει οὕτω κατασκευαζομένῃ, *whether it would be better for the state, supposing it to be thus constituted ;* the difference between this and *better for the state to be thus constituted* (οὕτω κατασκευάζεσθαι) being practically very slight.

8. It is more than doubtful whether λανθάνω, τυγχάνω, and φθάνω (887) ever have the infinitive in classic Greek. The passages

formerly cited for this are now generally emended, or the readings are
doubted : thus, in PLAT. Rep. 333 E, λαθεῖν ἐμποιῆσαι must be for
λαθεῖν ἐμποιήσας (Schneider), and in AR. Eq. 935, φθαίηs ἐλθεῖν,
and Nub. 1384, οὐκ ἔφθης φράσαι, Meineke reads ἐλθών and φράσας.
See Classen on THUC. iii. 82, ὁ φθάσας θαρσῆσαι (?).

II. PARTICIPLE IN INDIRECT DISCOURSE.

904. The participle is used with verbs signifying *to see,*
to hear or *learn, to perceive, to know, to be ignorant of, to re-*
member, to forget, to show, to appear, to prove, to acknowledge,
and with ἀγγέλλω, *to announce,* in a sense approaching that
of the infinitive in indirect discourse. Here each tense of
the participle represents the corresponding tense of the
indicative or optative. (See 687.)

The participle may belong to either the subject or the
object of these verbs, and agree with it in case. *E.g.*

Μέμνημαι αὐτὸν τοῦτο ποιήσαντα, *I remember that he did this*
(ἐποίησεν) ; μέμνημαι τοῦτο ποιήσας, *I remember that I did this*
(ἐποίησα). Οἶδε τούτους εὖ πράξοντας, *he knows that they will*
prosper ; οἶδε αὐτὸς εὖ πράξων, *he knows that he himself will prosper.*
Εἴ κ᾽ αὐτὸν γνώω νημερτέα πάντ᾽ ἐνέποντα, *if I shall find that he*
tells all without fault. Od. xvii. 549. Ὁρῶ δέ μ᾽ ἔργον δεινὸν ἐξειργα-
σμένην, *and I see that I have done a terrible deed.* SOPH. Tr. 706.
Ἡμεῖς ἀδύνατοι ὁρῶμεν ὄντες τῇ οἰκείᾳ μόνον δυνάμει περιγενέσθαι,
we see that we are unable, etc. (ἀδύνατοί ἐσμεν). THUC. i. 32. Ἤκουσε
Κῦρον ἐν Κιλικίᾳ ὄντα, *he heard that Cyrus was in Cilicia.* XEN. An.
i. 4, 5. Περὶ τῆς χώρας, ὅτι ἤκουον δῃουμένην, *because they heard*
that it was suffering from ravages. Ib. v. 5, 7. Ὅταν κλύῃ τινὸς
ἥξοντ᾽ Ὀρέστην, *when she hears from any one that Orestes is coming.*
SOPH. El. 293. Πυθόμενοι Ἀρταξέρξην νεωστὶ τεθνηκότα, *learning*
that Artaxerxes had recently died. THUC. iv. 50 ; so HDT. vi. 23. Ἐπεὶ
πρὸς ἀνδρὸς ᾔσθετ᾽ ἠδικημένη. EUR. Med. 26. Ἤισθοντο τοὺς
μετ᾽ Ἀριστέως ἐπιπαριόντας. THUC. i. 61. Διὰ τὴν Ἰλίου ἅλωσιν
εὑρίσκουσι ἐοῦσαν τὴν ἀρχὴν τῆς ἔχθρης (see 883). HDT. i. 5.
Ἐπειδὰν γνῶσιν ἀπιστούμενοι, *when they find out that they are*
distrusted. XEN. Cyr. vii. 2, 17. Ἤιδεσαν Σωκράτην αὐταρκέστατα
ζῶντα. Id. Mem. i. 2, 14. Ἐν πολυτρόποις γὰρ ξυμφοραῖς ἐπίστανται τραφέντες. THUC. ii. 44. Διαβεβλημένος οὐ μανθάνεις.
HDT. iii. 1. Ἐννοοῦμαι φαῦλος οὖσα. EUR. Hipp. 435. Ἐννοήσας
γένος ἐπιεικὲς ἀθλίως διατιθέμενον. PLAT. Criti. 121 B. Τίς οὕτως
εὐήθης ἐστὶν ὑμῶν ὅστις ἀγνοεῖ τὸν ἐκεῖθεν πόλεμον δεῦρο ἥξοντα ;
DEM. i. 15. Μέμνημαι Κριτίᾳ τῷδε ξυνόντα σε (i.e. ξυνῆσθα).
PLAT. Charm. 156 A. Μεμνήμεθ᾽ ἐς κίνδυνον ἐλθόντες μέγαν (i.e.
ἤλθομεν). EUR. Hec. 244. Ἐπιλελήσμεθ᾽ ἡδέως γέροντες ὄντες. Id.

Bacch. 188. Ἐπιδείξω δὲ τοῦτον οὐ μόνον ὡμολογηκότα εἶναι τὸν Μιλύαν ἐλεύθερον (with six other participles, perfect, aorist, and present). DEM. xxix. 5. Ὁ πόλεμος οὗτος δηλώσει μείζων γεγενημένος αὐτῶν (i.e. μείζων γεγένηται). THUC. i. 21. Εἰ φανήσεται ταῦθ' ὡμολογηκὼς, παρά τε τοῦ Δημοφῶντος τὰς τιμὰς εἰληφὼς, αὐτός τε . . . ἀπογράψας, οἰκῶν τε τὴν οἰκίαν, κ.τ.λ. DEM. xxvii. 16. Εὐθὺς ἐλεγχθήσεται γελοῖος ὤν. XEN. Mem. i. 7, 2. Οὕτως ὁμολογουμένη οὖσα δούλη καὶ ἅπαντα τὸν χρόνον αἰσχρῶς βιοῦσα, when it was thus admitted that she was a slave and was all the time living a life of disgrace. ISAE. vi. 49. Εἰ μὴ ἐξήγγειλε προσιὸν τὸ στράτευμα, had he not reported that the enemy was advancing. XEN. Hell. vii. 5, 10. Ἀπηγγέλθη Φίλιππος ὑμῖν Ἡραῖον τεῖχος πολιορκῶν, it was reported to you that he was besieging, etc. DEM. iii. 4.

Compare the examples of ὁρῶ, ἀκούω, and similar verbs here given with those of the same verbs under 884, in which the participle is not in indirect discourse.

See other examples of the participle in indirect discourse under 687, where examples of the participle with ἄν may be found (see also 213-216).

905. When one of these verbs has for its object an accusative of the reflexive pronoun referring to its subject, the participle generally agrees with the reflexive. Thus we may have either δείξω ἐμαυτὸν τοῦτο πεποιηκότα, *I shall show that I have done this*, or δείξω τοῦτο πεποιηκώς.

906. The participle of an *impersonal* verb in this construction stands alone in the neuter singular. The following includes both the personal and the impersonal construction:—

Πειράσομαι δεῖξαι καὶ μετὸν τῆς πόλεως ἡμῖν καὶ πεπονθότα ἐμαυτὸν οὐχὶ προσήκοντα, *I shall try to show not only that we have rights in the city, but also that I have suffered*, etc. DEM. lvii. 1. (The direct discourse is μέτεστι τῆς πόλεως ἡμῖν, καὶ πέπονθα αὐτός. Compare 876.)

907. The participle is used in the same way in a personal construction with δῆλός εἰμι and φανερός εἰμι, in preference to an impersonal expression. So with ἐπάϊστος γίνομαι in Herodotus. *E.g.*

Δῆλός τ' ἦν οἰόμενος, κ.τ.λ., *it was evident that he thought*, etc. XEN. An. ii. 5, 27. (This is equivalent to δῆλον ἦν ὅτι οἴοιτο. See 899; 912.) Ἀπικόμενοι μὲν φανεροί εἰσι ἐς Ὄασιν πόλιν, *it is evident that they came to the city Oasis*. HDT. iii. 26. Ὡς ἐπάϊστος ἐγένετο τοῦτο ἐργασμένος, *when it became known (heard of) that he had done this*. Id. ii. 119.

Similar is the participle with φανερὸν ποιῶ; as φανερὸν πᾶσιν ἐποίησαν οὐκ ἰδίᾳ πολεμοῦντες, *they made it evident to all that they were not fighting for themselves*. LYCURG. 50.

908. When σύνοιδα and συγγιγνώσκω have a dative of the *reflexive* referring to the subject, a participle may stand either in the dative agreeing with the reflexive, or in the nom inative agreeing with the subject; as σύνοιδα ἐμαυτῷ ἠδικημένῳ (or ἠδικημένος), *I am conscious to myself that I have been wronged.* *E.g.*

Ἐγὼ οὔτε μέγα οὔτε σμικρὸν ξύνοιδα ἐμαυτῷ σοφὸς ὤν. PLAT. Ap. 21 B. Ἐμαυτῷ ξυνῄδειν οὐδὲν ἐπισταμένῳ. Ib. 22 D.

909. When the participle of indirect discourse belongs to an infinitive depending on a verb with an object dative to which the participle refers, the participle stands in the dative. *E.g.*

Συμβέβηκε τοῖς προεστηκόσι καὶ τἄλλα πλὴν ἑαυτοὺς οἰομένοις πωλεῖν πρώτους ἑαυτοὺς πεπρακόσιν αἰσθέσθαι, *it has been the lot of those who were in authority and who thought they were selling everything except themselves, to find that they have sold themselves first.* DEM. xviii. 46.

910. Some verbs which regularly have the infinitive or ὅτι and ὡς in indirect discourse occasionally take the participle. *E.g.*

Νόμιζε ἄνδρα ἀγαθὸν ἀποκτείνων, *think that you are putting to death a good man.* XEN. An. vi. 6, 24. Ἀνεβήσετο ἐρεοῦσα φίλον πόσιν ἔνδον ἐόντα. Od. xxiii. 1. Θανόντ' Ὀρέστην νῦν τε καὶ πάλαι λέγω. SOPH. El. 676. See O. C. 1579; EUR. Hel. 1076. Οὐ Τρωὰς γυνὴ τεκοῦσα κομπάσειεν ἄν ποτε, i.e. *none could boast that she was the mother (of such children),* ἔτεκον being the direct form. EUR. Tro. 477. Μετὸν ἄν ποτε λέγοιτο. PLAT. Phil. 22 E. Σμέρδιν μηκέτι ὑμῖν ἐόντα λογίζεσθε. HDT. iii. 65. Οὐ γὰρ εὐτυχῶν ἀρνήσομαι, *for I will not deny that I am happy.* EUR. Alc. 1158. So ἀρνεῖ κατακτάς; Id. Or. 1581.

911. The participle ὤν is sometimes omitted in indirect discourse. *E.g.*

Σὺ δὲ σῶς ἴσθι (sc. ὤν), *but know that you are safe.* SOPH. O. C. 1210. Εἰδὼς εὐτρεπεῖς ὑμᾶς (sc. ὄντας). DEM. iv. 18; so iv. 41. Ἄγγελλε πασῶν ἀθλιωτάτην ἐμέ (sc. οὖσαν). EUR. Hec. 423.

912. The verbs included in 904 may also be followed by a clause with ὅτι or ὡς in indirect discourse. When δῆλόν ἐστιν and φανερόν ἐστιν are used impersonally, they regularly take ὅτι or ὡς. *E.g.*

Ἤισθετο ὅτι τὸ Μένωνος στράτευμα ἤδη ἐν Κιλικίᾳ ἦν. XEN. An. i. 2, 21. Αἰσθάνεσθε ὡς ἀθύμως ἦλθον. Ib. iii. 1, 40. Ἀκούοντες ὅτι οὗτος πολίζει τὸ χωρίον. Ib. vi. 6, 4. Τοσοῦτόν γ' οἶδα κἀμαυτὴν, ὅτι ἀλγῶ. SOPH. El. 332. Ταῦτα ἴσασιν ὅτι φύσει τε καὶ τύχῃ γίγνεται. PLAT. Prot. 323 D. Δῆλον (sc. ἐστίν) ὅτι οὕτως ἔχει. XEN. An. i. 3, 9. Φανερὸν δὲ ὅτι οὔτ' ἂν Θραξὶν οὔτε Σκύθαις ἐθέλοιεν ἂν διαγωνίζεσθαι. Id. Mem. iii. 9, 2. Τοῦτο φανερὸν, ὡς . . . λέγομεν. PLAT. Soph. 237 D.

913. Verbs signifying *to remember* or *to know* may have ὅτε, *when*, and the indicative, to emphasise the temporal relation. *E.g.*

Εἰ γὰρ μέμνησαι ὅτ᾽ ἐγώ σοι ἀπεκρινάμην, *for if you remember (the time) when I answered you*, etc. PLAT. Men. 79 D. Οἶσθ᾽ ὅτε χρυσέοις ἐφάνη σὺν ὅπλοις. EUR. Hec. 112. So Il. xv. 18. (See 519, end.)

Infinitive with the Verbs of § 904.

914. Many of the verbs which regularly have the participle in indirect discourse (904) may also take the infinitive in nearly or quite the same sense.

1. Ἀκούω, πυνθάνομαι, and αἰσθάνομαι, which have the participle both in indirect discourse (904) and in the other construction (884-886), sometimes take the infinitive in indirect discourse, in a sense differing little, if at all, from that of the participle. *E.g.*

Ἀκούω δὲ καὶ ἄλλα ἔθνη πολλὰ τοιαῦτα εἶναι, *I hear that there are also many other such nations.* XEN. An. ii. 5, 13. (Πολλὰ τοιαῦτα ὄντα would apparently mean the same.) So Mem. iv. 2, 4. Ἀκούω αὐτὸν ἐρεῖν, *I hear that he will say.* DEM. xix. 202. (Compare SOPH. El. 293, under 904.) Πυνθανόμενος τὸν Θουκυδίδην κτῆσίν τε ἔχειν καὶ ἀπ᾽ αὐτοῦ δύνασθαι ἐν τοῖς πρώτοις. THUC. iv. 105. So DEM. xix. 201. Αἰσθανόμενος αὐτοὺς μέγα παρὰ βασιλεῖ Δαρείῳ δύνασθαι. THUC. vi. 59.

2. Ὁρῶ has the participle in both constructions (904; 886), but the infinitive (of indirect discourse) only in THUC. viii. 60 (according to Kühner, § 484, 2): ἑώρων οὐκέτι ἄνευ ναυμαχίας οἷόν τε εἶναι ἐς τὴν Χίον βοηθῆσαι, where Krüger brackets εἶναι.

3. Ἀγγέλλω may have the infinitive in indirect discourse, in place of the regular participle (904). *E.g.*

Ὁ Ἀσσύριος εἰς τὴν χώραν αὐτοῦ ἐμβαλεῖν ἀγγέλλεται, *is reported to have invaded his country.* XEN. Cyr. v. 3, 30.

4. Ὁμολογῶ, *to admit* or *grant*, is but rarely followed by the participle (904), and generally takes the infinitive of indirect discourse. *E.g.*

Ὁμολογεῖται πρὸς πάντων κράτιστος δὴ γενέσθαι θεραπεύειν (τοὺς φίλους). XEN. An. i. 9, 20. (See 136.)

5. Φαίνομαι, *to appear*, which generally takes the participle in indirect discourse (904), sometimes has the infinitive. The distinction generally holds that φαίνεται σοφὸς ὤν means *he is manifestly wise*, while φαίνεται σοφὸς εἶναι means *he seems to be wise;* but in some cases the two constructions cannot be distinguished in sense. *E.g.*

Tῇ φωνῇ σαφῶς κλαίειν ἐφαίνετο, *by his voice he seemed plainly to be weeping* (but he really was not). XEN. Symp. i. 15. Compare καί ὐφι εὔνοος ἐφαίνετο ἐών, *and he was plainly well disposed towards them*, HDT. vii. 173. But see also AESCH. Ag. 593, πλαγκτὸς οὖσ᾽ ἐφαινόμην, *I appeared to be crazed*, said by Clytemnestra of herself, after she was shown to have been right. Τοῦτό μοι θειότατον φαίνεται γενέσθαι, *this seems to me to have been a most wonderful event.* HDT. vii. 137.

915. Other verbs of this class (904) may be used in a peculiar sense, in which they have the infinitive not in indirect discourse. Others, again, allow both constructions of the infinitive; while γιγνώσκω and εὑρίσκω have the infinitive in three different senses.

1. Μανθάνω, μέμνημαι, and ἐπιλάνθανομαι, in the sense of *learn, remember,* and *forget to do* anything, take the ordinary object infinitive. *E.g.*

Ἐπεὶ μάθον ἔμμεναι ἐσθλὸς αἰεὶ καὶ πρώτοισι μετὰ Τρώεσσι μάχεσθαι, *since I learned to be brave,* etc. Il. vi. 444. Τοὺς προδότας γὰρ μισεῖν ἔμαθον. AESCH. Prom. 1068. So XEN. An. iii. 2, 25. Μεμνήσθω ἀνὴρ ἀγαθὸς εἶναι, *let him remember to be a brave man.* Ib. iii. 2, 39 (with ὤν it would mean *let him remember that he is a brave man*). Μεμνήσονται δεῦρο ἀποπέμπειν. Id. Cyr. viii. 6, 6. Ἐπελαθόμην τοὺς καδίσκους ἐκφέρειν, *I forgot to bring out the urns.* AR. Vesp. 853. Ὀλίγου ἐπελαθόμεθ᾽ εἰπεῖν. PLAT. Rep. 563 B.

2. (*a*) Οἶδα and ἐπίσταμαι, which regularly have the participle in indirect discourse, take the ordinary infinitive in the sense of *know how* to do anything. *E.g.*

Μὴ· ψεύδε᾽, ἐπιστάμενος σάφα εἰπεῖν, *do not be false, when you know how to speak truly.* Il. iv. 404. Οἶδ᾽ ἐπὶ δεξιά, οἶδ᾽ ἐπ᾽ ἀριστερὰ νωμῆσαι βῶν. Il. vii. 238. Προβάλλεσθαι δ᾽ ἢ βλέπειν ἐναντίον οὔτ᾽ οἶδεν οὔτ᾽ ἐθέλει. DEM. iv. 40. So EUR. Hipp. 729, Med. 664. Εἴκειν δ᾽ οὐκ ἐπίσταται κακοῖς, *she knows not how to yield to troubles.* SOPH. Ant. 472; so Aj. 666; EUR. Hipp. 996.

(*b*) But these verbs in the sense *to know* or *to believe* sometimes take the infinitive (like the participle) in indirect discourse. This is rare in prose, except with ἐπίσταμαι, *to believe,* in Herodotus. *E.g.*

Ἴσθι τὰ σκλήρ᾽ ἄγαν φρονήματα πίπτειν μάλιστα, *know that too stubborn spirits are most apt to fall* (like πίπτοντα). SOPH. Ant. 473. (Οἶδα with the participle follows in 477.) Εὖ νῦν ἐπίστω τῶνδέ μ᾽ αἰσχύνην ἔχειν. Id. El. 616; so O. T. 690, Ant. 1092; AESCH. Pers. 337. Εὖ ἴσθι τοῦτον ἰσχυρῶς ἀνιᾶσθαι. XEN. Cyr. viii. 3, 44; so viii. 7, 12. Ἐπιστάμενοι τότε τελευτῆσαι, *believing that he* (Cyrus) *had then perished.* HDT. i. 122; so iii. 66, 134, and 140, vii. 172. See ἴσθι μήποτ᾽ ἂν τυχεῖν, SOPH. Ph. 1329; and τόδ᾽ ἴσθι, μὴ γῆμαι, EUR. Med. 593; cf. I. A. 1005.

3. Γιγνώσκω, besides its construction with the participle in indirect discourse (904), has three uses with the infinitive :—

(a) In the meaning *to decide* or *judge*, with the infinitive in indirect discourse ; as τὸ δ᾽ ἴσον ἀνταπόδοτε, γνόντες τοῦτον εἶναι τὸν καιρόν, *making up your minds that this is that time*, etc., THUC. i. 43 ; so HDT. ix. 71 ; XEN. An. i. 9, 17.

(b) In the meaning *to determine* or *resolve*, with the ordinary object infinitive ; as Ἀλυάττεα ἔγνωσαν δοῦναι τὴν θυγατέρα Ἀστυάγεϊ, *they decided that Alyattes should give his daughter to Astyages*, HDT. i. 74 ; so XEN. Hell. iv. 6, 9, ἔγνω διώκειν, and iii. 1, 12 ; ISOC. xvii. 16.

(c) Occasionally in the meaning *to learn* (ἔγνων), with the object infinitive, like μανθάνω and μέμνημαι (1) ; as ἵνα γνῷ τρέφειν τὴν γλῶσσαν ἡσυχωτέραν, *that he may learn to keep his tongue more quiet*, SOPH. Ant. 1089.

4. Δείκνυμι and other verbs signifying *to show*, besides the participle in indirect discourse (904), may take an object infinitive in the sense *to show how* to do anything. *E.g.*

Ἀπέδειξαν οἱ ἡγεμόνες λαμβάνειν τὰ ἐπιτήδεια, *the guides instructed them to take provisions*. XEN. An. ii. 3, 14. Διαιτητήρια τοῖς ἀνθρώποις ἐπεδείκνυον τοῦ μὲν θέρους ἔχειν ψυχεινά, τοῦ δὲ χειμῶνος ἀλεεινά, *I taught the men to keep their dwellings cool in summer and warm in winter*. Id. Oec. ix. 4.

5. Δηλῶ sometimes has the infinitive (like the regular participle, 904) in indirect discourse ; and sometimes in the sense of *command* (*make known*) it has the ordinary object infinitive. *E.g.*

Δηλοῖς γὰρ αὐτὸν σωρὸν ἥκειν χρημάτων ἔχοντα, *for you indicate that he has come with a heap of money*. AR. Pl. 269. Δηλοῦντες προσίεσθαι τὰ κεκηρυγμένα, *showing that they accepted the terms which were announced*. THUC. iv. 38. Κηρύγματι ἐδήλου τοὺς ἐλευθερίας δεομένους ὡς πρὸς σύμμαχον αὐτὸν παρεῖναι, *he proclaimed that those who wanted freedom should come to him as to an ally*. XEN. Ag. i. 33.

6. (a) Εὑρίσκω, which has two constructions with the participle (883 ; 904), occasionally has the infinitive in indirect discourse. *E.g.*

Εὕρισκε πρῆγμά οἱ εἶναι ἐλαύνειν ἐπὶ τὰς Σάρδις, *he found that he must* (πρῆγμά μοι ἐστι, *mihi opus est*) *march to Sardes*. HDT. i. 79 : so i. 125, vii. 12. See PLAT. Leg. 699 B.

(b) The middle may take the ordinary object infinitive in the sense of *discover how* to do anything. *E.g.*

Οὐδεὶς λύπας εὕρετο παύειν, *no one ever found out how to stop pains*. EUR. Med. 195.

(c) The middle may also have the infinitive in the sense of *procure by asking. E.g.*

Παρὰ δὲ σφίσι εὕροντο παρὰ Παυσανίεω ἑστάναι Ποτιδαιητέων τοὺς παρέοντας, *they gained (the favour) from Pausanias that those who were present from Potidaea should stand next to themselves.* HDT. ix. 28.

Ὡς with the Participle in Indirect Discourse.

916. The participle in indirect discourse may be preceded by ὡς, which implies that the thought of the participle is expressed as that of the leading subject, or as that of some person prominent in the sentence. (See 864.) When this is already implied in the context, as it often is, ὡς adds only emphasis to the expression. Thus ἴσθι ταῦτα οὕτως ἔχοντα means *know that this is so;* but ἴσθι ὡς ταῦτα ἔχοντα means *know that (as you may assume) this is so,* i.e. *be assured that this is so. E.g.*

Ὡς μηδὲν εἰδότ' ἴσθι μ' ὧν ἀνιστορεῖς, *understand (that you must look upon) me as knowing nothing of what you seek.* SOPH. Ph. 253. Ὡς μηκέτ' ὄντα κεῖνον ἐν φάει νόει, *think of him as no longer living.* Ib. 415. Ὡς ταῦτ' ἐπίστω δρώμεν', οὐ μέλλοντ' ἔτι, *understand that (as you may assume) these things are going on, etc.* Ib. 567. Ταῦτα γῇ τῇδ' ὡς τελῶν ἐφαίνετο. Id. O. C. 630. Καὶ τοῦτο ἐπιστάσθω Κροῖσος, ὡς ὕστερον ἁλοὺς τῆς πεπρωμένης, *and let Croesus understand this, that he was captured later than it was fated for him to be.* HDT. i. 91. Ὡς μὴ 'μπολήσων ἴσθι τὴν ἐμὴν φρένα, *be assured that you will not buy me off from my determination.* SOPH. Ant. 1063. Δηλοῖς δ' ὥς τι σημανῶν νέον, *you show that you have something new in your mind to disclose.* Ib. 242. Δῆλός ἐστιν ὥς τι δρασείων κακόν, *it is very plain that he wishes to do some harm.* Id. Aj. 326. Δῆλος ἦν Κῦρος ὡς σπεύδων, *Cyrus showed that he was in haste.* XEN. An. i. 5, 9. Δῆλοι ἔσεσθε ὡς ὀργιζόμενοι τοῖς πεπραγμένοις, *you will show that you are angry.* LYS. xii. 90. Πατέρα τὸν σὺν ἀγγελῶν ὡς οὐκ ἔτ' ὄντα, *(he comes) to announce that your father is no more.* SOPH. O. T. 956. (In vs. 959, the messenger himself says εὖ ἴσθ' ἐκεῖνον θανάσιμον βεβηκότα.) The force of ὡς here can seldom be well expressed in English.

917. In place of the participle with ὡς in indirect discourse, we may have a circumstantial participle with ὡς in the genitive or accusative absolute, followed by a verb to which the participle would naturally be the object. *E.g.*

Ὡς ὧδ' ἐχόντων τῶνδ' ἐπίστασθαί σε χρή, *you must understand that this is so ;* lit. *believing this to be so, you must understand (it is so).* SOPH. Aj. 281 ; see Schneidewin's note. By an entirely different construction this comes practically to the same meaning as ὡς ὧδ' ἔχοντα τάδ' ἐπίστασθαί σε χρή. Ὡς τοίνυν ὄντων τῶνδέ σοι μαθεῖν πάρα, *in the belief that this is so, you may learn it*, i.e. *you may learn that this is so.* AESCH. Prom. 760. Ὡς πολέμου ὄντος παρ᾽ ὑμῶν ἀπαγγελῶ; *shall I announce from you that there is war?* lit. *shall I make a report from you on the assumption that there is war?* XEN. An. ii. 1, 21. Ὡς πάνυ μοι δοκοῦν, οὕτως ἴσθι, *know that I think so very decidedly;* lit. *in the belief that this seems so to me, understand accordingly.* Id. Mem. iv. 2, 30. Ὡς ἐμοῦ ἀγωνιουμένου, οὕτως γίγνωσκε, *know that I shall contend.* Id. Cyr. ii. 3, 15.

918. Ὡς with the participle in the genitive or accusative absolute, used as in 917, may depend on verbs or expressions which do not take the participle without ὡς in indirect discourse. *E.g.*

Ὡς οὐκέτ᾽ ὄντων τῶν τέκνων φρόντιζε δή, *think of it, that your children are no longer living,* lit. *knowing that your children are no longer living, think of it.* EUR. Med. 1311. Ὡς καὶ τῶν στρατιωτῶν καὶ τῶν ἡγεμόνων ὑμῖν μὴ μεμπτῶν γεγενημένων, οὕτω τὴν γνώμην ἔχετε, *be of this mind, that both your soldiers and their leaders have been free from blame.* THUC. vii. 15. Ὡς ἐμοῦ οὖν ἰόντος ὅπῃ ἂν καὶ ὑμεῖς, οὕτω τὴν γνώμην ἔχετε, *be of this opinion, that I shall go wherever you do.* XEN. An. i. 3, 6. Ὡς τοίνυν μὴ ἀκουσομένων, οὕτως διανοεῖσθε, *make up your minds then that we shall not hear;* lit. *knowing then that we shall not hear, so make up your minds.* PLAT. Rep. 327 C. Ἐν τούτοις μὲν ὡς διδακτοῦ οὔσης τῆς ἀρετῆς λέγει, *here he speaks of virtue as a thing that can be taught.* Id. Men. 95 E. Ὑποθέμενοι ὡς τούτου οὕτως ἔχοντος, προΐωμεν, *having premised that this is so, let us proceed.* Id. Rep. 437 A. Διανοηθέντες ὡς ἰόντων ἁπάντων ἀεὶ καὶ ῥεόντων, *thinking of all things as moving and in flux.* Id. Crat. 439 C. Οὕτω σκοπῶμεν, ὡς τάχ᾽ ἄν, εἰ τύχοι, καὶ τούτων κἀκείνων συμβάντων, *let us look at the case, feeling that both this and that might perhaps happen if it should so chance;* lit. *with the idea that both this and that might perhaps happen if it should so chance, let us look at it in this light.* DEM. xxiii. 58. Ὡς δέον αὐτὸν τεθνάναι. Id. xxi. 70.

919. Verbs of *saying* and *thinking* which do not take the participle in indirect discourse sometimes have the participle (in the accusative or nominative) with ὡς, which in some cases approaches very near indirect discourse, and in others is more like a circumstantial participle. *E.g.*

Φροντίζεθ᾽ ὡς τούτοις τε καὶ σοφωτέροις ἄλλοισι τούτων πλείοσιν μαχούμενοι, *consider that you will have to fight with these*, etc. SOPH. El. 1370 (cf. EUR. Med. 1311, quoted in 918). Λέγουσιν ἡμᾶς ὡς ὀλωλότας, *they speak of us as lost.* AESCH. Ag. 672. Ὡς οὐκ ὑπείξων οὐδὲ πιστεύσων λέγεις; *do you speak with a resolution not to yield or to believe?* SOPH. O. T. 625. Καμβύσης Ἴωνας μὲν καὶ Αἰολέας ὡς δούλους πατρωίους ἐόντας ἐνόμιζε, *he thought of Ionians and Aeolians as his father's slaves.* HDT. ii. 1. Ὡς στρατηγήσοντα ἐμὲ μηδεὶς λεγέτω, *let no one speak of me as the one who is to be general.* XEN. An. i. 3, 15. Ἐδόκει πολλὰ ἤδη ἀληθεῦσαι τοιαῦτα, τὰ ὄντα

τε ὡς ὄντα καὶ τὰ μὴ ὄντα ὡς οὐκ ὄντα, *he was thought to have
already reported truly many such occurrences, (reporting) what was real as
real, and what was unreal as unreal.* Ib. iv, 4, 15. Ὅταν ὡς πετό-
μενοι ἐν τῷ ὕπνῳ διανοῶνται, *when in their sleep they fancy themselves
flying.* PLAT. Theaet. 158 B.

CHAPTER VII.

VERBAL ADJECTIVES IN -τέος AND -τέον.

920. The verbal in -τέος is used in both a personal and an impersonal construction.

921. In the personal construction, the verbal is always passive in sense. It expresses *necessity* (like the Latin participle in -*dus*) and agrees with its subject in case. This construction is, of course, restricted to transitive verbs. *E.g.*

ʼΩφελητέα σοι ἡ πόλις ἐστί, *the city must be benefited by you.* XEN. Mem. iii. 6, 3. Ἄλλας (ναῦς) ἐκ τῶν ξυμμάχων μεταπεμπτέας εἶναι (ἔφη), *he said that others must be sent for.* THUC. vi. 25. Οὐ γὰρ πρὸ τῆς ἀληθείας τιμητέος ἀνήρ, *a man must not be honoured before the truth.* PLAT. Rep. 595 C. Ὁμοίας φησὶν ἁπάσας εἶναι καὶ τιμητέας ἐξ ἴσου. Ib. 561 C. Φράζοντες ὡς οὔ σφι περιοπτέη ἐστὶ ἡ Ἑλλὰς ἀπολλυμένη. HDT. vii. 168.

922. The substantive denoting the agent is here in the dative. Εἰμί is often omitted.

923. In the impersonal construction (which is the more common), the verbal is in the neuter of the nominative singular (sometimes plural), with ἐστί expressed or understood. The expression is equivalent to δεῖ, (*one*) *must*, with the infinitive active or middle of the verb to which the verbal belongs.

This construction is practically active in sense, and allows transitive verbals to have an object in the same case which would follow their verbs. The agent is generally expressed by the dative, sometimes by the accusative. *E.g.*

Ταῦτα ἡμῖν (or ἡμᾶς) ποιητέον ἐστί, we must do this, equivalent to ταῦτα ἡμᾶς δεῖ ποιῆσαι. Οἰστέον τάδε, we must bear these things. EUR. Or. 769. Πειστέον τάδε (sc. σοί), you must obey in this (— δεῖ πείθεσθαι). SOPH. Ph. 994. 'Απαλλακτέον αὐτοῦ (τοῦ σώματος), καὶ αὐτῇ τῇ ψυχῇ θεατέον αὐτὰ τὰ πράγματα (= δεῖ ἀπαλλάττεσθαι αὐτοῦ, καὶ τῇ ψυχῇ θεᾶσθαι τὰ πράγματα), we must free ourselves from it (the body), and with the soul itself we must contemplate things themselves. PLAT. Phaed. 66 E.   Φημὶ δὴ διχῇ βοηθητέον εἶναι τοῖς πράγμασιν ὑμῖν, I say that you must give assistance in two ways. DEM. i. 17.   Τί ἂν αὐτῷ ποιητέον εἴη; what would he be obliged to do? XEN. Mem. i. 7, 2.   'Εψηφίσαντο πολεμητέα εἶναι (= δεῖν πολεμεῖν), they voted that they must go to war. THUC. i. 88.   Τὴν χώραν, ἐξ ἧς αὐτοῖς ὁρμωμένοις πολεμητέα ἦν. Id. vi. 50.   Οὔτε μισθοφορητέον ἄλλους ἢ τοὺς στρατευομένους, οὔτε μεθεκτέον τῶν πραγμάτων πλείοσιν ἢ πεντακισχιλίοις. Id. viii. 65.   (Here both the accusative and the dative of the agent are found : see 926.)   'Ημῖν δὲ ξύμμαχοι ἀγαθοὶ, οὓς οὐ παραδοτέα τοῖς 'Αθηναίοις ἐστὶν, οὐδὲ δίκαις καὶ λόγοις διακριτέα μὴ λόγῳ καὶ (ἡμᾶς) αὐτοὺς βλαπτομένους, ἀλλὰ τιμωρητέα ἐν τάχει καὶ παντὶ σθένει (= οὓς οὐ δεῖ ἡμᾶς παραδοῦναι, κ.τ.λ.). Id. i. 86.   'Ιτέον ἂν εἴη θεασομένους (sc. ἡμᾶς), it would be best for us to go and see her. XEN. Mem. iii. 11, 1. Οὐδενὶ τρόπῳ φαμὲν ἑκόντας ἀδικητέον εἶναι. PLAT. Crit. 49 A. 'Ατὰρ οὐ γυναικῶν οὐδέποτ' ἔσθ' ἡττητέα ἡμῖν (= οὐ γυναικῶν δεῖ ἡττᾶσθαι), but we must never be beaten by women. AR. Lys. 450. So SOPH. Ant. 678.

It will be seen that this construction admits verbals of both transitive and intransitive verbs.

924. The Latin participle in -dus is used in the same personal construction as the Greek verbal in -τέος ; as epistula scribenda est, ἐπιστόλη γραπτέα ἐστίν, a letter must be written.

The impersonal construction is found in Latin, but generally only with verbs which do not take an object accusative, as Eundum est tibi (ἰτέον ἐστί σοι),—Moriendum est omnibus,—Bello utendum est nobis (τῷ πολέμῳ χρηστέον ἐστὶν ἡμῖν), we must employ war. See Madvig's Latin Grammar, § 421.

Occasionally the earlier Latin uses even the object accusative, like the Greek ; as Aeternas quoniam poenas in morte timendum est, LUCR. i. 112.

925. A sentence sometimes begins with an impersonal verbal in -τέον and is continued with an infinitive, the latter depending on δεῖ implied in the verbal. E.g.

Πανταχοῦ ποιητέον ἃ ἂν κελεύῃ ἡ πόλις καὶ ἡ πατρὶς, ἢ πείθειν αὐτήν. PLAT. Crit. 51 B.

926. The dative and the accusative of the agent are both allowed with the verbal in -τέον (or -τέα); although the equivalent δεῖ with the infinitive has only the accusative.   Thus we can say τοῦτο ἡμῖν ποιητέον or τοῦτο ἡμᾶς ποιητέον, but only τοῦτο ἡμᾶς δεῖ ποιεῖν.

APPENDIX.

I.

THE RELATION OF THE OPTATIVE TO THE SUBJUNCTIVE AND OTHER MOODS.

In the chapter on the general view of the moods, no attempt was made to assign to either the subjunctive or the optative a single "fundamental idea" from which all the uses of the mood could be derived, except so far as the idea of futurity was shown to belong essentially to the subjunctive in all its most primitive uses. It would be impossible to include under one fundamental idea all the actual uses of any mood in Greek, except the imperative; for even the indicative is used to express unfulfilled conditions, unaccomplished wishes, and unattained purposes, none of which can be brought under the ideas of "declaration" or "absolute assertion" commonly attributed to this mood. Again, it is not to be expected that the true fundamental idea of any mood should include all its uses in a developed language; for the fortunes of language often depend on causes which are quite independent of the original essence of the forms employed, and which seldom can be referred to invariable laws of thought. The same idea can be expressed in two cognate languages by different moods : as *he would have seen* is εἶδεν ἄν in Greek and *vidisset* in Latin, while in Sanskrit it would be expressed by a past augmented future equivalent to the Greek ἔμελλεν ὄψεσθαι (see § 428). Even within the Greek itself, we have *if he were wise* expressed by εἰ σοφὸς εἴη in Homer and by εἰ σοφὸς ἦν in Attic; and in Homer, both οὐκ ἄν ἔγνως and οὐκ ἄν γνοίης can mean *you would not have discerned*, while the latter can mean also *you would not discern* (in the same future sense as in Attic).

One doctrine of the original meaning of the Greek subjunctive and optative has gained such general approval of late, that it is entitled to special consideration. This teaches that the fundamental idea of the subjunctive is *will*, and that of the optative is *wish*. In the subjunctive, the idea of will appears especially in exhortations and prohibitions and in expressions of purpose. It can also be used to explain the subjunctive in protasis, by understanding ἔλθῃ in ἢν ἔλθῃ to mean originally *let him go, suppose him to go* (in some case). But before we can decide that will is the fundamental idea of the subjunctive, or even that it is a necessary and essential part of the idea of this mood, we must ask, first, whether it is essential to those uses of the subjunctive which we have a right on other grounds to call the most primitive; and, secondly, whether there is any other idea equally essential and equally primitive, from which the idea of will could have been evolved more simply and naturally than this could have been evolved from the idea of will.

The subjunctive nowhere bears more distinct marks of primitive simplicity than when it appears in Homer as a simple future; as in οὐ γάρ πω τοίους ἴδον ἀνέρας οὐδὲ ἴδωμαι, *for never yet have I seen such men, nor shall I ever see them*, Il. i. 262, and in καί ποτέ τις εἴπῃσιν, *and some one will say*, Il. vi. 459, followed by ὥς ποτέ τις ἐρέει in vs. 462, referring to the same thing. See other examples in § 284. In this sense it is negatived by οὐ, like an indicative; and it may be modified by κέ or ἄν, like the future indicative in Homer, and thus acquire a potential sense (see §§ 285 and 286). It is seldom that any modal form (except a plain indicative) is found so free from associations which might affect its meaning and conceal its original character. It has, moreover, its exact counterpart in Sanskrit in the Vedic subjunctive, which is negatived by nâ, the equivalent of οὐ.[1] This simple subjunctive has no element of will. It expresses what the speaker regrets as readily as what he is resolved to do. Thus in both the examples above quoted, the subjunctive expresses an act which is decidedly contrary to the speaker's will and wish. This subjunctive and the future indicative run parallel in all their constructions, and the former expresses will only so far as the latter does. The only character that is beyond question in this subjunctive is its reference to future time, and if we were left to this use alone, we should have no hesitation in designating the subjunctive as a form expressing futurity like a future tense. As this use cannot be deduced from the subjunctive as an expression of will, let us see whether the opposite process, the evolution from the simple future meaning of the uses in which will appears, is any easier and does any less violence to the principles of the language.

The use of the subjunctive which strikes every one as coming next in simplicity to the Homeric construction just described is seen in exhortations, like ἴωμεν, *let us go*, and (in its negative form) in prohibitions, like μὴ ἴωμεν, *let us not go*, μὴ εἴπητε τοῦτο, *do not say this*. This use of the subjunctive is found also in Sanskrit, and its negative is there generally (though not always) mâ', the equivalent of μή. It thus appears that the marked distinction which is seen in the early Greek between ἴωμεν, *we shall go*, and ἴωμεν, *let us go*, in both positive

[1] See Delbrück, *Syntaktische Forschungen*, i. (*Conjunctiv und Optativ*), pp. 23-25.

and negative forms, was probably inherited from an ancestral language, so that we need not seek for the development of this distinction within the Greek itself. It is obvious that the future element is equally strong in both expressions, while the hortatory subjunctive also expresses will. Now it is much more natural to suppose that a future form expressing exhortation or prohibition originated in a form expressing mere futurity, than that the merely future form originated in the exhortation or prohibition. We cannot derive οὐκ ἴδωμαι, *I shall not see*, from μὴ ἴδωμαι, *let me not see*. But it is by no means impossible that, in some language which was a common ancestor of Greek, Latin, and Sanskrit, subjunctive (i.e. originally future) forms came to be used to express both commands and prohibitions; that, when these imperative expressions became distinguished from the subjunctive in its ordinary future sense, they adopted the negative (the ancestor of *mâ'* and μή) which was used with similar imperative forms, though this use of the negative might not at first be very rigid ; and that thus μή ἴωμεν, in the sense *let us not go*, became established in early Greek as opposed to οὐκ ἴωμεν, *we shall not go*. In Sanskrit, however, the use of *mâ'* in such cases was less fixed, and here *na'* (the equivalent of οὐ) is sometimes found with the subjunctive in prohibitions.[1] This last is what we should have if in χειρὶ δ' οὐ ψαύσεις ποτέ, *you shall never touch me*, Eur. Med. 1320, we could substitute an Homeric subjunctive (e.g. ψαύσῃς) for the future indicative. The cases of μή with the future in prohibitions given in § 70, like μὴ βουλήσεσθε εἰδέναι, *do not wish to know*, Dem. xxiii. 117, are too few to be of much weight in the discussion ; but they seem to show an abortive tendency to establish the future indicative with μή by the side of the subjunctive in prohibitions. What the future could do in an imperative sense is shown by examples like πάντως δὲ τοῦτο δράσεις, *but by all means do this*, Ar. Nub. 1352, and others quoted in § 69 ; but the natural negative here was οὐ, not μή, as in οὐ ψαύσεις above.

If the origin of the interrogative subjunctive in appeals (§ 287) and of its negative μή has been correctly explained in §§ 288 and 291, this is merely an interrogative form of the subjunctive in exhortations and prohibitions, and calls for no special discussion here. The origin of the use of the subjunctive with οὐ μή is still too uncertain to give this construction much weight in determining the essential character of the subjunctive. If the view of this construction which is advocated in this work (see Appendix II.) is accepted, the form is an offshoot of the prohibitory subjunctive. If it is thought to be an original construction, expressing a strong denial or prohibition by its own force, the subjunctive appears in its original future force. Whatever theory we may have of the origin of this subjunctive, the form is interchangeable in use with the future indicative.

In dependent sentences, the subjunctive is used in two constructions, —in so-called final clauses, and in conditional sentences. In negative

---

[1] See Delbrück, *Conjunctiv und Optativ*, p. 112.

final constructions with μή, the subjunctive was originally prohibitive (§§ 262, 307); in positive clauses with the final particles, it expresses something aimed at, that is, an object of will. But here, as in independent sentences, to derive the more complex from the more simple is far more natural than the reverse. Further, in all final constructions the future indicative may be used in the same sense as the subjunctive; this could hardly be done if the subjunctive contained an essential element of will which is wanting in the future. Again, the subjunctive is very common in final constructions after past tenses, where the optative is the regular form (318); it cannot be supposed that the idea of will is present in such final clauses when they have the subjunctive (as they generally do in Thucydides) and is absent when they have the optative (as is more common in Xenophon). In conditional sentences, although we may explain the subjunctive as originally hortatory, ἤν ἔλθῃ meaning *let him come (we will suppose)*, it is more natural to refer this use to the primitive use of the subjunctive as a simple future, εἴ κεν ἔλθῃ (or εἰ ἔλθῃ), *in case he shall come*, making a supposition of a future event of which the Homeric ἔλθῃ, *he will come*, might make a statement (see §§ 11 and 398). We thus avoid the necessity of explaining the indicative and the subjunctive in protasis on different principles. As each of the various tenses of the indicative with εἰ expresses a supposition in the time which it naturally denotes (§ 3, c), so the subjunctive is a natural form to express a future supposition. Thus, as εἰ γενήσεται τοῦτο supposes what γενήσεται τοῦτο states, εἰ γένηται τοῦτο naturally supposes what (in the older language) γένηται τοῦτο, *this will happen*, states. As the former cannot be explained by the idea of will, it seems unnecessary and illogical to introduce this idea to account for the latter. What has been said of ordinary conditional sentences applies also to relative conditions.

The only use of the subjunctive in conditions which cannot be derived from the simple future meaning is that in general suppositions; but the undeveloped state of this construction in Homer and other considerations make it highly probable, if not certain, that this is a use of the subjunctive which grew up within the Greek language itself at a comparatively late period, and that it is not one of the primitive uses of the mood. (See §§ 11, b, 400, 401.)

It is certain that no trace of the subjunctive as a mood of will can be seen in its actual use in conditional sentences. Thus ἤν τὴν πόλιν ἔλωσι could always be said as properly by the friends as by the enemies of a city, by the besieged as well as by the besiegers. In Il. iii. 71, ὁππότερός κε νικήσῃ, spoken by Priam, is, as an expression, perfectly neutral as regards the hope or desire of victory. It may be said with truth, that the primitive meaning of a verbal form is apt to be weakened, or even to disappear, in actual use. But is it logical to assume a lost meaning to account for an expression, when the meaning which remains accounts for it satisfactorily without external help? When we find ἤν ἔλωσι τὴν πόλιν actually expressing a mere future supposition, with no idea of will, in all periods of the language, and

when we find ἕλωσι meaning *they will capture* in the earliest period
that we know, why should we assume an original idea of will (which
was afterwards lost) in ἢν ἕλωσι to account for its actual meaning ?
The view of the conditional sentence here adopted is confirmed by
paratactic conditions like the following : θύσεις δὲ τὴν παῖδ᾽ · ἔνθα
τίνας εὐχὰς ἐρεῖς; EUR. I. A. 1185, where θύσεις makes a supposition,
supposing you shall sacrifice the girl, which would generally be expressed
by εἰ θύσεις or ἢν θύσῃς : so ἀδικεῖ τις ἑκών and ἐξήμαρτέ τις ἄκων,
both expressing suppositions, DEM. xviii. 274.[1]

On these grounds we may feel justified in regarding the subjunctive
as originally and essentially a form for expressing future time, which
the Greek inherited, with its subdivision into an absolute future
negatived by οὐ and a hortatory future negatived by μή, and used
in independent sentences.

The name *optative* mood (ἔγκλισις εὐκτική), which was invented
by grammarians long after the usages of the language were settled,
designated the mood by the only use which it then had in independent
sentences without ἄν, that of *wishing*. It is evident that this name
in itself is no ground for assuming that wishing was the primitive
function, or even an essential function, of the optative, any more than
the name of the subjunctive (ἔγκλισις ὑποτακτική) would lead us to
assume dependence as an original or necessary characteristic of that
mood. We have already mentioned the theory that the optative is
the mood of *wish*, as the complement of that which makes the subjunctive the mood of *will*. This theory finds no support in the
potential use of the optative with or without κέ or ἄν, which is the
only independent use of the optative except in wishes and exhortations.
Surely ἀπόλοιτο ἄν, *he would perish*, can never have been developed
from ἀπόλοιτο, *may he perish*, for the former is no more likely to be
said by one who wishes the death of a person than by one who fears
it, and there is nothing in the addition of ἄν or κέ which can reasonably
be supposed to change a form, which in itself expresses wish, to a neutral
form or even to one expressing what is feared. The fundamental distinction in negative sentences between μὴ ἀπόλοιτο and οὐκ ἄν ἀπόλοιτο (or οὐκ ἀπόλοιτο) is still more significant. Nor can any support
for the theory be found in dependent final constructions or in indirect
discourse. No one would see a distinction of will and wish in ἴδῃ and
ἴδοι in ἔρχεται ἵνα ἴδῃ τοῦτο and ἦλθεν ἵνα ἴδοι τοῦτο, or in φοβοῦμαι
μὴ ἔλθῃ and ἐφοβήθην μὴ ἔλθοι,—not to speak of ἦλθεν ἵνα ἴδοι
τοῦτο and ἦλθεν ἵνα ἴδῃ τοῦτο. Still less would any one dream of
looking for wish in the optative in εἶπεν ὅτι ἔλθοι, *he said that he
had come*, or in ἤρετο εἴ τις εἴη σοφώτερος. In all these dependent
constructions, the optative is only the representative of the subjunctive
or indicative when these are, as it were, transferred to the past by depending on a verb of past time ; but, if wish were the fundamental idea
of the optative, we should hardly expect this to vanish so utterly, since

---

[1] See C. F. Hermann, *de Protasi Paratactica*, p. 7.

the essential character of the optative would naturally be especially marked where it is used by a fixed principle of the language as a substitute for an indicative or a subjunctive.

The only strong argument for the theory that the optative is primarily the mood of wish is found in the optative with εἰ in protasis. It is maintained that a gradual development of this conditional form from the simple optative in a wish can be actually seen in Homer. The strongest and most attractive statement of this argument is given by Lange in his elaborate, but unfortunately unfinished, treatise on the particle εἰ in Homer.[1] Delbrück's treatment of the optative in his *Syntaktische Forschungen*, vol. i., is based on this doctrine. When Lange states (p. 485) that, of 200 examples of εἰ with the optative in Homer, 136 are expressions of wish, the majority seems decisive ; although we may even here withhold our judgment until we examine the majority and also see what the minority of 64 have to say. The majority of 136 is made up as follows :—

1. Ordinary wishes with εἰ γάρ, εἴθε (αἲ γάρ, αἴθε), or εἰ, like αἴθ᾽ οὕτως, Εὔμαιε, φίλος Διὶ πατρὶ γένοιτο, Od. xiv. 440 ; αἲ γὰρ οὕτως εἴη, Il. iv. 189 ; εἴθ᾽ ὡς ἡβώοιμι, βίη δέ μοι ἔμπεδος εἴη, Il. xi. 670. (Of these there are 38 cases.)

2. Cases in which a wish with εἰ and the optative (like the expressions just quoted) is followed by an apodosis expressing a consequence which would follow the fulfilment of the wish. Thus the last example in 1 appears in Il. vii. 157 with such an apodosis :—

εἴθ᾽ ὡς ἡβώοιμι, βίη δέ μοι ἔμπεδος εἴη·
τῷ κε τάχ᾽ ἀντήσειε μάχης κορυθαίολος Ἕκτωρ.

If we put a comma at the end of the first verse, we have a full conditional sentence. In many cases it is doubtful which punctuation is correct. Lange includes under this head even such sentences as Il. vii. 28, ἀλλ᾽ εἴ μοί τι πίθοιο, τό κεν πολὺ κέρδιον εἴη, and Od. xx. 381. (Of these there are 28 cases.)

3. Ordinary conditional sentences, in which the fusion between the optative with εἰ expressing a wish (i.e. supposing something that is desired) and a *following* apodosis with κέ or ἄν is said to be complete, as in Il. xiii. 485 :—

εἰ γὰρ ὁμηλικίη γε γενοίμεθα τῷδ᾽ ἐπὶ θυμῷ,
αἶψά κεν ἠὲ φέροιτο μέγα κράτος ἤ κε φεροίμην.

(Of these there are 19 cases, against 18 otherwise similar cases in which the optative with εἰ supposes something not desired.)

4. Cases of which the following are examples :—

ἤλυθον, εἴ τινά μοι κληηδόνα πατρὸς ἐνίσποις, Od. iv. 317.

---

[1] *Der Homerische Gebrauch der Partikel EI*, von Ludwig Lange, des vi. Randes der Abhandlungen der philologisch-historischen Classe der Königl. Sächsischen Gesellschaft der Wissenschaften No. 4. Lange himself, nevertheless, believes the optative to be originally the mood of " Einbildungskraft," not of wish.

πάπτηνεν δ' ἀνὰ πύργον 'Αχαιῶν, εἴ τιν' ἴδοιτο
ἡγεμόνων, ὅς τίς οἱ ἀρὴν ἑτάροισιν ἀμύναι, Il. xii. 333.
Such examples are variously explained, but the protasis generally refers
to something that is desired. (Of these there are 43 cases.)

5. Ordinary conditional sentences in which εἰ with the optative
expressing a wish follows an apodosis; as in Il. xxii. 20, ἢ σ' ἂν
τισαίμην, εἴ μοι δύναμίς γε παρείη. These differ from those in 3
only in the position of the protasis. (Of these there are 8 cases of
wishes, against 33 in which no wish is implied, of which last 17 are
concessive.)

The minority of 64 examples, in which εἰ with the optative does
not express a wish, is made up of the 18 dissenting cases under 3, the
33 under 5 which contain no wishes, 5 exceptional cases (as Lange
views them) under 4 (2 with doubtful readings), and 8 cases of ὡς εἰ
with the optative in similes, like ἴσαν ὡς εἴ τε πυρὶ χθὼν πᾶσα
νέμοιτο, Il. ii. 780.

It will be seen that the strength of the argument lies in the gradual
development of the optative conditional sentence which is supposed to
appear in 1, 2, and 3. This is further enforced by reference to cases
in which the simple optative in a wish (without any form of εἰ) is
followed by an apodosis, like the equivalent optatives with εἰ in 2,
thus showing the absence of a conditional force in the latter. See
Od. xv. 180 :—

οὕτω νῦν Ζεὺς θείη, ἐρίγδουπος πόσις "Ηρης·
τῷ κέν τοι καὶ κεῖθι θεῷ ὡς εὐχετοῴμην.

Since the two clauses are grammatically independent here, it is argued
that they must be equally so in the examples in 2.

The whole argument is based on the important assumption that the
optative with εἰ, εἰ γάρ, etc. in a wish is the same in origin with the
simple optative in a wish, so that εἰ γένοιτο τοῦτο and γένοιτο τοῦτο
both come to mean may this be done in the same way, by a wishing
power inherent in the optative itself; and from this it is argued that
εἰ γένοιτο τοῦτο as a protasis is used in a more primitive and natural
sense when what is supposed is desired by the speaker than when it
is not. Unless we assume this as proved, and reject the opposite
alternative which makes the optative with εἰ in a wish a protasis with
a suppressed apodosis, we have no right to count the examples in 1 and
2 as evidence that the optative with εἰ denotes a wish by its own
nature ; for it would be reasoning in a circle to quote these as proof
that the optative itself denotes wish, in a discussion which aims at
establishing the nature and meaning of the optative in these very
expressions. Again, the real nature of the 43 conditions with εἰ
and the optative in 4 is in question in this discussion ; and it is inad-
missible here to assume at the outset that they express wish in themselves and then to use them as evidence that wishing is the original
function of the optative. Proof is needed, therefore, that the optatives
in 1, 2, and 4 (that is, in 109 of the 136 wishing optatives in Homer)

actually express wish by their own force, so that they can properly be used as independent testimony here. Until at least a reasonable presumption in favour of this view is established, we are without evidence that there is any such gradual development of the optative condition as is claimed. We must therefore depend at present on the only cases about which no doubts exist, the complete conditional sentences in 3 and 5, to determine whether the optative with εἰ involves the idea of wish without regard to the nature of its apodosis. If it should be found that the idea of wish preponderates in these optatives, we should have a convincing proof that the same is true of the optatives in 1, 2, and 4, whether these are viewed as protases or as original wishes. A slight inspection of Lange's statistics will show that the question is not to be settled in this simple way. Of the 37 optatives in 3, 19 suppose something that is wished for, while 18 do the opposite. Of the 41 in 5, only 8 suppose desirable things, while 33 do not. Therefore, in the 78 plain cases of εἰ with the optative in conditions in Homer, we find only 27 expressing wishes. If we confine ourselves to the cases in 3, where the protasis precedes, we find as equal a division as is possible (19 : 18), showing very plainly that even here wish has nothing whatever to do with the form of expression. Indeed, if we take εἰ with the optative in protasis by itself, what is there to indicate that it involves a wish? It cannot be doubted that this form is the equivalent of the English *if he should go* and *if we should see him;* and who would attempt to find any such idea as wish in these expressions? Unless we are prepared to maintain that *if we should be saved* expresses the original idea of the English construction better than *if we should perish,* we must be slow to assert that εἰ σωθεῖμεν gives the spirit of the Greek optative better than εἰ ἀποθάνοιμεν. We must remember also the large class of conditional relative sentences which have the optative. This optative cannot be explained on any different principle from the optative with εἰ, and yet who would profess to find anything like the idea of wish in ὅ τις ῥέζοι, Od. i. 47, ᾧ μὴ εἴη, xi. 490, or in Il. vi. 330, 521, xiii. 344, xiv. 248? I give the first six examples that I meet.

It is obvious at once that we must recur to the examples in 1 and 2, and see whether these establish any such strong presumption as will justify us in making wish the fundamental idea of the optative with εἰ, *notwithstanding* the fact that a large majority of the optatives in protasis in Homer have a contrary meaning.

In dealing with the examples in 1 and 2, it will be assumed that εἰ, εἴθε, εἰ γάρ, and αἰ, αἴθε, αἰ γάρ all have the same origin, and involve the same particle εἰ or αἰ which is used in protasis.[1] The question in regard to the wishes in 1 amounts to this : is it more probable that the optative here is merely the wishing optative, preceded by a sort of exclamatory particle εἰ,[2] so that γένοιτο and εἰ γένοιτο are merely

---

[1] See Lange, pp. 311, 312 ; and footnote to § 379 of this work.
[2] Lange, p. 484, calls εἰ "eine zur Einleitung von Wünschen und Fallsetzungen geeignete *interjectionsartige* Partikel." See also p. 565.

different forms of an exclamation, *O may it be done!*—or that εἰ γένοιτο
in a wish is the same as εἰ γένοιτο in protasis, meaning *if it should only
be done,* deriving its force as a wish from the unconscious suppression
of an apodosis like *how happy I should be* or *it would be well?* The
difficulty of explaining εἰ in an ordinary protasis like εἰ ἦλθεν, *if he
came,* as in any sense exclamatory is a great obstacle in the way of
Lange's view ; but his alternative is equally hard, to make εἰ in a wish
radically different from εἰ in a protasis. In the incomplete state of
Lange's work, it is impossible to see how successfully he would have
surmounted this difficulty. But, apart from this, we are compelled
on his theory to believe that the parallel construction of εἰ γάρ and
εἴθε with the past tenses of the indicative in wishes is radically
different in principle from that of εἰ etc. with the optative. The former
is a later construction ; but is it possible that the traditions of so fixed
an expression as εἰ with the optative in wishes could have so utterly
vanished that, while εἰ γὰρ γένοιτο, *may it be done,* had no conditional
force, εἰ γὰρ ἐγένετο τοῦτο, *O that this had been done,* was felt as
conditional ? It is impossible to explain εἰ γὰρ ἐγένετο except as an
elliptical protasis, since there is no form of wish like ἐγένετο (alone)
corresponding to γένοιτο, *may it be done.* Even if we could suppose
that εἰ γὰρ ἐγένετο was formed ignorantly on the analogy of εἰ γὰρ
γένοιτο, it would be incredible that μὴ γένοιτο should not have
engendered a corresponding μὴ ἐγένετο.

But why is it thought necessary or probable that γένοιτο and εἰ
γὰρ γένοιτο should have had the same origin ? If we can trust our
feelings in the use of our own language, it is beyond doubt that our
expressions of wish, like *may help come* and *O if help should* (or *would*)
come! are entirely independent constructions, and also that the latter
is a condition with its conclusion suppressed. Why should we not
accept the same simple distinction in the Greek forms, and admit that
the Greek had two ways of expressing a future wish, one by the simple
optative, the other by a protasis with its apodosis suppressed ? Absolute
proof is, of course, impossible in such a case ; but it is surely safe to
maintain that no such strong presumption is established in favour of
identity of construction in γένοιτο and εἰ γένοιτο in wishes, as to make
it probable that εἰ γένοιτο in protasis was originally a form of wish, in
face of the fact that only a small proportion of Homer's undoubted
protases with εἰ and the optative express wishes.

But it may be said that the peculiar examples of half-formed
conditional sentences in 2 (p. 376) establish the theory of the development of the conditional optative out of a wish. But this connecting
link loses its value, when it is seen that it connects merely one construction, in which the wishing force of the optative is at least questionable,
with another in which there is no positive evidence of any wishing
force at all. If the ordinary theory of the suppression of an apodosis
with εἰ γὰρ γένοιτο in a wish is correct, we must suppose that the
suppressed apodosis was seldom felt in a definite form of words any
more than it is with our *O if he would come.* But it might sometimes

happen that an actual expression of a definite result of the fulfilment
of a wish would suit the case better than the uncertain reference to a
fulfilment, which the mere clause with *if* suggests. We have an
excellent illustration of this when a wish is repeated as a protasis in
almost the same words, and is then followed by an apodosis. See Od.
iii. 217-223 (quoted in § 730), where εἰ γάρ σ' ὣς ἐθέλοι is first a
simple wish, and then is repeated as εἴ σ' οὕτως ἐθέλοι, with the
apodosis τῷ κέν τις, etc. naturally following. The oft-recurring verse
εἴθ' ὣς ἡβώοιμι, βίη δέ μοι ἔμπεδος εἴη appears in Il. xi. 670, xxiii.
629, and Od. xiv. 468 (if Bekker is right in omitting vss. 503-506) as
a simple wish with no addition; but in Il. vii. 157 it stands as a
repetition of the wish contained in vss. 132, 133, αἰ γὰρ ἡβῷμ' ὣς,
etc., and is followed by the apodosis τῷ κε τάχ' ἀντήσειε μάχης κορυθαίολος Ἔκτωρ. In the other examples, we have simply the wish *O
if I were young again*, with its vague unexpressed apodosis ; but in Il.
vii. 157 the result is expressed in the definite form, *then would Hector
meet his match.* See Od. xvii. 496 and xv. 536 (quoted in § 730), in
both of which a definite apodosis expressing a result takes the place of
the usual suppressed conclusion. A distinction of optatives with εἰ
into wishes and suppositions, based on the wishing or non-wishing
nature of the verb, is often arbitrary. Thus Lange quotes, among his
" paratactic " wishes followed by an apodosis in a distinct sentence
(that is, half-developed conditional sentences), Il. xvii. 102 :—

εἰ δέ που Αἴαντός γε βοὴν ἀγαθοῖο πυθοίμην,
ἄμφω κ' αὖτις ἰόντες ἐπιμνησαίμεθα χάρμης,

while he gives as an ordinary conditional sentence Il. xxiv. 653 :—

τῶν εἴ τίς σε ἴδοιτο θοὴν διὰ νύκτα μέλαιναν,
αὐτίκ' ἂν ἐξείποι Ἀγαμέμνονι ποιμένι λαῶν.

His ground for distinction is merely that the former expresses a
wish, while the latter does not. Even if both sentences were held to
be simply conditional (as they probably are), it would still be claimed
that the optative is used in a more legitimate and primitive sense in
the former than in the latter. But is not the patent fact that there is
really no essential distinction between these two optatives with εἰ (taken
as conditions) a strong argument against the whole doctrine which
derives the optative in protasis from the optative in wishes ?

As to the 43 examples in 4, in which the optative with εἰ obviously
stands without any expressed apodosis, I must refer to the discussion
of these in §§ 486-493, where they are explained as protases which
contain within themselves an implied clause of purpose as the apodosis.
Whoever will compare the examples of the optative in § 488 with those
of the subjunctive in § 487, or those of the optative in Delbrück's *Conjunctiv und Optativ*, pp. 236-238, with those of the subjunctive in
pp. 171-175, will probably be satisfied that the greater part of these
optatives represent original subjunctives, which are regularly used in
this sense after primary tenses, while the original optatives that occur
after primary tenses in this construction are not more frequent than

they are in ordinary protasis in Homer (see §§ 499-501). Thus βῆ
Πάνδαρον διζήμενος εἴ που ἐφεύροι, *he went seeking Pandarus, in case
he should find him anywhere* (i.e. *to find P if haply he might*), Il. v. 167,
represents an original form βαίνω Πάνδαρον διζήμενος, ἤν που ἐφεύρω.
This is true, whatever theory we hold as to the nature of the condition
here. Again, this form is equally adapted to suppositions which are
not objects of wish or desire ; as in Thuc. vi. 100, πρὸς τὴν πόλιν, εἰ
ἐπιβοηθοῖεν, ἐχώρουν, *they marched towards the city, in case the enemy
should rush out* (*to be ready to meet them if they should rush out*). So in
Od. xxii. 381 :—

πάπτηνεν δ' Ὀδυσεὺς καθ' ἑὸν δόμον, εἴ τις ἔτ' ἀνδρῶν
ζωὸς ὑποκλοπέοιτο ἀλύσκων κῆρα μέλαιναν,

where Ulysses is said to have searched the house, *in case any one of the
suitors should still be alive and be concealed* (i.e. *to find any such*). This
is quite as natural an expression as Il. xii. 333, πάπτηνεν εἴ τιν' ἴδοιτο
ἡγεμόνων, where the protasis supposes something desired. The idea
of purpose which these sentences imply makes it natural that the supposition should be a desirable one in the majority of cases ; but no
independent support for the theory we are discussing can be found in
them.

We come then to the following conclusions. The theory that wish
is the fundamental idea of the optative finds no support in conditional
sentences with εἰ and the optative in Homer, for among 78 full sentences
of this class, only 27 express suppositions which are desired by the
speaker. The other optatives with εἰ which are said to express wishes
stand without apodosis, and the nature of these expressions is itself in
question in this discussion. As the presence of the idea of wish in the
optative in ordinary conditions would have been a strong proof that the
same idea is inherent in these other optatives, so the conspicuous
absence of wish in the former creates a presumption against its existence
in the latter ; for it appears that, even if the optative with εἰ in wishes
does express the wish by its own natural force, this force has not
passed over into the ordinary optative in protasis, even in Homer.
We have to consider, therefore, whether in spite of this presumption
it can be established that the optative is the mood of wish, or that the
two forms of optative in wishes (with and without εἰ) are identical in
origin and construction. The theory of their identity obliges us to
believe that εἰ is a sort of exclamatory particle ; whereas the older view,
which has the authority of Aristarchus (§ 723), that the optative with εἰ
in wishes is a protasis with a suppressed apodosis, avoids this difficulty
by making the form of wish the same as that of protasis. The new
theory also compels us to explain the past tenses of the indicative with
εἰ and the optative with εἰ in wishes on different principles. The cases
in 2 (p. 376) of an optative with εἰ in a wish followed by an apodosis
in a separate sentence are easily explained by supposing an actual
apodosis to be expressed in them, where commonly only a general idea
of satisfaction (like καλῶς ἂν ἔχοι) is understood. The cases of εἰ with

the optative without an apodosis in 4 are to be explained by the implied
apodosis : they are not necessarily expressions of desire, and the optative here generally represents an original subjunctive.

As a negative result, we do not find in the Homeric examples
as a whole any satisfactory proof that wish is the fundamental idea, or
even an essential idea, of the optative.

For the original meaning of the optative we must go, not to the
developed wish, still less to the developed potential construction with
ἄν or to the protasis with εἰ, but rather to certain simpler and less
decided expressions, a few of which remain in Homer. In Il. iv. 17-19
we have a full conditional sentence,

εἰ δ' αὖ πως τόδε πᾶσι φίλον καὶ ἡδὺ πέλοιτο,
ἦ τοι μὲν οἰκέοιτο πόλις Πριάμοιο ἄνακτος,
αὖτις δ' Ἀργείην Ἑλένην Μενέλαος ἄγοιτο.

This may be translated, *and if moreover this should be welcome and pleasing
to all, king Priam's city may continue to be a dwelling-place, and Menelaus
may take Argive Helen home again.* But οἰκέοιτο and ἄγοιτο (without
κέ or ἄν) here do not make the usual potential apodosis, nor do they
express a wish ; and yet a very slight change in the thought would
make them either of these. With κέ or ἄν added, the meaning would
be *Priam's city would continue to be,* etc. ; without ἄν, in the ordinary
language it would be *may Priam's city continue to be,* etc. The same
general result happens to be expressed in other passages in various
ways. In Il. iii. 71-75 Paris proposes the duel with Menelaus, and
says :—

ὁππότερος δέ κε νικήσῃ κρείσσων τε γένηται,
κτήμαθ' ἑλὼν εὖ πάντα γυναῖκά τε οἴκαδ' ἀγέσθω·
οἱ δ' ἄλλοι φιλότητα καὶ ὅρκια πιστὰ ταμόντες
ναίοιτε Τροίην ἐριβώλακα, τοὶ δὲ νεέσθων
Ἄργος ἐς ἱππόβοτον.

Here ἀγέσθω is used with the same general idea in mind as ἄγοιτο in
iv. 19, and ναίοιτε is like οἰκέοιτο. This example would rather lead
us to understand both ἄγοιτο and οἰκέοιτο as wishes. But in iii. 255
we have τῳ δέ κε νικήσαντι γυνὴ καὶ κτήμαθ' ἔποιτο, where τῷ
νικήσαντι is equivalent to ὁππότερός κε νικήσῃ in 71, and ἔποιτό κε
is potential, though expressing the same general idea as ἀγέσθω and
ἄγοιτο above. Also, in iii. 256 we have ναίοιμεν (like ναίοιτε in 74)
and νέονται (as future). Again, in iii. 138 Iris says to Helen τῷ δέ
κε νικήσαντι φίλη κεκλήσῃ ἄκοιτις, where κεκλήσῃ κε is potential,
referring to the same result as ἔποιτό κε, ἄγοιτο, and ἀγέσθω. These
passages show a use of the optative without κέ which comes very near
to that of the optative with κέ, and also to that of the imperative and
of the future (with and without κέ). This neutral use of the optative
is generally called " concessive."

In other cases, the optative without κέ has a more decided potential
force ; as in Il. xxiii. 151, νῦν δ' ἐπεὶ οὐ νέομαί γε φίλην ἐς πατρίδα
γαῖαν, Πατρόκλῳ ἥρωι κόμην ὀπάσαιμι φέρεσθαι, *I would fain send.*

So in Il. xv. 45, αὐτάρ τοι καὶ κείνῳ ἐγὼ παραμυθησαίμην, I should advise him. In Il. xxi. 274, ἔπειτα δὲ καί τι πάθοιμι may be either then let mo suffer anything (i.e. let me perish), or then would I suffer anything : that the latter is the true meaning is made more probable by xix. 321, οὐ μὲν γάρ τι κακώτερον ἄλλο πάθοιμι, for nothing else that is worse could I suffer, where οὐ shows that the optative is potential. On the other hand, in Il. xxiv. 148, μηδέ τις ἄλλος ἅμα Τρώων ἴτω ἀνήρ· κῆρύξ τίς οἱ ἔποιτο γεραίτερος, i.e. let no other of the Trojans go with him; only let an elder herald accompany him (or a herald may accompany him), the general sense and the preceding imperative seem to show that ἔποιτο is hortatory. Compare Il. iii. 407, μηδ᾽ ἔτι σοῖσι πόδεσσιν ὑποστρέψειας Ὄλυμπον, between two pairs of imperatives, where μηδέ shows the nature of the expression. Again, in Il. vi. 164, τεθναίης, ὦ Προῖτ᾽, ἢ κάκτανε Βελλεροφόντην, we may doubt whether τεθναίης means you must die or may you die (i.e. die), although the connexion with κάκτανε leads us to the latter interpretation : here also compare Il. iii. 407. The tendency is not very strong in either direction in these passages, as is plain from the difficulty which we sometimes feel in deciding which the direction actually is in a given case.[1]   But as the potential and the wishing forms are generally clearly distinguished in Homer, we must look upon the few neutral expressions that we find as relics of an earlier stage of the language, in which the optative without κέ or ἄν was freely used in the sense of οἰκέοιτο and ἄγοιτο in Il. iv. 18, 19. Such expressions could not be used in negative sentences, at least after οὐ and μή were established in their regular force, as the use of either negative would at once decide the character of the sentence.   In the earlier language ἔλθοιμι and ἴδοιμι, I may go and I may see, probably corresponded to the subjunctives ἔλθω and ἴδω, I shall go and I shall see, as weaker forms for expressing future time.   But both moods had inherited another use, by which ἔλθω and ἴδω meant let me go and let me see, while ἔλθοιμι and ἴδοιμι meant may I go and may I see.   The reasons given above, for thinking a derivation of the hortatory subjunctive from the simple future expression more probable than the reverse, apply equally to the corresponding uses of the optative.

In these neutral optatives, of which Il. iv. 18, 19 gives the most striking examples, we probably come nearest to the primitive use out of which the two most common uses of the independent optative

---

[1] To show the uncertainty that exists concerning some of these optatives in the minds of modern scholars, I give some of the most recent translations of four of them.

Il. vi. 164 : You may as well die, Monro ; I pray that you may die, Leaf (ed.) ; Die, Proetus, Leaf (transl.) ; Du wirst selbst sterben müssen, Delbrück.

Il. xxiii. 151 : I may as well give, Monro ; "The optative expresses a wish," I should like to give it, may I be allowed to give it, Leaf ; I may give, Myers ; Ich werde mitgeben, Delbrück.

Il. xxi. 274 : I am ready to suffer, Monro ; Perish ; then let come what may, Leaf ; After that let come to me what may, Myers.

Il. xxiv. 149 : Only a herald may follow, Monro ; I permit a herald to go with him, Leaf ; Let some older herald attend on him, Myers.

(potential and wishing) were developed. Before the Homeric period these two uses were already established, the potential with its mark of κέ or ἄν and its negative οὐ, and the wishing with no external mark and its negative μή. It is hardly possible that the first potential use of the optative was marked by κέ or ἄν, for we find undoubted potential optatives in Homer without either of these particles (see § 240), and even in Attic poetry such indefinite expressions as οὐκ ἔσθ᾽ ὅστις, οὐκ ἔσθ᾽ ὅπως, etc. have the optative without ἄν (§ 241). Although the early Greek, even in Homer, did not always use κέ or ἄν with the potential optative, there is no evidence that it ever failed to distinguish the wishing optative in negative sentences by the use of μή, while the potential was always negatived by οὐ. The Sanskrit optative, which must have had a common origin with the Greek, appears in its earliest use in the state in which we have supposed the early Greek optative to have been, i.e. used both in a potential sense and in wishes without any particle like κέ or ἄν, and occasionally in a neutral or concessive sense. But while the negative ná (= οὐ) is always found in the potential use, we have both má᾽ (= μή) and ná in wishes and similar expressions in which the Greek has only μή.[1] The same peculiarity

[1] See Delbrück, Conj. u. Opt. pp. 26, 194, 198, 199. Whitney, who agrees generally with Delbrück in deriving the other uses of the Sanskrit optative from the idea of wish or desire, says of the actual use of the mood (Sanskrit Grammar, § 573): "But the expression of desire, on the one hand, passes naturally over into that of request or entreaty, so that the optative becomes a softened imperative; and on the other hand, it comes to signify what is generally desirable or proper, what should or ought to be, and so becomes the mode of prescription; or, yet again, it is weakened into signifying what may or can be, what is likely or usual, and so becomes at last a softened statement of what is." Again, in § 574: "Subjunctive and optative run closely parallel with one another in the oldest language in their use in independent clauses, and are hardly distinguishable in dependent." In § 575: "The difference between imperative and subjunctive and optative, in their fundamental and most characteristic uses, is one of degree. . . . There is, in fact, nothing in the earliest employment of these modes to prove that they might not all be specialised uses of forms originally equivalent—having, for instance, a general future meaning." In § 581: "In all dependent constructions, it is still harder even in the oldest language to establish a distinction between subjunctive and optative: a method of use of either is scarcely to be found to which the other does not furnish a practical equivalent."

The original relation of the Sanskrit subjunctive and optative here stated closely resembles what I believe to have been the original relation of the Greek subjunctive and optative, the optative being essentially a sort of weaker subjunctive, both expressing essentially the same ideas. My own view would, I think, agree substantially with that suggested by Delbrück (Syntaktische Forschungen, iv. p. 117) as an alternative to his earlier view presented in his Conjunctiv und Optativ (vol. i. of the same work) eight years before: "Eine andere Möglichkeit wäre, in beiden Modi den futurischen Sinn zu finden, und zwar im Conj. die Bezeichnung der nahen, im Opt. die der ferneren Zukunft. Unter dieser Voraussetzung müsste die von mir Synt. Forsch. i. gewählte Anordnung gänzlich umgestaltet werden." I was, of course, not aware of this important concession of Delbrück when I suggested in the same month (August, 1879), in my Greek Grammar, p. 258, the relation of the optative to the subjunctive which is advocated in the present work.

Since the above was written, Delbrück in his Alt-Indische Syntax has

has been noticed in the use of negatives with the subjunctive (p. 373).

It is probable that at some early period the Greek had two parallel uses of the subjunctive and optative in independent sentences, as follows :—

ἔλθω, I shall go (neg. οὐ), or let me go (neg. μή)
ἔλθῃς, thou wilt go („   ), or go thou   („   )
ἔλθῃ, he will go   („   ), or let him go („   )
ἔλθοιμι, I may or might go (neg. οὐ), or may I go   (neg. μή)
ἔλθοις, thou mayest or mightest go („   ), or mayest thou go („   )
ἔλθοι, he may or might go („   ), or may he go   („   )

Although the Greek which is best known to us did not use the second and third persons of the subjunctive in a hortatory sense, there can be little doubt that such a use existed in the earlier language, as appears from the use in Sanskrit and in Latin, and from the Greek prohibitions with μή. (See § 258.) In an Elean inscription we find two cases of the third person : τὸ δὲ ψάφισμα . . . ἀνατεθᾷ ἐν τὸ ἱαρὸν τῶ Διὸς τῶ Ὀλυμπίω, and (voted) that the decree be set up, etc. ; and also ἐπιμέλειαν ποιήαται (subj.) Νικόδρομορ ὁ βωλογράφορ, that N. have charge, etc.[1]

Both moods alike developed a distinct potential use, which was distinguished from the other by κέ or ἄν; and in Homer we have forms like ἔλθω κε and ἔλθῃ κε parallel with ἔλθοιμί κε and ἔλθοι κε, all negatived by οὐ. The potential subjunctive, however, did not survive the Epic period, while the potential optative became fixed in the language. The future indicative also developed a potential form with κέ or ἄν, which appears to have survived the potential subjunctive, at least in the colloquial language. The English has no form except its vague I may take to express the various shades of meaning denoted by ἐλοῦμαί κε, ἔλωμαι, ἔλωμαί κε, and ἐλοίμην, which once stood between ἐλοῦμαι, I shall take, and ἐλοίμην ἄν, I should take. (See § 399.) The subjunctive, therefore, in its two chief uses in independent sentences, from which all others are derived, was originally accompanied by a weaker future form, the optative, expressing the same idea less distinctly and decidedly.

Let us now see how this weaker subjunctive (or future) form enters into the various dependent constructions, that is, into conditional and final sentences and indirect discourse.

The only dependent construction in which the optative is an original form, not representing another mood after a past tense, is that of protasis (including the conditional relative clause, but excluding the past generic

expressed an opinion (in contradiction to his earlier view, discussed above), that the potential and wishing functions of the optative are distinct in their origin.
[1] Delbrück, Synt. Forsch. iv. p. 117, quotes these passages from Cauer (No. 116). In p. 118 he says of this use : " Es ist nicht zu bezweifeln, dass dieser Conjunctiv-Typus im Griechischen ausstarb, weil der Imperativ dem Bedürfniss genügte." See also i. p. 20.

condition). Here we see the same relation between ἐὰν (or εἰ) ἔλθω and εἰ ἔλθοιμι, *if I shall go* and *if I should go*, as between the original ἔλθω, *I shall go*, and ἔλθοιμι, *I may* (or *might*) *go*, the optative being a less distinct and vivid form for presenting a future supposition, it may be for presenting the same supposition which has already been presented by the subjunctive. The distinction, whatever it may be thought to be, is that which appears in our distinction of *shall* and *should*, and there will always be differences of opinion as to the exact nature of this.[1] The objections to deriving this form of condition from the optative in wishes have already been considered. On the theory that the protasis is an offshoot of the conditional relative clause (see § 398), we should understand εἰ ἔλθω as meaning originally *in case* (i.e. *in the case in which*) *I shall go* or *may go*, and εἰ ἔλθοιμι *in case I should go* or *might go,—should* and *might* being here merely weakened forms of *shall* and *may*. (Homeric optatives referring to the present are discussed below.)

In the whole class of final sentences, in which the subjunctive and optative are probably the only primitive forms, the optative always represents a dependent subjunctive in the changed relation to its leading verb in which it is placed when this verb is changed from present or future to past time, a change which we represent by our change from *may* to *might* or from *shall* to *should*; as ἔρχεται ἵνα ἴδῃ τοῦτο, *he comes that he may see this*, ἦλθεν ἵνα ἴδοι τοῦτο, *he came that he might see this*, etc. The thought in the dependent clause is in both cases what would be expressed originally by ἵνα ἴδω, adapted to different circumstances; and the original subjunctive (ἵνα ἴδῃ) could always be retained, even after past tenses, and by some writers it was generally retained (§§ 318-321). The change is, in fact, the same which is made in indirect discourse when the leading verb is past, since a past final clause always expresses the past thought of the leading subject (§ 703). This relation to indirect discourse is especially clear when the future indicative is used after primary tenses, with the future optative corresponding to it after past tenses.

The optative of indirect discourse has much wider relations, which were greatly extended as the language developed. Here the optative represents not merely the subjunctive but also the indicative in the changed relation in which these are placed by a change of the leading verb from present or future to past time, the tenses of the optative (with some restrictions) representing the corresponding tenses of either subjunctive or indicative at pleasure, the present including also the imperfect. In the development of the language, the want of an optative

---

[1] For an attempt to make this distinction more clear and to remove some difficulties concerning it, see my paper on "Shall and Should in Protasis and their Greek Equivalents," in the *Transactions of the Am. Phil. Assoc. for* 1876, pp. 87-107, and in the English *Journal of Philology*, vol. viii. no. 15, pp. 18-38. I have there given the best answer in my power to the objection that my explanation of the optative in protasis as "less distinct and vivid" than the subjunctive lacks distinctness; this answer is, briefly, that my statement is as distinct as the distinction itself to which it refers.

form to represent the future indicative was felt, and the future optative was added to the verb to supply the need, appearing first in Pindar. In Homer, this use of the optative is imperfectly developed, as the optative with ὅτι or ὡς in a quotation representing a simple indicative is still unknown (§ 671). Still the Homeric language has most of the other constructions of indirect discourse, including the optative in indirect questions representing both the indicative and the subjunctive. This optative in Homer appears (as we should expect) more as the correlative of the subjunctive than as that of the indicative. In indirect discourse, as in final constructions, the optative is not absolutely demanded after past tenses; and in some writers the original indicatives and subjunctives are more common (§ 670). The future optative, as a new form, is always less freely used than the older tenses.

In final constructions and in indirect discourse the optative appears as a subjunctive or indicative (as it were) transferred to the past, and it here has many points in common with the Latin imperfect and pluperfect subjunctive. In Homer, moreover, the present optative is regularly used in present unreal conditions and conclusions, and both present and aorist optative with κέ occasionally refer to the past like the imperfect and aorist indicative with κέ or ἄν. These uses, taken in connexion with the secondary terminations of the optative, might lead us to think that the optative was originally a past expression, so that καί νύ κεν ἔνθ᾽ ἀπόλοιτο, and now ⸱ ⸱ would have perished there, Il. v. 311, would represent the regular use of the primitive optative, instead of being (as is commonly thought) a rare exception. Against this view, however, there are many considerations to be urged.

1. The optative is fully established in Homer in wishes and conditions as a future expression, and also in *present* unreal conditions, the imperfect indicative here being still confined (like the aorist) to the past. In *past* unreal conditions the optative never appears in protasis, and only rarely in apodosis, the aorist indicative being already established here before Homer. Thus, while οὐκ ἂν γνοίης in Il. v. 85 means *you would not have discerned*, it would commonly mean, even in Homer, *you would not discern* (as future), and the common Homeric expression in Il. v. 85 would be οὐκ ἂν ἔγνως. The evidence of the Homeric language, therefore, shows that the present optative is the original form in present unreal conditions and conclusions and in present unattained wishes, but is opposed to the view that the optative was ever regularly past.

2. It is hardly possible that the past unreal conditional preceded in development the ordinary future supposition. Every primitive language must have needed expressions like *if he should go he would see this* before it ventured upon *if he had gone he would have seen this*. If now we suppose that οὐκ ἂν γνοίης had originally the sense *you would not have discerned*, we must assume that the Greek expressed this idea before it could express *you would not discern* (future), for the language never had any other form to express the latter. We cannot hesitate, therefore, to find in the common future meaning of οὐκ ἂν γνοίης the

original force of the expression, and to look upon the occasional
reference to the past as a relic of an early attempt to express *you
would not have discerned* by a form already appropriated to another
use.

3. The Homeric optative in conditional sentences agrees remarkably
with the Sanskrit in both the future and the present use, the Sanskrit
optative being used both in future and in unreal present conditions
and conclusions, but not in past conditions or conclusions. This seems
to show that the Greek inherited the two principal Homeric uses of
the optative, (1) in future conditions and wishes, and (2) in *present*
unreal conditions and unattained wishes, while, so far as our evidence
goes, the occasional use of the optative in past potential expressions is
an extension of its use beyond its hereditary limits made by the early
Greek itself.

4. The argument drawn from the past tenses of the Latin subjunctive will not apply to Greek conditional sentences, for here the present
and perfect subjunctive in Latin (not the imperfect and pluperfect)
correspond to the Greek optative in its most frequent use, and in the
older Latin these primary tenses sometimes express present unreal
conditions.

The most natural view seems to be, that the primitive optative,
before it came into the Greek language, was a weak future form, like
he may go and *may he go*, from which on one side came its potential
and its future conditional use, and on the other side its use in exhortations and wishes. These uses would naturally all be established
before there was any occasion to express either an unreal condition or
an unattained wish. The need of a form for present unreal conditions and present unattained wishes would naturally come next, and
the present optative was made to include these also, no practical
difficulty being caused by having a single form for *it would be* as both
present and future, none being felt in Homer and none being now felt
in English. In this state the optative probably came into the Greek,
before any attempt was made to extend its use to past unreal conditions.
When a form was required for these, the optative may have been used
at first, on the analogy of present unreal conditions ; but here the
serious difficulty of using ἀπόλοιτό κε for *he would have perished* when
it was already familiar in the sense *he would perish* (hereafter) probably
prevented the establishment of this usage. Before our evidence begins,
the past tenses of the indicative were firmly established in past unreal conditions, while the optative was here a rare exception, even in
apodosis, and was never used in protasis. But no attempt was yet
made to dislodge the present optative from present unreal conditions
or the corresponding wishes, although the use of ὤφελον or ὤφελλον
in Homer shows that a past indicative in a present sense was not
absolutely repugnant even to the early usage. But afterwards a new
tendency prevailed, and the imperfect indicative took the place of the
optative in present unreal conditions, still retaining its older use (with
the aorist) in past conditions. The Greek, Sanskrit, and Latin appear

to have developed their expressions of past unreal conditions independently. The Sanskrit, which seldom needed such a form, used its past future, as the Greek occasionally used ἔμελλον with the infinitive (see § 428).

The optative in past general suppositions only represents the corresponding subjunctive transferred to the past. This is, moreover, not to be treated as a primitive use of the optative, for reasons which apply also to the generic subjunctive (see §§ 11, b, and 17).

If the optative, at the time of its origin in some ancestral language, ever actually existed as a past form, as its terminations certainly seem to indicate, no effect has come down to the Greek from this remote origin, except perhaps the use of the optative to represent the subjunctive (and afterwards the indicative) transferred to the past in final constructions and indirect discourse. Even here, its relation to the subjunctive, which is probably all that is primitive in this use, is substantially that of a "remoter future," as it is in independent sentences and in protasis.

II.

ON THE ORIGIN OF THE CONSTRUCTION OF οὐ μή WITH THE SUBJUNCTIVE AND THE FUTURE INDICATIVE.[1]

THE origin of the construction of οὐ μή has never been satisfactorily explained. While there is a general agreement as to the meaning of the two forms of expression in which this double negative occurs, that (1) οὐ μὴ γένηται or οὐ μὴ γενήσεται is *it will not happen*, and (2) οὐ μὴ καταβήσει is *do not come down*, there is great diversity of opinion as to the manner in which these meanings are obtained from the Greek expressions, and still greater as to the origin of the constructions themselves. Most scholars have explained expressions of *denial* with οὐ μή and those of *prohibition* on entirely different theories, which involve different views of the functions of the negatives in the two forms. The explanation of the expressions of denial (like οὐ μὴ γένηται) which has gained most favour is that of an ellipsis after οὐ of a verb or other form denoting fear, on which μὴ γένηται depends ; so that the full form would be οὐ δέος ἐστὶ μὴ γένηται, *there is no fear that it will happen.* Since a strong argument for this ellipsis is the existence of such examples as οὐ φόβος μή σε ἀγάγω, XEN. Mem. ii. 1, 25, and οὐχὶ δέος μή σε φιλήσῃ, AR. Eccl. 650, which, by omitting φόβος and δέος, would become οὐ μή σε ἀγάγω and οὐχὶ μή σε φιλήσῃ, it can hardly be said that this is supposed to be one of the unconscious ellipses which are no longer felt in actual use. This explanation,

---

[1] Reprinted, with a few changes, from the *Harvard Studies in Classical Philology*, vol. i. pp. 65-76.

however, does not help to account for the prohibitions in the second person, like οὐ μὴ καταβήσει, for there is no freak of language by which οὐ δέος ἐστὶ μὴ καταβῇς or even οὐ δέος ἐστὶ μὴ καταβήσει (if we can suppose such an expression) could be transformed into οὐ μὴ καταβήσει, in the sense *do not come down*. The prohibitions have, therefore, generally been explained, on Elmsley's theory, as interrogative ; and οὐ μὴ καταβήσει; is supposed to mean *will you not not come down?* i.e. *do not come down*. All subjunctives that are found in these prohibitions, as in οὐ μὴ σκώψῃς μηδὲ ποιήσῃς, AR. Nub. 296, have generally been condemned since Brunck and Elmsley, and such subjunctives are seldom seen in recent editions of the dramatists.

But all attempts to explain these constructions of οὐ μή on different theories lead to fatal difficulties. We cannot make all the prohibitions interrogative, nor can we change all the prohibitory subjunctives to futures without violence to the text; nor are all cases of οὐ μή with the second person of the subjunctive or of the future prohibitory. The following examples show a complete transition from one of the uses of οὐ μή to the other, and yet no line of distinction, on which different theories of construction can reasonably be based, can be drawn between any two of them :—

Οὖτοι σ' Ἀχαιῶν, οἶδα, μή τις ὑβρίσῃ, *no one of the Achaeans, I am sure, will insult you.* SOPH. Aj. 560.   Οὔ σοι μὴ μεθέψομαί ποτε, *I never will follow you.* Id. El. 1052.   Κοὐχὶ μὴ παύσησθε, *and you will not cease.* AR. Lys. 704.   Ἀλλ' οὔ ποτ' ἐξ ἐμοῦ γε μὴ πάθῃς τόδε, *but you shall never suffer this from me.* SOPH. El. 1029.   Οὐ μή ποτ' ἐς τὴν Σκῦρον ἐκπλεύσῃς, *you shall never sail off to Scyros.* Id. Ph. 381.   Οὐ μὴ σκώψῃς . . . ἀλλ' εὐφήμει, *do not jeer* (i.e. *you shall not jeer*), *but hold your tongue.* AR. Nub. 296 (this cannot be interrogative).   Οὐ μὴ προσοίσεις χεῖρα μηδ' ἅψει πέπλων, *do not bring your hand near me, nor touch my garments.* EUR. Hipp. 606 (generally made interrogative).

It should be made a first requisite of any theory that it shall explain all these cases on the same general principle.

A preliminary question to be settled, if possible, is whether οὐ and μή merely combine to make a single strong negative, or whether οὐ as an independent adverb negatives μή and the verb taken together. The difficulty either of conceiving οὐ and μή as forming a single strong negative, as οὐ and οὐδέν or μή and μηδέν often do, or of understanding how μὴ γένηται, which by itself cannot mean *it will not happen*, can be strengthened by οὐ into an expression *with* this very meaning, has made it impossible to defend the former view on any recognised principle, even when it was adopted for want of something better, as in the earlier editions of the present work. The supposed analogy of μὴ οὐ forming a single negative with the infinitive will hardly hold as a support of this ; for, while we cannot have a sentence like οὐχ ὅσιόν ἐστι μὴ οὐ βοηθεῖν continued by an infinitive with οὐδέ (e.g. by οὐδὲ ἀμύνεσθαι), we frequently have sentences like οὐ μὴ καλεῖς με μηδὲ κατερεῖς τοὔνομα, where μηδέ continues the prohibition without repeating οὐ, showing the distinct force of each part of this double negative. But this only brings out more emphatically the perplexing question that lies at the basis of the whole discussion. If οὐ is an independent negative, as by every principle of Greek negatives it should be, what does it negative? It is clear that there is only one active negative in οὐ μὴ γένηται, it will not happen; and οὐ μὴ σκώψῃς, do not jeer, surely does not have one more active negative than μὴ σκώψῃς.[1]

It seems obvious, therefore, that if οὐ is an independent negative in οὐ μὴ γένηται, the negative force of the μή must in some way be in abeyance, as otherwise the two simple negatives would make the sentence as a whole positive. We may naturally turn for a suggestion here to the principal form of expression in which the negative force of μή seems to be in abeyance,—to Plato's favourite subjunctive with μή as a form of cautious assertion, as μὴ φαῦλον ᾖ, I think it will prove to be bad, Crat. 425 B. (See § 264 and the examples.) Such expressions are, practically, cautious affirmative statements, the fear that something may prove true having by usage softened into a suspicion, and this again into an idea of probability or possibility, so that μὴ φαῦλον ᾖ, which originally meant may it not prove bad (as I fear it may), has come to mean I suspect it may prove bad, and finally, I think it will prove bad or it will probably prove bad. The expression, however, always retains at least the implication that the fact thus stated is an object of apprehension to some one, though it has lost all of its original reference to such apprehension on the part of the speaker.[2] If now a writer wished to express the negative of one of these cautious assertions, in which the original force of μή has practically disappeared, he would say, for example, οὐ μὴ φαῦλον ᾖ, it will not prove to be bad. We thus have a simple explanation of such sentences as οὐ μὴ οἷός τ᾿ ᾖς, you will not be able, PLAT. Rep. 341 B, and οὐ μὴ δυνατὸς ὦ, I shall not be able, Id. Phil. 48 D, the former being the negative of μὴ οἷός τ᾿ ᾖς, I suspect you will be able, the latter of μὴ δυνατὸς ὦ, I suspect that I

---

[1] The idea suggested rather than advocated by Gildersleeve (American Journal of Philology, iii. pp. 203, 205), that οὐ is an independent negative, nay, while μή introduces a question which expects a negative answer, was evidently held by some of the copyists of the best Mss. of Aristophanes or by their predecessors: thus, Rav. and several Paris Mss. have οὔ μὴ σκώψῃς (or σκώψῃς) in Nub. 296 ; Ven. 474 has οὔ· μὴ ληρήσῃς in Nub. 367, and οὔ· μὴ λαλήσεις in 505. See the Ms. readings given in Transactions of the American Philological Association for 1869-70, p. 52.

[2] I give the following passages of Plato, with Jowett's translation, to illustrate this idiom :—

Ἄλλως δὲ συνείρειν μὴ φαῦλον ᾖ καὶ οὐ καθ᾿ ὁδόν, ὦ φίλε Ἑρμόγενες, if they are not, the composition of them, my dear Hermogenes, will be a sorry piece of work, and in the wrong direction. Crat. 425 B. Ἀλλὰ μὴ ὡς ἀληθῶς, τὸ τοῦ Ἑρμογένους, γλίσχρα ᾖ ἡ ὁλκὴ αὕτη τῆς ὁμοιότητος, ἀναγκαῖον δὲ ᾖ καὶ τῷ φορτικῷ τούτῳ προσχρῆσθαι, τῇ ξυνθήκῃ, but the force of resemblance, as Hermogenes says, is a mean thing ; and the mechanical aid of convention must be further employed. Ib. 435 C. Μὴ οὐδὲν ἄλλο σκεπτέον ᾖ, the only question which remains to be considered is, etc. Crit. 48 C.

shall be able. So, by prefixing οὐ to μὴ ἀναγκαῖον ᾖ, *it may be necessary,* we have οὐ μὴ ἀναγκαῖον ᾖ, *it will not be necessary.* (See footnote, p. 394.)

This use of μή with the independent subjunctive in Plato, is, however, confined to the present subjunctive, and generally to ᾖ (or ἔχῃ with an adverb), while οὐ μή generally has the aorist subjunctive or the future indicative, and only rarely the present subjunctive, even in Plato. (See examples in § 295.) Still, the successful application of the principle to the few present subjunctives which are like those above quoted indicates that we are on the right track.

The independent subjunctive with μή is by no means confined to the Platonic construction above mentioned, although this is its chief representative in Attic Greek. It is familiar in Homer in expressions of apprehension combined with a desire to avert the object of fear; as μὴ δὴ νῆας ἕλωσι, *may they not seize the ships (as I fear they may),* Il. xvi. 128. (See § 261.) In such expressions sometimes the fear itself and sometimes the desire to avert the danger is more prominent; see Od. v. 415 : μή πώς μ᾽ ἐκβαίνοντα βάλῃ λίθακι προτὶ πέτρῃ κῦμα μέγ᾽ ἁρπάξαν, μελέη δέ μοι ἔσσεται ὁρμή, i.e. *I fear that some wave may dash me upon a rock as I am emerging from the sea, and my effort will* (then) *be in vain* (the clause of fear being merged in a direct statement). See also Il. ii. 195, xviii. 8 ; Od. v. 356, xvi. 255. Between Homer and Plato, we find only eight cases of independent μή (or μὴ οὐ) with the subjunctive ;[1] but in these we can see the transition from Homer's clause of apprehension to Plato's cautious assertion. (See § 264.) In four of these cases, the speaker expresses fear and a desire to avert its object. These are EUR. Alc. 315, μὴ σοὺς διαφθείρῃ γάμους,—Or. 776, μὴ λάβωσί σ᾽ ἄσμενοι,—H. F. 1399, ἀλλ᾽ αἷμα μὴ σοῖς ἐξομόρξωμαι πέπλοις,—Rhes. 115, μὴ οὐ μόλῃς πόλιν. In the other four we see either the cautious assertion found in Plato or a near approach to it. In HDT. v. 79, we have ἀλλὰ μᾶλλον μὴ οὐ τοῦτο ᾖ τὸ μαντήιον, but *I suspect rather that this will prove not to be the meaning of the oracle* (precisely Plato's usage). Cases of μὴ οὐ of course illustrate this use of μή with the subjunctive equally with those of the simple μή. In EUR. Tro. 982, Hecuba says to Helen, μὴ οὐ πείσῃς σοφούς, *I suspect you will not convince wise people,* with the same sarcastic tone which is in Plato's μὴ οὐκ ᾖ διδακτὸν ἀρετή, *I suspect it will prove that virtue is not a thing to be taught,* Men. 94 E (said by Socrates, who is arguing that virtue is οὐ διδακτόν). In AR. Eccl. 795, most editions have μὴ γὰρ οὐ λάβῃς ὅποι (sc. ταῦτα καταθῇς, where the Mss. give an impossible λάβοις), *I suspect you will not find a place to put them down,* with the same affectation of anxiety as in the two preceding examples. In XEN. Mem. iv. 2, 12, we have one of the rare interrogative forms of the subjunctive with μή, in which Euthydemus says to Socrates, μὴ οὖν οὐ δύνωμαι (v. l. δύναμαι) ἐγὼ τὰ τῆς δικαιοσύνης ἔργα διηγήσασθαι; *do you suspect that I shall be*

---

[1] I depend here on Weber's statistics, given in his *Entwickelungsgeschichte der Absichtssätze.*

(or *am*) *unable to explain the works of Justice?* He adds, καὶ νὴ Δι'
ἔγωγε τὰ τῆς ἀδικίας, *I assure you, I can explain those of Injustice.*
Here the spirit of the expression is the same as in the other cases.
Compare the similar interrogatives in Plato : Phaed. 64 C, Rep. 603
C, Parm. 163 D, Sisyph. 387 C. But for the eight cases of independent μή that have been quoted, we should never know that the
construction existed between Homer and Plato. We have good ground
for believing that it remained as a colloquial idiom in the language,
though it seldom appeared in literature until Plato revived it and
restored it to common use as a half-sarcastic form of expressing mildly
a disagreeable truth. In Plato, the construction is not confined to
this peculiar sense, for we find cases in which honest apprehension is
expressed as in the older use. Weber quotes Euthyd. 272 C, μὴ τοῖν
ξένοιν τις ταὐτὸ τοῦτο ὀνειδίσῃ, *I am afraid some one may insult the
two strangers in this same way* (or *let no one insult them, as I fear some
one may*) ; also Symp. 193 B, καὶ μή μοι ὑπολάβῃ, *I hope he will not
answer me ;* and Leg. 861 E, μὴ τοίνυν τις οἴηται.
    It appears, therefore, that the independent subjunctive with μή
was in good use in the fifth century B.C. in the two senses illustrated
by EUR. Or. 776, μὴ λάβωσί σε, *I fear they may seize you,* and by
EUR. Tro. 982, μὴ οὐ πείσῃς σοφούς, *I suspect you will fail to convince
wise people.* From the persistence of the original meaning, even in
Plato, we may probably assume that the expression more frequently
included the idea of apprehension which is essential to it in Homer.
But the other examples show that μὴ λάβωσί σε must have been in
equally good use in the sense *I suspect they will seize you* (implying no
apprehension). If now we suppose οὐ to be prefixed to μὴ λάβωσί
σε, we shall have οὐ μὴ λάβωσί σε, which could be said with the
meaning *I am not afraid that they will seize you,* and equally well
with the meaning *they shall not seize you.* The former sense agrees
precisely with that of some of the older uses of οὐ μή with the subjunctive. If the strange example from Parmenides (vs. 121) is genuine,
we have οὐ μή ποτέ τίς σε βροτῶν γνώμῃ παρελάσσῃ, *there is no
danger that any mortal will surpass you in wisdom.* In AESCH. Sept.
38 (one of the oldest cases, 467 B.C.), οὔ τι μὴ ληφθῶ δόλῳ, *I have no
fear of being caught by any trick,* we can easily understand οὐ μὴ ληφθῶ
as the negative of μὴ ληφθῶ, *I fear I may be caught.* So in Parmenides
we have the negative of μή τίς σε παρελάσσῃ, *I fear some one may
surpass you.* Οὐ μή τις ὀνειδίσῃ would be a natural negative of μή
τις ὀνειδίσῃ, *I fear some one may insult,* in PLAT. Euthyd. 272 C. So,
where there is no denial of apprehension, οὐ μὴ πάθῃς τόδε, *you shall
not suffer this,* SOPH. El. 1029, may be the negative of μὴ πάθῃς τόδε,
I suspect you will suffer this ; and οὐ μὴ ἐκπλεύσῃς, Id. Phil. 381, may
be the negative of μὴ ἐκπλεύσῃς, *I suspect you will sail away.* So οὐ
μὴ ναῦς ἀφορμίσῃ (Kirchoff, -σῃς) χθονὸς, πρὶν ἄν, etc., *you shall not
move your ships from the shore, until,* etc., EUR. I. T. 18, will be the
negative of μὴ ναῦς ἀφορμίσῃ, *I suspect you will move your ships.*
These expressions with οὐ μή were always colloquial, as were also (at

least in Attic Greek) the expressions with μή and the subjunctive from which they are here supposed to have sprung.[1]

If it is thought that the limited number of cases of independent μή with the subjunctive not implying apprehension do not justify the assumptions which have been based on them, it is easy to see how the change from the denial of an apprehension to the denial of a suspicion might have taken place within the οὐ μή construction itself. If we suppose such expressions as οὐ μὴ ληφθῶ and οὐ μή τίς σε ὑβρίσῃ to have been established as the negatives of μὴ ληφθῶ, *I fear I may be caught*, and μή τίς σε ὑβρίσῃ, *I fear some one may insult you*, they must soon have fallen out of this relation to the parent forms, and have been felt in use to be mere future negative assertions, so that they could not long be restricted to sentences in which apprehension was implied. Thus, οὐ μὴ ναῦς ἀφορμίσῃ χθονός would soon become as natural to those who used these forms as the older οὐ μή τίς σε ὑβρίσῃ. According to this view, οὐ μή with the subjunctive would come into the language in the sense of a denial of an apprehension, which is essentially the same general sense as that supposed by the theory of an ellipsis of δέος ἐστίν. But there is a great advantage in dispensing with this troublesome and improbable ellipsis, and deriving the meaning from the sentence as it stands. There is surely no more ground for assuming this ellipsis here than in the independent subjunctive with μή, which is an older construction than the dependent subjunctive with μή. And if we accept μή τίς σε ὑβρίσῃ as a complete construction, without the help of δέος ἐστίν, it is absurd to invent an ellipsis to explain οὐ μή τίς σε ὑβρίσῃ as a shorter form for οὐ δέος ἐστὶ μή τίς σε ὑβρίσῃ. In fact, dispensing with this ellipsis removes the most fatal objection to the view of the sentence on which the old theory was based.

[1] It may perhaps be urged, in opposition to the view here presented, that οὐ μὴ λάβωσί σε, *they will not seize you*, cannot be the negative of μὴ λάβωσί σε in its sense of *I suspect they will seize you*, or even in that of *I fear they may seize you*, because the regular negative of this is μὴ οὐ λάβωσί σε, as we may call μὴ οὐ πείσῃς σοφούς (EUR. Tro. 982) the negative of μὴ πείσῃς σοφούς. But οὐ in μὴ οὐ πείσῃς negatives only the verb, whereas οὐ in οὐ μὴ πείσῃς would negative the whole expression μὴ πείσῃς. Μὴ οὐ πείσῃς is a cautious negative, meaning *I suspect you will not convince them*, corresponding in a certain way to μὴ πείσῃς, *I suspect you will convince them*. But οὐ μὴ πείσῃς would be the true negative of μὴ πείσῃς, denying it absolutely, in the sense *there is no ground for suspicion that you will convince them*, or (sometimes) *there is no fear that you will convince them*, i.e. *you will not convince them*. There is all the difference in the world between suspecting a negative (*e.g.* suspecting that something will not happen) and negativing a suspicion (*e.g.* denying that there is any suspicion that something will happen). Surely no one could understand μὴ οὐ δυνατὸς ὦ, *I suspect I shall not be able*, as the negative of μὴ δυνατὸς ὦ, *I suspect I shall be able*. The real negative is much rather οὐ μὴ δυνατὸς ὦ, *there is no chance that I shall be able*, in PLAT. Phil. 48 D. The negative power of οὐ in negativing μὴ λάβωσί σε in its sense of *I fear they may seize you* is perhaps still more apparent. Whereas μὴ οὐ λάβωσί σε in this sense would mean *I am afraid they may not seize you*, οὐ μὴ λάβωσί σε would mean *I do not fear* (or *there is no danger*) *that they will seize you*, which is felt as a strong negative, *they will not seize you*.

In whichever of the two ways above suggested the subjunctive with οὐ μή came to express a simple future denial, it was only natural that the Attic Greek should soon begin to use the future indicative in place of the subjunctive in the same sense. Thus we have in SOPH. El. 1052, οὔ σοι μὴ μεθέψομαί ποτε, and in AR. Ran. 508, οὐ μή σ' ἐγὼ περιόψομαι, both expressing denial. At this stage all recollection of the original clause with μή and the subjunctive must have been lost, as there was no corresponding clause with μή and the future indicative in common use, of which οὐ μή with the future could be the negative. A most striking proof of the entire loss of this tradition is given by examples of indirect quotation of οὐ μή with the future. In SOPH. Ph. 611 we have τά τ' ἄλλα πάντ' ἐθέσπισεν, καὶ τἀπὶ Τροίας πέργαμ' ὡς οὐ μή ποτε πέρσοιεν εἰ μὴ τόνδε ἄγοιντο, the direct form being οὐ μή ποτε πέρσετε ἐὰν μὴ τόνδε ἄγησθε. In XEN. Hell. i. 6, 32, εἶπεν ὅτι ἡ Σπάρτη οὐδὲν μὴ κάκιον οἰκιεῖται αὐτοῦ ἀποθανόντος, the future indicative is retained in an otherwise similar construction. In EUR. Ph. 1590, we find εἶπε Τειρεσίας οὐ μή ποτε, σοῦ τήνδε γῆν οἰκοῦντος, εὖ πράξειν πόλιν, representing οὐ μή ποτε εὖ πράξει. We could not explain οὐ μὴ πράξειν as an independent expression on any theory, either with or without an ellipsis. Such forms show the advanced stage which the construction of οὐ μή had reached. (See § 296.)

We find in the Roman comic poets a few cases of neque with haud in the same clause, forming a single negative. Such are PLAUT. Bacch. 1037, Neque ego haud committam ut, si quid peccatum siet, fecisse dicas de mea sententia ; and TER. Andr. 205, Neque tu haud dices tibi non praedictum. Neque haud may fairly be supposed to be a translation of οὐδὲ μή in a Greek original. If it is, it shows that the Roman poet understood οὐ μή with the subjunctive or the future indicative as a simple expression of denial.

When οὐ μή with the future indicative had been established as a regular form of future denial, the second person singular probably began to be used as a form of prohibition. As the future could be used in positive commands in an imperative sense, as in πάντως δὲ τοῦτο δράσεις, but by all means do this, AR. Nub. 1352, it could also take the simple οὐ in prohibitions, as in χειρὶ οὐ ψαύσεις ποτε, you shall not touch me with your hand, or do not touch me, EUR. Med. 1320. (See § 69.) The dramatists soon introduced the new form with οὐ μή into such prohibitions, generally with the future indicative, but occasionally with the more primitive subjunctive. Thus οὐ μὴ κατα-βήσει had the sense of do not come down, derived from you shall not come down, as οὐ ψαύσεις (above) from meaning you shall not touch came to mean do not touch. One of the strongest objections to the older views of the forms with οὐ μή is that they generally require a distinct explanation of this prohibitory construction. Elmsley's theory of a question with two negatives, explaining οὐ μὴ καταβήσει; as will you NOT NOT come down? hence do not come down, was stated in the Quarterly Review for June 1812, and in his note to EUR. Med. 1120

(1151 Dind.). Many who do not adopt Elmsley's theory in full still accept the interrogative form, and these sentences are now generally printed as questions. Long before Elmsley, the famous "Canon Davesianus" had proscribed all sigmatic aorist subjunctives with οὐ μή as well as with ὅπως μή. This edict removed nearly or quite all the troublesome subjunctives that would have opposed Elmsley's view, and left only the future indicative in his doubly-negatived questions, which of course required an indicative. This again set up an artificial distinction in form between the prohibitory construction allowing only the future indicative, and the other construction allowing both subjunctive and future indicative.

But it has been more and more evident in later years that this distinction in form between the two constructions cannot be maintained. It was seen by Brunck, before Elmsley's interrogative theory appeared, that it would be absurd to distinguish sentences like ταῦτα οὐ μή ποτ' ἐς τὴν Σκῦρον ἐκπλεύσῃς ἔχων, *you shall never sail away to Scyros with these arms*, SOPH. Ph. 381, from οὐ μὴ καταβήσει, *you shall not come down*, AR. Vesp. 397. He therefore wrote ἐκπλεύσεις in the former, with the note "soloece vulgo legitur ἐκπλεύσῃς." But ἐκπλεύσεις proved to be even a greater solecism than ἐκπλεύσῃς was thought to be, for the only classic future of πλέω is the middle πλεύσομαι or πλευσοῦμαι, and ἐκπλεύσει will not suit the verse. So ἐκπλεύσῃς had to be restored. Again, while almost all the sentences containing a prohibition with οὐ μή, followed by a positive command with ἀλλά or δέ, could admit of Elmsley's punctuation and interpretation,—as οὐ μὴ λαλήσεις ἀλλ' ἀκολουθήσεις ἐμοί; AR. Nub. 505, explained as *won't you not talk nonsense and follow me?*—another passage of the Clouds resisted both of these and also the prescribed form. In 296, the Mss. have οὐ μὴ σκώψῃς μηδὲ ποιήσῃς ἅπερ οἱ τρυγοδαίμονες οὗτοι· ἀλλ' εὐφήμει. Brunck emended this without hesitation to οὐ μὴ σκώψεις μηδὲ ποιήσεις, with the note "soloece vulgo σκώψῃς . . . ποιήσῃς." But there was no place for Elmsley's interrogative mark, which could not stand after the imperative, and could not be inserted after οὗτοι without implying that the other sentences (like Nub. 505 above) were wrongly punctuated. The emendation σκώψεις was as unfortunate as ἐκπλεύσεις, as the future of σκώπτω is σκώψομαι, not σκώψω, so that a further emendation to σκώψει was needed. In this battered condition, and with no interrogative mark to help the interpretation, the passage usually appears, even in the latest editions. (See §§ 298, 300, 301.) So long as it is proposed to explain these prohibitions and the ordinary denials with οὐ μή on entirely different theories, with nothing common to the two constructions, it may not seem unreasonable to force a few examples like Nub. 296 and 367 into conformity with the general usage. But on any theory which makes no distinction in construction between the prohibitions and the other negative expressions of denial or refusal (for example, between οὐ μὴ ἐκπλεύσῃς, *you shall not sail away*, and οὐ μὴ καταβήσει, *do not come down*, i.e. *you shall not come*

down), there is no more reason for objecting to οὐ μὴ σκώψῃς than to
οὐ μὴ ἐκπλεύσῃς. An occasional subjunctive, like οὐ μὴ σκώψῃς or
οὐ μὴ ληρήσῃς, is indeed no more than we should naturally expect
in a construction which had its origin in the subjunctive. In such
expressions, further, the analogy of the equivalent μὴ σκώψῃς and μὴ
ληρήσῃς would tend to make the aorist subjunctive unobjectionable
and perfectly natural. A reference to the list of passages quoted on
page 390 will show the inconsistencies into which every one must fall
who attempts to explain the prohibitions and the clauses of denial on
different theories. We cannot separate οὐ μὴ σκώψῃς from οὐ μὴ
ἐκπλεύσῃς in construction, nor the latter from οὐ μὴ πάθῃς, nor this
again from οὐ μή τις ὑβρίσῃ, on any consistent principle of interpretation.[1]

Sentences of one class have been claimed as decisive witnesses in
favour of the interrogative theory. They are represented by οὐ
θᾶσσον οἴσεις, μηδ᾽ ἀπιστήσεις ἐμοί; *will you not more quickly extend
it* (your hand), *and not distrust me?* SOPH. Tr. 1183. These are undoubted questions, but there is no construction with οὐ μή in them.
They consist of one question with οὐ, implying an affirmative answer,
will you not extend your hand? and another with μή, implying a
negative answer, *and you will not distrust me, will you?* The compound of the two has the general sense expressed in the first translation above. (See § 299 and the examples.)

In conclusion, we may sum up the result of the investigation as
follows. The original construction of οὐ μή with the subjunctive was
developed as a negative form of the independent subjunctive with μή,
which had already become an expression of apprehension with desire
to avert its object, even if it had not passed into the stage of a
cautious assertion ; in either case, the real negative force of μή was
in abeyance. The aorist subjunctive is the most common form here,
the present being less frequent. This form of future denial next
admitted the future indicative in the same sense as the subjunctive.
The second person singular of this future with οὐ μή was used by the
dramatists as a prohibition, without abandoning the sense which the
future can always have in both positive and negative commands. In
these prohibitions the future indicative, in which they had their
origin, is generally used ; but the subjunctive occasionally occurs,
being analogous to the ordinary aorist subjunctive with μή in prohibitions ; *e.g.* μὴ σκώψῃς supporting οὐ μὴ σκώψῃς.[2]

---

[1] For a further discussion of the form of the sentences with οὐ μή, in connexion with that of clauses with ὅπως and with the Canon Davesianus, see
Trans. of the Am. Phil. Assoc. for 1869-70, pp. 46-55.

[2] Since this paper was written, I have seen that Kvičala, in two articles
on οὐ μή in the *Zeitschrift für die oesterreichischen Gymnasien for* 1856, proposed an explanation of οὐ μή with the subjunctive, which at one important
point came very near the view now presented. He states two (apparently
theoretical) meanings which he supposes μὴ θάνῃς to have had at some
period (zwei Bedeutungsentwickelungen) : one, " Du wirst doch wol am Ende,
trotzdem dass ich es abzuwehren suche, sterben ; " the other, " Ich fürchte,

III.

STATISTICS OF THE USE OF THE FINAL PARTICLES.

The following tables are based on the statistics given by Dr. Philipp Weber in his *Entwickelungsgeschichte der Absichtssätze*.

1. Statistics of the use of the Final Particles in pure final clauses by different authors.

	Ὄφρα.	Ὄφρα κε or ἄν.	Ἵνα.	Ὡς.	Ὡς ἄν or ὡς κε.	Ὅπως.	Ὅπως ἄν with Subj.[1]
Homer . .	223	14	145	24 [2]	38	9	
Hom. Hymns	8	1 (opt.)	5	...	2 (opt.)		
Hesiod . .	10	...	11	3	3		
Pindar . .	11	...	...	3	1 (opt.)	1	
Aeschylus .	...	...	2	23	11	11	5 [3]
Sophocles .	...	...	14	52	5	31	2
Euripides .	...	...	71	182	27	19	7
Aristophanes	...	...	183	3 [4]	14	18 [5]	24
Herodotus .	...	...	107	16	11	13 [6]	5
Thucydides .	...	...	52	1	1	114	
Xenophon .	...	...	213	83	8 [7]	221	14
Plato . .	...	...	368	1	...	23	25
Ten Orators .	...	...	579 [8]	3 or 4 [9]	...	42	12
Demosthenes	...	...	253	...	...	14	4

dass du doch wol (trotz meiner Abwehr) sterben werdest." By prefixing οὐ to μὴ θάνῃς in these meanings, he arrives at two uses of οὐ μή with the subjunctive. The second meaning comes so near the independent subjunctive with μή in Homer, that it is surprising that neither this nor the equally important μή in Plato is mentioned. But no use is made of the advantage here gained in explaining οὐ μή with the future indicative, either in prohibitions or in denials. The prohibitions are made interrogative, οὐ μὴ δυσμενὴς ἔσει; being explained as "Nicht wahr?—du wirst doch nicht feindselig seyn?" The future of denial is explained simply as developed from the interrogative future, as a form of reply to this, by leaving out the interrogative element.

[1] For ὅπως ἄν with the optative in Attic Greek, see § 330.
[2] Omitting Od. xxi. 201. [3] In Agam. 364 ὅπως has the optative with ἄν.
[4] Two of these occur in Lysistr. 1265, 1305, in the Χορὸς Λακώνων : the third is in Eccl. 286.
[5] Including 10 with future indicative.
[6] Ὅκως. See Weber's erratum for his p. 130.
[7] Omitting Cyr. viii. 3, 2 (see p. 400, footnote), and Xenophon's peculiar cases of ὡς ἄν with the optative (see § 326, 2). See Appendix IV.
[8] Weber omits Dinarchus in p. 185 (see his p. 182).
[9] Dem. xxiv. 146 is omitted, as ὡς cannot be final there. The only sure examples of ὡς final in the orators are Ant. v. 53, vi. 15 ; And. i. 99. Lys. xxviii. 14 is probably corrupt (see *Am. Jour. Phil.* vi. p. 56).

2. Statistics of the use of the four Final Particles in pure final clauses in the Iliad and the Odyssey.

		SUBJ.	FUT. IND.	OPT.	
Ὄφρα (pure)	Il. Od.	89 82	2 2	22......Il. 113 26......Od. 110	
		171	4	48	——223
Ὄφρα κε	Il. Od.	1 6	... ...	1......Il. 2 0......Od. 6	
		7		1	— 8
Ὄφρ᾽ ἄν	Il. Od.	2 3	... ...	0......Il. 2 1......Od. 4	
		5		1	— 6

Total cases of ὄφρα 237

Ἵνα (pure)	Il. Od.	45 48	... ...	22......Il. 67 30......Od. 78	
		93		52	—145 (total)
Ὥς (pure)	Il. Od.	10 2	... ...	6......Il. 16 6......Od. 8	
		12		12	— 24
Ὥς κε	Il. Od.	11 9	... ...	0......Il. 11 5......Od. 14	
		20		5	— 25
Ὥς ἄν	Il. Od.	3 6	... ...	1......Il. 4 3......Od. 9	
		9	·	4	— 13

Total cases of ὡς 62

Ὅπως (pure)	Il. Od.	0 1	0 1	2......Il. 2 5......Od. 7	
		1	1	7	— 9 (total).

3. Examples of ὡς and ὅπως in object clauses in Homer after verbs of *planning, trying*, etc. (see § 341).

Simple ὡς with subjunctive : Il. ii. 4 (some read opt.), Od. v. 24. (*2*.) Ὥς κε with subjunctive : Il. iv. 66 (= 71), ix. 112, xv. 235, xxi. 459; Od. i. 205, ii. 168, 316, 368, v. 31, vii. 192. (*10*.)

Simple ὅπως with subjunctive : Il. iii. 19, 110, xvii 635, 713, Od. i. 77, xiii. 365, 386. (*7*.) Ὅπως κε with subjunctive : Od. i. 270, 295, iv. 545; so Il. ix. 681, if this is subjunctive. (*4*.)

'Ὡς with optative : Il. ix. 181; Od. vi. 112. (2.) Ὅπως with optative : Il. xiv. 160, xxi. 137, xxiv. 680; Od. iii. 129, viii. 345, ix. 420, 554, xi. 229, 480, xv. 170, 203. (11.) Weber cites ὅππως κεν σόῳς in Il. ix. 681 as optative, and omits Od. iii. 19 as a suspected verse.

The following verbs are used to introduce this construction in Homer : φράζομαι and its compounds, 14 times ; βουλεύω and βουλὴν εἰπεῖν, 5 times ; πειρῶ, 5 times ; μερμηρίζω, 4 times ; ὁρμαίνω and λίσσομαι, each twice ; and νοέω, λεύσσω, μῆτιν ὕφηνον, and μνήσομαι, each once. (36.)

IV.

XENOPHON'S PECULIAR USE OF ὡς, ὡς ἄν, AND ὅπως ἄν IN FINAL AND OBJECT CLAUSES.

In Final Clauses.

I. (Ὡς and ὡς ἄν.)   1. It is well known that Xenophon is almost the only writer of Attic prose who uses ὡς freely in the final constructions. Weber's statistics (p. 398) show that while ὡς is the favourite final particle in tragedy, it is hardly found in Aristophanes, Thucydides, Plato, and the Orators. Xenophon forms a strange exception to the prose usage, having ὡς or ὡς ἄν in 91 of his pure final clauses. There is nothing peculiar in his use of final ὡς with either subjunctive or optative, as it merely takes the place of another final particle.

2. In his use of ὡς ἄν in final clauses, however, several peculiarities appear, which show that Xenophon felt the original force of ὡς as a relative adverb of manner (§ 312).   The following examples occur.[1]

(a) Of eight cases of ὡς ἄν with the subjunctive, six are normal, while two show the relative force of ὡς :—

Ἐᾶσαι χρὴ τοὺς ἄνδρας τὸ μέτριον ἀποκοιμηθῆναι, ὡς ἂν δύνωνται ὑπνομαχεῖν, that they be able to fight against sleep. Cyr. ii. 4, 26. Ὡς δ᾽ ἂν μάθῃς, ἀντάκουσον. An. ii. 5, 16. Ἀλλ᾽ ἕπεσθαι χρὴ καὶ προσέχειν τὸν νοῦν, ὡς ἂν τὸ παραγγελλόμενον δύνησθε ποιεῖν. An. vi. 3, 18. So Cyr. viii. 7, 9 ; Ag. xi. 1 ; Eques. iv. 4.

Ὡς ἂν δύνηταί σοι ὁ στρατὸς ἕπεσθαι, τῷ μέσῳ τῆς σπουδῆς ἡγοῦ, lead on at a medium rate of speed, that the army may be able to follow you. Cyr. ii. 4, 28.   (The analogy of the following cases of the optative may justify the translation, lead at a rate at which the army may be able to follow you.)   Αἱ μὲν κνῆμαι εἰς μέγεθος οὐ μάλα αὔξονται,

---

[1] See Weber, p. 224, where the examples of the optative with ὡς ἄν are also given.   Weber cites Cyr. viii. 3, 2 as an example of the subjunctive ; but this section has ὡς ἂν ἐξαγγείλῃ as a relative clause, but no final clause.   I have added Cyr. vii. 5, 81 and Eques. ix. 3 to the examples of the optative given by Weber.

πρὸς δὲ ταύτας ὡς ἄν συμμέτρως ἔχῃ συναυξέται καὶ τὸ ἄλλο σῶμα, i.e. *the rest of the* (horse's) *body grows so as to be in the right proportion to the legs.* Éques. i. 16. These two cases are (as Weber says of those of the optative) on the line between final and consecutive sentences. The original relative and conditional force of ὡς (§ 312, 2) can here be plainly seen.

(*b*) The original relative force of ὡς, *as*, is much more apparent when ὡς ἄν takes the optative in Xenophon with a potential force, especially after primary tenses. These examples occur :—

Προσφέρουσιν ὡς ἄν ἐνδοῖεν τὸ ἔκπωμα εὐληπτότατα τῷ μέλλοντι πίνειν, *they offer the cup in the most convenient way in which they can present it for the one who is to drink* (lit. *as they can present it most conveniently*). Cyr. i. 3, 8. Ὣς δ' ἄν καὶ οἱ πόδες εἶεν τῷ ἵππῳ κράτιστοι, εἰ μέν τις ἔχει ῥάῳ ἄσκησιν, ἐκείνη ἔστω, *if any one has any easier exercise for keeping the horse's feet as strong as possible.* Hipp. i. 16. So also Eques. ix. 3 : οὕτως αὖ εἰς τὸ θᾶττον (χρὴ) προάγειν, ὡς ἄν μάλιστα λανθάνοι αὐτὸν ὁ ἵππος εἰς τὸ ταχὺ ἀφικνούμενος.

Ὁ Ἀρμένιος ἐφοβεῖτο, ὅτι ὀφθήσεσθαι ἔμελλε τὰ βασίλεια οἰκοδομεῖν ἀρχόμενος, ὡς ἄν ἱκανὰ ἀπομάχεσθαι εἴη, *beginning to build his palace so that it would be capable of defence (in a manner in which it would be).* Cyr. iii. 1, 1. Ἔδοξεν αὐτῷ τοῦτο ποιῆσαι, ὡς ὅτι ἥκιστα ἄν ἐπιφθόνως σπάνιός τε καὶ σεμνὸς φανείη, *to do this so that he would appear, etc.* Cyr. vii. 5, 37. (Here the separation of ἄν from ὡς makes the potential nature of φανείη ἄν especially plain.) Εἰ ὧν μὲν μάλιστα ἄνθρωποι ἐπιθυμοῦσιν ὁ δαίμων ταῦτα ἡμῖν συμπαρεσκεύακεν, ὡς δ' ἄν ἥδιστα ταῦτα φαίνοιτο αὐτός τις αὐτῷ ταῦτα παρασκευάσει, κ.τ.λ., *if, while God has helped to provide for us what men most desire, any one will then provide these for himself so that they would appear most agreeable to him, etc.* Cyr. vii. 5, 81. Συντεταγμένον μὲν οὕτως ἦγε τὸ στράτευμα ὡς ἄν ἐπικουρεῖν μάλιστα ἑαυτῷ δύναιτο, ἡσύχως δὲ ὥσπερ ἄν παρθένος ἡ σωφρονεστάτη προβαίνοι, *he led the army so ordered that it would be best able to help itself, and as quietly as the most modest maiden would walk.* Ag. vi. 7. (Compare this with Cyr. ii. 4, 28 under *a,* and compare ὡς ἄν and ὥσπερ ἄν here.) See § 329, 2, for similar cases in Demosthenes.

II. (Ὅπως.) Xenophon's favourite final particle is ὅπως, but there is nothing peculiar in his use of it in pure final clauses with either subjunctive or optative. He further uses ὅπως ἄν with the subjunctive like other Attic writers (see examples in § 328).

With the optative he uses ὅπως ἄν in four cases with a distinct final and an equally distinct potential force. These examples are quoted in § 330. The only other case is THUC. vii. 65.

IN OBJECT CLAUSES AFTER VERBS OF *striving* ETC.

Xenophon is more peculiar in his use of ὡς, ὡς ἄν, and ὅπως ἄν in these clauses than in pure final clauses. Here he generally uses ὅπως with the future indicative, subjunctive, and optative, and occasionally ὅπως ἄν with the subjunctive, like other Attic writers (see examples in §§ 339 and 348). But he distinctly violates Attic usage by having ὡς (in the sense of ὅπως) with both subjunctive and future indicative, and with the present, aorist, and future optative; also ὡς ἄν with both subjunctive and optative and ὅπως ἄν with the optative; and further by allowing the optative with ὡς ἄν and ὅπως ἄν to follow both primary and secondary tenses. His use of ὡς ἄν and ὅπως ἄν with the optative, especially after primary tenses, shows strongly the original relative and interrogative force of ὡς and ὅπως.

The examples of the exceptional uses are these.

(Ὡs.) Ἐπιμελοῦνται ὡς ἔχῃ οὕτως. Oec. xx. 8. Σκοπείτω τὰ ἔμπροσθεν, ὡς μηδὲν ἡμᾶς λάθῃ, *let him keep a look-out in front, to see that nothing escapes us*. An. vi. 3, 14. Πῶς δ᾽ οὐ (χρὴ) φυλάξασθαι ὡς μὴ καὶ ἡμᾶς ταὐτὸ δυνασθῇ ποιῆσαι; Hell. ii. 3, 33. Ἐπεμέλοντο ὡς μὴ κωλύοιντο πορεύεσθαι, *they took care that they should not be prevented from marching*. Cyr. vi. 3, 2. Ἐπεμελήθη ὡς τύχοιεν πάντων τῶν καλῶν. Cyr. vii. 3, 17.[1]

Ὡς δὲ καλῶς ἕξει τὰ ὑμέτερα, ἐμοὶ μελήσει (like the regular ὅπως ἕξει). Cyr. iii. 2, 13. Ἐπεμελήθη ἦ ὅπως φῦλόν τι ἀποστήσεται ἦ ὅπως τὸ ἀποστὰν μὴ ἀπόληται ἦ ὡς καὶ βασιλεὺς μὴ δυνήσεται πράγματα παρέχειν (two regular cases of ὅπως with one case of ὡς). Ag. vii. 7. Προεῖπον ὡς μηδεὶς κινήσοιτο μηδὲ ἀνάξοιτο. Hell. ii. 1, 22.

(Ὡς ἄν.) *Subj.* Τὸ ὅσα ἂν γνῷ ἀγαθὰ εἶναι ἐπιμελεῖσθαι ὡς ἂν πραχθῇ. Hipp. ix. 2. Οὐ φέρει καρπὸν ἢν μή τις ἐπιμελῆται ὡς ἂν ταῦτα περαίνηται. Ibid.

Opt. Ἐπιμέλονται ὡς ἂν βέλτιστοι εἶεν οἱ πολῖται, *they take care that (of the way by which) the citizens may be the best*. Cyr. i. 2, 5. Ἐπιμελούμενος τούτου ὡς ἂν πραχθείη, *seeing how this could be done*. Cyr. i. 6, 23. So Hipp. i. 12; Eques. ix. 3. Ἢν γνῶσιν (αὐτὸν) δυνάμενον παρασκευάζειν ὡς ἂν πλέον ἔχοιεν τῶν πολεμίων, πρὸς δὲ τούτοις κἀκεῖνο λάβωσιν εἰς τὴν γνώμην ὡς οὔτ᾽ ἂν εἰκῇ οὔτ᾽ ἄνευ θεῶν ἡγήσαιτ᾽ ἂν ἐπὶ πολεμίους, πάντα ταῦτα πιθανοτέρους ποιεῖ. Hipp. vi. 6. (Compare ὡς ἂν πλέον ἔχοιεν, *to provide means by which they could be superior*, with ὡς οὐκ ἡγήσαιτ᾽ ἄν, *to get the idea that he would not lead*, indirect discourse).

Ὡς ἂν ἀσφαλέστατά γε εἰδείην ὁπόσον τὸ στράτευμά ἐστιν ἐποίουν, *I took the course by which I should know most accurately the size of the army*. Cyr. vi. 3, 18. Αἰσθανόμενος (αὐτὴν) ἀντεπιμελουμένην ὡς καὶ εἰσιόντι εἴη αὐτῷ τὰ δέοντα, καί, εἴ ποτε ἀσθενήσειεν, ὡς μηδενὸς ἂν δέοιτο,

---

[1] See also ὡς with the subjunctive in An. iii. 1, 35 and 41; Cyr. i. 6, 24; Hell. v. 4, 33; Oec. vii. 34 (*bis*), xx. 4 (*bis*) and 16; Rep. Lac. xiv. 4; and ὡς with the optative in An. i. 1, 5; Cyr. v. 1, 18, vi. 3, 4, viii. 1, 42; Hell. iii. 4, 15, v. 2, 1 and 5; Ages. i. 19 and 22 and 23, ii. 31; Rep. Lac. iii. 3. This list includes all object clauses with simple ὡς not given above. All Weber's examples of these clauses in Xenophon which have ὡς with the future, ὡς ἄν with the subjunctive or optative, or ὅπως ἄν with the optative are quoted or cited in the text above, except Cyr. vii. 5, 81, which is classed with final clauses in p. 401.

ἐκ πάντων τούτων ἡλίσκετο ἔρωτι. Cyr. v. 1, 18. (Here the protasis εἴ ποτε ἀσθενήσειεν causes the change from ὡς with the simple optative to the potential ὡς μηδενὸς ἂν δέοιτο, in which the separation of ἄν from ὡς is to be noticed.) Ἐκπεπονημένους ὡς ἂν κράτιστοι εἶεν, *thoroughly trained to be the best* (in the way in which they would be best). Hell. vi. 4, 28. So Cyr. v. 2, 2 ; Rep. Lac. vi. 1. ("Ὅπως ἄν *with Opt.*) Three examples after primary tenses are especially peculiar. Κελεύεις με ἐπιμελεῖσθαι ὅπως ἂν μὴ παντάπασιν ἀληθῶς πένης γένοιο, *you bid me see how you could escape becoming in truth absolutely poor.* Oec. ii. 9. Σκοπῶ ὅπως ἂν ὡς ῥᾷστα διάγοιεν, ἡμεῖς δ' ἂν μάλιστα ἂν εὐφραινοίμεθα θεώμενοι αὐτούς, *I try to see how they might live the easiest lives, and how we might take most delight in beholding them.* Symp. vii. 2. Τί οὐ τὴν δύναμιν ἔλεξας, ὅπως εἰδότες πρὸς ταῦτα βουλευσόμεθα ὅπως ἂν ἄριστα ἀγωνιζοίμεθα, *that we might take counsel* (§ 324) *how we might fight the best.* Cyr. ii. 1, 4. Here belongs also PLAT. Lys. 207 E, προθυμοῦνται ὅπως ἂν εὐδαιμονοίης (349).

Εἰσῆλθεν ἐπιβουλεύσας ὅπως ἂν ἀλυπότατα εἴποι. Cyr. i. 4, 13. Σκοπῶν δ' αὖ ὅπως ἂν καὶ ἡ πᾶσα ἀρχὴ κατέχοιτο καὶ ἄλλη ἔτι προσγίγνοιτο, ἡγήσατο. Cyr. vii. 5, 70. So iv. 2, 34, viii. 1, 14 and 47. Ἐλογιζόμεθα ὡς ἱκανὸν εἴη εἴ τις δύναιτο ἐπιμεληθῆναι ὅπως ἂν καλὸς κἀγαθὸς γένοιτο. Cyr. i. 6, 7. (Was the oratio recta here ὅπως ἂν γένηται ?) Ἐβουλεύετο ὅπως ἂν μὴ βαρὺς εἴη τοῖς ξυμμάχοις. Hell. iii. 2, 1. So vii. 1, 33 ; An. iv. 3, 14, v. 7, 20. Πάντ' ἐποίησεν ὅπως ἂν δι' ἐκείνου ἐγκριθείη. Hell. iv. 1, 40. Τῷ μὲν θεῷ οὐδὲν ἐκοινώσαντο ὅπως ἂν ἡ εἰρήνη γένοιτο, αὐτοὶ δὲ ἐβουλεύοντο. Hell. vii. 1, 27.

V.

ON SOME DISPUTED POINTS IN THE CONSTRUCTION OF ἔδει, χρῆν, ETC. WITH THE INFINITIVE.[1]

SUPPLEMENT TO §§ 415-423.

THE familiar construction by which ἔδει, χρῆν or ἐχρῆν, εἰκὸς ἦν, προσῆκεν, ἐξῆν, and other imperfects denoting *obligation, propriety,* or *possibility,* are used with the infinitive in an idiomatic sense, the whole expression becoming a form of potential indicative, and generally implying the opposite of the action or the negation of the infinitive, has already been explained in §§ 415-423. Some additional remarks, however, seem necessary, to guard against prevailing misapprehensions.

The important distinction between this idiomatic construction and the use of these imperfects as ordinary past tenses (§ 417) is generally

---

[1] Many parts of this paper are identical with the article with the same title in the *Harvard Studies in Classical Philology*, vol. i. pp. 77-88.

indicated only by the context, and not by the words themselves. It may even be doubtful in some cases which meaning is intended. Thus, in DEM. xviii. 190, τί τὸν σύμβουλον ἐχρῆν ποιεῖν; οὐ . . . ἐλέσθαι; nothing in the words shows whether the action of ἐλέσθαι is real or not ; but the following τοῦτο τοίνυν ἐποίησα shows that the questions refer merely to a past duty which the speaker actually performed. Indeed, the idiomatic use of ἔδει etc. with the infinitive may be found in the same sentence with the ordinary use of these imperfects as past tenses without reference to any condition. A familiar case is in the New Testament, MATTH. xxiii. 23, ταῦτα δὲ ἔδει ποιῆσαι κἀκεῖνα μὴ ἀφεῖναι, these (the weightier matters of the law) ought ye to have done, and yet not to have left the others (taking tithes) undone. This is equivalent to two sentences, ταῦτα ἔδει ὑμᾶς ποιῆσαι, ye ought to have done these (which ye did not do), and ἐκεῖνα ἔδει ὑμᾶς μὴ ἀφεῖναι, ye were right in not leaving those undone (which ye did not leave undone). We have a decisive proof of the idiomatic use when the present infinitive with ἔδει etc. refers to present time, as when χρῆν σε τοῦτο ποιεῖν means you ought to be doing this (but are not) ; for these words without the potential force could mean only it was (once) your duty to do this. This use of a past tense to express present time, which is found in Greek, Latin, and English (§ 417), is an important characteristic of this idiom.

It is generally laid down as an absolute rule that in this idiom the opposite of the infinitive is always implied. See Krüger, § 53, 2, 7, where the usual formula is given, that with ἔδει τοῦτο γίγνεσθαι we must understand ἀλλ᾽ οὐ γίγνεται, but with ἔδει ἂν τοῦτο γίγνεσθαι we must understand ἀλλ᾽ οὐ δεῖ. This principle was first formulated, I believe, by G. Hermann.[1] It covers nearly all the ordinary cases, and has generally been found to be a convenient working rule, though many passages show that it is not of universal application. The following three classes of examples show the need of a more flexible formula.

(1) In the following cases the opposite of the leading verb is implied far more than that of the infinitive, the action of the latter in the first case being emphatically affirmed :—

HDT. i. 39 (χρῆν σε ποιέειν τὰ ποιέεις), DEM. ix. 6, xxxiii. 37, and EUR. Med. 490 (reading συγγνωστὸν ἦν). These are quoted and discussed in § 422, 1.

(2) In concessive sentences introduced by καὶ εἰ, even if, οὐδ᾽ εἰ, not even if, or εἰ, although, which contain unreal conditions, the action

---

[1] See Hermann, de Particula Ἄν, i. 12. In discussing SOPH. Elec. 1505, χρῆν δ᾽ εὐθὺς εἶναι τήνδε τοῖς πᾶσιν δίκην, Hermann says : " Χρῆν dicit, quia oportere indicat sine condicione : nec potest opponi, ἀλλ᾽ οὐ χρή : nam si oportet, quomodo potest non oportere ? At non omnia fiunt, quae oportebat. Itaque quod opponere potes, aliud est : ἀλλ᾽ οὐκ ἔστι."
The "opposite" implied in a negative expression of this kind (even when the negation belongs to the leading verb) is an affirmative. Thus οὐ προσῆκεν ἐλθεῖν, he ought not to have gone, implies ἀλλ᾽ ἦλθεν, as ἔδει τούτους μὴ ζῆν implies ἀλλὰ ζῶσιν.

or negation of the apodosis must be distinctly affirmed (§ 412, 3). Here, therefore, the common formula cannot be applied. See ISOC. xviii. 19, and ISAE. vi. 44, quoted in § 422, 2 ; and the following. Καὶ γὰρ ἄνευ τούτων (i.e. καὶ εἰ μὴ εἴχετε τούτους) ἐξῆν τοι ποιέειν ταῦτα, i.e. *even if you had not all mankind with you, you could still do what you now do.* HDT. vii. 56. (Here ταῦτα ποιέειν is of course affirmed.) Εἰ γὰρ ἦν ἅπασι πρόδηλα τὰ μέλλοντα γενήσε- σθαι, . . . οὐδ᾽ οὕτως ἀποστατέον τῇ πόλει τούτων ἦν, i.e. *Athens ought not even then to have withdrawn from this policy,* which she followed (ἀποστατέον ἦν = ἀποστῆναι ἔδει). DEM. xviii. 199. See also DEM. xv. 28. Εἰ γὰρ μηδὲν εἴχετε τῶν ἄλλων λογίσασθαι, μηδ᾽ ἐφ᾽ ὑμῶν αὐτῶν οἷοί τε ἦτε ταῦτα συνεῖναι, ἦν ἰδεῖν παράδειγμα Ὀλυνθίους τουτουσί, *for although you had no other cases to consider, and could not learn this lesson in your own experience, you might have seen an example in these Olynthians.* Id. xxiii. 107.

These examples are important as showing that there is nothing in an expression like ἐξῆν σοι ποιεῖν τοῦτο, even in its idiomatic sense, which *necessarily* involves the denial of the action of ποιεῖν.

(3) In some concessive examples, in which the apodosis ought to be affirmed, we find the action of the infinitive denied. See SOPH. O. T. 255, THUC. i. 38, ISOC. xii. 71, quoted in § 422, 2. These are important as showing that the real apodosis in these expressions with ἔδει etc. is not to be found in the infinitive *alone.*

It is well known that the imperfects in question (without ἄν) can be used with the infinitive in two ways,—(a) alone, with no protasis expressed or implied except the condition which is contained in the expression itself, as in ἔδει σε ἐλθεῖν, *you ought to have gone ;* and (b) as the apodosis of an unreal condition, as in εἰ οὗτός σε ἐκέλευσεν, ἔδει σε ἐλθεῖν, *if he had commanded you, you should have gone.* It will be noticed that all the examples quoted above under (1) and (2) are of the latter class, for in HDT. vii. 56, ἄνευ τούτων represents εἰ μὴ εἴχετε τούτους. If now we take the apodoses of these sentences apart from their protases, we shall find that no one of them can then have the meaning which it now has. For example, in HDT. i. 39, χρῆν σε ποιέειν τὰ ποιέεις would not be Greek at all as a potential expression, for χρῆν σε ποιέειν would mean *you ought to do* (something which you do not do). In DEM. xxxiii. 37, ἐνῆν αἰτιάσασθαι by itself would mean *he might have charged me* (but did not). Οὐκ ἐξῆν αὐτῷ δικάζεσθαι (ISOC. xviii. 19) could mean only *he could not maintain a suit as he does ;* that is, it would mean nothing without a protasis. Οὐ προσῆκεν αὐτοὺς Εὐκτήμονος εἶναι (ISAE. vi. 44) by itself would mean *they ought not to belong to E.'s house as they do.* Οὐκ ἀποστατέον ἦν (DEM. xviii. 199) alone would mean *she ought not to have withdrawn as she did.* So ἦν ἰδεῖν παράδειγμα (Id. xxiii. 107) would mean *you might have seen* (but you did not see) *an example.* (Compare DEM. xxviii. 10, τὴν διαθήκην ἠφανίκατε, ἐξ ἧς ἦν εἰδέναι τὴν ἀλήθειαν, *the will, from which we might know the truth.*)

When these potential expressions without ἄν stand alone, they always imply the opposite of the action or the negation of the infinitive ; so that εἰκὸς ἦν σε τοῦτο παθεῖν by itself can mean only *you would properly have suffered this* (but you did not). This is necessary because the equivalent of this form, τοῦτο ἂν ἔπαθες εἰ τὸ εἰκὸς ἔπαθες, always involves οὐκ ἔπαθες τοῦτο, since τοῦτο and τὸ εἰκός are here made identical, and τὸ εἰκὸς ἔπαθες is denied. When, however, one of these expressions is made the apodosis of an unreal condition external to itself, it may be so modified by the new condition as no longer to imply the opposite of the infinitive as before. This is the case with the four examples under (1), in which we certainly do not find οὐ ποιέεις, ἄλλο λέγει καὶ συμβουλεύει, οὐκ ᾐτιάσατο, and οὐκ ἠράσθης implied in the form of expression. The apparent paradox here is explained by the principle stated in § 511, that when several protases, not co-ordinate, belong to the same sentence, one always contains the leading condition, to which the rest of the sentence (including the other conditions) forms the conclusion ; and when this leading condition is unreal, it makes all subordinate past or present conditions also unreal, so far as the supposed case is concerned, without regard to their own nature. A sentence like this, *If you had been an Athenian, you would have been laughed at if you had talked as you did*, shows the principle clearly. This has become the relation of the unreal protasis involved in εἰκὸς ἦν σε τοῦτο παθεῖν, when this expression is made the apodosis of a new unreal condition. Thus, when χρῆν σε ποιέειν in HDT. i. 39, which by itself could admit only an unreal object, follows εἰ ὑπὸ ὀδόντος εἶπε τελευτήσειν με, even τὰ ποιέεις can be its object, and the whole can mean *if the dream had said I was to perish by a tooth, you would do what you now do if you did what was right.* The new chief protasis that has come in has changed the whole relation of the old implied protasis to the sentence as a whole.

It is often difficult to express in English the exact force of these expressions, even when no external protasis is added, and the opposite of the infinitive (not that of the leading verb) is therefore implied. Thus, a common translation of DEM. xviii. 248, οὐδ' ἀγνωμονῆσαί τι θαυμαστὸν ἦν τοὺς πολλοὺς πρὸς ἐμέ, it *would have been no wonder if the mass of the people had been somewhat unmindful of me* (Westermann translates *entschuldbar gewesen wäre*), would seem to require ἦν ἄν. But the strength of the apodosis lies in the infinitive, and the meaning (fully developed) is, *the mass of the people might have been somewhat unmindful of me* (ἠγνωμόνησαν ἄν τι) *without doing anything wonderful* (i.e. *if they had done a very natural thing*). With θαυμαστὸν ἂν ἦν there would have been an undue emphasis thrown upon θαυμαστόν. In PLAT. Rep. 474 D, ἄλλῳ ἔπρεπεν λέγειν ἃ λέγεις is equivalent to ἄλλος ἔλεγεν ἂν πρεπόντως ἃ λέγεις, *another would becomingly say what you say*, the opposite of λέγειν being implied. Ἔπρεπεν ἂν λέγειν would have caused a change of emphasis, but would have substantially the same general meaning, *it would have been becoming for another to say what you say.* See also DEM. xviii. 16, xlv. 69, and

PLAT. Euthyd. 304 D, quoted in § 419 ; and the discussion of EUR. Med. 490 in § 422, 1.

We have seen that we cannot make the denial of the action of the infinitive an absolute test of the proper use of the form without ἄν where there is an external protasis added to the condition implied in the expression itself. The examples last quoted show that we cannot make the denial of the leading verb an absolute test of the proper use of the form with ἄν. In fact, this idiom is too flexible and too dependent on the momentary feeling of the speaker or writer to subject itself to any such strict rules as are usually forced upon it. The following rules seem to me to be as exact as the Greek usage warrants.[1]

1. The form without ἄν is used when the infinitive is the principal word, on which the chief force of the expression falls, while the leading verb is an auxiliary which we can express by *ought, might, could,* or by an adverb.

2. On the other hand, when the chief force falls on the necessity, propriety, or possibility of the act, and not on the act itself, the leading verb has ἄν, like any other imperfect in a similar apodosis.

Examples of the form with ἄν are generally regular. See those quoted in § 423.[2]   A standard case is DEM. iv. 1, εἰ τὰ δέοντα οὗτοι συνεβούλευσαν, οὐδὲν ἄν ὑμᾶς νῦν ἔδει βουλεύεσθαι, *if these had given you the necessary advice, there would be no need of your deliberating now.*   Here, as in all the ten examples of ἔδει ἄν quoted by La Roche, we find ἔδει ἄν in its meaning *there would be* (or *would have been*) *need,* whereas in the form without ἄν we generally have ἔδει in the sense of *ought,* expressing *obligation* and not *necessity.*   Of course, the idea of necessity is incompatible with that of an act not done.   If La Roche's statistics are complete here, we see that the Greeks almost always expressed obligation or propriety, and generally expressed possibility, by the form without ἄν, reserving ἔδει ἄν for the idea of necessity, and ἐξῆν ἄν for a few cases in which the idea of possibility was to be made specially emphatic.

It is not surprising, under these circumstances, that the form without ἄν should often be used where we are at first inclined to think ἄν

---

[1] When an external protasis is added, there is no necessity for any denial of the action of the apodosis at all (see § 412). But this denial, though not essential, is generally implied in the apodosis of an unreal condition, and the apodosis (as a whole) happens to be denied in all the cases of the construction of ἔδει etc. with the infinitive which are discussed here. No notice is taken, therefore, of the principle of § 412 in this discussion.

[2] See La Roche on "ἄν bei ἔδει und ἐξῆν" in the *Zeitschrift für die oesterreichischen Gymnasien* for 1876, pp. 588-591. He professes to give all the cases ; but his twenty-one examples of ἔδει ἄν include eleven in which ἔδει has the genitive of a noun and no infinitive. Omitting these, we have only ten of ἔδει ἄν with the infinitive : THUC. i. 74 , LYS. Frag. 56 (88 Scheibe) ; ISOC. xv. 17 ; ISAE. iv. 4 ; DEM. iv. 1 ; PLAT. Rep. 328 C, Theaet. 169 E, Gorg. 514 A, Alc. i. 119 B ; DEM. lvii. 47 (only the last three affirmative) ; with four of ἐξῆν ἄν : LYS. iv. 13, Frag. 47 (79 Scheibe) ; ISAE. x. 13 ; DEM. xxiv. 146. He finds χρῆν ἄν only in LYS. xii. 48, where he proposes to omit ἄν, overlooking χρῆν ἄν προσδοκῆσαι in DEM. xviii. 195. Both of these passages are discussed below, pp. 409, 410.

is required. It must be remembered that the real apodosis here is not
the central infinitive alone, but this infinitive modified by the idea of
obligation, propriety, or possibility in the leading verb, that is, conditioned by the implied protasis which the expression includes (see §
420). This modification may be so slight as to leave the infinitive
the only important word in the apodosis ; in this case the opposite of
the infinitive is generally implied, as it always is when no protasis is
added : thus, Eur. Med. 520, χρῆν σ᾽, εἴπερ ἦσθα μὴ κακὸς, πείσαντά
με γαμεῖν γάμον τόνδε, implies ἀλλ᾽ οὐκ ἐγάμεις πείσας με. It may
be so great as to make the idea of obligation etc. a prominent factor
in the apodosis, still stopping short of the point at which this favourite
Greek idiom was abandoned and an ordinary apodosis with ἄν was
substituted in its place. The Greeks preferred the form without ἄν
almost always where we can express the apodosis by the verb of the
infinitive with *ought, might*, or *could*, or with an adverb, although we
sometimes find it hard to express the combined idea in English without giving undue force to the leading verb. Sometimes, when the
idea of obligation, propriety, or possibility is specially prominent in
the apodosis, although no ἄν is used, the opposite that is suggested
combines this idea with that of the infinitive. This is the case with
the examples in (1), in which the distinction between the two forms
is very slight and of little practical account. In Hdt. i. 39, the
apodosis is *you would then properly do what you now do* (or *you would
then, if you did what you ought, do what you now do*), implying *now you
do not do this properly.* With χρῆν ἄν it would have been *it would
then be your duty to do what you now do*, the chief force being transferred from the act to the duty or necessity. Still, this change might
have been made without otherwise affecting the sense. In Dem. ix. 6,
the apodosis is *in that case the speaker would properly talk of nothing else
than this* (implying *now he may properly talk of another matter*) ; whereas
with ἔδει ἄν it would be *there would then be no need of his talking of
anything else*, with greater emphasis on the ἔδει and with a change of
meaning. In Dem. xxiii. 37, ἐνῆν αἰτιάσασθαι means *he might then
possibly have accused me*, implying *he could not possibly accuse me as it
was ;* with ἐνῆν ἄν it would have been *it would then have been possible
for him to accuse me*, the emphasis being transferred with no other
change of sense. The same is true of Eur. Med. 490. Likewise, in
Isoc. xviii. 21, the apodosis, *in that case we ought not to wonder at him*
or *we should not properly wonder at him*, is equivalent to οὐκ ἂν ἐθαυ-
μάζομεν ἀξίως, with the opposite implied, *now we do wonder at him
properly* (νῦν θαυμάζομεν ἀξίως). This combination of two ideas in an
apodosis of this kind is analogous to that which we often find in an
ordinary apodosis with ἄν ; thus, in Isoc. vi. 87, οὐχ οὕτω δ᾽ ἂν προθύμως ἐπὶ τὸν πόλεμον ὑμᾶς παρεκάλουν, εἰ μὴ τὴν εἰρήνην ἑώρων
αἰσχρὰν ἐσομένην, *I should not exhort you with all this zeal to war, did
I not see*, etc., the apodosis which is denied includes οὕτω προθύμως.
      A striking illustration of the modification of the infinitive in an
apodosis of this kind by the force of the leading verb may be seen in

the examples under (3). Here in concessive sentences, in which the apodosis must be affirmed, we find the action of the infinitives denied. This shows that the infinitive alone is not the real apodosis. In SOPH. O. T. 255, the actual apodosis is *you would not properly leave the guilt unpurged* (implying *you do not properly leave it*). In THUC. i. 38, the apodosis is *they would fairly have yielded* (implying *they did not yield, but it was fair that they should*). In ISOC. xii. 71, it is *they would deservedly have received*, = ἔτυχον ἂν ἀξίως (implying that it was only *undeservedly* that they *failed to receive* the reward). The remarks that have been made above apply also to the concessive sentences in (2), in which nothing in the apodosis is denied. Here, too, the form with ἄν might have been used by transferring the force of the expression from the infinitive to the leading verb.

It has been seen that ἔδει ἄν with the infinitive differs from ἔδει without ἄν in meaning as well as in the balance of emphasis. On the other hand, ἐξῆν ἄν differs from ἐξῆν only in the latter respect. See ISAE. x. 13, τῷ μὲν πατρὶ αὐτῆς, εἰ παῖδες ἄρρενες μὴ ἐγένοντο, οὐκ ἂν ἐξῆν ἄνευ ταύτης διαθέσθαι, i.e. *in that case he would not have been permitted* (by law) *to leave his daughter out of his will ;* and DEM. xxiv. 146, οὔτε γὰρ ἂν ἐξῆν ὑμῖν τιμᾶν ὅτι χρὴ παθεῖν ἢ ἀποτῖσαι, i.e. *if this law were passed, you would not have the power* (which you now have) *of assessing penalties.* Compare with these ISOC. xviii. 19, οὐκ ἐξῆν αὐτῷ δικάζεσθαι, *he could not* (in that case) *maintain a suit*, where ἐξῆν ἄν would only give more emphasis to the possibility, which is done in the preceding examples. For the ordinary use of ἐξῆν and the infinitive see PLAT. Crit. 52 C, ἐξῆν σοι φυγῆς τιμήσασθαι εἰ ἐβούλου, *you might have proposed exile as your penalty if you had wished to* (implying only οὐ φυγῆς ἐτιμήσω).

It remains to discuss two passages in which χρῆν ἄν occurs, with a view to La Roche's disbelief in the existence of this form (see footnote 2, p. 407). In DEM. xviii. 195, we have χρῆν and χρῆν ἄν in close succession, with no essential change in meaning except the difference in emphasis above mentioned. The sentence is : εἰ μετὰ Θηβαίων ἡμῖν ἀγωνιζομένοις οὕτως εἵμαρτο πρᾶξαι, τί χρῆν προσδοκᾶν εἰ μηδὲ τούτους ἔσχομεν συμμάχους ; . . . καὶ εἰ νῦν τριῶν ἡμερῶν ἀπὸ τῆς Ἀττικῆς ὁδὸν τῆς μάχης γενομένης τοσοῦτος κίνδυνος καὶ φόβος περιέστη τὴν πόλιν, τί ἄν, εἴ που τῆς χώρας ταὐτὸ τοῦτο πάθος συνέβη, προσδοκῆσαι χρῆν ; i.e. *when it was fated that we should fare as we did with the Thebans on our side, what ought we to have expected (which we did not find ourselves expecting) if we had not secured even these as allies ? And, if so great danger and terror surrounded the city when the battle was fought two or three days' journey from Attica, what should we have had to expect (which we did not really have to expect) if this calamity had occurred within our own country ?* Here the unreal supposition of not having secured the Thebans as allies, or (its probable consequence) the battle of Chaeronea having been fought in Attica, suits either form of apodosis, τί χρῆν προσδοκᾶν ; or τί ἂν χρῆν προσδοκῆσαι ; the expectation itself in the former case, and the

necessity for the expectation in the latter, being specially emphasised.
It is hard to believe that the orator felt any important change in the
general force of his question when he added ἄν in the second case.
In LYS. xii. 32, we have, addressed to Eratosthenes, χρῆν δέ σε,
εἴπερ ἦσθα χρηστός, πολὺ μᾶλλον τοῖς μέλλουσιν ἀδίκως ἀποθανεῖ-
σθαι μηνυτὴν γενέσθαι ἢ τοὺς ἀδίκως ἀπολουμένους συλλαμβά-
νειν, *if you had been an honest man, you ought to have become an informer
in behalf of those who were about to suffer death unjustly, much rather than
(and not) to have arrested (as you did) those who were doomed to perish
unjustly;* but in 48, referring to the same man and the same acts, the
orator says εἴπερ ἦν ἀνὴρ ἀγαθός, ἐχρῆν ἄν πρῶτον μὲν μὴ παρανόμως ἄρχειν, ἔπειτα τῇ βουλῇ μηνυτὴν γενέσθαι, κ.τ.λ., *if he had
been an honest man, he would have had, first, to abstain from lawlessness
in office, and, next, to come before the Senate as an informer,* etc. La
Roche proposes to omit ἄν in the second passage, because it would be
absurd to suppose that ἀλλ᾿ ἐχρῆν is implied in the sense that *E. had
a right to be lawless in office* (" *er durfte παρανόμως ἄρχειν* ") because he
was not honest. What is implied is rather ἀλλ᾿ οὐκ ἐχρῆν μὴ παρανόμως ἄρχειν, i.e. *not being an honest man, he did not have to abstain
from lawlessness in office,* etc., which we can understand without absurdity. The passage, like so many sentences of this class, is simply
an argument to prove that E. was not honest. *If he had been honest*
(it is said), *he would have had to do certain things* (which, it is implied,
all honest men do); *but he did not do these* (as is stated, εἰς τὴν ἀρχὴν
καταστὰς ἀγαθοῦ μὲν οὐδενὸς μετέσχεν, ἄλλων δὲ πολλῶν); *therefore
he was not honest.* There is a slight slip in showing (in the words last
quoted) that he *did not do* the things in question, and not that *he did
not have to do* them; so that of the two constructions, χρῆν in 32 and
ἐχρῆν ἄν in 48, the former is more strictly logical. This use of ἐχρῆν
ἄν is the counterpart of that of χρῆν, ἔδει, ἐνῆν, and θαυμαστὸν ἦν
in the passages quoted above (1), where the forms with ἄν might have
been used.

The Latin follows precisely the same principle as the Greek in the
use of such imperfects as *debebat, licebat* (= χρῆν, ἐξῆν), and *deberet,
liceret* (= χρῆν ἄν, ἐξῆν ἄν), with reference to present time. But
when such expressions are past, the Latin uses *debuit* or *debuerat* in
the sense of χρῆν, and *debuisset* for χρῆν ἄν, both with the present
infinitive; while the Greek keeps the imperfect in all cases. See
CIC. Phil. ii. 99, Quem patris loco, si ulla in te pietas esset, *colere
debebas* (= χρῆν σε φιλεῖν), *you ought to love (but you do not);* and
Cluent. 18, Cluentio ignoscere debebitis quod haec a me dici patiatur;
mihi ignoscere *non deberes* si tacerem (= οὐ ἄν σε ἐμοὶ συγγιγνώσκειν
χρῆν εἰ ἐσίγων), *it would not be right for you to pardon me if I were
silent.* In the former case the emphasis falls on *colere;* in the latter
on *non deberes,* which is in strong antithesis to *debebitis.* See also CIC.
Verr. ii. 5, 50: Qui ex foedere ipso navem vel usque ad Oceanum, si
imperassemus, *mittere debuerunt,* ei, ne in freto ante sua tecta et domos
navigarent, . . . pretio abs te ius foederis et imperii condicionem

redemerunt, *they who were bound by the very terms of the treaty, if we had commanded it, to send a ship even into the Ocean,* etc. So far as any opposite is implied here, it is not that of *mittere,* but rather something like what is implied in the examples in (1), like *they did not have to send.* Mittere debuissent (ἔδει ἂν πέμψαι) would mean *they would have been bound to send.* In Latin, as in Greek and English, the peculiar force of the past tense of the indicative with the infinitive is purely idiomatic.

VI.

In a paper on *The Extent of the Deliberative Construction in Relative Clauses in Greek,* in the Harvard Studies in Classical Philology, vol. vii. (1896), pp. 1-12, I have reviewed the recent discussion on this subject, and have maintained the following points, on which I agree substantially with Professor Hale's paper in the Transactions of the American Philological Association, xxiv. pp. 156-205.

1. Οὐκ ἔχω, οὐκ ἔστι with the dative, and similar expressions, in the sense of ἀπορῶ, may be followed by a deliberative subjunctive in an indirect question ; as οὐκ ἔχω ὅ τι εἴπω or οὐκ ἔχω τί φῶ, *I know not what to say, non habeo quod* (or *quid*) *dicam,* ὅ τι here being purely interrogative like τί. This subjunctive can become an optative after a past tense or another optative ; as οὐκ εἴχομεν ὅτου ἐπιλαβοίμεθα, DEM. xxxv. 25. Besides the examples in 677 we have the following. Οὐκ ἔχοιμεν ἂν ὅποι σωθῶμεν and οὐχ ἔξουσιν ὅποι φύγωσιν, XEN. An. ii. 4, 19 (involving ποῖ σωθῶμεν ; and ποῖ φύγωμεν ;). Ἐμοὶ γὰρ οὐκέτ᾽ ἐστὶν εἰς ὅ τι βλέπω (εἰς τί βλέπω ;), SOPH. Aj. 514. So ὅπου τεθῇ, EUR. H. F. 1245 ; ὅποι φύγω, OREST. 722 ; δι᾽ ὅ τι . . . πολεμήσωμεν, ANDOC. iii. 16 ; ὅπως ὠφελοίη, XEN. Hellen. i. 4, 15. In AR. Eq. 1320, τίν᾽ ἔχων φήμην ἀγαθὴν ἥκεις, ἐφ᾽ ὅτῳ κνισῶμεν ἀγυιάς; we probably have an indirect question representing ἐπὶ τίνι (*in whose honor* or *for what*) κνισῶμεν ἀγυιάς; depending on the idea *what have you to report to us?* or *can you tell us?*

In all these we find no case parallel to the Homeric ἡγεμόν᾽ ὅπασσον, ὅ κέ με κεῖσ᾽ ἀγάγῃ, Od. xv. 310.

2. Expressions like οὐκ ἔχει ὅ τι εἴπῃ, *he has nothing to say,* give rise by analogy to ἔχει ὅ τι εἴπῃ, *he has something to say,* though in the latter there is really no indirect question. See examples in § 572, 1.

3. A further extension of the deliberative usage leads to the subjunctive and optative in clauses introduced by true relatives with distinct antecedents, when these depend on expressions implying doubt, perplexity, or ignorance. See examples in § 572, 2. Thus, in οὐ γὰρ ἄλλον οἶδ᾽ ὅτῳ λέγω, we cannot distinguish the modal force of the subjunctive from that in οὐ γὰρ οἶδ᾽ ὅτῳ ἄλλῳ λέγω, the subjunctive being deliberative in both. The former is the result of

a simple evolution, by which a relative clause derives its modal force from an interrogative form. Whatever final force is felt in the expression comes from the intimate relation between the deliberative and the hortatory subjunctive (see § 291). See A. Sidgwick in the Classical Review for 1891, p. 148. We have the evolution actually going on in XEN. An. i. 7, 7, where μὴ οὐκ ἔχω ὅ τι δῶ is interrogative and μὴ οὐκ ἔχω ἱκανοὺς οἷς δῶ is purely relative, while the modal force of δῶ must be the same in both. See also XEN. Hellen. i. 3, 21, SOPH. Phil. 692, THEOC. xxv. 218. In AESCH. Prom. 470, LYS. xxiv. 1, ISOC. xxi. 1, we may call the dependent clause an indirect question, depending directly on the idea I cannot (could not) see. See Tarbell in Classical Review for 1891, p. 302.

4. While most of the optatives quoted in this discussion are simply explained as correlatives of the deliberative subjunctive, a very different problem is presented by the examples in § 573. In SOPH. Tr. 903, κρύψασ᾽ ἑαυτὴν ἔνθα μή τις εἰσίδοι, we cannot suppose an Attic construction like κρύψω ἐμαυτὴν ἔνθα μή τις εἰσίδῃ, for we should certainly find εἰσόψεται, as in SOPH. Aj. 658, κρύψω τόδ᾽ ἔγχος ἔνθα μή τις ὄψεται. (For an occasional future optative, see § 574.) In AR. Ran. 97, ὅστις λάκοι clearly expresses purpose, and we cannot think of substituting ὅστις λάκῃ for it ; and ὅστις φθέγξεται, the true Attic expression, is found in the next verse : the latter decides the force of ὅστις λάκοι. It would seem that the optative, which is further removed than the subjunctive from the original deliberative construction, took another step in the process of "extension," and gave us a few such expressions as have been quoted. Another case of final optative is PLAT. Rep. 398 B, ὃς . . . μιμοῖτο καὶ . . . λέγοι. In Rep. 578 E, εἴ τις θεῶν ἄνδρα θείη εἰς ἐρημίαν, ὅπου αὐτῷ μηδεὶς μέλλοι βοηθήσειν, if some God should put a man in a desert, where there should be nobody likely to help him, we might take the second clause as either final or conditional ; it probably combines a final with a conditional force, expressing the purpose of putting the man into a desert and also continuing the condition of the preceding clause.

In SOPH. Phil. 279-282, ὁρῶντα (past) ναῦς βεβῶσας, ἄνδρα δ᾽ οὐδέν᾽ ἔντοπον (sc. ὄντα), οὐχ ὅστις ἀρκέσειεν οὐδ᾽ ὅστις συλλάβοιτο, I formerly classed the optatives with those in § 573 ; but it now seems to me that οὐδεὶς ἔντοπός ἐστιν ὅστις ἀρκέσῃ would be as natural as ἐμοὶ γὰρ οὐκέτ᾽ ἐστὶν εἰς ὅ τι βλέπω in Aj. 514, and I have therefore included this passage with the examples under § 573, 2.

INDEX TO THE EXAMPLES

N.B.—The references are made to the *Sections* of the Book.

TYRTAEUS.

XENOPHON.

Anabasis.

LATIN AUTHORS.

ADDITIONAL EXAMPLES
1910

GREEK INDEX.

and ὅπως in Hom. 341, 342, 343, ὅπως ἄν in Attic 348, ὡς ἄν in Xen. 351¹, ὡς ἄν once in Herod. 347. Epic use w. subj. in potential sense and in apod. 201¹, 285, 452, 235, 399, 401. Regularly omitted when conditional subj. becomes opt. after past tenses 667⁴, 689², rarely retained 692, 702, 649. See Subjunctive. With Optative. In potential sense and in apod. 202, 232, 233, 234, 455, 531, never w. fut opt. 203, 459; rarely omitted 240-242. In protasis: εἴ κε (once εἴ περ ἄν) in Hom. 460; w. pot. opt. in present cond. 409, 458, 506; εἰ or εἴ κε, if haply, in case that, in Hom. 488, 491. With conditional relative and opt. in Hom. 542; w. pot. opt. in Attic 557; ὅτε κε in a past gen. cond. in Hom. 542; εἰσόκε w. opt., once in Hom., 616. Πρὶν ἄν w. opt. 649. In final clauses w. ὡς and ὄφρα in Hom. and w. ὡς and ὅκως in Herod. 329¹ (cf. 358), ὡς ἄν in Attic (w. pot. opt.) 329², ὅπως ἄν (w. pot. opt.) 330; in object clauses w. ὡς and ὅπως in Xen. (w. pot. opt.) 351² (see Appendix IV.), ὅπως ἄν (once) in Plato 349, ὅκως ἄν in Herod. 350; after verbs of fearing w. μή and pot. opt. 368. See Optative.

With Infinitive, always potential or in apodosis, 204; chiefly in indirect discourse 211, 479¹, 683 (see examples), 751; sometimes in other constructions 211, 212; w. pres. infin. 205, w. perf. 206, w. aor. 207, w. fut. (rare in Attic) 208; rare in early poets 209; repres. iterative impf. or aor. w. ἄν 210; w. infin. and article 212, 794. Expressions like δοκεῖ τις ἄν w. infin., how to be translated 754.

With participle, always potential or in apodosis 213, never in protasis 217, 224; w. pres. partic. 214, w. aor. 215, w. fut. (rare) 216; in indirect discourse 479¹, 687 (see 904); never in Homer or Pindar 213 (end).

With subj., closely joined to particle or relative word 218, 381, 522; w. indic. or opt., joined to emphatic word 219; separated from its verb by οἴομαι, δοκέω, etc. 220. Never begins sentence or clause 222. Repeated w. same verb 223, 225; not repeated in co-ordinate clauses

226. Without verb, potential 227, w. rel. or εἰ 228. Retained in indirect discourse after past tenses w. potential (seldom w. conditional) forms 667⁴. Τάχ' ἄν, perhaps, 221. Ἄν(ᾶ), conjunction, for εἰ ἄν, 192², 381, 382. See Εἰ.

Ἀναίνομαι, uses w. partic. and infin. 881 (end).

Ἀναιρέω, give oracular response, w. pres. and aor. infin. 98: see Θεσπίζω and Χράω.

Ἀνέχομαι w. partic. 879, w. infin. 903².

Ἄνοια and ἀνόητος w. negative force, followed by μὴ οὐ w. infin., 817 (cf. 647).

Ἀνύσας, quickly, 837.

Ἄξιον ἦν w. infin. without ἄν, potential, 415, 416: see Ἔδει.

Ἀπεικάσαι as absol. infin. 778.

Ἀποδείκνυμι w. participle 898.

Ἀποκάμνω w. partic. 881, w. infin. 903³.

Ἀποφήνασθαι w. ὡς, as absolute infin. 778.

Ἄρα, rare in indirect questions 665¹.

Ἀρκέω w. participle 899.

Ἄρτι w. temporal participle 858.

Ἄρχομαι (Hom. ἄρχω) w. partic. 879, w. infin. 903⁴. Ἀρχόμενος, at first, 834.

Ἀσμένῳ τινὶ εἶναι 900.

Ἅτε w. causal participle 862.

Αὐτάρ (like δέ) in apodosis 512.

Αὐτίκα w. temporal participle 858.

Ἀχθομένῳ τινὶ εἶναι 900.

Ἄχρι and μέχρι, until, 514, 611, 612; used like ἕως 618; w. subj. without ἄν 620. Ἄχρι οὗ and μέχρι οὗ 619.

Βαίνω w. infin. of purpose 772; βῆ and ἔβαν (βάν) w. partic. 895.

Βεβηκέναι as present 49.

Βελτίων εἰμί w. partic. 899.

Βούλει or βούλεσθε w. interrogative subj. 287, 288.

Βουλεύω w. ὅπως or ὡς and subj. or opt. (Hom.) 341-343.

Βούλομαι w. fut. infin. (rare) 113, w. infin. and ἄν 211. Βουλομένῳ τινὶ εἶναι 900. See Ἐβουλόμην.

Γεγονέναι, to be, 49.

Γιγνώσκω w. partic. 904, w. infin. (three uses) 915³.

Δέ in apodosis 512, 513, 564.

Δεδογμένον as accus. absol. 851.

Δείκνυμι w. partic. 904, w. infin. 915⁴.

Δεῖν omitted in ὀλίγου δεῖν and μικροῦ δεῖν 779 *b*.

Δεινόν ἐστιν εἰ 494.

Δέον as accus. absol. 851.

Δεῦρο or δεῦτε w. imperative 251, w. subj. 255.

Δῆλός εἰμι w. partic. 907. Δῆλόν ἐστιν (impersonal) w. ὅτι or ὡς 912.

Δηλῶ w. partic. 904, w. infin. (two uses) 915 5.

Διαλανθάνω w. partic. 888.

Διαλιπὼν χρόνον, *after a while*, and διαλείπων χρόνον, *at intervals*, 834.

Διατεινάμενος and διατεταμένος, *with all one's might*, 837.

Διατελέω w. participle 879.

Δίδωμι, *offer*, 25, imperfect of 36.

Δίκαιος w. infin., used personally, 762. Δίκαιον ἦν w. infin. without ἄν, potential, 415, 416 : see ῎Εδει.

Δικαίως containing a protasis 472, 239.

Διόπερ, causal 712.

Διότι, causal, *because*, 712 ; *that*, in indirect quotations, 663 3, 710 2 ; w. infin. by assimilation (Herod.) 755.

Δοκέω w. infin., usually in personal constr., 754, w. infin. and ἄν 754. Δοκεῖ and ἔδοξε w. infin., not in indirect discourse, 99, ἔδοξε in laws etc. 99, 750. Δοκοῦν and δόξαν as accus. absol. 851. Δοκεῖν as absol. infin. (w. ὡς δοκεῖν, ἐμοὶ δοκεῖν, etc.)· 778 ; ὥς γε δόξαι 778. Separating ἄν from its verb 220 1.

'Εάν, conjunction, for εἰ ἄν, 192 2, 381, 382. See Εἰ.

'Εβουλόμην w. infin. without ἄν, potential, 425 ; ἐβουλόμην ἄν (*vellem*) 246, 426.

῎Εγκειμαι w. partic. 897.

'Εγνωκέναι as present 49.

῎Εδει, χρῆν, and other imperfects (see 416) w. infin. without ἄν, in potential sense 415-422 (see Contents); as simple expression of past necessity etc. 417. ῎Εδει ἄν etc., how distinguished from ἔδει (alone) etc. 420, 423 (see Appendix V.).

'Εθέλοντί τινι εἶναι 900.

Εἰ, *if*, introduces protasis 378 ; relation to αἰ 379 (and footnote) ; forms of εἰ combined with ἄν and κέ (ἐάν, ἄν, ἤν, εἴ κε, αἴ κε, εἰ ἄν) 200, 381, 382, 450 : for the use of these see ῎Αν. Origin of conditional forms discussed 898 ; great variety in early Greek, 399, 400.

With present and past tenses of Indicative (simple supposition) 402 ;

w. fut. indic. in future suppos. 447-449, in present suppos., of intention or expectation, 407, 408 ; w. potential indic. (w. ἄν) 409, 506 ; w. secondary tenses of indic. in unreal cond. 410, 411, once εἴ κε w. aor. indic. in Hom. 437. After verbs of *wonder*, *indignation*, etc. 494, 495.

With Subjunctive (without ἄν or κέ). In future cond., in Hom. 453, rarely in Attic poets 454 ; in general cond., regularly in Hom. 468, always in Pindar 469, sometimes in other lyric poets 470, rarely in Attic poets 471. Relation of εἴ κε w. subj. to simple εἰ in Hom., and possible origin of the two uses, 401.

With Optative. In future cond. 455, 456, representing subj. w. ἐάν of direct form in indirect discourse after past tenses 457, 667 4, 689 2, 694 1 ; w. pot. opt. (w. ἄν) 409, 458, 506 ; in past general cond. 462-466, only once in Homer 468. Εἰ (in Hom. sometimes εἴ κε), *if haply*, *in case that*, w. opt., w. apodosis implied in protasis, in Homer 488, 491, in other Greek 489, 490. After past tenses of verbs expressing *wonder*, indignation, etc. (also indic.) 495, 697. In future wishes (generally εἴθε or εἰ γάρ) 721, 723 (end).

With Infinitive in indirect discourse, by assimilation (Herod.) 755.

Εἰ γάρ and εἴθε in future wishes 721, 723, in present or past unattained wishes 731-733 ; in Homer (also αἰ γάρ and αἴθε) in present unattained wishes 739. With ὤφελον etc. in present and past unattained wishes (poetic) 734, 736. Εἰ δ' ἄγε 251, 474. Εἰ δὲ μή, *otherwise*, 478. Εἰ δ' οὖν or εἰ δέ (sc. μή) 478. Εἰ μή, *except*, without verb, 476. Εἰ μὴ διὰ τοῦτο 476 3. Εἰ μή εἰ 476 4. Πλὴν εἰ 477.

Εἰ, *whether*, in indirect questions 665, 669, 362, 376, 497, even w. subj. 677, 680. Negative οὐ or μή 667 5. In alternative questions, εἰ . . . εἴτε or εἰ . . . ἤ, *whether . . . or*, 665. See Indirect Questions under Indirect Discourse.

Εἰδέναι or ὡς (ὅσον, ὅ τι) εἰδέναι as absolute infin. 778.

Εἴθε in wishes : see Εἰ γάρ (under Εἰ).

Εὑρίσκω w. partic., not in indirect discourse 883, in ind. disc. 904 ; w. infin. in ind. disc. 915⁶. Εὑρίσκομαι (mid.) w. infin. (in two uses) 915⁶.

Εὗτε, causal, 712, 713 (end).

'Εφ' ᾧ and ἐφ' ᾧτε w. infin. 610 -, w. fut. indic. 610².

"Εφην w. infin. without ἄν, expressing unrealised past intention, 429.

'Εφορῶ (ἐπεῖδον) w. partic. 885, w. aor. partic. (not past) 148.

'Εχρῆν or χρῆν w. infin. without ἄν, potential, 415, 416 : see Ἔδει.

"Εχω w. partic. as periphrastic perf. 47, εἶχον as pluperf. 48 ; see 831. Ἔχει (or οὐκ ἔχει) ὅ τι εἴπῃ etc. 572. Ἔχων, continually, 837, with, 844.

"Εως (Hom. εἷος and εἵως), while and until, 611. While, as ordinary relative : see Relative sentences. Until, meaning of clauses with 611, 612 ; w. indic., of definite past action 613¹, w. secondary tenses, of result not attained, 613² ; w. subj., of supposed future case 613³ ; w. opt., by assimilation, in future sense 613⁴ ; w. subj. and opt. in general suppositions 613⁵ ; w. subj. and opt. w. final force 614¹, 698 ; w. opt. in Odyssey, with special final force, 614². With subj. without ἄν 620 ; w. ἄν (retained from original subj.) w. opt. in indirect discourse 702.

Ἤ, than, after comparative w. infin. 764ᵃ, sometimes w. ὥστε or ὡς 764ᵇ.

Ἤ, or, 665¹ ; see Πότερον, and Εἰ, whether. Ἤ πρίν w. infin. 631 : see Πρίν.

Ἤ or ἤέ, whether (Hom.), 665².

Ἤ or ἦε, or (Hom.), 665².

Ἤδη w. gnomic aorist 156, w. temporal partic. 855.

Ἡδίων εἰμί w. partic. 899.

Ἡδομένῳ τινί εἶναι 900.

Ἥκω as perfect 27, imperf. of 37 ; w. infin. of purpose 772 ; w. partic. 895.

Ἠμφιέσθαι, wear, 49.

Ἤν, for εἰ ἄν, 381, 382 : see Εἰ.

Ἦν 39, 415, 416 : see Εἰμί.

Ἥρμοττεν w. infin. without ἄν, potential, 415, 416 : see Ἔδει.

Ἡττῶμαι as perfect 27.

Θαμίζω w. partic. 891.

Θαῦμα w. infin. 766.

Θαυμάζω εἰ 494.

Θέλω w. fut. infin. (irregular) 113.

Θέλεις or θέλετε w. interrog. subj. (poetic) 287, 288 ; w. ἵνα and subj. in later Greek 288. Modern θέλετε νά (and θά) w. subj. 288. Θέλοντί τινι εἶναι 900.

Θεσπίζω w. pres. or aor. infin., as verb of commanding, 98. See 'Αναιρέω and Χράω.

Θνητὸν ὄντα, one who is a mortal, of both sexes 827ᵇ.

Ἰδεῖν and ὁρᾶν, in appearance, 768 ; ἰδεῖν as absolute infin. (w. ὡς ἰδεῖν, ὅσον ἰδεῖν, etc.) 778.

Ἰθέως (Ionic) w. temporal partic. 858.

Ἴθι w. imperative 251, w. subj. 255.

Ἱκανός w. infin. 758 ; ἱκανός εἰμι w. partic. 899.

Ἵνα, final particle, 302, 311 ; w. subj. and opt. 317, 318-323 ; never w. fut. indic. 324 ; never w. ἄν or κέ 325 (w. footnote) ; without verb 331 ; w. secondary tenses of indic. 333 ; after λίσσομαι (Hom.) 357, similar use in New Test. and Latin 357. As adv., where, w. ἄν 325 (footnote).

Κά, Doric for κέ, 381 : see Ἄν.

Καθίζω w. partic. 898.

Καίπερ (Hom. also καί . . . περ) or καί w. partic. of opposition or limitation 859, 860.

Καίτοι w. partic. like καίπερ (rare) 861.

Καλὸν (κάλλιον, κρεῖττον, κράτιστον) ἦν w. infin. without ἄν, potential, 415, 416 (see Ἔδει) ; w. protasis in place of infin. 433.

Κατανεύω ὡς w. subj. (Hom.) 359.

Κατατείνας, earnestly, 837.

Κέ (κέν), relation to ἄν, 194, 401 : see Ἄν.

Κεκλῆσθαι, to be called, 49.

Κεκτῆσθαι, to have, 49.

Κελεύεται w. infin. in laws etc. 750.

Κινδυνεύω and κίνδυνός ἐστιν w. μή and subj. and opt. 365, w. infin. 375, 747. 'Εκινδύνευσα and κίνδυνος ἦν w. infin. without ἄν, potential, 427ᵃ, with ἄν 427ᵇ.

Κλαίων, to one's sorrow, 837 : cf. Χαίρων.

Κρατέω, am victorious, 27.

Κρείσσων εἰμί w. partic. 899.

Κυρέω and συγκυρέω w. partic. 889 145.

Λαβών, with, 844.

Λαθών, *secretly*, 837.

Λανθάνω w. partic. 887, 892, w. aor.
partic. 144, 146 (see Aorist Participle) ; reversal of constr. w. partic.
893 ; probably never w. infin. 903⁶.

Λέγω w. ὅτι or ὡς or w. infin. in indirect quotations 753¹, generally w.
ὅτι or ὡς in active voice 753¹ ; w.
infin. as verb of commanding 99,
753³. Ὡς λέγειν as absol. infin.
777².

Λήθω (poetic) w. partic. 888, 146.

Λίσσομαι w. ὅπως and subj. and opt.
(Hom.) 356, w. ἵνα and subj. (Hom.
and N. Test.) 357.

Λοιπὸν ἦν w. infin. and τό, potential
without ἄν, 431.

Μανθάνω w. partic. 904, w. infin.
915¹.

Μέλλω w. infin. as periphrastic future
73, 75, 111, tense of infin. (generally pres. or fut.) 74. Imperf. w.
infin. as past future 76 ; w. infin.
without ἄν, expressing unrealised
past intention 428ᵃ, Sanskrit construction compared 428 (footnote) ;
ἔμελλον ἄν (once) 428ᵇ.

Μέλλον as accus. absolute 851.

Μέμνημαι as present 49 ; w. partic.
904, w. infin. 915¹ ; μέμνημαι ὅτε
913.

Μένω w. partic. (poetic) 880.

Μερμηρίζω w. ὅπως or ὡς and subj. and
opt. (Hom.) 341-343.

Μεταμέλον as accus. absol. 851.

Μεταξύ w. temporal partic. 858.

Μέχρι, used like ἕως, 618 ; μέχρι οὗ
619. See Ἄχρι.

Μή, conditional, prohibitory, and final
negative particle : final use derived
from prohibitory 262ᵇ, 307 ; distinguishing prohibitory subj. from
subj. as simple future, and opt. in
neg. wishes from potential opt., 6,
8, 13, 234 : see Appendix I.
  In independent sentences. With
subj. and imperative in prohibitions 255, 258, 259, w. interrog.
imperat. 253 (end) ; w. subj. expressing apprehension with desire
to avert object, chiefly in Homer
261, sometimes in other Greek 264 ;
in cautious assertions (chiefly in
Plato), w. subj. 265, 266 (sometimes
in dependent clause 267), w.
indic. 269, sometimes interrog. 268,
269 ; w. interrog. subj. 287, 291,
even when affirmative answer is
implied 293 ; w. fut. indic. and

potential opt. used in sense of
interrog. subj. 292. Ὅπως μή w.
fut. indic. in prohibitions 271, 272,
w. fut. indic. or subj. implying
desire to avert something (like μή,
261) 278, 279, w. subj. in cautious
assertions (like μή, 265) 280 ; ὅπως
μή once with perf. indic. (as pres.)
282 ; subj. w. ὅπως μή 283, 278, 280.
With indic. in oaths 686.
  In final clauses etc. Μή becomes
a final from a prohibitory particle,
lest, that, 302, 307, 310 ; gradually
gives place to final particles w. μή
in negative final clauses 315 (w.
footnote) ; regular neg. adv. w.
final particles 305, but οὐ used after
μή itself 305, 306 ; μή . . . μή rare
306. In pure final clauses, w. subj.
and opt. 317, w. subj. after past
tenses 318-321, rarely w. fut. indic.
324, never w. ἄν 325. In object
clauses, for ὅπως μή, w. subj. (rarely
w. fut. indic.) 354. After verbs of
fearing, w. subj. and opt. 365, w.
pres. subj. denoting what may *prove*
to be object of fear 365 (end), 92 (cf.
perf. subj. in 103), after verbs like
ὁρῶ and οἶδα 366 ; w. fut. indic.
(seldom) 367, w. potential opt. w.
ἄν 368 ; w. pres. and past tenses of
indic. 369, μή not interrog. here 369
(footnote 1). In consecutive relative
clauses w. fut. indic. 576 ; w. ὥστε
and infin. 582, 584, 606, but seldom
(for οὐ) in indirect discourse 594,
595 ; w. ὡς (for ὥστε) 608 ; w. ἐφ'
ᾧ and ἐφ' ᾧτε 610.
  In protasis 383 ; exceptional cases
of οὐ 384-387. In cond. rel. clauses
518, 520. In causal rel. clauses
(also conditional) 580, 581.
  In indirect discourse w. finite
moods, when negatived by μή in
direct form, 667⁵ (for infin. and
partic. see below).
  Regular neg. of infin., except in
indirect discourse, 685 (end) ; sometimes μή for οὐ w. infin. and partic.
of ind. disc. 667⁵, 685, 688 ; regular
w. infin. after verbs of *hoping, ex-*
pecting, swearing, etc. 685. With
infin. after negative expressions,
strengthening negation of leading
verb, 815¹, 807, 809, 811, 812 ; w.
infin. in negative sense 808, 813 (see
Μή οὐ).
  With all participles expressing a
condition 832, 841 : see 472, 823.

Μὴ ὅτι and μὴ ὅπως (elliptical)

707, 708. Μή ὅτι w. indic. (rare) 686.

See Οὐ μή and Μὴ οὐ.

Μὴ οὐ, regular negative of final and prohibitory expressions introduced by μή, 263, 305 (cf. 815 [2]); in independent sentences 263, 264, 265, 269 ; in pure final clauses (rare) 305, 306 ; regular after verbs of *fearing* 270, 306, 365. With infin. (when this is already negatived by μή) after neg. leading verb 815 [2], 816, after neg. idea in leading clause 817 : see 807, 809, 811, 814 ; w. partic. 818 ; w. nouns 819. Forms one syllable in poetry 820.

Μικροῦ δεῖν, *almost*, 779 [a]; without δεῖν 779 [b].

Νικῶ as perfect 27.

Νομίζω in indirect discourse, w. infin. 683, rarely w. neg. μή (for οὐ) 685 ; w. aor. infin. referring to the future (exceptional and doubtful) 127 ; w. partic. 910.

῝Ο, neuter of ὅς, used in Homer like ὅτι, *that*, in indirect quotations, 663 [1], 709 [1], 671 (footnote) ; causal, *because*, 712, 713.

Ὀθούνεκα, causal 663 [3], 712 ; in indirect quotations 663 [3], 710 [1]. See Οὕνεκα.

Οἶδα w. partic. in indirect discourse 904, 687 ; w. infin. not in ind. disc. 915 [2 (a)], in ind. disc. 915 [2 (b)]. Οἶδ' ὅτι, οἶσθ' ὅτι, *I am sure*, etc. 705. Separating ἄν from its verb 220 [1]; οὐκ οἶδ' ἂν εἰ or οὐκ ἂν οἶδ' εἰ, w. indic. and opt. 220 [2]. Οἶσθ' ὃ δρᾶσον 253.

Οἴομαι or οἶμαι w. infin. in indirect discourse 683, rarely w. neg. μή (for οὐ) 685 ; w. aor. infin. referring to the future (exceptional and doubtful) 127 ; separating ἄν from its verb 220 [1].

Οἷον and οἷα w. causal participle 862.

Οἷος w. infin. 759. Οἷός τ' ἦν w. infin. without ἄν, potential, 415, 416 : see ῝Εδει.

Οἴχομαι as perf. 27, imperf. of 37 ; w. partic. 895.

Ὀλίγου δεῖν, *almost*, 779 [a]; without δεῖν 779 [b].

῝Ολλυμαι as perfect 27, imperf. of 37.

῝Ολωλα, *I shall perish*, 51.

Ὁμοῖος w. infin. (Hom.) 769.

Ὁμολογέω w. infin. in indirect dis-

course 914 [4], tense of infin. 136 ; w. partic. 904.

Ὁπόταν, for ὁπότε ἄν, 192 [2], 522.

Ὅποτε, relative, 514 (cf. 313 [1]) ; causal 712, 713 ; meaning *until* (Hom.) 553, 698 ; w. peculiar final force in predictions (Hom.) 571.

Ὅπου (ὅκου), causal, 712, 713 (end).

Ὅπως, originally relative adv., then indirect interrog. 313. With independent fut. indic. in commands etc. (ὅπως μή in prohibitions) 271-277, rarely ὅπως μή (but not ὅπως) w. subj. 283, 364 ; ὅπως μή w. fut. indic. or subj. implying desire to avert something 278, 279, w. subj. in cautious assertions 280, once w. perf. indic. (as pres.) 282.

As final particle 302, 313. In pure final clauses w. subj. and opt. 317-321, rarely w. fut. indic. 324 ; w. secondary tenses of indic. 333, 334, 336, never w. ἄν 335 ; ὅπως ἄν w. subj. 313 [3], 328, 200, w. opt. 329, 330. In object clauses after verbs of *striving*, etc. w. fut. indic. and opt. (sometimes w. pres. or aor. subj. and opt.) 339, 340 ; similar use of ὅπως or ὡς in Homer w. subj. and opt. 341 (examples in Appendix III. 3), w. κέ 341, 343 ; w. fut. indic., subj., and opt. after verbs of *asking*, *commanding*, etc. 355 ; w. fut. indic. after δεῖ σε 360 ; w. subj. and opt. after λίσσομαι (Hom.) 356 ; ὅπως ἄν w. subj. (Attic) 348, ὅπως ἄν w. opt. 349, 351 [2]; ὅκως ἄν w. opt. (Herod.) 350 ; Xenophon's use of ὅπως ἄν and ὡς ἄν 351 (see also Appendix IV.). Dawes's Canon 364 (cf. 363). After verbs of *fearing* : ὅπως μή (for simple μή) w. fut. indic., subj., and opt. 370 ; ὅπως or ὡς, *that*, in indirect discourse, w. pres. or fut. indic. 371. With fut. indic. (Hom.) as indirect interrog. 344, 351 [2]. In consecutive rel. sentences w. fut. indic. 578. In indirect quotations (like ὡς) 663 [2], 706. Οὐχ ὅπως and μὴ ὅπως, elliptical, 707, 708.

Ὁρῶ (εἶδον) w. partic. not in indirect discourse 885, 886, w. aor. partic. (not past) 148 ; in ind. disc., w. partic. 904, 914 [2], 886, w. infin. 914 [2]. Ὁρᾶν and ἰδεῖν, *in appearance*, 768 (cf. 766).

Ὅσος w. infin. 759. Ὅσον and ὡς w. absolute infin. 778. Ὅσον μή, *except*, 550.

Τί μαθών; and τί παθών; wherefore? why? 839ᵃ; dependent form, ὅ τι μαθών and ὅ τι παθών, because, 839ᵇ.
Τί οὐ in exhortations, w. aor. in future sense, 62.
Τί πάθω; 290.
Τίκτω, to be mother of, in tragedy, 27.
Τλάω w. partic. (poetic) 880, w. aor. partic. (not past) 148; w. infin. 903².
Τὸ νῦν εἶναι 781.
Τὸ τήμερον εἶναι, to-day, 781.
Τὸ τί ἦν εἶναι 781.
Τοῖος, τοιόσδε, τοιοῦτος and τόσος, without rel., w. infin. (Hom.) 760.
Τοιοῦτος οἶος and τοσοῦτος ὅσος w. infin. 759.
Τολμῶ w. partic. (poetic) 880, w. infin. 903².
Τότε or τότε ἤδη w. temporal partic. 855.
Τυγχάνω w. partic. 887, w. aor. partic. 144, 146 (see Aorist Participle); reversal of constr. w. partic. 893; prob. never w. infin. 903⁸.

Ὑπέρ w. τοῦ and infin. in final sense 802.
Ὑπάρχω w. predicate partic. 830.
Ὑπῆρχεν w. infin. without ἄν, potential, 415, 416: see Ἔδει. Τὰ ὑπάρχοντα, resources, as subst. 828.
Ὑπομένω w. partic. 879, w. infin. 903².
Ὕστερον ἤ w. infin., like πρότερον ἤ or πρίν, once in Thuc., 655.

Φαίνομαι w. partic. 904, w. infin. 914⁵; two uses distinguished 914⁵.
Φανερός εἰμι and φανερὸν ποιῶ w. partic. 907; φανερόν ἐστιν (impersonal) w. ὅτι or ὡς 912.
Φέρε w. imperat. 251, w. subj. 255, 257, w. ὅπως and fut. indic. 276.
Φερόμενος, with a rush, 837. Φέρων, hastily, 837, with, 844.
Φεύγω as perfect 27.
Φημί w. infin. in indirect quotations 683, 753¹, in Hom. 671 (end); rarely w. neg. μή 685; very seldom w. ὅτι or ὡς 753²; w. aor. infin. referring to the future (exceptional and doubtful) 127. Separating ἄν from its verb 220¹.
Φθάνω in leading clause emphasising following πρίν 660, φθάνω . . . ἤ w. infin. (Herod.) 661. With partic. 887, w. aor. partic. 144, 146 (see Aorist Participle); reversal of constr. w. partic. 893; probably

never w. infin. 903⁸. Φθάσας, before, 837. Οὐκ ἄν φθάνοις (φθάνοιτε) w. partic. 894.
Φράζομαι w. ὅπως or ὡς and subj. or opt. (Hom.) 341-343. Φράζειν and φράσαι w. ὡς as absol. infin. 777².

Χαίρων, with impunity, 837. See Κλαίων.
Χαλεπός w. negative force, followed by μή οὐ, 817.
Χράω, to give oracular response, w. pres. or aor. infin. (as verb of command) 98. See Ἀναιρέω and Θεσπίζω. Χρῆσθαι w. ὡς as absol. infin. 778. Χρώμενος, with, 844.
Χρῆν w. infin. without ἄν, potential, 415-422 (see Contents); as simple expression of past necessity 417; χρῆν ἄν 420, 423 (see Appendix V.): see Ἔδει.
Χρονίζων, for a long time, χρονισθείς, after a time, 834.

Ὤν, partic. of εἰμί, omitted; as circumstantial partic. 875, supplementary 902, in indirect discourse 911. See Participle.
Ὡς, relative adv. of manner, derivation of 312¹; for its use as rel. see Relative sentences. In Homeric similes 543-549: see Ὡς ὅτε. In comparisons (Hom.) 869, 871: see Ὡς εἰ.
Becomes final particle 312, 302; use in pure final clauses, w. subj. and opt. 317, 318, w. fut. indic. (rare) 324, w. ἄν or κέ and subj. 200, 325, 326, w. ἄν or κέ and opt. 329, w. secondary tenses of indic. 333; in object clauses after verbs of planning etc. in Homer w. subj. and opt. (subj. generally w. κέ) 341, 342, relics of this usage in other Greek 347, ὡς ἄν w. subj. and opt. in Xen. 351 (see Appendix IV.), ὡς μή in neg. obj. clauses 353 (cf. 352), peculiar uses of ὡς in Hom. 358, 359. Ὡς ἄν w. subj. (independent) 281. Final ὡς seldom in Attic prose, except in Xen., 312³ (see Appendix III. 1, and IV.).
In consecutive sentences (used like ὥστε) w. infin. and finite moods 608, 609.
Introducing indirect quotations (orig. = how) 663², earliest use 671; use in substantive clauses generally 664¹; w. indic. and opt.

ENGLISH INDEX.

N.B.—The references are made to the *Sections.*

itself, 96 ; how distinguished from pres. infin. 97 ; after χράω etc. 98 ; after λέγω, *to command, δοκεῖ, it seems good, ἔδοξε, it is enacted,* etc. 99 ; after verbs of *hoping, expecting, promising, swearing,* etc. (in fut. sense) 100, 136 ; after αἴτιός εἰμι 101. In indirect discourse, repres. aor. indic. 126, rarely and irreg. ref. to future time 127 ; as secondary tense 189. Gnomic aor. infin. 159.

Participle, ordinary use of, 143 ; as primary or secondary tense 190. With λανθάνω, τυγχάνω, and φθάνω 887, time of partic. 144, 146 ; w. συμπίπτω 145, 890 ; w. περιορῶ, ἐφορῶ, ὁρῶ, ἀκούω, etc., not relatively past, 148, 884, 885 ; w. noun, like infin. w. subject, not past, 149, 829 ᵇ ; denoting that in which action of past verb consists, not past, 150, 845 ; peculiar use w. ὁμολογέω etc. 151. In indirect discourse 904 (see 886) ; gnomic aor. partic. 159. Attributive aor. partic. absolutely (though not relatively) past 152 (cf. 141).

For uses with ἄν or κέ, see Ἄν.

Apodosis defined 378, 520 ; negatived by οὐ 383. Forms of, in simple pres. and past conditions 403 ; in fut. cond. 445 ; in pres. and past unreal cond. 410, 411, action not necessarily denied in last case 412, w. aor. indic. w. ἄν sometimes not past 414. With potential force without ἄν, in ἔδει, χρῆν, etc. w. infin. 415, 416. Expressed in infin. or partic. 479, 552, in a verbal noun 480. Omitted for effect 482 ; repres. by ἄν without verb 227, 483, 484 ; implied w. ὡς εἰ and ὥσπερ εἰ 485, 868, 869 (cf. 475). Contained in protasis 486-493 (see Contents). Introduced by δέ, ἀλλά, or αὐτάρ 512, 513.

Assimilation in conditional relative clauses 558-563 : w. subj. and opt. referring to future 558, variable in general conditions 563 ; w. past tenses of indic. in unreal cond. 559.

Causal sentences 712-719 (see Contents) ; see also 377, 699. Causal relative sentences (w. neg. οὐ) 580, sometimes conditional also (w. neg. μή) 580, 581. Causal participle 838, w. ὡς 864, 865, w. ἅτε and οἷα

or οἷον 862, rarely w. ὥσπερ 874, w. ὥστε (Herod.) 863.

Caution, verbs of, w. μή and subj. or opt. 365 : see *Fearing.* With infin. (sometimes infin. w. μή) 374.

Commands, expr. by imperative 18, 250, by fut. indic. 69.

Comparative w. ἤ and infin. 764 ᵃ, sometimes w. ὥστε or ὡς 764 ᵇ.

Conditional sentence, parts of 378 ; possible origin of 398-401 ; classification of 388-397 ; forms of 378-513 : see Contents ; and for details see Εἰ, Indicative, Subjunctive, and Optative.

Conditions, particular and general, 394, 395, 397. Present and past, w. indic., in simple suppos. 402, w. suppos. contrary to fact 410, Homeric usages in latter 434-443. Future, w. subj. 444-446, w. fut. indic. 447-449, Homeric usages in 450-454 ; w. opt. 455-459, Homeric usages in 460, 461. General pres. and past cond. w. subj. and opt. 462-466, w. indic. 467, Homeric and poetic usages in 468-471. Hom. pres. cond. w. opt. 438, 439. Mixed constructions 498-509 : see Contents. For relative conditions, see Relative sentences.

Consecutive clauses with relatives 575-579 : see Relative clauses (consecutive). With ὥστε 582-607 ; w. ὡς 608, 609 ; w. ἐφ' ᾧ and ἐφ' ᾧτε 610 : see Ὥστε, Ὡς, and Εφ' ᾧ.

Danger, expressions of, see *Fearing,* verbs of.

Dative of agent, w. verbals in -τέος 922 ; dative or accus. w. verbals in -τέον (-τέα) 926.

Dawes's Canon, 363, 364.

Dependence of moods and tenses, general principles of 165, 166. For details, see Contents for §§ 167-191.

Dependent moods, as opposed to indicative, 1.

Direct quotations, distinguished from indirect 662 ; sometimes introduced by ὅτι or ὡς 711.

Exhortations w. imperative 18, 250 ; w. first person of subj. 255-258, other persons of subj. not generally used 258 ; w. opt. (poetic) 725, 13, 234 ; w. ὅπως and fut. indic. 271-275.

Fearing, verbs of, w. μή and subj.

and opt. 303, 365, 366 ; in neg. expressions w. μὴ οὐ 365, 305, 306, 264 (end), rarely μή . . . μή 306 ; development of construction 262, 307, 309 ; w. fut. indic. (rare) 367 ; w. μή or ὅπως μή and fut. opt. 367, 131 ; w. μή and potential opt. w. ἄν 368 ; w. μή and pres. or past tenses of indic. 308, 369 ; w. ὅπως μή (for simple μή) 370 ; w. ὅπως or ὡς (neg. οὐ) in indirect discourse 371 ; w. fut. infin. (indir. disc.) 372 ; w. pres. or aor. infin. 373, 747 ; w. εἰ in indir. questions 376 ; w. causal ὅτι 377.

Final clauses (pure), w. ἵνα, ὡς, ὅπως, ὄφρα, and μή, 302, 303, distinguished from object clauses w. ὅπως 303, 304 ; development of 262, 307-316 ; negatives in 305, 306 ; simple μή in neg. final clauses displaced by final particles w. μή 315 (cf. 310). With subj. and opt. 317, w. subj. after past tenses 318-321 ; w. opt. after primary tenses, irregular and doubtful 322, when leading verb implies past 323 ; w. fut. indic. (never w. ἵνα) 324 ; w. past tenses of indic. 333, 334, never w. ἄν 335, indic. in same final clause 336. With ὡς, ὅπως, and ὄφρα, w. ἄν or κέ and subj. 325-328, w. ἄν or κέ and opt. 329, 330: for Xen. see also Appendix IV. Without leading verb expressed 332. Ἵνα τί; 331.

For relative clauses of purpose, see Relative sentences.

For clauses w. ὅπως etc. after verbs of striving etc., see Object clauses.

Finite moods, as opposed to the infin., 1.

Future. Indicative, expressing future time 19, 63, relatively future time in final constr. and indirect discourse 64 ; may repres. action in duration, occurrence, or inception 65 ; in gnomic sense 66 ; expr. general truth hereafter to be recognised 67 (cf. 40) ; in questions of doubt, like interrog. subj., 68, w. neg. μή 292[1] ; in 2nd person, expr. concession or command, 69 ; rarely in prohibitions w. μή 70 ; periphrastic form w. μέλλω and infin. 73-76. With ὅπως μή in exhortations and prohibitions (independent) 271-277 (see Ὅπως) ; w. ὅπως μή expr. desire to avert (also subj.)

278, 279, 283. In final clauses (rarely) for subj. w. ὡς, ὅπως, ὄφρα, μή, 324 ; in object cl. w. ὅπως (regularly) 339, 340, in Homer chiefly w. interrog. ὅπως 344, in Herod. and Xen. w. ὡς 347, 351 ; after verbs of fearing, seldom w. μή 367, oftener w. ὅπως μή 370, w. ὡς or ὅπως as indirect discourse (neg. οὐ) 371. In conditions : w. εἰ in future suppositions (like subj. w. ἐάν) 447-449, in pres. suppos. 407, 408 ; not regular in fut. rel. cond. 530, but allowed in pres. 527. In rel. clauses of purpose (neg. μή) 565, also after past tenses 566, seldom in Hom. 570 ; w. rel. denoting result aimed at (neg. μή) 576 ; in consecutive cl. w. ὥστε 601, w. ὡς 608, w. ἐφ' ᾧ and ἐφ' ᾧτε 610.[2] In indirect discourse after past tenses for fut. opt. 670[b].

With οὐ μή 294 : see Appendix II. In clauses of denial, future sometimes used for subj. 295, also in dependent constructions 296. In prohibitions, future regular form 297-301. See Οὐ μή, and Contents under §§ 294-301.

In dependent moods (only opt. and infin.), used chiefly in indirect discourse, repres. fut. indic. of direct form, and in infin. w. μέλλω, 111.

Optative, in indirect discourse, repr. fut. indic. 128, 669[2] ; w. ὅπως after past verbs of striving etc. 130, 339, rarely w. μή or ὅπως μή after verbs of fearing 131, 367, doubtful in final clauses 132, never w. ἵνα 133 ; never in protasis or apodosis (except in indirect discourse for fut. indic.) 459 ; never w. ἄν 203 ; rarely in rel. clauses of purpose 134, 574 ; w. ὥστε by assimilation 604 ; once w. οὐ μή in indirect quotation w. ὡς 296[a]. First used by Pindar 129.

Infinitive, chiefly in indirect discourse, repres. fut. indic. 135, 683, 689 ; w. verbs of hoping, expecting, promising, swearing, etc. (also pres. and aor. infin.) 136. Irregular use not in indir. disc., for pres. or aor., 112, 113. With μέλλω, forming periphrastic future 73, 111, w. past tenses of μέλλω as past fut. 76, 567.

Participle 153 ; expressing purpose 840 ; used in present (not in future) conditions 473.

and ὡς (neg. οὐ) as indirect discourse 371. See 3 ᵇ.

In protasis 3-5 : pres. and past tenses in simple suppositions 402-406 ; fut. of pres. intention etc. 407, 408, fut. w. εἰ in fut. suppos. (like subj. w. ἐάν) 447-449, in Hom. also w. εἰ κε 451 ; secondary tenses in pres. and past unreal cond. (w. ἄν in apodosis) 4, 410, 411, relation of tenses here 413, aor. in apodosis sometimes not past 414, imperf. always past in Hom. 435 ; potential indic. w. εἰ as protasis 409, .506 ; present and past tenses in general cond. for subj. and opt. 405, 467. In relative clauses w. definite antecedent 519.   In conditional rel. clauses : in simple pres. and past cond. 525, 526 ; fut. of pres. intention etc. 527, not in fut. cond. 530 ; secondary tenses in unreal cond. 528, 559, 560 ; pot. indic. w. cond. relative 557 ; for subj. and opt. in general rel. cond. 534, 535 ; w. rel. after general negatives 536 ; in parenthetic rel. clauses 537 ¹. In Homeric similes w. ὡς or ὡς ὅτε 547, 548, 549.

In consecutive sentences : w. ὥστε, expressing actual result, 601, distinguished from infin. 582, 583, 584 ; indic. and infin. in same sentence 603 (see ῞Ωστε) ; w. ὡς 608, 609 ; fut. w. ἐφ᾽ ᾧ and ἐφ᾽ ᾧτε 610 ². In consec. rel. sentences (w. neg. οὐ) 575, fut. (w. neg. μή) 576. In causal sentences (w. neg. οὐ) 713, 715 ; causal potential indic. 717 ; in causal rel. sentences (neg. οὐ or μή) 580, 581. With ἕως, until, of definite past actions (generally aor.) 613 ¹, secondary tenses, of result not attained, 613 ² ; w. ἄχρι and μέχρι 618, 619 ; w. ἐς ὅ and ἐς οὗ (Herod.) 616 ; w. ἔστε 617 ; w. ὄφρα 615 : see ῞Εως etc. With πρίν 622, 623, 624 ; not in Homer 625, except w. πρίν γ᾽ ὅτε 636 ; in early poets 632 ; in Attic poets 633 ; in prose 634, 635 ; of result not attained 637. With πρίν ἤ 651, 652. With πρότερον ἤ 653, 654.

In indirect discourse 3 ᵃ, 667 ¹, ², after primary tenses 669 ¹, allowed after past tenses 669 ², 670 ; imperf. and pluperf. generally retained after past tenses 672, imperf. sometimes changed to pres. opt. 673 ; aor. retained from dependent clauses of

direct form 667 ¹, 689 ³, rarely changed to opt. 693, 694 ² ; all past tenses w. ἄν and in unreal cond. retained 667 ², 681 ; pres. and perf. changed to imperf. and pluperf. after past tenses in Homer 671, 674 ¹, sometimes in other Greek 674 ², 691, 701. See Indirect Discourse.

Secondary tenses in present or past unattained wishes 5, 720, 731, 732, 740 ; never without εἴθε or εἰ γάρ 733 ; never in Homer 732, 735. See Wishes and ῎Ωφελον.

For the uses of the Indicative with ἄν or κέ, see ῎Αν. For future indic. w. οὐ μή, see Οὐ μή and Future.

Indirect Discourse 662-710 : see Contents for these sections. Indirect and direct quotations distinguished 662. Extent of term indirect discourse or oratio obliqua 666, 694, of term infinitive in indirect discourse 684. Indirect quotations, how introduced 663 ; indirect questions, how introduced 665. General principles of construction 667, use of ἄν 667 ⁴, negatives 667 ⁵ ; indirect quotations and questions in apposition w. pronoun like τοῦτο 668.

Indirect Quotation of simple sentences. Introduced by ὅτι or ὡς 667 ¹,² : indic. (without ἄν) in direct forms, and indic. or opt. in indirect, 669, both moods in same quotation 670 ; imperf. and pluperf. retained without change 672, but imperf. may be changed to pres. opt. (imperf. opt.) 673 ; constr. imperfectly developed in Hom. 671 ; pres. and perf. changed to imperf. and pluperf. in Hom. 674 ¹, sometimes in Attic 674 ² ; independent opt. following opt. w. ὅτι or ὡς 675 ¹, sometimes foll. other forms 675 ² ; opt. after a pres. tense implying former expression of thought 676 ; indic. or opt. w. ἄν unchanged in quot. 667 ², 681, likewise potential. indic. without ἄν 682. Introduced by infinitive 683, 751, sometimes w. neg. μή (for direct οὐ) 685, 667 ⁵ ; by participle 687, 904, sometimes w. μή 688, 667 ⁵. See Infinitive and Participle.

Indirect Quotation of complex sentences : general principles of construction 689 ; different moods in same quotation 690 ; pres. or perf. indic. in dependent clause of